BUSINESS

BUSINESS

Robert J. Hughes
Richland College

Jack R. Kapoor
College of DuPage

HOUGHTON MIFFLIN COMPANY

BOSTON *Dallas   Geneva, Illinois   Lawrenceville, New Jersey   Palo Alto*

Dedication

To Peggy Hughes

To Theresa Kapoor and Karen, Kathy, and Dave Kapoor

Credits

Cover

Original photograph, Black Star/Boisverd; color alteration by Color Response, Inc.

Line Art

Omnigraphics, Inc., unless otherwise credited.

Chapter One

Text 7 "Department Store" reprinted from *The Book of Firsts* by Patrick Robertson. Copyright © 1974 by Patrick Robertson. Used by permission of Clarkson N. Potter, Inc., and Michael Joseph. 19 "Cash Register" reprinted from *The Book of Firsts* by Patrick Robertson. Copyright © 1974 by Patrick Robertson. Used by permission of Clarkson N. Potter, Inc., and Michael Joseph. **Art** 20–21 Peter Marzio, ed., *A Nation of Nations* (New York: Harper & Row, 1976). Copyright © 1976 Smithsonian Institute.

Chapter Two

Text 51 "Adopting a Dump" from *Business Today,* Fall 1983, page 20. By permission. **Art** 45 U.S. Bureau of the Census, "Table 55. Work Experience in 1982—Civilians 15 Years Old and Over, by Total Money Earnings in 1982, Race, Spanish Origin, and Sex," *Statistical Abstract of the United States 1984* (Washington, D.C.: Government Printing Office, 1983), pp. 197–199. 46 Bureau of Labor Statistics, U.S. Department of Labor, *Perspectives on Working Women: A Databook* (Washington, D.C.: Government Printing Office, October 1980), p. 52. 54 Lowell G. Rein, "Is Your (Ethical) Slippage Showing?" *Personnel Journal* 59 (September 1980): pp. 740–743. Reprinted with the permission of *Personnel Journal*, Costa Mesa, California: all rights reserved.

Chapter Three

Text 62 Apple Computer Company, Third Quarter Report, July 27, 1983. By permission. 77 Extract from "Texaco Wins FTC's Nod to Acquire Getty after Agreeing to Shed Certain Properties" by Jeanne Saddler reprinted by permission of *The Wall Street Journal,* © Dow Jones & Company, Inc. 1984. All rights reserved. **Art** 64 U.S. Bureau of Census, "Tables 887 and 888," *Statistical Abstract of the United States 1984* (Washington, D.C.: Government Printing Office, 1983), p. 532. 67 U.S. Bureau of the Census, "Tables 887 and 888," *Statistical Abstract of the United States 1984* (Washington, D.C.: Government Printing Office, 1983), p. 532. 68 R. Robert Rosenberg et al., *College Business Law* (New York: McGraw-Hill, 1978) p. 408. Copyright 1978 McGraw-Hill Book Company. Reproduced with permission. 72 *Chicago Sun-Times*, February 7, 1983, p. 50. Chicago Sun-Times, Field Enterprises, Inc., © News Group Chicago Inc., 1983. Map by Char Searl. Reprinted with permission of the *Chicago Sun-Times.*

Chapter Four

Text 88 Adapted from "A Bit of Old-Style Imagination Leads to a High Tech Success," by Carrie Dolan, reprinted by permission of *The Wall Street Journal,* © Dow Jones & Company, Inc. 1983.

Credits continued on p. 650.

Printed in the U.S.A.
Library of Congress Catalog Card Number: 84-80374
ISBN: 0-395-35587-7

DEFGHIJ-D-8987

Preface

Each day thousands of very successful people participate in our business system because they *want* to. For these people, the chance to make money, to compete, and to grow makes business exciting and makes the work of learning about business worthwhile. As the authors of *Business,* we have worked to create a book that encourages the same motivation in students and employs that motivation in instruction.

As teachers of business, we have found that it's hard to have students learn about business in the same way that people who participate in it do. During thirty years of teaching, we have worked with thousands of students and with many different textbooks. Invariably, no matter which text we have chosen, it has created a one-dimensional experience that leaves the students wondering why they should want to participate.

Out of our day-to-day teaching experiences, we set goals for ourselves as authors:

1. to create a textbook that conveys the excitement and enthusiasm that successful business people feel about their work;
2. to create a multi-faceted teaching and learning system that would be effective and efficient enough to allow the professor time to teach the students how it really feels to do business.

We believe we've accomplished these goals by developing a multi-level instructional system that maximizes both the ease of learning the subject and of teaching it.

THE TEXT

The heart of this collection is, of course, the text. We have designed *Business* to be the most readable and visually exciting text on the market. Its best features are its organization, coverage of topics, and presentation.

Organization

Business is organized around the traditional functional areas of American business. Part 1 provides the framework for understanding the development and structure of American business. Parts 2, 3, 4, 5, and 6 correspond to the areas of management and organization, human resources management, marketing, finance, and information resources. Part 7 on the business environment deals with fast-changing legal and regulatory issues and the importance of international trade in the world today.

All the parts are self-contained; they may be assigned in any sequence, a feature that allows the instructor to organize the course according to his or her preference.

Coverage of Topics

In addition to the full treatment given to the functional areas of business, we give extended coverage to a number of emerging trends and areas of growing importance. Among these are transnational companies, our increasingly service-oriented economy, personal investment, changing demographic patterns and their effect on marketing, and the importance of small business. The epilogue suggests the future shape and course of American business and focuses on personal career planning aids for the student.

Presentation

The text has an informal, readable style. Furthermore, every line of text has been carefully edited to ensure that ideas are explained clearly and that there is a well-defined transition from one idea to the next. A chapter outline, an overview, learning objectives, and a classic business case are used to introduce each chapter. Within each chapter concrete examples and real-world applications illuminate major topics. Thought-provoking inserts occur regularly to add to student interest. A summary, key terms, review questions, discussion questions, exercises, and two cases end each chapter. The end-of-chapter activities give students a chance to use data and explore ideas. The ending cases provide the opportunity to analyze real companies engaged in issues the chapter has discussed.

We believe that the specialized vocabulary of business deserves special attention. Therefore, on first mention in text, key terms appear in boldfaced type and are immediately defined. The student's business vocabulary is strengthened by highlighting key terms at the end of the chapter. Finally, there is a complete glossary at the back of the book.

The art program of *Business* is strong enough instructionally to amount to a mini-course in itself. Together with the captions, the art explains key concepts and real-world applications and can serve the student as both a preview and review of each chapter. The drawings explain ideas in a manner that appeals to memory and understanding as well as the eye. You can turn to pages 39, 79, 120, 149, 256, 330, and 512 for immediately recognizable examples of this type of visual instruction.

ENRICHMENT MATERIALS

We have designed the following enrichment materials to give students the chance to learn about business in the way it feels to participate in business today.

- *Business Year,* a business news magazine containing 60 articles researched in business and news publications. *Business Year* was created to accompany the text and to provide students with an inside view of contemporary business.
- *Enterprise,* a computer simulation by Jerald Smith, University of Louisville, Kentucky. This game provides student players with simulated real-world experience in business decision making.
- *Investing in Business,* a student project manual that engages the student in making practical decisions about personal investments. This investment project allows students to whet their appetites at making money work for them.
- *Opening a Business,* a student project manual that involves the student in facing the practical

steps of starting and operating a business. This business project teaches students what it takes to start a business in their own community.
- *Careers in Business,* a student project manual that engages the student in detailed planning of a career in business. This employment game starts students in the techniques of acquiring a job and building a career. It motivates and instructs students in their first real business concern.

RETENTION AND REINFORCEMENT MATERIALS

We have designed the following materials to provide multi-level reinforcement of concepts in the text.

- *Study Guide* by Kathryn Hegar, Mountainview College. The study guide provides students with several formats for reviewing and mastering the material. For each chapter of *Business,* there are sections on: grasping main ideas, meeting chapter objectives, visiting businesses (as well as doing other exercises), and reviewing intensively through an array of questions (true and false, matching, completion, and essay). Some chapters have sections to "beef up" the student's knowledge with additional practical knowledge not included in the text.
- *Business Micro Study,* a microcomputer version of the *Study Guide.*

TEACHING MATERIALS

We have provided the following resource materials to make teaching as efficient as possible for expert and novice alike.

- *Instructor's Resource Files* by John Beem, College of DuPage. This is a uniquely organized library of materials useful in teaching *Business.* For each chapter it provides a clearly worded overview and introduction; a brief outline; objectives; a detailed lecture outline in large type; relevant "At Issue" discussion topics with pros and cons already researched; chapter quizzes;

solutions to all end-of-chapter materials; a list and description of relevant films; sample business forms and papers; and approximately 100 test questions categorized by difficulty. All these materials are organized into a file for each chapter so that the instructor does not have to "prepare" the preparation or carry around a lot of extra materials. The test bank of over 2,200 items was prepared by Jimmy McKenzie, Northeast Campus of Tarrant County Junior College District. In addition to questions for each chapter, there are test questions summarizing each part, or group of chapters.

☐ *100 Color Transparencies.* The transparencies provide dramatic presentation of concepts in each chapter as well as additional lecture ma-terial related to the chapter but not found in the text.

TESTING AND EVALUATION MATERIALS

Computer technology has had a profound effect on higher education as well as business. One of its more profound uses is in the evaluation stage of instruction. We have provided the following programs to help instructors, especially those with large numbers of students.

☐ *Computerized Test Item File,* a test preparation program available for micro- or mainframe computers.
☐ *GPA: Grade Performance Analyzer,* a record-keeping system for use with microcomputers.

Acknowledgments

We gratefully acknowledge the many reviewers who read the manuscript in its various stages of development and offered so many useful suggestions and recommendations. Their help was invaluable.

James O. Armstrong, II
John Tyler Community College

Robert W. Bitter
Southwest Missouri State University

James Boyle
Glendale Community College

Lyle V. Brenna
Pikes Peak Community College

Harvey S. Bronstein
Oakland Community College

Edward Brown
Sinclair Community College

Clara Buitenbos
Pan American University

Richard M. Chamberlain
Lorain County Community College

J. Michael Cicero
Highline Community College

Harris D. Dean
Lansing Community College

Wayne H. Decker
Memphis State University

William M. Dickson
Green River Community College

Robert Ek
Seminole Community College

Carleton S. Everett
Des Moines Area Community College

Arlen Gastineau
Valencia Community College

Robert Googins
Shasta College

Joseph Gray
Nassau Community College

Ricky W. Griffin
Texas A & M University

John Gubbay
Moraine Valley Community College

Rick Guidicessi
Des Moines Area Community College

Ronald Hadley
St. Petersburg Junior College

Richard D. Hartley
Solano Community College

Donald Hiebert
Northern Oklahoma College

Marie R. Hodge
Bowling Green State University

James L. Hyek
Los Angeles Valley College

Betty Ann Kirk
Tallahassee Community College

Clyde Kobberdahl
Cincinnati Technical College

Robert Kreitner
Arizona State University

R. Michael Lebda
DeVry Institute of Technology

George Leonard
St. Petersburg Junior College

Chad Lewis
Everett Community College

William M. Lindsay
Northern Kentucky University

Paul James Londrigan
Charles Stewart Mott Community College

Fritz Lotz
Southwestern College

Robert C. Lowery
Brookdale Community College

Jack McDonough
Menlo College

Sheldon A. Mador
Los Angeles Trade and Technical College

John Martin
Mt. San Antonio Community College

Charles Morrow
Cuyahoga Community College

W. Gale Mueller
Spokane Community College

Robert J. Mullin
Orange County Community College

Jerry Novak
Alaska Pacific University

Dennis Pappas
Columbus Technical Institute

Roberta F. Passenant
Berkshire Community College

Clarissa M. H. Patterson
Bryant College

Donald Pettit
Suffolk County Community College

Norman Petty
Central Piedmont Community College

Gloria D. Poplawsky
University of Toledo

William M. Pride
Texas A & M University

John Roisch
Clark County Community College

Karl C. Rutkowski
Pierce Junior College

P. L. Sandlin
East Los Angeles College

John E. Seitz
Oakton Community College

J. Gregory Service
Broward Community College, North Campus

Richard Shapiro
Cuyahoga Community College

Anne Smevog
Cleveland Technical College

John Spence
University of Southwestern Louisiana

Nancy Z. Spillman
President, Economic Education Enterprises

J. Stauffer
Ventura College

W. Sidney Sugg
Lakeland Community College

Raymond D. Tewell
American River College

Theodore F. Valvoda
Lakeland Community College

Frederick A. Viohl
Troy State University

Loren K. Waldman
Franklin University

Larry Williams
Palomar College

Gregory J. Worosz
Schoolcraft College

Contents

CHAPTER SIX

Creating the Organization *142*

PART 4

Marketing 281

CHAPTER ELEVEN

An Overview of Marketing 282

Product and Price *310*

Wholesaling, Retailing, and Physical Distribution *336*

CHAPTER FOURTEEN

Promotion 352

PART 5

Finance and Investment 391

CHAPTER FIFTEEN

Money, Banking, and Credit 392

CHAPTER SIXTEEN

PART 7

The Business Environment 559

CHAPTER TWENTY-ONE

Business Law 560

EPILOGUE

Our Future, Your Future 636

PART

1
American Business Today

This introductory part of Business *is an overview of American business. We begin with an examination of the American business system, its basis, and its function within our society. Then we discuss the responsibilities of business as a part of that society. Next we move to an important and very practical aspect of business: how businesses are owned and by whom. Finally, because the vast majority of businesses are small, we look at American small business in some detail. Included in this part are:*

CHAPTER

ONE
Foundations of Business

Everyone seems to have something to say about business, good or bad and right or wrong, perhaps because business really is everyone's business. Anyone who has ever made a purchase, worked at a job, or even seen an advertisement has been involved with business. And business is involved in almost everything we do throughout our lives, from the first diaper to the last resting place. In Chapter 1, we shall look briefly at what business is and how it got that way. After studying the chapter, you should understand:

1. *The primary objective of business, and its risks and rewards*
2. *The four main ingredients of laissez-faire capitalism*
3. *How the three basic economic questions are answered in a free-market economy*
4. *How supply and demand determine price in competitive markets*
5. *The origins and development of our modified capitalist business system*
6. *The roles that households, businesses, and governments play in our business system*

Consider this:

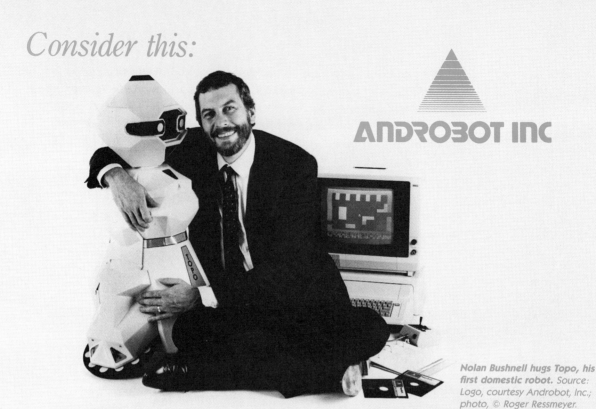

ANDROBOT INC

Nolan Bushnell hugs Topo, his first domestic robot. *Source: Logo, courtesy Androbot, Inc.; photo, © Roger Ressmeyer.*

Nolan Bushnell was president and owner of Atari, Inc., when that firm produced and marketed the first successful video games. These early devices played only a single game, but they were an instant hit with both arcade and home game players. Atari's sales and earnings grew rapidly, as did the value of the company itself. In 1976 Bushnell sold his ownership of Atari to Warner Communications, a firm that was primarily in the entertainment field. As part of the sale, Bushnell agreed not to compete against Warner in the video games business for seven years.

A year later, in 1977, the first cartridge-driven home video games were introduced. Buyers could use the new units to play a variety of games—rather than just one—merely by inserting different cartridges in the game console. Again the sales of Atari units rose sharply, and every purchaser of an Atari console became a potential customer for Atari cartridges—the video game software.

Soon the production of cartridges became more profitable than the production of consoles. Other firms, including Mattel Inc. (Intellivision), and Coleco Industries (Colecovision), began to market consoles and software to capture part of this profitable and growing market. And such firms as Activision (established by several former Atari employees) began to produce cartridges that could be used on Atari and other consoles. These firms were competing only in the more profitable software market; in effect, they were skimming the cream! They left the more costly and less profitable production of hardware to the large, established firms that had sufficient resources.

The console manufacturers continued to produce software, of course, but they also developed and marketed improved hardware—each trying to outdo the others in the kinds of games their products could play and in the variety of uses of their consoles. As a result of this competition among hardware manufacturers, console prices began to tumble. The Atari 2600 console (Atari's first cartridge-driven unit) sold for close to $200 at the end of 1979, but just before Christmas of 1983 it could be purchased for around $50 (after a manufacturer's rebate of $30). The prices of cartridges, however, remained steady or increased slightly in the same time period.

Nolan Bushnell was not sitting still while all this was going on. He had an idea, and the money from the sale of Atari, Inc., gave him the means to finance it. The result was Pizza Time Theatre, Inc., the home of Chuck E. Cheese—a chain of combination pizza restaurants and video arcades. The first Pizza Time Theatre was opened in California in 1978, and there are now about 200 of them around the country. Sales and profits soared in the first few years, but now they are declining. This decline may have resulted from the novelty wearing off, the fact that the theatres appeal mainly to children, or competition from another chain called ShowBiz Pizza Places. ShowBiz began in 1980 and features large, animated robot characters designed to appeal to a slightly older audience.[1]

Bushnell's agreement not to compete with Warner Communications ended in late 1983, and the industry is waiting to see what he has planned for his pizza-and-video arcades and for video games in general. But meanwhile, Bushnell has founded still another business, Androbot, Inc., to produce domestic robots. The first robots, called Topo, are now available. Although they are fairly primitive, they are mobile, are able to "learn" to move around a home or office without bumping into the furniture, and are capable of "speech" in English and almost any other language. Later, more sophisticated robots are expected to be able to communicate directly with people. Like home video consoles, they are designed to accept a variety of software.[2]

Perhaps the most important characteristic of American business is the freedom of individuals to start a business, to buy or sell ownership shares in a business, and to sell a business outright. Within certain limits imposed mainly to ensure public safety, the owners of a business can produce any product or service they choose and sell it at any price they set. This system of business, in which individuals decide what to produce, how to produce it, and at what price to sell it, is called **free enterprise**. It is rooted in our traditional and Constitutional right to own property.

This American system of free enterprise, for example, ensured the right of Nolan Bushnell to sell Atari, Inc., and then to launch Pizza Time, Androbot, and the several other companies he is associated with (see Figure 1.1). It also gave to Warner Communications the right to purchase Atari; to Mattel, an established toy and game manufacturer, the right to get into the video game

Figure 1.1 *Nolan Bushnell, the Entrepreneur. Thanks to the free enterprise system, Nolan Bushnell was able to found three different companies—and to leave them whenever he wished.*

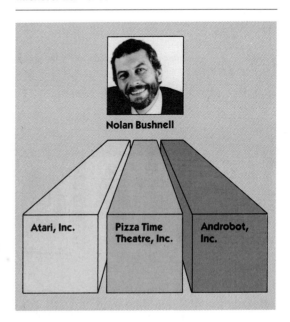

Nolan Bushnell

Atari, Inc. Pizza Time Theatre, Inc. Androbot, Inc.

business; and to the founders of Activision, the right to leave their jobs at Atari and create a firm whose product is sold in direct competition with one of Atari's products.

Competition such as that between Activision and Atari is a necessary and extremely important by-product of free enterprise. Because any individual can enter just about any business at any time, there are sure to be a number of firms offering similar products. But a potential customer will be satisfied with owning only one such product—say, a Topo or an RB5X robot—and does not usually purchase both. Each of the firms offering these similar products must therefore try to convince the potential customer to buy its particular product rather than a similar one made by somebody else. In other words, these firms must compete with each other for sales. Business **competition**, then, is essentially a rivalry among businesses for sales to potential customers. In free enterprise, it works to ensure the efficient and effective operation of American business. Competition also ensures that a firm will survive only if it serves its customers well. In March 1984, Pizza Time Theatres, Inc.—and Chuck E. Cheese—filed for bankruptcy. Two months later,

the management of Pizza Time met with the owners of ShowBiz Pizza Place to discuss the possibility of combining their businesses. Both parties hope that together they can form a strong, profitable business.

BUSINESS: A DEFINITION

Business is the organized effort of individuals to produce and sell, for a profit, the goods and services that satisfy society's needs. The general term *business* refers to all such efforts within a society (as in "American business") or within an industry (as in "the steel business"). However, *a business* is a particular organization, such as Eastern Airlines or Sunnyside Country Store & Gas Pumps, Inc.

The Organized Effort of Individuals

No person or group of persons actually organized American business as we know it today. Rather, over the years individuals have organized their own particular businesses, for their own particular reasons. All these individual businesses, and all the interactions between these businesses and

Figure 1.2 *Combining Resources. The effective combination of all four resources is necessary for a business to be successful.*

| material resources | human resources | financial resources | information resources | business |

their customers, have given rise to what we call American business.

A person who risks his or her time, effort, and money to start and operate a business is called an **entrepreneur**. To organize a business, an entrepreneur must combine four kinds of resources: material, human, financial, and informational. *Material* resources include the raw materials used in manufacturing processes, as well as buildings and machinery. *Human* resources are the people who furnish their labor to the business in return for wages. The *financial* resource is the money required to pay employees, purchase materials, and generally keep the business operating. And *information* is the resource that tells the managers of the business how effectively the other resources are being combined and utilized (see Figure 1.2).

Businesses are generally of three types. Manufacturing businesses (or *manufacturers*) are organized to process various materials into tangible goods, such as delivery trucks or towels. *Service businesses* produce services, such as haircuts or legal advice. And some firms—called *middlemen*—are organized to buy the goods produced by manufacturers and then resell them. For example, the General Electric Company is a manufacturer that produces clock radios and stereo "boxes," among other things. These products may be sold to a retailing middleman such as K mart, which then resells them to consumers in its retail stores. **Consumers** are individuals who purchase goods or services *for their own personal use* rather than to resell them.

Satisfying Needs

All three types of businesses may sell either to other firms or to consumers. In both cases, the ultimate objective of every firm must be to satisfy the needs of its customers. People generally don't buy goods and services simply to own them; they buy products to satisfy particular needs. People generally don't buy an automobile solely to store it in a garage; we do, however, buy automobiles to satisfy our need for transporta-

The first department store was the Marble Dry Goods Palace opened on Broadway by Alexander Turney Stewart in 1848. Stewart had been a poorly paid schoolmaster in Ireland before he emigrated to New York in 1823 and set up his own business. At the time of its erection, the Marble Dry Goods Palace was the largest shop in the world, extending the whole length of a city block. By 1876, the year of his death, Stewart's company had an annual turnover of $70 million a year, and his personal fortune was estimated at $80 million. A man of few personal attractions, he was never known to have given away any of his vast wealth.

Source: Patrick Robertson, *The Book of Firsts* (New York: Bramhall House, 1974) p. 48.

tion. Some of us may feel that this need is best satisfied by an air-conditioned Mercedes Benz with stereo cassette player, automatic transmission, power seats and windows, and remote-control side mirrors. Others may believe that a Ford Escort with a stick shift and an AM radio will do just fine. Both products are available to those who want them, along with a wide variety of other products that satisfy the need for transportation.

When the businesses that produce and sell goods and services understand their customers' needs and work to satisfy these needs, they are usually successful. But when firms lose sight of their customers' needs, they are likely to find the going rough. This is exactly what happened in the mid-1970s, when American auto manufacturers produced big, gas-guzzling cars and tried to sell them to consumers who needed fuel-efficient transportation. Consumers simply said "No, thanks" to Detroit and proceeded to buy smaller, more efficient foreign cars by the tens of thousands. The American auto makers didn't recover from the resulting sales slump until they produced what their customers wanted.

Some businesses, called middlemen, buy goods from manufacturers and sell them to consumers. Herman's Sporting Goods, a middleman, sells running shoes supplied by W. R. Grace. Source: Courtesy of W. R. Grace & Co.

Business Profit

In the course of normal operations, a business receives money (sales revenue) from its customers in exchange for goods or services. It must also pay out money to cover the various expenses involved in doing business. If the firm's sales revenue is greater than its expenses, it has earned a profit. More specifically, as shown in Figure 1.3, **profit** is the amount of money that remains after all business expenses have been deducted from sales revenue. (A negative profit, which results when a firm's expenses are greater than its sales revenue, is called a *loss*.)

The profit earned by a business becomes the property of its owners. So in one sense profit is the return, or reward, that business owners receive for producing goods and services that consumers want.

Profit is also the payment that business owners receive for assuming the considerable risks of ownership. One of these is the risk of not being paid. Everyone else—employees, suppliers, and lenders—must be paid before the owners. And if there is nothing left over (if there is no profit), there can be *no* payments to owners. A second risk that owners run is the risk of losing whatever they have put into the business. A business that cannot earn a profit is very likely to fail, in which case the owners lose whatever money, effort, and time they have invested. For entrepreneurs like Nolan Bushnell, the challenge of business is to earn a profit in spite of these risks.

THE ECONOMICS OF BUSINESS

Economics is the study of how wealth is created and distributed. By *wealth* we mean anything of value, including the products produced and sold by business. "How wealth is distributed" simply means "who gets what."

According to economic theory, every society must decide on the answers to three questions:

1. *What* goods and services—and how much of each—will be produced?
2. *How* will these goods and services be produced? (That is, who will produce them and which resources will be used to do so?)
3. *For whom* will these goods and services be produced? (This is the question "Who gets what?")

The way in which a society answers these questions (as shown in Figure 1.4), determines the kind of economic system, or **economy**, that society has chosen. In the United States, our particular answers have provided us with a *mixed* economy, which is based on laissez-faire capitalism, or private enterprise. Our free-enterprise business system is the practical application—the everyday workings—of this economic system.

Laissez-Faire Capitalism

Laissez-faire capitalism stems from the theories of Adam Smith, a Scot. In 1776, in his book *The Wealth of Nations,* Smith argued that a society's interests are best served when the individuals within that society are allowed to pursue their own self-interest.

> Every individual endeavors to employ his capital so that its produce may be of greatest value. . . . And he is in this led by an INVISIBLE HAND to promote an end which was no part of his intention. By pursuing his own interest he frequently promotes that of Society more effectually than when he really intends to promote it.

In other words, Smith believed that each person should be allowed to work toward his or her

own economic gain, without interference from government. In doing so, each person would unintentionally be working for the good of society as a whole. And society would benefit most when there was the least interference with this pursuit of economic self-interest. Government should therefore leave the economy to its citizens. The French term *laissez faire* implies that there shall be no interference in the economy; loosely translated, it means "let them do" (as they see fit). The features of laissez-faire capitalism are summarized on page 12 in Figure 1.5.

Private Ownership of Property Smith argued that the creation of wealth (including products) is properly the concern of private individuals, not of government. Hence the resources that are used to create wealth must be owned by private individuals. Economists recognize three categories of resources: *land,* including all natural resources; *labor,* which is the work performed by people; and *capital* or *capital goods,* a category that includes all the buildings, machinery, tools,

Figure 1.3 *The Relationship Between Sales Revenue and Profit*

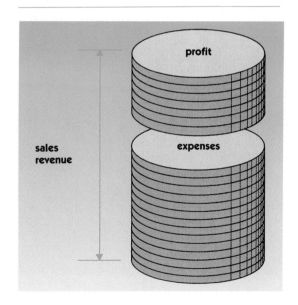

and equipment that are used in the actual production of goods and services. We have referred to these resources as material, human, and financial resources, and we shall continue to do so. (Nowadays, business people use the term **capital** to mean both capital goods and the money needed to purchase them. The private ownership and use of both kinds of capital give us the names *capitalism* and *private enterprise* for our economic system.)

Smith argued further that the owners of all three economic resources should be free to determine how these resources are used. They should also be free to enjoy the income and other benefits that they might derive from the ownership of these resources.

Figure 1.4 *The Basic Questions of the Economic System. How these three questions are answered determines the economy of every society.*

WHAT   goods and services will be produced?

HOW   will these goods and services be produced?

WHO   will receive these goods and services?

Economic Freedom   Smith's economic freedom extends to all those involved in the economy. For the owners of land and capital, this freedom includes the right to rent, sell, or invest their resources and the right to use their resources to produce any product and offer it for sale at the price they choose. For workers, this economic freedom means the right to accept or reject any job they are offered. For all individuals, economic freedom includes the right to purchase any good or service that is offered for sale by producers. These rights, however, do not include a guarantee of economic success. Nor do they include the right to harm others during the headlong pursuit of one's own self-interest.

Competitive Markets   A crucial part of Smith's theory is the competitive market composed of large numbers of buyers and sellers. (For now, think of a market as the interaction of the buyers and sellers of a particular type of product or resource, like shoes or secretarial skills. We shall discuss a more limited concept of market in Chapter 11.) Economic freedom ensures the existence of competitive markets, because sellers and buyers can enter markets as they choose. Sellers enter a market to earn profit, rent, or wages; buyers enter a market to purchase resources and want-satisfying products. Then, in a free market, sellers compete for sales and buyers compete for available goods, services, and resources.

This freedom to enter or leave a market at will has given rise to the name **free-market economy** for the capitalism that Smith described.

Limited Role of Government   In Smith's view, the role of government should be limited to providing defense against foreign enemies, ensuring internal order, and furnishing public works and education. With regard to the economy, government should act only as rule maker and umpire. As rule maker, government should provide laws that ensure economic freedom and promote competition. As umpire, it should act to settle disputes arising from conflicting interpretations of its laws. Government, according to Adam Smith, should have no major economic responsibilities beyond these.

What, How, and For Whom in the Free-Market Economy

Smith's laissez-faire capitalism sounds as though it should lead to chaos, not to answers to the three basic economic questions. How can millions of individuals and firms, all intent only on their own self-interest, produce an orderly economic system? One response might be simply, "They can and they do." Most of the industrialized nations of the world exhibit some form of modified capitalist economy, and these economies do work. A better response, however, is that these millions of individuals and firms actually provide very concrete and detailed answers to the three basic questions.

What to Produce? This question is answered continually by consumers as they spend their dollars in the various markets for goods and services. When consumers buy up every Cabbage Patch doll Coleco can produce, as they did late in 1983, they are casting "dollar votes" for more Cabbage Patch dolls. They are telling resource owners to produce more of this product and more of the capital goods with which the product is manufactured. In the gas shortage in the early 1970s, consumers began buying Datsuns and Toyotas rather than Fords and Chryslers. Losing these "dollar votes" meant a significant loss of profits for the U.S. auto industry. Chrysler Corporation almost went bankrupt and had to receive financial aid from the U.S. government to stay in business. Conversely, when consumers refuse to buy a product at its going price, they are voting against the product, telling producers to either reduce the price or ease off on production. In each case, consumers are giving a very specific answer concerning a very specific product.

How to Produce? The two parts of this question are answered by producers as they enter various

markets and compete for sales and profits. Those who produce for a particular market answer the question "Who will produce?" simply by being in that market. Their answer, of course, is "We will."

Competition within various markets determines which resources will be used. To compete as effectively as possible in the product markets, producers try to use the most efficient (least-cost) combination of resources. When a particular resource can be used to produce two or more different products, then producers must also compete with each other in the market for that resource. And, if the price of one needed resource becomes too high, producers will look for substitute resources—say, plastics in place of metals. The resources that will be used to produce are those that perform their function at the least cost.

For Whom to Produce?   In a market economy, goods are distributed to those who have the money to purchase them. This money is earned by individuals as wages, rents, profit, and interest—that is, as payment for the use of economic resources. Money is thus a medium of exchange, an artificial device that aids in the exchange of resources for goods and services (Figure 1.6). The distribution of goods and services ("who gets what") therefore depends on the *current prices* of economic resources and of the various goods and services. And prices, in turn, are determined by the balance of supply and demand.

PLANNED ECONOMIES

Before we discuss the workings of supply and demand in a market economy, we shall look

quickly at two other economic systems that contrast sharply with the capitalism of Adam Smith. These systems are sometimes called **planned economies**, because the answers to the three basic economic questions are determined, at least to some degree, through centralized government planning.

Socialism

In a *socialist* economy, the key industries are owned and controlled by the government. Such industries usually include transportation, utilities, communications, and those producing important materials such as steel. (In France, the major banks are in the process of being *nationalized,* or transferred to government control. Banking, too, is considered extremely important to a nation's economy.) Land and raw materials may also be the property of the state in a socialist economy. Depending on the country, private ownership of real property and smaller or less vital businesses

Figure 1.5   *The Features of Laissez-Faire Capitalism. New York's Park Row in the 1850s featured dozens of new shops full of ready-made merchandise. Source: The Bettmann Archive.*

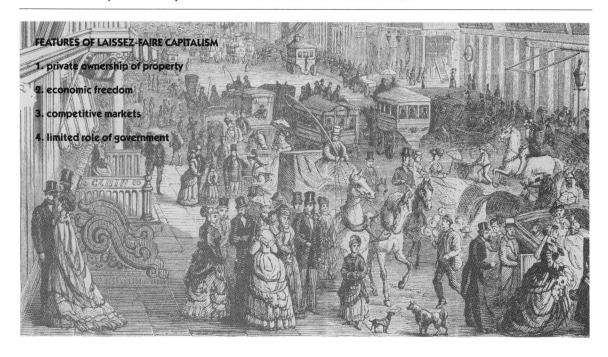

FEATURES OF LAISSEZ-FAIRE CAPITALISM

1. private ownership of property

2. economic freedom

3. competitive markets

4. limited role of government

is permitted to varying degrees. People usually may choose their own occupations, but many work in state-owned industries.

What to produce and how to produce it are determined in accordance with national goals, which are based on projected needs, and the availability of resources—at least for government-owned industries. The distribution of goods and services is also controlled by the state to the extent that it controls rents and wages. Among the professed aims of socialist countries are the equitable distribution of income, the elimination of poverty and the distribution of social services such as medical care to all who need them, smooth economic growth, and elimination of the waste that supposedly accompanies capitalist competition.

Britain, France, Sweden, and India are democratic countries whose mixed economies include a very visible degree of socialism. Other, more authoritarian countries may actually have socialist

economies; however, we tend to think of them as communist because of their almost total lack of freedom.

Communism

If Adam Smith was the father of capitalism, Karl Marx was the father of communism. In his writings (during the mid-nineteenth century), Marx advocated a classless society whose citizens together owned all economic resources. He believed that such a society would come about as the result of a class struggle between the owners of capital and the workers whom they had exploited. All workers would then contribute to this *communist* society according to their ability and would receive benefits according to their need.

The Soviet Union, the People's Republic of China, Cuba, North Vietnam, and the Eastern European countries are generally considered to have communist economies. Almost all economic

Figure 1.6 *The Circular Flow in Smith's Laissez-Faire Economy. The use of money enhances the exchange of goods and services for resources, gives rise to the resource and product markets, and helps answer the question "For whom to produce?"*

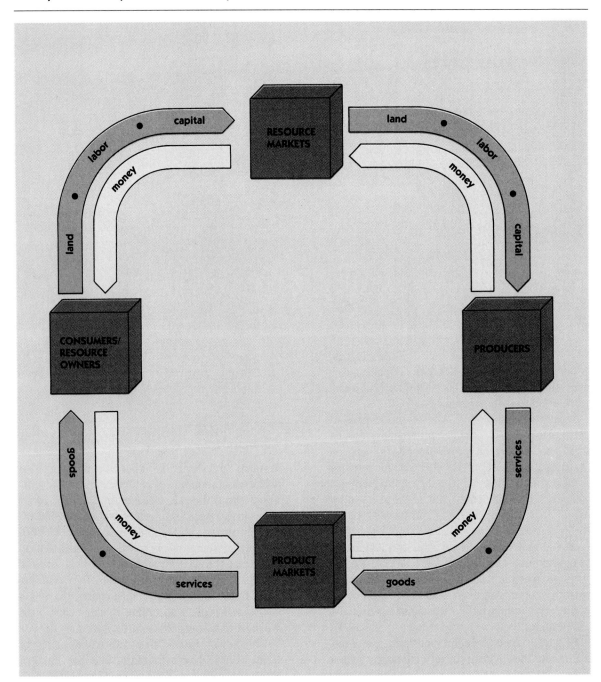

resources are owned by the government in these countries. The basic economic questions are answered through centralized state planning, which sets prices and wages as well. In this planning, the needs of the state generally outweigh the needs of its citizens. Emphasis is placed on the production of capital goods (such as heavy machinery) rather than on the products that consumers might want, so there are frequent shortages of consumer goods. Workers have little choice of jobs, but special skills or talents seem to be rewarded with special privileges. Various groups of professionals (bureaucrats, university professors, and athletes, for example) fare much better than, say, factory workers.

The so-called communist economies thus seem to be far from Marx's communism, but rather to practice a strictly controlled kind of socialism. (There is also a bit of free enterprise here and there. For example, communist China's planners recently decided to allow farmers to raise some crops for sale in free markets.) However, like all real economies, these economies are neither pure nor static. Every operating economy is a constantly changing mixture of various idealized economic systems. Some, like ours, evolve slowly. Others change more quickly, through either evolution or revolution. And, over many years, an economy may move first in one direction—say, toward capitalism—and then in the opposite direction. It is impossible to say whether any real economy will ever closely resemble Marx's communism.

SUPPLY, DEMAND, AND COMPETITION

As we have noted, a free-market system implies competition among sellers of products and resources. Economists recognize four different degrees of competition, ranging from an ideal complete competition to no competition at all. These are pure competition, monopolistic competition, oligopoly, and monopoly.

Pure Competition

Pure (or perfect) competition is the complete form of competition. **Pure competition** is the market situation in which there are many buyers and sellers of a product, and no single buyer or seller is powerful enough to affect the price of that product. Note that this definition includes several important ideas. First, we are discussing the market for a single product—say, bushels of wheat. (The definition also applies to markets for resources, but we'll limit our discussion here to products.) Second, all sellers offer essentially the same product for sale; a buyer would be just as satisfied with seller A's wheat as with that offered by seller B or seller Z. Third, all buyers and sellers know everything there is to know about

In communist and socialist economies, there is less emphasis on production of consumer goods. This often leads to shortages. Source: © Lou Jones.

the market (including, in our example, the prices that all sellers are asking for their wheat.) And fourth, the market is not affected by the actions of any one buyer or seller.

In such a situation, every seller would do best by asking the same price that every other seller is asking. Why is this so? Suppose one seller wanted 50 cents more than all the others per bushel of wheat. That seller would not be able to sell a single bushel, because buyers could—and would—do better by purchasing wheat from the competition. On the other hand, a firm that was willing to sell below the going price would sell all its wheat quickly. But that seller would lose sales revenue (and profit), because buyers are actually willing to pay more.

In pure competition, then, sellers—and buyers as well—must accept the going price. But who

or what determines this price? Actually, everyone does. The price of each product is determined by the actions of *all buyers and all sellers together,* through the forces of supply and demand. It is this interaction of buyers and sellers, working for their best interest, that Adam Smith referred to as the "invisible hand" of competition. Let us see how it operates.

Supply and Demand in Pure Competition

The **supply** of a particular product is the quantity of the product that producers are willing to sell at each of various prices. Supply is thus a relationship between prices and the quantities offered by producers. Producers are rational people, so we would expect them to offer more of a product for sale at higher prices and to offer less of the product at lower prices.

The **demand** for a particular product is the quantity that buyers are willing to purchase at each of various prices. Demand is thus a relationship between prices and the quantities purchased by buyers. Buyers, too, are usually rational, so we would expect them—as a group—to buy more of a product when its price is low and to buy less of the product when its price is high. (This is exactly what happened when the price of gasoline rose so dramatically in the middle and late 1970s. People drove less, joined or organized car pools, and used public transportation in order to reduce their purchases of gasoline. They began to buy more of it only when its price dropped somewhat.)

Of course, neither sellers nor buyers exist in a vacuum. What they do is interact within a market. (Recall our working definition of *market*.) And there is always one certain price at which the quantity of a product that is demanded is exactly equal to the quantity of that product that is produced. Suppose producers are willing to *supply* 2 million bushels of wheat at a price of $5 per bushel and that buyers are willing to *purchase* 2 million bushels at a price of $5 per bushel. In other words, supply and demand are in balance, or *in equilibrium,* at the price of $5. Therefore, if suppliers produce 2 million bushels then no one who is willing to pay $5 per bushel will have to go without wheat, and no producer who is willing to sell at $5 per bushel will be stuck with unsold wheat.

Obviously, $5 per bushel is the "going price" at which producers should sell their 2 million bushels of wheat. Economists call this price the *equilibrium price* or *market price.* Under pure competition, the **market price** of any product is the price at which the quantity demanded is exactly equal to the quantity supplied.

In theory and in the real world, market prices are affected by anything that affects supply and demand. The *demand* for wheat, for example, might change if researchers suddenly discovered that it had very beneficial effects on users' health.

Then more wheat would be demanded at every price. The *supply* of wheat might change if new technology permitted the production of greater quantities of wheat from the same amount of acreage. In that case, producers would be willing to supply more wheat at each price. Either of these changes would result in a new equilibrium and a new market price. Other changes that can affect competitive prices are shifts in buyer tastes, the development of new products that satisfy old needs, and fluctuations in income due to inflation or recession. For example, generic or "no-name" products are now available in supermarkets. Consumers can satisfy their needs for products ranging from food to drugs to paper products at a lower cost, with quality comparable to brand name items. Kellogg was recently forced to lower the price of its very popular cornflakes because of competition from generic products.

Monopolistic Competition

Pure competition is only a theoretical concept. Some specific markets (such as auctions of farm products) may come close, but no real market exhibits perfect competition. However, many real markets are examples of monopolistic competition. **Monopolistic competition** is a market situation in which there are many buyers along with relatively many sellers who differentiate their products from the products of competitors. The various products available in a monopolistically competitive market are very similar in nature, and they are all intended to satisfy the same need. However, each seller attempts to make its product somewhat different from the others by giving the product a brand name, through unique packaging or design, by offering services such as free delivery or a "lifetime" warranty, or in any of various other ways. Digital Equipment Corporation gives a free one-year service contract to people who buy its personal computer systems. This is one way that Digital can differentiate its products from those of competing computer companies like IBM and Apple.

Though all brie cheeses are essentially the same, it is the job of advertisers to try to differentiate their particular product by some means in order to persuade consumers to buy. *Source: Courtesy of Besnier USA, Inc.*

Product differentiation is a fact of life for the producers of many consumer goods, from soaps to clothing to personal computers. The individual producer sees what looks like a mob of competitors, all trying to chip away at its market. (Actually, monopolistic competition is characterized by fewer sellers than pure competition, but there are enough sellers to ensure a highly competitive market.) By differentiating its product from all similar products, the producer obtains some limited control over the market price of its product. For example, the current prices of the detergents All, Cheer, Fab, and Tide are each different from the others; under pure competition, the price of all laundry detergents would simply be the equilibrium price of laundry detergent.

Oligopoly

An **oligopoly** is a market situation (or industry) in which there are few sellers. Generally these sellers are quite large, and sizable investments are required to enter into their market. For this reason, oligopolistic industries tend to remain oligopolistic. Examples of oligopolies are the American automobile, steel, and aluminum industries.

Because there are few sellers in an oligopoly, each seller has considerable control over price. At the same time, the market actions of each seller can have a strong effect on competitors' sales. If one firm reduces its price, the other firms in the industry usually do the same to retain their share of the market. If one firm raises its price, the others may wait and watch the market for a while, to see whether their lower price tag gives them a competitive advantage, and then eventually follow suit. All this wariness usually results in similar prices for similar products. In the absence of much price competition, product differentiation becomes the major competitive weapon; this is very evident in the advertising of the major American auto manufacturers.

Monopoly

A **monopoly** is a market (or industry) with only one producer. Because only one firm is the supplier of a product, it has complete control over price. However, no firm can set its price at some astronomical figure just because there is no competition; the firm would soon find that there is no sales revenue, as well. Instead, the firm in a monopoly position must consider the demand for its product and set the price at the most profitable level.

The few monopolies in American business don't have even that much leeway in setting prices because they are all carefully regulated by government. Each of them operates in a **natural**

monopoly, an industry that requires a huge investment in capital and within which any duplication of facilities would be wasteful. Most monopolies in America are public utilities, such as we find in electric power distribution. They are permitted to exist because the public interest is best served by their existence, but they operate under the scrutiny and control of various state and federal agencies.

Except for such regulated monopolies, federal laws prohibit not only monopolies but also attempts to form them. The Sherman Antitrust Act of 1890 made any such attempt a criminal offense, and the Clayton Antitrust Act of 1914 prohibited a number of specific actions that could lead to monopoly. The goal of these and other antitrust laws is to ensure the competitive environment of American business.

THE DEVELOPMENT OF AMERICAN BUSINESS

American business and the American economy developed together with the nation itself. All three have their roots in the knowledge, skills, and values that were brought to this country by the earliest settlers. Refer to Figure 1.7 for an overall view of the relationship between our history and economy, and some of the major inventions that had an influence on them.

The Colonial Period

The first settlers in the New World were concerned mainly with providing themselves with the necessities—food, clothing, and shelter. Almost all families lived on farms, and the entire family worked at the business of surviving.

The colonists did indeed survive, and eventually they were able to produce more than they consumed. They used their surplus for trading, mainly by barter, among themselves and with the English trading ships that called at the colonies. As this trade increased and capital was accumulated, small-scale business enterprises began to

The first cash register was patented by James J. Ritty of Dayton, Ohio, on 4 November 1879. Ritty owned a saloon on Main Street in Dayton, and constant pilfering by his bartenders so undermined his health that he took a sea voyage to Europe to recover. While on board the liner his attention was attracted by a machine used to record the number of revolutions made by the propellers; it was this that gave him the idea from which the basic principle of the cash register is derived. After taking out the patent he continued to work on improvements and in 1884 the National Cash Register Co. was formed to exploit his invention.

Source: Patrick Robertson, *The Book of Firsts* (New York: Bramhall House, 1974) p. 33.

appear. The predominant form of ownership was the *sole proprietorship,* a business owned by only one individual. Most of these firms produced farm products, primarily rice and tobacco for export. Other industries that had been founded by 1700 were shipbuilding, lumbering, fur trading, rum manufacturing, and fishing. These industries too produced mainly for export. Trade with England grew, but British trade policies heavily favored British merchants.

About 90 percent of the population was still engaged in farming. As late as the Revolutionary War period, farm families were engaged primarily in meeting their own needs. Some were able to use their skills and whatever time they had left over to work under the domestic system of production. The **domestic system** was a method of manufacturing in which an entrepreneur distributed raw materials to various homes, where families would process them into finished goods. The goods were then offered for sale by the merchant entrepreneur.

During and after the Revolutionary War, Americans began to produce a wider variety of goods, including gunpowder, tools, hats, and cutlery.

Later, after the War of 1812, domestic manufacturing and trade became much more important as trade with England and other nations declined. The timing may be coincidental, but American industry began to grow in earnest just when Adam Smith's economic theory was becoming widespread. In any case, private ownership of resources and free enterprise were already a part of American political and business life.

The Industrial Revolution

In 1790 a young English apprentice mechanic named Samuel Slater decided to sail to America. At this time, to protect the English textile industry, British law forbade the export of machinery, technology, and skilled workers. To get around the law, Slater painstakingly memorized the plans for Arkwright's water-powered spinning machine and left England disguised as a farmer. A year later he set up a textile factory in Pawtucket, Rhode Island, to spin raw cotton into thread. Slater's ingenuity resulted in America's first use of the **factory system** of manufacturing, in which all the materials, machinery, and workers required to manufacture a product are assembled in one place.

By 1814 Francis Cabot Lowell had established a factory in Waltham, Massachusetts, to spin, weave, and bleach cotton all under one roof. He organized the various manufacturing steps into one uninterrupted sequence, hired professional

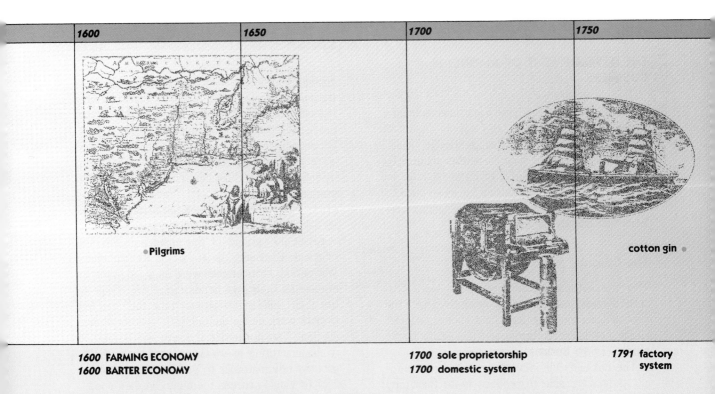

| 1600 | 1650 | 1700 | 1750 |

•Pilgrims

cotton gin •

1600 **FARMING ECONOMY**
1600 **BARTER ECONOMY**

1700 sole proprietorship
1700 domestic system

1791 factory system

managers, and was able to produce 30 miles of cloth each day! In doing so, Lowell seems to have made use of another concept put forth by Adam Smith: specialization. **Specialization** is the separation of a manufacturing process into distinct tasks and the assignment of different tasks to different individuals. Its purpose is to increase the efficiency of industrial workers.

With Lowell's factory the Industrial Revolution, which had already started in England, arrived in America. The three decades from 1820 to 1850 were the golden age of invention and innovation in machinery. The cotton gin of Eli Whitney greatly increased the supply of cotton for the textile industry. Elias Howe's sewing machine became available to convert materials into clothing. The agricultural machinery of John Deere and Cyrus McCormick revolutionized farm production.

At the same time, new means of transportation greatly expanded the domestic markets for American products. The Erie Canal was opened in the 1820s. Soon, thanks to Robert Fulton's engine, steamboats appeared that could move up-

Figure 1.7 *Time Line Showing the Development of American Business from the Pilgrims to the Present. Notice how invention and innovation naturally led to changes in transportation. This in turn caused a shift to more of a manufacturing economy. Source:* A Nation of Nations, *Peter Marzio, ed., Harper & Row Publishers. Copyright © 1976 Smithsonian Institution.*

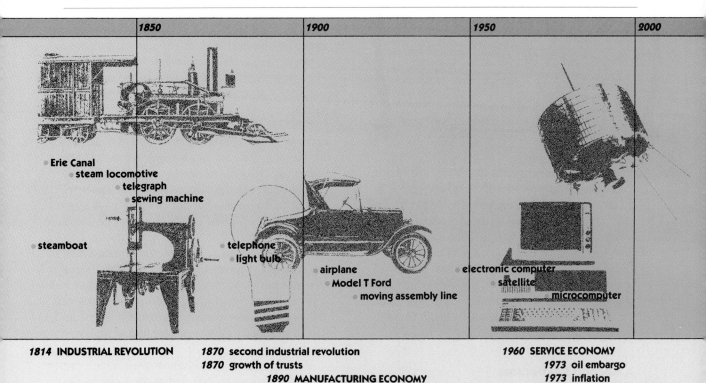

| 1850 | 1900 | 1950 | 2000 |

- Erie Canal
  - steam locomotive
    - telegraph
    - sewing machine
- steamboat
  - telephone
  - light bulb
    - airplane
    - Model T Ford
      - moving assembly line
- electronic computer
  - satellite
    - microcomputer

1814 **INDUSTRIAL REVOLUTION**
1870 second industrial revolution
1870 growth of trusts
1890 **MANUFACTURING ECONOMY**
1917 World War I
1918 large corporations
1918 **MODERN BUSINESS**
1930 Great Depression
1941 World War II
1960 **SERVICE ECONOMY**
1973 oil embargo
1973 inflation

The prosperity of the 1920s encouraged the public to buy high-priced items on credit. Unfortunately, the bubble would burst all too soon. *Source: Courtesy of Loftis Brothers and Co.*

stream against the current; they were able to use the rivers as highways for hauling bulk goods. In the 1830s and 1840s, the railroads began to extend the existing transportation system to the west, carrying goods and people much farther than was possible by waterways alone. Between 1860 and 1880 the number of miles of railroad track tripled; by 1900 it had doubled again. The phenomenal growth of the railroads in these four decades paralleled the industrial growth that the railroads had fostered.[3]

A Second Revolution

Many business historians view the period from 1870 to 1900 as the second industrial revolution; certainly, many of the characteristics of our modern business system took form during these three decades. In this period, for example, the nation shifted from a farm economy to a manufacturing economy. The developing oil industry provided fuel for light, heat, and energy. Greatly increased immigration furnished the labor for expanded production. New means of communication brought sophistication to banking and finance. All the tools of industrialization were at hand and Smith's private enterprise was put to work. The United States became not only an industrial giant but a leading world power as well.

Industrial growth and prosperity continued well into the twentieth century. Henry Ford's moving assembly line, which brought the work to the worker, refined the concept of specialization and spawned the mass production of consumer goods. By the 1920s the automobile industry had begun to influence the entire economy. The steel industry, which supplies materials to the auto industry, grew along with it. The oil and chemical industries grew just as fast and provided countless new synthetic products—new ways to satisfy society's wants. And the emerging airplane and airline industries promised better and faster transportation.

Fundamental changes occurred in business ownership and management as well. The largest businesses were no longer each owned by one individual; instead, ownership was in the hands of thousands of corporate shareholders who were willing to invest in—but not to operate—a business. A new breed of business professional emerged to manage the huge and growing corporations. To prepare these business managers, colleges and universities began to offer degree programs in accounting, production, industrial engineering, and marketing. New philosophies of business management and personnel relations focused attention on human problems and employee morale.

Certain modern marketing techniques are products of this era, too. Large corporations developed new methods of advertising and selling. Time payment plans made it possible for the average consumer to purchase costly durable goods, such as automobiles, appliances, and furnishings. Advertisements counseled the public to "buy now and pay later." A higher standard of living was indeed created for most people—but it was not to last.

The Great Depression

The "roaring twenties" ended with the sudden crash of the stock market in 1929 and the near collapse of the economy. The Great Depression that followed in the 1930s was a time of misery and human suffering. The unemployment rate varied between 16 and 25 percent in the years 1931 through 1939, and the value of goods and services produced in America fell by almost half. Business investment came to a complete halt. People lost their faith in business and its ability to satisfy the needs of society without government interference.

After the election of President Franklin D. Roosevelt, the federal government devised a number of programs to get the economy moving again. In implementing these programs, the government got deeply involved in business for the first time—as both a regulator of business activity and a provider of social services to individuals. Many business people opposed this government intervention, but they reluctantly accepted the fact that they were no longer operating within a purely capitalist economy.

Recovery and Beyond

The economy was on the road to recovery when World War II broke out in Europe in 1939. The need for vast quantities of war materials—first for our allies and then for the American military as well—spurred business activity and technological development. This rapid economic pace continued after the war, and the 1950s and 1960s witnessed both increasing production and a rising standard of living. **Standard of living** is a loose, subjective measure of how well off an individual or a society is, mainly in terms of want satisfaction through goods and services.

In the mid-1970s, however, a shortage of crude oil, along with constantly rising prices for petro-

Not only did the stock market crash and hundreds of firms go out of business, but even the banks failed during the Depression. Unhappy crowds formed outside a branch of the Bank of the United States, which closed in December 1930. Source: AP, Wide World Photos.

leum products, led to a new set of problems for business. Petroleum products supply most of the energy required to produce goods and services and to transport goods around the world. As the cost of petroleum products increased, the cost of energy increased along with it, and the cost of goods and services increased as well. The result was **inflation**, a general rise in the level of prices, at a rate well over 10 percent per year. Interest rates also increased dramatically, so borrowing by both businesses and consumers was reduced. Business profits fell as the consumer's purchasing power was eroded by inflation and high interest rates, and unemployment reached alarming levels.

These problems seem now to have been solved—at least partially. The inflation rate, interest rates, and unemployment have all declined. Consumers have become more willing to spend money, and business people are cautiously optimistic. Production is again increasing. In 1983, for example, the gross national product of the

U.S. economy rose to over $3.5 trillion ($3,500,000,000,000). The **gross national product** (GNP) of a nation is the total value of all goods and services produced by that nation in a certain period of time, usually one year. Services, as a matter of fact, have become a dominant part of our economy. Since well over half of the American workforce is involved in service industries, ours is often called a **service economy**. (Service economy is discussed more fully in Chapter 7.) If GNP is any indication at all of a country's standard of living, then ours is high and moving higher.

OUR BUSINESS SYSTEM TODAY

So far we have looked at several different aspects of our business system. Its theoretical basis is the laissez-faire economic system of Adam Smith. However, our real-world economy is not so "laissez-faire" as Smith would have liked, because government participates as more than umpire and rule maker. Ours is, in fact, a **mixed economy**, one that exhibits elements of both capitalism and socialism.

We also looked at the development of our business system. Again we saw government participation, which began in earnest during the Great Depression of the 1930s and has generally increased since those years, for a variety of economic and social reasons. Our business system is still guided by the interplay of buyers and sellers, but obviously the role of government must also be taken into account.

In today's economy, then, the three basic economic questions (what, how, and for whom) are answered by three groups:

1. *Households,* made up of consumers who seek the best value for their money and the best prices for the economic resources they own
2. *Businesses,* which seek to maximize their long-term profits
3. *Federal, state, and local governments,* which seek to promote public safety and welfare and to serve the public interest

The interactions among these three groups are shown in Figure 1.8, which is actually Figure 1.6 with government included.

Households

Households are both consumers of goods and owners of the productive resources of land, labor, and capital. (These resources are also called the **factors of production** to emphasize their importance in the creation of wealth.) As *resource owners,* the members of households provide businesses with the means of production. In return, businesses pay rent, wages, and interest, which households receive as income.

As *consumers,* household members use this income to purchase the goods and services produced by business. Today almost two-thirds of our nation's GNP consists of **consumer goods**: products purchased by individuals for personal consumption. (The remaining one-third is purchased by business and government.) This means that consumers, as a group, are the biggest customer of American business. So it should come as no surprise that business does as consumers wish. And, as we saw earlier, consumers make their wishes known through their "dollar votes."

Business

Like households, businesses are engaged in two exchanges. They exchange money for the factors of production, and they use these resources to produce goods and services. Then they exchange their products for sales revenue. This sales revenue, in turn, is exchanged for additional resources, which are used to produce and sell more products. So the circular flow of Figure 1.8 is continuous: Business pays *wages, rent, and interest* which becomes *household income* which becomes *consumer spending* which becomes *sales revenue* which again becomes *wages, rent, and interest.* And so on.

Along the way, of course, business owners would like to remove something from the circular flow in the form of profits. And households try to

Figure 1.8 *The Circular Flow in Our Modified Capitalist System Today*

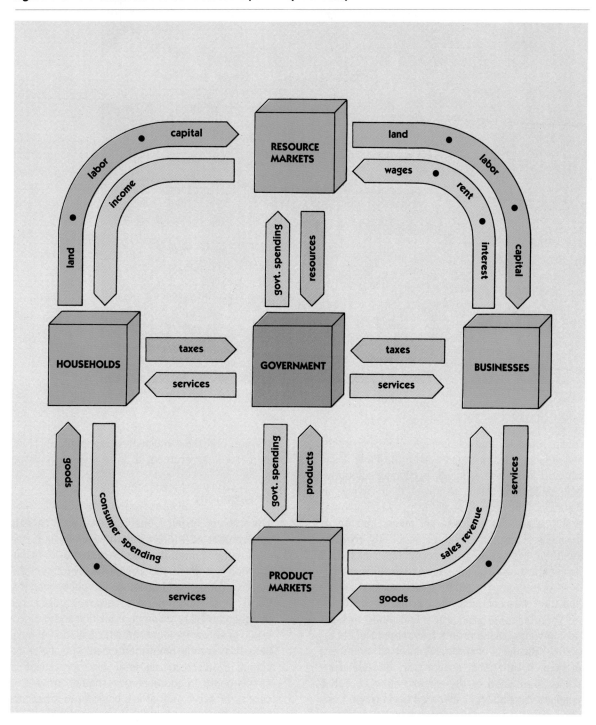

retain some income as savings. But are profits and savings really removed from the flow? Usually not! When the economy is running smoothly, households are willing to invest their savings in business. They can do so directly, by buying ownership shares in business or lending money to business. They can also invest indirectly, by placing their savings in bank accounts; banks then invest these savings as part of their normal business operations. In either case, savings usually find their way back into the circular flow.

When business profits are distributed to business owners, these profits become household income. (Business owners are, after all, members of households.) And, as we saw, household income is retained in the circular flow as either consumer spending or invested savings. So business profits, too, are retained in the business

system, and the circular flow is complete. How, then, does government fit in?

Government

The framers of our Constitution desired as little government interference with business as possible. At the same time, the Preamble to the Constitution set forth the responsibility of government to protect and promote the public welfare. Local, state, and federal governments discharge this responsibility through regulation and the provision of services. Government regulation of business has already been mentioned; specific regulations are discussed in detail in various chapters of this book. In addition, government provides a variety of services that are considered important but either (1) would not be produced by private firms in a free-enterprise system or (2) would be produced only for those who could afford them. Among these services are

- National defense
- Police and fire protection
- Welfare payments and retirement income
- Education
- National and state parks, forests, and wilderness areas
- Roads and highways
- Disaster relief
- Unemployment insurance programs
- Medical research
- Development of purity standards for foods and drugs

This list could go on and on, but the point is clear: Government is deeply involved in business life. To pay for all these services, governments collect a variety of taxes from households (such as personal income taxes and sales taxes) and from businesses (corporate income taxes).

Figure 1.8 shows this exchange of taxes for government services. It also shows government's spending of tax dollars for the resources and products required to provide these services. In other words, government, too, returns all its income to the business system through the resource and product markets. The circular flow of business activity, including government, is thus complete and self-contained. That is, the system works.

Actually, with government included, our so-called circular flow looks more like a combination of several flows. And in reality it is. The important point is that, together, the various flows make up a single unit—a complete system that effectively provides answers to the basic economic questions.

THE CHALLENGES AHEAD

There it is—the American business system in brief. When it works well, it provides jobs for those who are willing to work, a standard of living that few countries can match, and almost unlimited opportunity for personal advancement. But, like every other system devised by humans, it is far from perfect. Our business system may give us prosperity, but it also gave us the Great Depression of the 1930s and the economic problems of the 1970s and early 1980s. And, in spite of the economic recovery of 1983, at the end of that year 9 million Americans who wanted jobs couldn't find them. At the same time, almost 12 percent of the population had incomes below the government-designated poverty level.

The system obviously can be improved. It may need no more than a bit of fine tuning, or it may require something more extensive. Certainly there are plenty of people who are willing to tell us exactly what *they* think it needs. But these people provide us only with conflicting opinions. Who is right and who is wrong? Even the experts can't agree.

The experts do agree, however, that several key issues will challenge our business system over the next decade or two. Some of the questions to be resolved are:

- How much government involvement in our economy is necessary for its continued well-being? In what areas should there be less involvement? In what areas, more?
- How can we balance national growth with the conservation of natural resources and the protection of our environment?
- How can we evaluate the long-term economic costs and benefits of various existing and proposed government programs?
- How can we hold down inflation and yet stimulate the economy to provide jobs for all who want to work?
- How can we preserve the benefits of competition in our American economic system and still meet the needs of the less fortunate?

The answers to such questions are anything but simple. Yet they will directly affect our own future, our children's future, and that of our nation. Within the American economic and political system, the answers are ours to provide.

Chapter Review

SUMMARY

Business is the organized effort of individuals to produce and sell, for a profit, the goods and services that satisfy society's needs. Four kinds of resources—material, human, financial, and informational—must be combined to start and operate a business. The three general types of businesses are manufacturers, service businesses, and middlemen.

Profit is what remains after all business expenses are deducted from sales revenue. It is thus the payment that business owners receive for assuming the risks of business: primarily the risk of not receiving payment and the risk of losing whatever has been invested in the firm. Most often, a business that is operated in such a way as to satisfy its customers earns a reasonable profit.

An economic system is a means of deciding what goods and services will be produced, how they will be produced, and for whom they will be produced. The pure laissez-faire capitalism of Adam Smith is an economic system in which these decisions are made by individuals and businesses as they pursue their own self-interest. In a laissez-faire capitalist system, the factors of production are owned by private individuals, and all individuals are free to use (or not to use) their resources as they see fit; prices are determined by the workings of supply and demand in competitive markets; and the economic role of government is limited to being the protector of competition.

Four degrees of competition among sellers are recognized by economists. Ranging from most competitive to least are: pure competition, monopolistic competition, oligopoly, and monopoly.

Planned economies are those in which government, rather than individuals, owns the factors of production and provides the answers to the three basic economic questions. Socialist and communist economies are—at least in theory—planned economies. In the real world, however, no economy attains "theoretical perfection."

Since its beginnings in the seventeenth century, American business has been based on private ownership of property and freedom of enterprise. And from this beginning, through the Industrial Revolution of the early nineteenth century, to the phenomenal expansion of American industry in the nineteenth and early twentieth centuries, our government maintained an essentially laissez-faire attitude toward business. However, during the Great Depression of the 1930s, the federal government began to provide a number of social services to its citizens. Government's role in business has been expanded continually since that time.

Our economic system is thus a mixed economy—capitalism cut with some socialism. Our present business system is called modified capitalism; it is essentially capitalist in nature, but government takes part in it along with households and businesses. In the circular flow that characterizes our business system, households and businesses exchange resources for goods and services, using money as the medium of exchange. Government collects taxes from businesses and households and uses tax revenues to purchase the resources and products with which to provide its services.

The American business system is not perfect by any means, but it does work reasonably well. We shall discuss some of its problems in the next chapter, wherein we examine the role of business as a part of American society.

KEY TERMS

You should now be able to define and give an example relevant to each of the following terms:

free enterprise

competition

business

entrepreneur

consumers

profit

economics

economy

laissez-faire capitalism

capital

free-market economy

planned economy

pure competition

supply

demand

market price

monopolistic competition

oligopoly

monopoly

natural monopoly

domestic system

factory system

specialization

standard of living

inflation

gross national product

service economy

mixed economy

factors of production

consumer goods

QUESTIONS AND EXERCISES

Review Questions

1. What is meant by free enterprise? Why does free enterprise naturally lead to competition among sellers of products?
2. Describe the four resources that one must combine to organize and operate a business. How do they differ from the economist's factors of production?
3. Describe the relationship among profit, business risk, and the satisfaction of customers' needs.
4. What distinguishes consumers from other buyers of goods and services?
5. Describe the four main ingredients of a laissez-faire capitalist economy.
6. What are the three basic economic questions? How are they answered in a capitalist economy? In a planned economy?
7. Identify and compare the four forms of competition that are recognized by economists.
8. Explain how the market price of a product is determined under pure competition.
9. Trace the steps that led from farming for survival in the American colonial period to today's mass production.
10. Why is the American economy called a mixed economy?
11. Outline the economic interactions between government and business in our business system. Outline those between government and households.
12. What basic rights are accorded to individuals and businesses in our modified capitalist business system?

Discussion Questions

1. When Nolan Bushnell agreed not to compete against Warner Communications in the video game market for seven years, did he violate the concept of free enterprise? Did Warner violate it by asking Bushnell not to compete?

2. Why did the price of video game cartridges remain steady while the price of consoles like the Atari 2600 fell drastically?
3. Does one individual consumer really have a voice in answering the three basic economic questions?
4. Discuss this statement: Business competition encourages efficiency of production and leads to improved product quality.
5. What factors caused American business to develop into a modified capitalist system rather than some other type of system?
6. Is gross national product really a reliable indicator of a nation's standard of living? What might be a better indicator?
7. In our business system, how is government involved in answering the three basic economic questions? Does government participate in the system or interfere with it?

Exercises

1. Choose a type of business that you are familiar with or interested in. Then list the *specific* material, human, financial, and informational resources that you would have to combine to start such a business.
2. Cite four methods (other than pricing) that American auto manufacturers use to differentiate their products. (The best way to do this is to scan their magazine and newspaper ads.) Rate these methods from least effective to most effective, using your own judgment and experience.
3. A retailing middleman like K mart does not process goods in any way, yet it helps satisfy consumer wants. List and explain several ways in which it does so.

CASE 1-1

What's Happening in China?

The planned economy of the People's Republic of China isn't really in trouble, but it has been moving very slowly. Chinese planners are faced with high youth unemployment, low productivity, and inefficiency in state-run factories. In an attempt to get things going, planners have lately instituted a number of reforms; these changes tend to shift China's economy away from the strict state ownership and control that had previously characterized it:

□ Farming. Farmland is still owned by the state, but small plots (about 1½ acres each) are assigned to individual farm families. In return for exclusive use of its plot, each family must deliver a certain output to the state. Any surplus output may be sold by the family in urban markets, at what is essentially the going price—determined by supply and demand.
□ State-owned factories. Except in strategic industries, factory managers now have some freedom to plan production and sell excess output (as farm families can). They may determine the number of employees to hire and what wages to pay them; and they may offer bonuses to more productive workers. Moreover, management may decide how to spend the money that remains after all expenses are paid—the money that is called *profit* in capitalist economies.
□ Private firms. Small privately owned enterprises are not only tolerated, but are also encouraged—through interest-free loans and temporary tax exemptions. Most of these new businesses seem to be started by young people who are unwilling to take jobs in the state-run factories. The Chinese entrepreneurs (such as Zhen Zhi Cheng, who sells barbecued geese to commuters in the city of Guangzhou) may earn more than factory managers.

□ Advertising! New Chinese advertising—mostly through billboards and neon signs—generally promotes factories and industrial goods. (A very popular ad at present is one for ball bearings.) Representatives of a Madison Avenue advertising firm were recently invited to China to discuss their field with government marketing officials.

Chinese planners are thus looking to individual initiative and private enterprise to help solve their country's economic problems. Each of these changes is, by itself, relatively small in scale. But together, they seem to add up to something that might be called "rice-bowl capitalism."[4]

1. Which features of capitalism are evident in the reforms instituted by Chinese planners?
2. Why would Chinese planners be interested in Madison Avenue type advertising for the products of state-run factories—which have no competition?

CASE 1-2
The Manhattan Company

One of the oldest existing firms in the United States began as the Manhattan Company in 1799. In that year, the city and state of New York authorized the firm to supply pure water to New York City, which was in the midst of a yellow-fever epidemic. The firm was organized by a group of citizens led by the political rivals Aaron Burr and Alexander Hamilton.

Hamilton did not, however, know that Burr had more on his mind than supplying water. Burr wanted to develop a bank that could challenge two large banks that were run by Hamilton's political allies. Without Hamilton's knowledge, Burr had a seemingly harmless clause inserted in the charter that permitted the Manhattan Company to engage in other business with excess funds.

Not surprisingly, the managers of the Manhattan Company soon found that the water-supply system would not require all their capital. So, within six months of its founding, the firm had opened the Bank of the Manhattan Company on Wall Street. Burr's deception fueled the antagonism that already existed between Hamilton and Burr. Their dispute was settled forever in 1804, when Burr killed Hamilton in a duel.

Meanwhile, the bank became quite successful, but the water-supply operation did not. In 1808, the Manhattan Company was permitted to sell the water system to New York City and concentrate on banking.

One hundred forty-seven years later, the Bank of Manhattan was merged with the Chase National Bank. The result of that merger—the Chase Manhattan Bank—was once the largest bank in the United States. Now, however, it has slipped to third place (see Table 15.1).[5]

1. What type of business is the Chase Manhattan Bank? What are its goods or services?
2. Are banks needed in non-capitalist economies? Explain.

CHAPTER TWO

Social Responsibility in Business

Let's suppose that we are all perfectly responsible citizens. Among other things, we vote at election time; we don't lie, cheat, or steal; we don't litter; we're blind to the color of our neighbor's skin; and when we see someone in trouble, we do our best to help. Can we forget all this once we enter the business world? Do we have a greater responsibility to the profit motive than to society? At one time, many thought the answer to these questions might be yes, but most have realized that they were mistaken. In this chapter, you will see why. After studying the chapter, you should understand:

1. *The background for present concern about the social responsibility of business*
2. *The reasons for the consumer movement, and some of its results*
3. *How present employment practices are being used to counteract past abuses*
4. *The various types of pollution, their causes, and their cures*
5. *The factors involved in business ethics*
6. *The steps a business should take in implementing its awareness of its social responsibility*

Consider this:

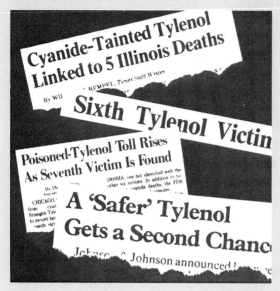

You walk into a drugstore, buy a bottle of cough medicine or headache tablets, carry it home, and take the recommended dosage. How can you be sure the drug you took is safe—that the contents of the bottle haven't been tampered with? Americans found themselves asking this question when seven people in the Chicago area died after taking Extra-Strength Tylenol capsules laced with cyanide.

The tragedy began on September 29, 1982, when 12-year-old Mary Ann Kellerman of Elk Grove Village took a Tylenol capsule for a sore throat. A short time later she died. The next day, Adam Janus collapsed after taking Tylenol capsules at his home in Arlington. He was rushed to a hospital but he, too, died. His brother Stanley and his sister-in-law Theresa went to Adam's house, where they took Tylenol capsules to ease headaches brought on by shock and grief. Both collapsed and were rushed to the same hospital. At this point, one of the doctors at the hospital suspected poisoning and called in a team of medical examiners.

After analyzing Extra-Strength Tylenol capsules taken from the Janus home, the medical examiners concluded that the capsules had been pulled apart and the medication replaced with deadly cyanide.

The management of Johnson & Johnson, the manufacturer of Tylenol, immediately saw that the Tylenol crisis was a major public health problem as well as a threat to the company. They made a series of quick and responsible decisions intended to safeguard the general public. James E. Burke, chairman of the board, took charge of efforts to get to the bottom of the problem.

It soon became clear that the tampering had occurred after the capsules had left the company's plants. Nevertheless, Burke suggested to the FBI and the U.S. Food and Drug Administration (FDA) that Tylenol be recalled—removed from store shelves throughout the country. Government officials argued against this action. They feared that a recall would encourage the perpetrators to believe they had brought a major corporation to its knees. The FDA also argued that a recall could cause even more public anxiety than it would relieve.

The next day, however, after a "copycat" poisoning in California, Johnson & Johnson issued a voluntary recall of over 31 million bottles of Tylenol with a retail value of over $100 million. In addition, through the various advertising media, the firm urged consumers to return any Tylenol they had on hand; everyone who did so would receive a full refund, even for a partially used package.

In the weeks that followed, executives at Johnson & Johnson were forced to decide whether to scrap Tylenol or try to rebuild the product's image. They decided to bring Tylenol back, even though marketing experts believed it would be impossible for the product to regain its former top position in the market.

Burke appointed a group of key executives to oversee the company's comeback effort. The first problem was to devise a tamper-proof container, and Johnson & Johnson came up with a new triple-sealed package. Johnson & Johnson then hired a major advertising firm, Young and Rubicam, to determine consumer attitudes toward Tylenol.

Polls taken by the advertising firm yielded the following information:

- 87 percent of Tylenol users said they realized the maker of Tylenol was not at fault
- 61 percent still said they were not likely to buy Tylenol in the future
- 50 percent said they would not buy Tylenol *tablets,* even though it was the capsules that had been altered

Next the company aired a series of 60-second advertisements on network television for 4 days. In these ads, Dr. Thomas N. Gates, Johnson & Johnson's medical director, said, "The company will reintroduce capsules in new tamper-proof containers as quickly as possible. Tylenol has had the trust of the medical profession and 100 million Americans for over 20 years. We value that trust too much to let any individual tamper with it. We want you to continue to trust Tylenol."[1]

Johnson & Johnson then placed over 75 million coupons, each worth $2.50 toward Tylenol products, in Sunday newspapers. From the beginning, the company knew it would have to rely on heavy coupon and television advertising if Tylenol were to make a comeback.

Six months later, Johnson & Johnson had spent millions but Tylenol sales were on the way up. Despite the doomsday predictions of marketing experts, Tylenol's market share had increased from 4 percent to 24 percent, which was just 11 percent below its share when the bizarre killings began.[2]

Tylenol's quick sales rebound is a result of restored public confidence due to responsible decision making by management. Johnson & Johnson acted first in the interest of public safety—to ensure that no more murders were committed with Tylenol capsules. Only after that goal was accomplished did it turn to the task of rebuilding Tylenol's reputation and sales.

If the decision to bring Tylenol back was a profitable one, the profit is well deserved. Johnson & Johnson spent millions of dollars to live up to what it saw as its responsibility to consumers. Consumers, in turn, are now giving evidence of renewed confidence by purchasing Tylenol products.

Social responsibility is the recognition that business activities have an impact on society, and the consideration of that impact in business decision making. Obviously, social responsibility costs money. It is perhaps not so obvious—except in isolated cases—that social responsibility is good business. Consumers eventually find out which firms are acting responsibly and which are not. And, just as easily as they cast their dollar votes *for* Tylenol, they can vote against the firm that is polluting the air or waterways, against the food product that contains the insecticide EDB, and against the company that survives mainly through bribery.

Today most managers regard the cost of social responsibility as a business expense, just like the cost of wages or rent. Unfortunately, to some the cost still is not worth the return. But to increasing numbers of firms, social responsibility is an essential part of business operations.

THE EVOLUTION OF SOCIAL RESPONSIBILITY

Business is far from perfect in many respects, but its social responsibility record today is much better than in past decades. In fact, present demands for social responsibility have their roots in outraged reaction to the abusive business practices of the early 1900s.

An assembly line at Ford's Highland Park Plant required workers to stand for long periods and work practically breathing over the shoulder of the next person. Source: Courtesy of the Educational Affairs Department, Ford Motor Company.

Social Responsibility Before the 1930s

During the first quarter of the twentieth century, businesses were free to operate pretty much as they chose. Government protection of workers and consumers was minimal. This was indeed a period of laissez-faire business conditions; people either accepted what business had to offer or they did without.

Working Conditions Before 1930 working conditions were often deplorable by today's standards. The average workweek was in excess of 60 hours for most industries, and there was no minimum wage law. Employee benefits such as paid vacations, medical insurance, and paid overtime were almost nonexistent. Work areas were crowded and unsafe, and industrial accidents were the rule rather than the exception.

In an effort to improve working conditions, employees organized and joined labor unions. But during the early 1900s, businesses—with the help of government—were able to use such weapons as court orders, force, and even the few existing antitrust laws to defeat the attempts of unions to improve working conditions.

Consumer Rights Then as now, most people in business were honest people who produced and sold decent products. However, some business owners, eager for even greater profits, engaged in misleading advertising and sold shoddy and unsafe merchandise.

During this period, consumers were generally subject to the doctrine of **caveat emptor**, a Latin phrase meaning "let the buyer beware." In other words, "what you see is what you get," and too bad if it's not what you expected. Consumers who were victims of unscrupulous business practices could take legal action, but going to court was very expensive and consumers rarely won their cases. Moreover, there were no consumer groups or government agencies to publicize their discoveries and hold sellers accountable for their actions.

In such an atmosphere, government intervention to curb abuses by business would seem almost inevitable. But there was as yet no great public outcry for such intervention.

Government Regulation   Prior to the 1930s, most people believed that competition and the action of the marketplace would correct abuses in time. Government became involved in day-to-day business activities only when there was an obvious abuse of the free-market system.

Six of the more important federal laws passed between 1887 and 1914 are described in Table 2.1. As you can see, these laws were aimed more at encouraging competition than at correcting business abuses, although two of them did deal with the purity of food and drug products. Such

laws did little to curb abuses that occurred on a regular basis.

Social Responsibility After the 1930s

The collapse of the stock market on October 29, 1929, triggered the Great Depression and years of economic problems for the United States. As we noted in Chapter 1, U.S. production fell by almost one-half, and up to 25 percent of the nation's work force was unemployed. At last public pressure mounted for government to "do something" about the economy and about worsening social conditions.

When Franklin Roosevelt was elected President in 1933, he instituted programs in both areas. Laws were passed to correct what many viewed as the monopolistic abuses of big business, and various social services were provided for individuals. These massive federal programs have become the precedent for increased government involvement in the dealings between business and American society.

As government involvement has increased, so has everyone's awareness of the social responsibility of business. Today business owners are concerned about the return on their investment in business, but at the same time most of them demand ethical behavior from professional busi-

Table 2.1 *Early Government Regulations that Affected American Business*

Government Regulation	Major Provisions
Interstate Commerce Act (1887)	First federal act to regulate business practices; provided regulation of railroads and shipping rates
Sherman Antitrust Act (1890)	Prevented monopolies or mergers where competition was endangered
Pure Food and Drug Act (1906)	Established limited supervision of interstate sale of food and drugs
Meat Inspection Act (1906)	Provided for limited supervision of interstate sale of meat and meat products
Federal Trade Commission Act (1914)	Created the Federal Trade Commission to investigate illegal trade practices
Clayton Act (1914)	Eliminated many forms of price discrimination that gave large businesses a competitive advantage over smaller firms

ness managers. In addition, employees demand better working conditions, and consumers want safe, reliable products. Various advocacy groups echo these concerns and also call for careful consideration of our delicate ecological balance. Managers must therefore operate in a complex business environment—one in which they are just as responsible for their managerial actions as for their actions as individual citizens. Figure 2.1 illustrates the change in emphasis in the business environment before and after the 1930s.

TWO VIEWS OF SOCIAL RESPONSIBILITY

Government regulation and public awareness are *external* forces that have increased the social responsibility of business. But business decisions are made *within* the firm—and there, social responsibility begins with the attitude of management. Two contrasting philosophies, or models, define the range of management attitudes toward social responsibility.

The Economic Model

According to the traditional concept of business, a firm exists to produce quality goods and services, earn a reasonable profit, and provide jobs. In line with this concept, the **economic model** of social responsibility holds that society will benefit most when business is left alone to produce and market profitable products.

To the manager who adopts this traditional attitude, social responsibility is someone else's job. After all, stockholders invest in a corporation to earn a return on their investment, not because the firm is socially responsible, and the firm is legally obliged to act in the economic interest of its stockholders. Moreover, profitable firms pay taxes that are used to meet the needs of society. Thus managers who concentrate on profit feel that they fulfill their social responsibility indirectly, through the taxes paid by their firms.

The Socioeconomic Model

In contrast, some managers believe they have a responsibility not only to stockholders but also to customers, employees, suppliers, and the general public. This broader view is referred to as the **socioeconomic model** of social responsibility. It places emphasis not only on profits, but also on the impact of business decisions on society.

Recently, increasing numbers of managers and firms have adopted the socioeconomic model, and they have done so for at least three reasons: First, business is dominated by the corporate form of ownership, and the corporation is a creation of society. If a corporation doesn't perform as a good citizen, society can and will demand changes. Second, many firms are beginning to take pride in their social responsibility records. Colgate-Palmolive, for example, has stated that a firm that does business in a community must return something to that community.[3] Third, many business people feel it is best to take the initiative in this area. The alternative may be legal action brought against the firm by some special-interest group; in such a situation, the firm may lose control of its activities.

The Pros and Cons of Social Responsibility

The merits of the economic and socioeconomic models have been debated for years by business owners, managers, consumers, and government officials. Each side seems to have four major arguments to reinforce its viewpoint.

Arguments for Increased Social Responsibility
Proponents of the socioeconomic model maintain that a business must do more than simply seek profits. To support their position, they offer the following arguments:

1. Business cannot ignore social issues because it is a part of our society.

Figure 2.1 *The Business Environment Before and After 1930. The owners of businesses were very powerful prior to 1930, and government, consumers, and workers had little or no influence. After 1930, several different groups were able to affect the way businesses were managed.*

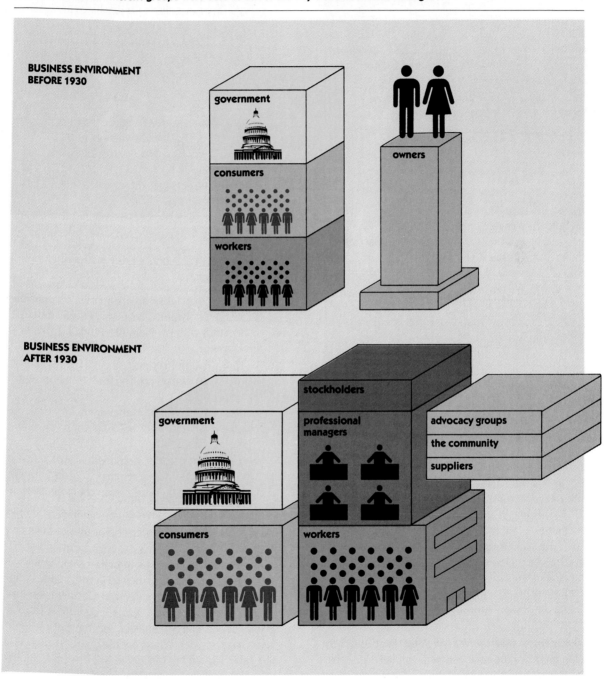

Research into orphan drugs costs companies a great deal and does not guarantee results, but several companies consider this type of research to be a part of their social responsibility. *Source: Courtesy of A. H. Robins.*

Social responsibility also takes the form of contributions to cultural institutions. *Source: Courtesy of the Minnesota Orchestra Association.*

people want. To support their position, they argue as follows:

1. Business managers are primarily responsible to business owners, so management must be concerned with providing a return for owners' investments.
2. Corporate time, money, and talent should be used to maximize profits, not to solve society's problems.
3. Social problems affect society in general, so business should not be expected to solve these problems.
4. Social issues are the responsibility of officials who are elected for that purpose and who are accountable to the voters for their decisions.

These arguments are obviously based on the assumption that the primary objective of business is to earn profits, whereas government and social institutions should deal with social problems.

Table 2.2 compares the economic and socioeconomic viewpoints in terms of business emphasis. Nowadays, few firms are either purely economic or purely socioeconomic in outlook; most have chosen some middle ground between the two. However, our society generally seems to want—and even to expect—some degree of social responsibility from business. Thus, within

2. Business has the technical, financial, and managerial resources that are needed to tackle today's complex social issues.
3. By helping resolve social issues, business can create a more stable environment for long-term profitability.
4. Socially responsible decision making by business firms can prevent increased government intervention, which would force businesses to do what they fail to do voluntarily.

Arguments Against Increased Social Responsibility

Opponents of the socioeconomic model argue that business should do what it does best: earn a profit by manufacturing and marketing products that

this middle ground, businesses are tending toward the socioeconomic view. In the next several sections, we shall look at some results of this tendency in four specific areas: consumers' rights, employment practices, environmental quality, and business ethics.

CONSUMERISM

Consumerism consists of all those activities that are undertaken to protect the rights of consumers in their dealings with business. Consumerism has been with us to some extent since the early nineteenth century, but the movement came to life only in the 1960s. It was then that President John F. Kennedy declared that the consumer was entitled to a new "bill of rights," as shown in Figure 2.2.

The Four Basic Rights of Consumers

Kennedy's consumer bill of rights consisted of the rights to safety, to be informed, to choose, and to be heard. These four rights are the basis of much of the consumer-oriented legislation that was passed during the last twenty years. They also provide an effective outline of the objectives and accomplishments of the consumer movement.

The Right to Safety The right to safety means that products purchased by consumers must

- Be safe for their intended use
- Include thorough and explicit directions for proper use
- Have been tested by the manufacturer to ensure product quality and reliability

There are several reasons why American business firms must be concerned about product safety. Federal agencies such as the Food and Drug Administration and the Consumer Product Safety Commission have the power to force those businesses that make or sell defective products to take corrective actions. Such actions include offering refunds, recalling defective products, issuing public warnings, and giving reimbursement to consumers—all of which can be expensive. Second, consumers and the government have been winning an increasing number of product-liability lawsuits against sellers of defective products. Moreover, the awards in these suits have been getting bigger and bigger. Another major reason for improving product safety is the consumer's demand for safe products. People will simply stop buying a product that they believe is unsafe or unreliable.

The Right to Be Informed The right to be informed means that consumers must have access to complete information about a product before

Table 2.2 *A Comparison of the Economic and Socioeconomic Models as Implemented in Business*

Economic Model: Primary emphasis is on			Socioeconomic Model: Primary emphasis is on
1. Production	M	G	1. Quality of life
2. Exploitation of natural resources	I	R	2. Conservation of natural resources
3. Internal, market-based decisions	D	O	3. Market-based decisions, with some community controls
4. Economic return (profit)	D	U	4. Balance of economic return and social return
5. Firm's or manager's interest	L	N	5. Firm's and community's interest
6. Minor role for government	E	D	6. Active government involvement

Source: Adapted from Keith Davis, William C. Frederick, and Robert L. Blomstrom, *Business and Society: Concepts and Policy Issues* (New York: McGraw-Hill, 1980) p. 9. Used by permission of McGraw-Hill Book Company.

they buy it. Detailed information about ingredients must be provided on food containers, information about fabrics and laundering methods must be attached to clothing, and lenders must disclose the true cost of borrowing the money that they make available so that customers can purchase merchandise on credit.

In addition, manufacturers must inform customers about the potential dangers of using their products. When they do not, they can be held responsible for personal injuries suffered because of their products. Sometimes such warnings seem excessive, but they are necessary if user injuries (and resulting lawsuits) are to be avoided.

Figure 2.2 The Consumer "Bill of Rights." Source: Photo for 1, James Scherer; photo for 3, courtesy of E. I. du Pont de Nemours and Company; photo for 4, courtesy of Victor F. Weaver, Inc.

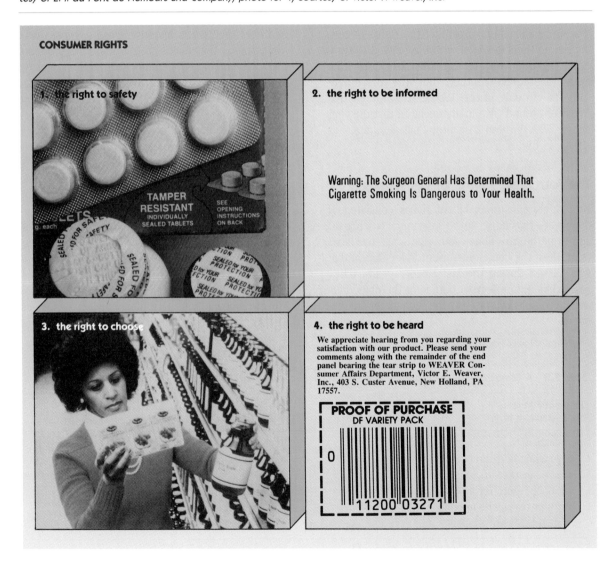

CONSUMER RIGHTS

1. the right to safety

TAMPER RESISTANT
INDIVIDUALLY SEALED TABLETS

SEE OPENING INSTRUCTIONS ON BACK

2. the right to be informed

Warning: The Surgeon General Has Determined That Cigarette Smoking Is Dangerous to Your Health.

3. the right to choose

4. the right to be heard

We appreciate hearing from you regarding your satisfaction with our product. Please send your comments along with the remainder of the end panel bearing the tear strip to WEAVER Consumer Affairs Department, Victor E. Weaver, Inc., 403 S. Custer Avenue, New Holland, PA 17557.

PROOF OF PURCHASE
DF VARIETY PACK

0   11200 03271

The Right to Choose The right to choose means that consumers have a choice of products, offered by different manufacturers and sellers, to satisfy a particular need. The government has done its part by encouraging competition through antitrust legislation. The more competition there is, the greater the choice available to consumers.

Competition and the resulting freedom of choice provide an additional benefit for consumers: They work to reduce the price of goods and services. Consider the electronic calculators that are so popular today. The Bowmar Brain, one of the first calculators introduced, carried a retail price tag in excess of $150. The product was so

Table 2.3 *Major Federal Legislation Passed Since 1960*

Government Regulation	Main Provisions
Federal Hazardous Substances Labeling Act (1960)	Required warning labels on household chemicals if they are highly toxic
Color Additives Amendment (1960)	Required manufacturers to disclose when colorings are added to foods
Kefauver-Harris Drug Amendments (1962)	Established testing practices for drugs and required manufacturers to label drugs with generic names in addition to trade names
Cigarette Labeling Act (1965)	Required manufacturers to place standardized warning labels on all cigarette packages and advertising
Fair Packaging and Labeling Act (1966)	Called for all products sold across state lines to be labeled with net weight, ingredients, and manufacturer's name and address
Motor Vehicle Safety Act (1966)	Established standards for safer cars
Wholesome Meat Act (1967)	Required states to inspect meat (but not poultry) sold within the state
Flammable Fabrics Act (1967)	Strengthened flammability standards for clothing, to include children's sleepwear in sizes 0 to 6X
Truth in Lending Act (1968)	Required lenders and credit merchants to disclose the full cost of finance charges in both dollars and annual percentage rate
Land Sales Disclosure Act (1968)	Provided protection for consumers from unscrupulous practices in interstate land sales
Child Protection and Toy Act (1969)	Banned from interstate commerce toys with mechanical or electrical defects
Credit Card Liability Act (1970)	Limited credit-card holder's liability to $50 per card and stopped credit-card companies from issuing unsolicited cards
Fair Credit Reporting Act (1971)	Required credit bureaus to provide summary credit reports to consumers regarding their own credit files; also provided for correction of incorrect information
Consumer Product Safety Commission Act (1972)	Established the Consumer Product Safety Commission
Trade Regulation Rule (1972)	Established a "cooling-off" period of 72 hours for door-to-door sales
Fair Credit Billing Act (1974)	Amended the Truth in Lending Act to enable consumers to challenge billing errors
Equal Credit Opportunity Act (1974)	Provided equal credit opportunities for males and females and for married and single individuals
Amendment to Equal Credit Opportunity Act (1976)	Prevented discrimination based on race, creed, color, religion, age, and income when granting credit
Fair Credit Collection Practices Act (1977)	Outlawed abusive collection practices by third parties

profitable that Texas Instruments, Rockwell International, and many other firms began to compete with Bowmar. As a result, calculators can now be purchased for under $10.

The Right to Be Heard This fourth right means that someone will listen and take appropriate action when consumers complain. Actually, management began to listen to consumers after World War II, when competition between businesses that manufactured and sold consumer goods increased. One way to get a competitive edge was to listen to consumers and provide the products they said they wanted and needed. Today, businesses are listening even more attentively, and many larger firms have consumer relations departments that the buying public can easily contact via toll-free phone numbers.

Other groups listen too. Most large cities and some states have consumer affairs offices to act on the complaints of citizens. The Better Business Bureau (BBB) was one of the first *private* groups to back individual consumers. Although the BBB is an association of business people, its major purpose is to help consumers resolve complaints or take action against firms that engage in unethical business practices. The BBB also records the details of each complaint for future reference. Potential customers can call the BBB to request information about a specific business. The BBB will tell callers whether there have been complaints against the business and, if so, how they were resolved.

Recent Developments in Consumerism

The greatest advances in consumerism have come through federal legislation. Some recent laws that have a direct bearing on your rights as a consumer are listed and described in Table 2.3.

In addition, most business people have come to realize that they ignore consumer issues only at their peril. Managers know that improper handling of complaints can mean lost sales, bad publicity, and lawsuits.

EMPLOYMENT PRACTICES

We have seen that a combination of managers who subscribe to the socioeconomic view of business's social responsibility and significant legislation enacted to protect the buying public has resulted in considerable broadening of the rights of consumers. The last two decades have seen similar progress in affirming the rights of employees to equal treatment in the work place.

Everyone who works for a living should have the opportunity to land a job for which he or she is qualified and to be rewarded on the basis of ability and performance. This is an important issue for society, and it also makes good business sense. Yet, over the years, this opportunity has been denied to members of various minority groups. A **minority** is a group of people singled out on the basis of race, age, religion, sex, or national origin for prejudicial, or selective, unfavorable treatment.

The federal government responded to the outcry of minority groups during the 1960s and 1970s by passing a number of laws forbidding job discrimination. (These laws are discussed in Chapter 9 in the context of human resources management.) Now, more than twenty years since passage of the first of these (the Civil Rights Act of 1964), abuses still exist. An example is the disparity in income levels for whites, blacks, and Hispanics, as illustrated in Figure 2.3. Lower incomes and higher unemployment rates also affect Native Americans, handicapped persons, and women.

Responsible managers have instituted a number of programs to counteract the results of discrimination.

Affirmative Action Programs

An **affirmative action program** is a plan designed to increase the number of minority employees at all levels within an organization. The objective of such programs is to ensure that minorities are represented within the organization in approximately the same proportion as in the

Figure 2.3 *Comparative Income Levels. Percentages have been rounded up or down to the nearest whole number.*

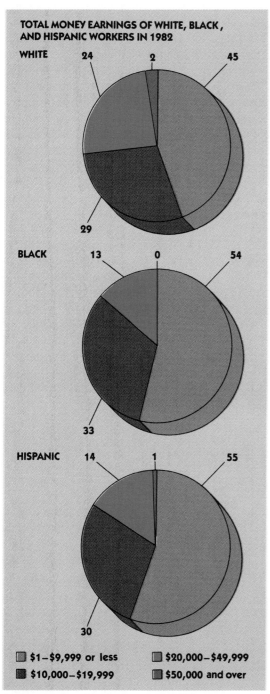

TOTAL MONEY EARNINGS OF WHITE, BLACK, AND HISPANIC WORKERS IN 1982

WHITE   24   2   45
29

BLACK   13   0   54
33

HISPANIC   14   1   55
30

■ $1–$9,999 or less   ■ $20,000–$49,999

■ $10,000–$19,999   ■ $50,000 and over

Source: "Work Experience in 1982—Civilians 15 Years Old and Over. . . ." *Statistical Abstract of the United States 1984,* U.S. Bureau of the Census.

An affirmative action program is a plan to increase the number of minority employees at all levels within an organization. Source: Courtesy of Monsanto Co.

surrounding community. They encompass all areas of human resources management: recruiting, hiring, training, promotion, and pay.

Unfortunately, affirmative action programs have been plagued by two problems. The first involves quotas. In the beginning, many firms pledged to recruit and hire a certain number of minority members by a specific date. To achieve this goal, they were forced to consider only minority applicants for job openings; if they hired non-minority workers, they would be defeating their own purpose. But the courts have ruled that such quotas are unconstitutional even though their purpose is commendable. They are, in fact,

a form of discrimination called *reverse discrimination.*

The second problem is that not all business people are in favor of affirmative action programs, although most have been reasonably successful. Managers not committed to these programs can "play the game" and still discriminate against workers. In order to help solve this problem, Congress created (and later strengthened) the **Equal Employment Opportunity Commission** (EEOC), a government agency with the power to investigate complaints of discrimination and the power to sue firms that practice employment discrimination.

Figure 2.4 *The Relative Earnings of Male and Female Workers. For over 30 years, women have consistently earned only about 60 cents for each dollar earned by a man. Source:* Perspectives on Working Women: A Databook, *U.S. Department of Labor Statistics, October, 1980, p. 52.*

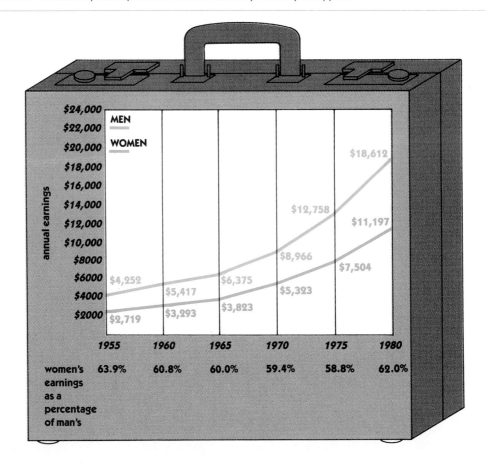

	1955	1960	1965	1970	1975	1980
women's earnings as a percentage of man's	63.9%	60.8%	60.0%	59.4%	58.8%	62.0%

The threat of legal action has been necessary to persuade some corporations to amend their hiring and promotion policies, but the discrepancy between men's and women's salaries has not really been affected, as illustrated in Figure 2.4. In 1973 American Telephone & Telegraph (AT&T) signed a consent decree to correct racial and sexual imbalances in what was the nation's largest private employer. The results:

- The number of women in middle and upper-level management rose from 9 percent in 1972 to 17 percent in 1978
- During the same period, the company's employment of minority women rose from 79,000 to 96,000, and that of minority men from 31,000 to 43,000
- Women are now working in traditionally male-dominated crafts, and men are working as operators and clerks—jobs traditionally reserved for women.[4]

Sometimes programs like AT&T's are painfully slow. But equal employment opportunity is no longer simply a good idea—because now it's the law.[5]

Training Programs for the Hard-Core Unemployed

For some firms, social responsibility extends far beyond placing a help-wanted ad in the local newspaper. These firms have assumed the task of helping the **hard-core unemployed**: workers with little education or vocational training and a long history of unemployment. In the past such workers were often routinely turned down by personnel managers, even for the most menial jobs.

Obviously such workers require training; just as obviously this training can be expensive and time-consuming. To share the costs, business and government have joined together in a number of cooperative programs. One particularly successful partnership is the **National Alliance of Businessmen** (NAB), a joint business–government program to train the hard-core unemployed.

The NAB is sponsored by participating corporations, whose executives contribute their talents to do the actual training. The government's responsibilities include setting objectives, establishing priorities, offering the right incentives, and providing limited financing. Is the program effective? The NAB's statistics show that, since 1968, some 40,000 executives have contributed services valued at $20 million and provided jobs for more than 3.5 million people who were unable to find jobs for themselves.[6]

CONCERN FOR THE ENVIRONMENT

The social consciousness of responsible managers and the encouragement of a concerned government have also made the public and the business community partners in a major effort to reduce environmental pollution, conserve natural resources, and reverse some of the worst effects of past negligence in this area.

Pollution is contamination of our water, air, or land through the actions of people in an industrialized society. For several decades, environmentalists have been warning us of the dangers of industrial pollution. Unfortunately, business and government leaders either ignored the problem or weren't concerned about it until pollution became a threat to life and health in America. Consider the following incidents:

- The Center for Disease Control found that more than 400 out of 1000 children who lived near a lead smelting plant in Kellogg, Idaho, had dangerously high levels of lead in their bodies. These children experienced serious learning deficiencies and faulty memories as a result of the lead contamination.[7]
- In 1978 more than 200 families were evacuated from Love Canal near Niagara Falls, New York, because toxic industrial wastes began to surface after having been buried there for 30 years. Two years later, another 700 Love Canal families were relocated because of the same problem.

□ The herbicide 2,4,5-T was linked to birth defects, miscarriages, and nervous disorders after it was used to destroy brush around timber in California. A number of local residents also claimed that the chemical had poisoned water, killed livestock, and destroyed crops. As a result, the EPA imposed a temporary ban on the herbicide.[8]

These are not isolated cases. Such situations, occurring throughout the United States, have made pollution a matter of national concern. Today Americans expect business and government leaders to take swift action to clean up our environment—and to keep it clean.

Effects of Environmental Legislation

As in other areas of concern to our society, legislation and regulations play a crucial role in pollution control. A quick glance at the laws outlined in Table 2.4 will show the scope of current environmental legislation. Of major importance was creation of the **Environmental Protection Agency** (EPA), the federal agency charged with enforcing laws designed to protect the environment.

Once they are aware of the problem of pollution, most firms respond to it rather than waiting to be cited by the EPA. But some owners and managers take the position that environmental standards are too strict. (Loosely translated, this means that compliance with present standards is too expensive.) Consequently, it has often been necessary for the EPA to bring legal action to force firms to install antipollution equipment and clean up waste storage areas.

Experience has shown that the combination of environmental legislation, voluntary compliance, and EPA action can succeed in cleaning the environment and keeping it clean. However, much still remains to be done.

Water Pollution Improved water quality is not only necessary, but it is also achievable. Consider Cleveland's Cuyahoga River. A few years ago the river was so contaminated by industrial wastes that it burst into flames one hot summer day! Now, after a sustained community cleanup effort, the river is pure enough for fish to live in.

Such improvement does cost money, and money is not easily available in many cases. New York City dumps nearly 200 million gallons of raw sewage into nearby rivers and harbors each day. The real problem is not unwillingness to stop polluting, but rather the cost of building a sewage treatment plant large enough to be effective.

Table 2.4 *Summary of Major Environmental Laws*

Government Act	Major Provisions
National Environmental Policy Act of 1970	Established the Environmental Protection Agency (EPA) to enforce federal laws that involve the environment
Clean Air Amendment of 1970	Provided stringent automotive, aircraft, and factory emission standards
Water Quality Improvement Act of 1970	Strengthened existing water pollution regulations and provided for large monetary fines against violators
Resource Recovery Act of 1970	Enlarged the solid-waste disposal program and provided for enforcement by the EPA
Water Pollution Control Act Amendment of 1972	Established standards for cleaning navigable streams and lakes and eliminating all harmful waste disposal by 1985
Resource Conservation and Recovery Act of 1976	Required federal regulation of potentially dangerous solid-waste disposal
Clean Air Act Amendment of 1977	Established new deadlines for cleaning up polluted areas; also required review of existing air-quality standards

In Clear Creek Valley, Colorado, Coors has taken extensive measures to ensure high quality air. The company voluntarily installed sophisticated equipment to monitor its impact on the environment and has been able to reduce substantially its emissions. Source: Courtesy of Adolf Coors Company, Golden, Colorado.

Today acid rain, which results from sulfur emitted by smokestacks in industrialized areas, is destroying many lakes and reservoirs. The sulfur combines with moisture in the atmosphere to form acids that are carried far from their point of origin by winds. The acids fall to earth in rain, which finds its way to streams and then to rivers and lakes. To solve the problem, investigators must first determine where the sulfur is being emitted. The expenses that this vital investigation and cleanup entail are going to be high. The human costs of having ignored the problem so long may be higher still.

Air Pollution Usually two or three factors combine to form air pollution in any given location. The first is large amounts of carbon monoxide and hydrocarbons emitted by many motor vehicles concentrated in a relatively small area. The second is the smoke and other pollutants emitted by manufacturing facilities. These two factors can be eliminated to a large extent through pollution control devices on cars, trucks, and smokestacks. Over the past ten years, private industry has spent more than $50 billion on emission control devices, "scrubbers," and other antipollution devices.

The third factor that contributes to air pollution—one that cannot be changed—is weather and geography. The Los Angeles basin, for example, combines just the right weather and geographic conditions for creating the dense smog that exists there more than one hundred days each year. Together, the three factors produce a multibillion-dollar health problem by polluting the air we breathe.

How effective is air pollution legislation? Most authorities agree that there has been a lot of progress. For example, in 1975 Chicago, Louisville, and Philadelphia all experienced more than 140 days during which air pollution reached unhealthful levels. By 1981 the number of unhealthful days had been reduced to fewer than 40 per year in all three cities.

Land pollution is taking its toll everywhere. The EPA investigates toxic waste sites, like this one involving PCBs, and helps determine how the site will be cleaned up. Source: Holt Confer, Uniphoto.

Land Pollution   Air and water quality may be improving, but land pollution is still a serious problem in many areas. The fundamental issues are (1) how to restore damaged or contaminated land at a reasonable cost and (2) how to protect unpolluted land from future damage.

The land pollution problem has been worsening over the past few years, as modern technology has continued to produce more and more chemical and radioactive waste. This country's 54,000 manufacturers produce an estimated 40 to 60 million tons of contaminated oil, solvents, acids, and sludges each year. When this is added to the wastes produced by service businesses, utility companies, hospitals, and others, the result is about 1 ton of waste each year for each man, woman, and child in the United States.[9] Other causes of land pollution include strip mining of coal, nonselective cutting of forests, the development of agricultural land for housing and industry, and garbage disposal.

To help pay the enormous costs of cleaning up land polluted with chemical and industrial wastes, Congress created a $1.6 billion Superfund in 1980. Originally, money was to flow into the Superfund from a tax paid by 800 oil and chemical companies that produce toxic waste. Then the EPA was to use the money in the Superfund to finance the cleanup of hazardous waste sites across the nation. To replenish the Superfund, the EPA had two options: It could sue the companies that were guilty of dumping chemicals at specific waste sites. Or it could negotiate with guilty companies and thus completely avoid the legal system. During the early 1980s, officials at the EPA came under fire because they preferred negotiated settlements. Critics referred to these settlements as "sweetheart deals" with industry. They felt the EPA should be much more aggressive in reducing land pollution in the United States.

Noise Pollution   Excessive noise caused by traffic, aircraft, and machinery can do physical harm to humans. Research has shown that people who are exposed to loud noises for long periods of time can suffer permanent hearing loss. The Noise Control Act of 1972 established noise emission standards for aircraft and airports, railroads, and interstate motor carriers. The Act also provides funding for noise research at state and local levels.

Noise levels can be reduced by two methods. The source of noise pollution can be isolated as much as possible. (Thus many metropolitan airports are located outside the city, in a rural setting.) And engineers can modify machinery and equipment to reduce noise levels. If it is impossible to reduce industrial noise to acceptable levels, workers should be required to wear earplugs to guard against permanent hearing damage.

Who Should Pay for a Clean Environment?

Government and business are spending at least $50 billion each year to reduce pollution. The

Adopting a Dump

Some companies want their landfills cleaned up so much—and so efficiently—that they are trying to take the law into their own hands. The CMA calls it "adopting a dump," whereby a company takes responsibility for cleaning up an orphaned or multi-party waste site. Often, frustrated by EPA bureaucracy and litigation, a company may seek to get the situation over with and determine responsibility later. According to DuPont Executive Vice President William G. Simeral, "It doesn't matter whether your company or mine has anything to do with a specific site. We are all being tarred with the same brush. It also doesn't matter whether a given site poses a genuine health hazard; the public perceives one."

For example, Stauffer Chemical Company had negotiated with government officials in Woburn, Mass., to give Stauffer the responsibility for cleaning up the site, with cost apportionment to follow. "We thought," states Mr. Jaeschke, "that this would serve everyone's interests best, rather than protracted litigation." He sites the danger of assigning all costs to those companies which step forward. The Woburn site, whose cleanup should be completed by 1986, contains waste dumped over the past century on a plot several hundred acres large.

Similarly, DuPont and several other companies have reached a settlement with the EPA to clean up a site in Seymour, Ind. Occidental and DuPont evaluated their sites for potential problems, and the latter is voluntarily digging up polymer wastes disposed of legally in Iowa in the 1930s and burning them or storing them at approved RCRA sites in order to avoid future problems.

Many chemical company executives feel that the efficiency and quality of cleanup might be improved if companies were more involved, for they possess resources and project experience. The EPA's Lee M. Thomas believes that even if companies were left to conduct cleanup on their own, "most would probably do a pretty responsible job."

Source: *Business Today,* Fall 1983.

---

economic unit of *U.S. News & World Report* estimates that $690 billion will be spent between 1980 and 1989 to create a cleaner environment. (See Table 2.5).

To make matters worse, much of the money required to purify the environment is supposed to come from already depressed industries, such as the steel industry. And some firms have discovered that it is cheaper to pay a fine than to install expensive pollution control equipment. (One firm has declared bankruptcy in anticipation of lawsuits arising from a related problem: health hazards attributed to the firm's asbestos products.)

Who, then, will pay for the environmental cleanup? Many business leaders believe that tax money should be used to clean the environment and keep it clean. They reason that business is

Table 2.5   The Cost of a Better Environment

Estimates of how much will be spent in 1980–89 to combat pollution, stated in constant 1982 dollars to discount the effects of inflation—

Air pollution	$393 bil.
Water pollution	$228 bil.
Solid-waste pollution	$ 22 bil.
Land reclamation	$ 19 bil.
Noise	$ 11 bil.
Toxic substances	$ 11 bil.
Drinking water	$ 4 bil.
Pesticides	$ 2 bil.
Total Cost, 1980-89	$690 bil.

Outlays in the 1980s—more than two thirds to be spent by industry—will exceed those of the '70s by 53 percent.

Source: Ronald A. Taylor, "Cleaner Air and Water," *U.S. News & World Report,* February 28, 1983, p. 27.

not the only source of pollution, so business should not be forced to absorb the entire cost of the cleanup. On the other hand, environmentalists believe that the cost of proper treatment and disposal of industrial wastes is an expense of doing business. In either case, consumers are likely to pay a large part of the cost—either as taxes or in the form of higher prices for goods and services.

BUSINESS ETHICS

Perhaps it is in the area of business ethics that the socioeconomic perspective on the social responsibility of business comes into sharpest focus.

Ethics is the study of right and wrong and of the morality of choices made by individuals. An ethical decision or action is one that is "right" according to some standard of behavior. **Business ethics** (sometimes referred to as *management ethics*) is the application of moral standards to business decisions and actions.

Business ethics has become a cause for public concern because of recent cases of unethical behavior. In this regard, two questions are relevant to today's business world: "What pressures affect the ethics of decision making in business?" and "Should business be more ethical?"

Pressures Influencing Ethical Decision Making

Business ethics involves relationships between a firm and its investors, customers, employees, creditors, and competitors. Each group has specific concerns, and each exerts some type of pressure on management.

□ *Investors* want management to make intelligent financial decisions that will boost sales, profits, and the return on their investments
□ *Customers* expect that a firm's products will be safe, reliable, and reasonably priced
□ *Employees* want to be treated fairly in hiring, promotion, and compensation

□ *Creditors* expect that bills will be paid on time and that the accounting information furnished by the firm will present an accurate picture of its finances
□ *Competitors* expect that the firm's marketing activities will accurately portray its products

When business is good and profit is high, it is relatively easy for management to respond to these expectations in an ethical manner. However, managers' concern for ethics can dwindle under the pressure of low or declining profit. It is in such circumstances that ethical behavior is most likely to be compromised.

Expanding international trade has also led to an ethical dilemma for many American firms. In some countries, bribes and payoffs are an accepted part of business, but the U.S. government frowns on this practice. In 1977, the government passed the Foreign Corrupt Practices Act, which prohibits these types of payments, but it is hard to enforce this act. Government agencies have prosecuted several firms for these "illegal payoffs," in spite of the fact that there is as yet no international code of business ethics. The U.S. Justice Department is currently investigating cases that involve improper payments to officials in South Korea and Mexico. With no international laws or ethics codes, these cases are difficult to investigate. Much of the evidence and many of the people are overseas and cannot be prosecuted effectively.

Should Business Be More Ethical?

Most authorities agree that there is room for improvement in business ethics. A more difficult question is whether business can be made more ethical in the real world. The majority of responses to this question suggest that government, trade associations, or individual firms establish acceptable levels of behavior.

The government can do so by passing more stringent regulations. But regulations require enforcement, and the unethical business person always seems to be able to "slip something by" without getting caught. Increased regulation may

"It's Wonderful, But Can I Keep It?"

Gifts under the corporate Christmas tree can sometimes be Pandora's boxes wrapped in pretty paper. Everyone likes to get presents, but gifts to business people from outside business contacts often represent more than just a simple expression of gratitude. They present moral dilemmas.

"Generally, I would say it is better not to give *or* receive at Christmas," says Laurence J. Stybel, a general partner at Stybel Peabody Associates, a Boston consulting firm, and an assistant professor of management at Babson College. Stybel is not the role model for the *Grinch that Stole Christmas*; he is talking about the ethical problems that arise when business people accept gifts from their customers or vendors.

"A purchasing manager, for example, should be forbidden to accept gifts," says Stybel, who adds that he has never had the opportunity to return a gift from one of his clients. "There should be no shadow of a doubt."

But quite a few companies—and the IRS—apparently believe that this is a $24.99 dilemma—you only have to worry if the ticket gets steeper. And a Gallup study shows that a significant percentage of business people believe that half or more of their colleagues do exchange expensive Christmas presents with vendors. And finally, there's the evidence of a whole flourishing industry catering to corporate gift giving.

Within some companies, gift swapping among persons whose relationship is strictly business creates no more of a problem than deciding what to buy. Expecially when what is swapped is little more than a company calendar or a pen. But at worst, and especially when the value of the gifts escalates, it could represent payola and an invitation to continue a working relationship regardless of its real value to the company.

Source: Douglas M. Balley, The Ethics of Corporate Gifts, *New England Business*, December 5, 1983, p. 23.

help, but it surely cannot solve the entire ethics problem.

Trade associations can provide (and some have provided) ethical guidelines for their members to follow. These organizations of firms within a particular industry are also in a position to exert pressure on members that stoop to questionable business practices. However, enforcement varies from association to association, and because trade associations exist for the benefit of their members, very strong measures may be self-defeating.

Perhaps the most effective way to encourage ethical behavior in business is for each firm to establish a corporate code of ethics. A **corporate code of ethics** is simply a guide to acceptable and ethical behavior. Of course, it would be impossible to cover every situation in such a code, but general guidelines should be sufficient for most employees. Specific details could deal with prohibited practices such as bribery.

In the final analysis, business ethics can be high only if the personal ethics of business people are high. The test shown in Figure 2.5 may tell you something about your own business ethics. Try it now, to see how you would rate. Remember, though, that a test cannot duplicate a real business situation. If you were a manager, your decisions might be complicated by pressure from a variety of sources, including your own desire to retain your job or to "move up" in the company.

Even if employees want to act ethically, it may be difficult to do so. Unethical practices often become ingrained in an organization. Employees with high personal ethics may then take a controversial step called whistle blowing. **Whistle blowing** is informing the press or government officials about unethical practices in your firm. Naturally this step can have serious repercussions for the employee, yet those who take it feel that the benefit to society outweighs any personal consequences they may suffer.

Figure 2.5   How Ethical Are You?

Many situations in day-to-day business are not simple right-or-wrong questions, but rather fall into a gray area. To demonstrate the perplexing array of moral dilemmas faced by 20th-century Americans, here is a "nonscientific" test for slippage. . . . Don't expect to score high. That is not the purpose. But give it a try, and see how you stack up.

(In the space at the right of each statement, mark a 0 (zero) if you strongly disagree, a 1 if you disagree, a 2 if you agree, and a 3 if you strongly agree.)

1. Employees should not be expected to inform on their peers for wrong-doings. ____
2. There are times when a manager must overlook contract and safety violations in order to get on with the job. ____
3. It is not always possible to keep accurate expense account records; therefore, it is sometimes necessary to give approximate figures. ____
4. There are times when it is necessary to withhold embarrassing information from one's superior. ____
5. We should do what our managers suggest, though we may have doubts about its being the right thing to do. ____
6. It is sometimes necessary to conduct personal business on company time. ____
7. Sometimes it is good psychology to set goals somewhat above normal if it will help to obtain a greater effort from the sales force. ____
8. I would quote a "hopeful" shipping date in order to get the order. ____
9. It is proper to use the company WATS line for personal calls as long as it's not in company use. ____
10. Management must be goal-oriented; therefore, the end usually justifies the means. ____
11. If it takes heavy entertainment and twisting a bit of company policy to win a large contract, I would authorize it. ____
12. Exceptions to company policy and procedures are a way of life. ____
13. Inventory controls should be designed to report "underages" rather than "overages" in goods received. ____
14. Occasional use of the company's copier for personal or community activities is acceptable. ____
15. Taking home company property (pencils, paper, tape, etc.) for personal use is an accepted fringe benefit. ____

If your total score is:

0 Prepare for canonization ceremony	16–25 Average ethical values
1– 5 Bishop material	26–35 Need moral development
6–10 High ethical values	36–44 Slipping fast
11–15 Good ethical values	45 Leave valuables with warden

SOURCE: Adapted from "Is Your (Ethical) Slippage Showing?" by Lowell G. Rein, *Personnel Journal*, September 1980. Reprinted with the permission of *Personnel Journal*, Costa Mesa, California; all rights reserved.

IMPLEMENTING THE SOCIAL RESPONSIBILITY CONCEPT

A firm's decision to be socially responsible is a step in the right direction—but only a first step. The firm must then develop and implement a tangible program to reach this goal. The factors that affect a particular firm's social responsibility program include its size, financial resources, past record in the area of social responsibility, and competition. But above all, the program must have total commitment or it will fail.

Initiating a Social Responsibility Program

An effective program for social responsibility takes time, money, and organization. In most cases, four steps are involved in developing and implementing such a program.

Commitment of Top Executives Without the support of top executives, any program will soon falter and become ineffective. As evidence of their commitment to social responsibility, top managers should develop a policy statement that outlines key areas of concern. This statement "sets the tone" (one of positive enthusiasm) and will later serve as a guide for other employees as they become involved in the program.

Planning Next a committee of managers should be appointed to plan the program. Whatever the form of their plan, it should deal with each of the issues described in the policy statement. If necessary, outside consultants can be hired to help develop the plan.

Appointment of a Director After the social responsibility plan is established, a top-level executive should be appointed to direct the organization's activities in implementing it. This individual should be charged with recommending specific policies and helping individual departments understand and live up to the social responsibilities that the firm has assumed. Depending on the size of the firm, the director may require a staff to handle the program on a day-to-day basis.

The Westinghouse Beverage unit supports many community programs including minority, cultural, environmental, and youth activities. Source: Courtesy of Westinghouse Electric Corporation.

The Social Audit The director of the program should prepare a social audit for the firm at specified intervals. A **social audit** is a comprehensive report of what an organization has done, and is doing, with regard to social issues that affect it. This document provides the information that is needed for evaluation and revision of the social responsibility program. Typical subject areas include human resources, community involvement, the quality and safety of products, business practices, and efforts to reduce pollution and improve the environment. The information included in a social audit should be as accurate and as quantitative as possible, and it should reveal both positive and negative aspects of the program.

Funding the Program

We have noted several times that social responsibility costs money. Thus a program to improve social responsibility must be funded just like any other program. Funding can come from three sources: (1) Management can pass the cost on to consumers in the form of higher prices. (2) The corporation may be forced to absorb the cost of the program if, for example, the competitive situation does not permit a price increase. In this case, the cost is treated as a business expense and profit is reduced. (3) The federal government may pay for all or part of the cost through special tax reductions or other incentives.

Chapter Review

SUMMARY

In a socially responsible business, management realizes that its activities have an impact on society, and that impact is considered in the decision-making process. Before the 1930s neither workers, consumers, nor government had much influence on business activities; as a result, business gave little thought to its social responsibility. All this changed with the Great Depression. Government regulation and a new public awareness combined to create a demand that businesses act in a socially responsible manner.

According to the economic model of social responsibility, society benefits most when business is left alone to produce profitable goods and services. According to the socioeconomic model, business has as much responsibility to society as it has to its owners. Most managers adopt a viewpoint somewhere between these two extremes.

Four areas of social concern to business are consumerism, employment practices, the environment, and business ethics. The consumer movement has generally demanded—and received—attention from business in the areas of product safety, product information, product choices through competition, and the resolution of complaints about products and business practices.

Legislation and public demand have prompted business to correct past abuses in employment practices—mainly with regard to minority groups. Affirmative action and training of the hard-core unemployed are two types of programs that have been used successfully.

Industry has contributed to the pollution of our land and water through the dumping of wastes, and to air pollution through vehicle and smoke-stack emissions. This contamination can be cleaned up and controlled, but the big question is who will pay for it. Present cleanup efforts are funded partly by government tax revenues, partly by business, and, in the long run, by consumers.

Management today is under pressure from business owners, customers, employees, creditors, and competitors. Pushed and pulled by such diverse demands, some managers compromise personal ethics in their business dealings. An organizational code of ethics can help ensure ethical business behavior and can reinforce in the business setting the high personal ethics of most employees.

A program to implement social responsibility in a business begins with total commitment by top management. The program should be carefully planned, and a capable director should be appointed to implement it. Social audits should be prepared periodically as a means of evaluating and revising the program. Programs may be funded through federal incentives or through price increases.

In this chapter and in Chapter 1, we have used the general term *business owners* and the more specific term *stockholders*. In the next chapter, wherein we discuss the various forms of business and business ownership, you will see who these people are.

KEY TERMS

You should now be able to define and give an example relevant to each of the following terms:

social responsibility

doctrine of *caveat emptor*

economic model of social responsibility

socioeconomic model of social responsibility

consumerism

minority

affirmative action program

Equal Employment Opportunity Commission

hard-core unemployed

National Alliance of Businessmen

pollution

Environmental Protection Agency

ethics

business ethics

corporate code of ethics

whistle blowing

social audit

QUESTIONS AND EXERCISES

Review Questions

1. How and why did the American business environment change after the Great Depression?
2. What are the major differences between the economic model of social responsibility and the socioeconomic model?
3. What are the arguments for and against increased social responsibility for business?
4. Describe and give an example of each of the four basic rights of consumers.
5. There are more women than men in the United States. Why, then, are women considered a minority with regard to employment?
6. What is the goal of affirmative action programs? How is this goal achieved?
7. What is the primary function of the Equal Employment Opportunity Commission?
8. How do businesses contribute to each of the four forms of pollution? How can they avoid polluting the environment?
9. Our environment *can* be cleaned up and kept clean. Why haven't we simply done so?
10. Why might an individual with high ethical standards act less ethically in business than in his or her personal life?
11. How would an organizational code of ethics help ensure ethical business behavior?
12. Describe the steps involved in developing a social responsibility program within a firm.

Discussion Questions

1. Why would consumers go back to Extra-Strength Tylenol capsules after some capsules had been poisoned?
2. Do you think Johnson & Johnson's actions during the Tylenol crisis indicate that the firm acts responsibly with regard to other social issues as well? Explain.

3. Overall, would it be more profitable for a business to follow the economic model or the socioeconomic model of social responsibility?
4. Why should business take on the task of training the hard-core unemployed?
5. To what extent should the blame for vehicular air pollution be shared by manufacturers, consumers, and government?
6. How can an employee take an ethical stand regarding a business decision when his or her superior has already taken a different position?
7. Why is there so much government regulation involving social responsibility issues? Should there be less?

Exercises

1. Research and report on one case in which the EEOC or the EPA successfully brought suit against one or more firms. Give your own evaluation of the merits of the case.
2. Write out four "guidelines" that can be included as part of the code of ethics that prevails at your school or at a firm where you have worked.
3. List some items that should be included in a social audit for a small business other than a retail store.

CASE 2-1
Comparable Worth at Westinghouse

Women are paid less than men, even when they do comparable work. According to the U.S. Department of Commerce, women earn about 60 cents for every dollar that men earn, at the same job.

The problem of unequal pay became obvious early in the 1960s. In fact, the Equal Pay Act of 1963 and Title VII of the Civil Rights Act of 1964 were passed partly to eliminate such discrimination in compensation. Yet obvious abuses continue to surface, as in the 1972 case brought by the International Union of Electrical Workers against Westinghouse Electric Corporation. The union traced the company's male–female wage disparity—about 20 percent in similar jobs—to a 33-year-old manager's manual which said, in essence, that women were to be paid less because they were women. Now, decades later, equal pay for equal work is still a dream.

To make the dream a reality, union negotiators and women's groups are pushing a new idea commonly referred to as "comparable worth." According to this concept, workers performing different jobs should receive the same pay if the skill required, the effort expended, the responsibility entailed, and the working conditions are the same for both jobs. When comparable worth is used as a basis for determining wages, jobs are broken down into individual components called factors. Points are assigned to each factor by supervisors, professional job evaluators, or management consultants. The "worth" of a job is then the total number of points assigned to all its factors. People who hold jobs with similar "comparable worth" should earn comparable pay.

For example, suppose a male has the job of maintenance worker, rated at 1465 points and a female has a clerical job rated at 1480 points. The female clerk should earn slightly more than the male maintenance worker.

Comparable worth seems to be an equitable solution to the probelm, and its future looks promising. It has already become part of the bargaining process between labor negotiators and employers: Comparable worth was a major issue in American Telephone & Telegraph's 1983 labor contract negotiations. According to AT&T's Kenneth Ross, "When more than half the students in college are women and more than half the people in law school and medical school are women, this issue is not going to go away."[10]

1. What impact might the use of comparable worth have on male employees' salaries?
2. Is equality of pay sufficent evidence of a firm's commitment to equitable employment practices? Explain.

CASE 2-2
Nestlé Re-examines Its Social Role

For years, Nestlé S.A. was severely criticized for encouraging mothers in underdeveloped countries to feed their children prepared infant formula instead of breast milk. The International Nestlé Boycott Committee was organized to fight Nestlé's marketing tactics through boycotts.

The boycott committee charged that Nestlé, a Swiss firm, promoted infant formula as superior to mother's milk; distributed free samples to people unfamiliar with bottle feeding; and supplied samples to institutions to encourage them to start newborns on formula. Powdered formula lacks the infection-fighting antibodies of breast milk, so that children in poorer countries were weakened by drinking formula. Moreover, uneducated mothers poisoned their infants by mixing the powder with contaminated water. Researchers generally agreed that breast milk is better by far for almost all newborns.

Initially, Nestlé viewed its promotion methods as "standard." As the controversy continued, however, management took a look at its social responsibility. This self-examination led to policy changes within the Nestlé organization. With regard to the marketing of infant formula, Nestlé agreed to revise its promotion practices in underdeveloped countries. It also financed the independent Nestlé Infant Formula Audit Commission to keep tabs on its infant formula marketing activities worldwide. Nestlé also endorsed the World Health Organization's code for marketing infant formulas, an outgrowth of the controversy.

According to one company spokesman, Nestlé has become a stronger firm "more sensitive" to social concerns.[11] Certainly, it is gratified that the international boycott has been lifted.

1. How does this case parallel the development of social responsibility in business generally?
2. Would you have joined one of the campaigns to "crunch Nestlé"? Why or why not?

CHAPTER THREE

The Forms of Business Ownership

Who owns what in American business? Walk into your neighborhood shoe store, and the owner will probably wait on you or be close at hand. Walk into your nearest K mart store, and a hundred thousand owners may be glad you did—but probably none of them will be in sight. As you will see in this chapter, the difference lies in the way the two businesses are owned. After studying the chapter, you should understand:

1. *The basic differences among the three most common forms of business ownership: sole proprietorships, partnerships, and corporations*

2. *The advantages and disadvantages of these three forms of ownership*

3. *How a corporation is formed, who owns it, and who is responsible for its operation*

4. *The basic structure of a corporation, and how corporations grow*

5. *How the special types of corporations differ from the more typical open or close corporation*

6. *Three additional forms of ownership: cooperatives, joint ventures, and syndicates*

Consider this:

In 1976 two young engineers got together to work on an idea for a small computer for personal use. Steven Jobs, then 21, and Stephen Wozniak, then 26, spent 6 months designing a prototype and 40 hours building it. Their idea worked—and they soon had an order for 50 of their personal computers.

With that first order in hand, they were practically in business. The only thing missing was resources. Jobs and Wozniak became the labor force, and Jobs' garage became their manufacturing site. To raise capital to buy the materials they needed, they sold a used Volkswagen van and a programmable calculator for $1350.

Now they *were* in business—and, like every other business, theirs needed a name. They searched for one that would express the simplicity they were aiming for in the design and use of their computer. Jobs and Wozniak finally decided on the name "Apple" for both the computer and their company.

That first Apple computer was sold in kit form to electronics hobbyists. It was so successful that neither Jobs' garage nor the firm's capital was large enough to keep up with the market demand. Realizing that they had a product with great commercial and social value, Jobs and Wozniak sought professional help in managing their firm.

A friend introduced them to Mike Markkula, Jr., who had been a successful marketing manager for two semiconductor companies—Intel Corporation and Fairchild Camera & Instrument Corp. Both had enjoyed dynamic growth under his leadership.

After researching the personal computer market and assessing Apple Computer's chances, the three men developed a set of plans for the firm. They considered both its immediate need for capital, management expertise, and marketing and such future needs as technical innovation and software development. Initial financing came from Markkula and a group of investors that included Venrock Associates and Arthur Rock and Associates.

Apple Computer was incorporated in 1977. It remained a private corporation until December 1980, when 4.6 million shares of common stock were offered and sold to the public. In May 1981, there was another offering of 2.6 million shares of common stock.

In only six years, Apple grew from a two-man operation into an international corporation employing more than four thousand people and producing annual sales of more than $1 billion.

Posting revenues of $583 million for fiscal 1982, Apple Computer, Inc., became the youngest company ever to join the ranks of *Fortune's* five hundred largest U.S. industrial corporations. In fiscal 1983, Apple's sales were $982.7 million.

Mike Markkula served as Apple's president and chief executive officer from March 1981 to April 1983. Today he is a member of the firm's board of directors and is involved in long-range strategic and technological planning. Among his concerns is competition from a number of firms that have recently decided to enter the personal computer market—perhaps motivated largely by Apple's success. The newest entry is IBM, the "big name" in computers, with its PC and PCjr.[1]

Source: Logo and photo, Apple Computer, Inc.

When people like Jobs and Wozniak start a business, they create something of value. In many cases, the immediate value is quite small: Apple Computer was worth only $1350 in cash at the start. But Apple's assets also included two clever engineer-entrepreneurs and an idea that was worth millions of dollars.

The people who start businesses must decide how their "something of value" will be owned. Should it be made part of their own personal assets, like a car or a house, for which they are responsible? Or should it be entirely separate from their personal finances? And should they retain ownership of the whole business, or exchange part of that ownership for such assets as capital resources?

Obviously the answers to these questions depend on the particular situation. And the answers change as the situation changes. Toward the end of the nineteenth century, Richard Sears was the sole owner of a small business in the midwest. Later this business became a partnership known as Sears, Roebuck and Company. And eventually Sears, Roebuck became a corporation owned by thousands of stockholders.

The three most common forms of business ownership in the United States are the sole proprietorship, the partnership, and the corporation (see Figure 3.1). In terms of ownership, corporations are generally the most complex, and sole proprietorships are the simplest. In terms of organization, however, all three usually start small and simple. And some, like Apple Computer, grow and grow.

SOLE PROPRIETORSHIP

A **sole proprietorship** is a business that is owned (and usually operated) by one person. Sole proprietorship is the oldest and simplest form of business ownership, and it is the easiest to start. In most instances, the owner (the *sole* proprietor) simply decides that he or she is in business and begins operations. Some of the largest of today's corporations, including Ford Motor Company,

H.J. Heinz Company, and J.C. Penney, started out as tiny—and, in many cases, struggling—sole proprietorships.

As you can see in Figure 3.1, there were over 12.1 million sole proprietorships in the United States in 1983. In that year they accounted for three-fourths of the country's business firms. Sole proprietorships are most common in retailing, agriculture, and the service industries. Thus the specialty clothing shop, the corner grocery, and the television repair shop down the street are likely to be sole proprietorships.

Most of the advantages and disadvantages of sole proprietorship arise from the two main characteristics of this form of ownership: simplicity and individual control.

Advantages of Sole Proprietorship

Ease and Low Cost of Formation and Dissolution

No contracts, agreements, or other legal documents are required to start a sole proprietorship. Most are even established without an attorney. A state or city license may be required for certain *types* of businesses that are regulated in the interest of public safety, such as running a restaurant. But beyond that, a sole proprietor does not pay any special start-up fees or taxes. And there are no minimum capital requirements.

If the enterprise does not succeed, or the owner decides to enter another line of business, he or she can close the firm as easily as it was opened. Creditors must be paid, of course. But the owner does not have to go through any legal procedure before hanging up an "Out of Business" sign.

Retention of All Profits

All profits earned by a sole proprietorship become the personal earnings of its owner. This provides the owner with a strong incentive to succeed—perhaps the strongest incentive—and a great deal of satisfaction when the business does succeed. It is this direct financial reward that attracts many entrepreneurs to the sole proprietorship form of business.

Flexibility

The sole owner of a business is completely free to make decisions about the firm's operations. Without asking or waiting for anyone's approval, a sole proprietor can switch from retailing to wholesaling, move a shop's location, or open a new store and close an old one.

A sole owner can also respond to changes in market conditions much more quickly than the operators of other forms of business. Suppose the sole owner of an appliance store finds that many customers now prefer to shop on Sunday afternoons. He or she can make an immediate change in business hours to take advantage of that information (provided that state laws allow such stores to open on Sunday). The manager of one store in a large corporate chain may have to seek the approval of numerous managers before making such a change. Furthermore, a sole proprietor can quickly switch suppliers to take advantage of a lower price, whereas such a switch could take weeks in a more complex business.

Possible Tax Advantages

The sole proprietorship's profits are taxed as personal income of the owner. Thus a sole proprietorship does not pay the special state and federal income taxes that corporations pay. (As you will see later, the result

Figure 3.1 *The Relative Percentages of Sole Proprietorships, Partnerships, and Corporations in the U.S.* Source: Adapted from The Statistical Abstract of the U.S. 1984 *U.S. Bureau of the Census, p. 532.*

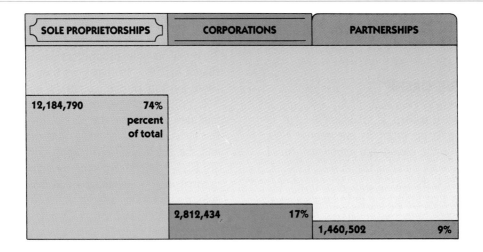

of these special taxes is that a corporation's profits are taxed twice. A sole proprietorship's profits are taxed only once.)

Secrecy   Sole proprietors are not required by federal or state governments to publicly reveal their business plans, profits, or other vital facts, so competitors cannot get their hands on this information. Of course, sole proprietors must report certain financial information on their personal tax forms, but that information is kept secret by the taxing authority.

Disadvantages of Sole Proprietorship

Unlimited Liability   **Unlimited liability** is a legal concept that holds a sole proprietor personally responsible for all the debts of his or her business. This means there is no legal difference between the debts of the business and the debts of the proprietor. If the business should fail, the owner's personal property—including house, savings, and other assets—could be seized (and sold if necessary) to pay creditors.

Unlimited liability is thus the other side of the owner-keeps-the-profits coin. It is perhaps the major factor that tends to discourage would-be entrepreneurs from going into business for themselves.

Lack of Continuity   Legally, the sole proprietor *is* the business. If the owner dies or is declared legally insane, the business essentially ceases to exist. In many cases, however, the owner's heirs take over the business and continue to operate it, especially if it is a profitable enterprise.

Limited Ability to Borrow   Banks and other lenders are usually unwilling to lend large sums to sole proprietorships. Only one person—the sole proprietor—can be held responsible for repaying such loans, and the assets of most sole proprietors are fairly limited. Moreover, these assets may already have been used as the basis for personal borrowing (a mortgage loan or car loan) or for short-term credit from suppliers. Lenders also worry about the lack of continuity of sole

Most boutiques and small stores are sole proprietorships, if for no other reason than they are easy to form and to dissolve. Source: Philip Jon Bailey, The Picture Cube.

proprietorships: Who will repay a loan if the sole proprietor is incapacitated?

The limited ability to borrow can keep a sole proprietorship from growing. It is the main reason why many business owners change from the sole proprietorship to some other ownership form when they need relatively large amounts of capital.

Limited Business Skills and Knowledge   In Parts 2, 3, 4, and 5 we will see managers perform a variety of functions (including planning, organizing, and controlling) in such areas as finance, marketing, personnel, and operations. Often the

Cornell McBride and Therman McKenzie formed a partnership ten years ago that has since become the eleventh-largest black-owned business in the U.S.—M & M Products Company. Source: Courtesy M & M Products Company.

sole proprietor is the sole manager as well—in addition to being a salesperson, buyer, accountant, and, on occasion, janitor.

Even the most experienced business owner is unlikely to be expert in performing all these tasks in all these areas. The business can suffer in those areas wherein the owner is less knowledgeable, unless he or she obtains the necessary expertise by hiring assistants or consultants.

Lack of Opportunity for Employees The sole proprietor may find it hard to attract and keep competent help. Potential employees may feel that there is no room for advancement in a firm whose owner assumes all managerial responsibilities. And when those who *are* hired are ready to take on added responsibility, they may find that the only way to do so is to quit the sole proprietorship and either work for a larger firm or start up their own business.

Beyond the Sole Proprietorship

The major disadvantages of a sole proprietorship stem from its one-person control—and the limited amount that one person can do in a working day. One way to reduce the effect of these disadvantages (while retaining many of the advantages) is to have more than one owner. This provides more time to manage, more management expertise, and more capital and borrowing ability.

PARTNERSHIP

The Uniform Partnership Act, which has been adopted by many states, defines a **partnership** as an association of two or more persons to act as co-owners of a business for profit. Thus, about ten years ago, two young black pharmacists named Cornell McBride and Therman McKenzie each put up $250 and, together, went into business making a hair spray for black men. They worked from the tiny basement of McBride's three-room house, mixing their first batch in a 55-gallon drum and stirring it with a pool cue. Today their M & M Products Company is an extremely successful firm. It is the eleventh largest black-owned business in the United States, employs nearly 400 people, and spends about $4 million each year on advertising alone.

In 1983 there were approximately 1.5 million partnerships in the United States. As shown in Figure 3.2, partnerships accounted for $292 billion in receipts. Note, however, that this form of ownership is much less common than the sole proprietorship and the corporation. In fact, partnerships represent only about 9 percent of all American businesses.

Although there is no legal maximum, most partnerships have only two partners. Often the partnership represents a pooling of special talents, particularly in such fields as law, accounting, advertising, real estate, and retailing. A sole proprietor may also take on a partner for the purpose of obtaining more capital.

Types of Partners

All partners need not be equal. Some may be fully active in running the business, whereas others may have a much more limited role.

General Partners   A **general partner** is a person who assumes full co-ownership of a business. Like sole proprietors, general partners are responsible for operating the business. They also assume unlimited liability for its debts, including debts that have been incurred by any other general partner without their knowledge or consent. The Uniform Partnership Act requires that every partnership have at least one general partner. This is to assure that the liabilities of the business are legally assumed by at least one person.

General partners are active in day-to-day business operations, and each partner can enter into contracts on behalf of all the others. Each partner is taxed on his or her share of the profit—in the same way a sole proprietor is taxed. (The partnership itself pays no income tax.) If one general partner withdraws from the partnership, he or she must give notice to creditors, customers, and suppliers in order to avoid future liability.

Limited Partners   A **limited partner** is a person who contributes capital to a business but is not active in managing it; his or her liability is *limited* to the amount that has been invested. In return for their investment, limited partners share in the profits of the firm.

Not all states allow limited partnerships. In those that do, the prospective partners must file formal articles of partnership. They must publish a notice regarding the limitation in at least one newspaper. And they must ensure that at least one partner is a general partner. The goal of these requirements is to protect the customers and creditors of the limited partnership.

The Partnership Agreement

Some states require that partners draw up *articles of partnership* and file them with the secretary of state. Articles of partnership are a written agreement listing and explaining the terms of the partnership. Even where it is not required, an oral or written agreement among partners is legal and can be enforced in the courts. A written agreement is obviously preferred, because it is not subject to lapses of memory.

Figure 3.3 shows a typical partnership agreement. The articles generally describe each partner's contribution to, share of, and duties in the business. They may also outline each partner's responsibilities—who will do the accounts, who will manage sales, and so forth. They also spell out how disputes will be settled and how one partner may buy the interests of others.

Figure 3.2   *Total Sales Receipts Earned by American Businesses in 1980.* *Source: Adapted from* Statistical Abstract of the United States, 1984, *U.S. Bureau of the Census.*

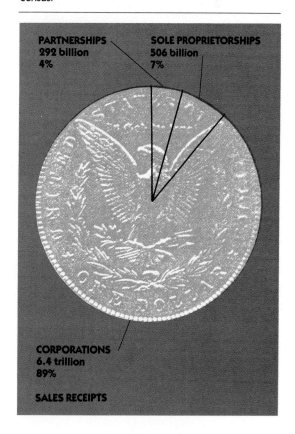

PARTNERSHIPS
292 billion
4%

SOLE PROPRIETORSHIPS
506 billion
7%

CORPORATIONS
6.4 trillion
89%

SALES RECEIPTS

Figure 3.3 *Articles of Partnership Source: R. Robert Rosenberg et al., College Business Law (New York: McGraw-Hill, 1978), p. 408. Copyright 1978 McGraw-Hill Book Company. Reproduced with permission.*

Date
Identity of Partners

This agreement made and entered into this eighth day of August 1986. between Steven Clark, of the City of Jersey City, County of Hudson, State of New Jersey, and Allan King, of the City of Elizabeth, County of Union, State of New Jersey.

WITNESSETH:

Nature of the Business

ONE. The parties, Steven Clark and Allan King, agree to become partners in the aircraft maintenance and operation business.

Name and Location of Firm

TWO. The business of the partnership shall be conducted under the firm name, Clark & King, Aircraft Specialists, at 100 Journal Square, Jersey City, N.J.

Duration of Partnership

THREE. The partnership shall begin on the date that this agreement is executed and shall continue for a term of five years thereafter.

Investments of Partners

FOUR. Each partner shall contribute to the capital of the partnership the sum of Twelve Thousand Dollars ($12,000). These contributions shall be without interest.

Sharing of Profits and Losses

FIVE. All profits resulting from the business shall be divided equally between the partners, and all losses incurred by the business also shall be borne equally by them.

Accounts of Business

SIX. Proper books of account shall be kept of all transactions relating to the business of the partnership.

At the end of each calendar year, a full inventory shall be prepared; a statement of the business made; the books closed; and the account of each partner credited or debited, as the case may be, with his proportionate share of the net loss. A statement of the business may be made at such other times as the partners agree on.

Partners' Drawings

SEVEN. Each partner may draw from the business, for his own use, a sum not to exceed One Thousand Dollars ($1,000) a month, to be withdrawn at such times as he may choose.

Duties of Partners

EIGHT. During the continuance of this partnership, each partner agrees to devote his entire time and attention to the business and to engage in no other business enterprise without the written consent of the other.

Restraints on Partners

NINE. Neither party shall, without the written consent of the other, become surety or bondsman for anyone.

Termination of Partnership

TEN. At the termination of this partnership, a full inventory and balance sheet shall be prepared; the debts of the business shall be discharged; and all property then remaining shall be divided equally between the partners.

In witness whereof, the parties have hereunto set their hands and seals the day and year first above written.

In the presence of

_____ L.S.

_____

_____ L.S.

Advantages of Partnership

Ease and Low Cost of Formation   Like sole proprietorships, partnerships are relatively easy to form. The legal requirements are often limited to registering the name of the business and purchasing whatever licenses are needed. It may not even be necessary to consult an attorney, except in states that require written articles of partnership. However, it is generally a good idea to get an attorney's help in forming a partnership.

Availability of Capital and Credit   Partners can pool their funds, so that their business has more capital than would be available to a sole proprietorship. This additional capital, coupled with the general partners' unlimited liability, can form the basis for a good credit rating. Banks and suppliers may be more willing to extend credit or grant sizable loans to such a partnership than to an individual owner.

This does not mean that partnerships can easily borrow all the money they need. Many partnerships have found it hard to get long-term financing, simply because lenders worry about projects that take years to earn a profit. But, in general, partnerships have greater assets and so stand a better chance of obtaining the loans they need.

Retention of Profits   As in a sole proprietorship, all profits belong to the owners of the partnership. The partners share directly in the financial rewards, so they are highly motivated to do their best to make the firm succeed.

Personal Interest   General partners are very much concerned with the operation of the firm—perhaps even more so than sole proprietors. After all, they are responsible for the actions of all other general partners, as well as for their own.

Combined Business Skills and Knowledge
Partners often have complementary skills. If one partner is weak in, say, finances, another may be stronger in that area. Moreover, the ability to discuss important decisions with another concerned individual often takes some of the pressure off everyone and leads to more effective decision making.

Possible Tax Advantages   Like sole proprietors, partners are taxed only on their individual income from the business. The special taxes that corporations must pay are not imposed on partnerships.

Disadvantages of Partnership

Unlimited Liability   As we have noted, each general partner is personally responsible for all debts of the business, whether or not the particular partner incurred those debts. General partners thus run the risk of having to use their personal assets to pay creditors. Limited partners, however, risk only their original investment.

Lack of Continuity   Partnerships are terminated in the event of the death, withdrawal, or legally declared insanity of any one of the general partners. However, that partner's ownership share can be purchased by the remaining partners. In other words, the law does not automatically provide that the business shall continue, but the articles of partnership may do so. For example, the partnership agreement may permit surviving partners to continue the business after buying a deceased partner's interest from his or her estate. However, if the partnership loses an owner whose specific skills cannot be replaced, it is not likely to survive.

Effects of Management Disagreements   The division of responsibilities among several partners means the partners must work together as a team. They must have great trust in each other. If partners begin to disagree about decisions, policies, or ethics, distrust may cloud the horizon. Such a mood tends to get worse as time passes—often to the point where it is impossible to operate the business successfully.

Frozen Investment It is easy to invest money in a partnership, but it is sometimes quite difficult to get it out. This is the case, for example, when remaining partners are unwilling to buy the share of the business that belongs to the partner who is leaving. To prevent such difficulties, the procedure for buying out a partner should be included in the articles of partnership.

In some cases, a partner must find someone outside the firm to buy his or her share. This may or may not be a problem, depending on how successful the business is.

Beyond the Partnership

The advantages of a partnership over a sole proprietorship are due mainly to the added capital and expertise of the partners. However, some of the basic disadvantages of the sole proprietorship also plague the general partnership. Unlimited liability and restraints on capital resources and borrowing, for example, can hinder a partnership's growth. A third form of business ownership, the corporation, overcomes some of these disadvantages.

THE CORPORATION

Perhaps the best definition of a corporation was given by Chief Justice John Marshall in a famous decision in 1819. A corporation, he said, "is an artificial being, invisible, intangible, and existing only in contemplation of the law." In other words, a **corporation** is an artificial person created by law, with most of the legal rights of a real person. These include the right to start and operate a business, to own or dispose of property, to borrow money, to sue or be sued, and to enter into binding contracts. Unlike a real person, however, a corporation exists only on paper.

There were about 2.8 million corporations in the United States in 1983. They comprised only about one-seventh of all businesses, but they accounted for nine-tenths of all sales revenues and

over three-quarters of all business profits. Table 3.1 lists the twenty-five largest industrial corporations in the United States at the end of 1983, ranked according to sales.

Corporate Ownership

The shares of ownership of a corporation are called its **stock**. The people who own a corporation's stock—and thus own part of the corporation—are called its **stockholders**, or sometimes its *shareholders*. Once a corporation has been formed, it may sell its stock to individuals. It may also issue stock as a reward to key employees in return for certain services, or as a return to investors (in place of cash payments).

A **private** or **close corporation** is a corporation whose stock is owned by relatively few people and is not traded openly (that is, in stock markets). A person who wishes to sell the stock of such a corporation generally arranges to sell it *privately,* to another stockholder or a close acquaintance. As an example, Mr. and Mrs. DeWitt Wallace owned virtually all the stock of *Reader's Digest,* making it one of the nation's largest private corporations.

A **public** or **open corporation** is a corporation whose stock is traded openly in stock markets and can be purchased by any individual. Exxon, the largest industrial company in the U.S., is a public corporation. Most large firms are open corporations, and their stockholders may number in the millions. For example, AT&T is owned by over 3.3 million shareholders.

Forming a Corporation

The process of forming a corporation is called **incorporation**. The people who actually start the corporation are its *incorporators*. They must make several decisions about the corporation before and during the incorporation process.

Where to Incorporate A business is allowed to incorporate in any state it chooses. Most small and medium-sized businesses are incorporated in the state where they do the most business. However, the founders of larger corporations, or of those that will do business nationwide, may compare the benefits provided to corporations by various states. Some states are more hospitable than others, and some offer low taxes and other benefits to attract new firms. Delaware is acknowledged as offering the most lenient tax structure. A huge number of firms (more than 75,000) have incorporated in that state, even though their corporate headquarters may be located in one of the larger cities of another state. Figure 3.4 shows the best and worst "business climates" among the states, according to one group of experts.

An incorporated business is called a **domestic corporation** in the state in which it is incorporated. In all other states where it does business, it is called a **foreign corporation**. Sears, Roebuck and Company, for example, is incorporated in New York, where it is a domestic corporation.

Table 3.1   The Twenty-Five Largest U.S. Industrial Corporations, Ranked by Sales

Rank 1983	Rank 1982	Company	Sales (in billions of dollars)	Assets (in billions of dollars)
1	1	Exxon (New York)	88.6	63.0
2	2	General Motors (Detroit)	74.6	45.7
3	3	Mobil (New York)	54.6	35.1
4	5	Ford Motor (Dearborn, Mich.)	44.4	23.9
5	6	International Business Machines (Armonk, N.Y.)	40.2	37.2
6	4	Texaco Inc. (Harrison, N.Y.)	40.1	27.2
7	8	E.I. du Pont de Nemours (Wilmington, Del.)	35.4	24.4
8	10	Standard Oil (Indiana) (Chicago)	27.6	25.8
9	7	Standard Oil of California (San Francisco)	27.3	24.0
10	11	General Electric (Fairfield, Conn.)	26.8	23.3
11	9	Gulf Oil (Pittsburgh)	26.6	21.0
12	12	Atlantic Richfield (Los Angeles)	25.1	23.3
13	13	Shell Oil (Houston)	19.7	22.2
14	15	Occidental Petroleum (Los Angeles)	19.1	11.8
15	14	U.S. Steel (Pittsburgh)	16.9	19.3
16	17	Phillips Petroleum Company (Bartlesville, Okla.)	15.2	13.1
17	18	Sun Company, Inc. (Radnor, Pa.)	14.7	12.5
18	20	United Technologies Corp. (Hartford)	14.7	8.7
19	19	Tenneco (Houston)	14.4	18.0
20	16	International Telephone & Telegraph (New York)	14.2	14.0
21	29	Chrysler (Highland Park, Mich.)	13.2	6.8
22	23	Procter & Gamble (Cincinnati)	12.5	8.1
23	25	R.J. Reynolds Industries (Winston-Salem, N.C.)	12.0	9.9
24	24	Getty Oil (Los Angeles)	11.6	10.4
25	21	Standard Oil (Ohio) (Cleveland)	11.6	16.4

Source: *Fortune 500*, April 30, 1984, issue, © 1984 Time Inc. All rights reserved.

In the remaining forty-nine states, it is a foreign corporation.

The Corporate Charter Once a "home state" has been chosen, the incorporators submit *articles of incorporation* to its secretary of state. If the articles of incorporation are approved, they become the firm's corporate charter. A **corporate charter** is a contract between the corporation and the state, in which the state recognizes the formation of the artificial person that is the corporation. Usually the charter (and thus the articles of incorporation) includes the following information:

- The firm's name and address
- The incorporators' names and addresses
- The purpose of the corporation
- The maximum amount of stock and the types of stock to be issued
- The rights and privileges of shareholders
- How long the corporation is to exist (usually without limit)

Each of these key details is the result of decisions that the incorporators must make as they organize the firm—before the articles of incorporation are submitted. Let us look at one area in particular: stockholders' rights.

Figure 3.4   The Best and Worst Business Climates. States are ranked best to worst, 1 to 48.
Source: Chicago Sun-Times, Field Enterprises, Inc. © News Group Chicago Inc., 1983. Map by Char Searl. Reprinted with permission of the Chicago Sun-Times.

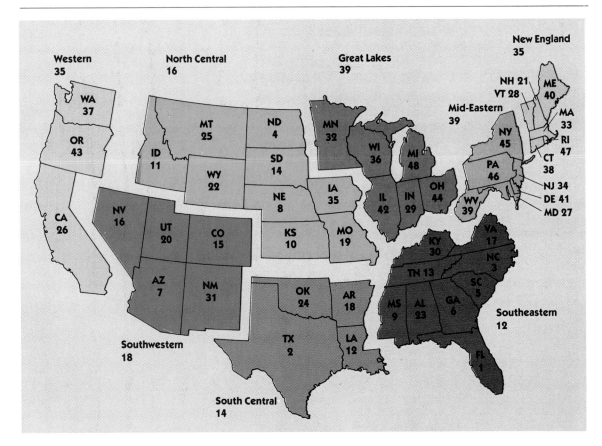

Stockholders' Rights   There are two basic kinds of stock (and some variations that are discussed in Chapters 16 and 17). Each type entitles the owner to a different set of rights and privileges. The owners of **common stock** may vote on corporate matters, but their claim on profit and assets is subsidiary to the claims of others. Generally, an owner of common stock has one vote for each share owned. The owners of **preferred stock** usually do not have voting rights, but their claim on profit and assets takes precedence over that of common-stock owners.

Perhaps the most important right of owners of both common and preferred stock is to share in the profit earned by the corporation. Other rights include being offered additional stock in advance of a public offering (*pre-emptive rights*); examining corporate records; voting on the corporate charter; and attending the corporation's annual stockholders' meeting, where they may exercise their right to vote.

Because common stockholders usually live all over the nation, very few actually attend the annual meeting. Instead, they vote by proxy. A **proxy** is a legal form that lists issues to be decided and requests that stockholders transfer their voting rights to some other individual or individuals. The stockholder registers his or her vote and transfers his or her voting rights simply by signing and returning the form.

In most cases, these voting rights are solicited only by the corporation's present management. Occasionally, however, a group of stockholders who are dissatisfied with management try to obtain the proxies of other stockholders in order to elect a new management team. Then a battle for proxies, between management and the dissatisfied stockholders, may take place. In 1983, a group of dissident stockholders of GAF Corporation organized the GAF Shareholders' Committee for New Management. As a result of a proxy fight, the old management team was defeated and one nominated by the committee was voted in.

Organizational Meeting   As the last step in forming a corporation, the original stockholders meet

The board of directors meets annually (sometimes more often) to set corporate goals and strategies for achieving those goals. Source: Courtesy of Emhart Corporation.

to elect its first board of directors. (Later, directors will be elected or re-elected at the corporation's annual meetings.) The board members are directly responsible to the stockholders for the way they operate the firm.

Corporate Structure

Board of Directors   The **board of directors** is the top governing body of a corporation, and, as we noted, directors are elected by the shareholders. A corporation is an artificial person, so it can act only through its directors, who represent the corporation's owners. Board members can be chosen from within the corporation or from outside it.

Directors who are elected from within the corporation are usually its top managers—the president and executive vice presidents, for example. Those who are elected from outside the corporation are generally experienced managers with proven leadership ability and/or specific talents

Figure 3.5 *The Hierarchy of Corporate Structure. Stockholders exercise a great deal of influence by their right to vote and elect directors.*

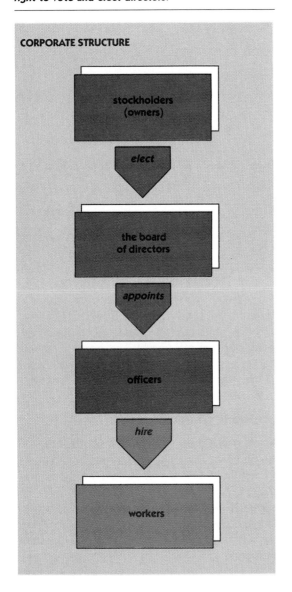

CORPORATE STRUCTURE

stockholders (owners)

elect

the board of directors

appoints

officers

hire

workers

that the organization seems to need. For example, Douglas A. Fraser, retired president of the United Auto Workers, served as a director on the board of the Chrysler Corporation. In smaller corporations, majority stockholders may also serve as board members.

The major responsibilities of the board of directors are to set company goals and develop general plans (or strategies) for meeting those goals. They are also responsible for the overall operation of the firm.

Corporate Officers The **corporate officers** (including the chairman of the board, the president, executive vice presidents, and the corporate secretary and treasurer) are appointed by the board of directors. These officers help the board make plans, carry out the strategies established by the board, and manage day-to-day business activities. Periodically (usually each month), they report to the board of directors. And once each year, at the annual meeting, the directors report to the stockholders. In theory, then, the stockholders are able to control the activities of the entire corporation through its directors (Figure 3.5).

Advantages of the Corporation

Limited Liability One of the most attractive features of corporate ownership is **limited liability**. Each owner's financial liability is limited to the amount of money she or he has paid for the corporation's stock. This feature arises from the fact that the corporation is itself a legal being, separate from its owners. If a corporation should fail, creditors have a claim only on the assets of the corporation, not on the personal assets of its owners.

Ease of Transfer of Ownership Let us say that a shareholder of a public corporation wishes to sell his or her stock. A telephone call to a stock broker is all that is required to put the stocks up for sale. There are usually willing buyers available for most stocks, at the market price. Ownership is transferred automatically when the sale is made, and practically no restrictions apply to the sale and purchase of stock.

When Managers Become Owners

Hanging on one wall of the president's office at Genesys Software Systems Inc. in Lawrence, Mass., is a picture frame that holds a mat with five openings. Three of the openings contain cancelled checks made out to Wang Laboratories Inc.; the largest is made out in the amount of $1 million. This is Lawrence J. Munini's version of the framed first dollar—that first, hard-won evidence that, yes, there is a going business here, and it belongs to me. When the fifth opening is filled with a final check made out to Wang in the amount of $1.4 million, Munini will have successfully completed the purchase of the Wang division he managed for more than 10 years.

Munini is one of a growing number of managers who have bought the divisions or companies or business segments they have managed from their former parent companies. The transactions can range from asset redeployment programs that affect dozens of units within a big company to sale or near-abandonment of operations that the parent company has decided are hopeless.

This spinning off is part of a deconglomeration phenomenon in American business, according to André Daniel-Dreyfus. Daniel-Dreyfus is a vice president at B. L. McTeague & Co., a Hartford-based investment banking firm that has worked with clients on both sides of management buy-outs. "We went through the conglomeration phase of the 60s; now we're doing the opposite, where large companies are looking at themselves, and they're spinning off a lot of the smaller businesses," says Daniel-Dreyfus. As a prime example, he cites General Electric Co., which last year spun off 200 businesses.

Source: Jane Simon, *New England Business*, Mar. 7, 1984, p. 30.

Ease of Raising Capital   The corporation is by far the most effective form of business ownership for raising capital. Like sole proprietorships and partnerships, corporations can borrow from lending institutions. However, they can also sell stock to raise additional sums of money. Individuals are more willing to invest in corporations than in other forms of business because of the limited liability that investors enjoy and because of the ease with which they can sell their stock.

Perpetual Life   Because a corporation is essentially a legal "person," it exists independently of its owners and survives them. Unless its charter specifies otherwise, a corporation has perpetual life. The withdrawal, death, or insanity of a key executive or owner is not cause for the corporation to be terminated. Sears, Roebuck and Company, incorporated almost a century ago, is the nation's largest retailing corporation, even though its original owners, Richard Sears and Alvah Roebuck, have been dead for decades.

Specialized Management   Typically, corporations are able to recruit more skilled and knowledgeable managers than proprietorships and partnerships. This is because they have more available capital and are large enough to offer considerable opportunity for advancement. Within the corporate structure, administration, personnel, finance, sales, and operations are placed in the charge of experts in these fields. As an example, Bechtel Power Corporation hired George P. Shultz, former Secretary of the Treasury under President Nixon, as its president.

Disadvantages of the Corporation

Difficulty and Expense of Formation   Forming a corporation is a relatively complex and costly process. An attorney must be hired to help fill out the necessary legal forms and apply to the state for a charter. Charter fees, attorney's fees, the costs of stock certificates and required record keeping, and other organizational costs must all

Not-for-profit organizations provide social, educational, religious, environmental, or other nonbusiness services to society. They are not in business for the purpose of earning a profit. *Source: Courtesy of National Wildlife Federation.*

Double Taxation Unlike sole proprietorships and partnerships, corporations must pay a tax on their profits. Then stockholders must pay a personal income tax on profits that are distributed to them. As a result, corporate profits are taxed twice—once as corporate income and again as the personal income of stockholders.

Lack of Secrecy Because public corporations are required to submit detailed reports to government agencies and to stockholders, they cannot keep their operations confidential. Competitors can study these required corporate reports, and they may use the information to compete more effectively. In effect, every public corporation has to share some of its secrets with its competitors.

SPECIAL TYPES OF CORPORATIONS

Most corporations are organized for the purpose of earning business profits. Of these, most are public corporations, although a number are privately owned. There are also various types of corporations that are organized for special purposes. Among these are government-owned, not-for-profit, and subchapter-S corporations.

Government-Owned Corporations

Government-owned corporations are owned and operated by local, state, or federal government. They usually provide a service that the business sector is reluctant or unable to offer. (It is doubtful, for instance, whether private enterprise could have marshaled the financial resources needed to put astronauts on the moon.) Profit is secondary in government-owned corporations. In fact, they may continually operate at a loss, particularly in the area of public transportation. Their main objective is to ensure that a particular service is available to citizens.

The U.S. Postal Service, the Tennessee Valley Authority (TVA), the National Aeronautics and Space Administration (NASA), and the Federal Deposit Insurance Corporation (FDIC) are all

be paid. These could amount to thousands of dollars for even a medium-sized corporation. The cost of incorporating, in both time and money, discourages many owners of smaller businesses from forming corporations.

Government Regulation Most government regulation of business is directed at corporations. A corporation must meet various government standards before it can sell its stock to the public. Then it must file many reports on its business operations and finances with local, state, and federal governments. In addition, the corporation must report periodically to its stockholders regarding various aspects of the business. Its activities are also restricted by law to those that are spelled out in its charter.

Texaco Wins FTC's Nod to Acquire Getty

Texaco, Inc. won Federal Trade Commission approval to acquire Getty Oil Co. with the provisional acceptance of a consent order requiring Texaco to shed two refineries and several other properties.

The commission's 4–1 vote cleared the way for Texaco to complete its $10.1 billion acquisition of Getty, the largest corporate merger in U.S. history.

Yesterday, Texaco said that it completed purchase of 56% of Getty's stock. Texaco bought 9.3 million common shares, or 11.8%, from the J. Paul Getty Museum and 35.1 million publicly held shares tendered for $125 a share. The purchases brought Texaco's holdings to 79.1 million shares.

An additional 31.8 million shares, or 40.2% of Getty, are being held in escrow for Texaco. Texaco will pay the Sarah C. Getty trust for those shares under a stock-purchase agreement.

The transaction moved ahead after the FTC accord and after a federal judge refused to grant a temporary restraining order that would have postponed the acquisition. A Getty dealer, Fairlawn Oil Service Inc., had filed the suit in Providence, R.I.

Under the agreement, Texaco must operate the two companies' oil-related assets separately until the FTC takes its final vote on the merger following a 60-day public comment period.

James Miller, FTC chairman, led the majority in accepting the proposed consent order. The agreement, he said, provides "important safeguards" against the anti-competitive effects that the agency said might otherwise have resulted.

Commissioner Michael Pertschuk, the sole opponent of the merger, said it will continue a trend toward the disappearance of medium-sized oil concerns. That trend, he said, will lead to tighter control of the industry by major companies and higher prices for consumers.

Source: Jeanne Saddler, *The Wall Street Journal*, February 14, 1984.

government-owned corporations. They are operated by the U.S. government. Most municipal buslines and subways are run by city-owned corporations.

In certain cases, a government will invite citizens or firms to invest in such a corporation as part owners. A business owned partly by the government and partly by private citizens or firms is called a **quasigovernment corporation**. Prominent examples are the Federal National Mortgage Association (Fannie Mae) and the Communications Satellite Corporation (Comsat).

Not-for-Profit Corporations

A **not-for-profit corporation** is a corporation that is organized to provide a social, educational, religious, or other nonbusiness service rather than to earn a profit. Various charities, museums, and private schools (including colleges) are organized in this way, primarily to ensure limited liability. The statutes of most states contain separate provisions dealing with the organization and operation of not-for-profit corporations.

In 1983 there were approximately 788,410 not-for-profit corporations in the United States.[2] These organizations do not issue stock certificates, because no dividends are paid and no one is interested in buying or selling their stock. They are also exempted from income taxes.

Occasionally, some not-for-profit organizations are inspired with entrepreneurial zeal. For example, the Children's Television Workshop netted $7.7 million in 1983 by licensing Sesame Street products. In the same year, the New York Museum of Modern Art sold air rights in Manhattan for $17 million to allow the construction of a private 44-story residential tower. The tax-free income from the sale helped finance a new wing, doubling the size of the museum.[3]

S-Corporations

If a corporation meets certain requirements, its directors may apply to the Internal Revenue Service for status as an S-corporation (formerly known as a subchapter-S corporation). An **S-corporation** is a corporation that is taxed as though it were a partnership. In other words, the corporation's income is taxed only as the personal income of shareholders.

Becoming an S-corporation can be an effective way to avoid double taxation while retaining the legal benefits of incorporation. Moreover, shareholders can personally claim their share of losses incurred by the corporation to offset their own personal income.

To qualify for this special status, the firm must meet the following criteria:

1. The firm must have no more than 35 shareholders.
2. The shareholders must be individuals or es-

tates, and they must be citizens or permanent residents of the United States.
3. There must be only one class of outstanding stock.
4. The firm must not own 80 percent or more of the stock of any other corporation.
5. Income from passive sources (such as interest, rent, and royalties) cannot exceed 25 percent of the firm's gross income. (However, there is no limit on passive income for new S-corporations formed after December 31, 1983.)

The characteristics of S-corporations are summarized and compared with those of other forms of doing business in Table 3.2.

CORPORATE GROWTH

Growth seems to be a basic characteristic of business. At least it is for those firms that can obtain the capital needed to finance growth. One reason for seeking growth has to do with profit: A larger firm generally has greater sales revenue and thus

Table 3.2 *Forms of Doing Business*

Characteristics	Sole Proprietorship	Partnership		Corporation	
		General	Limited	Regular	S-Corporations
Instrument of creation	None (Assumed name statement may be required.)	Agreement— oral or written	Written agreement— File certificate of limited partnership	Articles of incorporation	Same, but must file form 2553
Tax rates	Individual	Individual	Individual	Corporate	Individual
Organizational documents	None	Partnership agreement	Certificate of limited partnership agreement	Articles of incorporation, bylaws, minutes	Same
Limited liability	No	No	Yes	Yes	Yes
Recognition of losses	Owner	Partners	Partners	Corporation	Shareholders

Source: John A. Andersen, "The Business Entity That's Best For You" by John A. Andersen, *Panorama*, Number 13, Second Quarter, 1982. Reprinted by permission of Pannell Kerr Forster and the author.

greater profit. Moreover, in a growing economy, a business that does not grow is actually shrinking relative to the economy. And, for some executives, business growth is a means by which to boost their power, prestige, and reputation.

Should all firms grow? Certainly not until they are ready to grow. Growth poses new problems and requires additional resources that must first be available and must then be used effectively. The main ingredient in growth is capital—and, as we have noted, capital is most readily available to corporations. Thus, to a great extent, business growth means corporate growth.

Growth from Within

Most corporations grow by expanding their present operations. They may introduce and sell new but related products, such as Chrysler Corporation's van/station wagon or IBM's personal computers. They may also expand the sale of present products to new geographic markets or new groups of consumers. Converse, Inc., the athletic shoe manufacturer, now makes its well-known basketball shoe in colors such as pink and purple. Converse hopes to increase its growth by selling its products to a different, fashion-conscious group of consumers.[4]

Growth from within generally has very little impact on the firm, especially if it is carefully planned and controlled. For the most part, the firm continues to do what it has been doing (and what it has been successful at doing), but on a larger scale. Because this type of growth is anticipated, it can be gradual and the firm usually adapts to it easily.

External Growth

Another way for a firm to grow is by purchasing some other corporation. The purchase of one corporation by another is called a **merger**. The firm that is expanding simply buys the stock of the purchased corporation. (This is not always as simple as it sounds. In some cases, the management and stockholders of the firm targeted for acquisition are unwilling to let their company be-

come a subsidiary of the purchasing firm. The results may be greatly inflated stock prices, legal battles, and—at the least—general ill will between the two firms.) The underlying reason for growth by merger is that the merged companies can produce benefits for the shareholders that the individual companies could not have offered on their own. The 1981 merger between American Express and Shearson Loeb Rhoades (a large stock brokerage firm), illustrates this point. In

Figure 3.6 *The Three Different Types of Growth By Merger. When one company, such as an airline, acquires another airline, there is a horizontal merger. If the same airline were to buy out its catering service, a vertical merger would result. A conglomerate merger would result from the airline buying a sports firm.*

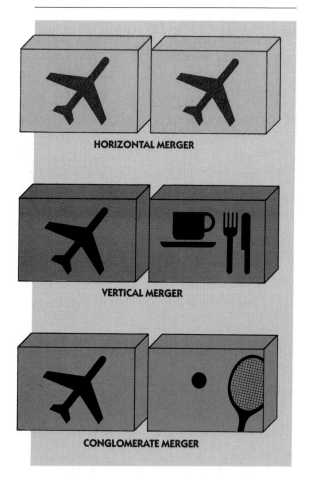

HORIZONTAL MERGER

VERTICAL MERGER

CONGLOMERATE MERGER

1983, Shearson's profits grew by 41 percent, and the 4000 brokers who work for Shearson now have access to the 17 million people who carry American Express cards. American Express now has the financial expertise of all the Shearson brokers at its disposal—increasing the benefits to each group.[5]

Horizontal Merger   A *horizontal merger* is a merger between firms that make and sell similar products in similar markets (see Figure 3.6). The recent purchase of National Airlines by Pan American World Airways is an example of a horizontal merger. The rash of mergers between large American oil companies in 1983 and 1984 is another. Horizontal mergers tend to reduce the number of firms in an industry—and thus reduce competition. For this reason, mergers may be looked over very carefully by federal agencies before they are permitted.

Firms may use horizontal mergers to accomplish goals other than growth. For example, the major goal of the oil company mergers was to acquire large petroleum reserves. It was actually less costly to obtain petroleum by buying a firm that owned oil than by exploring, drilling, and pumping oil from the ground.

Table 3.3   The Largest Mergers of 1983

	Acquiring Company	Acquired Company	Value of the Merger (in billions of dollars)	Type of Merger
1	Santa Fe Industries, Inc. (transportation and natural resources)	Southern Pacific Co. (transportation and natural resources)	2.3	horizontal
2	Xerox Corporation	Crum & Foster (insurance)	1.6	conglomerate
3	Diamond Shamrock (oil and gas)	Natomas Company (oil and geothermal energy)	1.5	horizontal
4	Phillips Petroleum Company	General American Oil Co. of Texas	1.1	horizontal
5	CSX Corporation (transportation and natural resources)	Texas Gas Resources (transportation and natural resources)	1.0	horizontal
6	Esmark (food and consumer products)	Norton Simon Inc. (food and consumer products)	0.9	horizontal
7	Southland (convenience retailing and gasoline sales)	Citgo Petroleum (oil refining)	0.9	vertical
8	Goodyear Tire and Rubber	Celeron Corp. (oil and gas)	0.8	vertical
9	Brown–Forman Distillers (alcoholic beverages)	Lenox, Inc. (china, jewelry, luggage)	0.4	conglomerate

Source: *Fortune*, January 23, 1984, p. 55. © 1984 Time Inc. All rights reserved.

Vertical Merger A *vertical merger* is a merger between firms that operate at different but related levels in the production and marketing of a product. Generally, one of the merging firms is either a supplier or a customer of the other. In December 1982, IBM agreed to purchase 12 percent of the stock of Intel Corporation, one of IBM's largest suppliers of semiconductors. This vertical merger should ensure that IBM has a steady supply of these devices for its computers.

Conglomerate Merger A *conglomerate merger* is a merger between firms in completely unrelated industries. In 1983 Xerox Corporation purchased Crum & Forster (an insurance firm), and Brown–Forman Distillers purchased Lenox, a producer of china. Both acquisitions were conglomerate mergers, and both enlarged the product base from which the purchasing firm receives its sales revenue.

Table 3.3 lists the nine largest mergers of 1983, along with their total values and the type of merger that each illustrates.

OTHER FORMS OF BUSINESS OWNERSHIP

Sole proprietorships, partnerships, and corporations are by far the most common forms of business ownership in the United States. Other forms of ownership do exist, however. And, like the nonstandard corporate forms, they are used primarily to serve the special needs of owners.

Cooperatives

A **cooperative** is an association of individuals or firms for the purpose of performing some business function for all its members. Members benefit from the activities of the cooperative, because it can perform its function more effectively than any member could by acting alone. For example, *buying cooperatives* are organized to purchase goods in bulk and then distribute them to members. The unit cost of the goods is lower

Cooperatives are most often found in agricultural industries. They are formed to facilitate certain business functions. Ocean Spray is a cooperative of about 700 cranberry growers and 100 citrus growers throughout the country. Source: Courtesy of Ocean Spray Cranberries, Inc.

than it would be if each member bought in a much smaller quantity.

Cooperatives are owned by their members, and they may or may not be incorporated. When they are, it is usually as nonprofit corporations. In either case, they generally have unlimited life; that is, a cooperative need not be dissolved when a member leaves the organization. Those that are incorporated also obtain such advantages as limited liability.

The members of a cooperative are charged membership fees, which cover its operating costs. In addition, members pay for the services of the cooperative as they use those services. In a buying cooperative, for example, members pay for the goods that they have ordered through the cooperative. Perhaps a small service charge is added to that cost. Cooperatives are not profit-making organizations, so surplus funds are either returned to the members or set aside to finance future needs.

Cooperatives may be found in all segments of our economy, but they are most prevalent in agriculture. Farmers make use of cooperatives to purchase supplies, to buy services such as trucking and storage, and to market their products. The trademark Ocean Spray, for example, is owned by Ocean Spray Cranberries, Inc., a cooperative of some 700 cranberry growers and more than 100 citrus growers throughout the country.

Joint Ventures

A **joint venture** is a partnership that is formed to achieve a specific goal or to operate for a specific period of time. Both the scope of the firm and the liabilities of the partners are limited. Once the goal is reached or the period of time elapses, the partnership is dissolved.

Corporations, as well as individuals, may form joint ventures. A number of these joint ventures were formed by major oil producers in the 1970s, to share the extremely high cost of exploring for offshore petroleum deposits.

Syndicates

A **syndicate** is a temporary association of individuals or firms, organized to perform a specific task that requires a large amount of capital. The syndicate is formed because no one person or firm is willing to put up the entire amount required for the undertaking. Like a joint venture, a syndicate is dissolved as soon as its purpose has been accomplished. However, the participants in a syndicate do not form a separate firm, as do the members of a joint venture.

Syndicates are most commonly used to underwrite large insurance policies, loans, and investments. Banks have formed syndicates to provide loans to developing countries, in order to share the risk of default. Stock brokerage firms usually join together, in the same way, to market a new issue of stock.

Chapter Review

SUMMARY

The three major forms of business are the sole proprietorship, the partnership, and the corporation. A sole proprietorship is a business that is owned by one person. In essence, the owner and the business are one. All business profits become the property of the owner, and all business debts are the responsibility of the owner. Sole proprietorship is the simplest form of business to enter, to control, and to leave. Perhaps for these reasons, about three-quarters of all American business firms are sole proprietorships.

A partnership is an association of two or more individuals who act as co-owners of a business for profit. Although partnership eliminates some of the disadvantages of sole proprietorship, it is the least popular of the major forms of business. Like sole proprietors, general partners are responsible for running the business and for all business debts. Limited partners receive a share of the profit in return for investing in the business. However, they are not responsible for business debts beyond the amount they have invested. A partnership agreement (or articles of partnership) is a written document setting forth the terms of a partnership.

Corporations are artificial beings created by law. These beings have the right to start and operate a business, to own property, and to enter into contracts. Although corporations comprise only one-seventh of all American businesses, they account for about nine-tenths of all business receipts. The largest businesses in the United States are organized as corporations.

Shares of ownership of a corporation are called stock, and owners are called stockholders. A corporation must be chartered, or formally recognized, by a particular state. Once the corporation has received a charter, its original stockholders elect a board of directors. The board of directors then elects or appoints corporate officers. Once each year, all stockholders have the right to vote for the firm's directors—either in person at the firm's annual meeting or by proxy.

Perhaps the major advantage of the corporate form is limited liability: Stockholders are not liable for the corporation's debts beyond the amount they have paid for its stock. Another important advantage is the perpetual life of the corporation. A major disadvantage is double taxation. The corporation's earnings are taxed once as corporate income and again as personal income (when earnings are distributed to stockholders). A corporation may grow by expanding its present operations or through merger—the purchase of another corporation.

The stock of public, or open, corporations is available to anyone who wants to buy it; the stock of private, or close, corporations is not. Government-owned corporations are used to provide particular services, such as public transportation, to citizens. Not-for-profit corporations are formed to provide social services rather than to earn profits, but they are not owned by governments. S-corporations are corporations that are taxed as though they were partnerships. Various restrictions apply to their formation.

Three additional forms of business ownership are the cooperative, the joint venture, and the syndicate. All are used by their owners to meet special needs, and each may be owned by either individuals or firms.

Whether they are sole proprietorships, partnerships, or corporations, most U.S. businesses are small. In the next chapter, we shall focus on these small businesses. Among other things, we shall examine the meaning of "small" as it applies to business and the place of small business in the American economy.

KEY TERMS

You should now be able to define and give an example relevant to each of the following terms:

sole proprietorship
unlimited liability
partnership
general partner
limited partner
stock
corporation
stockholder
private (close) corporation
public (open) corporation
incorporation
domestic corporation
foreign corporation
corporate charter
common stock
preferred stock
proxy
board of directors
corporate officers
limited liability
government-owned corporation
quasi-government corporation
not-for-profit corporation
S-corporation
merger
cooperative
joint venture
syndicate

QUESTIONS AND EXERCISES

Review Questions

1. What is a sole proprietorship? What are the major advantages and disadvantages of this form of business ownership?
2. How does a partnership differ from a sole proprietorship? Which disadvantages of sole proprietorship does the partnership tend to eliminate or reduce in effect?
3. Why is sole proprietorship the most popular form of business ownership? Why is partnership the least popular?
4. What is the difference between general partners and limited partners?
5. Explain the difference between:
   a. An open corporation and a close corporation.
   b. A domestic corporation and a foreign corporation.
   c. A government-owned corporation and a not-for-profit corporation.
6. Outline the incorporation process and describe the basic corporate structure.
7. What rights do stockholders have?
8. What are the major advantages and disadvantages of the corporate form of business ownership?
9. What are the primary duties of a corporation's board of directors? How are directors elected?
10. How is an S-corporation different from the usual open or close corporation?
11. Describe the three types of mergers.
12. Why are cooperatives formed? How do they operate?
13. In what ways are joint ventures and syndicates alike? In what ways are they different?

Discussion Questions

1. Apple Computer was a partnership until it was incorporated in 1977. It remained a close corporation until 1980, when its stock was sold to the public. What might have prompted Jobs and Wozniak to make these changes in the form of ownership of their firm?
2. Did Apple Computer grow internally, externally, or both? In what possible ways can Apple grow in the future? Explain.
3. If you were to start a business, which ownership form would you use? What factors might affect your choice of ownership form?
4. Why might an investor become a limited partner instead of purchasing the stock of an open corporation?
5. Discuss the following statement: "Corporations are not really run by their owners."
6. Is growth a good thing for all firms? How can management tell when the firm is ready to grow?
7. What kinds of services are provided by government-owned corporations? How might such services be provided without government involvement?

Exercises

1. Suppose you are a part-time employee working for the sole proprietor of a car wash. The owner has offered you a 29 percent partnership, and you are going to accept. Write out at least six articles of a partnership agreement that would cover your partnership.
2. You and your partner in the car wash of Exercise 1 have decided to incorporate. List the steps you would follow to form the corporation, and include specific decisions you must make at each step. Include at least six articles of incorporation (or, if you prefer, obtain and fill out a standard articles-of-incorporation form for your state).
3. Do some research on one of the mergers listed in Table 3.3, and determine the specific reasons why each of the two firms sought, or was agreeable to, the merger.

CASE 3-1

A Successful Expansion for Pabst

At the 1982 annual meeting of the Pabst Brewing Company, its president and chief executive officer, William F. Smith, Jr., told stockholders that that year was a critical one for the firm. According to Smith:

> While successfully withstanding a total of seven unsolicited takeover attempts by outside forces, we also reached an agreement for a merger with the G. Heileman Brewing Company. At the same time, we were able to initiate acquisition of the nation's seventh largest brewer, the Olympia Brewing Company, a move which gained for us additional volume of approximately 2.5 million barrels of beer.[6]

Two special stockholders' meetings were held on March 18, 1983. At one, Pabst stockholders voted to approve both the merger with Heileman and the acquisition of Olympia. At the other meeting, Olympia's stockholders approved the agreement with Pabst. Once both groups of owners had approved the Pabst–Olympia merger, this "long-awaited marriage of the two historic brewing companies" was completed.[7] Pabst Brewing Company borrowed over $35 million from banks to finance its purchase of Olympia.

According to Pabst's 1983 annual report to stockholders, revenues in 1982 were $758.6 million, based on 12,300,000 barrels sold. Net profit was $2.7 million, which came to 33 cents per share. Pabst declared a dividend of 10 cents per common share.[8]

1. Why would Pabst management decide to acquire Heileman and Olympia but to "withstand" seven merger attempts by other firms?
2. What reasons might the Pabst board of directors have for declaring a dividend of 10 cents per share—in spite of the fact that Pabst borrowed over $35 million to purchase Olympia?

CASE 3-2

Cargill, Inc.

Chances are you've never heard of Cargill, Inc., although it is one of the top 25 American firms in annual sales as well as this country's largest grain exporter. And Cargill's owners are quite satisfied with this lack of notoriety—for Cargill is also the nation's largest privately owned corporation. All of Cargill's stock is owned by members of two families (the Cargills and the MacMillans), the Cargill Foundation, and the firm's executives.

Cargill's primary business is to buy grain from farmers and sell it in domestic and foreign markets. In addition, the firm owns grain milling and crushing facilities and meat and soybean processing plants.

Because world grain prices can fluctuate widely, trading in grains is highly speculative; a wrong move may result in huge losses. During more than a century of grain trading, however, Cargill has developed the means for removing much of the risk from its operations. In part, this involves careful monitoring of the many factors that can affect grain prices. In addition, the firm makes use of a variety of trading strategies such as "hedging"—buying or selling for future delivery—to counter possibly unfavorable price changes.

Since Cargill is a close corporation, its managers are not obliged to reveal its trading secrets, or much else about the firm. Those who have visited its headquarters or facilities generally consider it to be a well-run firm. Recently, for example, the company instituted an innovative employee safety program that reduced the time lost through on-the-job accidents by 94 percent.[9]

1. In what ways is a close corporation like Cargill similar to a partnership? In what ways is it different?
2. If you were a Cargill stockholder, would you be for or against selling shares of the firm's stock to the public? Why?

CHAPTER

FOUR

Small Business in the United States

Before you go on to the next paragraph, stop for a moment and think of the name of a business—any business—producing or selling any product or service.

Chances are you thought of a corporate giant like IBM or General Motors or AT&T. These are the businesses that seem to make the news and whose names stick in our minds. Yet they make up a very small portion of the total number of businesses in the United States today. By far the largest proportion of American businesses are small— extremely small compared to firms like General Motors. Moreover, most workers in the United States are employed by small businesses, and we deal mainly with small businesses in our daily lives. Why, then, don't we think of a small local firm (like Dave's Superette or Jane's Cut & Curl) when we are asked to name a business? Perhaps because these firms are so very small, or because there are so many of them that we take them for granted.

In this chapter we shall not take small businesses for granted. Instead we shall look closely at this important business sector. After studying the chapter, you should understand:

1. *What a small business is and in what fields small businesses are concentrated*
2. *The people who start small businesses, how some succeed, and why many fail*
3. *The contributions of small business to our economy*
4. *The advantages and disadvantages of operating a small business*
5. *How the Small Business Administration helps small businesses*
6. *The concept of franchising, and the advantages and disadvantages of owning a franchise*

Consider this:

Roberta Williams programs new computer adventures.
Source: Logo and photo, courtesy of Sierra On-Line, Inc.

Kenneth Williams brought home an Apple II computer in 1980, and his wife Roberta took to it immediately. However, instead of using the available computer software, Mrs. Williams began to write stories for home computers. One of her first was a who-dun-it that included a spooky house, stolen jewels, and a killer. When she got tired of looking at only words on the screen, she drew pictures to go with the game.

The Williamses believed the game had commercial potential, and Kenneth was able to put it on a computer disk. They spent $200 on an advertisement in a computer magazine, just to see what would happen. What happened was that their game, "Mystery House," brought them $167,000 in sales during the last eight months of 1980.

Roberta Williams continued to write adventure story-games for the computer. Among the most popular are "Wizard and the Princess" and a game based on the movie *The Dark Crystal*. Because these games have plots, and players must solve a puzzle to win, they are different from the usual arcade games. According to Roberta, "It's like reading a story where you're the main character. You don't know how it's going to end. You just have to figure it out."[1]

In 1980 the Williamses were working out of a 10-by-10-foot den in their home. Today their company, Sierra On-Line, occupies 17,000 square feet of space in a small town next to Yosemite National Park. The firm has more than 130 employees (including Kenneth's former boss). In 1982 it posted sales exceeding $10 million, and sales were expected to double in 1983.

Besides computer games, Sierra On-Line produces educational and "home productivity" software programs that are used for record keeping and personal finance. Recently the firm announced that it was about to produce and market a $50 word processor called HomeWord. It also produces the arcade-style game "Frogger."

According to Kenneth Williams, the firm now has teams of specialists working on new products. (He plans to release about 300 new products this year.) Roberta Williams has 8 programmers at her disposal but prefers to work at home. Kenneth puts in long hours at the firm's facility. Until the middle of 1983, he tried to run the entire firm alone—without proper management training. Now, however, he has hired professionals in marketing, administration, and finance.

The Williamses began their business because it was fun. Today Mr. Williams says it is still fun, but it's also a lot of hard work.[2]

ierra On-Line grew from an idea into a $10 million business in less than three years. That kind of growth is phenomenal, even for the rapidly expanding computer software industry. In fact, most businesses start small, and those that survive usually remain small. They also provide a solid foundation for our economy—as employers, as suppliers and purchasers of goods and services, and as taxpayers.

SMALL BUSINESS: A PROFILE

The **Small Business Administration** (SBA) is a government agency that was created to assist, counsel, and protect the interests of small businesses in the United States. We shall discuss the SBA and the services it offers later in this chapter. For now, however, we are mainly concerned with its definition of a small business. According to the SBA, a **small business** is "one which is independently owned and operated for profit and is not dominant in its field."

How small must a firm be in order not to dominate its field? That depends on the particular business it is in. The SBA has developed specific "smallness" guidelines for the various industries. Its guidelines to smallness in different kinds of businesses are as follows:

- *Manufacturing:* A maximum number of employees ranging from 250 to 1500, depending on the particular industry
- *Wholesaling:* Maximum yearly sales ranging from $9.5 million to $22 million
- *Retailing:* Maximum yearly sales or receipts ranging from $2 million to $7.5 million
- *Construction:* Maximum average annual receipts of $9.5 million for the 3 most recent fiscal years
- *Special construction trades:* Maximum average annual sales ranging from $1 million to $2 million for the 3 most recent fiscal years
- *Agriculture:* Maximum annual receipts of $1 million
- *Service:* Maximum annual receipts ranging from $2 million to $8 million

A new standard, based only on number of employees, has been proposed but not yet adopted by the SBA.

Annual sales in the millions of dollars may not seem very small. However, for many firms, profit is only a few percent of total sales. Thus a firm may earn only $30,000 or $40,000 on yearly sales of $1 million—and that *is* small in comparison to the profits earned by most medium-sized and large firms. Moreover, most small firms have annual sales that are well below the limits the SBA has used in its definitions.

The Small-Business Sector

A surprising number of Americans take advantage of their freedom to start a business. There are, in fact, about 14 million businesses in this country. Around 90 percent are small, and many are new. Up to 8400 new businesses are started in a typical week![3]

At the same time that new firms are being created, others are going out of business. Statistically, over 70 percent of new businesses can be expected to fail. The primary reason for these failures is mismanagement due to a lack of business know-how.[4]

The makeup of the small-business sector is thus constantly changing. While some businesses are starting, others are closing shop. Still others are being acquired by larger firms. In spite of the high failure rate, many small businesses succeed modestly. Some, like Apple Computer, turn out to be extremely successful—to the point where they may no longer be considered small. Taken together, small businesses are also responsible for providing a high percentage of the jobs in the United States. According to some estimates, the figure is well over 60 percent.

Areas That Attract Small Business

Some industries, such as auto manufacturing, require huge investments in machinery and equipment. Businesses in such industries are big from the day they are started—if an entrepreneur or group of entrepreneurs can gather the capital required to start one.

By contrast, a number of industries require a low initial investment along with some special skills or knowledge. It is these industries that tend to attract new businesses. Growing industries, such as computer software, are attractive because of their sales and profit potential. However, knowledgeable entrepreneurs choose areas with which they are familiar, and these are most often the more established industries.

Small enterprise ranges from corner newspaper vending to the development of optical fibers. The owners of small businesses sell gasoline, flowers, and coffee to go. They publish magazines, haul freight, teach languages, and program computers. They make wines, movies, and high-fashion clothes. They build new homes and restore old ones. They fix appliances, recycle metals, and sell used cars. They drive cabs and fly planes. They make us well when we are ill, and they sell us the products of corporate giants.

Figure 4.1 *The Relative Proportion of Small Businesses by Industry.* **Small businesses are found in three major industries; most are in service and distribution.** *Source: Adapted from "Small Business in America," copyright © National Federation of Independent Business Research and Education Foundation.*

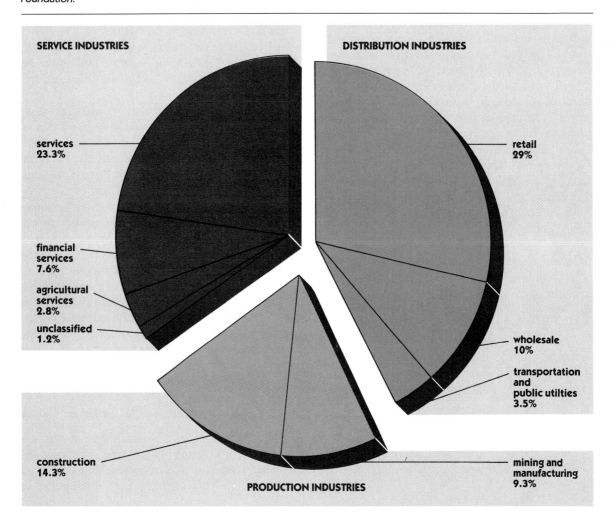

SERVICE INDUSTRIES

services
23.3%

financial services
7.6%

agricultural services
2.8%

unclassified
1.2%

construction
14.3%

PRODUCTION INDUSTRIES

DISTRIBUTION INDUSTRIES

retail
29%

wholesale
10%

transportation and public utilties
3.5%

mining and manufacturing
9.3%

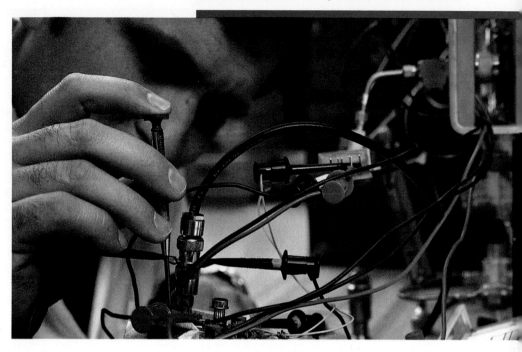

Most small manufacturers supply products to larger companies. Here a worker in a small plant assembles circuits for use in the computer industry. Source: © 1982 Lou Jones.

As Figure 4.1 shows, the various kinds of businesses are generally grouped in three broad categories: service industries, distribution industries, and production industries. Within these categories, small businesses tend to cluster in the service industries and in retailing.

Service Industries This category accounts for about 35 percent of all small businesses. Of these, about three-quarters provide such nonfinancial services as medical and dental care; watch, shoe, and TV repairs; hair cutting and styling; restaurant meals; and dry cleaning. About 8 percent of the small service firms offer financial services such as accounting, insurance, and investment counseling.

Distribution Industries This category includes retailing, wholesaling, transportation, and communications—industries that are concerned with the movement of goods from producers to consumers. Distribution industries account for approximately 42 percent of all small businesses.

Of these, almost three-quarters are involved in retailing, the sale of goods directly to consumers. Clothing and jewelry stores, pet shops, book stores, and grocery stores, for example, are all retailing firms. Slightly less than one-quarter of the small distribution firms are wholesalers. Wholesalers purchase products in quantity from manufacturers and then resell them to retailers.

Production Industries This last category includes construction, mining, and manufacturing industries. Only about 23 percent of all small businesses are in this group, mainly because these industries require relatively large initial investments. Small firms that do venture into production generally make parts and subassemblies for larger manufacturing firms or supply special skills to larger construction firms.

The People in Small Businesses

Small businesses are typically managed by the people who started and own them. Most of these

The Entrepreneur

Most of them are firstborns. When they read, they read nonfiction. In school, they weren't the brightest or the most popular either—not because they didn't want to be or couldn't have been, but because they had other things to do.

Most of them grew up in families where Mom was the boss. They don't tend to be hard drinkers. They like to talk to people, but not at parties. They go to bed when they can't stay awake any longer.

Who are these non-drinking, non-scholarly, restless loners? Why, entrepreneurs, of course.

These are just a few of the findings of a questionnaire put together by William A. Delaney, the president and chief executive officer of a $6 million software-engineering company and a self-styled expert in ways entrepreneurial.

It all started a few years ago when business was going so smoothly at Delaney's company, Analysis & Computer Systems Inc. of Bedford, Mass., that he found himself with something every entrepreneur seeks to be rid of—extra time on his hands. So Delaney began to write business articles in his spare time for the fun of it. Before long, the articles began to be published, and soon Delaney was writing books about running small businesses, and they too were published.

At the same time, Delaney began to collect articles about other entrepreneurs—what they wrote, said and thought about themselves and about each other. As he read more and more articles by and about entrepreneurs, Delaney began to notice some striking similarities among the personalities profiled, as well as in his own personality. To find out to what extent this apparent entrepreneurial personality existed, Delaney prepared a 60-question questionnaire. He sent the questionnaire to 150 chief executives of small, medium and large companies and to several military generals as well. (Delaney thinks that generals fit the entrepreneurial mold.) He requested anonymous answers and received 49 responses.

The answers confirmed Delaney's suspicions, and indicated some very definite similarities among entrepreneurs. More than 90%, for example, consider themselves aggressive, and most say they are authoritarian. They share an ability to think abstractly, and they sometimes hear inner voices—intuitive directives, really, that help them make decisions; most say they work better under pressure, and fully 100% report that they are healthy.

Source: Jane Simon, "So What Does It Take to Establish a Mark as an Entrepreneur?" *New England Business*, May 7, 1984, p. 46.

people have held jobs with other firms. The rest could have had such jobs if they had wanted them. Yet owners of small businesses would rather take the risk of starting and then operating their own firms, even if the money they make is less than the salaries they might otherwise earn.

The Entrepreneurs Researchers have suggested a variety of personal factors as reasons why individuals go into business. One that is often cited is the "entrepreneurial spirit"—the desire to create a new business. Other factors, such as independence, the desire to determine one's own destiny, and the willingness to find and accept a challenge certainly play a part. Background may come into play as well. In particular, researchers feel that people whose families have been in business (successfully or not) are most apt to start and run their own businesses. The age factor is important, too. People under 25 or over 40 less often start their own businesses (see Figure 4.2).

There must also be some motivation to start a business. One person may finally decide she has simply "had enough" of working and earning a profit for someone else. John DeLorean, for example, left a very prosperous and prestigious position at General Motors to start his own car manufacturing company. Another may lose his job for some reason and decide to start the business he has always wanted rather than seeking another job. Still another person may have an idea for a new product or a new way to sell an existing product. Or the opportunity to go into business may arise suddenly, perhaps when a good friend suggests a partnership. Lillian Katz was a young housewife in 1951, with a hardworking husband. An additional $50 a week in income would mean the difference between meeting expenses and living fairly well. Lillian paid $495 to advertise in *Seventeen* magazine, offering readers a matching belt and pocketbook. She received orders for $16,000 worth of goods. Based on her successful idea, Lillian Katz today is the entrepreneur who owns and runs Lillian Vernon, the mail-order catalogue firm, which has annual revenues of $100 million. [5]

In some people the motivation develops more slowly, as they gain the knowledge and ability required for success as a business owner. Knowledge and ability—especially management ability—are probably the most important factors involved. A new firm is very much built around the entrepreneur. The owner must be able to manage the firm's finances, its personnel (if there are any employees), and its day-to-day operations. He or she must handle sales, advertising, purchasing, pricing, and a variety of other business functions. The knowledge and ability to do so are most often

Figure 4.2 *How Old Is the Average Entrepreneur? People in all age groups become entrepreneurs, but almost 60 percent are between 25 and 40.* Source: Adapted from "Small Business in America," copyright © National Federation of Independent Business Research and Education Foundation.

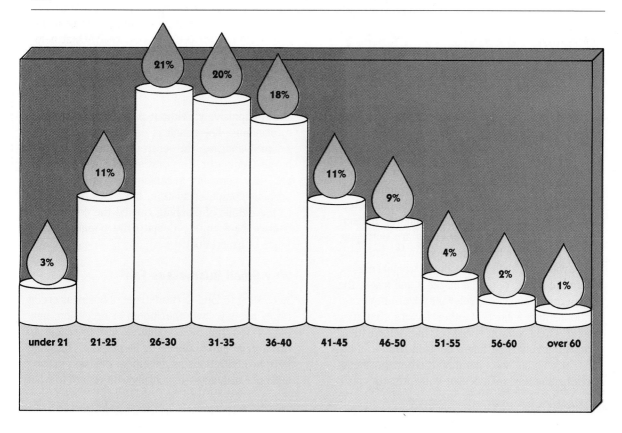

A variety of introductory courses can help the entrepreneur start his or her own business. *Source: Courtesy of The Boston Center for Adult Education.*

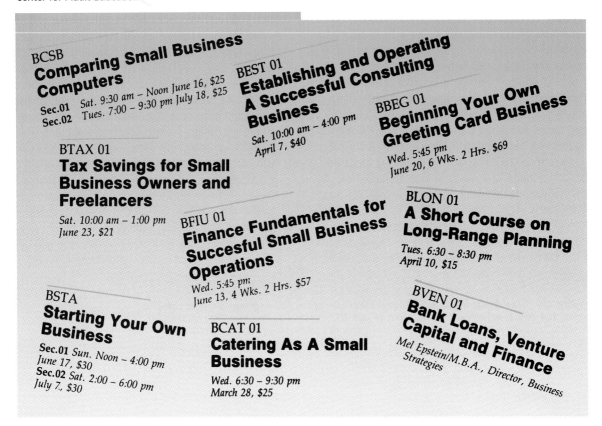

BCSB
Comparing Small Business Computers
Sec.01 Sat. 9:30 am – Noon June 16, $25
Sec.02 Tues. 7:00 – 9:30 pm July 18, $25

BEST 01
Establishing and Operating A Successful Consulting Business
Sat. 10:00 am – 4:00 pm
April 7, $40

BBEG 01
Beginning Your Own Greeting Card Business
Wed. 5:45 pm
June 20, 6 Wks. 2 Hrs. $69

BTAX 01
Tax Savings for Small Business Owners and Freelancers
Sat. 10:00 am – 1:00 pm
June 23, $21

BFIU 01
Finance Fundamentals for Succesful Small Business Operations
Wed. 5:45 pm
June 13, 4 Wks. 2 Hrs. $57

BLON 01
A Short Course on Long-Range Planning
Tues. 6:30 – 8:30 pm
April 10, $15

BSTA
Starting Your Own Business
Sec.01 Sun. Noon – 4:00 pm
June 17, $30
Sec.02 Sat. 2:00 – 6:00 pm
July 7, $30

BCAT 01
Catering As A Small Business
Wed. 6:30 – 9:30 pm
March 28, $25

BVEN 01
Bank Loans, Venture Capital and Finance
Mel Epstein/M.B.A., Director, Business Strategies

obtained through experience working for other firms in the same area of business.

Planning One other element of vital importance to those who start businesses is planning. Although this is not exactly a personal characteristic, entrepreneurs must be planners. In fact, they must be planners *before* they are entrepreneurs. Planning a business begins with gathering and evaluating data on resource requirements, operating costs, potential markets and sales, the competition, suppliers, relevant government regulations, and a host of other factors that may apply. Then, on the basis of this information, planning involves setting a detailed course of action for starting and operating the new business.

Unfortunately, many eager entrepreneurs push ahead impulsively, without paying much attention to planning. The result is often business failure. Adam Osborne, the entrepreneur behind Osborne Computer Corporation, is such an example. His company manufactured an innovative portable computer system, but a lack of attention to the details of planning caused the company to declare bankruptcy, despite the popular acceptance of its product.

Why Small Businesses Fail[6]

According to Dun & Bradstreet, a business credit rating agency, "whether boom or recession, nine out of ten [business] failures are traceable to managerial inexperience or ineptitude." Included here are both poor management decision making and poor planning—especially with regard to what products or services are to be offered and what markets are to be served. The agency lists the following specific reasons for business failure.

- *Lack of experience.* According to the available evidence, more than 50 percent of all entrepreneurs start their businesses in industries in which they already have some experience. But they may not have the variety of experience needed to manage all aspects of a business. And the 40 percent or so who do *not* have experience in the area they are entering may be in trouble from the start.
- *Lack of money.* Many new firms must be in business for several years before their revenue is high enough to cover expenses and provide a profit. Through poor planning, entrepreneurs may seek only enough capital to start such a business, but not enough to keep it going in this building-up period. Later they find it very difficult to raise the additional capital they need.
- *The wrong location.* Location—the right one— is of critical importance to a business. Many inexperienced persons choose the wrong location, often to save on expenses. A typical example is locating a new retail store in a community with a declining population. The rent may be right, but the customers are in the process of leaving!
- *Mismanagement of inventory.* Carrying improper merchandise, or inventory, is a common pitfall. Often the problem is not too much inventory, but rather too much of the wrong kind of merchandise on hand. Generally, inventory represents a debt on which interest must be paid; unsold merchandise is a drain on the business.
- *Poor credit-granting practices.* For a new or young business, the pressure to sell on credit is strong—especially when competing firms are granting credit. However, credit sales raise a whole new set of problems, which many young firms are not able to handle.
- *Poorly planned expansion.* Once a new business becomes successful, there is a tendency to expand it in order to make it even more successful. Slow, steady growth may be healthy for a fairly new firm; but fast, poorly planned, and undercapitalized growth can be disastrous.

Every day, and in every part of the country, people are in the process of planning or opening new businesses. Many of these businesses may not succeed. Others represent well-conceived ideas that are developed by entrepreneurs who have the experience, the resources, and the determination to make their businesses succeed. As these well-prepared entrepreneurs pursue their individual goals, our society benefits in many ways from their work and their creativity.

THE IMPORTANCE OF SMALL BUSINESSES IN OUR ECONOMY

This country's economic history is chock full of stories of ambitious men and women who turned their ideas into business dynasties. The Ford Motor Company started as one man with a new method for industrial production. Macy's can trace its beginnings to a pushcart in the streets of New York. Both Xerox Corporation and Polaroid Corporation began as small firms with a better way to do a job.

Providing Technical Innovation

Invention and innovation are among the foundations of our economy. The increases in productivity that have characterized the two hundred years of our history are all rooted in one principal source: new ways to do a job with less effort, at a lower cost. A National Science Foundation study covering the period 1953 to 1973 concluded that small firms produce about four times as many innovations per research-and-development dollar as medium-sized firms and about twenty-four times as many as the largest firms![7]

According to the U.S. Office of Management and Budget, more than half the major technological advances of this century originated with individual inventors and small companies. A sampling of those innovations is remarkable:

- air conditioning
- automatic transmission
- ball-point pen
- FM radio
- helicopter
- instant camera
- insulin
- jet engine
- penicillin
- power steering
- xerography
- zipper

Perhaps even more remarkable is the fact that many of these inventions sparked major new U.S. industries.

Providing Employment

Small businesses employ somewhat less than two-thirds of all nongovernment workers in this country. Between 1969 and 1976, however, these businesses accounted for virtually all *new* nongovernment employment. Among the small high-technology firms, the growth in hiring was nearly nine times that of other parts of our economy.[8] And this trend seems to be continuing.

Small business is thus capable of resolving the present unemployment problem. In fact, it has gone a long way toward doing so. William K. Eastham, chairman of the board of directors of the U.S. Chamber of Commerce, summarized the importance of small business in this regard by saying, "Historically, small business has created the bulk of the new jobs. If problems of unemployment are to be resolved, it is likely that we must depend on small business as a principal factor in the solution."[9]

Providing Competition

Small businesses challenge larger, established firms in many ways, causing them to become more efficient and more responsive to consumer needs. A small business cannot, of course, compete with a large firm across the board. But a number of small firms, each competing in its own particular area and its own particular way, together have the desired competitive effect. Thus a small producer of portable computers, a small producer of less expensive personal computers, and a small producer of computer software together add up to reasonable competition for the no-longer-small Apple Computer.

Filling Needs of Society and Other Businesses

Large firms must, by their nature, operate on a large scale. Many may be unwilling or unable to meet the special needs of smaller groups of consumers. Such groups create almost perfect markets for small companies, which can tailor their products to these groups and fill their needs profitably. A prime example is a firm that modifies automobile controls to accommodate handicapped drivers.

Small firms also provide a variety of goods and services to each other and to much larger firms. Sears, Roebuck and Company purchases merchandise from approximately 12,000 suppliers—and most of them are small businesses. General Motors relies on more than 32,000 companies for parts and supplies. And it depends on more than 11,000 independent dealers to sell its automobiles and trucks. Large firms generally buy parts and assemblies from smaller firms for one very good reason: It is less expensive than manufacturing the parts in their own factories. This lower cost is eventually reflected in the price that consumers pay for their products.

It is clear that small businesses are a vital part of our economy and that, as consumers and as members of the labor force, we all benefit enormously from their presence. Now let us look at the situation from the point of view of the owners of small businesses themselves.

THE PROS AND CONS OF SMALLNESS

Do most owners of small businesses dream of their firms growing into giant corporations—managed by professionals—while they serve only on the board of directors? Or would they rather stay small, in a firm where they have the opportunity (and the responsibility) to do everything that needs to be done? The answers depend on the personal characteristics and motivation of the individual owner. For many, the advantages of remaining small far outweigh the disadvantages.

Advantages of Small Business

Personal Relationships with Customers and Employees For those who like dealing with people, small business is the place to be. The owners of retail shops get to know many of their customers by name and to deal with them on a personal basis. Through such relationships, small-business owners often become involved in social, cultural, and political affairs within the community.

Relationships between owner–managers and employees also tend to be closer in smaller businesses. To many an employee, the owner is a friend and counselor as well as the boss.

These personal relationships also provide an important business advantage. The personal service offered to customers is a major competitive weapon of small business—one that larger firms try to match but often cannot. And close relationships with employees often help the small-business owner keep effective workers who might earn more with a larger firm.

Ability to Adapt to Change Being his or her own boss, the owner–manager of a small business does not need anyone's permission to adapt to change. An owner may add or discontinue merchandise or services, change store hours, and experiment with various price strategies in response to changes in market conditions. Moreover, through personal relationships with customers, the owners of small businesses quickly become aware of changes in people's needs and interests—as well as the activities of competing firms.

Simplified Record Keeping Many small firms need keep only a simple set of records. Such a system might consist of a checkbook, a cash receipts journal in which to record all sales, and a cash disbursements journal in which to record all amounts that are paid out.

Like most small businesses, this pushcart enterprise gives its operator independence, flexibility, and personal contact with customers. Source: © Ellis Herwig, The Picture Cube.

Independence Small-business owners don't have to punch in and out, bid for vacation times, take orders from superiors, or worry about being fired or laid off. They are the masters of their own destinies—at least with regard to employment. For many people, this is the one prime advantage of owning a small business.

Other Advantages Small-business owners also enjoy a number of the advantages of sole proprietorship, which are discussed in Chapter 3. These include being able to keep all profits, the ease and low cost of going into business and (if necessary) going out of business, and being able to keep information about one's business secret.

Disadvantages of Small Business

Risk of Failure As we have noted, small firms (especially newer ones) run a heavy risk of going out of business. About two out of three firms close their doors within four years of their founding. Older, well-established but small firms can be hit hard by a business recession, mainly because they do not have the financial resources they need to weather a really difficult period.

Limited Potential The small businesses that survive do so with varying degrees of success. Many small firms are simply means of making a living for the owner and his or her family. The owner may have some technical skill—as a hair stylist or an electrician does—and may have started business to practice his or her trade. Such a business is unlikely to grow much or earn large profits.

Other Disadvantages Some of the disadvantages of sole proprietorships apply to small businesses as well. Of primary concern are the limited ability to obtain capital, the generally unspecialized or limited management skills of owners, and the lack of opportunity for employees. With regard to capital, Figure 4.3 shows that most small-business financing comes out of the owner's pocket.

Figure 4.3 *Sources of Capital for Entrepreneurs. Small businesses get financing from various sources, but the most important is personal resources.* Source: Adapted from "Small Business in America," copyright © National Federation of Independent Business Research and Education Foundation.

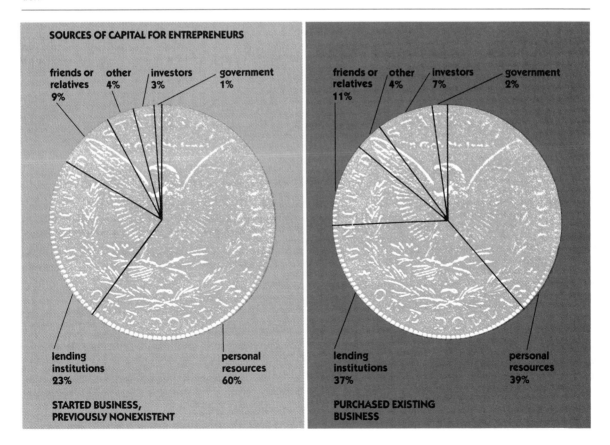

SOURCES OF CAPITAL FOR ENTREPRENEURS

friends or relatives 9%
other 4%
investors 3%
government 1%
lending institutions 23%
personal resources 60%

STARTED BUSINESS, PREVIOUSLY NONEXISTENT

friends or relatives 11%
other 4%
investors 7%
government 2%
lending institutions 37%
personal resources 39%

PURCHASED EXISTING BUSINESS

Although every person who considers starting a small business should be aware of the hazards and pitfalls we have noted, these brave souls need not feel that they must act alone. Politically and economically, the United States is dedicated to helping small businesses "make it." It expresses this aim most actively through the Small Business Administration.

THE SMALL BUSINESS ADMINISTRATION

The Small Business Administration (SBA) was created by Congress in 1953 to help people get into business and stay in business. The agency provides assistance to owners and managers of prospective, new, and established small businesses. Through more than one hundred offices throughout the nation, the SBA provides both financial assistance and management counseling. It helps small firms bid for and obtain government contracts, and it helps them prepare to enter foreign markets.

SBA Management Assistance

Statistics show that most failures in small business are due to poor management. For this reason, the SBA places special emphasis on improving the management ability of the owners and managers of small businesses. The SBA's Management Assistance Program is extensive and diversified. It includes free individual counseling, courses, conferences, workshops, and a wide range of publications.

Management Courses and Workshops The management courses offered by the SBA cover all the functions, duties, and roles of managers. The most popular of these courses is a general survey of eight to ten different areas of business management. In follow-up studies, business people may concentrate in depth on one or more of these areas, depending on their own particular strengths and weaknesses. The SBA also offers occasional one-day conferences. These are aimed at keeping owner–managers up to date on new management developments, tax laws, and the like.

Instructors may be teachers from local colleges and universities or professionals such as management consultants, bankers, lawyers, and accountants. Fees for these courses are quite small.

The SBA also invites prospective owners of small businesses to workshops, where management problems and good management practices are discussed. A major goal of these sessions is to emphasize the need for sufficient preparation before starting a new venture. Sometimes they serve to convince an eager but poorly prepared entrepreneur to wait until he or she is ready for the difficulties that lie ahead.

SCORE and ACE The **Service Corps of Retired Executives** (SCORE) is a group of retired business people who volunteer their services to small businesses through the SBA. The collective experience of SCORE volunteers spans the full range of American enterprise.

A small-business owner who has a particular problem can request free counseling from SCORE. An assigned counselor visits the owner in his or her establishment and, through careful observation, analyzes the business situation and the problem. If the problem is complex, the counselor may call on other volunteer experts to assist. Finally, the counselor offers a plan for solving the problem and helping the owner through any critical period.

The **Active Corps of Executives** (ACE) is a group of active managers who counsel small-business owners on a volunteer basis. ACE was established to supplement the services available through SCORE and to keep the SBA's management counseling as current as possible. ACE volunteers come from major corporations, trade associations, educational institutions, and professions.

Help for Minority-Owned Small Businesses Americans who are members of minority groups have had difficulty entering the nation's economic main-

Failures in small business can usually be traced to management problems. One source of free, specialized help is the Service Corps of Retired Executives. Source: Reprinted courtesy of SCORE (Service Corps of Retired Executives).

Call SCORE

SCORE is the Service Corps of Retired Executives. SCORE has 8,000 members throughout the United States and Trust Territories and together has more than 300,000 years of business experience — much of it dealing with growing businesses.

And the service is free!

SCORE is a counseling service of the U.S. Small Business Administration. You'll find SCORE listed in the phone book under SCORE, U.S. Small Business Administration. Or, if you like, inquire about SCORE at your local Chamber of Commerce.

stream. Raising money is a nagging problem for minority business owners, who may also lack adequate training. Members of minority groups are, of course, eligible for all SBA programs, but the SBA makes a special effort to assist those who want to start small businesses or expand existing ones.

Helping women become entrepreneurs is also a special goal of the SBA. Women make up more than half of America's population, but they own less than one-fourth of its businesses. In 1980 an SBA Assistant Administrator for Women's Business Enterprise was appointed, and programs directed specifically toward this minority group were expanded.

Small Business Institutes A **Small Business Institute** (SBI) is a group of senior and graduate students in business administration who provide management counseling to small businesses. SBIs have been organized on almost 500 college campuses as another way to help business owners. The students, who work in small groups, are guided by faculty advisors and SBA management-assistance experts. Like SCORE volunteers, they analyze and help solve the problems of small-business owners at their business establishments.

Small Business Development Centers Small **Business Development Centers** (SBDCs) are university-based groups that provide individual counseling and practical training to owners of small businesses. SBDCs draw from the resources of local, state, and federal government, private business, and the university. They can provide managerial and technical help, the results of research studies, and various other types of specialized assistance that are of value to small businesses.

SBA Publications The SBA issues management, marketing, and technical publications dealing with hundreds of topics that are of interest to present and prospective managers of small firms. Most of these publications are available from the SBA free of charge. Others can be obtained for a small fee from the U.S. Government Printing Office.

A summary of the various services offered by the SBA is illustrated in Figure 4.4.

SBA Financial Assistance

Small businesses seem to be constantly in need of money, for one reason or another. An owner may have enough capital to start and operate the business. But then he or she may require more money to finance increased operations during peak selling seasons, to pay for required pollution-control equipment, to mop up after a natural disaster such as a flood, or to finance an expansion. The SBA offers special financial assistance programs that cover all these situations. However, its primary financial function is to guarantee loans to eligible businesses.

Regular Business Loans Most of the SBA's business loans are actually made by private lenders, but repayment is partially guaranteed by the agency. That is, the SBA may guarantee that it will repay up to 90 percent of the loan if the borrowing firm cannot repay it. Guaranteed loans may be as large as $500,000, and repayment can take as long as 25 years. The average size of an SBA-guaranteed business loan is $102,000, and its average duration is about 8 years.

Until recently, a few loans were made directly to businesses by the SBA. (Under law, the SBA could not consider making a direct loan unless a private lender had already refused to lend the money, even with an SBA guarantee.) Funding for direct loans was not included in President Reagan's fiscal 1983 budget, so these loans were discontinued.

Small Business Investment Companies **Venture capital** is money that is invested in small (and sometimes struggling) firms that have the potential to become very successful. In many cases, only a lack of capital keeps these firms from rapid and solid growth. The people who invest in such firms expect that their investments will grow with the firms and become quite profitable.

The popularity of these investments has increased in the past five to ten years, but most new, small firms still have difficulty in obtaining venture capital. To help such firms, the SBA licenses, regulates, and provides financial assistance to **Small Business Investment Companies** (SBICs). These are privately owned firms that provide venture capital to small enter-

prises that meet their investment standards. SBICs are intended to be profit-making organizations. However, SBA aid allows them to invest in small businesses that would not otherwise attract venture capital.

Figure 4.4 *Services Offered by the SBA. The SBA offers a variety of managerial and financial aids to small business owners.*

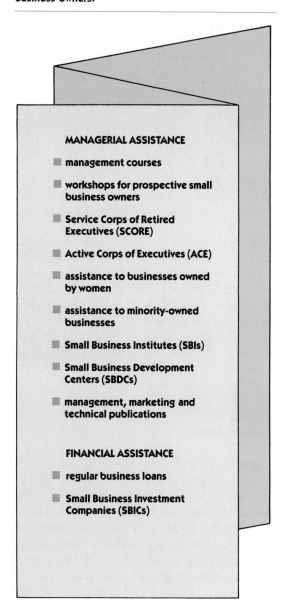

MANAGERIAL ASSISTANCE

- management courses
- workshops for prospective small business owners
- Service Corps of Retired Executives (SCORE)
- Active Corps of Executives (ACE)
- assistance to businesses owned by women
- assistance to minority-owned businesses
- Small Business Institutes (SBIs)
- Small Business Development Centers (SBDCs)
- management, marketing and technical publications

FINANCIAL ASSISTANCE

- regular business loans
- Small Business Investment Companies (SBICs)

Many fast-food chains, like Burger King, lease their outlets as franchises that offer the same products and services but are individually operated. *Source:* © 1979 Andy Levin , Black Star.

We have discussed the importance of the small-business segment of our economy. And we have weighed the advantages and drawbacks of operating a small business compared to a large one. But is there a way to achieve the best of both worlds? Can one preserve one's independence as a business owner while enjoying some of the benefits of "bigness"? Let's take a close look at franchising.

FRANCHISING

A **franchise** is a license to operate an individually owned business as though it were part of a chain of outlets or stores. Often the business itself is also called a *franchise*. Among the most familiar franchises are McDonald's and Kentucky Fried Chicken fast-food outlets, AAMCO Transmission and Midas muffler shops, and Holiday Inns. There are many other franchises with familiar names; this method of doing business has become

very popular in the last two decades or so. It is an attractive means of starting and operating a small business.

What Is Franchising?

Franchising, which is the actual granting of a franchise, is essentially a method of distributing goods or services. Suppose that you open a small business—the Salad Plate Sandwich Shop—selling salad sandwiches in Orlando, Florida. What you are distributing is quickly prepared meals for weight- and health-conscious people.

Now suppose your shop does extremely well. Perhaps this is because you serve your salads on any of sixteen different varieties of freshly baked breads, as well as on tacos. Rather than expand your shop, you open a second one at the other end of town. That shop does extremely well too, and you decide to open a third. However, by now Orlando probably has all the salad-sandwich shops it needs, so you open your third shop in Winter Haven. When this third shop also is an overnight

They Rescue Rockers From Heartbreak Hotels

A dozen years ago, Cindy Johnson and Jeri Jenkins, now both 30, were art students working part-time in a north Miami health food store when they were asked if they would like to cook for a rock musician who was recording in the city for three months. They didn't know who Stephen Stills was, but the job sounded good.

"They only wanted one person," Jeri says. "But we said, 'We'll cook, clean, shop, do everything.' We sold ourselves as a package."

Since that time, as more pop stars have retreated to south Florida to make records, Cindy and Jeri have incorporated. Their business, "Home at Last," provides temporary residences and a homey atmosphere to visiting pop and rock bands, businessmen, and foreign dignitaries. Happy clients include Yul Brynner, Anthony Newley, the BeeGees, Crosby, Stills and Nash, Neil Young, the Eagles, and George Harrison. The service finds homes (usually beachfront), cooks meals, provides laundry service, charters boats and jets and gets their musician clients to the studio on time. Cindy and Jeri now have a full-time staff of four, and they hire additional help as needed. The cost for a week of pampering can run from $500 for a small house to $3,500 for a mansion complete with cook, chauffeur, and maid. Their most valuable service, however, is priceless.

"Something we consciously tried to do was buffer them from the outside world," Cindy says. "One of the reasons they came to Miami was because nobody knew who they were. And we kept it very quiet."

Had it not been for the celebrities' hotline, "Home at Last" might never have prospered. After that initial three-month job, the women were back working at the health food store for three years when a call came on behalf of English rocker Eric Clapton. He needed a house and some everyday help. Besides finding him a Spanish style mansion, Cindy says, "We took care of him, pressed his clothes, got him to the studio on time, provided a pleasant atmosphere while he was recording. Working for Clapton got the business rolling."

Clapton was so pleased, he named his album *461 Ocean Boulevard* after his temporary address. Better still, he recommended the service to other producers, managers, recording artists, and agents. Business became so brisk, Jeri and Cindy left art school to set up their new enterprise full time.

"We really had to prove ourselves to get homes leased," Cindy says. "We have to maintain the houses better than the owners."

As their clientele grew, the women earned real estate licenses, and now sell homes to rock performers and other VIPs. They also conduct training sessions for others wanting to start similar businesses of their own.

Source: Scott R. Benarde, *Family Circle*, January 24, 1984, p. 10.

---

success, it begins to dawn on you that you have a profitable fast-food idea. Salad-sandwich shops could do well throughout Florida, and perhaps throughout the country!

Because of the success of your three shops, you expect to have no trouble raising the capital you need to open one or two more, then a few more after that, and so on up to a hundred or even more. On the other hand, you wonder whether you really want to own and operate ten or thirty or a hundred fast-food outlets. You're having enough trouble running from Orlando to Winter Haven and back to keep tabs on the three you already own.

At about this time Gary Smith, a young entrepreneur from Atlanta, Georgia, finally catches up

Computer Junkyards

Gone are the days when a junkyard was a junkyard. Now they are "salvage yards" and, at least in Phoenix, Denver, and Tucson, they list available car parts by computer. According to Steven Knight, president of Parts by Computer, a young firm backed by venture capital, 8 to 30 salvage yards in each of those towns now list parts on computers hooked up with insurance adjusters at companies like State Farm, Travelers, Allstate, American Family, and Farmers. The system boosts the salvage yards' sales, so Parts by Computer charges a monthly inventory-based advertising fee to list. The system finds parts about 50 percent of the time and insurance companies pay $3 or $4 for each "hit." According to Knight, the company grosses between $170,000 and $200,000 in Phoenix. Things are going so well, he says, that Parts by Computer may franchise. This year he expects to add four or five additional cities.

Source: *Forbes*, January 16, 1984, p. 8.

with you in the original Orlando shop. Over a salad-sandwich, he explains that he owns a luncheonette in Atlanta but is on vacation in Orlando. Salads are a big item in his shop, and he believes your salad-sandwiches would really draw a crowd. Smith wants to know where you get your very fresh bread and salad ingredients, and anything else you are willing to tell him about your business. And he is willing to pay you for the information. "Aha!" you say to yourself. "See me tomorrow evening," you say to him.

One week later, you and Smith have drawn up a franchising agreement. Although the agreement covers many additional details, it basically provides for the following: You, as the **franchisor**—that is, the individual or firm granting a franchise—will allow Smith to use your shop name and your method of doing business. You will also provide him with the necessary training. You will

sell him raw bread dough, salad ingredients, and special Salad Plate Sandwich Shop restaurant supplies. And you will furnish him with advertising materials. Smith, as the **franchisee**—that is, the person or firm purchasing a franchise—will redecorate his shop in the Salad Plate colors and design. He will also keep agreed-upon business hours, serve salad sandwiches exactly as they are served in your three shops, and purchase ingredients and supplies only from you. In addition he will pay you, for the franchise, both an initial fee and a royalty (a percentage of his monthly sales revenue).

You are now in the franchising business, as a distributor of restaurant supplies. To expand your business, you can sell additional franchises (especially if Smith is successful). If you wish, you can also open additional shops of your own or sell your three shops to other franchisees.

This is the essence of franchising, although the details vary from franchise to franchise. The franchisor supplies a known and advertised business name, the required training and materials, and a method of doing business. The franchisee supplies labor and capital, and she or he owns and operates the individual outlet. Table 4.1 lists some items that would be covered in a typical franchise agreement.

The Growth of Franchising

Franchising has been used since the early 1900s, primarily for filling stations and car dealerships. However, it has experienced enormous growth since the mid-1960s. This growth has generally paralleled the expansion of the fast-food industry—the industry in which franchising is used to the greatest extent.

Of course, franchising is not limited to fast foods. The International Franchise Association, the industry trade group, now lists its members in more than three dozen different *categories* of industries. Among those industries that have experienced the greatest growth (both in number of franchised establishments and in their sales) are real estate (Century 21), printing and copying (Kwik-Kopy Corp.), employment (Manpower,

Inc.), educational products and services (Evelyn Wood Reading Dynamics Institute), rental equipment (Taylor Rental), computer products and services (Entre), and restaurants (Tico Taco). Real estate sales provide an excellent example of the application of the franchising concept to an established industry. In 1975 there were about 3800 real estate franchises. By 1980 the number had increased to over 33,500. Among the newest are the Coldwell-Banker franchises licensed by Sears, Roebuck and Company.

In 1982 the U.S. Department of Commerce called franchising "a significant part of the U.S. economy" and cited a 5.6 percent increase in the net number of franchises over the previous year. This trend is expected to continue, at about 5 percent annually.

Franchised sales of goods and services reached an estimated $376 billion in 1982 and nearly $419 billion in 1983. Franchised establishments now account for 31 percent of all U.S. retail sales.

Are Franchises Successful?

Modern franchising is designed to provide a tested formula for success, along with ongoing advice and training. The success rate for businesses owned and operated by franchisees is significantly better than the success rate for other independently owned small businesses.

According to the Department of Commerce, fewer than 5 percent of franchisee-owned outlets have been discontinued since 1971. In 1981, the last year for which actual data are available, only about 3.8 percent of franchisee-owned outlets were discontinued—and many of these went out of business for reasons other than business failure.[10] Compared to the overall small-business

Table 4.1 *McDonald's Conventional Franchise as of September, 1981*

McDonald's (franchisor) provides:	Individual (franchisee) supplies:
1. Nationally recognized trademarks and established reputation for quality	1. Total investment of approximately $293,500 to $344,500 (depending on size). Includes initial fee of $12,500 and refundable security deposit of $15,000
2. Designs and color schemes for restaurants, signs, and equipment layouts	2. Approximate cash requirement of 40 percent of total investment
3. Formulas and specifications for certain food products	3. A minimum of 4 percent of gross sales annually for marketing and advertising
4. Proven methods of inventory and operations control	4. Payment of 11½ percent of gross sales monthly to McDonald's Corp.
5. Bookkeeping, accounting, and policies manuals specially geared toward a franchised restaurant	5. Kitchen equipment, seating, decor, lighting, and signs in conformity with McDonald's standards (included in total investment figure)
6. A franchise term of up to 20 years	6. Willingness to relocate
7. Thorough training program including 300 hours in a McDonald's restaurant and a 2-week Basic Operations Course	7. Taxes, insurance, and maintenance costs
8. A 2-week advanced management training program at Hamburger University	8. Commitment to assuring high quality standards and upholding McDonald's reputation
9. On-going regional support services and field service staff	
10. Research and development into labor-saving equipment and methods	
11. Monthly bulletins, periodicals, and meetings to inform franchisees about management and marketing techniques	

Source: *This Is McDonald's*, McDonald's Corporation, Oak Brook, Ill., September 1981. Used by permission.

failure rate of around 70 percent, this is an enviable record.

Nevertheless, franchising is not a guarantee of success for either franchisees or franchisors. Too rapid expansion, inadequate capital or management skills, and a host of other problems can cause failure for both. Thus, for example, the Dizzy Dean's Beef and Burger franchise is no longer in business.

Advantages of Franchising

To the Franchisor The franchisor gains fast and selective distribution of its products without incurring the high cost of constructing and operating its own outlets. The franchisor thus has more capital available to expand production and to use for advertising. At the same time, it can ensure, through the franchise agreement, that outlets are maintained and operated by its own standards.

Figure 4.5 *Types of Franchises, Ranked by Sales: 1982. Franchised businesses account for billions of dollars annually. Those that relate to the automobile industry bring in over 70 percent of all franchising revenues. In recent years, growth in franchising has paralleled growth in the fastfood industry. Source: U.S. Department of Commerce, Bureau of Industrial Economics.*

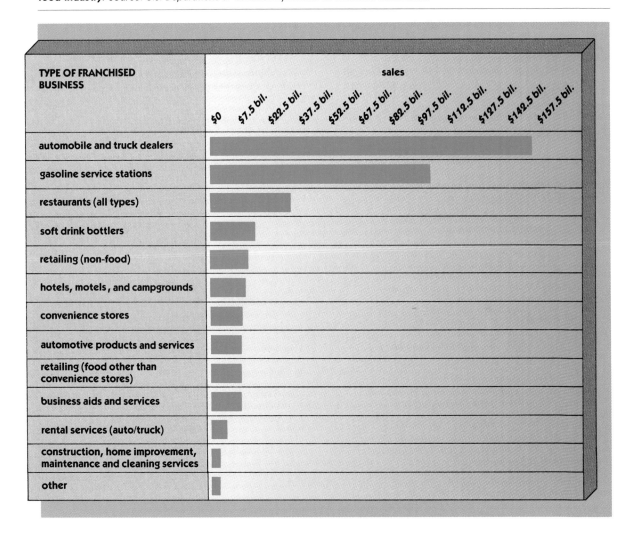

The franchisor also benefits from the fact that the franchisee, being a sole proprietor in most cases, is likely to be very highly motivated to succeed. The success of the franchise means more sales, which translate into higher royalties for the franchisor.

To the Franchisee   The franchisee gets the opportunity to start a business with limited capital and to make use of the business experience of others. Moreover, an outlet with a nationally advertised name, such as McDonald's, Dunkin' Donuts, or Avis, Inc., is often assured of customers as soon as it opens. Figure 4.5 ranks the different areas of business franchising according to sales.

If business problems arise, the franchisor gives the franchisee guidance and advice. This counseling is primarily responsible for the very high degree of success enjoyed by franchises. In most cases, the franchisee does not pay for such help.

The franchisee also receives materials to use in local advertising and can take part in national promotional campaigns sponsored by the franchisor. McDonald's and its franchisees, for example, constitute one of the nation's top twenty purchasers of advertising. Finally, the franchisee may be able to minimize the cost of advertising, of supplies, and of various business necessities by purchasing them in cooperation with other franchisees.

Disadvantages of Franchising[11]

The disadvantages of franchising mainly affect the franchisee, because the franchisor retains a great deal of control. The franchisor can dictate every aspect of the business: decor, the design of employees' uniforms, types of signs, and all the details of business operations. All Burger King french fries taste the same because all its franchisees have to make them the same way.

Franchise holders pay for their security. Usually there are a one-time franchise fee and continuing royalty and advertising fees, collected as a percentage of sales. Insty-Prints collects a non-refundable $8000 franchise fee, then a royalty of 3 percent of gross sales (payable monthly), and an additional 2 percent of sales for advertising materials.

Franchise operators also work hard. They often put in 10- and 12-hour days, 6 days a week. And in some fields, franchise agreements are not uniform: One franchisee may pay more than another for the same services.

Even success can cause problems. Sometimes a franchise is so successful that the franchisor opens its own outlet nearby, in direct competition. A spokesman for one franchisor says his company "gives no geographical protection" to its franchise holders and thus is free to move in on them.

The International Franchise Association advises prospective franchise purchasers to investigate before investing and to approach buying a franchise cautiously. Franchises vary widely in approach as well as in products. Some, like Dunkin' Donuts and Baskin-Robbins ice cream stores, demand long hours. Others, like Command Performance hair salons and Uncle John's restaurants, are earmarked for those who don't want to spend many hours at their store.

Chapter Review

SUMMARY

A small business is one that is independently owned and operated for profit and is not dominant in its field. The Small Business Administration (SBA) has developed guidelines that make this definition more specific and that determine whether a particular business is eligible for SBA aid.

There are about 14 million businesses in this country, and about 90 percent of them are small businesses. Small businesses provide more than 60 percent of the jobs in the United States, in spite of the fact that over 70 percent of new businesses can be expected to fail. More than half of all small businesses are retailing and service businesses.

Such personal characteristics as independence, desire to create a new enterprise, and willingness to accept a challenge may impel individuals to start small businesses. Various external circumstances, such as special expertise or even the loss of a job, can also supply the motivation to strike off on one's own. Lack of management experience and poor planning are the major causes of failure.

Small businesses have been responsible for a wide variety of inventions and innovations, some of which have given rise to new industries. Historically, small businesses have created the bulk of the new jobs and have mounted effective competition to larger firms. They have provided things that society needs, acted as suppliers of larger firms, and acted as customers of other businesses both large and small.

The advantages of smallness in business include independence, the opportunity to establish personal relationships with customers and employees, and the ability to adapt to changes quickly. The major disadvantages are the high risk of failure and the limited potential for growth.

The U.S. Small Business Administration was created in 1953 to assist and counsel the millions of small-business owners. The SBA offers management courses and workshops; managerial help, including one-to-one counseling through SCORE and ACE; various publications; and financial assistance through guaranteed loans and SBICs. It places special emphasis on aid to minority-owned businesses, including those owned by women.

Franchising is the granting of a license to operate an individually owned business as though it were part of a chain. The franchisor provides a known business name, a method of doing business, training, and assistance in merchandising and management. The franchisee contributes labor and capital, and she or he owns the individual franchise. Franchising has grown tremendously over the past 20 years. Franchised establishments now account for almost one-third of all retail sales in the United States and are found in a wide range of industries. Franchises have a failure rate of only about 5 percent.

A major advantage of franchising is fast and well-controlled distribution of the franchisor's products, with minimal capital outlay. In return, the franchisee has the opportunity to open a business with limited capital, to make use of the business experience of others, and to sell to an existing clientele. For this, the franchisee must usually pay both an initial franchise fee and a monthly royalty based on sales. He or she must also follow the dictates of the franchisor with regard to operation of the business.

This chapter ends our discussion of the foundations of American business. From here on, we shall be looking closely at various aspects of business operation. We begin, in the next chapter, with a discussion of management—what it is, what managers do, and how they work to coordinate the basic economic resources within a business organization.

KEY TERMS

You should now be able to define and give an example relevant to each of the following terms:

Small Business Administration

small business

Service Corps of Retired Executives

Active Corps of Executives

Small Business Institutes

Small Business Development Centers

venture capital

Small Business Investment Companies

franchise

franchising

franchisor

franchisee

QUESTIONS AND EXERCISES
Review Questions

1. What information would you need in order to determine whether a particular business is small according to SBA guidelines?
2. Which two areas of business generally attract the most small businesses? Why are these areas attractive to small business?
3. Distinguish among service industries, distribution industries, and production industries.
4. What kinds of factors impel certain people to start new businesses?
5. What are the major causes of small-business failure? Do these causes also apply to larger businesses?
6. Briefly describe four contributions of small business to the American economy.
7. What are the major advantages and the major disadvantages of smallness in business?
8. Describe five ways in which the SBA provides management assistance to small businesses.
9. Describe two ways in which the SBA provides financial assistance to small businesses.
10. Why does the SBA concentrate on providing management and financial assistance to small businesses?
11. Explain the relations among a franchise, the franchisor, and the franchisee.
12. What does the franchisor receive in a franchising agreement? What does the franchisee receive? What does each provide?
13. Cite one major benefit of franchising for the franchisor. Cite one major benefit for the franchisee.

Discussion Questions

1. Was Sierra On-Line eligible for SBA aid in 1982? What specific types of aid might it have required? Why?
2. Explain whether Sierra On-Line is typical of small businesses, in terms of:
   a. The people who start small businesses
   b. The contributions of small businesses to the economy
   c. The advantages and disadvantages that a small business offers
3. Most people who start small businesses know of the high failure rate and the reasons for it. Why, then, do they not take steps to protect their firms from failure? What steps should they take?
4. Are the so-called advantages of small business really advantages? Wouldn't every small-business owner like his or her business to grow into a large firm?
5. Do average citizens benefit from the activities of the SBA, or is the SBA only another way to spend our tax money?
6. Would you rather own your own business independently or become a franchisee? Why?

Exercises

1. For a sample of 25 small businesses in your community, calculate what percentage is in service industries, in distribution industries, and in production industries. Explain any major differences between your results and Figure 4.1.
2. Devise a plan for opening a new bicycle sales and repair shop in your community. Consider each of the items listed in the subsection on planning in this chapter. Also give some thought to how you will avoid the major causes of small-business failure.

CASE 4-1
Gibraltar Industries—How Big Is Small?

Remaining small is essential for Gibraltar Industries, Inc., a major supplier of fire-, chemical-, and heat-resistant clothing for the military. It is vital to be a small business because the Defense Department reserves 95 percent of apparel contracts for small businesses exclusively. If Gibraltar loses its status as a small business, it loses the prime source of its revenues!

Its competitors insist that the company is a big business posing as a small one to get contracts under the federal small-business set-aside program. The program is supposed to help small firms by reserving a "reasonable portion" of federal purchases for small businesses to bid on.

The SBA has had trouble deciding just how large or small Gibraltar is. At one point the SBA Size Appeals Board in Washington ruled that Gibraltar no longer qualified as a small business. It exceeded the 500-employee limit for apparel makers when 3 affiliated companies' labor forces were counted. But 3 weeks after the size board's ruling, the SBA re-certified the company as a small business, noting that it had "substantially" changed its relationships with the affiliates.

Lawyer Dennis Riley, who represents one of Gibraltar's rivals, has called these changes "a sham." He says that Gibraltar's maneuvers make a mockery of the set-aside program and the size standards. Gibraltar's chairman Wallace Forman says that he *must* maneuver like this or the company will lose a huge amount of income.

The set-aside "has become a sort of welfare program," Mr. Forman claims. "The recipients are trapped in it. If I tried to escape, I would starve to death."[12]

1. Should Gibraltar be allowed to bid on contracts that are set aside for small business?
2. Has the set-aside program become a "sort of welfare program" as Mr. Forman says?

CASE 4-2

The Flyaway Franchise Takes Off

Would-be skydivers who yearn to fly free, but are too chicken-hearted to take the plunge, can now get their thrills only 30 feet off the ground. The latest in simulated sports, Flyaway, built by real estate developer Marvin Kratter, 67, in Las Vegas, Nevada, has attracted over 10,000 customers since it opened in December.

After plunking down $10 for 5 minutes of floating time, fliers don inflatable suits, goggles, and helmets. Then, with ankles and arms crossed and backs arched, they leap from a platform into space.

A DC-4 propeller, mounted on a 600-horsepower engine, blasts a 120-mile-per-hour current of air upward through a grate in the floor. This cushion of air keeps the fliers airborne. To descend, a flier assumes an upright position, which offers less resistance to the wind.

Reportedly, most "fliers" crash into the padded walls or plummet into a safety net in a few seconds. Spectators can pay $2 to watch the show through windows in the sides of the silo-like building.

Since March, five franchisees have committed about $1 million each to Kratter's company (Airflite Associates, Las Vegas) for the right to open Flyaways in five states. At least five more are in negotiation.

Michael Murphy, a Miami stockbroker who is negotiating for a franchise in Fort Lauderdale, Florida, plans to give discounts for exercise club members. "It's a real aerobic workout," says Murphy, who compared his first Flyaway float to "being tied to the back of a car." Murphy and other franchisees are predicting they will make enough to recover their initial investment in 2 to 5 years.

Franchise fees range from $100,000 to $500,000, depending on territory size. The franchisee must also invest $500,000 to $700,000 for sites and construction costs and must pay $50,000 for insurance. A 6 percent royalty fee on gross annual revenues is collected by Kratter, who bought the patent and franchise rights from inventor Jean St. Germain in Quebec, Canada. Kratter (former owner of the Boston Celtics and New York's St. Regis hotel) and fifteen investors have put $3.5 million into the Las Vegas Flyaway, which they expect will bring in revenues of $1 million to $2 million the first year and be profitable in two years. They expect to make close to $10 million from the sale of franchises.[13]

1. If you had the capital required to buy a Flyaway franchise, what questions would you ask before becoming a franchise holder?
2. Where would you go to "investigate before investing" in this franchise?
3. What might be some of the advantages of owning such a franchise? What might be some of the drawbacks?

Career Profile

Lorraine Mecca "I knew I was good, but no one else seemed to know it," says 35-year-old Lorraine Mecca of Fountain Valley, California. After earning a degree in English education, Mecca taught in a junior high school for two years, then worked her way up from clerk to production coordinator in a Los Angeles distribution firm. In 1978, she gained $25,000 from a divorce settlement, but the future seemed to hold only the frustrations of being underpaid and undervalued. That's when she started Micro D.

Mecca became interested in the computer business when she began attending industry meetings with her new husband, Geza Csige, a computer dealer. Although she is not a technically oriented person, Mecca listened when her husband and others complained about the difficulty of getting certain fast-selling computer items, particularly accessories and software made to work with popular computers like the Apple.

Like most entrepreneurs, Mecca recognized an opening that a new company could fill. She saw a need for a wholesale computer accessories and software distributor in southern California, so she invested her time and money—she raised a total of $50,000—to start Micro D. Six years later, her holdings in the company are estimated to be worth well over $25 million.

The company began by selling accessories compatible with Apple computers to dealers on a wholesale basis. Because of her travels with her husband, Mecca already knew many area computer dealers and therefore already had a good prospective sales network. In its first year, Micro D totalled $3.5 million in revenues, and it now does well over $100 million in sales each year. It went public in 1983, has three branch offices around the country, and has expanded its product line to include IBM-compatible accessories.

After only a month, her husband saw that Mecca's business had much more promise than his and sold his store interests to join her venture. The wife and husband team has worked out well. Mecca feels lucky that she had a spouse to pay the bills while her company was getting off the ground. Csige is responsible for technical aspects of the business and is officially chairman of the company, although he owns no shares and receives an allowance from Mecca rather than a salary.

Mecca and Csige have not done it alone. They recognized that neither of them had the managerial experience necessary to run a large company, so they found professionals to fill their top management positions, and in 1982 they hired Linwood A. Lacy, an experienced, successful manager, to run the company for a year while they established the branch offices. They kept in constant touch with Lacy, learned from him and have avoided the problems faced by many entrepreneurs who are good at starting a business but not as good at running it.

Mecca has become aware of particular difficulties that women face as entrepreneurs. She has had to modify her instincts for dealing with people on a personal level in order to achieve a more businesslike manner. But she also feels that the relatively new computer industry is a good place for female entrepreneurs. "There's no old boy network," she says. And, as Mecca points out, running a big company is easier than working in many traditionally female-dominated professions, like teaching.

Mecca isn't done yet; she continues to see new opportunities all around her. She wants to write software and to pursue her interest in oceanography by developing nautical graphics to help yacht owners navigate by computer.

Like many of us, Mecca had felt unappreciated and unable to exploit many of her talents. But her own creative efforts have now earned her the admiration of the business community.[1]

CAREER PLANNING

The future looks bright for individuals who possess the training and skills needed to meet the technological challenges of the future. The courses that you take in college, your early employment experience, and early career exploration become increasingly important. To help you explore different employment opportunities and plan for your future, we have included profiles of successful business people, together with specific career information, at the end of each major part in *Business*. All career information is taken from the U.S. Department of Labor's *Occupational Outlook Handbook* for 1982–83 and 1984. It is presented in an easy-to-use grid format like the one below.

We have emphasized in each career section that the business environment is undergoing rapid changes. Your success in career planning will be based to some extent on your ability to adapt to these changes.

Part Two *Career Opportunities in Management and Organization*

The number in the salary column approximates the expected annual income after two or three years of service.

1 = $12,000–$15,000   2 = $16,000–$20,000   3 = $21,000–$27,000   4 = $28,000–$35,000   5 = $36,000 and up

Job Title	Educational Requirements	Salary Range	Prospects
Administrative management assistant	Two years of college; on-the-job experience	2	Gradual growth
1	**2**	**3**	**4**
Clerical supervisor	High school diploma; some college preferred	1–2	Greatest growth
Purchasing agent	Bachelor's degree in business; on-the-job experience helpful	3	Limited growth
Secretarial supervisor	High school diploma; on-the-job experience; some college preferred	2	Gradual growth

Column	Explanation		
1	This column lists common job titles that correspond to job opportunities in the employment world today. Entries are alphabetized for easy reference.	3	Salary ranges for each job title are included in this column. Of course, actual salary will be determined by employee qualifications, geographical differences in salary levels, and other factors.
2	Here, the general educational levels and degree requirements for each job title in column 1 are shown. In some cases, on-the-job experience is also necessary.	4	Employment prospects for each job title are indicated by a relative scale. In descending order, the scale ranges from greatest growth and gradual growth to limited growth and no growth.

PART

2
Management and Organization

This part of the book deals with the organization—the "thing" that is a business. We begin with a discussion of the functions involved in developing and operating an organization. Then we analyze the organization itself, to see what makes it tick. Next we put the two together, to examine the part of a business that is concerned with the conversion of material resources to products. Included in this part are:

Chapter 5 The Management Process
Chapter 6 Creating the Organization
Chapter 7 Operations Management

CHAPTER

FIVE
The Management Process

A Concorde SST airplane is a sleek structure, precisely engineered to accomplish its goal of speedy transatlantic flight. A business is a structure as well. Perhaps it is not so sleek, but it too is organized to accomplish a goal. Picture a Concorde speeding down the runway without its flight crew, and you'll have an idea of what a business would be like without its management. Both an airplane and a business must be carefully monitored and controlled by those who are responsible for its operation. This chapter is about managers—the people who run the day-to-day operation of organizations—and the work they do. After studying the chapter, you should understand:

1. *What management is and what managers do*
2. *The four basic management functions: goal setting and planning, organizing, leading, and controlling*
3. *The various kinds of managers, in terms of both level and area of management*
4. *The key management skills and the management roles in which these skills are used*
5. *The sources companies turn to for managers*
6. *Three important contemporary management theories: Theory Z, corporate culture, and management excellence*

Consider this:

In 1982 International Harvester (IH) sustained losses of almost $1.7 billion. The company's stock price plunged to a paltry $3 per share (from a figure of $45 per share in 1979). All signs indicated that the company was doomed. Now, however, IH is getting back on its feet again, and the firm may survive after all. For the most part, IH's almost miraculous turnaround was due to shrewd and effective management.

Historically, International Harvester had built its operations on the production of trucks and farm equipment. Several times the company had resisted both the temptation and the opportunity to branch out into other products. Instead management chose to focus its efforts within a fairly narrow area of business. As a result of this strategy, the hard times suffered by American farmers beginning in the 1980s had a direct and profound impact on IH: Farmers simply could not afford to buy as much new equipment as they had in the past. Farm equipment was one mainstay of the company, so it was no surprise that IH began to suffer as well.

In 1979, at the risk of displeasing IH's existing top management, the IH board of directors persuaded Archie McCardell to become chief executive officer for their firm. At the time McCardell was the second in command at Xerox Corporation. He in turn convinced Donald Lennox, a senior vice president at Xerox, to join the new management team at International Harvester.

In 1979 IH's workers went on strike against the firm. The strike, combined with the worsening economy, accelerated a downturn that included the farmers' economic problems and almost ruined the company. One devastating result was the $1.7 billion loss experienced by IH in 1982. There was every indication that the company would show continuing heavy losses in 1983.

McCardell was fired from his post and Lennox became president in mid-1982. Seven months later Lennox was named CEO and developed a plan for restoring the company's health. The core of this plan was a major cost-cutting program designed to stem the flow of financial resources out of the company. On the recommendation of IH's operations managers, Lennox closed several inefficient plants. Two-thirds of the work force was laid off. Certain subsidiaries—including a construction operation—were sold because they had been draining resources from the truck and farm-equipment operations. Altogether, Lennox cut operating expenses by $1 billion.

This series of maneuvers left IH in a much better position when the economy began its upswing in 1983. The truck group, for example, had shut down three old plants, trimmed its management structure, and adopted a Japanese inventory-management technique called "just-in-time." As a result the group was quite healthy by late 1983. Moreover, there was a good chance that changes in federal farm policies would dramatically increase farmers' buying power. This could revitalize the farm-equipment group as well.

Of course IH is not out of the woods yet. For example, the company's European operations are still in a shambles. Sales are still far down in Europe, where the company is facing increased competition from firms like Fiat. And IH is still paying off some $3.5 billion in debts. Finally, labor unions like the United Auto Workers (which represents approximately three-fifths of IH's 21,000 workers in the United States) want IH to restore several benefits that workers gave up to help the company pull through. Clearly, Lennox cannot afford to rest on his laurels.[1]

Source: Courtesy of International Harvester.

Without a doubt, management is one of the most exciting, challenging, and rewarding of professions. The men and women who manage business firms play an important part in shaping the world we live in. At International Harvester, for example, 33,000 jobs worldwide depended on whether management was able to solve the company's problems.

No doubt decisions that had been made throughout International Harvester's history contributed to its difficulties. But they were due in large part to present external forces: the inability of the firm's customers to purchase new farm machinery and the generally worsening economy. Because these difficulties affected the entire company, it was the responsibility of top management, which consists of the highest-ranking executives in the firm, to deal with them. They were also pressing problems that called for immediate action.

Donald Lennox was aided in his efforts by IH's operations managers and probably by other specialized managers as well. For example, the firm's financial managers were almost certainly involved. Depending on its size, an organization may employ a number of these specialized managers—people who are responsible for particular areas of management. An organization also includes managers at its several operational levels to coordinate resources and activities at those levels.

Must every organization employ all these managers in area after area and level upon level? Well, yes and no. A very large organization may actually field a battalion of managers, each responsible for activities on one particular level of one management area. On the other hand, the owner of a sole proprietorship may be the only manager in the organization. He or she then *is* all the managers we have described. He or she is responsible for all levels and areas of management (and probably for getting the mail out on time, as well).

What is important to an organization is not the number of managers it employs but the ability of these managers to achieve the organization's goals. As you will see, this task requires the application of a variety of skills to a wide range of functions and roles.

MANAGEMENT AND MANAGERS

Trying to describe the process of management is somewhat like trying to explain the universe. Both are made up of numerous parts, some highly visible and others more like abstract concepts or relationships. Nevertheless, we must start somewhere. We shall begin with the definition of management and a preliminary overview of what managers do.

What Is Management?

Management is the process of coordinating the resources of an organization so as to achieve the primary goals of the organization. As we saw in Chapter 1, most organizations make use of four kinds of resources: material, financial, human, and informational. (See Figure 5.1.)

Material resources are the tangible, physical resources that an organization uses. For example, General Motors uses steel, glass, and fiberglass to produce cars and trucks on complex machine-driven assembly lines. Both the assembly lines and the buildings that house them are material resources, as are the actual materials from which vehicles are built. A college or university uses books, classroom buildings, desks, and computers to educate students. And the Mayo Clinic uses beds, operating room equipment, and diagnostic machines to provide health care.

Financial resources are the funds that the organization uses to meet its obligations to various creditors. A Safeway store obtains money from customers at the check-out counters and uses a portion of it to pay the wholesalers from whom it buys the food we purchase. Citicorp, a large New York bank, borrows and lends money. A college obtains money in the form of tuition, income from its endowment, and state and federal grants. It uses the money to pay utility bills,

Figure 5.1 *The Four Main Resources of Management*

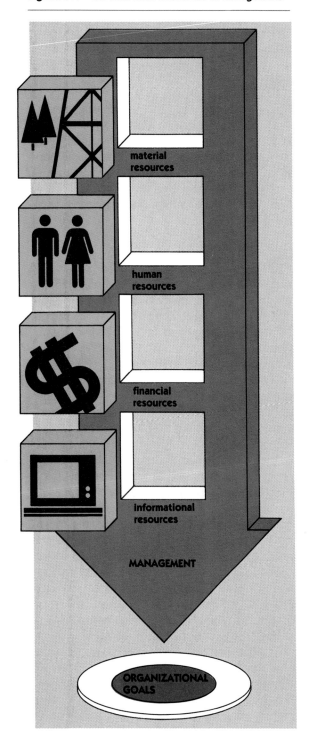

material resources

human resources

financial resources

informational resources

MANAGEMENT

ORGANIZATIONAL GOALS

insurance premiums, and teachers' salaries. Each of these transactions involves financial resources.

Perhaps the most important resource of any organization is its *human resource*—people. Delta Air Lines has clearly demonstrated its conviction that its people are its most important asset by maintaining a "no layoff" policy since 1957. This dedication to human resources has paid off in many ways. According to *The Wall Street Journal:*

> . . . the policy has generated an unusual degree of employee loyalty, which has helped the airline save money in other ways. Delta says it doesn't have to rehire and retrain workers during good times. And [in 1982], as a thanks for a pay increase, employees raised enough money to buy the company a $30 million airplane.[2]

Hospitals could not function without doctors, nurses, and orderlies. In fact, no organization can be an organization without people.

Finally, many organizations are increasingly finding that they cannot afford to ignore *information*. External environmental conditions—including the economy, consumer markets, technology, politics, and cultural forces—are all changing so rapidly that an organization that does not adapt will probably not survive. And, in order to adapt to change, the organization must know what is changing and how it is changing. Companies are finding it increasingly important to gather information about their competitors in today's business environment. Companies such as Ford Motor Company, Westinghouse Electric, and General Electric are known to collect information about their competition. These companies are technology based, but other types of companies collect this information as well: Chemical Bank, Kraft, and J. C. Penney also carefully monitor the activities of their competition.[3] As you will see in Part 6, information that is generated within the organization is just as important as this external information.

It is important to realize that these are only general categories of resources. Within each category are hundreds or thousands of more specific types, from which management must choose the set of resources that can best accomplish its goals. Consider, for example, the wide variety of skills and talents that people have to offer. Of these, Metro-Goldwyn-Mayer would certainly choose a different set of skills from, say, the American Red Cross. And a Burger King outlet would require still a different set. When we consider choices from all four categories, we end up with an extremely complex group of specific resources. It is this complex group of specific resources—and not simply "some of each" of the four general categories—that managers must coordinate so as to produce goods and services.

What Do Managers Do?

Managers engage in a multitude of activities as they go about the job of coordinating resources. Most of their time is spent communicating with other people, both within their own organizations and in other organizations. In fact, research on the work of managers indicates, on the average, they spend about 60 percent of their time in scheduled meetings, 22 percent of their time working at their desks, 10 percent of their time in unscheduled meetings, 6 percent of their time on the telephone, and the remaining time touring the work area.[4] (See Figure 5.2.) Of course these figures are averages, and the actual proportions vary considerably from one management situation to another. Still, it is obvious that managers spend much of their time interacting with other people. This conclusion is consistent with our observation that an organization's people are perhaps its most important resource.

Another interesting way to look at management is in terms of the functions that managers perform. These functions have been identified as goal setting and planning, organizing, leading and motivating employees, and controlling ongoing activities. We shall explore them in some detail in the next section.

BASIC MANAGEMENT FUNCTIONS

A number of management functions must be performed if any organization is to succeed. Some

Managers spend most of their time interacting with people in different ways. Typically, the amount of time they spend in the actual work area is relatively small. Source: Courtesy of Continental Group, Inc.

seem to be most important when a new enterprise is first formed, or when something is obviously wrong (as was the case with International Harvester in 1982). Others seem to be essentially day-to-day activities. In truth, however, all are part of the ongoing process of management.

First, goals must be established for the organization, and plans must be developed to achieve those goals. Next, managers must organize people and other resources into a logical and efficient "well-oiled machine" that is capable of accomplishing the goals that have been chosen. Third, managers must lead employees in such a way that they are motivated to work effectively to help achieve the goals of the organization. And finally, managers need to maintain adequate control to ensure that the organization is working steadily toward its goals.

For example, when Lee Iacocca took the reins at Chrysler Corporation, that firm was on the brink of bankruptcy. One of the first things Iacocca did was to establish a series of specific goals for sales growth and a strategy for achieving them. He changed the basic structure of the organization. Then he provided effective leadership by working for $1 a year until he had turned the company around. He also developed an elaborate control system to keep Chrysler on track.

These functions do not occur according to some rigid, preset timetable. Managers don't plan in January, organize in February, lead and motivate in March, and control in April. At any given time, managers are likely to be engaged in a number of functions simultaneously. However,

each of the functions tends to lead naturally to others. Figure 5.3 provides a visual framework for discussion of these management functions.

Goal Setting and Planning

As we have noted, goals must first be set for the organization. Then the manager must develop plans by which to achieve those goals.

Goal Setting   A **goal** is an end state that the organization is expected to achieve. **Goal setting**, then, is the process of developing—and committing an organization to—a set of goals. Every organization has goals of several types.

The most fundamental type of goal is the organization's **purpose**, which is the reason for the organization's existence. Texaco's purpose is to earn a profit for its owners. Houston Community College's purpose is to provide an education for local citizens. The purpose of the Secret Service is to protect the life of the President. The organization's **mission** is the means by which it is to fulfill its purpose. Apple Computer Company attempts to fulfill its purpose by manufacturing computers, whereas Ford Motor Company fulfills the same purpose (making a profit) by manufacturing cars. Finally, **objectives** are specific statements detailing what the organization intends to accomplish as it goes about its mission. For McDonald's, one objective might be that all customers will be served within two minutes of their arrival. Sears, Roebuck might adopt the objective that sales will be increased by 7 percent this year. For IBM, one objective might be that the delivery time for home computers will be reduced by two weeks next year.

Goals can deal with a variety of factors, such as sales, company growth, costs, customer satisfaction, and employee morale. They can also extend over various periods of time. A small manufacturer may focus primarily on sales objectives for the next six months, whereas Exxon may be more interested in objectives for the year 2000. Finally, goals should be established for every level in the organization. The president of the

Figure 5.2   How Managers Spend Their Time. *Source: Data from Mintzberg, "The Manager's Job,"* Harvard Business Review, *1975.*

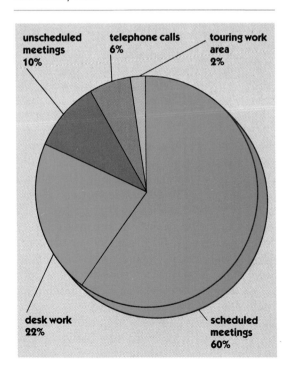

unscheduled meetings 10%

telephone calls 6%

touring work area 2%

desk work 22%

scheduled meetings 60%

company has a set of goals that he or she hopes to achieve. The head of a department also has a set of goals, as does an operating employee at the lowest level in the organization.

The goals developed for these different levels must be consistent with one another. However, it is likely that some conflict will arise. A production department, for example, may have a goal of minimizing costs. One way to do this is to produce only one type of product and offer no "frills." Marketing, on the other hand, may have a goal of maximizing sales. And one way to implement this goal is to offer prospective customers a wide range of products with many options available. As part of his or her own goal setting, the manager who is ultimately responsible for *both* departments must achieve some sort of balance between such competing or conflicting goals. This balancing process is called *optimization*.

The optimization of conflicting goals requires insight and ability. When faced with the marketing-versus-production conflict we have just described, most managers would probably not adopt either viewpoint completely. Instead, they might decide on a reasonably diverse product line offering only the most widely sought-after options. Such a compromise would seem to be best for the organization as a whole.

Planning Once goals have been set for the organization, managers must develop plans for achieving them. A **plan** is an outline of the actions by which the organization intends to accomplish its goals. The processes involved in developing plans are referred to as **planning**. Just as it has several goals, the organization should develop several types of plans.

An organization's **strategy** is its broadest set of plans and is developed as a guide for major policy setting and decision making. A firm's strategy defines what business the company is in or wants to be in and the kind of company it is or wants to be. When the Surgeon General issued a report linking smoking and cancer in the 1950s, top management at Philip Morris, Inc., recog-

nized that the company's very survival was threatened. Action was needed to broaden the company's operations. Major elements in the overall Philip Morris strategy were to purchase first the Miller Brewing Company and then Seven-Up and to aggressively promote the com-

Figure 5.3 *The Management Process. Note that management is not a step-by-step procedure, but a process with a feedback loop that represents a flow.*

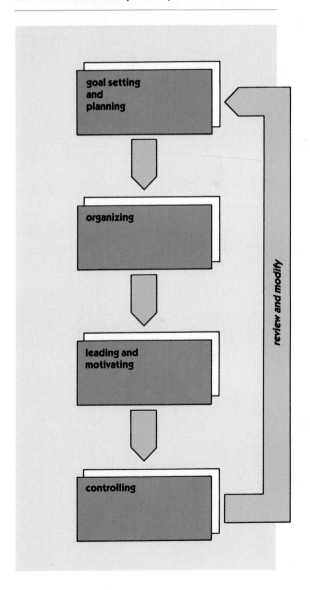

After the goals of an organization have been established, managers must develop plans that will achieve them.
Source: Courtesy of Harsco Corporation.

panies' products. As a result of its strategy, Philip Morris seems to have attained the goal of being less dependent on tobacco sales.

Most organizations also employ several narrower kinds of plans. **Tactical plans** are smaller-scale (and usually shorter-range) plans developed to implement a strategy. If a strategic plan will take five years to complete, the firm may develop five tactical plans, one covering each year. Tactical plans may need to be updated periodically as conditions and experience dictate. Their narrower scope permits them to be changed more easily than strategies.

Another category of plans is referred to as *standing plans*. These result from—and implement—decisions that have previously been made by management. A **policy** is a general guide for action in a situation that occurs repeatedly. A **standard operating procedure** (SOP) is a plan that outlines the steps to be taken in a situation that arises again and again. An SOP is thus more specific than a policy. For example, a Sears, Roebuck department store may have a policy of accepting deliveries only between 9 A.M. and 4 P.M. Standard operating procedure might then require that each accepted delivery be checked, sorted, and stored before closing time on the delivery day.

Organizing the Enterprise

After goal setting and planning, the second major function of the manager is organization. **Organizing** is the grouping of resources and activities to accomplish some end result in an efficient and effective manner. Consider the case of an inventor who creates a new product and goes into business to sell it. At first, he will probably do everything himself—purchase raw materials, make the product, advertise it, sell it, and keep his business records up to date. Eventually, as his business grows, he will find that he needs help. To begin with, he might hire a professional sales representative and a part-time bookkeeper. Later he might need to hire full-time sales personnel, other people to assist with production, and an accountant. As he hires each new person, he must decide what that person will do, to whom that person will report, and generally how that person can best take part in the organization's activities. We shall discuss these and other facets of the organizing function in much more detail in the next chapter.

Leading and Motivating

The leading and motivating functions are concerned with the human resources within the organization. **Leading** is the process of influencing people to work toward a common goal. **Motivating** is the process of providing reasons for people to work in the best interests of the organization. Together, leading and motivating are often referred to as *directing*.

We have already noted the importance of an organization's human resources. Because of this importance, leading and motivating are critical activities. Obviously, different people do things for different reasons—that is, they have different *motivations*. Some are primarily interested in earning as much money as they can. Others may be spurred on by opportunities to get ahead in the organization. Part of the manager's job, then, is to determine what things motivate his or her subordinates and to try to provide those things in a way that encourages effective performance.

Quite a lot of research has been done on both motivation and leadership. As you will see in Chapter 8, research on motivation has yielded very useful information. Research on leadership has been less successful. In spite of decades of study, no one has discovered a set of personal traits or characteristics that make a good leader.

We do, however, know something about leadership styles—how managers go about the function of leading. The *authoritarian* leader makes all the decisions and then tells subordinates what to do and how to do it. The *democratic* leader involves subordinates in most decisions and in the assignment of tasks. The *laissez-faire* leader maintains a "hands-off" attitude; he or she allows subordinates to work as they decide is best.

Managers lead and motivate employees to work toward their organization's goals. *Source: Courtesy of Pitney Bowes, photo by Gabe Palmer.*

Each of these styles has its advantages and its disadvantages. For example, democratic leadership can motivate employees to work effectively, because it is *their* decisions that they are implementing. On the other hand, the decision-making process takes time that subordinates would otherwise be devoting to their tasks. Actually, each of the three leadership styles can be effective. The style that is *most* effective depends on the interaction among the subordinates, characteristics of the work situation, and the manager's leadership style.

Controlling Ongoing Activities

Controlling is the process of evaluating and regulating ongoing activities to ensure that goals are achieved. To see how controlling works, consider a rocket launched by NASA to place a satellite in orbit. Do NASA personnel simply fire the rocket

Like the controllers at this television network center, managers must monitor the activities of their organization constantly. *Source:* © 1983 Henry Groskinsky.

and then check back in a few days to find out whether the satellite is in place? Of course not. The rocket is constantly monitored, and its course is regulated and adjusted as needed to get the satellite to where it should be. In a similar fashion, managerial control involves both close monitoring of the progress of the organization as it works toward its goals, and whatever regulating and adjusting are required to keep it on course.

For example, suppose that United Airlines established a goal of increasing its profit by 12 percent next year. To ensure that this goal is reached, United's management might monitor its profit on a monthly basis. After three months, if profit had increased by 3 percent, management might be able to assume that everything was going according to schedule. Probably no action would be taken. However, if profit had increased by only 1 percent after three months, some corrective action would be needed to get the firm on track. The particular action that was required

would depend on the reason for the low increase in profit.

The control function includes three steps. The first is the *setting of standards,* or specific goals to which performance can be compared. (Quantitative goals, such as United's 3 percent profit increase in three months, are perhaps the most useful.) The second step is *measuring actual performance* and comparing it with the standard. And the third step is *taking corrective action* as necessary. These steps must be repeated periodically until the primary goal is achieved.

KINDS OF MANAGERS

We noted earlier that managers—or at least the work of managers—can be viewed from two different perspectives: level within the organization and area of management. Here we shall use these two viewpoints to extend our discussion of management functions.

Levels of Management

For the moment, think of an organization as a three-story triangular structure (Figure 5.4). Each story corresponds to one of the three general levels of management: top managers, middle managers, and lower-level managers.

Top Managers **Top managers** are the small group of upper-level executives who guide and control the overall fortunes of the organization. In terms of planning, top managers are generally responsible for interpreting the organization's purpose and developing its mission. They also determine the firm's strategy and define its major policies. It takes years of hard work and determination, as well as talent and no small share of good luck, to reach the ranks of top management in large companies. Common titles associated with top managers are president, vice president, chief executive officer (CEO), and chief operating officer (COO).

Middle Managers There are more middle managers in most organizations than any other kind. **Middle managers** are those managers who implement the strategy and major policies that are handed down from the top level of the organization. They develop tactical plans and standard operating procedures, and they coordinate and supervise the activities of lower-level managers. Titles at the middle management level include division manager, department head, plant manager, and operations manager.

Lower-Level Managers **Lower-level managers** are those who coordinate and supervise the activities of operating employees. They spend most of their time working with and motivating their employees, answering questions, and solving day-to-day problems. Most lower-level managers are former operating employees who, owing to their hard work and potential, were promoted into management. And many of today's middle and top managers began their careers on this

lowest management level. Common titles for lower-level managers include office manager, supervisor, and foreman.

Areas of Management

Our triangular organizational structure can also be divided more or less vertically into areas of management specialization (Figure 5.5). The most common of these areas are finance, operations, marketing, personnel, and administration. Depending on its purpose and mission, an organization may include other areas as well—research and development, for example.

Financial Managers **Financial managers** are those managers whose primary responsibility is the organization's financial resources. Accounting and investment are specialized areas within financial management. Because financing affects the

Figure 5.4 *Management Levels Found in Most Companies. Middle managers are the largest group in most organizations. To implement the goals of any company requires the coordinated effort of all three levels of managers.*

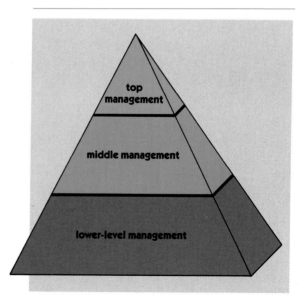

operation of the entire firm, many of the presidents of this country's largest companies are people who got their "basic training" as financial managers.

Operations Managers **Operations managers** are those people who create and manage the systems that convert resources into goods and services. Traditionally, operations management has been equated with manufacturing—the production of goods. Increasingly, however, we have come to realize that many of the techniques and procedures of operations management can be applied to the production of services and to a variety of nonbusiness activities. Like financial management, operations management has produced a good percentage of today's company presidents.

Marketing Managers **Marketing managers** are those who are responsible for facilitating the exchange of products between the organization and its customers or clients. Specific areas within marketing are marketing research, advertising, promotion, sales, and distribution. A fair number of today's company presidents have risen from the ranks of marketing management.

Personnel Managers **Personnel managers** are the people charged with managing the organization's formal human-resources programs. They engage in human-resources planning; design systems for hiring, training, and appraising the performance of employees; and ensure that the organization follows government regulations concerning employment practices. Because personnel management is a relatively new area of specialization in many organizations, there are not many top managers with a personnel background. However, this situation should change with the passage of time.

Administrative Managers **Administrative managers** (also called *general managers*) are managers who are not associated with any specific area but who provide overall administrative guidance and leadership. A hospital administrator is a good example of an administrative manager. He or she does not specialize in operations, finance, marketing, or personnel management but instead coordinates the activities of specialized managers in all these areas. In many respects, most top managers (like Donald Lennox at IH) are really administrative managers.

Whatever their level in the organization and whatever area of management they specialize in, successful managers generally exhibit certain key skills and are able to play certain managerial roles. But, as we shall see, some skills may be more critical at one level of management than at another.

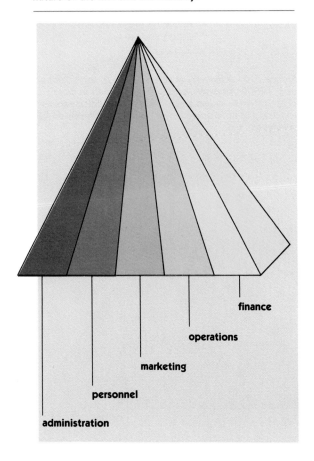

Figure 5.5 *Areas of Management Specialization. Other areas may have to be added, depending on the nature of the firm and the industry.*

finance

operations

marketing

personnel

administration

CHARACTERISTICS OF SUCCESSFUL MANAGERS

In general, successful managers are those who (1) possess certain important skills and (2) are able to use these skills in a number of managerial roles. Probably no manager is called upon to use any particular skill *constantly* or to play a particular role all the time. However, these skills and abilities must be available when they are needed.

Key Management Skills

The skills that typify successful managers tend to fall into five general categories: technical, conceptual, interpersonal, diagnostic, and analytic. See Figure 5.6.

Technical Skills **Technical skills** are the specific skills needed to accomplish specialized activities. They are the skills that engineers, lawyers, and machinists, for example, need to do their jobs. Lower-level managers (and to a lesser extent middle managers) need the technical skills that are relevant to the activities they manage. Although these managers may not have to perform the technical tasks themselves, they must be able to train subordinates, answer questions, and otherwise provide guidance and direction. In general, top managers do not rely on technical skills as much as managers at other levels. Still, understanding the technical side of things is an aid to effective management at every level.

Conceptual Skills A manager's **conceptual skills** are his or her ability to conceptualize and to think in abstract terms. Conceptual skills allow the manager to see the "big picture" and to understand how the various parts of an organization or an idea can fit together. In 1951 a man named Charles Wilson decided to take his family on a cross-country vacation. All along the way, the family was forced to put up with high-priced but shabby hotel accommodations. Wilson reasoned that most travelers would welcome a chain of moderately priced, good-quality roadside hotels.

You are no doubt familiar with what he came up with: Holiday Inns. Wilson was able to identify a number of isolated factors (existing accommodation patterns, the need for a different kind of hotel, and his own investment interests) to "dream up" the new business opportunity, and to carry it through to completion.

Conceptual skills are useful in a wide range of situations, including the optimization of goals described earlier. They appear, however, to be more crucial for top managers than for middle or lower-level managers.

Interpersonal Skills The **interpersonal skills** that managers need add up to the ability to deal effectively with other people, both inside and outside the organization. When all other things are equal, the manager who is able to relate to people, understand their needs and motives, and show genuine compassion will be more successful than the manager who is arrogant and brash and who doesn't care about others. Of course, there are always exceptions: The former CEO at In-

Figure 5.6 Key Management Skills. A strong manager needs to have developed all five skills to a high degree. Source: Photo, © 1984 T. Molinski.

- technical skills
- conceptual skills
- interpersonal skills
- diagnostic skills
- analytic skills

ternational Telephone and Telegraph had a terrible reputation for publicly humiliating subordinates who annoyed or disappointed him.

Diagnostic Skills **Diagnostic skills** are skills in assessing a particular situation and identifying its causes. The diagnostic skills of the successful manager parallel those of the physician, who assesses the patient's symptoms in order to pinpoint the underlying medical problem. We can take this parallel one step further, too. In management as in medicine, correct diagnosis is often critical in determining the appropriate action to take. All managers need to make use of diagnostic skills, but these skills are probably used most by top managers.

Analytic Skills All managers, regardless of level or area, need analytic skills. **Analytic skills** are used to identify the relevant issues (or variables) in a situation, to determine how they are related, and to assess their relative importance. Analytic skills often come into play along with diagnostic

skills. For example, a manager assigned to a new position may be confronted with a wide variety of problems that all need attention. Diagnostic skills will be needed to identify the causes of each problem. But first the manager must analyze the problem of "too many problems" in order to determine which problems need immediate attention and which ones can wait.

Managerial Roles

Research suggests that managers must, from time to time, act in ten different roles if they are to be successful.[5] (By "role" we mean a part that someone plays, as in the theater.) These ten roles can be grouped in three categories: decisional, interpersonal, and informational.

Decisional Roles As you might suspect, the **decisional roles** are those that involve various aspects of management decision making. In the role of *entrepreneur,* the manager is the voluntary initiator of change. For example, the manager who develops a new strategy or expands the sales force into a new market is playing the entrepreneur's role. A second decisional role is that of *disturbance handler.* A manager who settles a strike, or finds a new supplier of raw materials because there have been inventory shortages, is handling a disturbance. Third, the manager also occasionally plays the role of *resource allocator.* In this role, the manager might have to decide which departmental budgets to cut and which expenditure requests to approve. The fourth and last decisional role is that of *negotiator.* Being a negotiator might involve settling a dispute between a manager and the manager's subordinate or negotiating a new labor contract.

Interpersonal Roles By now you should realize that dealing with people is an integral part of the manager's job. The three **interpersonal roles** are the roles in which the manager deals with people. The manager may be called upon to serve as a *figurehead,* perhaps by attending a ribbon-cutting ceremony or taking an important client to

As he analyzes data with a subordinate for use in decision making, this manager performs all three types of managerial roles—decisional, interpersonal, and informational. Source: Courtesy of E. I. du Pont de Nemours and Company.

dinner. The manager may also have to play the role of *liaison* by serving as a go-between for two different groups. In this case, one of the two groups is the manager's own company. As a liaison, a manager might represent his or her firm at meetings of an industry-wide trade organization. Finally, the manager often has to serve as a *leader.* Playing the role of leader includes being an example for others in the organization, developing the skills and abilities of others, and working to motivate others.

Informational Roles **Informational roles** are those in which the manager either gathers or provides information. In the role of *monitor,* the manager actively seeks information that may be of value to the organization. For example, a manager who hears about a good business opportunity, or is told by subordinates that employees are contemplating a strike, is engaging in the role of monitor. The second informational role is that

of *disseminator.* In this role, the manager transmits key information to those who can make use of it. As a disseminator, our manager would tip off the appropriate marketing manager about the business opportunity and warn the personnel manager about the possible strike. The third informational role is that of *spokesperson.* In this role, the manager provides information to people outside the organization, such as the press and the public.

SOURCES OF MANAGERS

We have discussed a number of functions that managers must perform, skills they must use, and roles they must play. But where do they acquire the ability to do all this? We can best answer this question by turning it around and asking where organizations get management personnel. And we find that there are three primary sources of managers: lower levels in the organization, other organizations, and schools and universities (Figure 5.7).

Inside the Organization

You have probably heard about firms whose policy is to "promote from within." This simply means that, whenever a position needs to be filled, the firm makes a genuine effort to promote someone from a lower level in the firm to that position. There are two advantages of this approach. First, the person promoted from within is already familiar with how the organization operates, its strategy, its people, and most other facets of the organization. Second, promotion from within may increase job motivation for all employees. That is, if employees recognize that good work can lead to a promotion, they are more likely to work harder and better and to stay with the company rather than seeking advancement elsewhere.

On the other hand, promoting from within may limit innovation. The new manager may simply continue to do things the way the previous manager did them—the way they have always been done in the organization. Furthermore, at the time a particular position needs to be filled, there might not be anyone in the organization who is truly qualified for that position. Hence, even firms that seek to promote from within may have to hire someone from another organization occasionally.

Other Organizations

The practice of hiring managers from other organizations seems to be used particularly to fill top-management positions. Within the last few years, Avis and Coca-Cola have hired top exec-

Figure 5.7 Sources of Managers. Potential managers may be promoted from within, hired away from other companies, or hired directly from college.

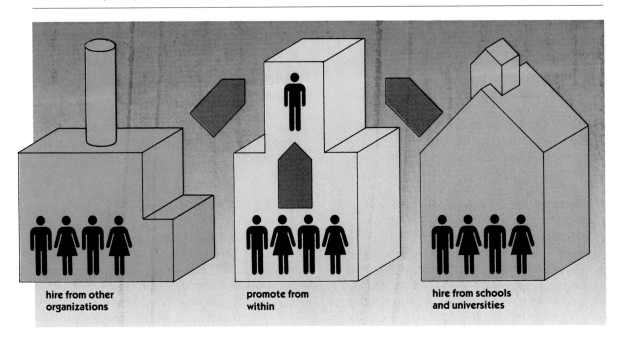

hire from other organizations

promote from within

hire from schools and universities

Most companies use some form of regular performance appraisal to evaluate the work and promotion prospects of managerial employees. Generally, a manager evaluates his own subordinates. But at Photocircuits, a New York manufacturer of printed circuit boards with 800 employees, managers and supervisors also get a regular performance review by their subordinates.

According to a report in *Management Review* (Vol. 71, No. 8), subordinates at Photocircuits first fill out a questionnaire designed to measure their immediate superiors' attitudes, performance, and relationships with colleagues. Some typical questions:

- Does your manager show interest in you as an individual?
- Is he or she a good listener who tries to understand your point of view?
- Does he or she make sure that you receive the training that you need?
- Is he or she fair and explicit in his or her assignments of work?
- Does he or she provide challenge in your job?
- Does he or she accept suggestions easily?
- Does he or she give criticism in a fair and considerate manner?

On a separate sheet, subordinates also summarize their supervisors' strong points and those that need improvement. The subordinate and the manager then meet to discuss the appraisal, after which both must sign it, with one copy going to the manager's superior.

Initially, many employees had difficulty being critical of their bosses, and their first evaluations tended to be uniformly glowing. But the company encouraged honest appraisals of everyone, starting with president John Endee, who was told by one subordinate that he was "too aggressive" and that he "frightened people." "This sort of program doesn't work in a climate of fear," says Endee. "It requires a lot of sensitivity on the part of a manager to encourage a subordinate's honesty."

The fear can work both ways. Some managers were fearful of being evaluated by those they supervised. But, as Endee explains, "Only managers who lack self-confidence in their abilities are afraid of criticism. After all, criticism of management occurs in every organization. Employees constantly criticize their boss—behind his back. The manager who has a problem—who needs to improve his behavior or attitude—will be made aware of this by the very people who can help him most." Asked whether the reverse-review policy might be a deterrent in recruiting new managers, Endee replied, "I hope so. Anyone unwilling to be evaluated, by anyone, would not work out well here."

Source: Berkeley Rice, "Reversing Performance Review," *Psychology Today,* March 1984, p. 80.

---

utives away from Hertz and Pepsi. Specialized executive employment agencies (sometimes unflatteringly called "head hunters") search out qualified personnel who may be interested in leaving their organization for a better job. The agencies then match these people with firms seeking top managers. Of course, many managers are hired by the more direct process of simply applying to the firm that has advertised an opening.

The primary advantages of hiring from the outside are that the applicant may be judged objectively, on the basis of his or her work record in the previous organization, and may bring new ideas and fresh perspectives to the hiring firm. On the other hand, the hiring firm may not be able to learn as much about the applicant as it might like. Also, hiring from outside may cause resentment among present employees.

The behavior patterns and decision-making practices of managers have been the focus of much recent business research. Source: Courtesy of Dow Jones and Company, photograph by Neil Selkirk.

Schools and Universities

The third important source of managers is school and university campuses. Most large companies—and many smaller ones as well—routinely interview prospective graduates who might be interested in working for them. Those who are hired usually go through a management training program before being assigned a position. The program acquaints them with the firm and its products and prepares them for higher-level positions in the firm. Hence, educational institutions provide a pool of management talent that the organization then develops further, with the eventual goal of promotion to higher management levels.

Even after potential managers leave school and begin their working careers, their education is often not finished. Many return to school for an advanced degree, such as the MBA (Master of Business Administration), or to receive specialized training through management development programs and seminars.

CONTEMPORARY MANAGEMENT THEORY

In recent years, there has been much interest in the development and application of new and innovative management theories. Three of the best-known and most influential new approaches to management are Theory Z and the theories of corporate culture and management excellence.

Theory Z

Japanese management practices and techniques have received much attention lately from managers and management theorists. One cause of this interest has been the difference in productivity trends in the United States and Japan. Simply defined, **productivity** is the average output per hour for all workers in the private business sector. In the United States, productivity increased at the rate of 3.2 percent per year from 1947 to 1966. The rate of increase dropped to half that figure during the years 1966 to 1976, and it declined even further to an annual growth rate of 0.7 percent per year from 1976 to 1981. By contrast, Japanese productivity increased by more than 12 percent per year until 1970 and is still increasing at a rate of 8 percent per year. This productivity is particularly visible in the Japanese automotive and electronics industries.

In the 1970s William Ouchi, a management professor at UCLA, began to study business practices in United States and Japanese firms.[6] He concluded that different types of management systems dominate in these two countries.

In Japan Ouchi found what he calls *Type J* firms. They are characterized by lifetime employment for employees, collective (or group) decision making, collective responsibility for the outcomes of decisions, slow evaluation and promotions, implied control mechanisms, nonspecialized career paths, and a holistic (or overall) concern for employees as people.

American industry is dominated by what Ouchi calls *Type A* firms, which follow a different pattern. They emphasize short-term employment, individual decision making, individual responsibility for the outcomes of decisions, rapid evaluation and promotion, explicit control mechanisms, specialized career paths, and a segmented concern for employees only as employees.

A few very successful American firms represent a blend of the Type J and Type A patterns. These *Type Z* organizations emphasize long-term employment, collective decision making, individ-

ual responsibility for the outcomes of decisions, slow evaluation and promotion, informal control along with some formalized measures, moderately specialized career paths, and a holistic concern for employees. Examples of Type Z firms are IBM, Eastman Kodak, and Hewlett-Packard.

Theory Z is the belief that some middle ground between Type A and Type J practices is best for American business. Perhaps the essence of Theory Z (and the main characteristic of Type Z firms) is a high level of employee involvement in decisions. Companies who follow Theory Z thus are able to take full advantage of all the human resources at their disposal. Ouchi and other proponents of Theory Z feel that it may help the United States regain its place as the world's primary industrial country. See Figure 5.8.

Figure 5.8 The Features of Theory Z. The best aspects of Japanese and American management theory combine to form the nucleus of Theory Z. *Source: Photo, courtesy of Merck & Co., Inc.*

TYPE J FIRMS (Japanese)

- lifetime employment
- collective decision making
- collective responsibility
- slow promotion
- implied control mechanisms
- nonspecialized career paths
- holistic concern for employees

TYPE A FIRMS (American)

- short-term employment
- individual decision making
- individual responsibility
- rapid promotion
- explicit control mechanisms
- specialized career paths
- segmented concern for employees

THEORY Z

- long-term employment
- collective decision making
- individual responsibility
- slow promotion
- informal control
- moderately specialized career paths
- holistic concern for employees

Corporate Culture

Another new idea that has attracted a great deal of interest among managers is the concept of corporate culture. A **corporate culture** is generally defined as the inner rites, rituals, heroes, and values of a firm. Rituals that might seem silly to an outsider can have a powerful influence on how the employees of a particular organization think and act. For example, new employees at Honda's Marysville, Ohio, manufacturing facility are encouraged to plant a small pine tree on the company's property. Symbolically, the growth of each employee's tree represents his or her personal growth and development at Honda.[7] Terrence Deal (a Harvard University professor) and Allan Kennedy (a management consultant) have identified several key types of cultures.[8] One is the *tough-guy, macho culture,* in which people act as rugged individualists who like to take chances. Another is referred to as the *work hard/play hard culture.* Here the emphasis is on fun and action with few risks. A third major form of corporate culture is the *bet-your-company culture.* In this corporate situation, the emphasis is on big-stakes decisions and gambles that may pay off far in the future. Finally, there is the *process culture,* in which the organization functions mechanically, with a lot of "red tape" and little actual exchange of information.

Corporate culture is generally thought to have a very strong influence on a firm's performance over time. Hence it is useful to be able to assess a company's culture. Common indicators of culture include the physical setting (building, office layouts, and so on), what the company itself says about its culture (in its advertising and public-relations news releases, for example), how the company greets its guests (does it have formal or informal reception areas?), and how employees spend their time (working alone in an office most of the time or spending much of the day working with others).

Deal and Kennedy believe that cultural change is needed when the company's environment is changing, when the industry is becoming more competitive, when company performance is mediocre, when the company is growing rapidly, and when the company is about to become a truly large corporation. Moreover, they believe that organizations of the future will look quite different from those of today. In particular, they predict that tomorrow's business firms will be made up of small task-oriented work groups, each with control over its own activities. These small groups will be coordinated through an elaborate computer network and held together by a strong corporate culture.

Management Excellence

The most recent new perspective on management theory focuses on excellence. The general concept of excellence is very difficult to define. However, Thomas Peters and Robert Waterman, in their book *In Search of Excellence,* say that excellence consists of things like making average employees feel like heroes and winners, giving employees a voice in how they do their work, and letting people control the quality of their own output.[9] **Management excellence**, then, is a

Figure 5.9 The Principal Features of Corporate Culture and Management Excellence. Compare aspects of these two theories with those of Theory Z.

CORPORATE CULTURE	MANAGEMENT EXCELLENCE
■ inner rites, rituals, heroes, and values have a strong influence on a firm's performance	■ creates an environment where employees feel like winners
■ several key types of culture: tough guy, work hard/play hard, bet-your-company, and process	■ gives employees a voice in how they do their work
■ culture must change when firm or its environment is changing	■ allows employees to control the quality of their output

point of view that promotes a feeling of excellence in employees. See Figure 5.9.

Examples of excellent companies include IBM and Procter & Gamble. At IBM, for example, sales quotas are purposely set so that 70 to 80 percent of all sales representatives can meet them. As a result, sales reps tend to feel like winners and to work even harder and more effectively. Contrast this with a firm that sets sales goals that only 30 percent of its representatives can meet. As a result, 70 percent of its sales reps cannot help but feel like failures and losers.

In many ways, the concept of management excellence builds on the ideas of Theory Z and corporate culture. All three emphasize the important role that people play in determining the success or failure of an organization.

Chapter Review

SUMMARY

Management is the process of coordinating the resources of an organization so as to achieve the primary goals of the organization. The resources that managers are concerned with are of four types—material, financial, human, and informational. As they go about their jobs, managers spend about 60 percent of their time in scheduled meetings, 22 percent at desk work, 10 percent in unscheduled meetings, and 6 percent on the telephone. Clearly, communicating with other people is the most important part of a manager's working life.

Managers perform four basic functions. The amount of time they devote to each depends on the situation of the firm and of the manager within the firm. First, managers engage in goal setting and planning (determining where the firm should be going and how to get there). Three types of plans, from the broadest to the most specific, are strategies, tactical plans, and standing plans. Next, managers organize resources and activities to accomplish results in an efficient and effective manner. Third, managers must lead and motivate others so as to inspire them to work in the best interest of the organization. Leadership styles run from the authoritarian "do it my way" style, through a more democratic "let's do it together" style, to the laissez-faire "do it your way" style. Finally, managers must control ongoing activities, through continual evaluation and regulation, to keep the organization on course as it pursues its goals.

Managers—or management positions—may be classified from two different perspectives. From the perspective of level, there are top managers, who control the fortunes of the organization; middle managers, who implement strategies and major policies; and lower-level managers, who supervise the activities of operating employees. From the viewpoint of area, managers most often deal with finance, operations, marketing, personnel, and administration.

Successful managers tend to possess a specific

set of skills and to fill ten basic managerial roles. Technical, conceptual, interpersonal, diagnostic, and analytic skills are all important, though the relative importance of each varies with the level of management. All the key managerial roles can be classified as decisional, interpersonal, or informational roles. Candidates for management positions learn their skills and roles in lower levels within the organization, other organizations, and schools and universities.

Contemporary management theory features three interrelated concepts. Theory Z involves a combination of Japanese and American management practices. The corporate culture theory focuses on the rituals, heroes, and values of the firm. The theory of management excellence is concerned with instilling a feeling of excellence in employees. All three theories stress the prime importance of people in the organization.

In the next chapter we shall examine the organizing function in some detail. We shall look specifically at various forms that organizations take and the management concepts that result in these forms. Like most things in management, the form of an organization depends on the organization's goals, strategies, and personnel.

KEY TERMS

You should now be able to define and give an example relevant to each of the following terms:

management	analytic skills
goal	decisional roles
goal setting	interpersonal roles
purpose	informational roles
mission	productivity
objectives	Theory Z
plan	corporate culture
planning	management excellence
strategy	
tactical plan	
policy	

standard operating procedure

organizing

leading

motivating

controlling

top managers

middle managers

lower-level managers

financial managers

operations managers

marketing managers

personnel managers

administrative managers

technical skills

conceptual skills

interpersonal skills

diagnostic skills

QUESTIONS AND EXERCISES
Review Questions

1. Define the term *manager* without using the word *management* in your definition.
2. What are the purpose and the mission of a neighborhood restaurant? of the Salvation Army? What might be reasonable objectives for these organizations?
3. How do a strategy, a tactical plan, and a policy differ? What do they all have in common?
4. What exactly does a manager organize, and for what reason?
5. Why are leadership and motivation necessary in a business where people are paid for their work?
6. Explain the steps involved in the control function.
7. How are the two perspectives on kinds of managers—that is, level and area—different from each other?
8. In what way are management skills related to the roles managers play? Provide a specific example to support your answer.
9. What are the advantages and disadvantages of promoting from within, compared to hiring new managers from outside the organization?
10. In what ways are Theory Z and the concept of management excellence alike?
11. What is meant by corporate culture?

Discussion Questions

1. Which of the four management functions are exemplified by the actions of Donald Lennox at International Harvester?
2. What reasons might the IH board of directors have had for looking outside the firm for a new CEO?
3. Does a healthy firm (one that is doing well) have to worry about effective management? Explain.
4. Which of the management functions, skills, and roles don't really apply to the owner–operator of a sole proprietorship?
5. Which leadership style might be best suited to each of the three general levels of management?
6. Do you think people are really as important to an organization as this chapter seems to indicate?

Exercises

1. You are the owner and only employee of a firm that you started this morning. Your firm is to produce and sell hand-sewn canvas work pants to clothing stores. (You, of course, are an expert tailor.)
   a. Write out your firm's purpose, its mission, and at least two of its objectives.
   b. Write out your firm's sales strategy and a tactical plan that follows from the sales strategy. Make sure the strategy is in keeping with your goals.
   c. Write out one sales policy to be followed by your firm, and one SOP that implements the policy.
2. Rate yourself on each of the five key management skills and on your proven ability to perform each of the four management functions. (Use a scale of from 1 to 5, with 5 highest.) Then, based on your ratings, explain why you would or wouldn't hire yourself for a lower-level management position.

CASE 5-1

Revlon, Inc.

Charles Revson started Revlon, Inc., in 1932. In four decades as head of the firm, he built his original $300 investment into a $600 million cosmetics business. In 1974, when Revson discovered that he had terminal cancer, he took two important steps. First, he established the goal of entering the scientific health-care industry. Second, he hired Michael Bergerac to be his replacement.

Bergerac took over the firm when Revson died in 1975. He immediately began to implement Revson's health-care goal through a series of acquisitions. Each business that was acquired by Revlon was expected to increase the firm's involvement in either the unregulated health-care products business or the ethical drugs business.

Bergerac had come to Revlon from ITT, a firm that practiced tight management control. He was shocked to find that little control was exercised at his new firm. For example, Revlon did not plan even five years in advance.

Bergerac soon instituted a number of controls throughout Revlon. Every part of the company now has its own annual budget—and the head of each department reports on its budget every month. Further, the department manager is expected to begin the report by pinpointing all potential trouble spots.

Revlon's new head also chairs monthly management meetings, similar to those he attended at ITT. At these meetings, the operating managers sit on one side of a table, and Bergerac and his staff sit on the other side. Each manager defends his or her business operations in front of all the other participants. A video monitor in the conference room displays the pertinent financial data as each operation is discussed.

To measure performance, Bergerac generally focuses on three financial indicators: earnings as a percentage of sales, earnings as a percentage of asset value, and manufacturing costs. He also places emphasis on performance in the areas of human resources, accounts receivable, and cost reduction.

During the five years after Bergerac took over, Revlon's sales increased at a rate of 24 percent per year; in 1980, sales reached $2.2 billion. The cosmetics group introduced such successful new products as "Charlie" and "Jontue." And, in the health-care business, sales increased from $197 million in 1974 to $1.1 billion in 1981. In fact, at the end of 1979 *Fortune* magazine named Revlon one of ten "American Business Triumphs" of the 1970s.

Sales leveled off in the early 1980s, however, primarily for three reasons. First, sales of cosmetics stopped their upward climb. Second, Revlon's new acquisitons have not been growing as fast as expected. And third, Revlon blundered in several areas of international marketing. Bergerac seems to feel, though, that the firm will soon be moving again. Overseas operations are being revamped; new cosmetics products are being developed; and research and development efforts in the health-care area are about to begin paying off. [10]

1. How would you characterize Michael Bergerac's leadership style? Why?
2. Do Bergerac's control techniques seem reasonable, given what you know about Revlon? Explain.

CASE 5-2

General Electric Company

General Electric Company (GE) consists of 250 individual businesses that produce a wide range of consumer and industrial products. The company has historically been one of this country's best managed firms, and a consistently profitable concern.

Lately, however, the firm has not always seemed to have a clear idea of what it is and where it is going. Often, management seemed to be attempting to do too many things at once. For example, one former chief executive involved the company in three risky ventures, all at the same time: nuclear energy, computers, and commercial jet engines. His successor sold the computer business to Honeywell in 1970. But as late as 1981, GE was still expecting that three new nuclear reactors would be built in this country each year although most planned facilities had been abandoned.

In mid-1981, John F. Welsh, GE's new chief executive officer, decided that the company must sharpen its focus and strengthen its position within each of its various product markets. He set an ambitious goal for each of GE's businesses—to become first or second in its industry, or achieve a distinct marketing advantage, within three to five years. He reasoned that such a goal was most easily accomplished during a period of slow economic growth like that of the early 1980s when decreased sales gave stronger companies like GE a greater competitive edge.

Welsh thus established the same clearly stated goal for each of GE's 250 businesses. Those that have no chance of reaching this goal are likely candidates for phasing out—although disposing of such businesses may be a problem. Moreover, it is expected that GE's reward structure will be changed. In particular, managers who achieve their goal will probably receive increased rewards.

On a company-wide basis, GE has chosen a number of areas for expansion. One of these is plastics. Another is medical equipment—particularly sophisticated diagnostic equipment. Still a third area in which GE wishes to establish a strong foothold is that of production automation—robots. It is this area that has generated the most enthusiasm among GE's managers. The firm presently produces robots under license from foreign manufacturers, but it expects to begin making its own shortly.[11]

1. Is the single goal established by Welsh for GE's businesses a reasonable and effective one? Should it have been modified to account for the particular characteristics of each of GE's businesses?
2. General Electric already dominates the light-bulb industry. As head of the company's light-bulb operation, how would you go about implementing the goal set by your new chief executive officer?

CHAPTER

SIX
Creating
the
Organization

We began the last chapter by comparing a business organization to a Concorde SST airplane. Both, we noted, are structures that must be managed so as to reach their goals. In Chapter 5 we were interested mainly in the management of the structure, but here we shall concentrate on the structure itself. Like the Concorde, a business must be well engineered—that is, organized—if it is to "get off the ground." Otherwise, management will have to spend so much time dealing with problems and conflicts that there will be little time left for the attainment of goals. After studying this chapter, you should understand:

1. What organizations are and what their organization charts show
2. Why job specialization is important, and why some firms are using less of it
3. The various bases for departmentalization
4. How decentralization follows from delegation
5. The span of management, and how it describes an organization
6. The distinction between line management and staff management
7. The three basic forms of organizational structure: bureaucratic, organic, and matrix
8. What the informal organization is

Consider this:

Over one hundred years ago, a young immigrant came to the United States from Bavaria, seeking to make his fortune. He had little success at first and was about to return home when he decided to try prospecting for gold in California. Things were not much better there until he recognized that his fellow prospectors had a need for sturdy, long-lasting work pants. He had found no gold, but he did have some talent as a tailor. Using the last of his financial resources, he bought several bolts of canvas and began to make heavy-duty pants for other prospectors. He eventually switched from canvas to denim and developed a unique riveting system to reinforce the major points of strain. His name? Levi Strauss.

The organization he founded, Levi Strauss & Company, has grown and prospered over the years. To date it has sold over one billion pairs of denim pants. The unique stitching on the pockets and the tab emblem are recognized around the world.

The company began to expand in a number of ways in the 1950s. White Levi's were introduced, the firm began to ship jeans to other countries, and the technology that led to permanent-press fabrics was developed. On into the 1970s, Levi Strauss & Company continued to expand and branch out. In 1977 the firm acquired Koracorp Industries Inc., a large manufacturer of women's wear, infant's clothing, and men's suits. The firm also introduced a line of athletic wear and western hats. Most recently, Levi's has started to sell to major department store chains like Sears, Roebuck and J. C. Penney.

Today Levi's is the largest apparel company in the world. Annual sales are approaching $3 billion, and the current product line is composed of over two thousand items. To cope with this com-plexity, Levi's has developed a very complex organizational structure.

At the corporate level there are three major divisions. One division is called Levi Strauss USA. It consists of three departments organized along product lines. Each department handles its own manufacturing, marketing, distribution, and financial activities. Several staff groups provide support services for all three departments and coordinate activities across departments. Decision making is also highly decentralized, and managers at lower levels have considerable decision-making latitude.

A second division is Levi Strauss International. As its name suggests, this division handles international activities. Departmentalization within this division is based on geographic location. The primary units are the Continental Europe, Northern Europe, Canada, Latin America, and Asia/Pacific

INSTANT GRATIFICATION

For those who just can't wait to wear
their new Levi's jeans, we offer Levi's Pre-Washed Denim.
Soft, comfortable, and already broken-in.
By the one company you'd trust to do it right.

Although Levi's principal product has remained the same, the firm's organization—and its advertising—have changed substantially over the last hundred years. Source: Logo and photos, courtesy of Levi Strauss & Co.

regional units. Each regional unit is organized like Levi Strauss USA.

Finally there is the New Business Group. This division handles all import and export activities and serves as a temporary home for new ventures. Each department head in this group reports directly to the president.[1]

This chapter is about organizing and organizational structure. At first Levi Strauss probably thought much more about the structure of work pants than about the structure of organizations. However, as his business grew, Strauss no doubt brought other people into his firm to help make and sell his famous pants. If not before, then certainly at that point, he had to consider his organization. The fact that Levi Strauss & Company has become the world's largest apparel company is evidence of the superb organizing ability of Strauss and his successors in the firm.

What do we know about the way Levi's is organized? If an organization is to grow, it must be organized for growth. Hence one of Levi's three major divisions is its New Business Group. You should also have noticed that Levi's other two major divisions are structured differently from each other—one by product line and the other by geographic region. Decision making is shared by all three levels of management; that is, the organization is decentralized. And finally, the departments within the USA and International divisions are supported by various staff groups.

Each of these structural arrangements is meant to help Levi's operate effectively. And each is the result of conscious decisions made by Levi's management—decisions that all managers must make as they seek the best possible structure for their own organization.

WHAT IS AN ORGANIZATION?

We used the term *organization* throughout Chapter 5 without really defining it, mainly because its everyday meaning is close to its business meaning. Here, however, let us agree that an **organization** is a group of two or more people working together in a predetermined fashion to achieve a common set of goals. A neighborhood grocery store owned and operated by a husband-and-wife team is an organization. Exxon Corporation, employing hundreds of thousands of workers world-wide, is also an organization in the very same sense. Both need to be organized, although

Exxon's organizational structure is vastly more complex than that of the grocery store.

An inventor who goes into business to produce and market a new invention adds people to his organization, and then decides what each will do, who will report to whom, and so on. These activities are the essence of organizing, or creating the organization. **Organizing**, we saw, is the process of grouping resources and activities to accomplish some end in an efficient and effective manner. Out of the organizing process comes an **organizational structure**, which is a fixed pattern of (1) positions within the organization and (2) relationships among those positions.

An **organization chart** is a diagram that represents the positions and relationships within an organization—that is, it reveals the company's organizational structure. An example of an organization chart is shown in Figure 6.1. What does it tell us?

Figure 6.1 *A Typical Corporate Organization Chart. A company's organization chart shows the managerial chains of command.*

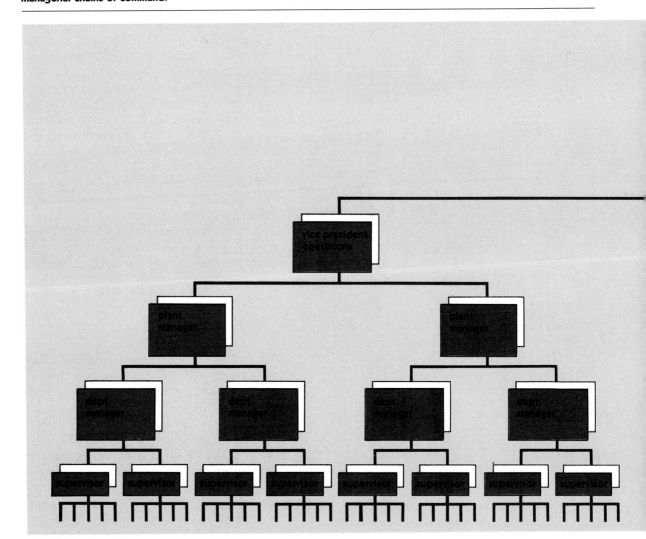

Each rectangle in the chart represents a particular position or person in the organization. At the top of the chart is the president; at the next level are the vice presidents. The solid vertical lines connecting the vice presidents to the president indicate that the vice presidents are in the chain of command. The **chain of command** is the line of authority that extends from the highest to the lowest levels of the organization. Moreover, each vice president reports directly to the president. Similarly, the plant managers, regional sales managers, and the accounting department managers report directly to the vice presidents.

The fact that the legal advisor, director of public affairs, and personnel director are shown with a connecting line, means that these people are not part of the direct chain of command. Instead, they hold *advisory* or *staff* positions. This difference will be made clear later in the chapter, when we discuss line and staff positions.

Most smaller organizations find organization charts useful. They clarify positions and reporting relationships for everyone in the organization, and they help managers track growth and change

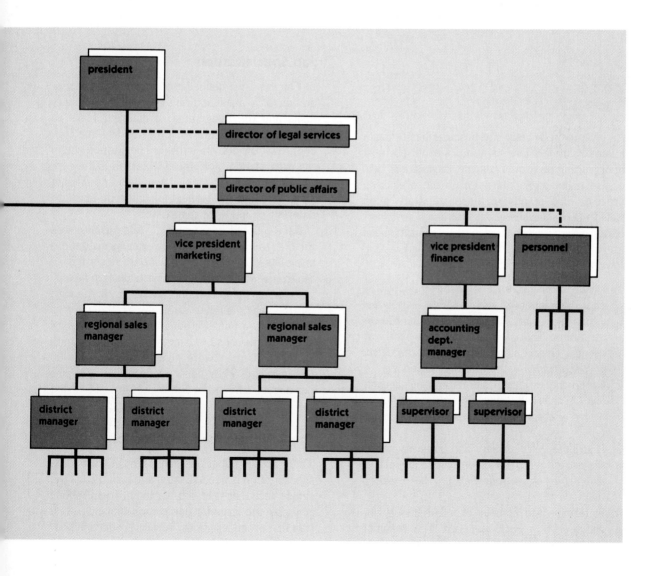

in the organizational structure. For two reasons, however, many large organizations do not maintain complete, detailed charts. It is difficult to chart accurately even a few dozen positions, much less the thousands that characterize larger firms. And larger organizations are almost always changing one part of their structure or another. A complete organization chart would probably be outdated before it was drawn.

In the next several sections we shall consider five major dimensions of organizational structure, most of which are not immediately apparent on the company's organization chart.

THE DIMENSIONS OF ORGANIZATIONAL STRUCTURE

An inventor who goes into business has to make a number of decisions as he goes about the task of organizing his firm. These decisions are all part of five major steps that sum up the organizing process. The results of these steps are often called the *dimensions of organizational structure,* because they are reflected in the organization and its organization chart. The five steps are as follows:

1. Divide the work that is to be done by the entire organization into separate parts, and assign those parts to positions within the organization. This step is sometimes called job design. The resulting dimension is the *degree of specialization* within the organization.
2. Group the various positions into manageable units. The result of this step is the *nature and degree of departmentalization* of the organization.
3. Distribute responsibility and authority within the organization. This step results in a particular *degree of centralization* for the organization.
4. Determine the number of subordinates who will report to each manager. The resulting dimension is called the *span of management.*

5. Distinguish between those positions whose occupants have direct authority and those that are support positions. This establishes the organization's *chain of command.*

JOB DESIGN

Until recently, the watchword in job design was specialization for worker efficiency. Now, however, the tide has turned. There seems to be a movement toward more variety in the design of jobs.

Job Specialization

In Chapter 1 we defined *specialization* as the separation of a manufacturing process into distinct tasks and the assignment of different tasks to different people. Here we are extending that concept to *all* the activities that are performed within the organization. **Job specialization** is the separation of all organizational activities into distinct tasks and the assignment of different tasks to different people (see Figure 6.2).

As we noted in Chapter 1, Adam Smith was the first to emphasize the power of specialization, in his book *The Wealth of Nations.* According to Smith, the various tasks in a particular pin factory were arranged so that one worker drew the wire for the pins, another straightened the wire, a third cut it, a fourth ground the point, and a fifth attached the head. Using this method, Smith claimed, 10 men were able to produce 48,000 pins per day. They could produce only 200 pins per day if each worker had to perform all 5 tasks!

The Rationale for Specialization

There are a number of reasons why at least some specialization is needed. First and foremost is the simple fact that the "job" of most organizations is simply too large for one person to handle. In a firm that produces goods, several production people may be needed. Others will be needed to sell

Figure 6.2 *Job Specialization. A task is divided into distinct parts. Each part is then assigned to a different worker.*

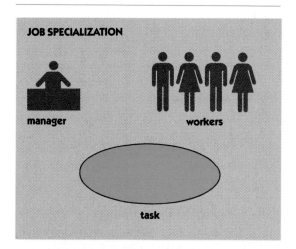

JOB SPECIALIZATION

manager — workers — task

When a job is divided into a number of separate smaller tasks each task can be performed more efficiently. On this assembly line food handlers fill only one section of each frozen-dinner tray. Source: Courtesy H. J. Heinz Company.

the product, still others to control the firm's finances, and so on.

Second, when a worker has to learn only a specific, highly specialized task, she or he should be able to learn to do it very efficiently. Third, the worker who is doing the same job over and over does not lose time changing from one operation to another, as the pin workers probably did when each was producing a complete pin.

Chapter 6   Creating the Organization   149

Risky Shifts

In our industrial society, the requirement that many workers change from one shift to another creates problems by disrupting the body's natural rhythms. Charles F. Ehret, a biologist at the Department of Energy's Argonne National Laboratory, points out that "when your body rhythms are upset, you are more likely to become ill. You are less alert, and you are more likely to make mistakes."

Based on his experience—35 years of studying natural rhythms in humans, laboratory animals, and protozoa—Ehret has found that the problems caused by shift changes can be lessened by proper diet and careful planning of meal and sleep times. He advises workers going from Friday's day shift (8 A.M. to 4 P.M.) to Monday's afternoon shift (4 P.M. to midnight) to:

Sleep late on Saturday and eat sparingly all day: soups, salads, fruits. Avoid carbohydrates.

Sleep late Sunday. Eat a big high-protein meal about 3 P.M. (breakfast time on Monday) and have a high-protein lunch about 8 P.M. (Monday's lunch time).

Eat a big, high-carbohydrate supper about 2 A.M. Monday. Go to bed about 7 A.M.

Source: *Psychology Today*, January 1984, p. 52.

Fourth, the more specialized the job, the easier it may be to design specialized equipment for those who do it. And finally, the more specialized the job is, the easier it is to train new employees when an employee quits or is absent from work.

Unfortunately, specialization can lead to some negative consequences as well. The most significant of these is the boredom and dissatisfaction that many employees feel when they do the same job over and over. Monotony can be deadening. Bored employees may be absent from work frequently, may not put much effort into their work, and may even sabotage the company. Because of these negative side effects, in recent years man-agers have begun to search for alternatives to specialization in the design of jobs.

Alternatives to Job Specialization

The three most frequently used antidotes to the problems that job specialization can breed are job rotation, job enlargement, and job enrichment.

Job Rotation **Job rotation** is the systematic shifting of employees from one job to another. For example, a worker may be assigned to a different job every week for four weeks and then return to the first job in the fifth week. The idea behind job rotation is to provide a variety of jobs so that workers are less likely to get bored and dissatisfied. Companies that use job rotation include Ford, Bethlehem Steel, and Prudential Insurance.

Unfortunately, many firms have had less than total success with job rotation. Often, each of the jobs to which a worker is shifted is itself narrow and boring. Therefore, although there may be a short period of revived interest after each new assignment, this interest wears off quickly. Still, job rotation is widely used, and it offers the added advantage of being an excellent tool for teaching employees new skills.

Job Enlargement In job rotation, the employee is shifted from job to job but the jobs are not changed. In **job enlargement**, on the other hand, the worker is given more things to do within the same job (see Figure 6.3). For example, under job specialization, each worker on an assembly line might connect three wires to the product as it moves down the line. After job enlargement, each worker might connect five wires. Unfortunately, the added tasks are often just as routine as those that the workers performed before the change. In such cases, enlargement may not be effective. American Telephone & Telegraph, IBM, and Maytag have all experimented with job enlargement.

Job Enrichment Job enrichment is perhaps the most advanced alternative to job specialization. Whereas job rotation and job enlargement do not really change the routine and monotonous nature of jobs, job enrichment does. **Job enrichment** is, in essence, providing workers with both more tasks to do and more control over how they do their work (see Figure 6.3). In particular, under job enrichment many controls are removed from jobs, workers are given more authority, and work is assigned in complete, natural units. Moreover, employees are frequently given new and challenging job assignments. These changes tend to increase the employee's sense of responsibility and provide motivating opportunities for growth and advancement. The company that uses job enrichment as an alternative to specialization faces extra expenses such as the costs of retraining. Among the companies that have used job enrichment are AT&T, IBM, General Foods, and Texas Instruments.

DEPARTMENTALIZATION

After jobs are designed, they must be grouped together into "working units" in keeping with the organization's goals. This process is called departmentalization. More specifically, **departmentalization** is the process of grouping jobs into manageable units according to some reasonable scheme. Several departmentalization schemes, or bases, are commonly used. And most firms—like Levi's—use more than one of them. The groups of positions that result from the departmentalization process are usually called *departments,* although they are sometimes known as units, groups, or divisions.

Departmentalization Bases

A **departmentalization basis** is the scheme or criterion according to which jobs are grouped into units. The most common bases are function,

Figure 6.3 *Alternatives to Job Specialization. Job rotation allows a worker to shift to another task every few weeks to help avoid boredom. In job enlargement, the worker performs more than one task. Job enrichment provides a worker with more authority and responsibility, thus improving motivation.*

JOB ROTATION

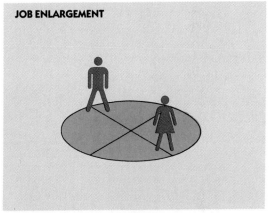

JOB ENLARGEMENT

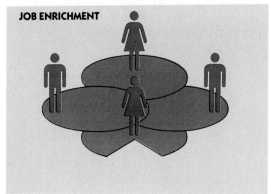

JOB ENRICHMENT

Figure 6.4 *The Four Bases of Departmentalization. The size of the firm and the industry influence how the jobs within the firm are grouped.*

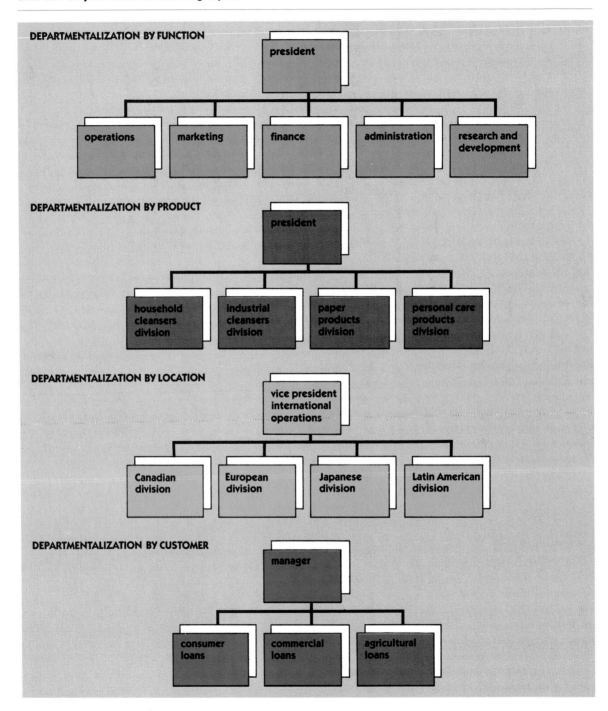

product, location, and customer. Figure 6.4 gives an example of each of these departmentalization bases.

By Function Departmentalization by function is the grouping together of all jobs that relate to the same organizational activity. Under this scheme, all marketing personnel are grouped together in the marketing department, all production personnel are grouped into the production department, and so on.

Most smaller and newer organizations base their departmentalization on function. Such grouping permits each department to be efficiently staffed by experts. Supervision is simplified because everyone is involved in the same kinds of activities. And coordination is fairly easy. On the other hand, this method of grouping jobs can lead to slow decision making, and it tends to emphasize the department rather than the organization as a whole.

By Product Departmentalization by product is the grouping together of all activities related to a particular product or product group. This scheme is often used by older and larger firms that produce and sell a variety of products. Each product department handles its own marketing, production, financial management, and personnel activities. For example, General Motors has separate departments (which it calls divisions) for Chevrolet, Buick, Oldsmobile, and each of the other major automobile lines it produces.

Departmentalization by product makes decision making easier and provides for the integration of all activities associated with each product or product group. However, it causes some duplication of specialized activities, such as finance, from department to department. And the emphasis is placed on the product rather than on the whole organization.

Digital Equipment Corporation, the second largest computer manufacturer in the world, was originally organized around eighteen separate product groups. Each product group competed with the others and became protective rather

than cooperative. Instead of working for the goals of the company, members of the product group were working for the good of the product group. As a result, the company's efficiency and profits suffered.

By Location Departmentalization by location is the grouping of activities according to the geographic area in which they are performed. Departmental areas may range from whole countries (for multinational firms) to regions within countries (for national firms) to areas of several city blocks (for police departments organized into precincts). Departmentalization by location allows the organization to respond readily to the unique demands or requirements of different locations. On the other hand, a large administrative staff and an elaborate control system may be needed to coordinate operations in many locations.

One of the ways that Ken Olsen, president of Digital, solved the problem of counterproductive product groups was to combine the twelve U.S. product groups into three regional management centers. This helped to clear up communication among different departments and consolidated much of the administrative paperwork, which had been slowing down important decisions.

By Customer Departmentalization by customer is the grouping of activities according to the needs of various customer groups. A car dealership, for example, may have one sales staff to deal with individual consumers and a different sales staff to work with corporate fleet buyers. The obvious advantage of this approach is that it allows the firm to deal with unique customers or customer groups. The biggest drawback is that a larger-than-usual administrative staff is needed.

Another part of Digital's reorganization was the assigning of the sales force to specific customers rather than to specific markets. Before the reorganization, as many as six salespeople, each from a different product group, could call on one large customer. The situation was confusing and frustrating for customers, and not very profitable for Digital.

Multiple-Bases Departmentalization

Few organizations exhibit only one departmentalization base. In fact, many firms make use of several different bases within a single organization (see Figure 6.5). Another example is General Motors (GM). As we have said, at the corporate level GM is departmentalized by product. Each GM division, in turn, is departmentalized by function; each has its own marketing, finance, production, and personnel group. The production group of one division might be further departmentalized by plant location, with each plant comprising an individual unit. Similarly, a divisional marketing group might be divided in such a way that one unit handles consumer sales and another handles fleet and corporate sales. Moreover, GM recently stated that it will realign its divisions into small-vehicle and large-vehicle groups.

All this adds up to the fact that multiple-bases departmentalization is the rule rather than the exception for larger firms. Like every management tool, departmentalization is used however and wherever it will benefit the organization most.

DELEGATION, DECENTRALIZATION, AND CENTRALIZATION

The third major step in the organizing process is to distribute power in the organization. Delegation is the act of distributing power from management to subordinates. The degree of centralization or decentralization of authority is determined by the overall pattern of delegation within the organization.

Figure 6.5 *Multiple-Bases Departmentalization. Most firms use more than one basis for departmentalization for efficiency and to avoid overlapping positions.*

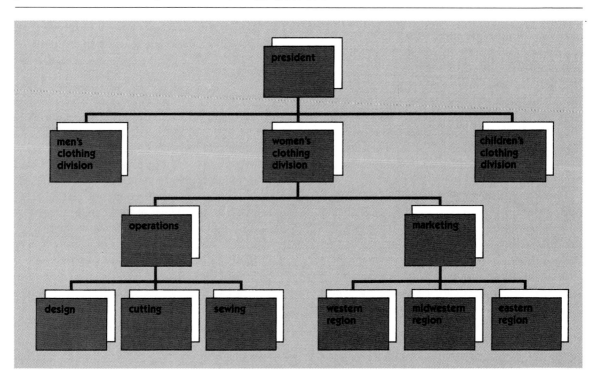

"All I need is a chair. I delegate everything."

Delegation of Authority

Delegation is the assigning of part of a manager's work and power to a subordinate (see Figure 6.6). No manager can do everything alone, so delegation is vital to the completion of a manager's work. Delegation is also important in developing the skills and abilities of subordinates. It allows those who are being groomed for higher-level positions to play increasingly important roles in decision making.

Steps in Delegation   Three steps are generally involved in the delegation process. First, the manager must *assign responsibility*. **Responsibility** is the duty to do a job or perform a task. Along with assigning responsibility the manager must *grant authority*. **Authority** is the power, within the organization, to accomplish an assigned job or task. This might include the power to

obtain specific information, order supplies, authorize relevant expenditures, and make certain decisions. Finally, the manager must *create accountability*. **Accountability** is the obligation of a subordinate to accomplish an assigned job or task.

Note that accountability is created but that it cannot be delegated away. Suppose we are responsible for performing some job. We, in turn, delegate part of the work to a subordinate. We nonetheless remain accountable to our immediate superior for getting the job done properly. If our subordinate fails to complete the assignment, we—not the subordinate—will be "requested" to account for what has become *our* failure.

Barriers to Delegation   For several reasons, managers may be unwilling to delegate work. One reason is that the person who delegates remains accountable for the work. Many managers are reluctant to delegate simply because they want to be sure that the work gets done properly. In other words, they just don't trust their subordinates. Another reason for reluctance to delegate stems from the opposite situation: A manager may fear that a subordinate will do the work so well that he or she will attract the approving notice of top management and will become a threat to the manager. Finally, some managers don't delegate because they are so disorganized that they simply can't plan and assign work in an effective way.

Decentralization of Authority

The general pattern of delegation throughout an organization determines the extent to which that organization is decentralized or centralized. An organization in which management consciously attempts to spread authority widely in the lower organization levels is said to be **decentralized.** An organization that systematically works to concentrate authority at the upper levels is said to be **centralized.**

A variety of factors can influence the extent to which a firm is decentralized. One is the external environment in which the firm operates. The more complex and unpredictable this environment is, the more likely it is that top management will let lower-level managers make important de-cisions. Another factor is the nature of the decision itself. The riskier the decision, the greater the tendency to centralize decision making. A third factor is the abilities of lower-level managers. If these managers do not have strong decision-making skills, top managers will be reluctant to decentralize. On the other hand, strong lower-level decision-making skills encourage decentralization. Finally, a firm that has traditionally practiced centralization is likely to maintain that centralization in the future, and vice versa.

Neither decentralization nor centralization is, in principle, either right or wrong. What works for one organization may or may not work for another. K mart, Toys "Я" Us, and McDonald's have all been very successful—and they all practice centralization. By the same token, decentralization has worked very well for General Electric, Du Pont, and Sears, Roebuck. Every organization must assess its own unique situation and then choose the level of centralization or decentralization that it feels will work best in that situation.

THE SPAN OF MANAGEMENT

The fourth major dimension of organizational structure, the **span of control** or **span of man-**

Figure 6.6 *Steps in the Delegation Process. A good manager must learn how to delegate if he or she is to be successful. No one can do everything alone.*

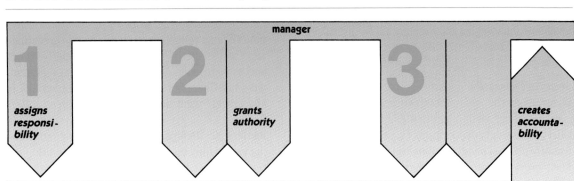

manager

1 assigns responsi-bility

2 grants authority

3 creates accounta-bility

subordinate

agement, is the number of subordinates who report directly to one manager. For hundreds of years, theorists have searched for an optimal span of management. When it became apparent that there is no perfect number of subordinates for a manager to supervise, they turned their attention to the more general issue of whether the span should be wide or narrow.

Wide and Narrow Spans of Control

A *wide span* of management exists when a manager has a large number of subordinates. *A narrow span* exists when the manager has only a few subordinates. Several factors (see Figure 6.7) determine the span that is better for a particular manager. Generally, the span should be narrow (1) when subordinates are physically located far from each other, (2) when the manager has a lot of work to do in addition to supervising subordinates, (3) when a great deal of interaction is required between supervisor and subordinates, and (4) when new problems arise frequently. The span of control may be wide (1) when the manager and the subordinates are very competent, (2) when the organization has a well-established set of standard operating procedures, and (3) when few new problems are expected to arise.

Figure 6.7 *The Span of Management. There are several criteria for deciding whether a firm uses a wide span of management, where several subordinates report to one manager, or a narrow span, where a manager has few subordinates.*

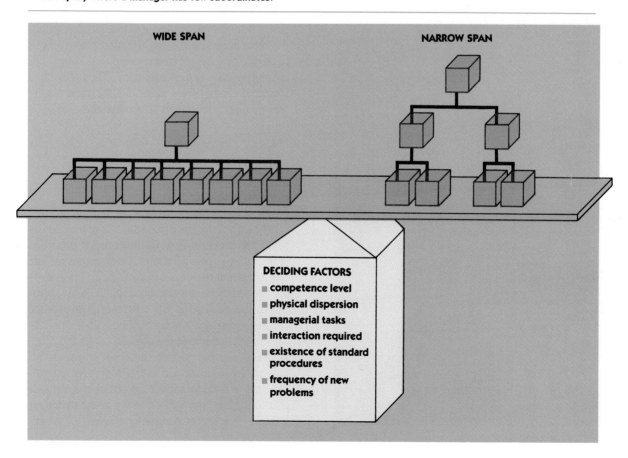

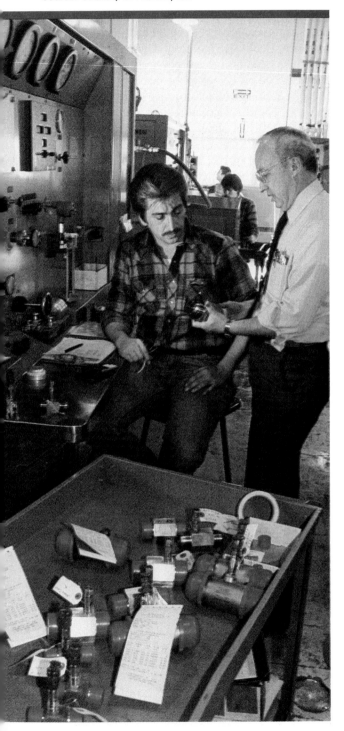

Line managers make decisions and give orders that contribute directly to the achievement of the organization's goals.
Source: Courtesy of AMETEK, Inc.

Organizational Height

Span of management has an obvious impact on relations between superiors and subordinates. And it has a more subtle but equally important impact on the height of the organization. **Organizational height** is the number of layers, or levels, of management in a firm. An organization with many layers of management is considered *tall,* whereas one with fewer layers is *flat.*

The span of management plays a direct role in determining the height of the organization. If spans of management are generally narrow, more levels are needed and the resulting organization is tall. If spans of management are wider, fewer levels are needed and the organization is flat.

In a taller organization, administrative costs are higher because more managers are needed. And communication among levels may become distorted because information has to pass up and down through more people. On the other hand, the managers in a flat organization may all have to perform more administrative duties simply because there are fewer managers. They may have to spend considerably more of their time supervising and working with subordinates.

LINE AND STAFF MANAGEMENT

Our last major organizational dimension is the chain of command (or line of authority) that reaches from the uppermost to the lowest levels of management. A **line management position** is one that is part of the chain of command and that shares in the direct responsibility for achieving the goals of the organization. A **staff management position**, by contrast, is a position created to provide support, advice, and expertise to someone who is in the chain of command. Staff positions are not part of the chain of command, and staff personnel are not specifically accountable for accomplishing the goals of the firm. A marketing executive is generally a line manager, because marketing is directly related to accomplishing the firm's purpose, mission, and objectives. A legal advisor, however, doesn't actively engage in profit-making activities but rather provides legal support to those who do. Hence the legal advisor occupies a staff position. See Figure 6.8.

Differences between Line and Staff Positions

Both line and staff managers are needed for effective management, but there are important differences between the two kinds of positions. The basic difference is in terms of authority. Line managers have *line authority*, which means that they can make decisions and issue directives that relate to the organization's goals. Staff managers, on the other hand, seldom have this kind of authority. Instead, they usually have either advisory authority or functional authority.

Advisory authority is simply the expectation that line managers will consult the appropriate staff manager when making decisions. (Even so, line managers generally don't have to follow the advice they get from staff managers). Functional authority is stronger, and in some ways it is like line authority. *Functional authority* is the authority of staff managers to make decisions and issue directives, but only about their own area of expertise. For example, a legal advisor can decide whether to retain a particular clause in a contract, but not what price to charge for a new product. Contracts are part of the legal advisor's area of expertise; pricing is not.

Line-Staff Conflict

For a variety of reasons, conflict between line managers and staff managers is fairly common in business. Staff managers often have more formal education and are sometimes younger (and perhaps more ambitious) than line managers. Line managers may perceive staff managers as a threat to their own authority. Or they may resent

the fact that they must depend on the expertise of a staff manager. For their part, staff managers may become resentful if their expert recommendations in public relations or personnel management, say, are not adopted by line management.

Fortunately, there are several ways to minimize the possibility of such conflict. One way is to integrate line and staff managers into one team working together on problems. Another is to ensure that the areas of responsibility of line and staff managers are clearly defined. And finally, line and staff managers can both be held accountable for the results of their activities.

Figure 6.8 Line and Staff Management. A line manager has a responsibility to achieve the company's goals and is in the direct chain of command. A staff manager supports and advises the line managers.

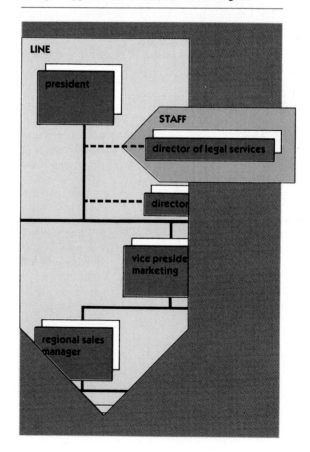

OTHER ELEMENTS OF ORGANIZATIONAL STRUCTURE

We have now discussed the five major dimensions of organizational structure. In this section we shall look at three other elements of organization: work schedules, committees, and coordination techniques. See Table 6.1.

Work Schedules

To most people, "work schedule" means the standard 9 A.M. to 5 P.M. forty-hour workweek. In reality, though, many people work on schedules that are quite different from this. Police officers, firefighters, restaurant personnel, airline employees, and medical personnel, for example, usually work on schedules that are far from standard. Some manufacturers also rotate personnel from shift to shift. And many professional people—such as managers, artists, and lawyers—work more than forty hours per week because they need the extra time to get their work done or simply because they want to.

In recent years, organizations have begun to experiment with alternative work schedules. One such schedule is called the compressed workweek. A **compressed workweek** is an arrangement whereby an employee works a full forty hours per week, but in fewer than the standard five days. The commonest variation is to have people work ten hours per day for four days and then give them a three-day weekend.

A second alternative work schedule is called the flexible workweek. A **flexible workweek** is an arrangement in which each employee chooses the hours during which he or she will work, subject to certain limitations. Typically the firm es-

Table 6.1 *Eight Dimensions of Organizational Structure*

Dimension	Purpose
Job Design	To divide the work performed by an organization into parts and assign each part a position within the organization. Job specialization, job rotation, job enlargement, and job enrichment are key elements in the job design process.
Departmentalization	To group various positions in an organization into manageable units. Departmentalization may be based on function, product, location, customer, or a combination of these.
Delegation	To distribute part of a manager's work and power to subordinates. A deliberate concentration of authority at the upper levels of the organization creates a centralized structure. A wide distribution of authority into the lower levels of the organization creates a decentralized structure.
Span of Management	To set the number of subordinates who report directly to one manager. A narrow span has only a few subordinates reporting to one manager. A wide span has a large number of subordinates reporting to one manager.
Line and Staff Management	To distinguish between those positions that are part of the chain of command and those that provide support, advice, or expertise to those in the chain of command.
Work Schedules	To assign the time in which a subordinate is to perform assigned responsibilities. A compressed workweek, a flexible workweek, and job sharing are three alternatives to the traditional 9 A.M. to 5 P.M. forty-hour workweek.
Committees	To accomplish a specific task by assigning it to a group of individuals within the organization.
Coordination Techniques	To coordinate organizational resources to minimize duplication and maximize effectiveness. Managerial hierarchy, rules and procedures, liaisons, and committees are four coordination techniques.

tablishes two bands of time: the *core time,* when all employees must be at work, and the *flexible time,* when employees may choose whether to be at work. The only condition is that every employee must work a total of eight hours per day. For example, the hours between 9 and 11 A.M. and 1 and 3 P.M. might be core time, whereas the hours between 6 and 9 A.M., between 11 A.M. and 1 P.M., and between 3 and 6 P.M. might be flexible time. This would give employees the option of coming in early and getting off early, coming in later and leaving later, or simply taking extra long lunch hours. But it would also ensure that everyone would be present at certain times, when conferences with supervisors and department meetings could be held.

Finally, some firms are experimenting with job sharing, which is similar to permanent part-time work in some ways. **Job sharing** is an arrangement whereby two people share one full-time position. One person may work from 8 A.M. to noon and the other from 1 to 5 P.M. Job sharing provides the security of a permanent job along with the flexibility of a part-time job. It is of special interest to parents who want more time with their children and people who simply desire more leisure time. For the firm, it provides an opportunity to attract highly skilled employees who might not be available on a full-time basis.

Committees

Several types of committees can be used within an organizational structure. An **ad hoc committee** is a committee created for a specific short-term purpose, such as reviewing the firm's employee benefits plan. Once its work is finished, the ad hoc committee is disbanded. A **standing committee** is a relatively permanent committee charged with performing some recurring task. A firm might establish a budget review committee, for example, to review departmental budget requests on an ongoing basis. Finally, a **task force** is a committee established to investigate a major problem or pending decision. If a firm were contemplating a merger with another company, it might form a task force to assess the pros and cons of the merger.

Committees offer some advantages over individual action. Their several members are, of course, able to bring more information and knowledge to the task at hand. Furthermore, committees tend to make more accurate decisions and to transmit their results through the organization more effectively. On the other hand, committee deliberations take much longer than individual action. Unnecessary compromise may take place within the committee. Or the opposite may occur as one person dominates (and thus negates) the committee process.

Coordination Techniques

Our final element of organization is the *coordination of organizational resources,* which is the integration of resources so as to minimize duplication and maximize effectiveness. Several coordination techniques have proved useful. One technique is simply to make use of the **managerial hierarchy**, which is the arrangement that provides increasing authority at higher levels of management. One manager is placed in charge of all the resources that are to be coordinated. She or he is able to coordinate them by virtue of the authority that accompanies her or his position.

Resources can also be coordinated through rules and procedures. For example, a rule can be created governing how a firm's travel budget is to be allocated. This particular resource, then, would be coordinated in terms of that rule.

In complex situations, more sophisticated coordination techniques may be called for. One approach is to establish a liaison. Recall from Chapter 5 that a liaison is a go-between—a person who coordinates the activities of two groups. Suppose Ford Motor Company is negotiating a complicated contract with a supplier of steering wheels. The supplier might appoint a liaison whose primary responsibility is to coordinate the contract negotiations. Finally, for *very* complex coordination needs, a committee (that is, a task force) could be established. Suppose Ford is in

Telecommuting—More Than a Fad

While still a new phenomenon, telecommuting may soon become a viable alternative to the traditional nine-to-five workday. More and more employees may find themselves working within sight of the kitchen table, instead of fighting the freeways every morning and evening.

According to a report in *Business Week*, 200 companies are now experimenting with some form of telecommuting, which makes use of computers and communications devices that enable employees to work at home. More than 30 firms, the report says, now have formal telecommuting programs. Marcia M. Kelly, president of Electronic Services Unlimited, predicts in the report that, within a decade, about 18 percent of the work force, or 18 million people, will be telecommuting.

Among the benefits of telecommuting, the most important must be the gains in productivity that the work-at-home movement may make possible. One expert quoted in the report notes that telecommuting can lead to productivity increases of up to 50 percent. Other advantages include saving on real estate expenses, since office space would be reduced, and tapping into labor pools such as the handicapped and mothers with young children.

Difficulties with working at home, the report notes, include employees' fear of losing touch with the office and possibly missing promotions, technical problems with the telecommuting equipment, and management worries about supervising from a distance. Kelly, however, in an interview for *The Generalist*, stresses that managers don't necessarily need to see employees to manage them. She also notes it may separate good managers from the bad, as telecommuting tends to magnify the weaknesses of ineffective managers. "People who are good managers in person," she says, "will be good managers at a distance."

Telecommuting also means that managers may need to pay more attention to organizing their work well, she says. In addition, it may point up the need for employee-manager interaction through regular meetings.

Kelly notes that while the number of employees who enter, then drop out of such programs is small, the new way of working is not for everyone. The odds of success become better, she says, "if people are extremely responsible, self-starters, and have a proven track record."

Source: *Management World*, March 1984, p. 23.

the process of purchasing the steering wheel supplier. In this case a task force might be appointed to integrate the new firm into Ford's larger organizational structure.

FORMS OF ORGANIZATIONAL STRUCTURE

Up to this point, we have focused our attention on the major dimensions and elements of organizational structure. In many ways, this is like discussing the important parts of a jigsaw puzzle one by one. Now it is time to put the puzzle together. In particular, we shall discuss three basic forms of organizational structure and characterize them in terms of the various dimensions and elements. These basic forms are the bureaucratic structure, the organic structure, and the matrix structure.

The Bureaucratic Structure

The term *bureaucracy* is often used in an unfavorable context, and it tends to suggest rigidity and red tape. This image may be a negative one, but it does capture something of the bureaucratic structure.

A **bureaucratic structure** is a management system based on a formal framework of authority that is carefully outlined and precisely followed. In terms of the major structural dimensions, a bureaucracy is likely to have the following characteristics:

1. A high level of job specialization
2. Departmentalization by function
3. Precise and formal patterns of delegation
4. A high degree of centralization
5. Narrow spans of management, resulting in a tall organization
6. Clearly defined line and staff positions, with formal relationships between the two

Perhaps the best examples of contemporary bureaucracies are government agencies, colleges, and universities. Consider the very rigid and formal college entrance and registration procedures. The reason for such procedures is to ensure that the organization is able to deal with large numbers of people in an equitable and fair manner. We may not enjoy them, but regulations and standard operating procedures do pretty much guarantee uniformity.

The biggest drawback to the bureaucratic structure is its lack of flexibility. The bureaucracy has trouble adjusting to change and coping with the unexpected. Because today's business environment is dynamic and complex, many firms have found that the bureaucratic structure is not appropriate.

The Organic Structure

An **organic structure** is a management system founded on cooperation and knowledge-based authority. It is much less formal than the bureaucracy and much more flexible. An organic structure tends to have the following structural dimensions:

1. A low level of job specialization
2. Departmentalization by product, location, or customer

3. General and informal patterns of delegation
4. A high degree of decentralization
5. Wide spans of management, resulting in a flat organization
6. Less clearly defined line and staff positions, with less formal relationships between the two

The organic structure tends to be more effective when the environment of the firm is complex and dynamic. This structure allows the organization to monitor the environment and react quickly to changes. It's fast on its feet. Of course, the organic structure requires more cooperation among employees than the bureaucracy does. Employees must be willing and able to work together in an informal atmosphere where lines of authority may shift according to the situation.

The Matrix Structure

The matrix structure is the newest and most complex organizational structure. Its hallmark is a multiple command system, in which individuals report to more than one superior at the same time. The **matrix structure** is the structure that results when product departmentalization is superimposed on a functionally departmentalized organization.

To see what this is like, first consider the usual functional arrangement, with people working in departments such as marketing and finance. Now suppose we assign people from these departments to a special group that is working on a new project as a team. This special group is really a product department. The manager in charge of the group is usually called a *project manager*. Any individual who is working with the group reports *both* to the project manager and to his or her superior in the functional department (see Figure 6.9).

A matrix structure usually evolves through four stages. At first the firm is organized simply as a functional structure. Then a smaller number of interdepartmental groups are created to work on especially important projects. Next more groups are created, and they become an integral and important part of the organization. Finally, the firm becomes what is called a *mature matrix*. In the mature matrix, project managers and functional managers have equal authority. Some employees float (or shift) from group to group without ever being "tied" to a particular functional department. Eventually the activities of the project teams become the major focus of the organization.

Many firms have experimented with matrix structures. Notable examples include Texas Instruments, Monsanto, and Chase Manhattan Bank. Matrix structures offer several advantages over the conventional organizational forms. Added flexibility is probably the most obvious advantage. Motivation also improves because people become more deeply committed to their special projects. Employees experience personal

development through doing a variety of jobs. And people communicate more as they become liaisons between their project groups and their functional departments.

There are also some disadvantages to the matrix structure. The multiple command system can cause confusion about who has authority in various situations. Like committees, groups may take longer to resolve problems and issues than individuals working alone. And, because more managers and support staff may be needed, a matrix structure may be more expensive to maintain than a conventional structure. All things considered, though, the matrix appears to offer a number of benefits to business. It is likely that in the future more and more firms will begin to explore and experiment with this innovative method of organization.

Figure 6.9 *A Matrix Organization. A matrix is usually the result of combining product departmentalization with function departmentalization. It is a complex structure wherein employees have more than one supervisor.* Source: Ricky W. Griffin, Management, p. 337.

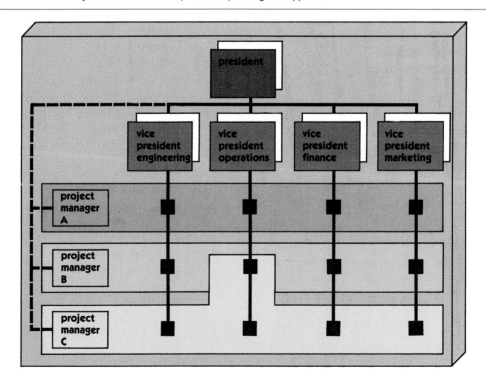

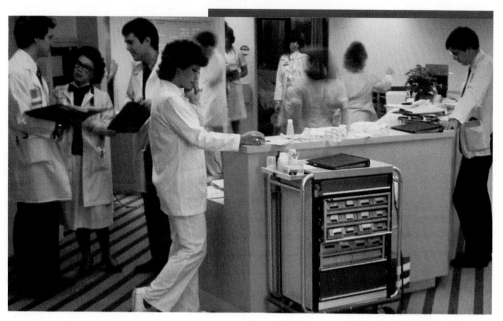

Informal groups based on personal relationships can be as important to an organization as its formal divisions. Source: Courtesy of Owens-Illinois.

THE INFORMAL ORGANIZATION

So far we have discussed the organization as a more or less formal structure consisting of positions and relationships among those positions. This is the organization that is shown on an organization chart. There is another kind of organization, however, one that does not show up on an organization chart. We shall define this **informal organization** as the pattern of behavior and interaction that stems from personal rather than official relationships. Firmly embedded within every informal organization are informal groups and the notorious grapevine.

Informal Groups

A formal group is one that is created by the organization to help accomplish the organization's goals. Such groups as departments, task forces, and committees are thus formal groups. On the other hand, an **informal group** is one that is created by the members of the group themselves to accomplish goals that may or may not be relevant to the organization. Workers may create

an informal group to go bowling, play softball, form a union, get a particular manager fired or transferred, or have lunch together every day. The group may last for several years or only a few hours.

Employees choose to join informal groups for a variety of reasons. Perhaps the main reason is that people like to be with others who are similar to themselves. The activities of a particular group may also be appealing. (A person who likes to bowl may be inclined to join a group of Thursday night bowlers.) Or it may be that the goals of the group appeal to the individual. (If a group has been formed to try to get the company to install a new cafeteria, and if a particular employee happens to think a new cafeteria is needed, he or she will probably join the group.) Others may join informal groups simply because they have a need to be with their associates and be accepted by them.

Informal groups can be powerful forces in organizations. They can restrict output, or they can help managers through tight spots. They can cause disagreement and conflict, or they can help boost morale and job satisfaction. They can show new people how to contribute to the organization, or they can help people get away with substandard performance. Clearly managers should be aware of these informal groups. Those who make the mistake of fighting the informal organization have a major obstacle to overcome.

The Grapevine

The **grapevine** is the informal communications network within an organization. It is completely separate from—and sometimes much faster than—the organization's formal channels of communication. Formal communication usually follows a path that parallels the organizational chain of command. By contrast, information can be transmitted through the grapevine in any direction—up, down, diagonally, or horizontally across the organizational structure. Subordinates may pass information to their bosses, an executive may relay something to a maintenance worker, or there may be an exchange of information between people who work in totally unrelated departments.

Grapevine information may be concerned with topics ranging from the latest management decisions to the results of today's World Series game to pure gossip. It can be important or of little interest. And it can be highly accurate or totally distorted and inaccurate.

How should managers treat the grapevine? Certainly they would be making a big mistake if they tried to eliminate it. Wherever people work together day in and day out, they are going to communicate. And even if a manager could eliminate informal communication at work, employees would still get together and talk outside the office. A more rational approach is to recognize the existence of the grapevine as a part—though an unofficial part—of the organization. For example, managers should respond promptly and aggressively to inaccurate grapevine information in order to minimize the damage that such misinformation might do. Moreover, the grapevine can come in handy when managers are on the receiving end of important communications from the informal organization.

Chapter Review

SUMMARY

Organizing is the process of grouping resources and activities to accomplish some end in an efficient and effective manner. The purpose of this process is to mold an organizational structure, which is a fixed pattern of positions and relationships. An organization chart is a diagram that represents the organizational structure. The five steps in the organizing process result in five basic dimensions of organizational structure. These are degree of job specialization, nature and degree of departmentalization, degree of centralization, the span of management, and the chain of command as determined by line-staff arrangements.

Job specialization is the separation of all the activities within the organization into smaller component parts. Several factors combine to make specialization a useful technique for designing jobs, but high levels of specialization may cause employee dissatisfaction and boredom. Techniques for overcoming these problems include job rotation, job enlargement, and job enrichment.

Departmentalization is the grouping of jobs into manageable units according to some reasonable scheme or basis. These bases include departmentalization by function, product, location, and customer. Because each of these bases provides particular advantages, most firms use different bases in different organizational situations.

Delegation is the assigning of part of a manager's work to a subordinate. It involves the assignment of responsibility, the granting of authority, and the creation of accountability. A decentralized firm is one that delegates as much power as possible to people in the lower management levels. In a centralized firm, on the other hand, power is systematically retained at the upper levels.

The span of management is the number of subordinates who report directly to a manager. Spans are generally characterized as wide (many subordinates per manager) or narrow (few subordinates per manager). Wide spans generally result in flat organizations (few layers of management); narrow spans result in tall organizations (many layers of management).

A line position is one that is in the organization's chain of command (line of authority), whereas a staff position is supportive in nature. Staff positions may carry some authority, but it usually applies only within staff areas of expertise.

Additional elements that must be considered in structuring an organization are work schedules, the use of committees, and techniques for achieving coordination among various groups within the organization.

There are three basic forms of organizational structure. The bureaucratic structure is characterized by formality and rigidity. The organic structure is characterized by flexibility. And the newer matrix structure may be visualized as product departmentalization superimposed on functional departmentalization.

The informal organization consists of social and personal interactions within the more formal organizational structure. Key aspects of the informal organization are informal groups created by the group members themselves and the grapevine, which is an informal information network. Managers must recognize the existence of the informal organization and can even learn to use the grapevine to their advantage.

In the next chapter, we shall apply these and other management concepts to an extremely important business function: the production of goods and services.

KEY TERMS

You should now be able to define and give an example relevant to each of the following terms:

organization
organizing
organizational structure
organization chart
chain of command
job specialization
job rotation
job enlargement
job enrichment
departmentalization
departmentalization basis
departmentalization by function
departmentalization by product
departmentalization by location
departmentalization by customer
delegation
responsibility
authority
accountability
decentralized organization
centralized organization
span of management (or control)
organizational height
line management position
staff management position
compressed workweek
flexible workweek

job sharing
ad hoc committee
standing committee
task force
managerial hierarchy
bureaucratic structure
organic structure
matrix structure
informal organization
informal group
grapevine

QUESTIONS AND EXERCISES

Review Questions

1. In what way do organization charts illustrate our definition of organizational structure?
2. What determines the degree of specialization within an organization?
3. Contrast the three alternatives to job specialization.
4. What are the major differences among the four departmentalization bases?
5. Why do most firms employ several departmentalization bases?
6. What three steps are involved in delegation? Explain each.
7. How does a firm's top management influence its degree of centralization?
8. How is organizational height related to the span of management?
9. What are the key differences between line and staff positions and the authority their occupants wield?
10. Describe three alternatives to the standard five-day, forty-hour workweek.
11. How may the managerial hierarchy be used to coordinate the organization's resources?
12. Contrast the bureaucratic and organic forms of organizational structure.
13. Which form of organizational structure would probably lead to the strongest informal organization? Why?

Discussion Questions

1. Which departmentalization bases does Levi Strauss & Company use for its three divisions? Why does it use these particular bases?
2. Would you characterize Levi's structure as bureaucratic, organic, or matrix? Why?
3. Explain how the five steps of the organizing process determine the dimensions of the resulting organizational structure. Which steps are most important?

4. Which kinds of firms would probably operate most effectively as centralized firms? as decentralized firms?
5. How do decisions concerning work schedules, the use of committees, and coordination techniques affect organizational structure?
6. How might a manager go about formalizing the informal organization?

Exercises

1. Draw the organization chart for Levi Strauss & Company, as far down the hierarchy as you can. List any assumptions you must make. (Note that Levi's "divisions" are actually what we defined as departments.)
2. Chart your own workweek and determine what type it is (standard, compressed, or flexible).

CASE 6-1

Decentralization at Beatrice Foods

Beatrice Foods is a very large but relatively unknown conglomerate (a company made up mostly of other, smaller companies). Even though Beatrice had sales of over $9 billion in 1982, few people outside the business world had even heard of the company. Altogether, however, the firm manufactures or sells over 9000 products organized into approximately 435 groups. Best known among these products are Samsonite luggage, Clark candy bars, and La Choy Chinese food.

At the present time, Beatrice is struggling with some major organizational problems. Beatrice has achieved its relatively large size by aggressively buying smaller companies and then retaining their existing management teams. Hence the company has practiced extreme decentralization. Each newly purchased firm continues to operate about as it did before it was purchased.

This extreme decentralization has caused some significant coordination problems for Beatrice. Top management is committed to maintaining decentralization, but the smaller firms are suffering from lack of staff support and poor coordination. For example, some of the firms Beatrice owns are too small to have a full-time marketing manager. Conglomerates faced with this situation typically establish a corporate marketing staff to assist these small firms. Beatrice, however, fears that such a staff would limit the power and authority it has traditionally given to subsidiaries.

A similar situation exists in the company's financial control staff. Conglomerates usually have a large staff to control and verify the financial reports and documents submitted by their subsidiaries. Beatrice maintains a very small financial control staff, which cannot possibly monitor all the subsidiaries at the same time.[2]

1. What departmentalization base is Beatrice using?
2. How might Beatrice resolve its dilemma of decentralization versus staff support?

CASE 6-2

Matrix Structure at Texas Instruments

Texas Instruments is the world's largest manufacturer of semiconductors. Annual sales usually exceed $3 billion. The electronics industry, in which Texas Instruments is a leader, operates in an extremely complex, volatile environment. Rapid technological breakthroughs make it crucial that firms anticipate and react to change quickly.

To cope with this uncertain environment, Texas Instruments has adopted a matrix structure. First, the firm created standard functional departments for such activities as engineering, production, finance, and marketing. These departments produce and market a full line of electronic components for other equipment manufacturers or for use in Texas Instruments products.

Overlying this structure are product-based departments that produce and market their own products. These departments, called product-customer centers (PCCs), design, produce, and market all new products. To spark creativity, Texas Instruments gave PCC managers responsibility for profits and losses in their departments, but not authority to issue directives to functional managers. The rationale was that if managers had to rely on persuasion, they would concentrate on making better products. Unfortunately, it didn't work. For example, the PCC in charge of digital watches needed a certain kind of chip in order to be competitive. But the functional departments refused to produce the chips because there wasn't enough of an outside market to make them profitable.

These problems have caused Texas Instruments to reconsider its matrix organization. Smaller PCCs are being dropped, and the managers of larger ones are being given more power.[3]

1. What are the reasons for the problems Texas Instruments has had with the matrix structure? How could these problems be solved?
2. Almost all electronics firms use the matrix structure. Why do you think they do?

CHAPTER SEVEN
Operations Management

This chapter describes the important area of management known as production management or operations management. It is through operations management that an organization creates the want-satisfying goods and services that—in essence—are its reason for being. Operations managers combine concrete and steel, investment dollars, construction workers, and blueprints to produce buildings. Operations managers also combined paper and ink, writers and editors, typesetters, presses, operating capital, and manuscript to produce the chapter you are now reading. After studying this chapter, you should understand:

1. *The nature of operations management*
2. *The conversion process, which transforms input resources into output goods and services*
3. *The need for product development, and the activities it includes*
4. *The elements of operations planning: design planning and operational planning*
5. *The four major areas of operations control: purchasing, inventory control, scheduling, and quality control*
6. *The reasons for recent trends in productivity, and some methods of enhancing productivity*

Consider this:

For decades, the American automobile industry generally had its own way with the car-buying public. General Motors, Ford, and Chrysler concentrated on building large cars, which produced big profit margins. The three firms were in the enviable position of having very little competition, except from each other. Prices rose steadily, quality rose at a considerably slower pace, and the three companies began to take their good fortune for granted. Further, generally poor relations between these giants of the industry and the United Auto Workers union led to antagonism between management and labor.

Some European and Japanese automobiles were being imported into the United States, but domestic firms felt there was little danger from this quarter. After all, most of the imports (especially those from Japan) were compacts, and the American public had never shown a liking for small autos.

In the mid-1970s, this all changed. The oil crisis and high gasoline prices altered the way car buyers looked at automobiles. Big cars were out, small cars were in, and the domestic firms were in trouble. This trouble didn't stem only from the high gasoline prices. By conservative estimates, the Japanese can produce a car for about $2000 less than American firms. Furthermore, the quality of those cars has generally been better than that attained by Detroit's big three. Even after import duties and shipping expenses are tacked onto the price, the Japanese have still been able to sell a better product for around $1500 less than its American counterpart.

How did this situation come about? Several factors have been cited. For example, wage rates in Japan have been better controlled. Workers there earn an average of almost $8 per hour less than workers in the United States. There is also more cooperation between management and labor. Employees in Japan play a much larger role in quality control, for example, than American workers.

The Japanese have pioneered an innovative inventory control system called "just-in-time." Pro-

Prodded by foreign competition, U.S. automakers have introduced new production methods such as the use of assembly-line robots. Source: Courtesy Chrysler Corporation.

duction schedules are set far ahead of time, but the required parts and subassemblies are scheduled to arrive at the assembly plant just as they are needed—just in time. As a result, the Japanese keep only $150 worth of parts in inventory for each car produced. American firms, by contrast, carry $775 worth of inventory for each car. These and related factors combine to give the Japanese a real advantage in the marketplace.

American firms have begun to fight back, however. They are paying considerably more attention to labor costs in general and to managerial labor costs in particular. General Motors is changing many long-standing policies that lavished a great deal of job security on managers. Ford has cut almost $4 billion from the cost of its salaried work force. Chrysler has virtually halved the number of its managers.

Detroit auto workers are also getting into the act through something called quality circles. A quality circle is a collection of workers who voluntarily meet once a week to solve quality-related problems the firm may be facing. Ford in particular has taken steps to overhaul its entire management structure. Decentralization is the watchword, and spans of control are being widened considerably. In early 1984, General Motors also announced a major change in its structure that will increase the visibility of its small cars and make them more competitive.

Better late than never, American companies are adopting the just-in-time inventory control techniques used in Japan. For example, the Ford Escort plant in Wayne, Michigan, sets its production schedules as far ahead as four weeks. Each night an operations manager at the plant orders the engines for the next day's assembly run from the Dearborn engine plant 20 miles away. The engines are shipped out in the proper sequence, so that they can be moved directly from the receiving dock to the assembly line.

Of course the battle is far from over. In the early 1980s, the Japanese auto makers became firmly entrenched in the American marketplace. Chrysler was pushed to the brink of bankruptcy, and Ford was severely hurt. Continued innovation and insightful management decision making will be needed if Detroit is ever again to rule the American roads.[1]

The problems experienced by the American auto industry point up the critical importance of operations management. The control of product quality, for example, is one of the prime responsibilities of operations managers. A firm that consistently produces goods or services of poor quality will, at the very least, lose customers in droves. In more extreme cases, faulty goods or services may involve a firm in costly legal difficulties.

Another key part of operations management is the effective use of resources—especially human resources—in the production of goods and services. The Detroit automakers have found that their operating employees are a valuable resource in more ways than one. Not only are workers producing cars, but they are also helping to solve quality control problems through such techniques as quality circles.

Inventory management is still another responsibility of operations managers. Every part that is stored for future use (such as on an auto assembly line) must be financed. And these financing costs eventually find their way into the price of the product, or else they eat away at profit. Scheduling control is closely allied to inventory control. The better the scheduling of incoming parts, the smaller the required inventory. The ideal is to have every part become available just when it is needed—just in time. Judging by the per-car parts-inventory dollar values that we have cited, Japanese manufacturers seem to be about five times closer to this ideal than American manufacturers.

Excessive inventory, poor scheduling, less than full use of resources, and even excess management all boil down to increased costs and thus too high a price. This high price and the lack of superior quality or fuel economy to make up for it caused American consumers to switch to Japanese cars in the 1970s. But, as we have seen, American manufacturers have begun to fight back, primarily through more effective operations management. Operations management is clearly a topic that warrants careful study.

PRODUCTION AND OPERATIONS MANAGEMENT

In Chapter 5, operations managers were described as the people who create and manage systems that convert resources into goods and services. In this chapter, we shall examine the activities that are part of the operations manager's job. In fact, we shall begin by defining operations management in terms of those activities. **Operations management** consists of all the activities that managers engage in for the purpose of creating goods and services.

This set of activities was once referred to as production management. However, at that time the term *production* was applied only to the manufacture of tangible goods. Then, as managers began to realize that many of their production techniques are just as relevant and useful to firms that produce services, such as insurance protection, the function came to be called production and operations management. The idea of produc-

Figure 7.1 The Conversion Process. The conversion process converts resources such as materials, finances, and people into useful goods and services. The conversion process is a crucial step in the economic development of any nation.

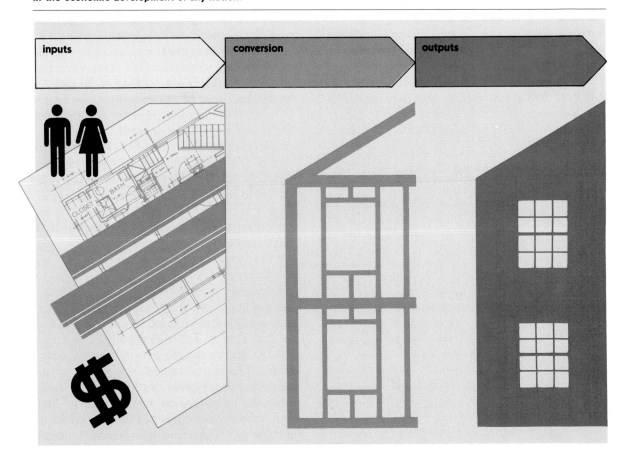

tion was also extended to include services. Thus **production** is now considered to be the process of converting resources into goods *or* services.

Finally, the phrase was shortened to *operations management,* and that's the phrase we shall use. When the word *production* creeps into our discussions, remember that we are using it in the enlarged sense. It includes the creation of both goods and services. And we shall use the word *products* to mean goods and services as well.

A number of activities are involved in operations management. First, the organization may engage in product development in order to come up with the goods and services it will produce. Next, production must be planned. As you will see, planning takes place both *before* anything is produced and *during* production. Finally, managers must concern themselves with the control of operations, to ensure that goals are being achieved. We shall discuss each of these major activities in the sections that follow. But first we need to take a closer look at the nature of production itself.

THE CONVERSION PROCESS

Production is the conversion of resources into goods and services. These resources are materials, finances, people, and information. The goods and services are varied and diverse. But how does the conversion take place? How does General Motors convert steel and glass, money from previous auto sales and stockholders' investment, production workers and managers, and economic and marketing forecasts into automobiles? How does Aetna Life and Casualty convert office buildings, insurance premiums, actuaries, and mortality tables into life insurance policies? They do so through the use of a particular conversion system, or a technology (Figure 7.1). A **technology** is a process used by a firm to transform input resources into output goods or services. And, as indicated by our Aetna example,

a technology need not involve heavy machinery and equipment.

The Nature of the Conversion

The conversion of inputs into outputs can be described in several ways. We shall limit our discussion to three: the focus of the conversion, its magnitude, and the number of technologies employed.

Focus By the *focus* of a conversion process we mean the resource or resources that comprise the major input. For example, for a bank like Citicorp, financial resources are of prime concern in the conversion process. A refiner such as Exxon concentrates on material resources. A college or university is primarily concerned with information. And a barber shop focuses on the use of human resources.

Magnitude The *magnitude* of a conversion is the degree to which the input resources are physically changed by the conversion. At one extreme lie such processes as the one by which Union Carbide Corporation produces Glad Wrap. Various chemicals in liquid or powder form are combined to form long, thin sheets of plastic Glad Wrap. Here the inputs are totally unrecognizable in the finished product. At the other extreme, American Airlines technology produces *no* physical change in its inputs. The airline simply transports people from one place to another.

Number of Technologies A single firm may employ one technology or many. In general, larger firms that make a variety of products use multiple technologies. For example, Sears, Roebuck & Co. manufactures some of its own products, buys other merchandise from wholesalers, and operates a credit division, an insurance company, and a property development division. Clearly a number of different conversion processes are involved in these activities. Smaller firms, by contrast, may operate in one fairly small and narrow

In recent decades, services, such as travel planning and transportation, have come to dominate the American economy. Source: © 1980 Michael Heron, Woodfin Camp.

market in which few conversion processes are required.

The Increasing Importance of Services

The application of operations management to the production of services has coincided with a dramatic growth in the number and diversity of service organizations. For example, only 28 percent of American workers were employed in service organizations in 1900. By 1950 this figure had grown to 40 percent, and by 1983 it had risen to 68 percent. Moreover, in 1962 approximately $58 billion was spent in this country for services. By 1982 this figure had increased to $350 billion. By any yardstick, service firms have become a dominant part of our economy. In fact, the American economy is now characterized as a service economy (Figure 7.2). A **service economy** is one in which more effort is devoted to the production of services than to the production of goods.

This rapid growth is the primary reason for the increased emphasis on production techniques in service firms. The managers of restaurants, dry cleaners, real estate agencies, banks, movie theaters, airlines, travel agencies, and other service firms have realized that they can benefit from the experience of manufacturers, construction firms, and retailers.

Now that we understand something about the conversion process as it is carried out to transform resources into goods and services, it is time to consider three major activities that are involved in operations management. These are product development, operations planning, and operations control (Figure 7.3).

PRODUCT DEVELOPMENT

No firm can produce a product until it has a product to produce. In other words, someone must first come up with a new way to satisfy a need—a new product or an improvement on an existing product. Only then will the firm be able to begin the variety of activities that make up operations management.

New-Product Development

Where do new products come from? How did we get electric pencil sharpeners and electronic word processors? We got them the same way we got light bulbs and automobile tires: from people working with new ideas and technical advances. Thomas Edison created the first light bulb and Charles Goodyear discovered the vulcanization process that led to tires. In the same way, scientists and researchers working in businesses and universities have produced many of the newer products that we may already have started to take for granted.

These activities are generally referred to as research and development (R&D). For our pur-

poses, **research and development** are an organized set of activities intended to identify new ideas and technical advances that have the potential to result in new goods and services.

In general, there are three types of R&D activities. *Basic research* consists of activities aimed at disclosing new knowledge. The goal of basic research is scientific advancement, without regard for its potential use in the development of goods and services. *Applied research,* on the other hand, consists of activities geared to disclosing new knowledge that has some potential use. And *development and implementation* are research activities undertaken to put new or existing knowledge to use in producing goods and services.

Figure 7.2 Service Industries. The growth of service firms has increased so dramatically that we live in what is now referred to as a service economy. Source: "Employees in Nonagricultural Establishments," Bureau of Labor Statistics, 1984.

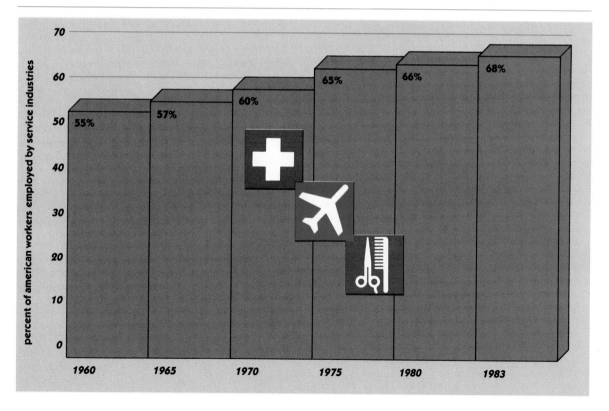

In order to create marketable new products, firms invest large sums of money in research and development. Source: Courtesy of Freeport-McMoRan, Inc.

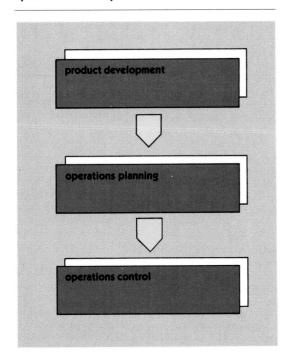

Figure 7.3 *Overview of Operations Management. In order to create goods and services, a firm researches product development, plans the production process, and sees that goals are achieved through an effective operations control system.*

The Costs of Research Research is costly. American businesses spend approximately $1 billion per year on basic research. In addition, the federal government spends about $2 billion each year on basic research. (Most federal research is done at colleges and universities and is funded through contracts or grants.) Businesses and the federal government also each spend around $3 billion per year on applied research. Finally, the federal government spends almost $11 billion per year, and businesses around $16 billion per year, on development and implementation (Figure 7.4).

The heavy emphasis on development stems from the risks involved in the three types of R&D. At one extreme, basic research is very risky. Scientists may work for months or even years and come up with nothing to show for their efforts. Applied research usually offers somewhat more promise of concrete results. At the other extreme, development and implementation are considerably less risky. Researchers are working with a "known quantity" and are simply trying to find uses for it.

R&D Organization Most firms organize their R&D activities as a staff function, either at the corporate level or within product-based departments. When R&D activities are placed at the corporate level, they are somewhat centralized. This arrangement allows the firm to concentrate research activities within one group, so that there is no duplication of effort among departments. However, a corporate R&D staff may not be sensitive to the needs of each separate department. Placing separate R&D staffs within product departments overcomes this problem. But costs are higher because R&D facilities must be duplicated for the various departments. Some firms try to combine the two approaches by centralizing basic research and some applied research but decentralizing the remaining R&D effort.

Recently several computer manufacturers banded together to establish a research partnership called the Micro Computer Consortium (MCC). Each firm contributed a fixed amount of money to operate MCC's research laboratory in

Austin, Texas. In return, the contributing firms have the right to exclusive use of any of MCC's results for three years. After that time, results may be licensed to other firms. This practice is widespread in Japan. The high cost of research and increased international business competition may encourage many more joint R&D ventures.

Product Extension and Refinement

When a brand new product is first marketed, its sales slowly increase from no sales at all. If the product is successful, annual sales increase more and more rapidly until they reach some peak. Then, as time passes, annual sales begin to decline, and they continue to decline until it is no longer profitable to market the product. (This

rise-and-decline pattern is called the *product life cycle*; it is seen in more detail in Chapter 12.)

If a firm sells only one product, when that product reaches the end of its life cycle, the firm too will die! To stay in business, the firm must, at the very least, find ways to extend or refine the want-satisfying capability of its product. Consider television sets. Since they were first introduced in the late 1930s, television sets have been constantly *refined*, so that they now produce clearer, sharper pictures with less dial twiddling. They are tuned electronically for better picture control and can even compensate for variations in room lighting and picture tube wear. During the same time, television sets were also *extended*. Full-color sets as well as black-and-white sets can be purchased. There are television-only sets

Figure 7.4   Types of Research. Both business and government spend billions of dollars on basic research, applied research, and development and implementation. *Source: Photo, courtesy of American Home Products Corporation.*

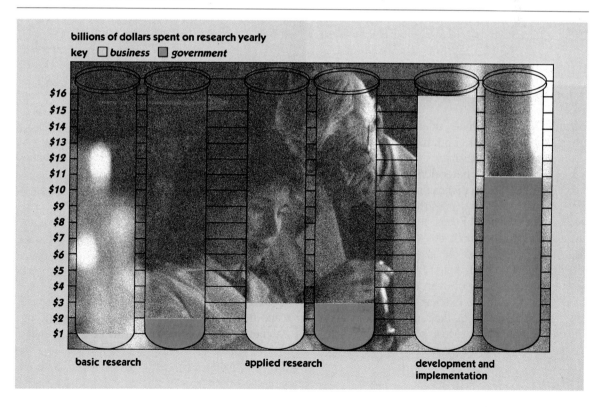

OPERATIONS PLANNING

Only a fraction of the many ideas for new products, refinements, and extensions ever get to the production stage. But for those that do, the next step in the process of operations management is operations planning. Operations planning involves two major phases: design planning and operational planning.

Design Planning

When the R&D staff at IBM recommended to top management that it produce and market an affordable personal computer, the company could not simply swing into production the next day. Instead, a great deal of time and energy had to be invested in determining what the new computer would look like, where and how it would be produced, what options would be included, and so on. These decisions are a part of design planning. **Design planning** is the development of a plan for converting a product idea into an actual commodity ready for marketing. This plan must, of course, be developed before a production facility is acquired or adapted. The major decisions involved in design planning deal with product line, capacity, technology, facilities, and human resources (Figure 7.5).

Product Line A **product line** is a group of similar products that differ only in relatively minor characteristics. During the design-planning stage, operations personnel must determine how many different product variations there will be. An automobile manufacturer needs to determine how many different models to produce, what major options to offer, and the like. A restaurant owner must decide how many menu items are best for him or her to list.

A wide product line (one with many choices and many options) has the most appeal to customers. However, it is also more costly than a narrower line, because variations lead to increased complexity during production. Hence the

and others that include video games, digital clocks, and telephones. Both manual control and remote control are available.

Each refinement or extension results in an essentially "new" product whose sales make up for the declining sales of a product that was introduced earlier. General Foods, for example, introduced Jell-O to the public 60 years ago. One of their newer products is still based on Jell-O. This relatively new product, Jell-O Pudding Pops, has been bringing in sales of over $100,000,000 annually. For most firms, extension and refinement are expected results of their development and implementation effort. Most often, they result from the application of new knowledge to existing products.

main purpose in deciding on the product line is to balance customer preferences against production costs. It is also important to identify the most effective combination of product alternatives. For this reason, marketing managers play an important role in making product-line decisions.

Each distinct product within the product line must be designed. **Product design** is the process of creating a set of specifications from which the product can be produced. The need for careful and complete design of tangible goods is fairly obvious; they cannot be manufactured without it. But services should be carefully designed as well, and *for the same reason*.

Required Capacity The **capacity** of a production facility is the amount of input the facility can process, or the amount of output it can produce, in a given time. (The capacity of an automobile assembly plant, for instance, might be 500,000 cars per year.) Operations managers—again working with the firm's marketing managers—must determine what the required capacity will be. This

determines the size of the production facility. Capacity planning is vitally important. If the facility is built with too much capacity, valuable resources (plant, equipment, and money) will lie fallow. If the facility offers insufficient capacity, capacity may have to be added later, which is much more expensive than building a large enough facility to begin with.

Suppose an automobile assembly plant is constructed with the capacity to produce 500,000 cars per year. If customers then want only 400,000 cars per year, 20 percent of the capital invested in the plant will be wasted. On the other hand, if customers want as many as 600,000 units per year, the company may have to build a costly addition onto the plant to produce all the cars it can sell.

Capacity means about the same thing to service businesses. The capacity of a restaurant is the number of patrons it can serve at one time. The capacity of a hospital is the number of patients it can care for at any one time (usually given as the number of beds in the hospital).

Figure 7.5 Design Planning. The design planning process uses a product line, plant capacity, technology, facilities, and human resources to create goods and services.

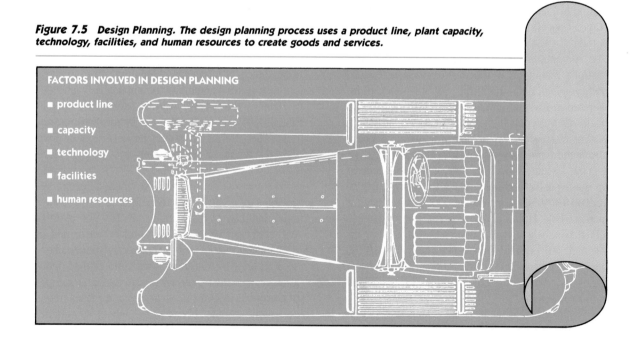

FACTORS INVOLVED IN DESIGN PLANNING

- product line
- capacity
- technology
- facilities
- human resources

Technology   A technology, as we saw earlier, is a process used to transform input resources into goods or services. During the design-planning stage, operations personnel must specify all the details of the processes that will be used.

A major decision for many contemporary operations managers is the degree to which *automation*—including industrial robots—should be enlisted in place of human labor. Here, there is a trade-off between high initial costs and low operating costs (for automation) and low initial costs and higher operating costs (for human labor). To a great extent, however, such decisions depend on the available technologies. A **labor-intensive technology** is one in which people must do most of the work. Home cleaning services and professional baseball teams, for example, are labor intensive. A **capital-intensive technology** is one in which machines and equipment do most of the work. An automated assembly plant is highly capital intensive.

Facilities   A very complex set of design-planning decisions deals with the facilities to be used in creating the products and services that the organization offers. Major decisions include the number of facilities to be used, their locations, and their layout.

Should all the required capacity be placed in one or two large facilities? Or should it be divided among several smaller facilities? In general, firms that market a wide variety of products find it more economical to have a number of smaller facilities. Firms that produce only a few products tend to have fewer but larger facilities. There are many exceptions to this general rule, and decisions concerning facility size must often be made in light of zoning and other restrictions.

In determining where to locate production facilities, operations managers need to consider a number of variables. These include

- The geographic locations of suppliers of parts and raw materials
- The location of major markets for their goods and services
- Transportation costs from suppliers and to various markets
- The availability of skilled and unskilled labor in various geographic areas
- Special requirements of the technologies used, such as great amounts of energy or water

The choice of a particular location often involves optimizing, or balancing, the applicable variables.

Finally, the **plant layout,** which is the arrangement of machinery, equipment, and personnel within the facility, must be determined. Two general types of plant layout are used (Figure 7.6).

The *process layout* is used when different sequences of operations are required for creating small batches of different products. The plant is arranged so that each operation is performed in a particular area, and the work is moved from area to area to match its own sequence of operations. An auto repair shop provides an example of a process layout. The various operations might be engine repair, body work, wheel alignment, and safety inspection. Each is performed in a different area. A particular car "visits" only areas where the kinds of work it needs are performed.

A *product layout* is used when all products undergo the same operations in the same sequence. The work stations are arranged to match the sequence of operations, and the work flows from station to station. An assembly line is the best example of a product layout.

Human Resources In many ways, human resources are more the concern of personnel managers than of operations managers, but the two must work together at the design-planning stage. Several design-planning activities affect the work of personnel managers. For example, suppose a sophisticated technology requiring special skills is called for. Personnel will have to recruit employees with the appropriate skills, or develop training programs, or both. And, depending on where facilities are to be located, arrangements may have to be made to transfer skilled workers to the new locations or to train local workers.

Personnel managers can also obtain valuable information on availability of skilled workers in various areas, wage rates, and other factors that may influence choices of technology and location.

Operational Planning

Once the production process and facilities have been designed, operations personnel must plan for their use. This **operational planning** is the development of plans for utilizing production facilities and resources. In contrast to the one-time-only design plans, operational plans are developed periodically for each facility. The objective of operational planning is to decide on a level of output for the facility. Four steps are required: (1) select a planning horizon, (2) estimate market demand, (3) compare demand with capacity, and (4) adjust output to match demand.

Select a Planning Horizon A **planning horizon** is simply the period over which a plan will be in effect. A common planning horizon for operational plans is one year. That is, operations personnel plan production output one year in advance. Before each year is up, they plan for the next.

A planning horizon of one year is generally long enough to average out seasonal increases and decreases in sales. At the same time, it is short enough for planners to adjust output to accom-

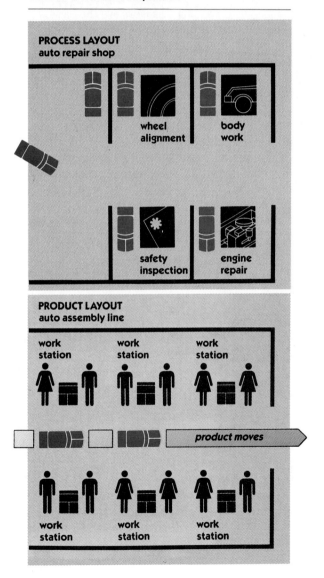

Figure 7.6 *Facilities Planning. The process layout is used when small batches of different products are created in a different operating sequence. The product layout is used when all products undergo the same operations in the same sequence.*

PROCESS LAYOUT
auto repair shop

wheel alignment

body work

safety inspection

engine repair

PRODUCT LAYOUT
auto assembly line

work station

work station

work station

product moves

work station

work station

work station

modate long-range sales trends. However, firms that operate in a rapidly changing business environment may find it best to select a shorter horizon to keep their operational planning current (Figure 7.7).

Estimate Market Demand The *market demand* for a product is the quantity that customers will demand at the going price. This quantity must be estimated for the period covered by the planning horizon. The sales forecasts and projections developed by marketing managers are the basis for market-demand estimates.

Compare Demand and Capacity The third step in operational planning is to compare the projected market demand with the facility's capacity to satisfy that demand. Again, demand and capacity must be compared over the same period—the planning horizon. One of three outcomes may result: demand may exceed capacity, capacity may exceed demand, or capacity and demand may be equal. If they are equal, the facility should be operated at full capacity. But if market demand and capacity are not equal, an adjustment may be called for.

Adjust Output to Demand When market demand exceeds capacity, several options are available to the firm. Output may be increased (to match demand) by operating the facility overtime with existing personnel, or by starting a second or third work shift. Another response is to subcontract a portion of the work out to other manufacturers. If the excess demand is likely to be permanent, the firm may expand the facility.

Another option that firms occasionally take is to ignore the excess demand and allow it to remain unmet. For several years, this strategy was used by the Adolph Coors Company. Gradually a mystique developed around Coors beer because it was not available in many parts of the country. Then, when the firm's brewing capacity was finally expanded, an eager market was waiting.

Figure 7.7 *Operational Planning. The objective of operational planning is to decide on the level of output for a facility.*

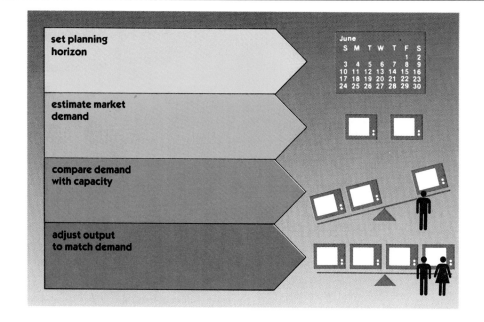

When capacity exceeds market demand, there are again several options. To reduce output temporarily, workers may be furloughed (laid off) and part of the facility shut down. Or the facility may be operated on a shorter-than-normal workweek for as long as the excess persists. To adjust to a permanently decreased demand, management may shift the excess capacity to the production of other goods or services. The most radical adjustment is to eliminate the excess capacity by selling unused facilities.

OPERATIONS CONTROL

So far we have discussed the development of a product idea and the planning that translates that idea into the reality of a production facility and determines the facility's level of output. Now it's time to push the "start button" to get the facility into operation.

While it is operating, the facility must be monitored and regulated—that is, controlled—to ensure that plans are being implemented and goals are being achieved. In this section we shall examine four important areas of operations control: purchasing, inventory control, scheduling, and quality control (Figure 7.8).

Purchasing

Purchasing consists of all the activities involved in obtaining required materials, supplies, and parts from other firms. The purchasing function is far from routine, and its importance should not be underestimated. For some products, purchased materials make up more than 50 percent of their wholesale cost.[2]

The objective of purchasing is to ensure that required materials are available when they are needed, in the proper amounts, and at minimum cost. In keeping with this objective, the two major functions of purchasing are supplier selection and purchase planning.

Supplier Selection Purchasing personnel should constantly be on the lookout for new or "back-

up" suppliers, even when their needs are being met by their present suppliers. It may become necessary to change suppliers for any of a variety of reasons. Or such problems as strikes and equipment breakdowns may cut off the flow of purchased materials from a primary supplier.

The choice of suppliers should result from careful analysis of a number of factors.

□ *Price.* Even tiny differences in price can add up to good-sized sums when large quantities are purchased. (A saving of 2 cents per unit on annual purchases of 100,000 units spells a yearly saving of $2000.) Moreover, some suppliers will give discounts on large purchases, and some may assume part or all of the cost of transportation. These arrangements are essentially price reductions. Purchasers should always take them into account.

□ *Quality.* The idea here is not necessarily to find the highest quality available. It is to buy materials at a level of quality that is in keeping with their intended use. The minimum acceptable quality is usually specified by product designers. Beyond that, purchasing personnel need to weigh quality against price, because higher quality usually costs more.

□ *Reliability.* An agreement to purchase high-quality materials at a low price is the purchaser's dream. But such an agreement becomes a nightmare if the supplier doesn't deliver. Purchasing personnel should check the reliability of potential suppliers as well as their ability to meet delivery schedules.

Figure 7.8 *Four Aspects of Operations Control. To implement the operations control system in any business requires the effective use of purchasing, inventory control, scheduling, and quality control by all managerial levels.*

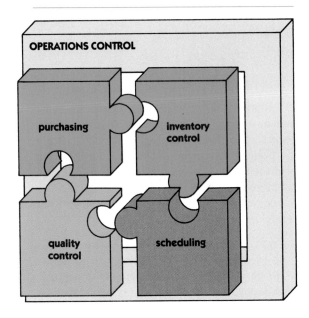

Purchase Planning If a production facility runs out of a part or material, it will probably have to shut down. And because costs such as rent, wages, and insurance expenses must still be paid, a shutdown can be expensive. However, large stockpiles of materials are also costly, because the money invested in stored materials does not contribute to the firm or its operations. The objective of purchase planning is to balance these two opposing factors—to ensure that sufficient purchased materials are on hand without paying excessive storage costs.

An important factor in purchase planning is lead time. **Lead time** is the time that elapses between placement of an order and receipt of that order. Various mathematical models based on lead time, costs, and required quantities can be used to optimize the timing of orders and to minimize ordering costs. One such model, the EOQ model (EOQ stands for economic order quantity), provides the least-cost order quantity via a simple arithmetic calculation.[3] Using this information, simple mathematical models can be used to determine when orders should be placed.

Inventory Control

Operations managers are concerned with three types of **inventories,** or stocks of goods and materials. *Raw-materials inventories* are stockpiles of materials that will become part of the product during the conversion process. These include purchased materials, parts, and subassemblies. The *work-in-process inventory* consists of products that have been partially completed but require further processing. *Finished-goods inventories* consist of completed goods that are awaiting shipment to customers.

Associated with each type of inventory are a *holding cost,* or storage cost, and a *stock-out cost,* the cost of running out of inventory. (We have already discussed these costs with regard to raw materials or purchased inventories. For work in process, the stock-out cost is the cost of the resulting shutdown or partial shutdown. For finished goods, the cost of running out is the resulting loss of sales.) **Inventory control** is the process of managing inventories in such a way as to minimize inventory costs, including both holding costs and potential stock-out costs.

Because large firms can incur huge inventory costs, much attention has been devoted to inventory control. The "just-in-time" system being used by Japanese (and now American) automakers is one result of all this attention. Another is computer-controlled inventory systems. For smaller firms, microcomputer-based systems can be used to keep track of inventories, provide periodic inventory reports, and alert managers to impending stock-outs. For larger firms, more complex computer-based systems maintain inventories of thousands of individual items, perform routine purchasing chores in accordance with a purchasing plan, and schedule the production of both subassemblies and finished goods.

What is most important, however, is not *how* inventories are controlled but the fact that they *are* controlled. Operations managers are responsible for making sure that sufficient inventories are on hand and that they are acquired at the lowest possible cost.

Scheduling

Scheduling is the process of ensuring that materials are at the right place at the right time. These "materials" may be raw materials, subassemblies, work in process, or finished goods. They may be moved from inventory to the work stations at which they are needed. They may move from station to station along an assembly line. Or they may arrive at work stations "just in time" to be made part of the work in process there. For finished goods, scheduling involves shipment to customers to fill orders and movement into finished-goods inventory.

As our definition implies, both place and time are important to scheduling. (This is no different from, say, the scheduling of classes. You cannot attend your classes unless you know both where and when they are held.) The *routing* of materials is the path, or sequence of work stations, that

the materials will follow. The *timing* specifies when the materials will arrive at each station, and perhaps how long they will remain there. Scheduling personnel may also be responsible for specifying which operations are to be performed at each work station, especially in plants that exhibit the process layout. They are also responsible for monitoring schedules (called *follow-up*) to ensure that the work flows according to schedule.

Scheduling Control via PERT The Program Evaluation and Review Technique (**PERT**) is a technique for scheduling a process or project and maintaining control of the schedule. PERT was developed for use in constructing the Polaris submarine in the late 1950s. It has since been applied successfully in a wide range of industries.

To use PERT, we begin by identifying all the major *activities* involved in the project. The completion of each activity is called an *event*. For example, building a house consists of such activities as pouring the foundation, erecting the frame, installing wiring and plumbing, putting on the roof, building the walls, and finishing the interior. The completion of each of these activities is an event.

Next we arrange the events in a sequence. In doing so, we must be sure that an event which must occur before another event in the actual process also occurs before that event in the sequence. For example, the frame of a house must be erected before wiring can be installed. Therefore, in our sequence, the event "frame erected" must precede the event "wiring installed."

Next we use arrows, representing activities, to connect events that must occur in sequence. We then estimate the time required for each activity and mark it on the corresponding arrow. The longest path through the sequence (the path that takes the longest time, from start to finish) is called the *critical path*. The activities on this path determine the minimum time in which the process can be completed. These activities are the ones that must be scheduled and controlled carefully. A delay in any one of them will cause a delay in completion of the project as a whole.

Figure 7.9 is a PERT diagram for the production of this book. The critical path runs from event 1 to event 4 to event 5 (which takes 12 weeks) rather than connecting events 1, 2, 3, and 5 (which takes only 10 weeks). It then runs through events 6, 8, and 9 to the finished book at event 10. Note that even a 6-week delay in preparing the cover will not delay the production process. However, *any* delay in an activity on the critical path will hold up publication. Thus, if necessary, resources could be diverted from cover preparation to, say, makeup of pages.

Quality Control

Quality control is the process of ensuring that goods and services are produced in accordance with design specifications for the product. These specifications should reflect the organization's goals and strategies regarding quality. Some

firms, such as Volvo and Neiman-Marcus, have built their reputations on quality. Customers pay more for their products in return for assurances of high quality. Other firms adopt a strategy of emphasizing lower prices along with reasonable (but not particularly high) quality.

As we saw at the beginning of this chapter, American automakers have recently adopted a strategy that calls for better quality in their products. The use of quality circles, groups of employees who meet on company time to solve problems of product quality, is one method of implementing this strategy at the operations level. Quality control circles have also been used successfully in some high technology companies, such as Digital Equipment Corporation. Increased effort is also being devoted to **inspection,** which is the examination of output to control quality.

Inspections are performed at various times during production, depending on both the process

Figure 7.9 *Simplified PERT Diagram for Producing this Book. A PERT diagram identifies the activities necessary to complete a given project, and arranges the activities based on the total time required for each to become an event. The activities on the critical path determine the minimum*

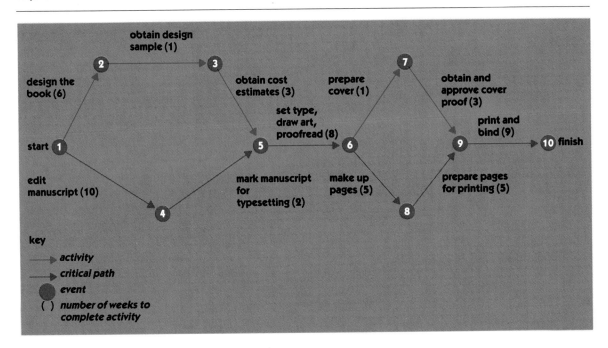

and the product. Purchased materials may be inspected when they arrive at the production facility. Subassemblies and manufactured parts may be inspected before they become part of a major assembly or finished product. And finished goods may be inspected before they are shipped to customers. Items that are within design specifications continue on their way. Those that are not within specs are removed from production.

The method used depends on the item that is being inspected. Visual inspection may be sufficient for products such as furniture and rug-cleaning services. Or one or two light bulbs may be tested out of every hundred produced. At the other extreme, complete X-ray inspection may be required for the vital components of airplanes and nuclear reactors.

The major objective of quality control is to see that the organization lives up to the standards that it has set for itself on quality. Quality control can also increase customer satisfaction, prevent product-safety problems, and decrease costs by reducing the size of the facility's scrap heap.

THE MANAGEMENT OF PRODUCTIVITY

We should not leave this chapter without discussing the management of productivity. Productivity concerns all managers, but it is especially important to operations managers. They are the people who must oversee the creation of the firm's goods and services. We define **productivity** as a measure of output per unit of time per worker. Hence, if each worker at plant A produces 75 units per day, and each worker at plant B produces only 70 units per day, the workers at plant A are more productive. If one bank teller serves 25 customers per hour and another serves 28 per hour, the second teller is more productive.

Productivity Trends

When we discussed Theory Z in Chapter 5, we noted that in recent years the productivity growth rate in the United States has fallen considerably behind that in other countries. American workers

Successful quality control requires careful inspection of goods at various stages in the production process. Source: Courtesy of Monsanto Company.

still produce more than their counterparts in most other industrialized countries, but our *rate of productivity growth* is lagging behind the productivity growth rates of many other world economic powers. Japan is a prime example, but productivity growth rates in West Germany and France are also exceeding that of the American worker. Moreover, specific American industries have been hit especially hard by sagging productivity. In the coal mining industry, productivity increased 6.6 percent each year from 1947 to 1966, but it

Another Look at Quality Circles

In their efforts to increase productivity, a growing number of manufacturing companies in the U.S. have introduced the Japanese model of "quality control circles"—small groups of workers, usually led by their supervisor, who meet regularly to discuss ways of improving team performance. But a study of QCC's in 29 companies by Matthew Goodfellow, a management researcher, found only 8 of them "successful" (as measured by the program's cost versus the value of gains in productivity), according to *Management Review* (Vol. 72, No. 9).

Woodruff Imberman, a management consultant, investigated the remaining 21 QCC's and found four major causes for failure:

1. In many companies, employees disliked—and even "hated"—management. Their animosity extended to the QCC's, which some employees saw as simply a management ploy to reduce overtime and perhaps cut the work force by increasing productivity.

2. Most companies did a poor job of selling QCC's. They relied on flip charts, booklets, and formal management presentations; managers had little personal contact with the workers themselves, who were left to wonder, "What's in it for me?"

3. The supervisors picked to lead the QCC's got some training in human relations and group dynamics, but they felt that little of it applied to the specific needs of their own departments.

4. Most companies regarded the QCC programs as merely a way of improving production techniques. They did not realize that QCC's cannot succeed without a change in management climate from the top down—a change that emphasizes the importance of human relations both among employees and between employees and management.

Source: Berkeley Rice, "Square holes for quality circles," *Psychology Today*, February 1984, p. 17.

---

has actually *declined* 3.5 percent each year since 1966. In petroleum refining, productivity growth was 4.2 percent per year between 1947 and 1966, but it has been only 2.3 percent per year since then. As a final example, drawn from the service sector, productivity in the air transportation industry grew 7.9 percent per year from 1947 to 1966, but it has grown only 4.4 percent per year since then.

Causes of Productivity Declines

No one is certain why these declines occurred, although several factors have been cited as possible causes. First, in recent years the United States has experienced major changes in the composition of its work force. In particular, many women and young people have entered the work force for the first time. The majority of these new entrants have relatively little working experience. Therefore their productivity might be lower than the average. As they develop new skills and experience, their downward influence on productivity trends should be minimized.

Another potential cause of stagnation in productivity is recent changes in industrial composition. (By *industrial composition* we mean the relative numbers of workers in various industries.) Specifically, many workers moved from agricultural jobs (which are low in productivity) to nonagricultural jobs (which are more productive) during the period beginning shortly after World War II and ending in the mid-1960s. This movement alone gave a boost to productivity growth. When it ended, productivity growth slowed down again.

There has also been a shift in the ratio of capital input to labor input in American industry. During the last decade, businesses have slowed their rate of investment in new equipment and technology. As workers have had to use increasingly outdated equipment, their productivity has naturally declined.

Another factor that may have contributed to the decline in productivity growth is a decrease in spending for research and development. The amount of money spent for R&D by government and industry, expressed as a percentage of gross national product, has been falling since 1964. As a result there have been fewer innovations and new products.

Finally, increased government regulation is frequently cited as a factor that has affected productivity. Federal agencies like the Occupational Safety and Health Administration (OSHA) and the Food and Drug Administration are increasingly regulating and intervening in business practices. Goodyear Tire and Rubber Company recently generated 345,000 pages of computer printout weighing 3200 pounds to comply with one new OSHA regulation! Further, the company spends over $35 million each year solely to meet the requirements of six regulatory agencies. These resources could increase productivity if they were invested elsewhere.

Improving Productivity

Several techniques and strategies have been suggested as possible cures for these downward productivity trends. Some involve the removal of major barriers to productivity growth. For example, research and development could be stimulated by tax credits or other inducements. Similarly, various government policies that may be hindering productivity could be eliminated, or at least modified.

Increased cooperation between management and labor could improve productivity. When unions and management work together, quite often the result is an improved situation for both.

In a related area, many managers believe that increased employee participation can enhance productivity. Employee participation is a primary

Quality circles are a Japanese innovation that has recently been adopted by many American firms. Employees meet during company time to discuss ways to achieve product quality. Source: Courtesy of BASF Wyandotte Corporation.

element in Theory Z. Another popular method of increasing participation is the quality circle now being used by a number of firms. As we have noted, a **quality circle** is a group of employees who meet periodically, on company time, to solve problems related to product quality. Quality circles are not only helpful in controlling quality. They also increase employee morale and motivation through employee participation in decision making.

Still another potential solution to productivity problems is to change the incentives for work. Many firms simply pay employees for their time, regardless of what or how much they produce. That is, employees are paid by the hour. As long as they produce at some minimal level, everything is fine. By changing the reward system so that people are paid for what they contribute, rather than for the time they put in, it may be possible to motivate employees to produce at higher levels.

Chapter Review

SUMMARY

Operations management consists of all the activities that managers engage in to create goods and services (products). Operations are as relevant to service organizations as to manufacturing firms. In fact, production is defined in such a way as to include the conversion of resources into either goods or services.

A technology is a process the firm uses to convert input resources into output goods or services. Conversion processes vary in terms of their major input (focus), the degree to which inputs are changed (magnitude), and the number of technologies employed in the conversion.

Operations management often begins with the research and product development effort. The results of R&D may be entirely new products or extensions and refinements of existing products. The limited life cycle of every product spurs companies to invest continuously in R&D.

Operations planning is planning for production. First, design planning is undertaken to address questions related to the product line, required production capacity, the technology to be used, the design of production facilities, and human resources. Next, operational planning focuses on the use of production facilities and resources. The steps in this periodic planning are (1) to establish the appropriate planning horizon, (2) to estimate market demand, (3) to compare demand and capacity, and (4) to adjust output to demand.

The major areas of operations control are purchasing, inventory control, scheduling, and quality control. Purchasing involves both selecting suppliers and planning purchases. Inventory control is the management of stocks of raw materials, work in process, and finished goods in such a way as to minimize the total inventory cost. Scheduling ensures that materials are at the right place at the right time—for use within the facility or for shipment to customers. Quality control ensures that products meet their design specifications.

In recent years, the productivity growth rate in this country has fallen behind the rates of productivity growth in many other industrialized nations. Several factors have been cited as possible causes for this trend, and managers have begun to explore techniques for overcoming it.

The next chapter treats a very important aspect of management in general and of productivity management in particular—employee motivation and morale. We shall discuss a number of major theories of employee motivation. And we shall see how managers try to boost motivation and morale through various reward systems.

KEY TERMS

You should now be able to define and give an example relevant to each of the following terms:

operations management

production

technology

service economy

research and development

design planning

product line

product design

capacity

labor-intensive technology

capital-intensive technology

plant layout

operational planning

planning horizon

purchasing

lead time

inventories

inventory control

scheduling

PERT

quality control

inspection

productivity

quality circle

QUESTIONS AND EXERCISES

Review Questions

1. List all the activities or functions that are involved in operations management.
2. In terms of focus, magnitude, and number, characterize the technologies used by a local pizza parlor, a dry-cleaning establishment, and an automotive repair shop.
3. Identify and briefly describe the two major aspects of product development.
4. What are the major elements of design planning?
5. What are the four steps in operational planning? What is its objective?
6. What is the difference between capacity and output?
7. Describe the two major functions of purchasing.
8. What are the costs that must be balanced and minimized through inventory control?
9. Explain in what sense scheduling is a *control* function of operations managers.
10. Who decides on the particular level of quality for a firm's products? How is that decision put into practice?
11. How might productivity be measured in a restaurant? in a department store? in a public school system?

Discussion Questions

1. Which areas of operations management, other than scheduling (just-in-time) and quality control (quality circles), might the American automobile industry investigate for solutions to its problems?
2. In what ways does the American automobile industry illustrate our discussion of productivity management?
3. Do certain kinds of firms need to stress particular areas of operations management? Explain.

4. Is it really necessary for service firms to engage in research and development? in operations planning and control?
5. How are the four areas of operations control interrelated?
6. Is operations management relevant to non-business organizations such as colleges and hospitals? Why?

Exercises

1. Assume you have decided to go into the business of assembling and selling desk lamps with built-in electronic calculators. Decide whether you would use a process layout or a product layout in your production facility. Then sketch the layout of the facility.
2. For the calculator lamp of Exercise 1, explain in detail what arrangements you would make in each of the four areas of operations control.
3. Draw a PERT diagram for the construction of a house, and identify the critical path. (Estimate reasonable times for the building activities listed in the chapter.)

CASE 7-1

John Deere Adopts FMS

A recent breakthrough in operations management is the flexible manufacturing system (FMS). FMS has three basic elements. First, computer-controlled machines process incoming materials. Second, industrial robots put parts into machines, take them out after processing, and move them to the next machine. Third, a computerized control system coordinates the entire operation.

FMS has two basic advantages over a conventional assembly line. The system takes advantage of the entire capacity of the facility by more efficiently routing work through the plant. And FMS provides considerably more flexibility. In a conventional system, machines and work stations are arranged in a fixed sequence. In FMS, the entire system can be rearranged easily, so even small batches can be processed efficiently.

FMS has been developed and popularized in Japan, where most automobile companies use it. In one plant, only 12 workers are needed during the day and only a guard is present at night. A conventional plant would require 215 employees, 4 times as many machines, and 3 months to make what this plant produces in one day!

In the United States, John Deere and Company is the only major firm to have adopted FMS. It recently invested $500 million in one of its tractor assembly plants. By combining FMS and the just-in-time inventory system, John Deere cut its inventory needs in half. It can produce a tractor in half the time required before, and it has more flexibility in reacting to market changes. The company is also planning a major push into the construction equipment industry to compete against J. I. Case and Caterpillar Tractor.[4]

1. Why do you think other American firms have been reluctant to adopt the concept of FMS?
2. What areas of operations management are affected most by FMS?
3. Is FMS applicable to service organizations? Explain.

CASE 7-2

Pizza Hut, Hut, Hut . . .

In 1977, when Pizza Hut was purchased by PepsiCo, Inc., for $340 million, it was the nation's largest pizza chain. But Pizza Hut's rapid growth in the preceding five years had produced problems along with size. The most pressing of these was a decline in the quality of both the food and the service. This resulted in a parallel decline in profit—from $52 million in 1977 to $22.4 million in 1979.

PepsiCo hired Donald N. Smith to solve Pizza Hut's problems. Smith, who was named head of the PepsiCo food-service division, had been responsible for such fast-food innovations as McDonald's breakfasts and Burger King's sandwiches.

To start, he put on an apron and worked at selected Pizza Hut outlets. While cooking pizza and serving customers, he was able to confirm reports of dirty facilities, slow service, and poor management. He also found that low pay and excessive paperwork were responsible for an 80 percent annual turnover among outlet managers. (One result of Smith's "on-the-job" training was the requirement that all top Pizza Hut executives spend some time working at local outlets.)

Smith then overhauled Pizza Hut's operations, almost across the board:

▫ New ovens were installed in Pizza Hut kitchens, to replace ovens that had been designed twenty years earlier. The new ovens cut pizza baking time in half.

▫ Managers' salaries were increased, and a streamlined bookkeeping system was installed. These steps helped reduce the annual manager turnover rate to 50 percent.

▫ Pan Pizza—a thick-crust pizza served in a deep pan—was introduced in 1980.

▫ Company-owned stores were redecorated in warmer, family-oriented wood tones. (The company owns about half the Pizza Hut outlets, and the rest are franchised.)

In addition, advertising expenditures were increased substantially; new advertising emphasized the *food* rather than the *fast* in fast food. And it was directed toward young families rather than teenagers.

By the end of 1981, Pizza Hut seemed to have turned around. The number of outlets had increased, and annual revenues had almost doubled—from $532 million in 1979 to over $1 billion in 1981. Annual sales per outlet, which had been less than $250,000 in 1979, were now $300,000.[5]

1. Which of Smith's changes actually dealt with activities that are the concern of operations management? Explain the connection in each case.

2. Is it reasonable for a fast-food producer to emphasize its food rather than its speed? Why or why not?

Career Profile

Clifton C. Garvin How do you become the head of the world's most prosperous company? Exxon's Clifton C. Garvin, like most of the huge energy company's recent top executives, was an engineer who rapidly climbed the well-worn rungs of the corporate ladder. He became Exxon's president in 1972 and its chief executive in 1975, when his predecessor, J. Kenneth Jamieson, reached 65. (Exxon does not bend its mandatory retirement rules, even for its chief executive officer.) Now approaching retirement himself, Garvin heads a company with yearly sales of over $100 billion.

Garvin grew up in Portsmouth, Virginia, graduated with a B.S. in chemical engineering from Virginia Polytechnic Institute in 1943, then spent two and a half years with the Army Corps of Engineers in the South Pacific. After the war he returned to VPI to get his master's degree. On the advice of an undergraduate classmate who was already working for Standard Oil Co. (New Jersey)—as Exxon was known until 1973—he applied for a job at Standard's Baton Rouge, Louisiana, refinery complex. At the refinery, traditionally a stepping stone for Exxon executives, he was spotted by Henry J. Voorhies, the refinery manager, who helped him to become within 10 years the operating superintendent of the refinery.

Garvin broadened his experience, working for Exxon in New York, Texas, Oklahoma, and California. While he was in LA he reported frequently to Houston, dealing with Kenneth Jamieson, who was to precede Garvin to the top. Garvin's next post gave him crucial experience of decision making at the highest level: he became executive assistant to Michael L. Haider, president and then chairman of the company. After this experience, he was made president of the company's chemical affiliates, first for the United States, then for the world. Under Garvin's leadership, the chemical divisions became among the company's most profitable.

In 1968, Garvin was named to Standard's board of directors, a move that assured him of a voice in all the major company decisions. Exxon is run largely by committee—no chief executive would make an important decision without consulting the management committee. Garvin's selection as company president in 1972 broadened and solidified his power, but he had already been party to key decisions for four years. One of Garvin's first responsibilities as new chief executive was to begin searching for his own successor. He was reminded of this task by a note from M. J. Rathbone, chief executive of a decade earlier, who wrote, "Your job right now is to develop some more Garvins. . . ."

To carry out this task, the management committee meets once a week with the expressed intent of locating and properly compensating rising managers within the company. And those managers are carefully picked and balanced. When Garvin moved up to chief executive, some observers were surprised by the selection of Howard C. Kauffmann as Exxon's new president. But Garvin explains it as a balancing act. "We deliberately set out to pick a man whose background is in exploration and production, where I have almost no experience. Anyone around here can tell you that Kauffmann and I don't always see eye to eye on everything, but we expect to complement one another." Exxon is famous for discovering and bringing along its new management as it did with Garvin, and the process is continuing.[1]

The figure in the salary column approximates the expected annual income after two or three years of service.

1 = $12,000–$15,000   2 = $16,000–$20,000   3 = $21,000–$27,000   4 = $28,000–$35,000   5 = $36,000 and up

Job Title	Educational Requirements	Salary Range	Prospects
Accounting manager	Bachelor's degree in accounting; on-the-job experience; master's degree in business administration preferred	3	Greatest growth
Administrative management assistant	Two years of college; on-the-job experience	2	Gradual growth
Clerical supervisor	High school diploma; some college preferred	1–2	Greatest growth
Food services manager	Two years of college or trade school; on-the-job experience	2	Gradual growth
General clerical employee	High school diploma; on-the-job experience; some college helpful	1–2	Gradual growth
Hospital administrator	Bachelor's degree in business or hospital administration; master's degree preferred	4	Gradual growth
Hotel manager	Some college helpful; bachelor's degree preferred	2–3	Limited growth
Industrial designer	Bachelor's degree; on-the-job experience	2–3	No growth
Industrial engineer	Bachelor's degree; on-the-job experience	3	Gradual growth
Management analyst	Bachelor's degree in management; on-the-job experience	2–3	Limited growth
Management trainee	Two years of college; bachelor's degree preferred	1–3	Gradual growth
Operations analyst	Bachelor's degree in math, statistics, or management	3	Greatest growth
Operations manager	Bachelor's degree in math, engineering, or management; several years of experience	3–4	Gradual growth
Operations research analyst	Bachelor's degree in math, statistics or computers	3	Gradual growth
Public relations manager	Bachelor's degree in business; on-the-job experience	3	Limited growth
Purchasing agent	Bachelor's degree in business; on-the-job experience helpful	3	Limited growth
Secretarial supervisor	High school diploma; on-the-job experience; some college preferred	2	Gradual growth
Shipping/receiving clerk	High school diploma	1–2	No growth
Systems analyst	College degree in business, math, or engineering	3	Greatest growth
Traffic manager	Some college; degree helpful	Varies widely	Limited growth

PART

3
The Human Resource

This part of Business is concerned with the most important and least predictable of all resources—people. We begin by discussing various ideas about why people behave as they do, paying special attention to the work environment. Then we apply these ideas to the management of the firm's work force. Finally, we look at organized labor in the United States and probe the sometimes controversial relationship between business management and labor unions. Included in this part are:

Chapter 8   People and Motivation in
Business
Chapter 9   Human Resources Management
Chapter 10 Union-Management Relations

CHAPTER

EIGHT
People and Motivation in Business

There was a time when managers used only two techniques to improve employee productivity. The first consisted of a five-cents-an-hour raise and a pat on the back—to show that increased productivity was appreciated. The second consisted of firing workers who didn't work hard enough and hiring substitutes who might work harder—to show that low productivity would not be tolerated. Nowadays, however, most managers realize that people are not machines. They know that there is a lot more to motivating workers than slapping on a little "oil" now and then and occasionally "replacing parts." In this chapter we shall examine both the theoretical and the practical aspects of motivation. After studying the chapter, you should understand:

1. The meaning of motivation

2. Some earlier perspectives on motivation: scientific management, Theory X, and Theory Y

3. The concept of Maslow's hierarchy of needs

4. The nature of Herzberg's two-factor theory

5. Three contemporary views of motivation: equity theory, expectancy theory, and reinforcement theory

6. The characteristics of effective reward systems, and several relatively new kinds of reward systems

7. Some techniques for increasing employee motivation

Consider this:

James Treybig is a founder and CEO of a company called Tandem Computers. Tandem is not very well known to the general public, primarily because it doesn't produce any consumer goods. However, Tandem and its products have a wide reputation in the business world.

The basis for this reputation is a remarkable computer system called the NonStop II™ system. The NonStop system is a very useful machine for firms that simply cannot afford a computer breakdown. One of the consequences of such a breakdown—or of the interruption of power to the computer—is the loss of all the information stored in the computer. Consider, for example, the chaos that would envelop an airline if a computer breakdown destroyed its passenger-reservations records. Picture the confusion in a hotel if all its advance room bookings were lost. Think of the effect on a bank or insurance company if all the records of last week's financial transactions disappeared.

The NonStop system provides an effective backup for firms that must depend on their on-line computer systems. Essentially, the NonStop system is two computers in one. Under normal circumstances, the work load is spread evenly between the two computers. If one fails, however, the other automatically takes over all current work in process. Moreover, a complex control system, which includes its own power source, protects all the data in the system, even if both computers shut down.

Although Tandem is only 10 years old, its annual sales already exceed $400 million. Treybig projects that its yearly sales volume will pass the $1 billion mark in 3 years.

Part of the success Tandem enjoys is attributable to its work force. Tandem is based in California's fabled "silicon valley," a string of high-tech firms extending from San Francisco to southern California. Loyal, hard-working employees are hard to find, and even harder to keep, in the silicon valley. New and growing firms pay premium salaries to attract good people, and most employees move from firm to firm often.

Treybig is very casual and relaxed, both as a

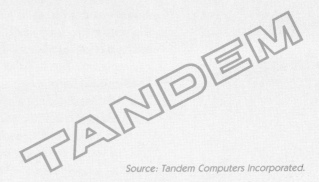

Source: Tandem Computers Incorporated.

person and as a manager. He has successfully translated his style of management into an innovative reward system that helps to maintain a high level of motivation among his employees. For one thing, flexible work schedules are the norm. For another, the work environment itself is very pleasant. Company headquarters is graced by a jogging track, a basketball court, and a swimming pool. Every Friday afternoon there is a big "beer bust" for all employees. The company even sponsored a male beauty contest judged by female employees.

Financial incentives have not been forgotten. Most employees are frequently offered valuable stock options. For someone who has been at Tandem since its beginning, the value of these options now exceeds $100,000.

Tandem Computers also has an open information system. All employees are given detailed information about the company's plans and methods of operation, for example. Treybig believes that having this information increases people's effectiveness within the firm and their loyalty to it. Because many Tandem employees also have a financial stake in the success of the company (through their stock options), this information is doubly motivating. It assures them that they are an important part of the firm, and it gives them the opportunity to help increase the value of their own stock holdings.

Not surprisingly, Tandem boasts a highly dedicated and motivated group of employees. Many say openly that Tandem is the best firm they have ever worked for and that they will never leave.[1]

In the early days of industrialization managers concentrated on productivity without paying attention to employees' needs. Since that time, research on employee motivation and morale has encouraged more sensitive management. Sources: (top) The Bettmann Archive; (bottom) Courtesy of Honeywell Inc.

Clearly, James Treybig recognized the value of Tandem's human resources. He has taken a number of steps to motivate and reward good performance.

Tandem provides incentives and benefits at a variety of levels. The swimming pool, jogging track, and basketball court, for example, help to satisfy employees' recreational needs. Not many people would go to work for a firm just because it has a swimming pool, but such an employee benefit would make few of them *unhappy*. Financial incentives—such as the stock option plan—are also carefully built into Tandem's reward system. And Treybig satisfies certain intangible needs by treating employees as an important element in the firm's success.

We shall be looking at various levels of needs and motivation later in this chapter. But what, exactly, is motivation? Most often, the term is used to explain people's behavior. Successful athletes are said to be highly motivated. A student who avoids work is said to be unmotivated. (From another viewpoint, the student might be thought of as motivated—to avoid work.)

We shall define **motivation** as the individual, internal process that energizes, directs, and sustains behavior. Motivation is the personal "force" that causes one to behave in a particular way. When we say that Tandem's stock option plan *motivates* employees, we mean that it activates this force or process within employees.

Tandem's employees are obviously satisfied with their jobs and with the company. Their dedication to the firm, and their feeling that Tandem is the best company they have ever worked for, are both indicators of high morale. An employee's **morale** is his or her attitude toward the job, his or her superiors, and the firm itself.

High morale—a positive attitude—results mainly from the satisfaction of needs on the job or as a result of the job. One need that might be satisfied on the job is the need for *recognition* as an important part of the organization. One need satisfied as a result of the job is the need for *financial security*. (Note that both these needs are recognized at Tandem Computers.) High morale, in turn, leads to the dedication and loyalty that are in evidence at Tandem, as well as to the desire to do the job well. Low morale can lead to shoddy work, to absenteeism, and to high rates of turnover, as employees leave to seek more satisfying jobs with other firms.

Motivation, morale, and the satisfaction of employees' needs are thus intertwined. Along with productivity, they have been the subject of much study since the end of the nineteenth century. Let us begin our treatment of motivation by outlining some landmarks of that early research.

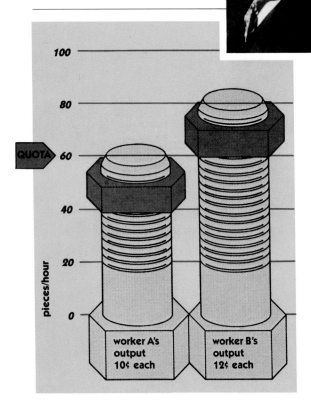

Figure 8.1 The Piece-Rate System. When workers exceeded their quota, they were rewarded by being paid at a higher rate per piece for all pieces produced.
Source: Photo, The Bettmann Archive.

HISTORICAL PERSPECTIVES ON MOTIVATION

Often, researchers begin a study with some fairly narrow goal in mind. But after they develop an understanding of their subject, they realize that both their goal and their research should be broadened. This is exactly what happened when early research into productivity blossomed into the more modern study of employee motivation.

Scientific Management

During the early part of the twentieth century, Frederick W. Taylor became interested in improving the efficiency of individual workers. This interest stemmed from his own experiences in manufacturing plants. It eventually led to **scientific management,** the application of scientific principles to management of work and workers.

One of Taylor's first jobs was with the Midvale Steel Company in Philadelphia. While he was there, he developed a strong distaste for waste and inefficiency. He also observed a practice that he called soldiering. Workers at Midvale "soldiered," or worked at a very slow pace, because they feared that if they worked faster they would run out of work and lose their jobs. Taylor realized that managers were not aware of the soldiering because they had no idea what the workers' productivity level *should* be.

Taylor later left Midvale and spent several years at Bethlehem Steel. It was there that he made his most significant contribution. In particular, he suggested that each job should be broken down into separate tasks. Then management should determine (1) the best way to perform these tasks and (2) the job output to expect when the tasks were performed properly. Next, management should carefully choose the best person for each job and train that person to do the job properly. Finally, management should cooperate with workers to ensure that jobs are performed as planned.

Taylor also developed the idea that most peo-

Studies by Elton Mayo (inset) at the Western Electric Company in Chicago revealed the importance of human factors, such as social acceptance and a sense of involvement, in motivating employees. *Source: Courtesy of Western Electric Corporation; inset, Courtesy of Baker Library, Harvard Business School.*

ple work only to earn money. He therefore reasoned that pay should be tied directly to output. The more a person produced, the more he or she should be paid. This gave rise to the **piece-rate system,** under which employees are paid a certain amount for each unit of output they produce. Under Taylor's piece-rate system, each employee was assigned an output quota. Those exceeding the quota were paid a higher per-unit rate for *all* units they produced (Figure 8.1).

Taylor's system was put into practice at Bethlehem Steel, and the results were dramatic. Average earnings per day for steel handlers rose from $1.15 to $1.88. (Don't let the low wages that prevailed at the time obscure the fact that this is an increase of better than 63 percent!) The average amount of steel handled per day increased from 16 to 57 tons.

Taylor's ideas were quite revolutionary for his day, and they had a profound impact on management practice. However, his view of motivation was soon recognized as overly simplistic and nar-

row. It is certainly true that most people expect to be paid for their work. But it is also true that people work for a variety of reasons other than pay. Simply increasing a person's pay may not increase his or her motivation.

The Hawthorne Studies

Between 1927 and 1932, two experiments were conducted by Elton Mayo at the Hawthorne plant of the Western Electric Company in Chicago. Their original objective was to determine the effect of the work environment on productivity.

In the first set of experiments, lighting in the work place was varied for one group of workers but not for a second group. Then the productivity of both groups was measured to determine the effect of the variations in light. To the amazement of the researchers, productivity increased for *both* groups. And for the group whose lighting was varied, productivity remained high until the light was reduced to the level of moonlight!

There are many ways managers inadvertently kill creativity in employees, according to Mo Edwards, president of Idea Development Assoc.

- ☐ Cutting off or ridiculing ideas.
- ☐ Always imposing budget limitations on new ideas.
- ☐ Overemphasizing end results so that ideas that don't sound like "sure things" never get tried.
- ☐ Using negative body language and saying "it will never work here."
- ☐ Ignoring ideas from "low status" employees.
- ☐ Keeping the work load so heavy and deadlines so tight there's no time to experiment.
- ☐ Taking employees' ideas and changing them before they can try them out their way.
- ☐ Imposing structure on what should be free-form brainstorming sessions.
- ☐ Asking the idea generator to "guarantee it will work before we try it."
- ☐ Worst of all: forming a committee to study the idea.

Source: "Killing Creativity," *Infosystems*, March 1984, p. 101.

The second set of experiments focused on the effectiveness of the piece-rate system in increasing the output of *groups* of workers. Researchers expected that output would increase, because faster workers would put pressure on slower workers to produce more. Again, the results were not as expected: Output remained constant, no matter what "standard" rates were set by management.

The researchers came to the conclusion that *human factors* were responsible for the results of the two experiments. In the lighting experiments, researchers had given both groups of workers a *sense of involvement* in their jobs merely by asking them to participate in the research. These workers—perhaps for the first time—felt as though they were an important part of the organization.

In the piece-rate experiments, each group of workers informally set the acceptable rate of output for the group. To gain the *social acceptance* of the group, each worker had to produce at that rate. Slower or faster workers were pressured to maintain the group's pace.

The Hawthorne studies showed that such human factors are at least as important to motivation as pay rates. From these and other studies, the *human relations movement* in management was born. Its premise was the assumption that employees who were happy and satisfied with their work would be motivated to perform better. Hence, management would do best to provide a work environment that maximized employee satisfaction.

Theory X and Theory Y

The concepts of Theory X and Theory Y were advanced by Douglas McGregor in his 1960 book *The Human Side of Enterprise.*[2] They are, in reality, sets of assumptions that underlie management's attitudes and beliefs regarding worker behavior.

Theory X is a set of assumptions that are generally consistent with Taylor's scientific management:

1. People dislike work and try to avoid it.
2. Because people dislike work, managers must coerce, control, and frequently threaten employees in order to achieve organizational goals.

Table 8.1 *Theory X and Theory Y Contrasted*

Area	Theory X	Theory Y
Attitude toward work	Indifference	Involvement
Control systems	External	Internal
Supervision	Direct	Indirect
Level of commitment	Low	High
Employee potential	Ignored	Identified
Use of human resources	Limited	Utilized

3. People generally must be led, because they have little ambition and will not seek responsibility. They are concerned mainly with security.

The logical outcome of such assumptions will be a highly controlled work environment—one in which the managers make all the decisions and the employees just take orders.

Theory Y, on the other hand, is a set of assumptions that are consistent with the human relations movement:

1. People do not naturally dislike work. In fact, work is an important part of their lives.
2. People will work toward goals that they are committed to.
3. People become committed to goals when it is clear that accomplishing the goals will bring personal rewards.
4. People often seek out and willingly accept responsibility.
5. Employees have the potential to help accomplish organizational goals.
6. Organizations generally do not make full use of their human resources.

Obviously this view is quite different from—and much more positive than—that of Theory X. McGregor argued that most managers behave in accordance with Theory X. But he maintained that Theory Y is more appropriate and effective as a guide for managerial action (Table 8.1).

The human relations movement and Theories X and Y increased managers' awareness of the importance of social factors in the work place. However, human motivation is a complex and dynamic process to which there is no simple key—neither money alone nor social factors alone. Rather, a variety of factors must be con-

sidered in any attempt to increase motivation. We turn now from research on human productivity to research that focused directly on human needs.

MASLOW'S HIERARCHY OF NEEDS

The concept of a hierarchy of needs was advanced by Abraham Maslow, a psychologist. Maslow assumed that humans are "wanting" beings who seek to fulfill a variety of **needs,** or personal requirements. Moreover, he assumed that these needs can be arranged in a sequence according to their importance. This sequence is known as Maslow's **hierarchy of needs** (Figure 8.2).

Figure 8.2 Maslow's Hierarchy of Needs. Maslow believed that people seek to fulfill five categories of needs, and that they must satisfy each level of needs, starting at the bottom, before proceeding to the next level.

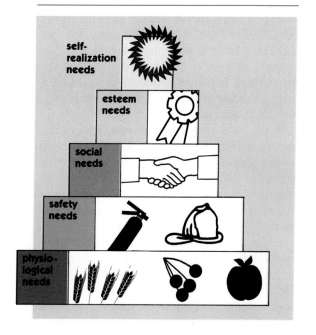

The theory of human needs developed by Abraham Maslow supplies some useful criteria for understanding employee motivation. Source: The Granger Collection.

At the most basic level are **physiological needs,** the things we require to survive. These include food and water, clothing, shelter, and sleep. In the employment context, these needs are usually satisfied through adequate wages.

At the next level are **safety needs,** the things we require for physical and emotional security. They may be satisfied through job security, health insurance, pension plans, and safe working conditions.

Next are the **social needs,** the human requirements for love and affection and a sense of belonging. To an extent, these can be satisfied through the work environment and the informal organization. But social relationships beyond the work place—with family and friends, for example—are usually needed too.

At the level of **esteem needs,** we require respect and recognition (the esteem of others) as well as a sense of our own accomplishment and worth (self-esteem). These needs may be satisfied through personal accomplishment, promotion to more responsible jobs, and various honors and awards.

At the uppermost level are **self-realization needs,** the needs to grow and develop as people and to become all that we are capable of being. These are the most difficult needs to satisfy, and the means of satisfying them tend to vary with the individual. For some people, learning a new skill, starting a new career after retirement, or becoming "the best there is" at some endeavor may be the way to satisfy the self-realization needs.

Maslow suggests that people work to satisfy their physiological needs first, then their safety needs, and so on up the "needs ladder." In general, they are motivated by the needs at the lowest (most important) level that so far remains unsatisfied. However, needs at one level do not have to be completely satisfied before needs at the next higher level come into play. If the majority of a person's physiological and safety needs are satisfied, that person will be motivated primarily by social needs. But any physiological and safety needs that remain unsatisfied will also be important.

Maslow's hierarchy of needs provides a useful way of viewing employee motivation, as well as a guide for management. By and large, American business has been able to satisfy workers' basic needs, but the higher-order needs present more of a problem. They are not satisfied in a simple manner, and the means of satisfaction vary from one employee to another.

HERZBERG'S THEORY

In the late 1950s, Frederick Herzberg interviewed two hundred accountants and engineers in the city of Pittsburgh. During the interviews, he asked them to think of a time when they had felt especially good about their jobs and their work. Then he asked them to describe the factor or factors that had caused them to feel that way. Next he did the same regarding a time when they had felt especially bad about their work. He was surprised to find that feeling good and feeling bad resulted from entirely different sets of factors. That is, low pay might have made a particular person feel bad, but it was not high pay that had made him or her feel good. Instead, it was some completely different factor.

Satisfaction and Dissatisfaction

Prior to Herzberg's interviews, the general assumption was that employee satisfaction and dissatisfaction lay at opposite ends of the same scale. People felt satisfied, dissatisfied, or somewhere between the two. Herzberg's interviews, however, convinced him that satisfaction and dissatisfaction may well be different dimensions altogether. One dimension might range from satisfaction to no satisfaction, and the other might range from dissatisfaction to no dissatisfaction. The idea that satisfaction and dissatisfaction are separate and distinct dimensions is referred to as the **motivation-hygiene theory** (Figure 8.3).

The factors that Herzberg found most frequently associated with satisfaction were achievement, recognition, responsibility, advancement and growth, and the work itself. These factors are generally referred to as **motivation factors** because their presence increases motivation. However, their absence does not necessarily result in feelings of dissatisfaction. When motivation factors are present, they act as *satisfiers*.

Factors cited as causing dissatisfaction were supervision, working conditions, interpersonal relationships, pay, job security, and company policies and administration. These factors, called **hygiene factors,** reduce dissatisfaction when they are present to an acceptable degree. However, they do not necessarily result in high levels of motivation. When hygiene factors are absent, they act as *dissatisfiers*.

Using Herzberg's Theory

Herzberg provides explicit guidelines for using the motivation-hygiene theory of employee motivation. He suggests that the hygiene factors must be present to ensure that a worker can function comfortably. But he warns that a state of *no dissatisfaction* never exists. In any situation, people will always be dissatisfied with something.

Managers should make hygiene as good as possible, but should then expect only short-term,

not long-term, improvement in motivation. Managers must work to provide the motivation factors, which will presumably enhance motivation and long-term effort.

One practical application of the motivation-hygiene theory is job enrichment, which is discussed in Chapter 6. Job enrichment provides or strengthens such motivation factors as achievement, recognition, and responsibility.

We should note in passing that employee pay has more effect than is explained by Herzberg's theory. His theory suggests that pay provides only short-term change and not motivation. Yet, in many organizations, pay provides recognition and reward for achievement—and recognition and achievement are both motivation factors. The ef-

Figure 8.3 *Motivation-Hygiene Theory. Herzberg's theory took into account that there were different dimensions to job satisfaction and dissatisfaction and that these factors did not overlap.*

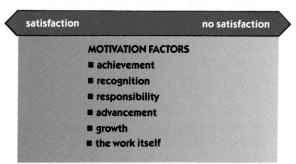

dissatisfaction	no dissatisfaction

HYGIENE FACTORS
- supervision
- working conditions
- interpersonal relationships
- pay
- job security
- company policies and administration

satisfaction	no satisfaction

MOTIVATION FACTORS
- achievement
- recognition
- responsibility
- advancement
- growth
- the work itself

fect of pay may depend on how it is distributed. If a pay increase does not depend on performance (as in across-the-board or cost-of-living raises), it may not motivate individuals. However, if pay is increased as a form of recognition (as in bonuses or awards), it may play a powerful role in motivating employees to higher performance.

CONTEMPORARY VIEWS ON MOTIVATION

Maslow's hierarchy of needs and Herzberg's two-factor theory are popular and widely known theories of motivation. Each is also a significant step up from the relatively narrow views of scientific management and Theories X and Y. But they do have one weakness: Each is an attempt to specify *what* motivates people, but neither explains *why* or *how* motivation is caused or how motivation is sustained over time. In recent years, managers have begun to explore three other models that take a more dynamic view of motivation. These are equity theory, expectancy theory, and reinforcement theory.

Equity Theory

The **equity theory** of motivation is based on the premise that people are motivated first to achieve and then to maintain a sense of equity. As used here, *equity* is the distribution of rewards in direct proportion to the contribution of each employee to the organization. Everyone need not receive the *same* rewards, but the rewards should be in accordance with individual contributions.

As individuals, the theory goes, we tend to implement the idea of equity as follows: First we develop our own outcome-to-input ratio. Inputs are the things we contribute to the organization, such as time, effort, skills, education, experience, and so on. Outcomes are the things we get from the organization, such as pay, benefits, recognition, promotions, and other rewards.

Next we compare this ratio to what we perceive as the outcome-to-input ratio for some other person. It might be a co-worker, a friend who works for another firm, or even an average of all the people in our organization. This person is called the "comparison other." Note that our perception of this person's outcome-to-input ratio may be absolutely correct or completely wrong. However, we believe it is correct.

If the two ratios are roughly the same, we feel that the organization is treating us equitably. In this case we are motivated to leave things as they are. However, if our ratio is the lower of the two, we feel underrewarded and are motivated to change things. We may (1) decrease our own inputs by not working so hard, (2) try to increase our total outcome by asking for a raise in pay, (3) try to get the comparison other to increase some inputs or receive decreased outcomes, (4) leave the work situation, or (5) do a new comparison with a different comparison other.

Equity theory is most relevant to pay as an outcome. Because pay is a very real measure of a person's worth to the organization, comparisons involving pay are a natural part of organizational life. Managers can avoid problems arising from inequity by doing everything possible to avoid inequity. For instance, they can make sure that rewards are distributed on the basis of performance and that everyone clearly understands the basis for his or her own pay.

Expectancy Theory

Expectancy theory, developed by Victor Vroom, is a very complex model of motivation that is based on a deceptively simple assumption. According to expectancy theory, motivation depends on how much we want something and on how likely we think we are to get it (Figure 8.4). Consider, for example, the case of three sales representatives who are candidates for promotion to one sales manager's job. Bill has had a very good sales year and always gets good performance evaluations. However, he isn't sure he wants the job because it involves a great deal more travel, longer working hours, and much more stress and pressure. Paul wants the job badly but doesn't think he has much chance of getting it. He has had a terrible sales year and gets only mediocre performance evaluations from his present boss. Susan wants the job as much as Paul, and she thinks she has a pretty good shot at it. Her sales have improved significantly this past year, and her evaluations are the best in the company.

Expectancy theory would predict that Bill and Paul are not very motivated to seek the promotion. Bill doesn't really want it, and Paul doesn't think he has much chance of getting it. Susan, on the other hand, is very motivated to seek the promotion, because she wants it *and* thinks she can get it.

Expectancy theory is complex because each action we take is likely to lead to several different outcomes, some that we may want and others that we may not want. For example, if people work hard and put in a lot of extra hours, several things may happen. They may get a pay raise, they may be promoted, they may have less time to spend with their families, they may have to cut back on their social life, and they may gain valuable new job skills.

For one person, the promotion may be paramount, the pay raise and new skills fairly impor-

tant, and the loss of family and social life of negligible importance. For someone else, the family and social life may be most important, the pay raise of moderate importance, the new skills unimportant, and the promotion undesirable because of the additional hours it would require. The first person would be motivated to work hard and put in extra hours, whereas the second person would not be at all motivated to do so. In other words, it is the entire bundle of outcomes, and the individual's evaluation of each outcome, that determines motivation.

Expectancy theory is difficult to apply, but it does provide several useful guidelines for managers. It suggests that managers must recognize that (1) employees work for a variety of different reasons; (2) these reasons, or expected outcomes, may change over time; and (3) it is necessary to show employees clearly how they can attain the outcomes they desire.

Reinforcement Theory

The contemporary motivation theory with perhaps the greatest potential for business application is reinforcement theory. **Reinforcement theory** is based on the premise that behavior that is rewarded is likely to be repeated, whereas

Figure 8.4 *Expectancy Theory. Vroom's theory is based on the idea that motivation depends on how much people want something and the likelihood of their achieving it.*

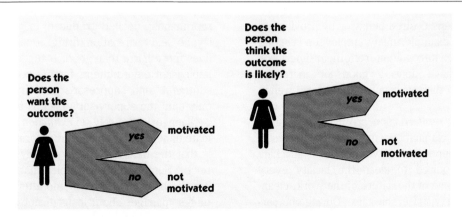

For three years, John Smith worked as a consultant for a business organization, reporting regularly to a company committee. To Smith, it was clear that the committee valued his services highly. In fact, the group had become thoroughly dissatisfied with him and was only waiting for his contract to expire so that they could replace him.

John Smith suffers from a syndrome that may be common in today's organizations—the delusion that one is well regarded. Fred H. Goldner, a former corporate executive, now a sociologist at Queens College, recently dubbed this phenomenon *pronoia*.

Writing in *Social Problems* (Vol. 30, No. 1), Goldner suggests that pronoia is the positive counterpart of paranoia. Whereas paranoids suffer from delusions of persecution, pronoids suffer from delusions of admiration. While paranoids think that people are saying bad things about them behind their backs, pronoids think that people are whispering their praises.

Goldner attributes pronoia to the ways in which organizations function and not to individual pathology. In modern organizations, a person's worth is typically measured by subjective assessments of others and not by objective criteria. But because of the evaluators' desire to be kind and especially to avoid confrontations, negative appraisals are likely to be expressed ambiguously and to be softened by compliments. Unfortunately, some people cannot discriminate between mere politeness and heartfelt praise. For the pronoid, even an exchange of pleasantries may be interpreted as an expression of friendship and support.

Source: Zick Rubin, "The invasion of the pronoids," *Psychology Today*, February 1984, p. 18.

behavior that has been punished is less likely to occur again.

Kinds of Reinforcement A *reinforcement* is an action that follows directly from a particular behavior. It may be a pay raise following a particularly large sale to a new customer, or a reprimand for coming to work late. Reinforcements can take a variety of forms and can be used in a number of different ways. A *positive reinforcement* is one that strengthens desired behavior by providing a reward. For example, many employees respond well to praise. Recognition from their supervisor after they have done a good job increases (strengthens) their willingness to perform well in the future.

A *negative reinforcement* strengthens desired behavior by eliminating an undesirable task or situation. Suppose that workers in a machine shop are required to clean the facility every month. Because of the nature of the work, cleaning up is a dirty, miserable task. During one particular month when the workers do an outstanding job at their normal work assignments, the boss hires a private maintenance service to clean up the facility. The employees will be motivated to work equally hard during the next month, in hopes of avoiding the unpleasant cleanup task again.

Punishment is an undesired consequence that follows from undesirable behavior. Common forms of punishment used in organizations include reprimands, docked (reduced) pay, disciplinary layoffs, and termination (firing). Punishment often does more harm than good. It tends to create an unpleasant environment, fosters hostility and resentment, and suppresses undesirable behavior only until the supervisor's back is turned.

Managers who rely on *extinction* hope to eliminate undesirable behavior by ignoring it. The idea is that the behavior will eventually become "extinct." Suppose, for example, that an employee has the habit of writing memo after memo to his or her manager about insignificant events. If the

manager doesn't respond to any of these memos, the employee will probably stop writing them; and the behavior will become extinguished.

Using Reinforcement The effectiveness of reinforcement depends on which type is used and how it is timed. Each of the four types is best in certain situations. However, many situations lend themselves to the use of more than one type. Generally, positive reinforcement is considered the most effective, and it is recommended when the manager has a choice.

Continual, repetitious reinforcement can become tedious for both manager and employees, especially when the same behavior is being reinforced over and over in the same way. At the start, it may be necessary to reinforce a desired behavior every time it occurs. However, once a desired behavior has become more or less established, occasional reinforcement seems to be most effective.

A number of firms have applied reinforcement theory in the work place. Procter & Gamble, Warner-Lambert, Ford Motor Company, and Emery Air Freight have all reported success with the systematic use of positive reinforcement to reward desired behavior. At Emery, for example, management felt that air-freight containers (used to consolidate many small shipments into fewer large ones) were not being utilized effectively. Through an innovative system based on positive reinforcement, Emery was able to increase container utilization from 45 percent of capacity to over 95 percent. As a result, Emery saved $3 million in the first three years of the program.

ORGANIZATIONAL REWARD SYSTEMS AND EMPLOYEE MOTIVATION

Up to now, we have focused our attention on theories and models of employee motivation. Many of these may be difficult for the practicing manager to apply. Those that are used generally become part of the organization's **reward system**, which is the formal mechanism for defining, evaluating, and rewarding employee performance. A reward system should motivate employees to work effectively in order to receive desired outcomes from the organization. It should also

Figure 8.5 *The Four Main Features of a Successful Reward System*

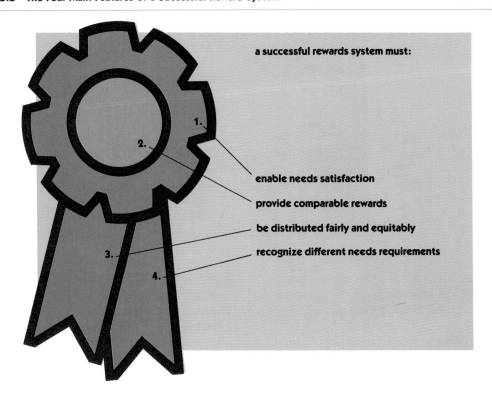

a successful rewards system must:

1. enable needs satisfaction
2. provide comparable rewards
3. be distributed fairly and equitably
4. recognize different needs requirements

have a positive impact on employee satisfaction and morale.

Effective Reward Systems

A reward system must accomplish four things if it is to be truly effective. First, it must enable people to satisfy their basic needs. In terms of Maslow's hierarchy of needs, for example, rewards should enable employees to satisfy the first two levels.

Second, an effective reward system should provide rewards comparable to those offered by other organizations. According to equity theory, employees at one firm will experience inequity if they think their outcome-to-input ratios are lower than those of employees at some other firm. This can result in decreased effort or increased turnover.

Third, rewards must be distributed fairly and equitably within the organization. People are more likely to compare themselves with others in their own firm than with workers elsewhere. Hence perceptions of equity come into play here as well. Moreover, a strong relationship between performance and reward is consistent with both expectancy theory and reinforcement theory.

Fourth, an effective reward system must recognize the fact that different people have different needs and may choose different paths to the fulfillment of those needs. Some people want economic gain, while others want more leisure time. Some people may want to earn more money by simply working longer hours in their current positions. Others may want to earn more money through promotions and new job opportunities (Figure 8.5).

New Kinds of Reward Systems

Money will always be an important part of the rewards employees expect. The two most commonly used monetary reward systems are fixed-rate systems and incentive systems. In *fixed-rate systems*, employees are paid a set amount for the work they do during some specified period—an hour, a day, a week, a month, or a year. In *incentive systems*, employees are paid a set amount for each unit they produce. Taylor's piece-rate system, which we described earlier, is an incentive system. The commission system, in which an employee is paid a percentage of his or her sales volume, is also an incentive system.

In their attempt to discover new and effective ways to enhance employee motivation, managers have begun to search for innovative reward systems. Among those now being explored are the all-salaried work force, the skill-based job-evaluation system, lump-sum salary increases, and the cafeteria benefits plan.

All-Salaried Work Force No member of an all-salaried work force punches a time clock or has a rigidly defined work schedule. Instead, every employee receives a guaranteed monthly salary, regardless of the time actually worked. Performance—rather than time—is the basis for this reward system, and employees are expected to get a certain amount of work done. If some employees need more time to complete their work, they are expected to put in that time without additional compensation, just as managers typically do. IBM, Dow Chemical, and Gillette are experimenting with the all-salaried work force.

Skill-Based Job Evaluation In conventional reward systems, all employees who do the same job are paid about the same amount, regardless of how well they perform. In the skill-based job-evaluation system, however, it is the person rather than the job that defines the compensation. If two people work at the same job, but one is considerably more skilled than the other, then the more skilled employee receives the higher pay. Usually a person's pay is adjusted upward for each new skill or job that she or he masters. Texas Instruments and General Foods have reported successful experiences with skill-based job-evaluation systems.

Table 8.2 *Types of Reward Systems*

Type	Description
Fixed	Employees are paid a set amount of money for the work they do during a specific time.
Incentive	Employees are paid a set amount of money for each unit produced. Taylor's piece-rate system and a commission sales position are two examples.
All-salaried work force	Employees receive a guaranteed monthly salary, regardless of the time actually worked. IBM, Dow Chemical, and Gillette are experimenting with this system.
Skill-based job evaluation	If two people work at the same job, but one is considerably more skilled than the other, then the more skilled employee receives the higher pay. Texas Instruments and General Foods have reported successful experiences with skill-based job-evaluation systems.
Lump-sum salary increases	Employees are allowed to take their entire pay raise in one lump sum at the beginning of the year and draw his or her "regular" pay the rest of the year. B. F. Goodrich, Aetna Life and Casualty, and Timex have all used variations of this plan.
Cafeteria benefits plan	Employees are allotted a certain amount of benefits money to "spend" as they see fit in the "benefits cafeteria." American Can Company and TRW have used this plan.

Lump-Sum Salary Increases In traditional reward systems, an employee who receives an annual pay increase is given part of the increase in each pay period. For example, suppose an employee on a monthly salary gets a 10 percent annual pay hike. He or she actually receives 10 percent of the former monthly salary added to each month's paycheck for a year. Companies that offer lump-sum salary increases give the employee the option of taking the entire pay raise in one lump sum at the beginning of the year. The employee then draws his or her "regular" pay for the rest of the year. The lump-sum payment is typically treated as an interest-free loan that must be repaid if the employee leaves the firm during the year. B. F. Goodrich, Aetna Life and Casualty, and Timex have all used variations of this plan.

Cafeteria Benefits Plan The usual reward system includes not only pay but also a set "package" of benefits. These may include health insurance, paid vacations, paid holidays, a retirement plan, life insurance, and other benefits. Some employ-

ees take advantage of all these benefits; others do not. Those who do not use certain benefits simply don't get them. For example, employees who choose not to take all their allotted vacation receive nothing in return; they just don't get all their vacation time.

Under the cafeteria benefits plan, employees are allotted a certain amount of benefits money to "spend" as they see fit in the "benefits cafeteria." They may use it to purchase whatever benefits they would like most. In a two-wage-earner family, one spouse might elect not to take health insurance (because the other spouse has a better plan) and to take additional vacation time instead. Similarly, a single employee with no dependents may by-pass life insurance in favor of other options.

Many employees like this approach, but it is quite costly to manage and administer. In spite of the cost, American Can Company and TRW have set up cafeteria benefits plans for their employees.

In 1983, a comprehensive flexible benefits

plan, similar to a cafeteria benefits plan, was instituted at Comerica, Michigan's second largest bank-holding company. The plan, called "Custom Comp," allows employees to customize their benefits compensation: medical insurance, life insurance, disability coverage, and vacation benefits. Each employee must take some coverage in each of the four categories, but the employee can set the level of coverage. Mellon Bank, PepsiCo, and Quaker Oats also use plans like Custom Comp.

Offering rewards (Table 8.2) is not the only way organizations can motivate employees. In the next section we will look at several other inducements to high performance.

KEY MOTIVATION TECHNIQUES

Several specific techniques have been developed to help managers boost employee motivation. Some of these have already been discussed in other contexts, but we will review them here.

Management by Objectives

Management by objectives (MBO) is a process in which a manager and his or her subordinates collaborate in setting goals. The primary purpose of MBO is to clarify the roles that the subordinates are expected to play in reaching the organization's goals. At the same time, MBO allows subordinates to participate in goal setting and in performance evaluation, thus increasing their motivation. Most MBO programs consist of a series of five steps (Figure 8.6).

The first step in setting up an MBO program is to secure the acceptance of top management. It is essential that top managers endorse and participate in the program if others in the firm are to accept it. The acceptance of top management also provides a natural starting point for educating employees in the purposes and mechanics of MBO.

Next, preliminary goals must be established. Top management also plays a major role in this

Figure 8.6 *The Five Steps Required for an Effective MBO Program*

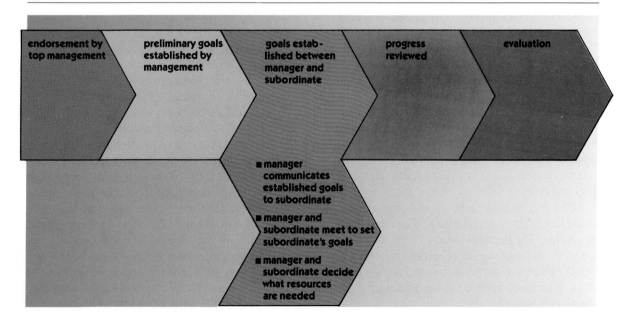

endorsement by top management

preliminary goals established by management

goals established between manager and subordinate

■ manager communicates established goals to subordinate

■ manager and subordinate meet to set subordinate's goals

■ manager and subordinate decide what resources are needed

progress reviewed

evaluation

activity, because the preliminary goals reflect the firm's mission and strategy. The intent is to have these goals filter down through the organization.

The third step, which actually consists of several smaller steps, is the essence of MBO. (1) The manager explains to subordinates that he or she has accepted certain goals for the group (manager plus subordinates) and asks subordinates to think about how they can help achieve these goals. (2) The manager later meets with each subordinate individually. Together, the two of them establish goals for the subordinate. Whenever possible, the goals should be measurable and should include a time within which they will be fulfilled (usually one year). K mart, for example, sets annual goals in terms of sales dollars per square foot of floor space. (3) The manager and the subordinate decide what resources the subordinate will need to accomplish his or her goals.

As the fourth step, the manager and each subordinate meet periodically to review the subordinate's progress. Goals may be modified during these meetings if circumstances have changed. For example, a sales representative may have accepted a goal of increasing sales by 20 percent. However, a new competitor may have entered the marketplace, making this goal unattainable. In light of this new information, the goal may be revised downward to 10 or 15 percent.

The fifth step in the MBO process is evaluation. At the end of the designated period, the manager and each subordinate meet again to determine which of the subordinate's goals were met, which goals were not met, and why. The employee's reward (in the form of pay raises, praise, or promotion) is based on the degree of goal attainment.

MBO has proved to be an effective motivational tool in many organizations. Tenneco, Black & Decker, Du Pont, General Foods, RCA, and General Motors have all reported success with MBO. Like any management technique, however, it must be applied with caution and in the right spirit if it is to work.

Job Enrichment

This concept was discussed in Chapter 6. There, we noted that job enrichment is an alternative to job specialization. It is an attempt to provide workers with variety in their tasks, and it accords them some responsibility for, and control over, their jobs. In this chapter we noted that Herzberg's motivation-hygiene theory is one basis for the use of job enrichment; that is, the added responsibility and control that job enrichment confers on employees increase their satisfaction and motivation.

Modified Workweeks

Modified workweeks were also discussed in Chapter 6. The compressed workweek, the flexible workweek, and job sharing were described as alternatives to traditional work schedules. Modified workweeks can also be used to enhance employee motivation. If an employee is permitted to decide when to work, he or she will develop a feeling of autonomy and professionalism. This, in turn, leads to increased motivation.

Employee Participation

Employee participation in decision making is frequently cited as a motivation-boosting technique. When employees are given a voice in determining what they will be doing and where the organization should be going, they develop a sense of involvement and commitment. This feeling should readily lead to enhanced motivation.

An increasingly popular method of soliciting employee participation is by applying Ouchi's Theory Z (Chapter 5)—and, in particular, quality circles. Recall from Chapter 7 that quality circles are groups of volunteer employees who meet to help solve problems related to product quality. This form of participation actually provides two advantages: increased employee motivation and solutions to organizational problems. At Jones & Laughlin Steel Corp. in Cleveland, labor-and-management participation teams have sought out and solved the more difficult production and maintenance problems.

Behavior Modification

This technique is based on reinforcement theory, which we discussed earlier in this chapter. As applied to management, **behavior modification** is the use of a systematic program of reinforcement to encourage desirable organizational behavior (Figure 8.7).

Use of the technique begins with the identification of target behavior—behavior that is to be changed. (It may be low production levels or a high rate of absenteeism, for example.) Existing levels of this behavior are then measured. Next, managers provide positive reinforcement in the form of rewards when employees exhibit the desired behavior (such as increased production or less absenteeism). Finally, the levels of the target behavior are measured again, to determine whether the desired changes have been achieved. If they have, the reinforcement is maintained in order to avoid extinction. However, if the target behavior has not changed in the desired direction, the reinforcement (reward) system must be changed to one that is likely to be more effective.

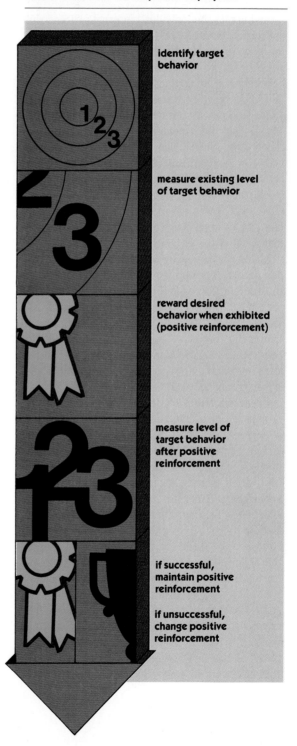

Figure 8.7 *Behavior Modification. Behavior modification is a motivation technique designed to reinforce desirable behavior on the part of employees.*

identify target behavior

measure existing level of target behavior

reward desired behavior when exhibited (positive reinforcement)

measure level of target behavior after positive reinforcement

if successful, maintain positive reinforcement

if unsuccessful, change positive reinforcement

Chapter Review

SUMMARY

Motivation is the individual, internal process that energizes, directs, and sustains behavior. One of the first approaches to employee motivation was Frederick Taylor's scientific management. Taylor believed that employees work only for money and that they must be closely supervised and managed. Douglas McGregor labeled this view Theory X and then described an alternative view called Theory Y. Theory Y is more in keeping with the results of the Hawthorne studies (which showed the importance of social processes in the work place) and with the human-relations movement (which was based on the idea that employees can be motivated to behave as responsible members of the organization).

Maslow's hierarchy of needs suggests that people may be motivated by five sets of needs. In order of decreasing importance, these needs are called the physiological, safety, social, esteem, and self-realization needs. People are motivated by the most important set (or level) of needs that remains unfulfilled. As needs at one level are satisfied, people move on to try to satisfy needs in the next level.

Frederick Herzberg found that satisfaction and dissatisfaction are influenced by two different sets of factors. Hygiene factors, including pay and working conditions, affect an employee's degree of dissatisfaction but do not affect satisfaction. Motivation factors, including recognition and responsibility, affect an employee's degree of satisfaction but do not affect the degree of dissatisfaction.

There are three major contemporary motivation theories. Equity theory maintains that people are motivated to obtain and preserve equitable treatment for themselves. Expectancy theory suggests that our motivation depends on how much we want something and how likely we think we are to get it. And reinforcement theory is based on the idea that people will repeat behavior that is rewarded and won't repeat behavior that is punished.

Effective reward systems must satisfy basic needs, they must be both externally and internally equitable, and they must recognize that people have a variety of needs. Traditional reward systems are based on fixed rate or incentives. Several new types of reward systems seem to provide additional motivation to employees.

Managers have a variety of techniques available for enhancing employee motivation. Key techniques include management by objectives, in which the manager and subordinate set goals for the subordinate together, and behavior modification, which is based on reinforcement theory. Also job enrichment, modified workweeks, and employee participation can be used to motivate employees.

The design of reward systems (and other personnel-related systems) is part of a broader set of activities called human resources management. These activities are the subject of the next chapter.

KEY TERMS

You should now be able to define and give an example relevant to each of the following terms:

motivation

morale

scientific management

piece-rate system

Theory X

Theory Y

needs

hierarchy of needs

physiological needs

safety needs

social needs

esteem needs

self-realization needs

motivation-hygiene theory

motivation factors

hygiene factors

equity theory

expectancy theory

reinforcement theory

reward system

management by objectives (MBO)

behavior modification

QUESTIONS AND EXERCISES
Review Questions

1. Compare the two earlier schools of thought on motivation: scientific management and Theory X versus the human-relations movement and Theory Y.
2. How did the results of the Hawthorne studies affect researchers' thinking about employee motivation?
3. What are the five sets of needs in Maslow's hierarchy? How are a person's needs related to motivation?
4. What are the two dimensions in Herzberg's motivation-hygiene theory? What kinds of things affect each factor?
5. According to equity theory, how does an employee determine whether he or she is being treated equitably?
6. According to expectancy theory, what two things determine motivation?
7. What is the basic premise of reinforcement theory?
8. What are the four attributes of an effective reward system?
9. What is the prime motivating factor in the all-salaried reward system? in the skill-based job-evaluation system?
10. Describe the steps involved in the MBO process.
11. What are the objectives of MBO? What do you think might be its disadvantages?
12. How does employee participation—as in quality circles—increase motivation?
13. Describe the steps in the process of behavior modification.

Discussion Questions

1. Some people argue that when Tandem Computers becomes a truly large organization, Treybig will not be able to continue offering the benefits and incentives he now provides. Do you agree or disagree? Why?
2. In what ways does Tandem's motivational system illustrate the various theories of employee motivation?
3. How might managers make use of the hierarchy of needs in motivating employees? What problems would they encounter?
4. Do the various theories of motivation contradict each other or complement each other? Explain.
5. What combination of motivational techniques do you think would result in the best overall motivation and reward system?
6. Reinforcement theory and behavior modification have been called demeaning because they tend to treat people "like mice in a maze." Do you agree?

Exercises

1. Analyze the system that is used in your school to motivate and reward students. Determine (a) the theory or theories on which it is based and (b) how it could be improved.
2. Suppose you are the owner of a neighborhood hardware store with two employees besides yourself. What motivational problems might you encounter? What techniques could you use to minimize these problems?
3. Devise a reward system for the hardware store of Exercise 2. Make sure it has all the attributes of an effective reward system *and* takes into consideration the hardware store "environment."

CASE 8-1

Motivating a Family Business

Bob Harrison is facing the biggest problem of his brief management career. Bob took over his father's prosperous manufacturing firm 18 months ago, after the elder Harrison died.

Mr. Harrison had been what some people might call a leader, but he wasn't much of a manager. For one thing, he refused to delegate. He personally hired all employees, determined their salaries, and stayed in close touch with each and every one. He kept few records. Salary information, for example, was recorded on a note pad he kept in a desk drawer. He did, however, earn a strong reputation for fairness. He told employees how they were doing, what their raises would be, and how they could do better next time.

Bob majored in business at the state university. He had just started with a large corporation when his father died, but he resigned to head the family business. Many employees knew Bob as a child, making it tense when he became their boss.

Bob buried himself in company records to learn as much as possible about the organization. He found that the company was not as financially healthy as everyone believed. On several occasions, the firm had barely been able to meet its payroll. Once Mr. Harrison had even used his own money to give an employee a small raise.

Bob took steps to restore the firm's financial health. First he announced a two-year wage freeze. He also terminated 10 percent of the firm's work force. To eliminate any resentment, he announced that he would cut his own 10 percent pay hike to only 5 percent.

Two weeks later absenteeism increased sharply. Production supervisors reported a decline in product quality and suspected vandalism in several machine breakdowns. Bob has also heard that employees are considering a strike.

1. Which motivation theories and concepts might explain what has happened at this firm?
2. What can Bob do to restore order?

CASE 8-2

RMI

RMI is a producer of titanium and titanium products, mainly for the aircraft industry. For a number of years, the firm's productivity and profit—and its employees' morale—had been well below standard. Then, in 1976, James Daniell was brought into the company as chief executive officer. Things began to change almost immediately; by 1979, RMI's *profit* was almost as large as its 1976 gross sales.

What Daniell brought to RMI was a strong orientation toward people—in particular, the firm's work force. His leadership style was simplicity itself: he enjoyed his job, and he did his best to see that hourly wage employees enjoyed theirs.

One part of his motivational program was smiles—on the company's logo, on signs throughout the plant, on workers' hard hats, and usually on "Big Jim" Daniell's face. He could often be found in the factory, joking or conversing with the firm's 2200 workers, calling each of them by his or her first name, and listening to what they had to say.

Other motivational techniques were just as simple and "cost-effective." When Daniell first arrived at RMI, the plant was dark and dingy; he and his employees brightened it up, even adding flowers. At that time, only he and a few key employees had reserved parking spaces in the company parking lot. Daniell gave all employees their own reserved spaces—with the employee's name on each spot. Suddenly, the parking lot, too, was a lot more pleasant—and cleaner—than it had been. Daniell also provided employees with an outdoor lunch area, where they could eat in a picnic-type setting, in the belief that even such simple changes have a direct effect on productivity.

The result, for workers, has been a very pleasant place to work—the best place in town, according to most. For the company, Daniell's new leadership has provided greatly increased productivity, revenues, and profits, and a tremendous decline in union grievances.

In 1982, Daniell told an interviewer that he hadn't taken a vacation in five years. "This is my hobby. I don't want to retire," he said. "I have a responsibility to 2200 families here."[3] He continued to bear that responsibility until his death in December 1983, at age 65.[4]

1. In what ways do Daniell's motivational techniques illustrate or contradict the various theories of motivation?
2. Big Jim Daniell was a former professional football player, the first captain of the Cleveland Browns. What connection might there be between this background and his effectiveness as RMI's chief executive officer?

CHAPTER

NINE
Human Resources Management

Human resources "Я" us, the people who work for a living. Manager or operating employee, full-time or part-time, permanent or temporary—any job at all includes membership in the unique and important league of human resources. Businesses couldn't do without us. As you saw in Chapter 8, they keep trying to develop better ways to motivate us. And, as you'll see in this chapter, they try just as hard to find, hire, train, and evaluate us. After studying this chapter, you should understand:

1. **The nature of human resources management**
2. **Some of the major legislation affecting human resources management**
3. **The steps in human-resource planning**
4. **The objectives and uses of job analysis**
5. **The processes of recruiting, employee selection, and orientation**
6. **The primary elements of employee compensation and benefits**
7. **The purposes and techniques of employee training, development, and performance appraisal**

Consider this:

Professional sports have certainly changed! There was a time when professionals played baseball, football, basketball, and other sports for their own pleasure and for the enjoyment of others. If they were able to throw a few dollars into the bargain, so much the better. In recent years, however, free agency, rival leagues, and escalating salaries have dramatically changed the complexion of things.

Team owners and players alike now see sports as a business. Owners seek to maximize their profits via hefty television contracts and higher ticket prices. Players seek to maximize their salaries by engaging agents and personal representatives. They also use two negotiating techniques that seem to be unique to sports: free agency and arbitration. The new relationships between owners and players have led to some strange circumstances. And no circumstances are more bizarre than those surrounding the practice of salary arbitration in professional baseball.

Arbitration began in 1974. Any player whose contract with a team has expired, and who has between two and six years of major league experience, is eligible for arbitration. Players who have gone through the free agent draft and who have more than six years of major league experience are also eligible for arbitration. Contracts for the next baseball season must be mailed to these players by December 20 of each year. Among other things, the contracts specify the team's salary offer. If a player does not want to accept his contract and the salary offer, he has until January 25 to file for arbitration. (If the contract is not mailed by December 20, the player is a free agent and may seek employment with any professional baseball team. If the player does not file for arbitration by January 25, he must accept the contract or drop out of baseball for one year.)

Even if a player files for arbitration, he and the club may still come to terms before the date of the arbitration hearing. At the hearing, which is usually held early in February, the player's agent and someone representing the team management present their cases to a federal arbitrator. The arbitrator then decides whether the player is to be paid his asking price or the last offer made by the team. There is no further appeal.

Some fairly dramatic salary changes have occurred in the last 10 years. In 1974 an infielder for the Oakland A's named Jack Heidemann filed for arbitration, asking for a salary of $15,600. He lost and received only $12,800, management's last offer prior to the hearing. In 1983 Texas Ranger infielder Buddy Samples filed for arbitra-

Well-known athletes such as Jim Rice are often candidates for free agency. Source: Rick Friedman, The Picture Cube.

tion and asked for a salary of $300,000. Management had originally offered $175,000 but then had increased its offer to $215,000 in an effort to sign Samples before the hearing. Samples lost the hearing but still got the $40,000 raise!

Arbitration cases can have unusual repercussions as well. Los Angeles Dodger pitcher Fernando Valenzuela, after only his second year in the league, asked for an increase from $330,000 to $1 million. The Dodgers offered $750,000. Valenzuela went to arbitration and won, which made him the third-highest-paid player in baseball history. Philadelphia Phillies pitcher Steve Carlton, who was a senior in high school when Valenzuela was born, was close to a contract agreement at the time (he was not eligible for arbitration). Upon hearing of the arbitrator's decision, Carlton angrily demanded that he be paid more money than Valenzuela. Philadelphia had little choice but to go along—to the tune of $4.15 million for 4 years.

Arbitration inevitably breeds conflict between a team's management and its players. If management says anything good about a player, the player's agent can use it in the arbitration hearing to justify the player's higher salary demands. Hence management must actually look for ways to downgrade the player. Yet, at the same time, it is in management's interest to motivate players to do their best. A winning season means added ticket revenues during the season and, perhaps, playoff and World Series revenues. It may also mean bonuses and other added income for players.

All in all, arbitration may lead to a situation in which the player cannot lose. But it takes its toll in strained relations between players and team management.[1]

Professional sports teams seem to do things in their own unique ways. But are these ways really unique? Or are they only exaggerations of ordinary business practices? For example, professional teams send out scouts to discover and interview potential team members. But other businesses use employment advertising and interviewers for the same purpose. Professional athletes have free agency and arbitration. But in other businesses, almost all employees are free agents—free to work where they will obtain the greatest reward. And labor arbitration is not unique to sports.

In other respects (including compensation, training, and player evaluation) the practices of professional teams parallel those of business in general. Again, these practices are exaggerated by the typically high salaries of professional athletes, the intense interest of sports fans, and daily reports by the news media. But they are all part of human resources management, and human resources management is a necessary function of every organization.

HUMAN RESOURCES MANAGEMENT: AN OVERVIEW

The human resource is not only unique and valuable; it is an organization's most important resource. It seems logical that the organization would expend a great deal of effort to acquire and utilize such a resource, and most organizations do. That effort is now known as *human resources management,* or HRM. It has also been called *staffing* and *personnel management.*

Human resources management consists of all the activities involved in acquiring, maintaining, and developing an organization's human resources. As the definition implies, HRM begins with acquisition—getting people to work for the organization. Next, steps must be taken to keep these valuable resources (they are the only business resources that can leave the organization at will). Finally, the human resources should be developed to their full capacity to contribute to the firm. (See Figure 9.1.)

HRM Activities

Each of the three phases of HRM—acquiring, maintaining, and developing human resources—consists of a number of related activities. Acquisition, for example, includes planning as well as the various activities that lead to the hiring of new personnel. Altogether, this phase of HRM includes five separate activities:

☐ *Human-resource planning,* to determine the firm's future human-resource needs
☐ *Job analysis,* to determine the exact nature of positions that are to be filled
☐ *Recruiting,* to attract people to apply for positions in the firm
☐ *Selection,* to choose and hire the most qualified applicants
☐ *Orientation,* to acquaint new employees with the firm

Figure 9.1 *Activities of Human Resources Management. HRM activities consist of all the efforts involved in acquiring, maintaining, and developing an organization's human resources.*

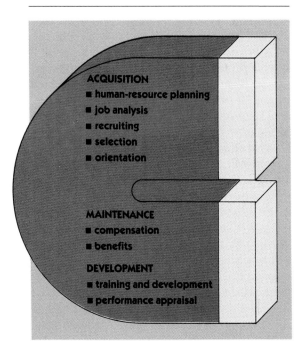

Maintaining human resources consists primarily of motivating employees to remain with the firm and to work effectively. Since motivation was discussed at length in Chapter 8, we shall concentrate here on some additional aspects of

☐ *Compensation and benefits,* to reward employee effort

The development phase of HRM is concerned with the improvement of employees' skills and the expansion of their capabilities. There are two important activities within this phase:

☐ *Training and development,* to teach employees new skills, new jobs, and more effective ways of doing their present jobs
☐ *Performance appraisal,* to assess employees' current and potential performance levels

These activities will be discussed in more detail shortly, when we have completed this overview of human resources management.

Responsibility for HRM

In general, human resources management is a shared responsibility of line managers and staff HRM specialists.

In very small organizations, the owner is usually both a line manager and the staff personnel specialist. He or she handles all or most HRM activities. As the firm grows in size, a personnel manager is generally hired to take over most of the staff responsibilities. As growth continues, additional staff positions are added as needed. In firms as large as, say, Bristol-Myers Company, HRM activities tend to be very highly specialized. There may be separate groups to deal with compensation, training and development programs, and the other staff activities.

Specific HRM activities are assigned to those who are in the best position to perform them. Human-resource planning and job analysis are usually done by staff specialists, with input from line managers. Similarly, recruiting and selection are generally handled by staff experts, although line managers are involved in the actual hiring decisions. Orientation programs are usually devised by staff specialists, and the orientation itself is carried out by both staff specialists and line managers. Compensation systems (including benefits) are most often developed and administered by the HRM staff. However, line managers recommend pay increases and promotions. Training and development activities are usually the joint responsibility of staff and line managers. Performance appraisal is the job of the line manager, although HRM staff personnel are likely to design the firm's appraisal system.

The Legal Environment of HRM

Legislation regarding personnel practices has been passed mainly to protect the rights of employees, to promote job safety, and to eliminate discrimination in the work place. Seven pieces of legislation and one set of executive orders are of primary concern. (See Figure 9.2.)

Title VII of the Civil Rights Act of 1964   This law applies directly to selection and promotion. It forbids organizations to discriminate in those areas on the basis of sex, race, color, religion, or national origin. Hence the purpose of Title VII is to ensure that employers make personnel decisions on the basis of employee qualifications only. As a result of this act, discrimination in employment (especially against blacks) has been sharply curtailed in this country.

The Equal Employment Opportunity Commission (EEOC) is charged with enforcing Title VII. If a person believes that he or she has been discriminated against, that person can file a complaint with the EEOC. The EEOC investigates the complaint. If it finds that the person has, in fact, been the victim of discrimination, it can take legal action on his or her behalf.

Age Discrimination in Employment Act   This Act was passed in 1967 and amended in 1978. Its general purpose is the same as that of Title VII—to eliminate discrimination. However, as the name implies, the Age Discrimination in Employ-

ment Act is concerned only with discrimination based on age. In particular, it outlaws personnel practices that discriminate against people between the ages of 40 and 69. (No federal law forbids discrimination against people younger than 40, but several states have adopted age-discrimination laws that apply to a variety of age groups.) Also outlawed are company policies that require employees to retire before age 70.

Fair Labor Standards Act   This Act, which was passed originally in 1938 and has been amended many times, applies primarily to wages. It establishes such things as minimum wages and overtime pay rates. Many managers and other professionals, however, are exempt from this law. Managers, for example, seldom get paid overtime when they work more than 40 hours in a week.

Equal Pay Act   This law, passed in 1963, overlaps somewhat with Title VII of the Civil Rights Act. The Equal Pay Act specifies that men and women who are doing equal jobs must be paid the same wage. Equal jobs are jobs that demand equal effort, skill, and responsibility and that are performed under the same conditions. Differences in pay are legal if they can be attributed to differences in seniority, qualifications, or performance. But women cannot be paid less (or more) for the same work solely because they are women.

Employee Retirement Income Security Act   This act was passed in 1974 to protect the retirement benefits of employees. It does not require that firms provide a retirement plan. However, it does specify that *if* a retirement plan is provided, it must be managed in such a way that the interests of employees are protected. It also provides federal insurance for retirement plans that go bankrupt.

Occupational Safety and Health Act   This law, passed in 1970, is concerned mainly with issues of employee health and safety. For example, the act regulates the degree to which employees can be exposed to hazardous substances. It also specifies the safety equipment that must be provided.

The Occupational Safety and Health Administration (OSHA) was created to enforce this act. Inspectors from OSHA investigate employee complaints regarding unsafe working conditions. They also make spot checks on companies operating in particularly hazardous industries, such as chemicals and mining, to ensure compliance with the law. A firm that is found to be in violation of federal standards can be fined heavily or even shut down.

National Labor Relations Act and Labor–Management Relations Act These laws are concerned with dealings between business firms and labor

Figure 9.2 *Federal Legislation That Focuses on Human Resources Management. These seven pieces of legislation have been passed to protect the rights of employees, promote job safety, and eliminate discrimination in the workplace.*

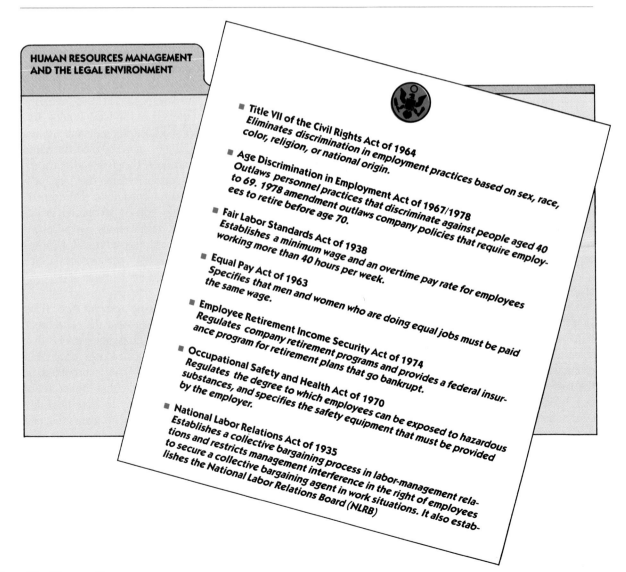

HUMAN RESOURCES MANAGEMENT AND THE LEGAL ENVIRONMENT

- **Title VII of the Civil Rights Act of 1964**
  Eliminates discrimination in employment practices based on sex, race, color, religion, or national origin.

- **Age Discrimination in Employment Act of 1967/1978**
  Outlaws personnel practices that discriminate against people aged 40 to 69. 1978 amendment outlaws company policies that require employees to retire before age 70.

- **Fair Labor Standards Act of 1938**
  Establishes a minimum wage and an overtime pay rate for employees working more than 40 hours per week.

- **Equal Pay Act of 1963**
  Specifies that men and women who are doing equal jobs must be paid the same wage.

- **Employee Retirement Income Security Act of 1974**
  Regulates company retirement programs and provides a federal insurance program for retirement plans that go bankrupt.

- **Occupational Safety and Health Act of 1970**
  Regulates the degree to which employees can be exposed to hazardous substances, and specifies the safety equipment that must be provided by the employer.

- **National Labor Relations Act of 1935**
  Establishes a collective bargaining process in labor-management relations and restricts management interference in the right of employees to secure a collective bargaining agent in work situations. It also establishes the National Labor Relations Board (NLRB)

unions. This general area is, in concept, a part of human resources management. However, because of its importance, it is often treated as a separate set of activities. We shall discuss both labor-management relations and these two acts in detail in Chapter 10.

Affirmative Action A series of executive orders, issued by the president of the United States, established the requirement for affirmative action in personnel practices. The requirement applies to all employers holding contracts with the federal government. It prescribes that such employers (1) actively encourage job applications from members of minority groups and (2) hire qualified employees from minority groups that are not fully represented in their organizations. Many firms that do not hold government contracts take part voluntarily in this affirmative-action program.

It is against this background of regulations and guidelines that human-resource planners must make decisions involving personnel recruiting and selection. But even before considering *whom* they need, they must forecast *how many*.

HUMAN-RESOURCE PLANNING

Human-resource planning is the development of strategies for meeting the firm's future human-resource needs. The starting point for this planning is the organization's overall strategic plan. From this, human-resource planners can forecast the firm's future demand for human resources. Next they must determine whether the needed human resources will be available; that is, they must forecast the supply of human resources within the firm. Finally, they have to take steps to match supply with demand.

Forecasting Human-Resource Demand

Forecasts of human-resource demand should be based on as much relevant information as planners can gather. The firm's overall strategic plan will provide information about future business

Standards for workplace safety set by the federal Occupational Safety and Health Administration are enforced by OSHA inspectors, who investigate employee complaints and make spot checks at potentially dangerous work sites.
Source: © Cary Wolinsky, Stock, Boston.

ventures, new products, and projected expansions or contractions of particular product lines. Information on past staffing levels, evolving technologies, industry staffing practices, and projected economic trends can also be very helpful.

All this information should be used to determine both the number of employees who will be required and their qualifications—including skills, experience, and knowledge. There are a variety of methods for forecasting specific personnel needs. In one simple method, personnel requirements are projected to increase or decrease in the same proportion as sales revenue. Thus, if a 30 percent increase in sales volume is projected over the next two years, a 30 percent increase in personnel requirements would be forecast over the same period. (This method can be applied to specific positions as well as to the work force in general. It is not, however, a very precise forecasting method.) At the other extreme are the elaborate computer-based personnel planning models used by some larger firms such as Exxon.

Forecasting Human-Resource Supply

The human-resource supply forecast must take into account both the present work force and any changes, or movements, that may occur within it. For example, suppose planners project that, in five years, the firm will need 100 more engineers than the 100 that are currently employed. They cannot simply assume that they will have to hire 100 engineers over the next five years. During that period, some of the firm's present engineers are likely to be promoted, leave the firm, or move to other jobs within the firm. Thus planners might project the supply of engineers in five years at 87, which means that a total of 113 (or more) would have to be hired.

Two useful techniques for forecasting human-resources supply are the replacement chart and the skills inventory. A **replacement chart** is a list of key personnel, along with possible replacements within the firm. The chart is maintained to ensure that top management positions can be filled fairly quickly in the event of an unexpected resignation or retirement. Some firms also provide additional training for those employees who might eventually replace top managers.

A **skills inventory** is a computerized data bank containing information on the skills and experience of all present employees. It is used to search for candidates to fill new or newly available positions. For a special project, a manager might be seeking a current employee with an engineering degree, at least six years of experience, and fluency in French. The skills inventory can identify quickly employees with such qualifications.

Matching Supply with Demand

Once they have forecasts of both the demand for personnel and the firm's supply of personnel, planners can devise a course of action for matching the two. When demand is forecast to be greater than supply, plans must be made to recruit and select new employees. The timing of these actions depends on the types of positions to be filled. Suppose we expect to open a new plant in five years. Along with other employees, a plant manager and 25 maintenance workers will be needed. We can probably wait quite a while before we begin to recruit maintenance personnel. However, because the job of plant manager is so critical, we may start searching for the right person for that position immediately.

When supply is forecast to be greater than demand, the firm must take steps to reduce the size of its work force. Several methods are available, although none of them is especially pleasant for managers or discharged employees. When the oversupply is expected to be temporary, some employees may be *laid off*—dismissed from the work force until they are needed again.

Perhaps the most humane method for making personnel cutbacks is through attrition. *Attrition* is the normal reduction in the work force that occurs when employees leave the firm. If these employees are not replaced, the work force eventually shrinks to the point where supply matches demand. Of course, attrition may be a very slow process—too slow to help the firm much.

Early retirement is another option that can sometimes be used. Under this method of reducing the size of the work force, people who are within a few years of retirement are permitted to retire early with full benefits. Depending on the age makeup of the work force, this may or may not reduce the staff enough. As a last resort, unneeded employees are sometimes simply *fired*. Because of its negative impact, this method is generally used only when absolutely necessary.

Even when human-resource planners know how many new employees the firm will need, one further step intervenes before these people can actually be hired. This step is job analysis.

JOB ANALYSIS

There is no sense in trying to hire people unless we know what we are hiring them for. In other words, we need to know the exact nature of a job before we can find the right person to do it.

Job analysis is a systematic procedure for studying jobs to determine their various elements and requirements. Consider the position of secretary, for example. In a large corporation, there may be 50 different kinds of secretarial positions. They all may be called "secretary," but each may be different from the others in the activities to be performed, the level of proficiency required for each activity, and the particular set of qualifications that the position demands. These are the things that job analysis focuses on.

The job analysis for a particular position typically consists of two parts—a job description and a job specification. A **job description** is a list of the elements that make up a particular job. It includes the duties the jobholder must perform, the working conditions under which the job must be performed, the jobholder's responsibilities (including number and types of subordinates, if any), and the tools and equipment that must be used on the job.

A **job specification** is a list of the qualifications required to perform a particular job. Included are the skills, abilities, education, and experience that the jobholder must have. (See Figure 9.3.)

The job analysis is the basis for recruiting and selecting new employees—for either existing positions or new ones. It is also used in other areas of human resources management, including evaluation and the determination of equitable compensation levels.

RECRUITING, SELECTION, AND ORIENTATION

In an organization with jobs waiting to be filled, HRM personnel need to (1) find candidates for those jobs and (2) match the right candidate with each job. Three activities are involved: recruiting, selection, and (for the new employees) orientation.

Recruiting

Recruiting is the process of attracting qualified job applicants. Because it is a vital link in a costly process (e.g., the average cost of hiring, moving, and training a computer programmer in 1981 was $60,000[2]), recruiting needs to be a systematic rather than haphazard process. One goal of recruiters is to attract the "right" number of applicants. The right number is enough to allow a good match between applicants and open positions, but not so many that matching them requires too much time and effort. For example, if there are five open positions and five applicants, the firm essentially has no choice. It must hire those five applicants (qualified or not) or the positions will remain open. At the other extreme, if several hundred people apply for the five positions, HRM personnel will have to spend weeks processing their applications.

Recruiters may seek applicants outside the firm, within the firm, or both. Which source is used generally depends on the nature of the position, the situation within the firm, and (sometimes) the firm's established or traditional recruitment policies.

Figure 9.3 *Job Description. A job description is a list of the elements that make up a particular position and the tasks that the employee is required to perform.*

MARTIN & MARTIN ENGINEERING CONSULTANTS, INC.	POSITION DESCRIPTION

Position: Accounts Payable Clerk   Date:

Reports to: Accounts Payable Supervisor   Analyst:

Division: Financial and Corporate Services   Approvals:

Department: Corporate Accounting

General Description This position is accountable for the timely processing of invoices in accordance with established procedures. Also, it is accountable for preparing the daily cash deposits, typing employee statements, and assisting the cashier.

Nature and Scope

This position reports directly to the Accounts Payable Supervisor who, in turn, reports to a Senior Accountant.

Workers in this position make up the Accounts Payable unit whose purpose is to process invoices received from all departments in accordance with established accounting procedures. These procedures include: (1) Checking the mathematical accuracy of the invoice. (2) Computing the amount of discount, if any. (3) Verifying the appropriateness of the information contained on the accounts payable sticker. (4) Completing the accounts payable sticker. (5) Verifying the appropriateness of the approval contained on the accounts payable sticker. (6) Batching and submitting invoices and checks to Comptroller for signature. (7) Proofreading the checks signed by the Comptroller. (8) Sending checks out. (9) Filing all documentation.

In addition to processing invoices, the worker is responsible for answering all inquiries received from vendors, following-up on overdue items when necessary, and responding to confirmation requests.

In preparing the daily cash deposit, the worker must post all checks to the cash receipt journal, total checks, prepare deposit slip, and send it to the bank.

The worker is also responsible for typing employee statements and assisting the cashier as deemed necessary. In this capacity, the worker may be asked to maintain the petty cash fund, balance journal vouchers and checks, issue stop payments, etc.

During the course of work the worker may speak to personnel throughout the company as well as outside vendors.

Principal Accountabilities

(1) Timely processing of invoices in accordance with established procedures. (2) Analyzing vendor statements, following up on overdue items. (3) Answering inquiries received from outside vendors. (4) Responding to audit confirmation requests. (5) Calculating cash discounts earned. (6) Preparing the daily cash deposit. (7) Typing employee statements.

External Recruiting **External recruiting** is the attempt to attract job applicants from outside the organization. Among the means that are available for external recruiting are newspaper advertising (Figure 9.4), recruiting on college campuses and in union hiring halls, applying to employment agencies, and soliciting the recommendations of present employees. In addition, many people who are looking for work simply apply at the firm's employment office.

Clearly, it is best to match the recruiting means with the kind of applicant being sought. For example, private employment agencies most often handle professional people, whereas public employment agencies (operated by state or local governments) are usually more concerned with operating personnel. Hence we might approach a private agency if we were looking for a vice president, but we would be more inclined to contact a public agency if we wanted to hire a machinist.

The primary advantage of external recruiting is that it enables the firm to bring in people with new perspectives and varied business backgrounds. It may also be the only way to attract applicants with the required skills and knowledge. On the other hand, external recruiting is often quite expensive, especially if private employment agencies must be used. External recruiting may also provoke resentment among present employees.

Figure 9.4 *Most Job Advertisements Include a Job Description as well as the Qualifications Required*

ACCOUNTS PAYABLE CLERK

Engineering consulting firm seeks versatile, experienced accounts payable clerk for processing invoices, preparing daily cash deposits, typing employee statements, and assisting the cashier. This challenging position requires thoroughness and an ability to follow established procedures. Experience with computerized systems is helpful. Competitive salary and benefits.

An Equal Opportunity Employer

Faked Credentials

More job candidates falsify their credentials today than in recent years, according to Thorndike Deland Assoc., a New York search firm.

Among 223 personnel officers polled, one-third say such deception has increased, while only one reports a decline. This problem is compounded by difficulty in checking references. Eighty-two percent of the respondents indicate that reference checking is troublesome, while 12 percent report their companies have had bad experiences recently, and plan to tighten hiring procedures.

The surveyed companies are most concerned with factors such as job performance and employment history (38 and 37 percent, respectively). Personality traits and interpersonal skills are third in importance (18 percent). Health and personal data each are cited as most important by fewer than 1 percent.

Job performance and personality (37 and 30 percent) are cited as the most difficult aspects to check, followed by salary history (15 percent).

Source: *Administrative Management*, December, 1982, p. 10.

Internal Recruiting **Internal recruiting** means considering present employees as applicants for available positions. Generally, current employees are considered for *promotion* to higher-level positions. However, employees may also be considered for *transfer* from one position to another at the same level.

Promoting from within provides strong motivation for current employees and helps the firm to retain quality personnel. General Electric, Exxon, Bell Telephone Laboratories, and Eastman Kodak are companies dedicated to promoting from within. (In cases where there is a strong union, the practice of *job posting,* or informing current employees of upcoming new openings, may be required by the union contract.) The primary disadvantage of internal recruiting is that promoting a current employee leaves another position to be filled. Not only does the firm still

Applicants for job openings may be recruited either internally among existing personnel or externally through advertising or other informational services, such as this job fair.
Source: © Chris Cross, Uniphoto.

incur recruiting and selection costs, but it must also train two employees instead of one.

In many situations, it may be impossible to recruit internally. For example, a new position may be such that no current employee is qualified to fill it. Or the firm may be growing so rapidly that there is no time to go through the reassigning of positions that promotion or transfer might require.

Selection

Selection is the process of gathering information about applicants for a position and then using that information to choose the most appropriate applicant. Note the use of the word *appropriate*. In selection, the idea is not to hire the person with the "most" qualifications, but rather to choose the applicant with the qualifications that are most appropriate for the job. The most commonly used means of obtaining information about applicants'

Figure 9.5 *Methods Commonly Used to Select Potential Employees. In the selection process several means may be used to determine the qualifications of candidates for a position. Information concerning the candidates is then carefully examined to narrow the pool of applicants to the single most appropriate person for the job.*

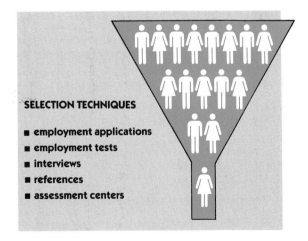

SELECTION TECHNIQUES

- employment applications
- employment tests
- interviews
- references
- assessment centers

qualifications are employment applications, tests, interviews, references, and assessment centers. (See Figure 9.5.)

Employment Applications   Nowadays, just about everyone who applies for anything must submit an application. You probably filled one out to apply to your school. Employment applications are useful in collecting factual information on a candidate's education, work experience, and personal history. (See Figure 9.6.) The data obtained from applications are usually used for two purposes: to identify candidates who are worthy of further scrutiny and to familiarize interviewers with applicants' backgrounds.

Many job candidates submit résumés to prospective employers, and some firms require them. A *résumé* is a one- or two-page summary of the candidate's background and qualifications, including the type of job the applicant is seeking. A résumé may be sent to a firm to request consideration for available jobs, or it may be submitted along with an employment application.

In recent years, a technique has been developed to determine the relative importance of information that is provided on applications and résumés. Current employees are asked which factors in their own backgrounds are most strongly related to their current jobs. Then these factors are given extra weight in assessing new applicants' qualifications to perform similar jobs.

Employment Tests   Tests that are given to job candidates usually focus on aptitudes, skills, abilities, or knowledge relevant to the job that is to be performed. Such tests (typing tests, for example) indicate how well the applicant will do on the job. Occasionally companies use general intelligence or personality tests, but these are seldom useful in predicting specific job performance.

At one time, a number of companies were criticized for using tests that were biased against members of certain minority groups—in particular, blacks. This practice of testing has largely been eliminated for two reasons. The test results were, to a great extent, unrelated to job perform-

Interviewing is almost always a part of the selection process. Ideally, an interview will give both the applicant and the interviewer a sense of how well each satisfies the other's requirements. Source: © 1984 Stacy Pick, Uniphoto.

ance. And to prove that they are not discriminating, firms must be able to demonstrate that the results of any tests they use are valid predictors of on-the-job performance. Applicants who believe they have been discriminated against in a test may file a complaint with the EEOC.

Interviews   The employment interview is perhaps the most widely used selection technique. Job candidates are usually interviewed by at least one member of the HRM staff and by the person for whom they will be working. Candidates for higher-level jobs may also meet with a department head or vice president and may have several additional interviews.

Interviews provide an opportunity for the applicant and the firm to learn more about each other. Interviewers can pose problems to test the candidate's abilities. They can probe employment history more deeply and learn something about the candidate's attitudes and motivation.

Figure 9.6 *A Typical Employment Application.* *Source: Courtesy of CBS Inc.*

CBS PERSONNEL RECORD

CBS POLICY AND FEDERAL AND STATE LAWS FORBID DISCRIMINATION BECAUSE OF AGE, COLOR, RACE, RELIGION, SEX OR NATIONAL ORIGIN. IF YOU ARE APPLYING FOR A POSITION IN THE FIELD OF BROADCASTING AND BELIEVE YOU HAVE BEEN DISCRIMINATED AGAINST FOR THE ABOVE, YOU MAY NOTIFY THE FEDERAL COMMUNICATIONS COMMISSION OR OTHER APPROPRIATE AGENCY. IN ADDITION, CBS POLICY FORBIDS DISCRIMINATION BASED ON SEXUAL ORIENTATION.

NOTE: WHERE AN ASTERISK (*) APPEARS, THE QUESTION NEED BE ANSWERED ONLY IF YOU ARE OFFERED A POSITION.

PERSONAL

Last Name	First	Initial	Today's date	Social Security number

Maiden Name*

Present address (Street, city, state, zip code)	Area code/Home telephone

Permanent address if different from above (Street, city, state, zip code)

Age*	Birth Date*	Are you a U. S. citizen? ☐ Yes ☐ No	Type visa	Shift Preferred

Do you have friends or relatives employed by CBS? — Friends ☐ Yes ☐ No — Relatives ☐ Yes ☐ No

Have you previously applied at CBS? ☐ No ☐ Yes When?

If yes, give name and relationship

Were you ever employed by CBS? ☐ No ☐ Yes From To

Have you been convicted of any law violation other than a minor traffic violation within the last 5 years? ☐ Yes ☐ No — Date — Place — Charge

Are you presently in good health? ☐ Yes ☐ No If "No", explain.

Applicant must pass a complete CBS physical examination as a condition of employment.

EMPLOYMENT

Business telephone number and extension where you can be reached — Position applied for — Salary desired $ — Date you could start

From Mo. Yr.	To Mo. Yr.	Previous employers (most recent first) Name / Address	Name of supervisor & title	Your position	Salary Beginning	Last	Reason for leaving

EDUCATION

From Mo. Yr.	To Mo. Yr.	Name and address of school	Type course or major	Graduate?	Degree	Year awarded
		Grammar				
		High or prep 1.				
		2.				
		Business or special				
		College 1.				
		2.				
		Graduate school				

U.S. MILITARY

From Mo. Yr.	To Mo. Yr.	Branch of service (If none, write "none")	Highest rank held	Date of discharge

Please complete reverse side

CBS 136 REV. 2/76 - FOR USE AT BROADCASTING LOCATIONS

CBS Personnel Record form used courtesy of CBS, Inc.

The candidate, meanwhile, has a chance to find out more about the job and the people with whom he or she would be working.

Unfortunately, interviewing may be the stage at which discrimination enters the selection process. For example, suppose a female applicant mentions that she is the mother of small children. Her interviewer may automatically (and mistakenly) assume that she would not be available for job-related travel. In addition, interviewers may be unduly influenced by irrelevant factors such as appearance. Or they may ask different questions of different applicants, so that it becomes impossible to compare candidates' qualifications.

Some of these problems can be solved through better interviewer training and the use of structured interviews. A *structured interview* is one in which the interviewer is given a prepared set of questions to ask. The firm may also consider using several different interviewers for each applicant, but that solution is likely to be a costly one.

References A job candidate is generally asked to furnish the names of references—people who can verify background information and provide personal evaluations of the candidate. Naturally, applicants tend to list only references who are likely to say good things about them. Thus personal evaluations obtained from references may not be of much value. However, references are often contacted to verify such information as previous job responsibilities and the reason why an applicant left a former job.

Assessment Centers A newer selection technique is the assessment center, which is used primarily to select current employees for promotion to higher-level management positions. Typically, a group of employees is sent to the center for two or three days. While they are there, these employees participate in a variety of activities designed to simulate the management environment and predict managerial effectiveness. Trained observers (usually managers) make recommendations regarding promotion pos-

sibilities. Although this technique is gaining popularity, the expense involved limits its use to larger organizations.

Orientation

Once all the available information about job candidates has been collected and analyzed, those involved in the selection decide which candidate they would like to hire. A job offer is extended to the candidate. If it is accepted, the candidate becomes an employee and starts to work for the firm.

Soon after a candidate joins the firm, he or she goes through the firm's orientation program. **Orientation** is the process of acquainting new employees with the organization. Orientation topics range from such basic items as the location of the company cafeteria to such concerns as various career paths within the firm. The orientation itself may consist of a half-hour, informal presentation by a personnel manager. Or it may be an elaborate program involving many different people and lasting several days or weeks.

In some firms, special orientation techniques

Tough Interviews

Speaking of job seekers, not many of them bring their mother to an interview or sit in the personnel manager's office guzzling wine from a goatskin. But some do, according to a survey of top hiring officials at 100 of the Fortune 1,000 companies.

The survey, commissioned by executive recruiter Robert Half of Palm Beach, Fla., and scheduled for publication later this year, included the question: "What was the most unusual thing that a candidate ever did at an interview?"

One executive recalled an applicant who "took a brush out of my purse, brushed his hair and left." Another told of a candidate who "bounced up and down on my carpet and told me that I was highly thought of by the company because I was given such a thick carpet." Another said he had to call the police when an applicant refused to leave until he was hired. Conversely, one executive was told by a candidate "that if he had known it was our company, he wouldn't have come."

And one applicant obviously wasn't taking any chances. Upon being offered a job, he asked the personnel manager to put on his suit jacket and repeat the offer—just to make it formal.

Source: *Wall Street Journal,* February 17, 1984, p. 33.

are used for both new and present employees. For example, Ford Motor Company conducts a three-month workshop for disadvantaged workers. The program acquaints these employees with efficient work habits, ways of getting to and from work, and the basic principles of money management. Atlantic Richfield in Dallas holds retirement seminars in its regional and district offices to keep its employees up to date on the latest retirement benefits.

Of course attracting and hiring new employees is of vital importance. Many prospective employees will decide whether to join the firm on the basis of our next topic, the compensation and benefits it offers.

COMPENSATION AND BENEFITS

In Chapter 8 we noted that an effective employee reward system must (1) enable employees to satisfy their basic needs, (2) provide rewards comparable to those offered by other firms, (3) be distributed fairly within the organization, and (4) recognize the fact that different people have different needs.

The firm's compensation system can be structured to fill the first three of these requirements. The fourth is more difficult; it must take into account the many differences among people. Most firms offer a number of benefits that, taken together, generally help provide for employees' varying needs.

Compensation Decisions

Compensation is the payment that employees receive in return for their labor. Its importance to employees is obvious. And, because compensation can account for up to 80 percent of a firm's operating costs, it is equally important to management. The firm's **compensation system**—the policies and strategies that determine employee compensation—must therefore be carefully designed to provide for employee needs while keeping labor costs within reasonable limits. For most firms, designing an effective compensation system requires making three separate management decisions. (See Figure 9.7.)

The Wage-Level Decision Management must first position the firm's general pay level relative to the pay levels of comparable firms. In other words, will the firm pay its employees less than, more than, or about the same as similar organizations? Most firms choose a pay level near the industry average. A firm that is not in good financial shape may pay less than the going rate. Large, prosperous organizations, by contrast, may pay a little more than average to attract and retain the most capable employees.

To determine what the average is, the firm may use wage surveys. A **wage survey** is a collection of data on prevailing wage rates within an industry or a geographic area. Such surveys are compiled by industry associations, local governments, personnel associations, and (occasionally) individual firms.

The Wage-Structure Decision   Next, management must decide on relative pay levels for all the positions within the firm. Will managers be paid more than secretaries? Will secretaries be paid more than custodians? The result of this decision (actually, it is a set of decisions) is often called the firm's *wage structure*.

The wage structure is almost always developed on the basis of a job evaluation. **Job evaluation** is the process of determining the relative worths of the various jobs within a firm. Most observers would probably agree that a secretary should make more money than a custodian, but how much more? Twice as much? One and one-half times as much? Job evaluation should provide the answers to such questions.

A number of techniques may be used to evaluate jobs. The simplest is to rank all the jobs within the firm according to their value to the firm. Of course, if there are more than a few jobs, this technique loses its simplicity very quickly. A more frequently used method is based on the job analysis. "Points" are allocated to each job for each of its elements and requirements, as set forth in the job analysis. For example, "college degree required" might be worth 50 points, whereas the need for a high school education might be allocated only 25 points. The more points a job is allocated, the more important it is presumed to be (and the higher its level in the firm's wage structure).

The Individual-Wage Decision   Finally, the specific payments that individual jobholders will receive must be determined. Consider the case of two secretaries working side by side. Job evaluation has been used to determine the relative level of their pay within the firm's wage structure. However, suppose one secretary has 15 years of experience and can accurately type 80 words per minute. The other has 2 years of experience and can type only 55 words per minute. In most firms, these people would not receive the same pay. Instead, a wage range would be established for the secretarial position. Suppose this range were $4.50 to $7 per hour. The more experienced and proficient secretary would then be paid an amount near the top of the range (say, $6.60 per hour).

Figure 9.7   Compensation Decisions. Management decides how competitive salaries will be with those of similar firms (wage level); the relative importance of different positions (wage structure); and the specific wages of each employee (individual wages).

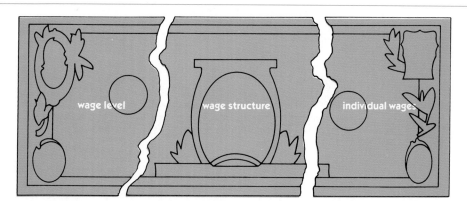

wage level   wage structure   individual wages

The less experienced secretary would receive an amount that was lower but still within the range (say, $5.25 per hour).

Two wage decisions actually come into play here. First the employee's initial rate must be established. It is based on experience, other qualifications, and expected performance. Later the employee may be given pay increases based on seniority and performance.

Types of Compensation

Hourly Wage   An **hourly wage** is a specific amount of money paid for each hour of work. People who earn wages are paid their hourly wage for the first 40 hours worked in any week. They are then paid one and one-half times their hourly wage for time worked in excess of 40 hours. (That is, they are paid "time and a half for overtime.") Workers in retailing and fast-food chains, on assembly lines, and in clerical positions are usually paid an hourly wage.

Weekly or Monthly Salary   A **salary** is a specific amount of money paid for an employee's work during a set calendar period, regardless of the actual number of hours worked. Salaried employees receive no overtime pay, but they do not lose pay when they are absent from work (within reasonable limits). Most professional and managerial positions are salaried.

Commissions   A **commission** is a payment that is some percentage of sales revenue. Sales representatives and sales managers are often paid entirely through commissions, or through a combination of commissions and salary.

Bonuses   A **bonus** is a payment in addition to wages, salary, or commissions. Bonuses are really extra rewards for outstanding job performance. They may be distributed to all employees or only to certain employees within the organization. Some firms distribute bonuses to all employees every Christmas. The size of the bonus depends on the firm's earnings and the particular employee's length of service with the firm. Other firms offer bonuses to employees who exceed specific sales or production goals. Kollmorgen Corporation of Stamford, Connecticut, is a large conglomerate that nurtures a feeling of smallness for the sake of its employees. One of the ways Kollmorgen maintains this feeling is to split any division that grows beyond a few hundred employees. Workers in that division receive a bonus for the good work that led to the growth and split; and then they return to a new division small enough to give each employee recognition.

Profit Sharing   **Profit sharing** is the distribution of a percentage of the firm's profit among its employees. The idea is to motivate employees to work effectively by giving them a stake in the

company's financial success. Some firms—including Sears, Roebuck—have linked their profit-sharing plans to employee retirement programs; that is, employees receive their profit-sharing distributions, with interest, when they retire. Olga Company, a maker of lingerie and underwear, places 20 to 25 percent of its annual pretax earnings in a profit-sharing plan for its employees.

Employee Benefits

Employee benefits are non-monetary rewards that are provided to employees. They consist mainly of services that are paid for by employers (such as insurance) and employee expenses that are reimbursed by employers (such as college tuition). Nowadays, the average cost of these benefits is over one-third of the total cost of wages and salaries. Thus a person who earns $15,000 a year is likely to receive, in addition, over $5000 worth of employee benefits.

Employee benefits take a variety of forms. *Pay for time not worked* covers such things as vacation time, holidays, and sick leave. *Insurance packages* may include health, life, and dental insurance for employees and their families. Some firms pay the entire cost of the insurance package, and others share the cost with the employee. The costs of *pension and retirement programs* may also be borne entirely by the firm or shared with the employee.

Some benefits are required by law. For example, employers must maintain *workmen's compensation insurance.* This insurance pays medical bills for injuries that occur on the job, and it provides income for employees who are disabled by job-related injuries. Employers also must pay for *unemployment insurance* and must contribute to each employee's federal *Social Security* account.

Other benefits provided by employers include *tuition-reimbursement plans, credit unions,* company *cafeterias* selling reduced-price meals, and various *recreational facilities.* We noted in Chapter 8 that Tandem Computers maintains a jogging track, a basketball court, and a swimming pool

A shining example of corporate child-care programs is that of Stride-Rite. Its program was started in 1971 as the result of a request for funds for a community preschool center.

Stride-Rite President Arnold Hiatt reasoned that a corporate contribution to such a center might as well benefit the company's employees, too. So half the children cared for by the facility must belong to Stride-Rite employees. The Boston center worked so well that in January, 1983, the company opened another in Cambridge, Mass.

Both centers derive their income in small part from the school lunch program and from the state department of social services' payments for many children from the community. Other funds come from Stride-Rite and tuition paid by parents. Stride-Rite's people pay a per-child cost of 10 percent of any weekly salary up to $250 and 15 percent beyond that. The annual tab for Stride-Rite, including both its subsidies to employees and its continuing contributions to the center: $150,000.

Arnold Hiatt sees the programs not only as an effective company benefit but also as a valuable contribution to the community. "Half the children are from the community, from very low income levels," he says. "They need a lot of help—medical, psychological and education—and they get it here."

Source: Carol Dilks, "Employers Who Help With the Kids," *Nation's Business,* February, 1984, p. 60.

for its employees. Tenneco provides an elaborate health facility for its Houston employees.

Employees generally want to improve their performance and their compensation as well. It is certainly in the firm's interest to provide opportunities for them to do so. Training and development, then, are important aspects of human resources management.

TRAINING AND DEVELOPMENT

Training and development are both aimed at improving employees' skills and abilities. However, the two are usually differentiated as follows: **Employee training** is the process of teaching operating and technical employees how to do their present jobs more effectively and efficiently. **Management development** is the process of preparing managers and other professionals to assume increased responsibility in both present and future positions. Thus training and development differ in who is being taught and in the purpose of the teaching. Both are necessary for personal and organizational growth. Companies that hope to stay competitive typically make huge commitments to employee training and development. In 1982, for example, IBM invested more than $500 million in employee education and training. Most new IBMers spend most of their first six weeks in company-run classes, and managers are required to take at least 40 hours of additional instruction a year.[3]

Training and Development Methods

A variety of methods are available for employee training and management development. Some of these methods may be more suitable for one or the other, but most can be applied to both.

- *On-the-job methods,* in which the trainee learns by doing the work under the supervision of an experienced employee
- *Vestibule training,* in which the work situation is simulated in a separate area so that learning takes place away from the day-to-day pressures of work
- *Classroom teaching* and *lectures,* methods that you probably already know quite well
- *Conferences* and *seminars,* in which experts and learners meet to discuss problems and exchange ideas
- *Role playing,* in which participants act out the roles of others in the organization, for better

understanding of these roles (primarily a management development tool)

Evaluation of Training and Development

Training and development are very expensive. The training itself costs quite a bit, and employees are usually not working—or are working at a reduced pace—during training sessions. To ensure that training and development are cost effective, the managers responsible should evaluate these efforts periodically.

The starting point for this evaluation is a set of verifiable objectives that were developed *before* the training was undertaken. Suppose a training program is expected to improve the skills of machinists. The objective of the program might be stated as follows: "At the end of the training period, each machinist should be able to process 30 parts per hour with no more than 1 defective part per 90 parts completed." This objective clearly specifies what is expected and how training results may be measured or verified. Evaluation then consists of measuring machinists' output and the number of defective parts produced, after the training.

The results of training evaluations should be made known to all those involved in the program—including trainees and upper management. For trainees, the results of evaluations can enhance motivation and learning. For upper management, the results may be the basis for making decisions about the training program itself.

Another form of evaluation—performance appraisal—is an equally important part of human resources management.

PERFORMANCE APPRAISAL

Performance appraisal is the evaluation of employees' current and potential levels of performance within the firm. It has three main objectives. First, performance appraisal allows a manager to let subordinates know how well they are doing

and how they can do better in the future. Second, it provides an effective basis for distributing rewards such as pay raises and promotions. Third, performance appraisal helps the organization monitor its employee selection and training and development activities. If large numbers of employees continually perform below expectations, the firm's selection process may need to be revised, or additional training and development may be required. Considering that experts believe that half of the three million employees who are fired each year in the U.S. are fired unfairly, managers are challenged to do a much better job of improving performance through performance appraisal. [4]

Common Evaluation Techniques

The various techniques and methods for appraising employee performance are either objective or judgmental in nature.

Objective Methods Objective appraisal methods make use of some measurable quantity as the basis for assessing performance. Units of output, dollar volume of sales, number of defective products, and number of insurance claims processed are all objective, measurable quantities. Thus an employee who processes an average of 26 claims per week is evaluated higher than one whose average is 19 claims per week.

Such objective measures cannot always be applied without some adjustment for the work environment. Suppose the first of our insurance claims processors works in New York City, whereas the second works in rural Iowa. Both must visit each client, perhaps because they are processing home-insurance claims. In this case the two may very well be equally competent and motivated. The difference in their average weekly output may be due entirely to the long distances that the Iowan must travel to reach clients' homes. Thus, a manager must take into account circumstances that may be hidden by a purely statistical measurement.

Figure 9.8 Performance Appraisal Form. Employees are evaluated using objective as well as judgmental criteria. *Source: R. Wayne Mondy and Robert M. Noe III, Personnel: The Management of Human Resources, Allyn and Bacon, 2d ed., p. 262.*

Employee's Name _____

Job Title _____

Department _____

Supervisor _____

Evaluation Period:
From _____ to _____

Instructions for Evaluation:
1. Consider only one factor at a time. Do not permit rating given for one factor to affect decision for others.
2. Consider performance for entire evaluation period. Avoid concentration on recent events or isolated incidents.
3. Remember that the average employee performs duties in a satisfactory manner. An above average or exceptional rating indicates that the employee has clearly distinguished himself or herself from the average employee.

Evaluation factors	Unsatisfactory. Does not meet requirements.	Below average. Needs improvement. Requirements occasionally not met.	Average. Consistently meets requirements.	Good. Frequently exceeds requirements.	Exceptional. Consistently exceeds requirements.
Quantity of work: Consider the volume of work achieved. Is productivity at an acceptable level?					
Quality of work: Consider accuracy, precision, neatness, and completeness in handling assigned duties.					
Dependability: Consider degree to which employee can be relied on to meet work commitments.					
Initiative: Consider self-reliance, resourcefulness, and willingness to accept responsibility.					
Adaptability: Consider ability to respond to changing requirements and conditions.					
Cooperation: Consider ability to work for and with others. Are assignments, including overtime, willingly accepted?					

Potential for future growth and development:
☐ Now at or near maximum performance in present job.
☐ Now at or near maximum performance in this job, but has potential for improvement in another job, such as:

_____

☐ Capable of progressing after further training and experience.
☐ No apparent limitations.

Employee statement: I agree ☐ disagree ☐ with this evaluation

Comments: _____

_____

_____

Employee	Date
Supervisor	Date
Reviewing Manager	Date

Judgmental Methods Judgmental appraisal methods are used much more frequently than objective methods. They require that the manager judge or estimate the employee's performance level, relative to some standard. (See the performance appraisal form in Figure 9.8.) In one such method, the manager ranks her or his subordinates from best to worst. This approach has a number of drawbacks, including the lack of any absolute standard.

Rating scales comprise the most popular judgmental appraisal technique. A *rating scale* consists of a number of statements. Each employee is rated on the degree to which he or she is described by each statement. For example, one statement might be "This employee always does high-quality work." The employee would be given a rating of any number from 5 down to 1, corresponding to gradations ranging from "strongly agree" to "strongly disagree." The ratings on all the statements are added together to obtain the employee's total evaluation.

Performance Feedback

No matter which appraisal technique is used, the results should be discussed with the employee soon after the evaluation is completed. The manager should explain the basis for present rewards and should let the employee know what he or she can do to be recognized as a better performer in the future. The information provided to an employee in such discussions is called performance feedback.

Many managers find it difficult to discuss the negative aspects of an appraisal. Unfortunately, they may ignore performance feedback or provide it in a very weak and ineffectual manner. In truth, though, most employees have strengths that can be emphasized while their weaknesses are discussed. An employee may not even be aware of his or her weaknesses and their consequences. If they are not pointed out through performance feedback, they cannot possibly be eliminated. Only through tactful, honest communication can the results of an appraisal be fully utilized.

Chapter Review

SUMMARY

Human resources management (HRM) is the set of activities involved in acquiring, maintaining, and developing an organization's human resources. Responsibility for HRM is shared by line and staff managers. A number of laws that affect HRM practices were passed to protect the rights and safety of employees.

Human-resource planning consists of forecasting the human resources that the firm will need and those that it will have available and then planning a course of action to match supply with demand. Attrition, layoffs, early retirement, and (as a last resort) firing can be used to reduce the size of the work force. Supply is increased through hiring.

Job analysis provides a job description and a job specification for each position within the firm. These serve as the basis for recruiting and selecting new employees. Candidates for open positions may be recruited from within or outside the firm. In the selection process, applications, resumés, tests, interviews, references, and assessment centers may be used to obtain information about candidates. This information is then used to select the most appropriate candidate for the job. Newly hired employees should go through a formal or informal orientation program to acquaint them with the firm.

In developing a system for compensating, or paying, employees, management must decide on the firm's general wage level (relative to other firms), the wage structure within the firm, and individual wages. Wage surveys and job analysis are useful in making these decisions. Employees may be paid hourly wages, salaries, or commissions. They may also receive bonuses and profit-sharing payments. Employee benefits, which are non-monetary rewards to employees, add about one-third to the cost of compensation.

Employee training and management development programs enhance the ability of employees to contribute to the firm. Several training techniques are available. Because training is expensive, its effectiveness should be evaluated periodically.

Performance appraisal, or evaluation, is used to provide employees with performance feedback, to serve as a basis for distributing rewards, and to monitor selection and training activities. Both objective and judgmental appraisal techniques are used. Their results must be communicated to employees if they are to help eliminate job-related weaknesses.

Early in this chapter we noted that relations between firms and labor unions are an extremely important part of human resources management, but are usually treated separately from HRM. In the next chapter, we shall discuss this topic in detail.

KEY TERMS

You should now be able to define and give an example relevant to each of the following terms:

human resources management

human-resource planning

replacement chart

skills inventory

job analysis

job description

job specification

recruiting

external recruiting

internal recruiting

selection

orientation

compensation

compensation system

wage survey

job evaluation

hourly wage

salary

commission

bonus

profit sharing

employee benefits

employee training

management development

performance appraisal

QUESTIONS AND EXERCISES

Review Questions

1. List the three main HRM activities and their objectives.
2. In general, on what basis is responsibility for HRM divided between line and staff managers?
3. How is a human-resource demand forecast related to the firm's organizational planning?
4. Describe the two techniques used in forecasting human-resource supply.
5. How do human-resource managers go about matching the firm's supply of workers with its demand for workers?
6. How are a job analysis, a job description, and a job specification related?
7. What are the advantages and disadvantages of external recruiting? of internal recruiting?
8. In your opinion, what are the two best techniques for gathering information about job candidates? Why?
9. Why is orientation an important HRM activity?
10. Explain how the three wage-related decisions result in a compensation system.
11. How is a job analysis used in the process of job evaluation?
12. Suppose you have just opened a new Ford auto sales showroom and repair shop. Which of your employees would be paid wages, which would receive salaries, and which would receive commissions?
13. What is the difference between the objective of employee training and that of management development?
14. Why is it so important to provide feedback after a performance appraisal?

Discussion Questions

1. To what extent are the three main HRM activities performed by the management of professional sports teams? Explain.
2. What kinds of conflicts can arise from the practice of salary arbitration in professional baseball? How would you resolve them?
3. Why are there so many laws relating to HRM practices? Which are the most important laws, in your opinion?
4. How accurately can managers plan for future human-resource needs?
5. How might a firm's recruiting and selection practices be affected by the general level of employment?
6. Are employee benefits really necessary? Why?
7. What actions would you take, as a manager, if an operating employee with six years of experience on the job refused ongoing training and ignored performance feedback?

Exercises

1. Construct a job analysis for the position of "entering first-year student" at your school.
2. Write a newspaper ad to attract applicants for the position of retail salesperson in your small business.
3. Describe the orientation procedure used by a firm that you have worked for or by your school. Then devise an *improved* procedure for that organization.

CASE 9-1

Lifetime Learning at SDU

Scandinavian Design is a chain of retail furniture stores, situated mainly in the Northeast. It sells primarily high-quality furniture made of such hardwoods as oak, teak, and rosewood—furniture with a clean, contemporary "Scandinavian" look. At a time when most general-line furniture stores are experiencing difficulties, Scandinavian Design is growing by about five stores per year. Sales were up 41 percent in 1982, and by more than 30 percent in 1983.

Usually, new employees of retail stores are trained on the job, by store managers or other experienced personnel. However, the rapid growth and unique product line of Scandinavian Design required something more. The answer was Scandinavian Design University, or SDU, a program of courses especially designed to provide all Scandinavian Design employees with the specialized knowledge and skills they need.

The first SDU sessions were held at three separate sites, in January 1983. About 200 of the firm's then 325 employees participated. All employees—from executives to stock clerks—took an orientation course and a product training course. Sales people took an additional course in the "College of Sales." Store managers took courses in the "College of Management"; and top executives attended the "Graduate School of Retailing."

The courses are informal, and they are designed to encourage student participation. They are given by two full-time and four part-time "professors" who have all managed Scandinavian Design stores in the past. Some outsiders question whether this managerial talent and experience should be kept away from the retail stores— especially since a fast-growing firm needs all the experienced managers it can get. But the trainees respond favorably to the knowledge and understanding of teachers who are familiar with Scandinavian Design's particular operation. Moreover,

the results of the training show that it is indeed worthwhile: After the first training session, the sales volumes of individual salespeople rose by 13 to 20 percent. And Scandinavian Design's annual sales revenue per square foot of retail space is more than six times the industry average.

The SDU courses are not the end of an employee's training. Robert Darvin, the president of Scandinavian Design, believes that learning is a lifetime endeavor. As "continuing education," the firm's headquarters sends memos and training tapes to each store every month. In addition, the stores hold their own training meetings, and employees occasionally visit suppliers' factories and warehouses.

All this training does not come cheap. Darvin estimates the 1984 cost at $600,000, or about 1 percent of 1983 gross sales. But he has no doubt that it is worth the expense. "Whatever we're spending," he says, "it isn't enough."[5]

1. What kinds of training methods might be used at SDU? How could the training be evaluated?
2. What effects might SDU have on the firm's other HRM activities and on its employees' motivation and morale?

CASE 9-2

HRM at IBM

Many people believe quality circles, career training, employee dress codes, and the encouragement of company loyalty through such benefits as lifetime employment and company country clubs have been the sole invention of Japanese industrialists, but they're not. They are part of a management style originated by Thomas Watson, Sr., who ran International Business Machines (IBM) from 1915 to 1956. The people who rebuilt the Japanese economy after World War II looked around for a model business—the most successful company that they could find. What they found was IBM.

Quality circles were instituted at IBM in the mid 1930s, when the firm's principal products were time clocks, tabulating machines, and card punchers—and when the first electronic computer was still almost two decades away. At the same time the position of foreman was eliminated. Instead, IBM had managers, whose prime responsibility was to ensure that workers had the tools, information, and advice they needed to do their jobs properly.

IBM has not laid off an employee since the early 1930s—not even during the very difficult Depression days of 1932 to 1934. And, even today, the firm hires new people expecting that they will stay through their entire business careers. Now—as then—much time, effort, and money (almost half a billion dollars in 1983 alone) goes into employee training. To a great extent, this emphasis on continuing professional development is what has enabled IBM to become and remain the leader of the computer industry.

Along with the training, IBM gives its employees a great deal of responsibility. Jobs are specifically designed to provide workers with the opportunity to contribute as much as they can to the firm. And employees are well compensated for their contributions: Salaries are usually the highest in the industry; employee benefits include membership in company country clubs for fees as low as $5 per year.

Watson also instituted a company dress code, banned the use of alcoholic beverages at company functions and discouraged it at other times, and even introduced company songs. These may have provoked joking by outsiders; however, along with Watson's other HRM techniques, they helped develop a sense of pride and loyalty within IBM. Both current and former employees still feel that same pride and loyalty. One ex-IBM employee, who now operates a competing firm, put it this way: "I still look back at IBM fondly and try to run my company by IBM standards."[6] Obviously, a lot of other people—including the Japanese industrialists—think IBM's standards are very much worthwhile.[7]

1. Does the combination of lifetime employment and continuing professional development make sense for American firms today? Explain.
2. If you were a human-resources manager at IBM, what qualities would you look for in recruiting and selecting new employees?

CHAPTER

TEN
Union-Management Relations

What is your perception of the relationship between labor unions and business management? Do you envision these two groups in constant combat over wages and working conditions—a battle that ends up in strike after strike? Then you should realize that the vast majority of union-management disputes are settled in days or weeks, without any loss of work time or productivity. And you may be surprised to learn that only about one-quarter of all American workers belong to unions. Yet labor unions are a powerful force in American business, and relations with unions are an important part of human resources management. In this chapter, we shall examine the various processes that make up union-management relations. After studying the chapter, you should understand:

1. *How and why labor unions came into being*
2. *The sources of unions' negotiating power: union membership and labor-relations legislation*
3. *The steps involved in forming a union, including the role of the National Labor Relations Board*
4. *The major issues covered in a union-management contract*
5. *The collective bargaining process*
6. *The major bargaining weapons and negotiating techniques available to unions and management*

Consider this:

If there is one prime example of union-management conflict, it is to be found in the historical relationship between the United Auto Workers (UAW) and the three American automobile giants (General Motors, Ford, and Chrysler). Fierce antagonism has characterized most of the dealings between this very large industry and what is one of the country's largest and strongest unions.

As a consequence of this long and bitter relationship, existing labor contracts contain clauses covering every imaginable circumstance. (This results from the union's seeking to protect its membership and from the auto companies' trying to give up as little power as possible.) For example, it was frequently stated in labor contracts that if an electrician needed to climb a ladder for some purpose, only another electrician could hold the ladder! Similarly, if a machine needed to be unplugged from an electrical outlet, a plant electrician had to be called. A member of management could not perform this simple task.

In the late 1970s and early 1980s, Chrysler was poised on the brink of bankruptcy. Drastic measures were needed to cut costs and restore profitability. One cost-cutting measure was to close a number of antiquated or marginally profitable facilities. The company's Hamtramck Assembly plant, Eight Mile Stamping plant, and Huber Foundry were all shut down in 1980. The Lynch Road Assembly plant and part of Mack Stamping plant were closed in 1981. In each case, the closing was accomplished with absolutely no cooperation and very little communication between management and labor. One day it was simply announced that a certain plant was to be closed down on a specified date.

One plant that remained open was Detroit Trim, a facility that produced seat covers for various Chrysler vehicles. For a while, however, it appeared that this plant too was doomed. A new cost-cutting system required that the cost of producing parts in a company-owned plant be compared with the cost of buying the same parts from an outside manufacturer. Then the less expensive method had to be used. For 1983 the estimated production costs at Detroit Trim were $51.5 million. The same amount of output could be bought for only $30.8 million from other companies which did not use UAW labor.

As rumors of the impending shutdown began to circulate, labor leaders decided to confront the problem head-on. Various meetings were arranged between members of the UAW and Chrysler management. Management agreed to prepare a plan to keep the plant open.

Meanwhile, the plant manager recognized a crucial point that neither side had been aware of. If the plant were closed, Chrysler would not save the full $20.7 million difference in product costs. Guaranteed management salaries, pension costs, and similar items would actually reduce the savings to only $11.4 million. At that point, Chrysler's management agreed to absorb $5 million of the potential savings *if* other ways could be found to make up the remaining $6.4 million.

Management and labor both came to realize that the plant was not very efficient. An excess of managers, wasteful work rules, and low production quotas were undermining productivity. A plan was developed to remedy this situation. First, the work force was to be cut from 709 to 528 employees. Specifically, the production staff would be reduced by 21 percent, the managerial staff by 25 percent, and the indirect-labor force (maintenance people, repair specialists, and the like) by 40 percent.

Second, the plant was to produce the same volume of output with the reduced work force. In particular, each worker was expected to produce from 15 to 28 percent more output than before. Work rules were also made more flexible: managers could unplug machines, and someone other than an electrician could hold a ladder for an electrician. For its part, management would assign only 1 foreman for each 30 employees (the previous span was 1 foreman for each 21 employees).

Union members accepted the plan by an overwhelming majority, and it was put into operation. As might be expected, there were some problems at first; for example, some workers had trouble reaching their new production quotas. Soon, however, the plant was operating pretty much as planned. Moreover, in some areas things worked out *better* than expected. Because of an increased market demand for Chrysler products, most production workers were able to keep their jobs. Rather than producing the same output with fewer workers, the plant was able to produce more with the same number of workers.

The cuts in the management staff and indirect-labor force were carried out as specified in the original plan.[1]

A **labor union** is an organization of workers acting together to negotiate their wages and working conditions with employers. In the United States, nonmanagement employees have the legal right to form unions and to bargain, as a group, with management. The result of the bargaining process is a *labor contract*, a written agreement that is in force for a set period of time (usually one to three years). The dealings between labor unions and business management, both in the bargaining process and beyond it, are called **union-management relations** or, more simply, **labor relations.**

The events that occurred at the Detroit Trim plant illustrate the two extremes of union-management relations. At one extreme continual distrust and even hostility between labor and management resulted in secrecy concerning vital information and in the formation of contracts that spelled out work procedures in the most minute detail.

At the other extreme is the spirit of cooperation that kept Detroit Trim in operation—and, at the same time, led to a hefty increase in productivity at that plant. (This cooperative spirit probably arose from the appointment of Douglas Fraser, president of the UAW, to the Chrysler board of directors in 1980. Such a step had seemed impossible before then, in view of the hostile relationship between the UAW and Chrysler. But Chrysler was in trouble and needed help from its unions. Fraser's directorship was part of the price of that help.)

There is, then, a dual relationship between labor and management. The two groups have different goals, which tend to place them at odds with each other. But these goals must be attained by the same means—through the production of goods and services. And, even at contract bargaining sessions, the two groups must work together to attain their goals. Perhaps mainly for this reason, antagonism now seems to be giving way to cooperation in union-management relations.

Before we examine how organized labor operates today, we should take a look at its roots in the history of the labor movement.

THE HISTORICAL DEVELOPMENT OF UNIONS

Until the middle of the nineteenth century, there was very little organization of labor in this country. Groups of workers did occasionally form a **craft union,** which is an organization of skilled workers in a single craft or trade. These unions were usually limited to a single city, and they often did not last very long. The first known strike in the United States involved a group of Philadelphia printers who stopped working over demands for higher wages. When the printers were granted a pay increase by their employers, the group disbanded.

Figure 10.1   Historical Overview of Unions. The total number of members for all unions has risen dramatically since 1869, when the first truly national union was organized. The dates of major events in the history of labor unions are singled out along the line of membership growth.
Source: U.S. Bureau of Labor Statistics.

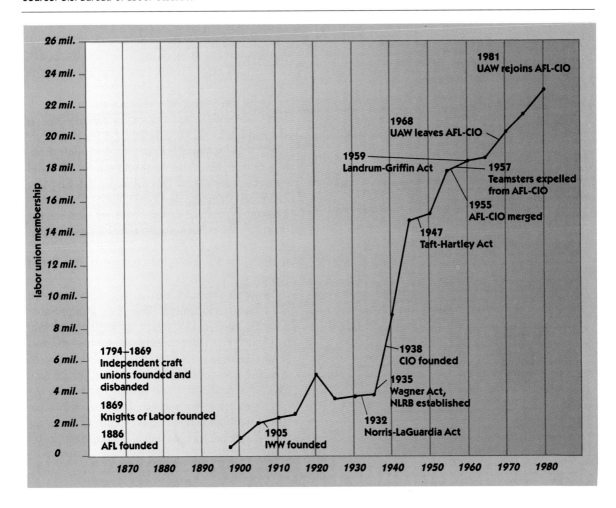

The growth of American manufacturing in the nineteenth century expanded the need for industrial workers and led to the formation of labor organizations. Source: Courtesy of the New York Historical Society, New York.

Early History

In the mid-1800s, improved transportation began to open new markets for manufactured goods. New manufacturing methods made it possible to satisfy those demands, and American industry began to grow. The Civil War and the continued growth of the railroads after the war led to further industrial expansion.

Large-scale production required more and more skilled industrial workers. As the skilled labor force grew, craft unions were formed in the more industrialized areas. From these craft unions, three significant labor organizations emerged. The first was the Knights of Labor. (See Figure 10.1 for a historical overview of unions and their patterns of membership.)

The Knights of Labor The *Knights of Labor* was formed as a secret society in 1869 by Uriah Stephens. One major goal of the Knights was to eliminate the depersonalization of the worker that

resulted from mass-production technology. Another was to improve the moral standards of both employees and society. The Knights of Labor was the first truly national labor union. Membership increased steadily, and by 1886 the Knights had approximately 700,000 members.

The moralistic goals of the Knights ultimately contributed to its downfall. The group's leaders concentrated so hard on social and economic change that they did not recognize the effects of technological change. Moreover, they assumed that all employees had the same goals—those of the Knights' leaders—and wanted social and moral reform.

The major reason for the demise of the Knights, however, was the Haymarket riot of 1886. At a rally (called to demand a reduction in the work day from ten to eight hours) in Chicago's Haymarket Square, a bomb exploded. Several police officers and civilians were killed or wounded. The Knights were not directly implicated, but they quickly lost public favor.

The American Federation of Labor In 1886 several leaders of the Knights joined with independent craft unions to form the *American Federation of Labor* (AFL). Samuel Gompers, one of the AFL's founders, became its first president. Gompers believed that the goals of the union should be those of its members rather than those of its leaders. Moreover, the AFL did not seek to change the existing business system, as the Knights of Labor had. Instead, its goal was to improve its members' living standards within that system.

Another major difference between the Knights of Labor and the AFL was in their positions regarding strikes. A **strike** is a temporary work stoppage by employees, calculated to add force to their demands. The Knights did not favor the use of strikes, whereas the AFL strongly believed that striking was an effective labor weapon. The AFL also believed that organized labor should play a major role in politics. As we will see, the AFL is still very much a part of the American labor scene.

The Industrial Workers of the World The *Industrial Workers of the World* (IWW) was created in 1905 as a radical alternative to the AFL. Among its goals was the overthrow of capitalism. This radical stance prevented the IWW from gaining much of a foothold. Perhaps its major accomplishment was to make the AFL seem less threatening, by comparison, to the general public and to business leaders.

Nevertheless, during the first two decades of

this century, both business and government attempted to keep labor unions from growing. This period is characterized by strikes and violent confrontations between management and unions. In steel works, garment factories, and auto plants, clashes took place in which striking union members fought bitterly against nonunion workers, police, and private security guards.

Between the World Wars

The AFL continued to be the major force in organized labor. By 1920 its membership included 75 percent of all those who had joined unions. Throughout its existence, however, the AFL had been unsure of the best way to deal with unskilled and semiskilled workers. Most of its members were skilled workers in specific crafts or trades. But technological changes during World War I had brought about a significant increase in the number of unskilled and semiskilled employees in the work force. These people sought to join the AFL, but they were not well received by its membership.

Some unions within the AFL did recognize the need to organize unskilled and semiskilled workers, and they began with the automotive and steel industries. The unions they formed were **industrial unions,** organizations of both skilled and unskilled workers in a single industry. Soon workers in the rubber, mining, newspaper, and communications industries were also organized into unions. Eventually these unions left the AFL and formed the *Congress of Industrial Organizations* (CIO).

During this same time (the late 1930s), there was a major upswing in membership—in AFL, CIO, and independent unions. Strong union leadership, the development of new negotiating tactics, and favorable legislation combined to increase total union membership to 9 million in 1940. At this point the CIO began to rival the AFL in size and influence. There was other rivalry as well: the AFL and CIO often clashed over which of them had the right to organize and represent particular groups of employees.

Recent History

Since World War II, the labor scene has gone through a number of changes. For one thing, during and after the war years there was a downturn in public opinion regarding unions. A few isolated but very visible strikes during the war caused public sentiment to shift against unionism.

Perhaps the most significant occurrence, however, was the merger of the AFL and the CIO. After years of bickering, the two groups recognized that they were wasting effort by fighting each other and that a merger would greatly increase the strength of both. The merger took place on December 5, 1955. The new union, called the *AFL-CIO,* had a membership of 16 million workers, which made it the largest union in the world. Its first president was George Meany, who served in that capacity until 1979.

ORGANIZED LABOR TODAY

The power of unions to negotiate effectively with management is derived from two sources. The first is their membership. The more workers a union represents within an industry, the greater its clout in dealing with firms operating in that industry. The second source of union power is the laws that guarantee unions the right to negotiate and, at the same time, regulate the negotiating process.

Union Membership

At present, union members account for a relatively small portion of the American work force. (As noted at the beginning of the chapter, about one-quarter of the nation's workers belong to unions.) Union membership is concentrated, however, in relatively few industries and job categories. Within these industries, unions wield considerable power.

The AFL-CIO is still the largest union organization in this country, boasting approximately 13,600,000 members. Those represented by the

AFL-CIO include actors, barbers, construction workers, carpenters, retail clerks, musicians, teachers, postal workers, painters, steel and iron workers, firefighters, bricklayers, and newspaper reporters. Clearly, this union represents a diverse membership. (See Figure 10.2, which shows the organization of this complex union.)

One of the largest unions not associated directly with the AFL-CIO is the Teamsters' union. The *Teamsters* were originally part of the AFL-CIO, but in 1957 they were expelled for corrupt and illegal practices. The union started out as an organization of professional drivers, but it has recently begun to recruit employees in a wide variety of jobs. Current membership is slightly below 2 million workers.

The *United Auto Workers* represents employees in the auto industry. The UAW too was originally part of the AFL-CIO, but it left the parent union—of its own accord—in 1968. Current membership in the UAW is around 1.5 million. For a while, the Teamsters' union and the UAW formed a semistructured partnership called the Alliance for Labor Action. This partnership was eventually dissolved, and the UAW again became part of the AFL-CIO in 1981.

Membership Trends

There has been a gradual decline in union membership during the past twenty years or so. To a great extent, this downward membership trend is due to the changing nature of business itself.

☐ Heavily unionized industries have been decreasing in size, or they have not been growing as fast as nonunionized industries. For example, recent cutbacks in the steel and auto industries have tended to reduce union membership. At the same time, the growth of high-tech industries has increased the ranks of nonunion workers.

☐ Many firms have moved from the heavily unionized northeast and Great Lakes regions to the less unionized southeast and southwest— the "Sunbelt." At the new plants, formerly unionized firms tend to hire nonunion workers.

☐ The largest growth in employment is occurring in the service industries, and these industries are typically not unionized.

☐ Management is providing benefits that tend to reduce employees' need for unionization. Increased employee participation and better wages and working conditions are goals of unions. When these benefits are already supplied by management, workers are less likely to join unions.

Unions are increasing the pace of their organizing activities in the Sunbelt and in the service industries. It remains to be seen whether they will be able to regain the prominence and power they enjoyed between the world wars and during the 1950s. There is little doubt, however, that they will remain a powerful force in particular industries. And their membership among professional and white-collar workers will probably increase.

The Legal Environment of Labor Relations

As we have noted, early efforts to organize labor were opposed by business. The federal government generally supported anti-union efforts through the court system, and in some cases federal troops were used to end strikes. Gradually, however, the government began to correct this imbalance through the legislative process.

Norris-LaGuardia Act The first major piece of legislation to secure rights for unions, the *Norris-LaGuardia Act* of 1932, was considered a landmark in labor-management relations. This act made it difficult for businesses to obtain court orders that banned strikes, picketing, or union membership drives. Previously, courts had issued such orders readily as a means of curbing union activities.

National Labor Relations Act This law, also known as the *Wagner Act,* was passed by Congress in 1935. It established procedures by which employees can decide whether they want to be

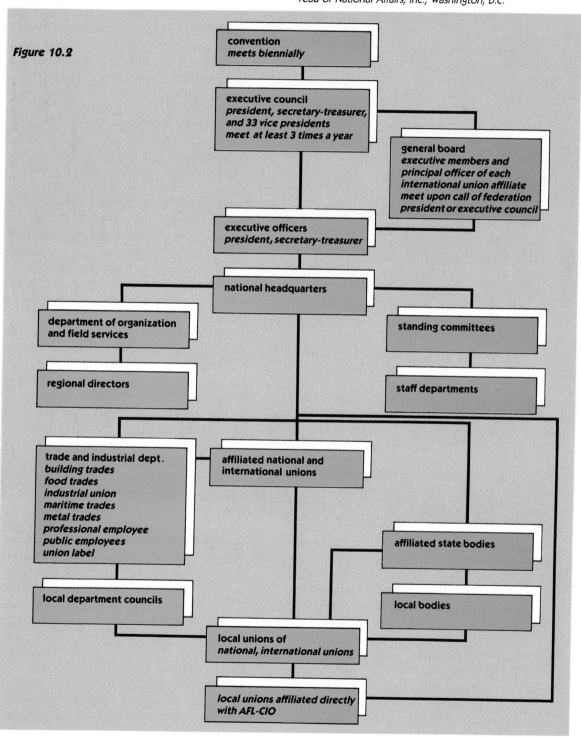

AFL-CIO Organization Chart. Like a big corporation, the AFL-CIO has organized its chain of command to best attain its goals as well as the goals of the various unions it represents. *Source: Courtney D. Gifford, ed., Directory of U.S. Labor Organizations, 1982–83 Edition, p. 7. Copyright © by The Bureau of National Affairs, Inc., Washington, D.C.*

Figure 10.2

convention
meets biennially

executive council
president, secretary-treasurer, and 33 vice presidents
meet at least 3 times a year

general board
executive members and principal officer of each international union affiliate meet upon call of federation president or executive council

executive officers
president, secretary-treasurer

national headquarters

department of organization and field services

standing committees

regional directors

staff departments

trade and industrial dept.
building trades
food trades
industrial union
maritime trades
metal trades
professional employee
public employees
union label

affiliated national and international unions

affiliated state bodies

local department councils

local bodies

local unions of
national, international unions

local unions affiliated directly with AFL-CIO

A Job For Life

For 300 employees at the Bethlehem Steel plant in Johnstown, Pa., having a job for life is no longer just a dream.

Since last July, mechanical workers in the bar, rod, and wire division have been protected from layoffs even during plant downturns.

"For the first time in their lives, these employees can plan for the future without fear of repeated layoffs," says Mark Reynolds, superintendent of labor relations for the division. "I think we've rewritten some labor history here."

Like Bethlehem, a growing number of employers in old-line, heavily unionized industries are starting to go along with contract demands by workers for far greater job security.

In return, companies are winning major work-rule concessions that allow the shifting of employees in and out of traditional job classifications and into areas where labor needs are greatest.

As a result, say analysts, unionized companies are achieving the kind of work-force flexibility that many nonunion employers have traditionally enjoyed and used to minimize—and often entirely eliminate—layoffs.

Source: Carey W. English, "Union's Latest Goal: A Job for Life," *U.S. News & World Report*, May 21, 1984, p. 74.

represented by a union. If they do, the Wagner Act requires that management negotiate with union representatives. It also forbids certain *unfair labor practices* on the part of management, such as firing or punishing pro-union workers, spying on union meetings, and bribing employees to vote against unionization.

Finally, the Wagner Act established the **National Labor Relations Board (NLRB)** to enforce the provisions of the law. The NLRB is primarily concerned with (1) overseeing the elections in which employees decide whether they will be represented by a union and (2) investigating complaints lodged by unions or employers.

Labor-Management Relations Act   The legislation of the 1930s sought to discourage unfair practices on the part of employers. As union membership and power grew, however, the federal government began to examine the practices of labor. Several long and bitter strikes, mainly in the coal and trucking industries in the early 1940s, led to a demand for legislative restraint on unions. As a result, in 1947 Congress passed the *Labor-Management Relations Act,* also known as the *Taft-Hartley Act,* over President Harry Truman's veto.

The objective of the Taft-Hartley Act is to provide a balance between union power and management power. It lists unfair labor practices that *unions* are forbidden to use. These include *not* bargaining with management in good faith, charging excessive membership dues, harassing nonunion workers, and using various means of coercion against employers.

The Taft-Hartley Act also gives management more rights during union organizing campaigns. For example, management may outline for employees the advantages and disadvantages of union membership, as long as the information it presents is accurate. Finally, the act gives the president of the United States the power to obtain a temporary injunction to prevent or stop a strike that endangers the national health and safety. An **injunction** is a court order requiring a person or group either to perform some act or to refrain from performing some act.

Landrum-Griffin Act   In the 1950s, Senate investigations and hearings exposed labor racketeering in unions and uncovered cases of bribery, extortion, and embezzlement among union leaders. Public pressure for reform resulted in the *Landrum-Griffin Act,* which was passed in 1959.

This law was designed to regulate the internal functioning of labor unions. Provisions of the law require unions to file annual reports with the U.S. Department of Labor regarding their finances, elections, and various decisions made by union officers. The Landrum-Griffin Act also ensures each union member the right to seek, nominate, and vote for each elected position in his or her union. It provides safeguards for union funds, and it requires management and unions to report the lending of management funds to union officers or members and to local unions.

The various pieces of legislation that we have reviewed here effectively regulate much of the relationship between labor and management once unions are established. The next section will show that forming a union at one's firm is also a carefully regulated process.

THE UNIONIZATION PROCESS

In order for a union to be formed at a particular firm, some employees of the firm must first be interested in being represented by a union. They must then take a number of steps to declare formally their desire for a union. To ensure fairness, most of the steps in this unionization process are supervised by the NLRB.

Why Some Employees Join Unions

Obviously, employees may have a variety of reasons for wishing to start or join a union. One commonly cited reason is to combat alienation. Some employees—especially those whose jobs are dull and repetitive—can begin to perceive of themselves as merely parts of a machine. They may feel that, at work, they lose their individual or social identity. Union membership is one way to establish contact with others in the firm.

Another common reason for joining a union is the perception that union membership increases job security. No one wants to live in fear of arbitrary or capricious dismissal from a job. Unions actually have only a limited ability to guarantee members' jobs, but they can help increase job security by using seniority rules.

Employees may also join a union because of dissatisfaction with one or more elements of their jobs. If they are unhappy with their pay, benefits, or working conditions, they may look to a union to correct the perceived deficiencies.

Some people join unions because of their personal background. For example, a person whose parents are strong believers in unions might be inclined to feel just as positive about union membership.

We should also note that there are situations in which employees *must* join a union to keep their jobs. Many unions try, through their labor contracts, to establish a union shop. A union shop is a firm whose new employees need not be union members but must join the union after a specified

Figure 10.3 Steps in Forming a Union. The unionization process consists of a campaign, authorization cards, a formal election, and certification by the National Labor Relations Board.

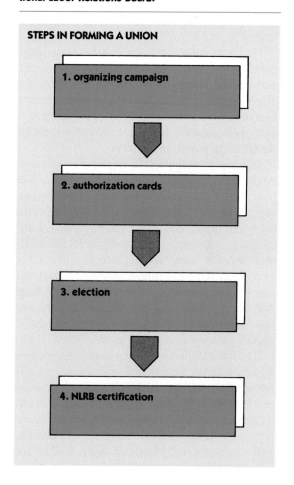

STEPS IN FORMING A UNION

1. organizing campaign

2. authorization cards

3. election

4. NLRB certification

probationary period. Thus everyone who accepts a job in a union shop must eventually become a union member. Under the Taft-Hartley Act, some states (mostly in the south), have established "right-to-work" laws, which prohibit the practice of union shops.

Steps in Forming a Union

The first step in forming a union is the *organizing campaign*. (See Figure 10.3.) Its primary objective is to develop widespread employee interest in having a union. To kick off the campaign, a national union may send organizers to the firm, in an attempt to develop this interest. Alternatively, the employees themselves may decide that they want a union. Then they contact the appropriate national union and ask for organizing assistance.

The organizing campaign can be quite emotional, and it may lead to conflict between employees and management. On the one hand, the employees who want the union are dedicated to its creation. On the other hand, management is extremely sensitive to what it sees as a potential threat to its power and control.

At some point during the organizing campaign, employees are asked to sign *authorization cards* (see Figure 10.4) to indicate—in writing—their support for the union. Because of various NLRB rules and regulations, both union organizers and company management must be very careful in their behavior during this authorization drive. For example, employees cannot be asked to sign the cards when they are supposed to be working. And management may not indicate in any way that employees' jobs or job security will be in jeopardy if they do sign the cards.

If at least 30 percent of the eligible employees sign authorization cards, the organizers generally request that the firm recognize the union as the employees' bargaining representative. Usually the firm rejects this request, and a *formal election* is held to decide whether or not to have a union. This election usually involves secret ballots and is conducted by the NLRB. The outcome of the election is determined by a simple majority of those eligible employees who choose to vote.

If the union obtains a majority, it becomes the official bargaining agent for its members. It may immediately begin the process of negotiating a labor contract with management. If the union is voted down, the NLRB will not allow another election for one year.

Several factors can complicate the unionization process. For example, the **bargaining unit,** which is the specific group of employees that the union is to represent, must be defined. Union organizers may want to represent all hourly employees at a particular site (such as all retail clerks in a department store). Or they may wish to represent only a specific group of employees (such as all electricians in a large manufacturing plant).

Another issue that may have to be resolved is that of **jurisdiction,** which is the right of a particular union to organize particular workers. Where jurisdictions overlap or are unclear, the employees themselves may decide who will represent them. In some cases, two or more unions may be trying to organize some or all of the employees of a firm. Then the election choices may be union A, or union B, or no union at all.

The Role of the NLRB

As we have indicated, the NLRB is heavily involved in the unionization process. Generally, the NLRB is responsible for overseeing the organizing campaign, conducting the election (if one is warranted), and certifying the results.

During the organizing campaign, both employers and union organizers can take steps to educate employees regarding the advantages and disadvantages of having a union. However, neither is allowed to use underhanded tactics or distort the truth. If violations occur, the NLRB can stop the questionable behavior, postpone the election, or set aside the results of an election that has already taken place.

The NLRB usually conducts the election within 45 days after the organizers submit the required number of signed authorization cards. A very high percentage of the eligible voters generally participate in the election, and it is held at the work place during normal working hours. In certain cases, however, a mail ballot or other form of election may be called for.

Certification of the election involves counting the votes and considering challenges to the election. After the election results are announced, management and the union organizers have five days in which to challenge the election. The basis for a challenge might be improper conduct prior to the election or participation by an ineligible voter. After considering any challenges, the NLRB passes final judgment on the election results.

Once union representation is established, union and management get down to the serious business of contract negotiations. Before we examine the process of collective bargaining, however, we should have some idea what issues are likely to be bargained over.

UNION-MANAGEMENT CONTRACT ISSUES

As might be expected, many diverse issues are negotiated by unions and management and are made a part of their labor contract. Unions tend to emphasize issues that are concerned with members' income and standard of living, and with the strength of the union. Management's primary goals are to retain as much control as possible over the operations of the firm and to maximize its strength relative to that of the union. The balance of power between unions and management varies from firm to firm.

Employee Pay

An area of bargaining that is central to union-management relations is employee pay. Three separate issues are usually involved: the forms of pay, the magnitude of pay, and the means by which the magnitude of pay will be determined.

Forms of Pay The primary form of pay is direct compensation—the wage or salary that an employee receives in exchange for his or her contribution to the organization. Direct compensation is, however, a fairly straightforward issue. Negotiators often spend much more of their time developing a benefits package for employees. And, as the range of benefits and their costs have escalated over the years, this element of pay has become increasingly important and complex.

We discussed the various employee benefits in Chapter 9. Of these, health, life, disability, and dental insurance are important benefits that unions try to obtain for their members. Deferred compensation, in the form of pension or retirement programs, is also a common focal point.

Other benefits commonly dealt with in the bargaining process include paid vacation time and holidays. Policy on paid sick leave may also be negotiated. Obviously, unions argue for as much paid vacation and holiday time as possible and for liberal sick-leave policies. Management naturally takes the opposite position.

Magnitude of Pay Of considerable importance is the magnitude, or amount, of pay that employees

Figure 10.4 Sample Authorization Card. Unions must have written authorization to represent employees.
Source: Courtesy National Labor Relations Board.

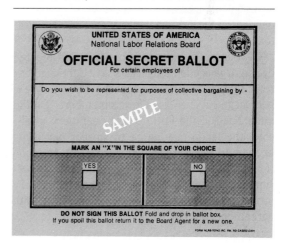

Keeping Unions Out

Cornelius P. Quinn is a senior partner, Management Education Center, Whitmore Lake, Michigan, a labor relations training and consulting firm. His work includes a stint representing the American Federation of Teachers, and as a teacher he gives a course on employee labor relations at the Williams School of Banking. Quinn offers a six-point program to head off a union effort:

1. Performance Review. Institute a systematic program through which employees are told how they are doing.
2. Upward Mobility. Announce a policy that allows people to expand their interests and move within the company. This includes job posting and training.
3. Regular Increases. Allow workers to depend on predictable pay raises that include cost-of-living adjustments.
4. Human Resources. Make sure your department is headed by a trained human resources expert.
5. Progressive Discipline. Oversee a program for graduated disciplinary action that requires good cause and documentation.
6. Communication. Schedule regular meetings, from one-on-one to departmental, with the goal of encouraging two-way communication and participatory management.

Source: "Keeping Unions Out," *United States Banker*, February 1984, p. 44.

will receive as both direct and indirect compensation.

The union attempts to ensure that pay is equitable with that received by other employees, both locally and nationally, in the same or similar industries. The union also attempts to include, in the contract, clauses that provide pay increases over the life of the agreement. The commonest is the *cost-of-living clause,* which ties periodic pay increases to increases in the cost of living, as defined by various economic statistics or indicators.

Of course, the magnitude of pay is also affected by the organization's ability to pay. If the firm has recently posted large profits, the union may expect large pay increases for its members. On the other hand, if the firm has not been very profitable, the union may agree to smaller pay hikes or even to a pay freeze. In an extreme situation (for example, when the firm is bordering on bankruptcy), the union may agree to pay cuts. Very stringent conditions are usually included with agreement to a pay cut.

As part of the comeback of the Chrysler Corporation in the late 1970s, its union employees accepted a pay cut. In 1983, when the firm earned a substantial profit, union members demanded and received comparable pay increases.

Bargaining with regard to magnitude also revolves around employee benefits. At one extreme, unions seek a wide range of benefits, entirely or largely paid for by the firm. At the other extreme, management may be willing to coordinate the benefits package but may want its employees to bear most of the cost. Again, factors such as equity (with similar firms and jobs) and ability to pay enter into the final agreement.

Pay Determinants Negotiators also address the question of how individual pay will be determined. For management, the ideal arrangement is to tie wages to each employee's productivity. As we saw, this method of payment tends to motivate and reward effort. Unions, on the other hand, feel that this arrangement can also create unnecessary competition among employees. They generally argue that employees should be paid—at least in part—according to seniority. **Seniority** is the length of time an employee has worked for the organization.

Determinants regarding benefits are also negotiated. For example, management may want to provide retirement benefits only to employees who have worked for the firm for a specified number of years. The union may want these benefits provided to all employees.

Working Hours

Of special interest relative to working hours is the matter of overtime. Federal law defines **overtime** as time worked in excess of forty hours in one week. And it specifies that overtime pay must be at least one and one-half times the normal hourly wage. Unions may attempt to negotiate overtime rates for all hours worked beyond eight hours in a single day. Similarly, the union may attempt to obtain higher overtime rates (say, twice the normal hourly wage) for weekend or holiday work. Still another issue is an upper limit to overtime, beyond which employees can refuse to work.

In firms with two or more work shifts, workers on less desirable shifts are paid a premium for their time. Both the amount of the premium and the manner in which workers are chosen for (or choose) particular shifts are negotiable issues. Other issues related to working hours are the work starting times and the length of lunch periods and coffee breaks.

Security

Security actually covers two issues: the job security of the individual worker and the security of the union as the bargaining representative of the firm's employees.

Job security is protection against the loss of employment. It is and probably always will be a major concern of individuals. As we noted earlier, the desire for increased job security is a major

reason for joining unions in the first place. In the typical labor contract, job security is based on seniority. If employees must be laid off or dismissed, those with the least seniority are the first to go. Some of the more senior employees may have to move to lower-level jobs, but they remain employed.

Union security is the protection of the union's position as the employees' bargaining agent. Union security is frequently a more volatile issue than job security. Unions strive for as much security as possible, but management tends to see an increase in union security as an erosion of its control.

Union security arises directly from its membership. The greater the ratio of union employees to nonunion employees, the more secure the union. In contract negotiations, unions thus attempt to establish various union-membership conditions. The most restrictive of these is the **closed shop,** in which workers must join the union before they are hired. This condition was outlawed by the Taft-Hartley Act, but several other arrangements are subject to negotiation:

☐ The **union shop,** in which new employees must join the union after a specified probationary period.
☐ The **agency shop,** in which employees can choose not to join the union but must pay dues to the union anyway. (The idea is that nonunion employees benefit from union activities and should help support them.)
☐ The **maintenance shop,** in which an employee who joins the union must remain a union member as long as he or she is employed by the firm.

Management Rights

Of particular interest to the firm are those rights and privileges that are to be retained by management. For example, the firm wants as much control as possible over whom it hires, how work is scheduled, and how discipline is handled. The union, on the other hand, would like some control over these and all other matters affecting its members. Interestingly, unions in the United States are making surprisingly rapid progress toward their goal of playing a more direct role in corporate governance. Recall that in exchange for union concessions that helped Chrysler fend off bankruptcy, Douglas Fraser, a high-ranking union official was given a seat on Chrysler's board of directors. He participated fully in all company business except labor-management strategy. Since that time, union employees have taken seats on a number of corporate boards including those of Eastern Air Lines, Pan Am, Weirton Steel, Rath Packing, Hyatt Clark Industries, and Commercial Lovelace Motor Freight.[2]

Grievance Procedures

A **grievance procedure** is a formally established course of action for resolving employee complaints against management. Virtually every labor contract contains one grievance procedure. Procedures vary in scope and detail, but most include the following four steps. (See Figure 10.5.)

Original Grievance The process begins with an employee who believes that he or she has been

Figure 10.5 *Steps in Resolving a Grievance. The employee grievance procedure for most organizations consists of four steps. Each step involves all the personnel at the preceding level plus at least one higher level person to try to resolve the problem. The final step is to go to a neutral third party, the arbitrator.*

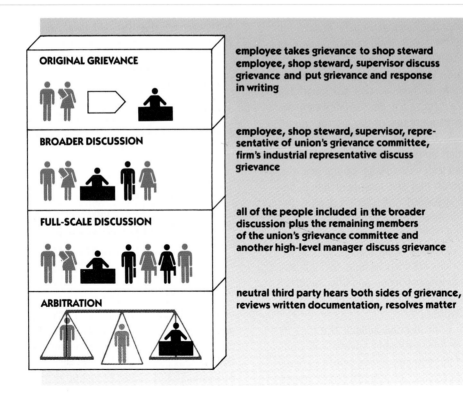

ORIGINAL GRIEVANCE — employee takes grievance to shop steward employee, shop steward, supervisor discuss grievance and put grievance and response in writing

BROADER DISCUSSION — employee, shop steward, supervisor, representative of union's grievance committee, firm's industrial representative discuss grievance

FULL-SCALE DISCUSSION — all of the people included in the broader discussion plus the remaining members of the union's grievance committee and another high-level manager discuss grievance

ARBITRATION — neutral third party hears both sides of grievance, reviews written documentation, resolves matter

treated unfairly, in violation of the labor contract. For example, an employee may be entitled to a formal performance review after six months on the job. If no such review is conducted, the employee may file a grievance. To do so, the employee explains the grievance to a **shop steward,** an employee who is elected by union members to serve as their representative. The employee and the steward then discuss the grievance with the employee's immediate supervisor. Both the grievance and the supervisor's response are put in writing.

Broader Discussion   In most cases the problem is resolved during the initial discussion with the supervisor. If it is not, a second discussion is held. Now the participants include the original parties (employee, supervisor, and steward), a representative from the union's grievance committee, and the firm's industrial-relations representative. Again a record is kept of the discussion and its results.

Full-Scale Discussion   If the grievance is still not resolved, a full-scale discussion is arranged. This discussion includes everyone involved in the broadened discussion, as well as all remaining members of the union's grievance committee and another high-level manager. As usual, all proceedings are put in writing. All participants are careful not to violate the labor contract during this attempt to resolve the complaint.

Arbitration   The final step in almost all grievance procedures is **arbitration,** in which a neutral third party hears the grievance and renders a binding decision. As in a court hearing, each side presents its case with the right to cross-examine witnesses. In addition, the arbitrator reviews the written documentation of all previous steps in the grievance procedure. Both sides may then give summary arguments and/or present briefs. The arbitrator then decides whether a provision of the labor contract has been violated and he or she proposes a remedy. The arbitrator cannot make any decision that would add to, detract from, or modify the terms of the contract. If it can be proved that the arbitrator exceeded the scope of his or her authority, either party may appeal the decision to the courts.

What actually happens when union and management "lock horns" over all the issues we have mentioned? We can answer this question by looking at the procedures involved in collective bargaining.

COLLECTIVE BARGAINING

Once a new union is certified by the NLRB, its first task is to establish its own identity and structure. It will immediately sign up as many members as possible. Then, in an internal election, members will choose officers and representatives (including the shop stewards and grievance committee members referred to earlier). A negotiating committee will also be chosen to begin **collective bargaining,** the process of negotiating a labor contract with management.

The First Contract

To prepare for its first contract session with management, the negotiating committee decides what position it will take on the various contract issues. The committee is likely to determine which issues are of most importance to the union's members. To the members of a newly formed union, the two most pressing issues might be a general wage increase and an improved benefits package.

The union then informs management that it is ready to begin negotiations, and a time and location are agreed on. Both sides continue to prepare for the session up until the actual date of the negotiations.

The negotiations are occasionally held on company premises, but it is commoner for the parties to meet away from the work place—perhaps in a local hotel. The union is typically represented by the negotiating committee and by one or more officials from the regional or national union office. The firm is normally represented by managers from the industrial-relations, operations, personnel, and legal departments. Each side is required by law to negotiate in good faith and not to stall or attempt to extend the bargaining proceedings unnecessarily.

The union normally presents its contract demands first. Management then responds to the union's demands, often with a counterproposal. The bargaining may move back and forth, from proposal to counterproposal, over a number of meetings. Throughout the process, union representatives constantly keep their members informed of what is going on and how the committee feels about the various proposals and counterproposals.

Each side clearly tries to "get its own way" as much as possible, but each also recognizes the need for compromise. For example, the union may begin the negotiations demanding a wage increase of $1 per hour but may be willing to accept 60 cents per hour. Management may initially offer 40 cents but may be willing to pay 75 cents. Eventually, the two sides will agree on a wage increase of somewhere between 60 and 75 cents per hour.

If an agreement cannot be reached, it is possible for the union to go on strike. Strikes are rare during a union's first contract negotiations. In most cases, the initial contract is eventually developed by the negotiating teams.

The final step in collective bargaining is **ratification,** which is approval of the contract by a vote of the union membership. If the membership accepts the terms of the contract, it is signed and becomes a legally binding agreement. If the contract is not ratified, the negotiators must go back and try to iron out a more acceptable agreement.

Later Contracts

A labor contract may cover a period of from one to three years or more, but every contract has an expiration date. As that date approaches, both management and union begin to prepare for new contract negotiations. Now, however, the entire process is likely to be much thornier than the first negotiation.

For one thing, the union and the firm have "lived with each other" for several years. There may have been some difficulties during this time, and issues may have arisen that each side sees as being of critical importance. Such issues can result in a great deal of emotion at the bargaining table, and they are often difficult to resolve. For another thing, each side has learned from the earlier negotiations. Each may take a harder line on certain issues and be less willing to compromise.

And then there is the contract deadline. As the expiration date of the existing contract draws near, each side feels pressure—real or imagined—to reach an agreement. This pressure may nudge the negotiators toward agreement, but it can also produce even greater difficulty in reaching an accord. Moreover, at some point during the negotiations, union leaders are likely to take a *strike vote*. This vote reveals whether union

Figure 10.6 Techniques Used by Labor and Management to Influence Negotiations

When negotiations fail and a strike is called, striking workers may picket to publicize their grievances and gain wider support. *Source:* © 1984 Martin Rogers, Uniphoto.

members are willing to strike in the event that a new contract is not negotiated before the old one expires. In almost all cases, this vote supports a strike. So the threat of a strike may add to the pressure mounting on both sides, as they go about the business of negotiating a new contract.

STRIKES, LOCKOUTS, AND OTHER NEGOTIATING TECHNIQUES

Both management and unions can draw on certain techniques to influence one another during contract negotiations. The most extreme are strikes and lockouts, but there are other, milder techniques as well. (See Figure 10.6.)

Strikes

Unions make use of strikes only in a very few instances, and it is almost always after an existing labor contract has expired. Even then, if new contract negotiations seem to be proceeding smoothly, a union does not actually start a strike. The union does take a strike vote, but the vote may be used primarily to show members' commitment to a strike if negotiations fail.

When union members do go out on strike, it is usually because negotiations seem to be stalled. A strike is simply a work stoppage: Employees do not report for work. In addition, striking workers engage in **picketing,** marching back and forth in front of their place of employment with signs informing the public that a strike is in progress. In doing so, they hope that (1) the public will be sympathetic to the strikers and will not patronize the struck firm; (2) nonstriking employees of the firm will honor the picket line and not report to work either; and (3) members of other unions will not cross the picket line (for example, to make deliveries or pickups) so as to restrict further the operations of the struck firm.

Obviously, strikes are expensive to both the firm and the strikers. The firm loses business and earnings during the strike. In fact, the main objective of a strike is to put financial pressure on the firm. At the same time, the striking workers lose the wages they would have earned if they had been at their jobs.

Unions try to support striking members as much as possible. Larger unions put a portion of their members' dues into a *strike fund.* The fund is used to provide financial support for striking union members.

At times, workers may go out on a **wildcat strike,** which is a strike that has not been approved by the union. In this situation, union leaders typically work with management to convince the strikers to return to work.

Other Union Weapons

Almost every labor contract contains a clause that prohibits strikes during the life of the contract. (This is why strikes usually take place after a contract has expired.) However, a union may strike a firm while the contract is in force if members believe that management has violated the terms of the contract. Workers may also engage in a **slowdown,** which is a technique whereby workers report to their jobs but work at a slower pace than normal.

A **boycott** is a refusal to do business with a particular firm. Unions occasionally bring this technique to bear by urging their members (and sympathizers) not to purchase the products of a firm with which they are having a dispute. A *primary* boycott, which is aimed at the employer directly involved in the dispute, can be a powerful weapon. *Secondary* boycotts, which are aimed at firms doing business with the employer, are prohibited by the Taft-Hartley Act.

Management Weapons

Management's most potent weapon is the lockout. In a **lockout,** the firm refuses to allow employees to enter the work place. Like strikes, lockouts are expensive for both the firm and its employees. For this reason they are rarely used, and then only in certain special circumstances. A firm that produces perishable goods, for example, may use a lockout if management believes its employees will soon go on strike. The idea is to stop production in time to ensure that there is minimal spoilage of finished goods or work in process.

Management may also attempt to hire strikebreakers. **Strikebreakers** are nonunion employees who perform the jobs of striking union members. This practice can result in violence when picketing employees confront the nonunion workers at the entrances to the struck facility. There is also the problem of finding qualified replacements for the striking workers. Sometimes management personnel will take over the jobs of strikers. Bell Telephone managers have done this on more than one occasion.

Mediation and Arbitration

Strikes and strikebreaking, lockouts and boycotts, all pit one side against the other. Ultimately one side "wins" and the other "loses." Unfortunately, the negative effects of such actions—including resentment, fear, and distrust—may linger for months or years after a dispute has been resolved.

More productive techniques that are being used increasingly are mediation and arbitration. These techniques may come into play before a labor contract expires or after some other strategy, such as a strike, has proved ineffective.

Mediation is the use of a neutral third party to assist management and the union during their negotiations. This third party (the mediator) listens to both sides, trying to find common ground for agreement. The mediator also tries to facilitate communication between the two sides, to promote compromise, and generally to keep the negotiations moving. At first the mediator may meet privately with each side. Eventually, however, his or her goal is to get the two to settle their differences at the bargaining table.

We have already encountered **arbitration** as the last stage of the union-management grievance procedure. It may also be used in contract negotiations when the two sides cannot agree on one or more issues. It should be noted that the arbitration step is a formal hearing, as in the grievance procedure. Here, the arbitrator hears the formal positions of both parties on outstanding, unresolved issues. He or she then analyzes these positions and makes a decision on the possible resolution of these issues. If both sides have agreed in advance that the arbitration will be binding, they must accept the arbitrator's decision.

Chapter Review

SUMMARY

A labor union is an organization of workers who act together to negotiate wages and working conditions with their employers. Labor relations are the dealings between labor unions and business management.

The first major union in the United States was the Knights of Labor, formed in 1869. The Knights were followed in 1886 by the American Federation of Labor and in 1905 by the radical Industrial Workers of the World. Of these three craft unions, only the AFL remained when the Congress of Industrial Organizations was founded as an industrial union between World War I and World War II. After years of bickering, the AFL and CIO merged in 1955. The largest union not affiliated with the AFL-CIO is the Teamsters' union.

At present, union membership accounts for only about one-quarter of the American work force, and it seems to be decreasing for various reasons. Nonetheless, unions wield considerable power in many industries—those in which their members comprise a large proportion of the work force.

Important laws that affect union power are the Norris-LaGuardia Act (which limits management's ability to obtain injunctions against unions), the Wagner Act (which forbids certain unfair labor practices by management), the Taft-Hartley Act (which forbids certain unfair practices by unions), and the Landrum-Griffin Act (which regulates the internal functioning of labor unions). The National Labor Relations Board, a federal agency that oversees union-management relations, was created by the Wagner Act.

Employees start or join unions for a variety of reasons, including alienation, concern about job security, and dissatisfaction with their jobs. The process by which a union is formed begins with an organizing campaign and ends with a formal election in which employees decide whether they want a union. The entire process is supervised by the NLRB, which also certifies the results of the election.

Once a union is established, it may negotiate a labor contract with management through the process called collective bargaining. Contract issues include employee pay and benefits, working hours, job and union security, management rights, and grievance procedures. As the expiration date of an existing contract approaches, management and the union begin to negotiate a new contract.

When contract negotiations do not run smoothly, unions may apply pressure on management through strikes, slowdowns, and boycotts. Management may counter by imposing a lockout or hiring strikebreakers. Less drastic techniques for breaking contract deadlocks are mediation and arbitration. In both, a neutral third party is involved in the negotiations.

This chapter ends our discussion of human resources. In the next part of the book, we shall examine the marketing function of business. We begin, in Chapter 11, by discussing the meaning of the term *marketing* and the various markets for products and services.

KEY TERMS

You should now be able to define and give an example relevant to each of the following terms:

labor union

labor relations

craft union

strike

industrial union

National Labor Relations Board (NLRB)

injunction

union shop

bargaining unit

jurisdiction

seniority

overtime

job security

union security

closed shop

agency shop

maintenance shop

grievance procedure

shop steward

arbitration

collective bargaining

ratification

picketing

wildcat strike

slowdown

boycott

lockout

strikebreakers

mediation

QUESTIONS AND EXERCISES

Review Questions

1. Briefly describe the history of unions in the United States.
2. How has government regulation of union-management relations evolved during this century?
3. For what reasons do employees start or join unions?
4. Describe the process of forming a union, and explain the role of the NLRB in that process.
5. List the major areas that are negotiated in a labor contract.
6. Explain the three issues involved in negotiations concerning employee pay.
7. What is the difference between job security and union security? How do unions attempt to enhance union security?
8. What is a grievance? Describe the typical grievance procedure.
9. What steps are involved in collective bargaining?
10. Why are strikes and lockouts relatively rare at the present time?
11. What are the objectives of picketing?
12. In what ways is mediation different from arbitration?

Discussion Questions

1. Chrysler and the UAW have been anything but cooperative during most of their relationship. Why did they agree to cooperate at the Detroit Trim plant? What did each side hope to gain?
2. How might collective bargaining between Chrysler and the UAW have been affected by the appointment of Douglas Fraser (head of the UAW) to the Chrysler board of directors? Explain.
3. Do unions really derive their power mainly from their membership and labor legislation? What are some other sources of union power?

4. Which labor contract issues are likely to be the easiest to resolve? Which are likely to be the most difficult?
5. Discuss the following statement: Union security means job security for union members.
6. How would you prepare for labor contract negotiations as a member of management? as head of the union negotiating committee?
7. Under what circumstances are strikes and lockouts justified in place of mediation or arbitration?

Exercises

1. Develop a labor contract to govern student-teacher relations in your school. Include at least four major issues.
2. Find two or more articles describing a recent strike.
   a. Try to determine the exact nature of the issue or issues on which negotiators could not agree.
   b. Determine how these issues were finally resolved.
   c. Explain how these issues could have been resolved without a strike.
3. Find a copy of a labor contract in your library. List the issues that are covered in the contract, and compare them with the issues cited in this chapter.

CASE 10-1

Unions at War and Peace

For years, St. Louis was a city of declining population and waning business strength. Although a number of factors contributed to this situation, one especially serious problem was the frequency of jurisdictional disputes among construction workers' unions.

The carpenters, pipefitters, iron workers, bricklayers, and other unions regularly quarreled over who would do what at various construction sites. Typically, one of two disputing unions would lose a particular work assignment, pull all its workers off the project, and go on strike. In some cases, only the work of that union was affected. In other cases, the entire project had to be shut down.

According to Anheuser-Busch, one of the city's largest firms, at least two jurisdictional strikes would occur during any given two-year project. Each strike might last days or weeks. In 1971, 13 days were lost when entire projects were shut down. Another 102 days were lost by individual unions that were out on strike.

In 1972, industry and labor leaders formed an alliance called Productivity and Responsibility Increase Development and Employment (PRIDE). The catalyst for PRIDE was the realization that each side needed the other. Both construction spending and jobs had dropped rapidly as many firms decided to build elsewhere, to avoid the large cost overruns that characterized St. Louis construction.

The unions vowed to end jurisdictional strikes and to eliminate unnecessary work practices. Management agreed to work harder at proper scheduling and to cooperate with the unions in making job assignments. A group of labor and management officials began to meet regularly to discuss current and potential problems.

The results of PRIDE have been impressive. Since 1972 there has been only one jurisdictional strike in St. Louis. Moreover, productivity has increased dramatically. One luxury hotel was recently completed at a cost of $71,000 per room. A comparable hotel in another city would cost from $80,000 to $85,000 per room. Similarly, the city's new convention center was completed three months early, at $864,000 below budget.[3]

1. What effects do such jurisdictional disputes have on union security and power?
2. Obviously, union construction workers earn less in total wages when they finish a project ahead of schedule and under budget. Why, then, should they work with management to do so?

CASE 10-2

Continental Airlines Sidesteps the Unions

The early 1980s were a bitter time for the airline industry. Braniff Airlines had folded, and several other airlines were flirting with bankruptcy. Following airline deregulation, many carriers had embarked on a near-disastrous course of action: They had cut their own income by engaging in fare wars, while their costs continued to soar.

One airline, Continental, found itself following in Braniff's footsteps in late 1983. However, rather than wait until all its resources were depleted before declaring bankruptcy, Continental shut down and filed while it still had some money in the bank. And just 56 hours after filing for court protection, the airline was flying again.

The company had used the protection of bankruptcy to get around its existing union contracts. Almost 4000 of the firm's 12,000 employees were hired back immediately—but at considerably reduced wages.

Three unions in particular were affected: the Air Line Pilots Association, the International Association of Machinists and Aerospace Workers, and the Union of Flight Attendants. Obviously, the three unions did not take Continental's course of action lightly. Their representatives claimed that they had already made substantial wage concessions and that the temporary shutdown was simply a ploy to get rid of the unions. Although federal judges sided with the airline, the unions called a general strike.

The first several weeks of the strike were filled with tension. The employees who went back to work were harassed by picketing ex-employees. The unions made several public statements in which they questioned the safety standards of the "new" airline. Eventually, however, the turmoil began to die down, and Continental turned its attention to other problems it must solve in order to survive.[4]

1. How could the unions have provided for such a possibility as Continental's bankruptcy in their contract negotiations?
2. Do you think Continental's actions were ethical? Why?

Career Profile

John Opel John Opel is "The Brain" who runs International Business Machines. He got his nickname because he is, as one IBM board member put it, "very possibly the brightest chief executive I've ever dealt with." Opel has spent his entire working life at IBM. Over the years he has held 19 positions in the company, posts ranging from manufacturing to press relations. In 1974 he became the company's president, and in 1981 he was chosen as its chief executive officer.

Opel grew up in Jefferson City, Missouri, where his father ran a hardware store. He went to local Westminster College, then to the University of Chicago from which he received a Master's of Business Administration degree. Back home, Opel immediately joined IBM as a salesperson.

IBM is known as a company that hires from within and that rewards long-term commitment. After a decade of success, Opel was moved to the company's headquarters in Armonk, New York, to become assistant to IBM's president, Tom Watson, Jr., son of the company's founder.

Opel describes himself as "a product of the culture of IBM, of the way we do things. The founder, Thomas Watson, Sr., had established IBM culture after his own image. He told employees what to wear (white shirts with their dark business suits and striped ties) and what to drink (no alcohol on or off the job), commissioned the writing of a company songbook and led gatherings of employees in singing the company's praises, and had his motto "Think" posted everywhere. Opel is cut from the old pattern. His shirts are white, his ties subdued, his shoes standard corporate cordovans. His manner is correct and restrained. He won't name the make of car he drives. A stand-up desk is the only unusual feature in his office.

Yet for all his conservative conformity, Opel has been successful as IBM's chief largely because he has been willing to shake the company up. In the 1970s, IBM had become big and complacent, lagging behind smaller, more innovative companies. Opel saw that IBM's highly centralized, structured management, while extremely efficient in some ways, did not allow enough room for innovation and creativity. Gradually he changed policy so that headquarters became responsible only for overall planning and control, not for short-term decisions. He established seven independent business units that operate like companies within a company. One of these groups, working virtually around-the-clock in Florida, produced the IBM Personal Computer (PC), which quickly became the industry standard and has challenged the Apple for the industry lead, despite Apple's four-year head start and huge success. The PC has signaled a departure from standard IBM practice in a number of ways. Many of its components were purchased from other companies, rather than made by IBM, and the company has opened retail stores to sell its products, rather than dealing only with corporate customers. In the 1980s, in large response to Opel's restructuring of management, IBM regained its position as chief innovator in the field. So although John Opel may still stand in his office as a perfect representative of what founder Thomas Watson would like in a chief executive, his managerial decisions have caused IBM to put on a new face and to regain its status as one of the best-run corporations in American history.

The figure in the salary column approximates the expected annual income after two or three years of service.

1 = $12,000–$15,000   2 = $16,000–$20,000   3 = $21,000–$27,000   4 = $28,000–$35,000   5 = $36,000 and up

Job Title	Educational Requirements	Salary Range	Prospects
Affirmative action coordinator	Some college; degree helpful	2–3	Gradual growth
Assembler	High school diploma	1	Limited growth
Blue-collar worker supervisor	High school diploma; some college helpful	2–3	Limited growth
Employment counselor	Degree in business or human relations management	3	Limited growth
Employment development specialist	Bachelor's degree in business or management; on-the-job experience	4	Limited growth
Industrial relations analyst	Bachelor's degree in business or management; on-the-job experience	3–4	Limited growth
Labor relations specialist	Bachelor's degree; on-the-job experience	4	Limited growth
Management services trainee—personnel	Two years of college; bachelor's degree helpful	1–3	Gradual growth
Mediator	Bachelor's degree; on-the-job experience	4–5	Limited growth
Personnel administrator	Bachelor's degree in personnel; master's degree helpful	3–4	Limited growth
Personnel interviewer	Some college; degree helpful	2	Limited growth
Personnel receptionist	High school diploma; on-the-job experience	1	Limited growth
Personnel worker	Some college; college degree preferred	2	Gradual growth
Procurement clerk	High school diploma	1–2	Limited growth
Records analyst	Bachelor's degree; on-the-job experience	2–3	Gradual growth
Regulatory inspector	High school diploma; some college preferred	2–3	Limited growth
Safety inspector	High school diploma; some college preferred	2–3	Limited growth
Salary and wage administrator	Some college; degree in personnel helpful	3	Limited growth
Social worker	College degree; graduate degree preferred	2–3	Limited growth
Training officer	Some college; degree helpful; on-the-job experience	2–3	Limited growth

PART

4
Marketing

The business activities that make up the firm's marketing effort are those that are most directly concerned with satisfying customers' needs. In this part, we discuss these activities in some detail. We begin with a general discussion of marketing and the market for consumer goods. Then, in turn, we discuss the four elements that are combined into a marketing program: product, price, distribution, and promotion. Included in this part are:

CHAPTER

ELEVEN

An Overview of Marketing

Picture some product—say, a pair of shoes—being inspected at the end of a production line in North Carolina. Now picture these shoes being purchased in a department store in, say, Duluth, Minnesota. Are they really the same pair of shoes in both cases? Although the shoes look the same, most business people would say they aren't the same at all. The shoes have been the object of some very important business activities between the time they were produced and the time they were purchased by the customer. Those activities, taken together, are called "marketing," and they have added "value" to the shoes. In this chapter, you will see what marketing entails and how it affects the goods and services you buy. After studying the chapter, you should understand:

1. *What marketing is, and how it creates utility for the purchasers of goods and services*
2. *The marketing concept, and how it is implemented*
3. *The importance of marketing information*
4. *How marketers pinpoint the markets for their products through market segmentation*
5. *The four ingredients of the marketing mix: product, price, distribution, and promotion*
6. *How a strategic marketing plan is developed*
7. *The major characteristics of the market for consumer products*

Consider this:

What does a firm do when its customers are so satisfied with its product that they seem to have no more needs for the firm to fill? For Eastman Kodak Company, the answer was to find a need that consumers didn't realize they had, then to develop a product to satisfy that need, and finally to show consumers that both the need and the need-satisfying product did indeed exist.

Eastman Kodak has been manufacturing photographic products for over a century. Although the firm produces a variety of cameras, its primary consumer products are film and photographic paper, products that generate repeat sales. All of Kodak's products have gained the reputation of high quality—a reputation that the company does not treat lightly. In fact, this quality seems to have been at least partly responsible for Kodak's dilemma.

To expand its sales of film and photographic paper, Kodak had worked diligently at increasing the number of consumers who own and use cameras. Over the years, the firm produced cameras that were easier and easier to use and took better and better photos. Cartridge-loading cameras, which were introduced in the 1960s, were the most popular. They are inexpensive and simple to use, and the "pocket" versions can be taken anywhere. Owners of these cameras were quite satisfied with them—to the extent that sales began to drop in 1978. According to one Kodak spokesman, "The reason for the decline was that consumers were generally very happy with the cameras they had at home."[1] In other words, consumers were so pleased with their present cartridge-loading cameras that they were not interested in buying improved versions.

Kodak chose not to wait until the product life cycle caught up with its cartridge cameras. In 1972 it began a program to determine *what else* its customers wanted—and to design and market a product to satisfy those wants.

Camera makers knew that inexpensive cartridge cameras could not take good photos in certain situations. Camera owners generally accepted this shortcoming, which did little to diminish their general satisfaction with the product. But Kodak's marketing personnel took on the

In Kodak's new camera, a film disc replaces the traditional roll. *Source: Courtesy of Eastman Kodak.*

tasks of (1) determining when, and where, consumers were *not* able to get good results and (2) providing a photographic system that would allow them to take satisfactory photos in these situations. The first task was accomplished through marketing research and studies of how people actually took photographs. The second called for a new look at photography fundamentals and for the development of faster and sharper color film, new lens-production technology, and special integrated control circuits. The entire process took approximately ten years. The product that resulted is Kodak's disc camera.

Through product testing in more than a thousand homes, Kodak's marketers determined which features of their new camera were most important to consumers, and these were made part of the final product design. These same features were emphasized in the advertising campaign for the new camera. They included the automatic flash, film advance, and focusing, all of which made taking pictures easier for amateurs. The features chosen for emphasis also included the ability to take photos under a wide variety of lighting conditions.

Kodak's product testing also led to the major

theme of its advertising: "You'll be able to take pictures you may have been missing before." This theme was the basis of Kodak's initial one-minute television commercials and half-minute follow-up commercials. Newspaper and magazine ads also emphasized the five-year warranty.

Three models of the disc camera were introduced early in 1982. Their retail prices ranged from $67.95 to $142.95. Some industry observers, who had been expecting a price tag around $40, were disappointed. Others were very much impressed with Kodak's new technology, which allows amateurs to take better pictures faster and with less worry about focus, lighting, and so on. Of particular interest were potential sales of Kodak's film disc and equipment for processing it.

"But the real test was in the marketplace," recalls John J. Powers, Kodak's vice president and director of marketing communications. "We set some very ambitious sales goals for 1982. Actual sales of film, cameras, and photofinishing equipment far exceeded our most optimistic projections."[2]

The creation and successful sales of this product are the result of extensive market research. Source: Courtesy of Eastman Kodak.

According to the American Marketing Association, **marketing** is "the performance of business activities that direct the flow of goods and services from producer to consumer or user." For Kodak, marketing began well before there was any actual flow of goods to direct. It was Kodak's marketing personnel who—through marketing research—discovered the need for a camera with certain features. No doubt these marketers worked with research and development personnel on the development of the disc camera. And, once the camera was designed, they were responsible for ensuring that it actually did satisfy that need.

Kodak's marketing effort thus began with the recognition of a need. Marketing personnel were involved in all activities related to filling this need, including product development. As we will see, this total involvement stems from a fairly new business perspective called the marketing concept.

When their product tests showed that the disc camera was a viable product, marketing personnel turned to more traditional marketing activities. They determined the number of models to be produced (the product line) and set the price of each model. They also decided to offer a five-year warranty with the disc camera. (This long warranty period implies both quality and worry-free picture taking for amateur photographers.) And they devised an advertising campaign that emphasized the satisfaction of customer needs through use of the disc camera.

These and many more activities, including the actual distribution and sale of products, are part of modern marketing. For the most successful firms, marketing begins well before a product is manufactured, and it ends only with satisfied customers. To fully understand customer satisfaction, we must explore the concept of utility, the value that marketing adds to consumer products.

UTILITY: THE VALUE ADDED BY MARKETING

We began this chapter by picturing a pair of shoes in two settings—first in a factory in North Car-

The marketing of public telephone service creates place utility through convenient location, time utility through 24-hour availability, and possession utility through coin and credit operation. Source: © 1984 T. Molinski.

olina and then in a department store in Minnesota. We noted that, to most business people, the difference in settings made a difference in the shoes. This difference is referred to as utility.

Utility is the power of a good or service to satisfy a human need. A lunch at a Ponderosa Restaurant, an overnight stay at a Hilton Inn, and a Ford Thunderbird all satisfy human needs. Each possesses utility. There are four kinds of utility. One of these is created by the production process, and three are created by marketing.

Form utility is utility that is created by converting production inputs into finished products. Our completed pair of shoes, waiting in the North

Carolina factory, certainly possesses form utility. If a customer for the shoes happened into the factory, the shoes could satisfy the customer's need for protection or warmth or fashionable footwear. Unfortunately, the customer for our pair of shoes is in Duluth, Minnesota.

The three kinds of utility that are created by marketing are place utility, time utility, and possession utility. **Place utility** is utility that is created by making a product available at a location where customers wish to purchase it. Our pair of shoes was given place utility when it was shipped to the department store in Duluth and displayed in the shoe department. Thousands of similar pairs of shoes were given place utility when they were distributed to other stores around the country.

Time utility is utility that is created by making a product available when customers wish to purchase it. For example, tennis shoes might be manufactured in December but not displayed until April, when consumers in Duluth start thinking about summer sports. By storing the shoes until they are wanted, the manufacturer or retailer provides time utility.

Possession utility is utility that is created by transferring title (or ownership) of a product to the buyer. For a product as simple as a pair of shoes, ownership is usually transferred by means of a sales slip or receipt. For such products as automobiles and homes, the transfer of title is a more complex process. Along with the title to its product, the seller transfers the right to use that product to satisfy a need. (See Figure 11.1.)

Time, place, and possession utility have real value in terms of both money and convenience. This value is created and added to goods and services through a wide variety of marketing activities—from the research indicating what customers want to the product warranties ensuring that customers get what they paid for. Overall, these marketing activities account for about half of every dollar spent by consumers. When they are part of an integrated marketing program that delivers maximum utility to the customer, most of us would agree that they are worth the cost.

Place, time, and possession utility are only the

most fundamental applications of marketing activities. In recent years, marketing has become much more a part of business philosophy. Marketing has become the marketing concept.

THE MARKETING CONCEPT

The process that led to Kodak's success with the disc camera seems as simple as it can be. First identify a consumer need. Then develop a product to satisfy the need. And finally, show potential customers that the product does actually fill their need. This process is an application of the marketing concept, or marketing orientation. As simple as it seems, American business took about 150 years to develop it.

Evolution of the Marketing Concept

From the start of the Industrial Revolution until the early twentieth century, business effort was directed mainly toward the production of goods.

Consumer demand for manufactured products was so great that manufacturers could almost bank on selling everything they produced. Business had a strong *production orientation,* in which emphasis was placed on increased output and production efficiency. Marketing was limited to taking orders and distributing finished goods.

The production orientation is still with us. It appears in the outlook of some individual firms and often in new industries. For example, the computer industry has been accused of worrying more about the production of hardware and software than about customers' needs. Computer advertisements stress RAM capacities, disk drives, monitor resolution, and IBM compatibility. But they don't tell the consumer how computers can satisfy human needs. According to James Morgan, Atari's new chairman, "The entire industry has missed the point. . . . The consumer does not know what to do with a computer."[3]

In the 1920s production began to catch up with demand. Now producers had to direct their efforts toward selling goods to consumers whose

Figure 11.1 *Types of Utility. Form utility is created by the production process, but marketing creates time, place, and possession utility.*

WANTED — One pair of size 8 shoes in Duluth immediately. Will pay $30.	can satisfy the need through	but cannot satisfy the need with
FORM UTILITY	size 8 shoes	size 10 shoes
PLACE UTILITY	size 8 shoes in Duluth	size 8 shoes in Los Angeles
TIME UTILITY	size 8 shoes in Duluth available now	size 8 shoes in Duluth, available next month
POSSESSION UTILITY	size 8 shoes in Duluth available now for $30	size 8 shoes in Duluth, available now for $50

basic wants were already satisfied. This new *sales orientation* was characterized by increased advertising, enlarged sales forces, and occasional high-pressure selling techniques. Manufacturers still produced the goods they expected consumers to want. Marketing still consisted primarily of taking orders and delivering goods, along with personal selling and advertising.

During the early 1950s, however, business people started to realize that even the best product and the most thoroughly proven sales techniques were not enough. Something else was needed if products were to sell as well as expected. It was then that business managers recognized that they were not primarily producers or sellers but rather were in the business of satisfying consumers' wants. They realized that the best strategy was first to determine what consumers need and then to develop, manufacture, and market goods and services that fill particular needs.

This **marketing orientation** (or **marketing concept**) is a total approach to marketing that includes the entire business organization in the process of satisfying customers' needs while achieving the organization's goals. (See Figure 11.2.) All the various functional areas—from product development through production to finance and, of course, marketing—are viewed as interrelated parts of a marketing system, rather than as separate parts of the firm.

The marketing process involves eight major business functions (see Table 11.1). Some of these a firm may hire another firm to perform;

but none of these functions can be eliminated if the marketing process is to be effective.

Implementing the Marketing Concept

The marketing concept has been adopted by many of the most successful business firms—Eastman Kodak, for example. Some firms, such as Ford Motor Company and Apple Computer, have gone through minor or major reorganizations in the process. The marketing concept is essentially a business philosophy, and anyone can say, "I believe in it." But to make it work, management must fully adopt and then implement it.

To implement the marketing concept, a firm must first obtain information about its customers and its potential customers. The firm must determine not only what customers' needs are but also how well those needs are being satisfied by its products and those of its competitors. It must ascertain how its products might be improved, what customers think of the firm and its marketing efforts, and so on.

The firm must then use this information to pinpoint the specific needs and potential customers toward which it will direct its marketing activities and resources. (Obviously, no firm can expect to satisfy all needs. And not every individual or firm can be considered a potential customer for every product manufactured or sold by a firm.) Next the firm must mobilize its marketing resources to (1) provide a product or service that will satisfy its customers, at a reasonable price that will earn it a profit; (2) promote the product

Figure 11.2 *Evolution of the Marketing Orientation*

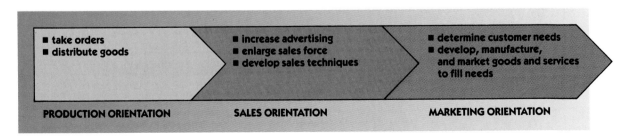

- take orders
- distribute goods

- increase advertising
- enlarge sales force
- develop sales techniques

- determine customer needs
- develop, manufacture, and market goods and services to fill needs

PRODUCTION ORIENTATION   **SALES ORIENTATION**   **MARKETING ORIENTATION**

so that potential customers will be aware of its existence and its ability to satisfy their needs; and (3) ensure that the product is distributed properly, so that it is available to customers.

Finally, the firm must again obtain marketing information—this time regarding the effectiveness of its efforts. Can the product be improved? Is it being promoted properly? Is it being distributed efficiently? Is the price too high? And the firm must be ready to modify any or all of its marketing activities on the basis of this feedback.

MARKETING INFORMATION

Accurate and timely information is the foundation of effective marketing—and, in particular, of the marketing concept. A wealth of marketing information is available, both within the firm and from outside sources, but this information must be gathered, analyzed, and put to use by marketing personnel.

There are two general approaches to collecting marketing information. A marketing information system provides information on a continuing basis, whereas marketing research is used to obtain information for specific marketing projects.

Marketing Information Systems

A **marketing information system** is a computer-based system for managing marketing information that is gathered continually from internal and external sources. A *computer* is essential to a marketing information system because of the amount of data that the system must accept, store, sort, and retrieve. Also essential is the *continual* collection of data, so that the system incorporates the most up-to-date information.

In concept (and with a computer), the operation of a marketing information system is extremely simple. Data from a variety of sources are fed into the system. For example, data from *internal* sources include sales figures; product and marketing costs; inventory levels; and activities of the sales force. Data from *external*

sources concern the firm's suppliers, middlemen, and customers; competitors' marketing activities; and economic conditions. All these data are stored and processed within the marketing information system. Its output is a flow of information

Table 11.1 Major Marketing Functions

Exchange Functions: All companies such as manufacturers, wholesalers, and retailers buy and sell in order to sell their merchandise.
1. **Buying** includes such things as obtaining raw materials to make products, knowing how much merchandise to keep on hand, and selecting suppliers.
2. **Selling** creates ownership utility, the transfer of title from seller to customer.

Physical Distribution Functions: These functions involve the flow of goods from producers to customers. Transportation and storage provide time utility and place utility and require careful management of inventory.
3. **Transporting** involves selecting a mode of transport that provides an acceptable speed of delivery at an acceptable price.
4. **Storing** goods is often necessary in order to sell them at the best selling time.

Facilitating Functions: These functions help the other functions take place.
5. **Financing** helps at all stages of marketing. In order to buy raw materials manufacturers often borrow from banks or receive credit from suppliers. Wholesalers may be financed by manufacturers and retailers may receive financing from the wholesaler or manufacturer. Finally, retailers often provide financing to customers.
6. **Standardizing** sets uniform specifications for products or services. **Grading** classifies products by size and quality, usually through a sorting process. Together standardization and grading facilitate production, transportation, storage, and selling.
7. **Risk taking**—even though competent management and insurance can minimize risks—is a constant reality of marketing because of such losses as bad debt expense, obsolescence of products, theft by employees, product-liability suits, and so on.
8. **Gathering market information** is a necessity for all marketing decisions.

in the form that is most useful for marketing decision making. Among this information might be daily sales reports by territory and product, forecasts of sales or buying trends, and reports on the effectiveness of particular marketing strategies. Both the information output and its form depend on the requirements of the individual firm. (See Figure 11.3.)

Marketing Research

Marketing research is the process of systematically gathering, recording, and analyzing data concerning a particular marketing problem. Thus marketing research is used in specific situations to obtain information that is not otherwise available to decision makers. It is an intermittent, rather than a continuous, source of marketing information.

Some general guidelines for conducting marketing research are given in Table 11.2. This procedure is particularly well suited to testing new products, determining various characteristics of consumer markets, and evaluating promotional activities. General Foods Corporation makes extensive use of marketing research—in the form of taste tests—to determine whether proposed new products will appeal to consumers.

Now that we know some of the ways in which firms compile marketing information, it is time to examine the idea of the market itself.

MARKETS AND MARKET SEGMENTATION

The word *market* has many meanings. We speak of the stock market, the money market, the col-

Figure 11.3 *Marketing Information System. Using a computer, the system compiles and converts information from inside and outside the company into a form useful for decision making.*

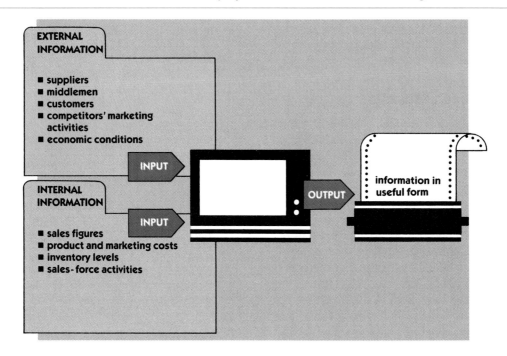

Table 11.2 *The Six Steps of Marketing Research*

1. Define the Problem	In this step, the problem is clearly and accurately stated in order to determine what issues are involved in the research, what questions to ask, and what types of solutions are needed. This is a crucial step that should not be rushed.
2. Make a Preliminary Investigation	The objective of preliminary investigation is to develop both a sharper definition of the problem and a set of tentative answers. The tentative answers are developed by examining internal information and published data, and by talking with persons who have some experience with the problem. These answers will be tested by further research.
3. Planning the Research	At this stage researchers know what facts are needed to resolve the identified problem and what facts are available. They make plans on how to gather needed but missing data.
4. Gather Factual Information	Once the basic research plan has been completed, the needed information can be collected by mail, telephone, or personal interview; by observation; or from commercial or government data sources. The choice depends on the plan and the available sources of information.
5. Interpret the Information	Facts by themselves do not always provide a sound solution to a marketing problem. They must be interpreted and analyzed so as to determine the choices that are available to management.
6. Reach a Conclusion	Sometimes the conclusion or recommendation becomes obvious when the facts are interpreted. However, in some cases, reaching a conclusion may not be so easy because of gaps in the information or intangible factors that are difficult to evaluate. If and when the evidence is less than complete, it is important to say so.

Source: Adapted from *Small Business Bibliography No. 9,* Small Business Administration, Washington, D.C.

lege market, and flea markets. People shop in the supermarket, and there was no market for Edsels.

For our purposes, a **market** consists of people who have a need, along with money and the desire and authority to spend it on goods and services. Thus people who would like to buy a 40-foot yacht, but cannot afford one, do *not* constitute a market for that product. However, executives earning more than $80,000 a year, with the time to devote to yachting, might make up one market for these yachts.

Market Segmentation

A firm that is marketing 40-foot yachts would not direct its marketing effort toward all those people who want (and can afford) a boat. Some may want a kayak or a canoe. Others may want a speedboat or an outboard-powered fishing boat. Still others might be looking for something resembling a small ocean liner. Any marketing effort that was directed toward such people would be wasted.

Instead the firm would direct its attention toward a particular portion, or segment, of the total market for boats. A **market segment** is a group of individuals or firms, within a market, that share one or more common characteristics. The process of dividing a market into segments is called **market segmentation**. In our example, one common characteristic, or *basis,* for segmentation might be "reason for wanting a boat." The firm would be interested primarily in that market segment whose reason for wanting a boat could lead to the purchase of a 40-foot yacht. Another basis for segmentation might be income; still another might be geographic location. Each of these variables has an effect on the type of boat an individual might purchase.

Marketers make use of a wide variety of segmentation bases. Those that are most commonly applied to consumer markets are shown in Figure 11.4. Each of them may be used as a single basis for market segmentation or in combination with other bases.

Target Markets

A **target market** is a market segment toward which a firm directs its marketing effort. A firm may have more than one target market for a particular product. For example, Ford Motor Company found that more than half of all Mustang owners are between 20 and 34 years old. However, a relatively large proportion are in the 45-to-54-year age bracket. Both of these age-segmented groups comprise target markets for Mustang marketers. In its marketing efforts, Ford also segments by sex, marital status, educational level, and income.[4] See Exhibits A and B, which show advertising by market segmentation.

On the other hand, a firm may develop different products for different target markets. (This strategy is very much in keeping with the marketing concept, in which marketing begins with the product.) Converse, Inc., manufacturer of athletic shoes, still targets the professional athlete as one of its primary markets, but it has introduced shoes and clothing to appeal to the "recreational athlete" as well.

The Consumer Market and the Industrial Market

One obvious, but nonetheless important, way to segment is according to whether the purchaser is a consumer or an industrial user. Consumers (the *consumer market*) purchase goods and services for their own personal use. Industrial users (the *industrial market*) purchase products to use in producing other products. Because these two groups purchase goods and services for different reasons, marketers use different marketing strategies to reach them.

Segmentation of the market at large into a

Figure 11.4 Common Market-Segmentation Bases. A company may select one common characteristic to identify a market segment. Source: Adapted from William M. Pride and O. C. Ferrell, Marketing, 3d ed., p. 46; photo, © 1983 Lou Jones.

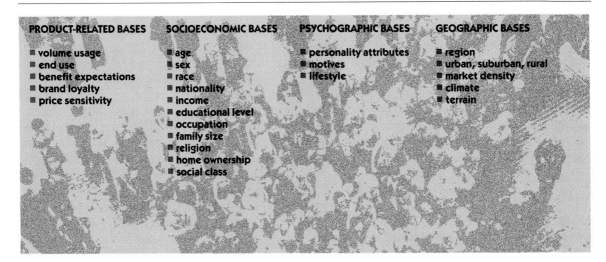

PRODUCT-RELATED BASES
- volume usage
- end use
- benefit expectations
- brand loyalty
- price sensitivity

SOCIOECONOMIC BASES
- age
- sex
- race
- nationality
- income
- educational level
- occupation
- family size
- religion
- home ownership
- social class

PSYCHOGRAPHIC BASES
- personality attributes
- motives
- lifestyle

GEOGRAPHIC BASES
- region
- urban, suburban, rural
- market density
- climate
- terrain

consumer market and an industrial market has led to a distinction between *consumer products* and *industrial products*. This distinction is not precise, however, and many products can fit in either category. For example, if a Brother Model 60 typewriter is purchased for use in a lawyer's office, it is an industrial good. If the same typewriter is purchased for household use, it is considered a consumer good.

Consumer Products A **consumer product** is a good or service that is intended primarily for personal or household use. Depending on *how these products are actually purchased* by the consumer, they are further classified as follows:

- **Convenience goods** are those that have a low unit price, are purchased frequently, and are purchased with a minimum of effort. These products (which include candy bars, milk, and newspapers) are sold in many outlets. Hence they are readily available to customers.
- **Shopping goods** are those that have a relatively high unit price, are purchased infrequently, and are usually purchased only after comparison with competing products. They are sold primarily in department stores, dealerships, and specialty stores. Personal computers, wide-screen television sets, automobiles, and furniture are included in this category.
- **Specialty goods** are those for which buyers

Some versatile industrial products, such as the laser, can be used in the production processes of many different industries. Source: Courtesy of Hitachi Corp.

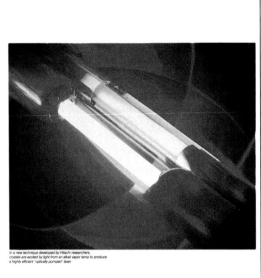

In a new technique developed by Hitachi researchers, crystals are excited by light from an alkali vapor lamp to produce a highly efficient "optically pumped" laser.

LASER

Almost a quarter of a century ago, Hitachi researchers began exploring how an exciting new form of light could be made to serve business and industry. The complex concept: Light Amplification by Stimulated Emission of Radiation. The legacy: "Laser," a beam with the ability to concentrate one million kilowatts of power in a single pulse.

Light that cuts, cures and communicates

Today, the results of Hitachi research are in use all around you. Laser diodes that can send your phone calls and business data across the country through hair-thin optical fiber. Laser memory systems capable of storing up to 40,000 pages of text on a single 12" disk. Laser-beam printers that can turn out a complete business letter in just 5 seconds. Digital-audio pickup devices for utterly distortion-free sound.

Our physicists have made significant improvements in laser technology. They have shrunk the size of the transmitter and increased output, accuracy and control. And they are experimenting with new materials capable of unleashing even greater potential.

In fact, we are constantly coming up with new methods of applying laser technology to products. One of the latest: A unique structure that boosts lasing power to the highest level ever obtained by a visible-light semiconductor laser.

These examples demonstrate a few of the ways in which Hitachi is improving upon basic technology. Then using it to create practical tools that meet your needs...and those of professionals in medicine, aerospace, and virtually every other field you can name.

The best of worlds is yet to come

Our vision of the future includes laser telecommunications networks that span the globe. Undersea tunneling and mining with laser excavating equipment. Satellite relay systems to carry transoceanic laser broadcast signals. And much, much more.

We'd like you to share in the benefits of our scientific research, covering the next generation of sensors, robots and other electronic devices. For improved business efficiency. For a higher quality of life. Two goals we've pursued for 74 years as part of our commitment to a better world through electronics.

WE BELIEVE LASERS ARE THE KEY TO PRECISION AND POWER

HITACHI

have a strong personal preference. For this reason, price is not a major purchase consideration. Specialty goods are purchased infrequently and often require that consumers make some extra effort to purchase them. They are sold in relatively few outlets, because consumers are willing to go to some trouble to buy them. Jewelry, cameras, gourmet foods, and many luxury items are classified as specialty goods.

Industrial Products An **industrial product** is a good or service that is intended primarily for use in producing other goods or services. For example, Kaypro purchases microcomputer chips to assemble into its computers. It also buys stationery for use by its employees. Both are industrial products.

Industrial products are often classified according to the way they will be used:

☐ Those that will become part of another product. Included here are *raw materials,* which have been mined or harvested but not processed; *process materials,* which have been partially processed; and *component parts,* which are ready for assembly. Examples are iron ore (a raw material), sheet steel (a process material), and automobile fenders (component parts).

☐ Those that are used in the production process but do not become part of a product. These include major equipment or *installations,* such as factories and blast furnaces, and smaller *accessory equipment,* such as hand tools.

☐ Those that are not directly associated with the production process. These industrial products include *supplies,* such as typewriter ribbons and lubricating oils, and *services,* such as janitorial or payroll services.

This classification scheme (or any other scheme) is far from foolproof. Many items cannot be classified accurately until they are actually put to use.

However, like the distinction between consumer and industrial goods, this scheme allows at least a first level of market segmentation based on product use.

Once market segmentation has identified various target markets, the firm faces the challenge of designing a marketing strategy appropriate for each. The several elements of such a strategy are known as the marketing mix.

THE MARKETING MIX

A business firm has control over four important elements of marketing—elements that it must combine in such a way as to reach its target market. These are the *product* itself, the *price* of the product, the means chosen for its *distribution,* and the *promotion* of the product. When they are combined, these four elements form a marketing mix. More specifically, a **marketing mix** is a combination of product, price, distribution, and promotion that is created to reach a particular target market. (See Figure 11.5.)

Figure 11.5 Marketing Mix. A marketing mix combines product, price, distribution, and promotion to reach a particular market. Source: Adapted from William M. Pride and O. C. Ferrell, Marketing, 3d ed., p. 19.

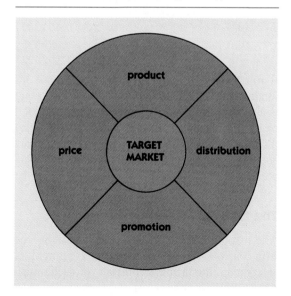

Slow Music Sells

Surprised by the size of your grocery bill? Try to remember what kind of music was playing the last time you shopped. During a nine-week test in a supermarket in the Southwest, a team of researchers arranged to have easy-listening music played in two tempos. On randomly assigned days the selections were slow (averaging 60 beats a minute) or fast (108 beats a minute). On up-tempo days, the store's gross receipts averaged $12,112, but on days when people shopped to a slower cadence, receipts were $16,740—a whopping increase of 38.2 percent.

The explanation? Researchers led by Ronald Milliman of Loyola University found that shoppers walked more slowly to tempered tunes, which presumably gave them time to browse and purchase more items. Reporting in *The Journal of Marketing* (Vol. 46, No. 3), Milliman says that when shoppers leaving the store were asked whether music had been played inside, 33 percent said they were not sure and 29 percent gave a flat "no."

Source: Carol Austin Bridgwater, *Psychology Today,* January, 1983, p. 56.

The firm can vary its marketing mix by changing any one or more of these ingredients. Thus a firm may use one marketing mix to reach one target market and a second, somewhat different marketing mix to reach another target market. Different products immediately result in different marketing mixes.

Marketers may develop a number of strategies with regard to each of the four elements of the marketing mix. *Product strategies* are concerned with the design of the product and with trade names, packaging, warranties, and the like. Thus Kodak's decision to produce three different models of the disc camera was a product strategy, as was its decision to offer purchasers a five-year warranty.

Although the forces that compose the marketing environment are usually uncontrollable, enterprising individuals may find ways to work around them. In Communist China, for instance, some improvised "free markets," based on competition, exist in spite of prevailing legal and political forces. Source: © Hiroji Kubota, Magnum.

Pricing strategies are concerned with both base prices and discounts of various kinds. They are developed to achieve particular goals, such as to maximize profit or even to make room for new models. The rebates offered by automobile manufacturers a few years ago were a pricing strategy developed to boost very low auto sales figures. Product and pricing strategies are discussed in detail in Chapter 12.

Distribution strategies are concerned not only with transportation and storage but also with the selection of middlemen. How many levels of middlemen should be involved in the distribution of a particular product? Should the product be distributed as widely as possible? Or should distribution be restricted to a few specialized outlets in each area? These and other questions related to distribution are considered in Chapter 13.

Promotional strategies are developed mainly to transmit product information to target markets. However, there are other uses of promotion—including image building. The various promotional goals, advertising strategies, and media are discussed in Chapter 14.

The "ingredients" of the marketing mix are controllable elements. The firm can vary each of them to suit its organizational goals, marketing goals, and target markets. As we extend our discussion to the firm's overall marketing plan, we will see that the marketing environment also includes a number of *uncontrollable* elements.

THE MARKETING PLAN

A **marketing plan** is an outline of actions intended to accomplish a specific set of marketing goals. The firm's marketing goals must be based on its organizational goals, and its marketing plan must be compatible with its marketing resources and the external environment in which it operates.

The External Marketing Environment

The marketing mix consists of elements that the firm controls and uses to reach its target market. In addition, the firm has control over such organizational resources as finances and information. These resources, too, may be used to accomplish marketing goals. However, the firm's marketing activities are also affected by a number of external—and generally uncontrollable—forces. These forces, which make up the external *marketing environment,* are as follows:

□ *Economic* forces—the effect of economic conditions on customers' ability and willingness to buy
□ *Societal* forces—including consumers' social and cultural values, the consumer movement, and environmental concerns
□ *Competitive* forces—the actions of competitors, who are in the process of implementing their own marketing plans

□ *Legal, political,* and *regulatory* forces—including government regulations and policies that affect marketing, whether or not they are directed specifically at marketing
□ *Technological* forces—in particular, technological changes that can cause a product (or an industry) to become obsolete almost overnight.

These forces are shown in Figure 11.6. Because they impinge on and affect the marketing mix, they cannot be ignored.

Strategic Market Planning

The development of a marketing plan begins with an assessment of the marketing environment. Marketers should gather and analyze all available

Figure 11.6 The Marketing Environment. A company's marketing activities are affected by external, largely uncontrollable forces as well as by the marketing mix it controls from inside the company. Source: Adapted from William M. Pride and O. C. Ferrell, Marketing, 3d ed., p. 19.

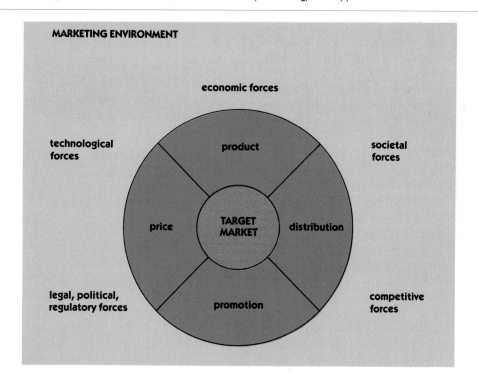

information concerning the marketing environment, the effectiveness of previous marketing programs or strategies, the firm's present and potential markets and their needs, and the availability of resources. Obviously, marketing research and the firm's marketing information system play an important role in this first stage of the planning process.

Next, particular and detailed marketing objectives should be formulated. These objectives should be developed in accordance with organizational goals. They must also be measurable and realistic—in line with both the marketing situation and the available resources.

Then a target market must be selected, and a marketing mix must be designed to reach that market. Here product, pricing, distribution, and promotion strategies need to be coordinated into a unified **marketing program,** which is a set of strategies aimed at accomplishing the firm's marketing objectives. And, as we have noted, the marketing program must be designed to operate effectively within the external marketing environment.

Finally, the marketing plan should include a means for monitoring and evaluating the operation of the marketing program. Again, both marketing research and the marketing information system come into play as monitoring tools. The information that is obtained may be used to evaluate the plan and modify it as necessary (and to the extent possible). This information will also be used to begin the next round of market planning.

We have described the marketing concept as it is. But is it as it should be? Or does it cost the consumer more than it is worth? The next section examines this issue briefly.

COSTS AND BENEFITS OF MARKETING

One of the major criticisms of American marketing is that it is costly and wasteful. Many critics feel that marketing costs are excessive when they make up as much as half the retail price of a consumer product. One of the major difficulties here is that marketing provides services, which are intangible and therefore hard to pinpoint. How much, exactly, is it worth to be able to buy Tylenol (and other over-the-counter drugs) in tamper-proof packages? What price would you put on the convenience of being able to purchase camera film in every city and town in this country? Such questions are difficult—perhaps impossible—to answer.

Here are some reasons for the general increase in marketing costs over the years.

1. Consumer demands for such services as conveniently located, pleasant shopping centers, wide assortments of attractively displayed merchandise, credit, merchandise-return privileges, guarantees and warranties, after-sale service, and free delivery all add to marketing costs.
2. Skyrocketing costs of energy, labor, transportation, packaging materials, labels, and most other inputs used by suppliers of goods and services have directly increased marketing costs.
3. Government regulations on packaging, labeling, grading, and a host of other marketing activities have increased the benefits of marketing, but they have increased its cost as well.

Though critics tend to focus on the costs of marketing, they do not deny that it serves a useful purpose. Some of the benefits of marketing activities include the following:

□ *Development of new or improved products.* Marketing research discovers consumers' changing needs and wants and translates them into new or modified products and services. The consumer gains through increased want satisfaction, often at lower prices.
□ *Creation of time, place, and possession utility.* Marketing provides goods and services where and when customers want them. Through fi-

School bus drivers in Atlanta figure out their routes by dipping into the data provided by a fledgling company in Lyme, N.H., seven miles north of Hanover. A San Francisco bank determined how to organize its branches with the help of the Lyme company. A Detroit automaker pinpointed the best spots for dealerships through the Lyme company.

The company is Geographic Data Technology Inc., founded in February 1980, employing 25. Donald F. Cooke, president, a sort of latter-day electronic-era Mercator, started GDT to "create a nationwide, machine-readable street map, essentially to put a street map of the entire country into the computer," says Woody Rothe, GDT's sales manager. The maps are being done county by county, town by town, street by street.

The job isn't done yet, but at this point, the country's 273 largest cities have all been mapped and translated into electronic dots that can be called up on a screen and then printed out as color maps. The downtown areas of these cities have been mapped, says Rothe, and "we're now in the fringe areas of the large cities; we're moving into the suburbs, adding all the suburban streets, putting them into the computer."

The main use of the maps is by marketing researchers of large corporations, which integrate the maps with other data—for example, census data on the number of people under the age of 35. The data-base maps and the data-base statistical information are, in effect, overlaid to do such things as picking locations for sales offices, plotting efficient delivery routes, or tracking acid rain. Besides corporations, customers are geographic service organizations that aid corporate clients, universities, government laboratories—anyone who wants to tie information in with geography. All that's needed is a computer, map-making software, data to use the map, and the map, which comes on a reel of computer tape.

The company is small, but very impressive. One boundary is a cartographic standard that was bought by the U.S. Census Bureau, and "in the case of that map, we have a monopoly," says Rothe. "For many of these maps, we have no competition. There's no one else capable of doing what we are doing."

That's why Atlanta school bus drivers turned to Lyme for help. But in Geographic Data Technology's home town of Lyme, the bus drivers have to fend for themselves; GDT has mapped every byway of Boston, but hasn't reached Lyme yet.

Source: Barbara Carlson, *New England Business*, December 5, 1983, p. 9.

nancing, marketing also permits consumers to own and use products well before they have accumulated the money to purchase these products outright. Marketing also provides a great deal of information (dealing with such things as product contents, use, and repair) that is valuable to purchasers.

□ *Creation of jobs.* The jobs provided by approximately 2,000,000 retailers, 400,000 wholesalers, 22,000 transportation companies, and thousands of advertising agencies are directly related to marketing.

□ *Improved standard of living.* Finally, by creating and delivering an immense variety of goods and services, marketing improves the standard of living.

Many issues involved in marketing arise in the marketing of both industrial and consumer goods. But it will be worthwhile, in the next section, to devote some attention specifically to the consumer—in short, to ourselves.

THE AMERICAN CONSUMER

In the remainder of this chapter, we shall briefly examine the market for consumer products. This market is extremely important to all marketers, for two reasons. American consumers possess tremendous purchasing power. And, perhaps more important, consumer buying patterns affect the markets for all goods—industrial goods as well as consumer goods.

To see this, we need only realize that the markets for industrial goods are *derived* from the markets for consumer goods. Without consumer goods, there would be no need for industrial goods. For example, suppose consumers stopped purchasing automobiles. The markets for sheet steel, automobile fenders, assembly plants, spark plug gauges, and a host of other industrial products would either shrink or disappear entirely.

A market consists of people with needs, money to spend, and the desire and authority to spend it. Let us look first at consumer income (the money) and then at consumer buying behavior (the spending).

Consumer Income

Purchasing power is created by income. However, as every taxpayer knows, not all income is available for spending. For this reason, marketers consider income in three different ways: **Personal income** is the income an individual receives from all sources *less* the Social Security taxes that the individual must pay. In 1983 total U.S. personal income was $2.9 trillion! The annual rate of increase in personal income at the end of that year was approximately 9.2 percent.[5]

Disposable income is personal income *less* all additional personal taxes. These taxes include income, estate, gift, and property taxes levied by local, state, and federal governments. About 6 percent of all disposable income is saved. On the average, about 60 percent is spent on such necessities as food, clothing, and shelter. In 1983 total U.S. disposable income was $2.3 trillion.[6]

Discretionary income is disposable income *less* savings and expenditures on food, clothing, and housing. Discretionary income is of particular interest to marketers, because consumers have the most choice in spending it. Consumers use their discretionary income to purchase items ranging from automobiles and vacations to movies and pet food. (Four of the largest producers of pet foods—General Foods, Nabisco, Carnation, and Quaker Oats—together sold more than $4 billion worth of dog and cat food in 1981.[7]) In 1983, total U.S. discretionary income was $758 billion.[8]

Americans are willing to spend not only present income but also income that they have not yet earned. In just one month—July 1983—consumers purchased $358 billion worth of durable goods on credit.[9] (*Durable goods* are goods whose usefulness extends over a relatively long period of time, such as automobiles and refrigerators.) Credit cards are one means of "buying now and paying later." About 70 percent of American households have at least one credit card. In December 1982, outstanding balances on all U.S. credit-card accounts totaled $75 billion.[10]

Consumer Buying Behavior

There has been a great deal of research regarding consumer buying habits and behavior. Psychologists, for example, have found that Maslow's hierarchy of needs has some application to buying behavior: People buy in such a way as to fill unsatisfied lower-level needs first. Social scientists have found that there are also social, economic, and cultural influences on the way people buy. We shall limit our discussion of buying behavior to the more obvious buying patterns.

Why Do Consumers Buy? If we eliminate deep psychological and social motivations for buying, we come up with a very simple answer to this question. Consumers buy because they would rather have a particular good or service than the money they have to spend to buy it! More specifically, consumers may choose to buy a given product for the following reasons:

1. *They have a use for the product.* Many items fill an immediate "use" need. A kitchen needs pots and pans; a family needs transportation; a student needs books.
2. *They like the convenience a product offers.* Such items as electric can openers and ice crushers are not essential, but they offer convenience and thus satisfaction.
3. *They believe the purchase will enhance their wealth.* People collect antiques or gold coins as investments as well as for enjoyment. Homeowners buy aluminum siding, awnings, and fences to add to the value of their property.
4. *They take pride in ownership.* Many consumers purchase the "latest" items (a Sony Walkman,

a cordless telephone, or a gold Rolex watch) because such products provide status and pride of ownership as well as utility.
5. *They buy for safety.* Consumers buy health, life, and fire insurance to protect themselves and their families. Smoke detectors, automatic appliance timers, traveler's checks, and similar products also provide safety and protection.

What Do Consumers Buy? Figure 11.7 shows how consumer spending is divided among various categories of products. As we have noted, the greatest proportion of disposable income is spent on food, clothing, and shelter. After these necessities have been provided, consumers tend to spend mostly on health care, transportation, recreation, and personal care. (A mere 1 percent of total disposable income amounts to around $24 billion, so none of the categories in Figure 11.7 is really small in terms of total dollars spent.)

Figure 11.7 Consumer Spending. What percentage of disposable income is spent on various categories of products? Source: Department of Labor, Bureau of Statistics, Survey of Consumer Expenditures, p. 17.

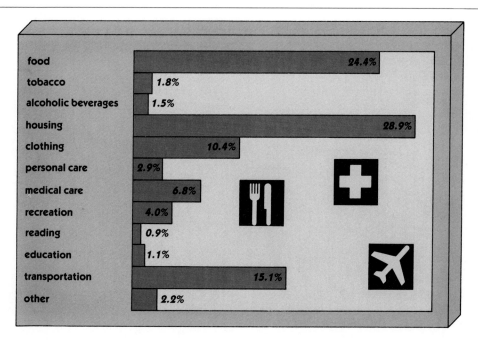

food 24.4%
tobacco 1.8%
alcoholic beverages 1.5%
housing 28.9%
clothing 10.4%
personal care 2.9%
medical care 6.8%
recreation 4.0%
reading 0.9%
education 1.1%
transportation 15.1%
other 2.2%

Where Do Consumers Buy?   Probably the most important factor that influences a consumer's decision on where to buy a particular product is his or her perception of the store. Consumers' general impressions of an establishment's products, prices, and sales personnel can mean the difference between repeat sales and lost business. Consumers distinguish among various types of retail outlets (such as specialty shops, department stores, and discount outlets), and they choose particular types of stores for specific purchases.

Many retail outlets go to a great deal of trouble to build and maintain a particular "image." Products that do not fit the image are not carried. For example, R. H. Macy and Company decided to stop selling Levi Strauss products in 1982, when Levi's began to distribute them through two mass merchandisers—J. C. Penney and Sears, Roebuck.

Consumers also select the businesses they pa-tronize on the basis of location, product assortment, and such services as credit terms, return privileges, and free delivery.

When Do Consumers Buy?   In general, consumers buy when buying is most convenient. Certain business hours have long been standard for establishments that sell consumer products. However, many of these establishments have stretched their hours to include evenings and Sundays (where local laws permit Sunday business). Ultimately, within each area, the consumers themselves control when they will do their buying.

Some Noteworthy Trends

American consumers are an especially dynamic group. They change their jobs and places of residence, their attitudes, and their lifestyles at a rate that would be alarming in most other coun-

Figure 11.8   U.S. Population by Age Groups. Projected population figures through the year 2000 reveal a trend toward increasing proportions of older people in America. Source: U.S. Bureau of the Census.

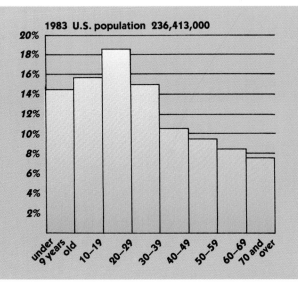

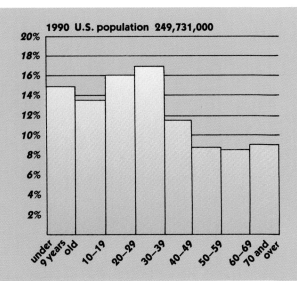

The image a store projects influences the kinds of consumers it will attract. The specialty goods and glamorous atmosphere of Neiman-Marcus (left) are calculated to appeal to the high-income shopper, while the sturdy, no-frills image of the J. C. Penney outlet (right) makes a bid for the practical buyer. *Sources: (left) © Eve Arnold, Magnum; (right) © Stan Ries, Leo deWys, Inc.*

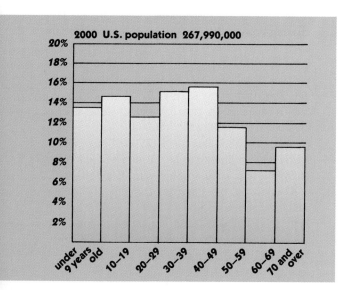

tries. Marketers, of course, must keep up with these changes. A shift in population from the cold north to the warm south and southwest, for example, affects both the marketing environment and the makeup of the firm's marketing mix. Let's outline several trends that researchers expect to be important to marketers over the next decade or so.

Growth in a Prime Spending Group Although the U.S. population is not growing very fast, its makeup is changing. In the next 15 years, there will be a large increase in the number of Americans between the ages of 25 and 44. For the first time in our history, the over-30 age group will become the dominant sector of society. (See Figure 11.8.)

The growing population of older Americans represents an expanding market in areas such as travel, recreation, and health care. Source: © 1983 Lou Jones.

Today there are about equal numbers of people above and below the age of 30. By 1990 there will be 124 people over the age of 30 for every 100 people below that age. And by the year 2000, the ratio will hit 145 to 100. In other words, the trend is toward an older America.

Marketing implications: It is expected that a large proportion of this affluent group will remain single or, if they marry, will remain childless. Single people and childless couples have quite different spending patterns from young couples with families. They are less likely to be homeowners; therefore they buy less furniture and fewer appliances and home furnishings. On the other hand, they spend more heavily on luxuries and leisure activities—travel, entertainment, restaurant meals, and recreation.

Sharp Decline in Teen-age Population The teen-age population is decreasing. By 1990 there will be about 6 million *fewer* teen-agers than there were in 1980. Many of the teen-oriented companies that flourished in the 1970s have already

begun to feel the pinch of the dwindling number of adolescents. Junior-apparel producers like Levi Strauss have reported declining earnings for the past few years. Many are currently redirecting their marketing efforts toward an older clientele.

Marketing implications: The market for youth-oriented products will obviously shrink. Soft drinks, snack foods, video games, records, denim clothing, certain cosmetics, and similar products are likely to be the hardest hit.

Increase in the Number of Senior Citizens The portion of the population that is aged 65 or older is now at 11.6 percent, is growing, and is expected to continue to grow. By the turn of the century, there will be 8 million *more* people over 65 than teen-agers.

Marketing implications: There has been a tendency to overlook this market because senior citizens have relatively small incomes and, according to market research, have passed the prime acquiring years. However, the over-65 population has become a growing market for many products and services—including travel, recreation, retirement housing, single-portion foods, special cosmetics, and health care.

A Better-Educated Population, with Greater Purchasing Power In 1975 about 23 million people over age 25 had attended or graduated from college. By 1990 this group is expected to grow to nearly 50 million. A U.S. Census Bureau study indicates that today's 18-year-old man who obtains a bachelor's degree can expect lifetime earnings of $1,190,000 to $2,700,000, compared with earnings of $861,000 to $1,870,000 for a man with a high school diploma. A man who does not complete high school would earn only $601,000.

A woman of the same age can expect earnings ranging from $381,000 to $800,000 with only a high school diploma and earnings ranging from $523,000 to $1,120,000 with a bachelor's degree. Without completing high school, she could expect to earn only $211,000.[11]

Marketing implications: A better-educated, more affluent population will mean increased demand for quality products and luxuries. It could also bring to advertising a more critical audience, more skeptical of product claims.

Greater Number of Working Women The number of women in the labor force has increased across the age spectrum, rising from 34 percent of the female population in 1950 to 52 percent in 1980. Today, about 67 percent of women between the ages of 18 and 34 are in the labor force, and they are there to stay.

Women's increased participation in the labor force has also added greatly to the number of two-income families in America and will continue to do so throughout the rest of the century. Since 1950 the number of two-earner families has more than tripled. These families now represent over 40 percent of all households. By 1990 they will represent at least 46 percent of all families.

Marketing implications: The working wife has been a key factor in the growth of the fast-food industry and the development of convenience appliances, such as the slow cooker and the microwave oven. The increase in female workers has also created the present day-care industry. Further growth over the next 10 years is anticipated for such products as convenience foods, women's clothing, cosmetics, grooming aids, and labor-saving appliances.

Shorter Workweek; More Leisure Time The average workweek decreased from 58 to 42 hours during the first half of this century. It has remained fairly stable ever since. However, the lengths of vacation periods and the number of paid holidays have continued to increase significantly. Paid vacations of 3 and 4 weeks are becoming more common. According to one research forecast, the 4-day workweek will become standard for major unionized U.S. industries by 1990.

Marketing implications: In 1977 the value of the leisure market was estimated at $150 billion. By 1980 it had doubled to $300 billion. Increased income, longer vacations, and a rise in the 25-to-44-year-old age group (those most committed to leisure pursuits) will continue to expand this market.

Chapter Review

SUMMARY

Marketing is the performance of business activities that direct the flow of goods and services from producer to consumer or user. Marketing creates time utility by making products available when customers want them. It creates place utility by making products available where customers want them. And it creates possession utility through the transfer of ownership of products to buyers.

From the start of the Industrial Revolution until the early twentieth century, business people stressed the production of goods. Then, from the 1920s to the early 1950s, their emphasis was on selling. During both periods, marketing received only limited attention. During the 1950s, however, the marketing concept or marketing orientation began to develop. Business people realized that they are not merely producers and sellers but are in the business of satisfying customers' needs. The marketing concept involves the entire business organization in the process of satisfying needs while accomplishing the organization's goals.

Implementation of the marketing concept begins and ends with marketing information—first to determine what customers need and later to determine how well the firm is filling the needs it has discovered. Marketing information may be stored and processed continually with a computer-based marketing information system. It is obtained on a project-by-project basis through marketing research.

A market consists of people with a need to fill, money to spend, and the desire and authority to spend it on want-satisfying goods and services. Market segmentation is the process of dividing a large, heterogeneous market into smaller "submarkets" or segments whose members share at least one common characteristic. A target market is a market segment toward which a firm directs its marketing effort. Segmentation permits a firm first to identify its target markets and then to reach them effectively.

At the most basic level, segmentation provides a market for consumer products and a market for industrial products. Consumer products may be classified as convenience, shopping, and specialty goods, depending on how they are purchased. Industrial goods may be classified according to how they are used.

A firm's marketing mix is the combination of product, price, distribution, and promotion that it uses to reach a target market. Marketing-mix strategies are incorporated into a marketing plan that is designed to achieve the firm's marketing goals. The various marketing activities may account for as much as half the retail price of consumer products. However, they benefit both purchasers and society at large in a variety of ways.

Personal income is the income an individual receives from all sources, after Social Security taxes have been paid. Disposable income is personal income less all other taxes. And discretionary income is what remains after savings and expenditures for necessities. American consumers spend this income on goods and services in the manner that best satisfies their individual needs. If marketers are effectively to serve this vast and affluent market, they must be aware of both consumer spending patterns and spending trends.

In the next chapter we shall discuss two elements of the marketing mix: product and price. Our emphasis will be on the development of product and pricing strategies as part of a marketing program.

KEY TERMS

You should now be able to define and give an example relevant to each of the following terms:

marketing
utility
form utility
place utility
time utility
possession utility
marketing concept (or orientation)
marketing information system
marketing research
market
market segment
market segmentation
target market
consumer product
convenience goods
shopping goods
specialty goods
industrial product
marketing mix
marketing plan
marketing program
personal income
disposable income
discretionary income

QUESTIONS AND EXERCISES

Review Questions

1. How, specifically, does marketing create place, time, and possession utility?
2. How is the marketing-oriented firm different from a production-oriented firm or a sales-oriented firm?
3. What is the difference between a marketing information system and a marketing-research project? How might the two be related?
4. What is the purpose of market segmentation? What is the relationship between market segmentation and the selection of target markets?
5. Explain the differences among the three types of consumer goods, classified according to buying pattern.
6. What are the four elements of the marketing mix? In what sense are they "controllable"?
7. Describe the external environment in which a firm's market plan must be implemented.
8. What steps are involved in developing a market plan? How do the marketing mix and the target market enter into market planning?
9. What benefits does marketing provide to purchasers of goods and services?
10. How are personal income, disposable income, and discretionary income related? Which is the best indicator of consumer purchasing power?
11. List five reasons why consumers make purchases. What need is satisfied in each case?
12. How might a marketing manager make use of information about consumer trends?

Discussion Questions

1. Were Kodak's marketers concerned with form utility as well as the other kinds of utility? Should they have been? Explain.
2. Explain how Kodak's success with the disc camera was a result of its ability "to select the right blend of [marketing-mix] elements to meet customer needs in specific situations."
3. Why is each of the following a marketing activity?
   a. The provision of sufficient parking space for customers at a suburban shopping mall
   b. The purchase (by a clothing store) of seven dozen sweaters in assorted sizes and colors
   c. The inclusion of nutrition information on the labels of food packages
4. How might adoption of the marketing concept benefit a firm? How might it benefit the firm's customers?
5. Is marketing information as important to small firms as it is to larger firms? Explain.
6. How does the external marketing environment affect the firm's marketing mix?

Exercises

1. Describe how a producer of computer hardware could apply the marketing concept.
2. Through library research, determine the distribution of income among American households in as much detail as possible. Then explain how you would use this information if you were marketing 40-foot yachts.
3. Explain how you would develop a marketing plan for an in-the-home rug and upholstery cleaning service. Describe the marketing information you would need, your marketing goals, the marketing environment, and the elements in your marketing mix.

CASE 11-1

Osborne Computer's Marketing Plan

In 1981 Adam Osborne had an idea—to produce a truly portable personal computer and sell it, along with a set of useful programs, at a relatively low price. In that year Osborne founded Osborne Computer Corporation to turn his idea into reality.

The firm's first computer, the Osborne 1, was a huge success. Orders poured in so fast that Osborne could not keep up with them. Other firms began to produce portable computers and to package software along with their hardware. Still, the Osborne 1 had the largest share of its market.

In early 1983 Osborne's dealers learned that the firm was soon to produce a new portable computer, the Executive. Osborne maintained that the new computer would not compete with the Osborne 1. However, many dealers canceled their orders for the original product in anticipation of the new one. Suddenly the company had almost no working capital, as sales of the Osborne 1 plummeted.

In addition Osborne did not anticipate and respond to a new rival in the personal computer market: IBM's PC. The PC quickly became the standard, and customers soon wanted hardware and software that could be used with IBM's entry in the personal computer sweepstakes. A number of Osborne's competitors responded quickly, but Osborne did not. Its products were not selling.

In early 1983, Osborne Computer Corporation employed more than 1000 people and was a $100 million-a-year success. At the end of that year, the firm had filed for bankruptcy.

Adam Osborne is back now, with a new software firm he calls Paperback Software. He expects Paperback to "bring software out of the high-priced, add-on market and turn it into a broad-based commodity" by selling computer programs at around $50 each. According to Osborne, "We are consumer-oriented, not technology-oriented."[12]

1. Was a lack of consumer orientation the main reason for the demise of Osborne Computer Corporation? Explain.
2. How could effective market planning have helped to prevent the failure of Osborne Computer Corporation?

CASE 11-2

McDonald's Marketing Segments

Marketers at the McDonald's Corporation believe that everyone is a potential customer for McDonald's food products. But they also understand that the American market for these products is far from uniform: different individuals patronize McDonald's outlets for different reasons, and they purchase different products to satisfy different tastes. McDonald's advertising reflects that understanding.

At the national level, McDonald's builds and maintains its image with general themes like "You deserve a break today." It also advertises individual products across the country. However, the proportion of the advertising that is devoted to each product varies, depending on regional preferences for that product. And national advertising may be directed toward a general audience, toward a particular minority group, or toward senior citizens or youngsters.

Regional advertising is conducted through 72 individual local agencies that understand local consumers, their preferences in foods, and the competition. For example, a specialized promotional effort was required in the southeast when the Egg McMuffin was introduced. Consumers there were not familiar with English muffins or eggs Benedict, the recipe on which the Egg McMuffin is based.

Further, McDonald's develops a specific market plan for every outlet. McDonald's marketers consider the business scope of an outlet to be the area within a three-mile radius of the outlet. The operator is expected to have an in-depth knowledge of that community and to use it in his or her marketing activities. [13]

1. List the specific segmentation bases used by McDonald's marketers. Now name some segmentation bases that are *not* used. How might these be useful or inappropriate?

2. As the operator of a McDonald's outlet, what information would you try to obtain before developing a market plan for your business? What might be the best ways of gathering this information?

CHAPTER

TWELVE
Product and Price

When we make a purchase, we exchange a certain amount of money for a certain product. The amount of money is called the price of the product, and the product is something that we expect will satisfy a need. If this all sounds very simple, it's because the exchange is meant to be simple. But both the product and its price reflect a variety of marketing decisions, which may not be simple at all. In this chapter we shall examine these two elements of the marketing mix and see how they are used to reach target markets. After studying the chapter, you should understand:

1. What a product is, and how a product line differs from a product mix
2. The product life cycle, and how it leads inevitably to the need for new-product development
3. The steps in new-product development
4. The uses and importance of branding, packaging, and labeling
5. The economic basis of pricing and the means by which sellers can control prices
6. Pricing goals and the methods that businesses use to implement them
7. The different strategies that may be applied in setting the basic prices of goods and services

Consider this:

In 1947 it was Slinky. In 1950 it was Silly Putty. Then there were Pet Rocks and Smurfs. But in 1983 the craze was the Cabbage Patch Kid, marketed by Coleco Industries.

Cabbage Patch Kids are homely cloth dolls with vinyl faces. They contain no motors, need no batteries, and do nothing but look lovable. Obviously, to the approximately 2.5 million people who purchased the Kids in 1983, lovable is enough.

The Cabbage Patch Kids are actually the creation of Xavier Roberts, an artist from Cleveland, Georgia. Roberts began to hand-produce the Kids—each one slightly different from the others—in 1977. Instead of selling the dolls, he "put them up for adoption" at prices ranging upward from $125. Each was sold with a name, a birth certificate, and a set of adoption papers. Prospective "parents" had to vow to love and care for their adopted Kids as part of a purchase ritual.

Coleco is the manufacturer of ColecoVision home video games and the Adam computer. The firm also produces tricycles for Strawberry Shortcake and Smurfs, two popular dolls. Roberts originally asked Coleco to produce the same things for the Cabbage Patch Kids, but Coleco sought and obtained a license to produce the Kids themselves.

Coleco's product testing indicated that the dolls appealed to adults as well as children, and to males as well as females. As a result, the firm modified its original advertising plans in order to include these groups. The firm also made arrangements with several Hong Kong manufacturers to mass-produce the Kids. Through the use of computers, the manufacturers were able to retain an important feature of the original Cabbage Patch Kids: each was still slightly different from all the others. Also retained was the "adoption package"—a name, a birth certificate, and adoption papers.

After showing off its Kids to retailers in early 1983, Coleco realized that it had a winner. Early orders indicated that the firm would sell about one million of the dolls in 1983. In addition to the doll itself, customers could purchase such related items as a stroller and a variety of clothing. Coleco also expected to market or license Cabbage Patch lunch boxes, T-shirts, games, and other items. Things looked great down at Coleco's Cabbage Patch.

The Kids were formally introduced to the public in June 1983. At the Boston Children's Museum, a group of school children took part in a mass adoption ceremony that was widely publicized by the news media. Over the next few months, magazines, newspapers, and television shows ran features on the dolls. (Not all the publicity was favorable. Spokespersons for several groups concerned about attitudes toward adoption and the self-image of adopted children leveled charges of exploitation and irresponsibility at Coleco.) Retail stores began to sell out and reorder the Kids. By the beginning of October, Coleco's entire projected 1983 production of Cabbage Patch Kids was spoken for. Stores began to ration their stock of the dolls. Production was increased, and Coleco chartered airplanes to bring in an additional 200,000 Kids per week from Hong Kong.

Still the demand grew faster than Coleco's ability to supply Cabbage Patch Kids. Crowds of frantic buyers pushed and shoved to get to some store counters, where the Kids were being sold only one or two hours per week. (That was how long each week's supply lasted.) Coleco stopped advertising the Kids; it no longer needed to buy advertising, with all the free publicity the dolls were getting. Several major stores began donating all or part of their meager allotment of dolls to hospitals and orphanages, rather than undergo the mob scenes that resulted from making any effort to sell them.

All in all, about 2.5 million Cabbage Patch Kids were sold by the end of December 1983. And, although the dolls were purchased primarily as Christmas gifts, the demand continued well into

Source: Logo courtesy of Coleco Industries, Inc.; photo, AP/
Wide World Photos.

1984. As late as April, potential buyers were still being turned away without dolls.

Coleco's Cabbage Patch Kids originally sold for $25 at retail stores, although the airlift was expected to raise the price by about $10. Just before Christmas 1983, some lucky (and enterprising) purchasers were able to resell their dolls—in "slightly cuddled condition"—for prices in excess of $200. And, for Roberts's original handmade dolls, owners were asking $1000 and more.

For Coleco, the Cabbage Patch success could not have come at a better time. According to company planning, the new Adam computer— selling for under $700—was to be Coleco's big moneymaker in 1983. But production problems cut an expected 1983 output of 500,000 computers down to around 125,000. And many of the units that *were* produced were returned because of mechanical difficulties. Although the Cabbage Patch Kids could not make up the sales revenue that had been expected from the Adam, they did brighten Coleco's Christmas just a bit.[1]

A **product** is everything that one receives in an exchange, including all tangible and intangible attributes and expected benefits. Thus the product "Cabbage Patch Kid" includes the doll itself, along with its name, birth certificate, and adoption papers. The uniqueness of the doll (no two Kids are exactly alike) is also part of the product, as is its homeliness, which almost begs children and adults to love the doll. The idea of adoption, rather than purchase, is another part of Coleco's product: according to psychologists, many children have the fantasy that they themselves were adopted. By adopting Cabbage Patch Kids, children are able to work out this fantasy in a healthy manner. Because this alleged benefit accrues to the purchaser of a Kid, it too is a part of the product.

As we noted in Chapter 1, a product may be a good or a service. A *good* is a real, physical thing that we can touch. A *service* is the result of applying human or mechanical effort to a person or thing. Basically, a service is a change we pay others to make for us. A real estate agent's services result in a change in the ownership of real property. A barber's services result in a change in one's appearance.

A product can also consist solely of an *idea.* For example, we might consult an attorney for ideas on how to collect a debt. Most often, though, ideas are included with a good or service. Thus we might buy a book (a good) that provides ideas on how to lose weight. Or we might join Weight Watchers, for both ideas on how to lose weight and help (services) in doing so.

Our definition of the term *product* is based on the concept of an exchange. In a purchase, the thing that is exchanged for the product is money—an amount of money equal to the *price* of the product. When the product is a good, the price may include such services as delivery, installation, warranties, and training. A good *with* such services is not the same product as the good *without* such services. In other words, sellers set a price for a particular "package" of goods, services, and ideas. When the makeup of that package changes, the price should change as well.

When a firm markets a number of essentially similar products, those products collectively are known as a product line. Exhibit A, below, shows one product line of a major food corporation. Source: Courtesy of General Mills, Inc.

In this chapter, we shall look first at products—both old and new—and then at the ways in which price enters into the firm's marketing mix.

PRODUCT LINE AND PRODUCT MIX

Coleco Industries markets electronic devices (ColecoVision and Adam computers) and Cabbage Patch Kids. But why would a home-electronics firm take on a product like soft dolls? Probably because marketing the dolls was in keeping with Coleco's corporate goals at the time when the firm had the opportunity to do so.

In Chapter 7, a **product line** was defined as a group of similar products that differ only in relatively minor characteristics. Generally, the products within a product line are related to each other in the way they are produced, marketed, or used. Parker Brothers, for example, manufactures and sells board games such as *Monopoly* and *Risk,* children's games such as *Winnie the Pooh,* electronic toys for children, and strategy games for adults. Exhibit A shows General Mills's line of breakfast cereals.

Many firms tend to introduce new products within existing product lines. This permits them to apply the experience and knowledge that they have acquired to the production and marketing of the new products. However, some firms, like Coleco, also develop entirely new product lines.

A firm's **product mix** consists of all the products that the firm offers for sale. Exhibit B shows part of the product mix of General Mills. Within that mix are *lines* of cereals, yoghurt, cookie and cake mixes, and baking products.

Two "dimensions" are often applied to a firm's product mix. The *width* of the mix is a measure of the number of product lines it contains. The *depth* of the mix is a measure of the number of individual products within each line. These are somewhat vague measures; we speak of a *broad* or a *narrow* mix, rather than a mix of exactly three or five product lines.

Many firms seek new products that will broaden their product mix, just as Coleco did with the Cabbage Patch Kids. By developing new product lines, they gain additional experience and expertise. Moreover, a firm achieves stability by operating within several different markets. Problems in one particular market do not affect a multiline firm nearly so much as they would affect a firm that depended entirely on a single product line.

Now let us turn our attention from the group of similar products that make up a product line to the individual product itself.

THE PRODUCT LIFE CYCLE

A firm grows by developing and marketing new products—that is, by increasing the depth or width of its product mix. But there is another reason, even more important than growth, for introducing new products: A business will eventually cease to exist if it does not continually market new products. Every product progresses through a **product life cycle,** which is a series of stages in which its sales revenue and profit increase, reach a peak, and then decline. A firm must have new products to take the place of declining older products. Otherwise, the firm's profit will disappear and the firm will fail.

The Stages of the Product Life Cycle

Generally the product life cycle is assumed to be composed of four stages—introduction, growth, maturity, and decline—as shown in Figure 12.1. Some products plunge through these stages rapidly, in a few weeks or months. Others may take years to go through each stage. Examples are Pet Rocks (a short-lived fad) and Parker Brothers' Monopoly game, which was introduced over 50 years ago and is still going strong.

Introduction In the *introduction stage,* consumer awareness and acceptance of the product are low. Sales rise gradually as a result of promotion and distribution activities, but initially high development and marketing costs result in low profit, or even in a loss. There are relatively few competitors. The price is often high, and purchasers are primarily people who want to be "the first on their block" to own the new product. The marketing challenge at this stage is to make potential customers aware of the product's existence and its features, benefits, and uses.

The assortment of products displayed in Exhibit B, below, represents a number of different product lines. Together, these constitute General Mills's product mix. Source: Courtesy of General Mills, Inc.

Growth In the *growth stage,* sales increase rapidly as the product becomes well known. Other firms have probably begun to market competing products. The competition and lower unit costs (due to mass production) result in decreased prices, but total profit (for the firm as well as the industry) tends to increase. To meet the needs of the growing market, the originating firm offers modified versions of its product and expands its distribution. Minnesota Mining and Manufacturing, the maker of Scotch Tape, developed a variety of tape dispensers, which made its product easier to use. General Foods Corporation, the maker of Jell-O, increased the number of Jell-O

In the decline stage of a product's life cycle, falling sales and profits may cause the manufacturer to discontinue the product completely. Source: © 1982 Lou Jones.

flavors from six to over a dozen. Promotion continues to be an important element of the marketing mix.

Maturity Sales are still increasing at the beginning of the *maturity stage,* but the rate of increase has slowed. Later in this stage the sales curve peaks, and profits begin to decline. Dealers simplify their product lines, markets are segmented more carefully, and price competition increases. The increased competition forces weaker competitors to leave the industry. Refinements and extensions of the original product appear on the market, and trade-ins become part of the purchase of new models.

Decline During the *decline stage,* the sales volume decreases sharply and the profit curve flattens out. The number of competing firms declines, and the only survivors in the marketplace are those firms that specialize in marketing the product. Production and marketing costs become the most important determinant of profit. Less profitable versions of the product may be elimi-nated from the product line, and eventually the firm may decide to drop the product entirely.

Using the Product Life Cycle

Marketers should be aware of the life-cycle stage of each product they are responsible for. And they should know how long the product is expected to remain in that stage. Both must be taken into account in making decisions about the marketing program for the product, the firm's overall marketing mix, and the introduction of new products. For example, Figure 12.1 shows that profit reaches a peak and then begins to decline while sales volume is still increasing. If a product is expected to remain in the maturity stage for a long time, a replacement product might be introduced between the peaks of the profit and sales curves. If the maturity stage is expected to be short, however, the new product should be introduced much earlier. Generally, firms should develop product strategies on the basis of the profit curve rather than the sales curve.

In introducing new products, a firm must be willing to take the chance of speeding up the decline of existing products. According to Robert A. Fox, president and chief operating officer of the Del Monte Corporation,

> This is a fact Procter & Gamble learned long ago. Only by introducing many detergents, each differently branded and competing with one another, has it built and maintained its dominance in that business. P&G knows that if an improvement is possible and they don't exploit it, it's only a matter of time until someone else will.
>
> Getting rid of the dead wood, especially for an old-line company, can be one of the hardest decisions to make. For many years, one of Del Monte's proudest claims was that it offered the broadest line of canned fruits and vegetables nationally, but the firm has faced up to the fact that today a claim like that costs more than it earns. Therefore in recent years, Del Monte has discontinued a number of products which could not achieve desired levels of sales volume and profitability. They were not clear failures, but neither were they clear winners.[2]

DEVELOPING NEW PRODUCTS

As we have noted, the introduction of new products is a matter of life or death for business firms. In Chapter 7 we discussed product development from the point of view of production. Now let us expand that viewpoint to encompass the entire marketing effort.

How New Is "New"?

New products are generally grouped into three categories on the basis of their degree of similarity to existing products. *Imitations* are products that are designed to be similar to—and to compete with—existing products of other firms. Examples are the various brands of fluoride toothpaste that were developed to compete with

Crest. Such "me too" products are not usually very successful, but a notable exception is Pepsi-Cola.[3]

Adaptations are variations of existing products that are intended for an established market. Freeze-dried coffee is a product adaptation. The refinements and extensions discussed in Chapter 7 are most often considered adaptations, although imitative products may also include some refinement and extension.

Innovations are entirely new products. They may give rise to a new industry (such as xerography or television) or revolutionize an existing one. Thus the introduction of sound tracks permanently changed the motion picture industry. Innovative products take considerable time, effort, and money to develop. They are therefore less common than adaptations and imitations.

Figure 12.1   Product Life Cycle. Graph shows sales volume and profits during the life cycle of a product. *Source: Adapted from William M. Pride and O. C. Ferrell, Marketing, 3d ed., p. 149.*

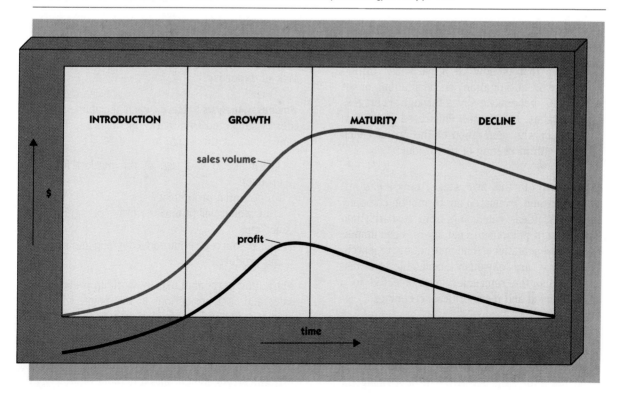

New York—Can successful young single adults find happiness with gourmet ice cream?

Can an ice cream marketer reach this growing market segment and addict them to its particular premium brand?

These questions are not as unrelated as they seem, according to Robert Heller, president of a newly formed social group called the Ice Cream Connoisseurs Club. The purpose of this group is not only to provide a way for singles—and non-singles—around the country to meet each other, but to promote the sale of premium ice cream.

Heller's theory is that this type of updated, more sophisticated ice cream social is a viable way to promote gourmet ice cream brands among the crowd that can—and will—pay the dollars for them.

"Very often, it is the young and upwardly mo-bile single who is willing to pay the price for the best product, whether it be a vacation, a home, or an ice cream cone," said Heller, who works for Newmark's Advertising Agency, New York.

"Getting together for ice cream is much less dangerous and more enjoyable to the palate than getting together over drinks," he explained. "I believe that ice cream is a catalyst for social communication because it conjures up images of childhood and reduces superficial and transitory behavior, which is characteristic of the bar scene," he added.

He told *Dairy Record* that since the club's inception last December, he has been in contact with a number of ice cream manufacturers and is interested in working with companies to set up a larger ice cream tasting event.

Source: *Dairy Record*, April, 1984, p. 42.

Stages in the Evolution of New Products

A product that is new to a particular firm—whether it is an imitation, an adaptation, or an innovation—generally evolves through six stages. These stages, which are illustrated in Figure 12.2, begin with generation of the product idea and end with marketing of the product.

Exploration   In this first stage, new ideas are generated and evaluated in terms of company objectives. Ideas can come from research and development personnel, customers, consultants, sales representatives, and marketing research. Those that are obviously unsuitable are discarded, and the remainder are subjected to a more detailed and more critical screening.

Screening   At this stage, ideas that are in line with company goals are screened to determine whether they are feasible. An important question is whether the firm is capable of developing the idea into a viable product. Sometimes a firm has to reject a good product simply because of its lack of expertise.

Business Analysis   Here, each feasible product idea is subjected to a marketing analysis. Important issues at this stage are

☐ The makeup and size of the market for the product
☐ Its potential profitability
☐ How well it will fit into the firm's present product mix
☐ The resources required to develop and market the product

Marketing personnel usually work up preliminary sales and cost projections at this point, with the help of R&D and production managers.

Development   At this stage, the product idea becomes a reality. The product and a production process are designed, and a number of *prototypes*

or samples are produced. At the same time, projections of costs, sales, and profit are refined. Issues involving brand name, packaging, warranties, and the like are resolved by marketing personnel.

Testing   Two types of tests are performed before the product is produced and marketed. First, the prototypes are tested for reliability, durability, convenience, and so on. If necessary, the product and the production process are modified on the basis of the results of this performance testing.

Second, the product is market-tested in one or more limited geographic markets that are typical of its overall expected market. Insofar as possible, all elements of the proposed marketing mix are duplicated in this test. Depending on the results of the test marketing—in terms of customer acceptance and profitability—the product may be modified and retested, abandoned, or advanced to the next and last stage.

Figure 12.2   *The Six Stages in the Evolution of a New Product*

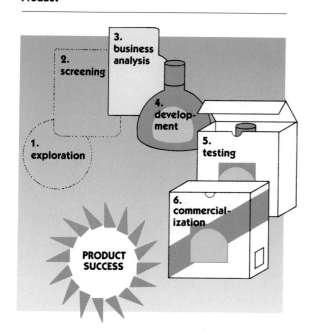

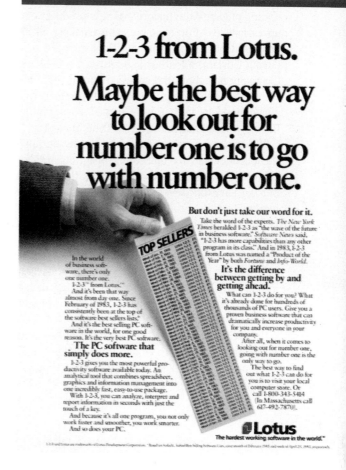

Commercialization   In this final stage, the product is launched into full-scale production and marketing. At this stage the company's reputation and resources are fully committed to the product.

Success or Failure?

On the average, only 1 out of 58 of those product ideas that pass beyond the exploration stage becomes a successful product. Most ideas are abandoned during screening and business analysis, which are the least costly stages. (Each succeeding stage is more expensive than the preceding stage.) And, of those that remain, only about 20 percent reach the commercialization stage.

Yet, in spite of this rigorous screening and testing of ideas, the majority of new products end up as failures. For example, after making an investment of $100 million, Du Pont stopped producing Corfam, a leather substitute. Ford Motor Company had about the same amount invested in the Edsel automobile before that product was abandoned. In fact, most "name" corporations have produced market failures. (See Table 12.1.)

Why does a new product fail? Mainly because the product and its marketing program are not planned and tested as completely as they should be. To save on development costs, a firm may market-test its product but not its entire marketing mix. Or a new product may be marketed before all the "bugs" have been worked out. Problems may show up in the testing stage, and yet the firm pushes ahead with full-scale marketing anyway, to try to recover its product development costs. And some firms try to market new products with inadequate financing.

In each case, at least one element of the marketing mix turns out to be defective, and potential customers are quick to find the flaws.

BRANDING, PACKAGING, AND LABELING

Three important features of a product (and particularly a consumer product) are its brand, its package, and its label. They may be used to identify the product with a successful product line or to distinguish it from existing products. They may be designed to attract customers at the point of sale or to provide information to potential purchasers. Because the brand, package, and label are a very real part of the product, they deserve careful attention during product planning.

What Is a Brand?

A **brand** is a name, term, symbol, design, or any combination of these that identifies a seller's products and distinguishes them from competitors' products.[4] A **brand name** is the part of a brand that can be spoken. It may include letters, words, numbers, and pronounceable symbols, as in Procter & Gamble. A **brand mark,** on the other hand, is the part of a brand that is a symbol or distinctive design, like Planters' "Mr. Peanut."

Table 12.1 *Examples of Modern Product Failures*

Food Items	Health and Beauty Aids	Other Products
Campbell's Red Kettle Soups	Colgate's Cue Toothpaste	Real (cigarettes)
Best Foods' Knoor Soups	Aerosol Ipana Toothpaste	Sylvania's Colorside TV Viewer
Post Cereals with Freeze-Dried Fruit	Bristol-Myers' Resolve Analgesic	Stanley Works' Garden Tool Line
	Scott Paper's Babyscott Diapers	Edsel
Gablinger's Beer	Nine Flags Men's Cologne	Du Pont's Corfam (leather substitute)
Hunt-Wesson's Suprema Spaghetti Sauce	Warner-Lambert's Reef Mouthwash	Golden Esso Extra
	Colgate's 007 Men's Cologne	Gillette's calculators and watches
Heinz's Great American Soup	Revlon's Super Natural Hairspray	Westinghouse's white goods*
Rheingold's California Gold Label Beer	Procter & Gamble's Hidden Magic Hairspray	Prestone Long-Life Coolant
		Corvair
Seagram's Four Roses Premium Light Whiskey	Crazy Legs (shaving cream for women)	Du Pont's 270 Material Dye Products
Gourmet Foods	Us (unisex deodorant)	
	Rely tampons	

* White goods are major home appliances, such as refrigerators, washing machines, dishwashers, ranges, and dryers.
Source: Reprinted with permission of Macmillan Publishing Company from *Essentials of Marketing* by Joel R. Evans and Barry Berman. Copyright © 1984 by Macmillan Publishing Company.

A **trademark** is a brand that is registered with the U.S. Patent and Trademark Office and thus is legally protected from use by anyone except its owner. Among the many registered trademarks are the shape of the Coca-Cola bottle and the CBS eye.

Brands are often classified according to who owns them: manufacturers or middlemen. A **manufacturer** (or **producer**) **brand,** as the name implies, is a brand that is owned by a manufacturer. The majority of foods, major appliances, and gasolines, as well as all automobiles, are sold with producer branding. So is much of today's clothing. Names such as Jonathan Logan, Calvin Klein, Bill Blass, and Gloria Vanderbilt are examples of producer brands that appeal both to department stores and to consumers. Many consumers prefer producer brands because they are nationally known, offer consistent quality, and are widely available.

A **middleman's** (or **store**) **brand** is one that is owned by an individual wholesaler or retailer. Among the better known store brands are Kenmore and Craftsman (owned by Sears, Roebuck) and KMC (owned by K mart). Owners of middleman's brands claim that they can offer their own brands at lower prices and earn greater profits by doing so. About one-third of all tire, food, and appliance sales are of store-branded items. Sears generates more than 75 percent of its sales through its own brands.

Consumer confidence is the most important element in the success of a branded product, whether the brand is owned by a producer or a middleman. Because branding identifies each product completely, consumers can easily repurchase products that provide satisfaction, performance, and quality. And they can just as easily ignore products that do not.

Generic products (sometimes called generic "brands") are products with no brand at all. Their plain white packages carry only the name of the product—applesauce, peanut butter, potato chips, or whatever—usually in black type. Usually, generics are produced by the major producers that manufacture name brands. Generics have

been available in supermarkets since 1977. They appeal mainly to consumers who are willing to sacrifice some quality or product consistency in return for a lower price.

Branding Strategies

The basic branding decision for any firm—producer or middleman—is whether or not to brand its products. A producer may market its products under its own brands, under middleman's brands,

The function of a brand name in distinguishing one product from others is lost if the name becomes generally applied to all products in a given category. *Source: Courtesy Xerox Corporation.*

You can't always take Roget's word for it.

We'd like to thank the people who publish a leading Roget's Thesaurus for taking the time and trouble to include Xerox. But we'd like to bring up a grammatical point.

The Xerox trademark is not a noun. Nor is it a verb. It is a proper adjective and should always be followed by a word or phrase describing one of our products. Such as Xerox copier, Xerox

word processor, Xerox electronic printing system, etc.

So please check your Thesaurus and, if necessary, make these corrections. And please feel free to use Xerox—the proper adjective—as a part of your speech.

That way you can be sure that when you ask for a Xerox product, you'll get only a Xerox product. And not just a synonym.

XEROX® is a trademark of XEROX CORPORATION.

---

as Virginia Slims are directed toward women and Marlboro toward men.

Family branding is the strategy in which a firm uses the same brand for all or most of its products. Sunbeam, General Electric, IBM, and Xerox use family branding for their entire product mixes. A major advantage of family branding is that the promotion of any one item that carries the family brand tends to help all other products with the same brand name. In addition, new products have a head start when their brand name is already known and accepted by consumers.

Brand names should be distinctive and easy to remember. However, they must also be carefully protected—both from competitors and, surprisingly, from excessive popularity. Many brand names have become the names of general classes of products because they were not adequately protected by their owners. Among these are cellophane, escalator, linoleum, nylon, thermos, harmonica, aspirin, and yo-yo.

At one point in the Watergate investigation, special prosecutor Leon Jaworski announced that transcripts of President Nixon's White House tapes were "*xeroxed.*" Attorneys from the Xerox Corporation took pains to correct him publicly: The transcripts were *photocopied,* because Xerox is a registered trademark and not a process.

Packaging

Packaging consists of all those activities involved in developing and providing a container for a product. The package is actually a vital part of the product. It can make the product more versatile, safer, or easier to use. Through its shape and what is printed on it, a package can influence purchasing decisions, and it can be used to implement branding strategies. (In the case of Pet Rocks, the package and the witty "care and feeding" instructions printed on it were probably more important in selling the product than the product itself. Inside was just a rock. And, for a follow-up product, *only* the package and labeling changed. The box now sported bars. For Wild Rocks, it had become a cage!)

---

or under both. A middleman may carry only producer brands, only its own brands, or both. Once either type of firm decides to brand, it chooses between two branding strategies: individual branding and family branding.

Individual branding is the strategy in which a firm uses a different brand for each of its products. For example, R.J. Reynolds Industries uses individual branding for its line of cigarettes, which includes Salem, Camel, Reyno, Vantage, Lucky Strike, and others. Individual branding offers two major advantages. A problem with one product will not affect the good name of the firm's other products. And the different brands can be directed toward different segments of the market,

Packages thus have both functional and marketing value. Their primary function is to protect the product, and they should be strong enough to do so. They should be easy to open and close, to store and reuse, and to dispose of or recycle.

With regard to marketing, packages should be attention-getters if they are to be displayed at the point of sale—as in supermarkets. Various sizes of packages may be used to reach particular target markets. Single-portion food packages for single-person households and the "giant economy size" for large families are examples. Such packages as reusable containers and no-drip bottles may also attract customers to particular products. See-through plastic packaging allows the customer to see the product before it is purchased and reduces theft. Both Lipton and Ocean Spray sell fruit juices aseptically packaged in boxes that do not need refrigeration.

Finally, the package can be used to inform customers about the product's contents, uses, advantages, features, and hazards.

Labeling

Labeling is the presentation of information on a product or its package. The *label* is the part that contains the information. It may include the brand name and mark and the registered-trademark symbol ®, package size and contents, product claims, directions for use and safety precautions, a list of ingredients, the name and address of the manufacturer, and the Universal Product Code symbol, which is used for automated checkout and inventory control.

A number of federal regulations specify information that *must* be included in the labeling for certain products.

- □ Garments must be labeled with the name of the manufacturer, country of manufacture, fabric content, and cleaning instructions.
- □ Nutrition labeling must be included with any food product for which a nutritional claim is made. This labeling must follow a standard format (see Exhibit C).

- □ Nonedible items such as shampoos and detergents must carry safety precautions as well as instructions for their use.
- □ The ingredients of food products must be listed in order, from the ingredient that constitutes the largest percentage of the product down to the one that makes up the least of it.

Such regulations are aimed at protecting the consumer from both misleading product claims and the improper (and thus unsafe) use of products.

Labels may also carry the details of written or express warranties. An **express warranty** is a written explanation of the responsibilities of the producer in the event that the product is found to be defective or otherwise unsatisfactory. Recently, as a result of consumer discontent (along with some federal legislation), firms have begun to simplify the wording of warranties and to extend their duration. Chrysler's 50,000-mile/5-year warranty is featured heavily in that firm's auto and truck advertising.

You pay *rent* for your apartment, *tuition* for your education, and a *fee* to your physician or dentist.

The airline, railway, taxi, and bus companies all charge you a *fare*; the local utilities call price a *rate*; and the local bank charges you *interest* for the money it loans.

The price for driving your car on Florida's Sunshine Parkway is a *toll*, and the company that insures your car charges a *premium*.

The great lecturer charges an *honorarium* to tell you about a government official who took a *bribe* to help a shady character steal *dues* collected by a trade association.

Clubs or societies to which you belong may make a *special assessment* to pay unusual expenses. A lawyer you use regularly may ask for a *retainer* to cover his services.

The "price" of an executive is a *salary*, the price of a salesman may be a *commission*, and the price of a worker is a *wage*.

Finally, although economists would disagree, many of us feel that *income taxes* are the price we pay for the privilege of making money.

Source: David J. Schwartz, "A Price by Any Other Name Is Still A Price," *Marketing Today* (New York: Harcourt Brace Jovanovich, 1977).

Of all the marketing decisions a firm must make, none is more crucial than pricing its products correctly. The rest of this chapter is devoted to considerations affecting pricing goals, pricing methods, and pricing strategies.

THE PRODUCT AND ITS PRICE

You should now realize that a product is more than a thing that we can touch or a change that we can see. It is, rather, a set of attributes and benefits that has been carefully designed to satisfy its market while earning a profit for the seller. But no matter how well a product is designed, it cannot perform its functions if it is priced incorrectly. Few people will purchase a product with too high a price, and a product with too low a price will earn no profit. Somewhere between too high and too low, there is a "proper," effective price for each product. In the remainder of this chapter, we shall see how businesses go about determining what the right price is.

The Meaning and Use of Price

The **price** of a product is the amount of money that the seller is willing to accept in exchange for the product, at a given time and under given circumstances. In most business situations the price is fixed by the seller. Suppose a seller sets a price of $10 for a particular product. In essence, the seller is saying, "Anyone who wants this product can have it here and now, in exchange for $10."

Each interested buyer then makes a very personal judgment regarding the utility of the product, often in terms of some dollar value. If a particular person feels that he will get at least $10 worth of want satisfaction (or value) from the product, he is likely to buy it. But if he feels that he can get more want satisfaction by spending the $10 in some other way, he will not buy it.

Price thus serves the function of *allocator*. First, it allocates goods and services among those who are willing and able to buy them. (As we noted in Chapter 1, the answer to the economic question "For whom to produce?" depends primarily on prices.) Second, price allocates financial resources (sales revenue) among producers according to how well they satisfy customers' needs. And third, price helps customers to allocate their own financial resources among various want-satisfying products.

Can Firms Control Their Prices?

Supply and Demand—Once Again In Chapter 1 we defined the **supply** of a product as the quantities of the product that producers are willing to sell at various prices. We can draw a graph of the supply relationship for a particular product—say, jeans—as shown in the top graph of Figure 12.3. Note that the quantity supplied by producers *increases* as the price increases (as we move to the right along this *supply curve*).

We also defined the **demand** for a product as the quantities that buyers are willing to purchase at various prices. We can also draw a graph of the demand relationship. This is done for the same product, jeans, in the middle graph of Figure 12.3. Note there that the quantity demanded by purchasers *increases* as the price decreases (as we move to the right along the *demand curve*).

As we noted in Chapter 1, the sellers and buyers of a product interact in the marketplace. We can show this interaction by superimposing the supply curve onto the demand curve for our product, as shown in the bottom graph of Figure 12.3.

The two curves intersect at point *E,* which represents a quantity of 15 million pairs of jeans and a price of $15 per pair. Point *E* is on the supply curve, so producers are willing to supply 15 million pairs at $15 each. Point *E* is also on the demand curve, so buyers are willing to purchase 15 million pairs at $15 each. Thus point *E* represents *equilibrium* within a purely competitive market for jeans. The equilibrium price is $15 per pair. If 15 million pairs are produced and priced at $15, they will all be sold. And everyone who is willing to pay $15 will be able to buy a pair of jeans.

Prices in the Real Economy In a (largely theoretical) system of pure competition, no producer has control over the price of its product: All producers must accept the equilibrium price. If they charge a higher price, they will not sell their products. If they charge a lower price, they will lose sales revenue and profits. In addition, the products of the various producers are indistinguishable from each other when a system of pure competition exists. Every bushel of wheat, for example, is exactly like every other bushel of wheat.

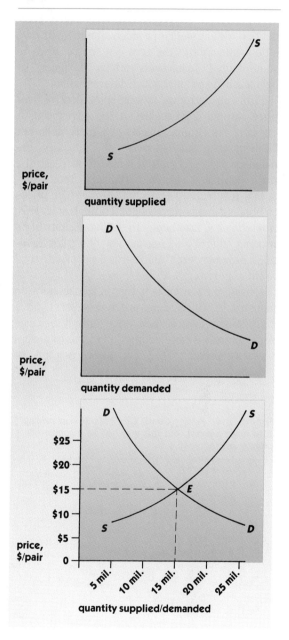

Figure 12.3 Supply Curve (top): *The upward slope (to the right) means that producers will supply more jeans at higher prices.* Demand Curve (middle): *The downward slope (to the right) means that buyers will purchase fewer jeans at higher prices.* Supply and Demand Curves Together (bottom): *Point E indicates equilibrium in quantity and price for both sellers and buyers.*

In the real economy, producers try to gain some control over price by differentiating their products from similar products. **Product differentiation** is the process of developing and promoting differences between one's product and all similar products. The idea behind product differentiation is to create a specific demand for the firm's product—to take the product out of competition with all similar products. Then, in its own little "submarket," the firm can control price to some degree. Jeans with various "designer" labels are a result of product differentiation.

Firms also attempt to gain some control over price through advertising. If the advertising is effective (as Brooke Shields apparently is in her "Calvins"), it will increase the quantity demanded. This may permit a firm to increase the price at which it sells its particular output.

In a real market, firms may also reduce prices to obtain a competitive edge. Through such *price competition,* a firm hopes to sell more units of its product, thereby increasing its total sales revenue. Although each unit earns less profit, total profit may rise.

Finally, the few large sellers in an oligopoly (an industry in which there are few sellers), have considerable control over price, mainly because each controls a large proportion of the total supply of its product. However, as we pointed out in Chapter 1, this control of price is diluted by each firm's wariness of its competitors.

Overall, then, firms in the real economy do exert some control over prices. How they use this control depends on their pricing goals and their production and marketing costs, as well as on the workings of supply and demand in competitive markets.

PRICING GOALS

Before management can set prices for a firm's products, it must decide what it expects to accomplish through pricing. That is, management must set pricing goals. And these goals must be in line with both organizational goals and marketing goals.

Of course, one objective of pricing is to make a profit, but this need not be a firm's primary objective. One or more of the following may be just as important. (See Figure 12.4.)

Survival

A firm may have to price its products in such a way as to survive—either as an organization or as a factor in a particular market. This usually means that the firm will cut its price to attract customers, even if it then must operate at a loss. Of course, such a goal can't be pursued on a long-term basis. Consistent losses would cause the business to fail.

Just to remain in the air transportation market, in the fall of 1983 the failing Continental Airlines offered a top fare of $49 on all its nonstop flights. Although this low price was extremely attractive to the public, it was not, however, greeted with delight by competing airlines. Nevertheless, Continental's management felt it was necessary for survival.

Profit Maximization

Many firms may state that their goal is to maximize profit, but this goal is impossible to define

Figure 12.4 Pricing Goals. One objective of pricing is to make a profit, but this may not be a company's primary pricing goal.

PRICING GOALS

■ survival
■ profit maximization
■ return on investment
■ market share
■ status quo

(and thus impossible to achieve). What, exactly, is the "maximum" profit? How does a firm know when it has been reached? Firms that wish to set profit goals should express them as either specific dollar amounts or percentage increases over previous profits. For example, Campbell Soup Company's pricing goal is to post a 15 percent annual increase in earnings.[5]

Target Return on Investment

The *return on an investment* (ROI) is the amount that is earned as a result of that investment. Some firms set an annual percentage ROI as their pricing goal. ConAgra, the parent company for Banquet Foods and other subsidiaries, considers rate of return the single most significant measure of operating performance. The company's objective is to earn an average after-tax ROI in excess of 20 percent.[6]

Market-Share Goals

A firm's *market share* is its proportion of total industry sales. Some firms attempt, through pricing, to maintain or increase their share of the market. In 1982 Ford Motor Company used pricing to increase its share of the European car market to a record 12.4 percent.[7] And, to protect their market shares against Continental Airlines, both United Airlines and Frontier Airlines cut their own fares to match Continental's $49 fare.

Status Quo Pricing

Some firms are guided, in pricing their products, by a desire not to "make waves," especially in industries where price stability is important. If such a firm can maintain its profit or market share by simply meeting the competition—charging about the same price as competitors for similar products—then it will do so.

Usually the strongest competitor, called the *price leader,* sets its price first; other firms in the industry then follow suit. In the automobile industry, General Motors is usually the price leader. When GM announced a 2 percent increase in price for its 1984 model cars, its three American competitors followed with their own price increases.

PRICING METHODS

Once a firm has developed its pricing goals, it must select a pricing method and strategies to reach that goal. The pricing method provides a "basic" price for each product. Pricing strategies are then used to modify the basic price, depending on pricing goals and the market situation.

Two factors are important to every firm engaged in setting prices. The first is recognition that the market, and not the firm's costs, ultimately determines the price at which a product will sell. The second is awareness that costs and expected sales can be used only to establish some sort of *price floor,* a minimum price at which the firm can sell its product without incurring a loss.

We shall look at three kinds of pricing methods: cost-based, demand-based, and competition-based pricing.

Cost-Based Pricing

In the simplest form of cost-based pricing, the seller first determines the total cost of producing (or purchasing) one unit of the product. The seller then adds an amount to cover additional costs (such as insurance or interest) and profit. The amount that is added is called the **markup.** The total of the cost and of the markup is the selling price of the product.

Many smaller firms calculate the markup as a percentage of their total cost. Suppose, for example, that the total cost of manufacturing and marketing 1000 portable stereos is $100,000. This works out to $100 per unit. If the manufacturer wants a 20 percent profit, the selling price will be $100 plus 20 percent of $100, or $120 per unit.

Markup pricing is easy to apply, and it is used by many businesses (mostly retailers and whole-

In cost-based pricing, the seller decides on a markup percentage that may set the price below or above the level that the market will bear. Source: © 1984 T. Molinski.

salers). However, it has two major flaws. The first is the difficulty of determining an effective markup percentage. If this percentage is too high, the product may be overpriced for its market; then, too few units may be sold to return the total cost of producing and marketing the product. On the other hand, if the markup percentage is too low, the seller is "giving away" profit that it could have earned simply by assigning a higher price. In other words, the markup percentage needs to be set to account for the workings of the market, and that is very difficult to do.

The second problem with markup pricing is that it separates pricing from other business functions. The product is priced *after* production quantities are decided on, *after* costs are incurred, and almost without regard for the market or the marketing mix. To be most effective, the various business functions should be integrated. *Each* should have an impact on *all* marketing decisions.

Demand-Based Pricing

There are several ways to include product demand in the pricing process. They range from the simple but dangerous method of experimenting with several prices to complex methods involving intricate and detailed calculations. Somewhere between these two extremes is a pricing method based on *breakeven analysis*.

For any product, the **breakeven quantity** is the number of units that must be sold in order for the total revenue (from all units sold) to equal the total cost (of all units sold). **Total revenue** is the total amount received from sales of the product. We can estimate projected total revenue as the selling price multiplied by the number of units sold.

The costs involved in operating a business can be broadly classified as either fixed costs or variable costs. **Fixed costs** are costs that are incurred no matter how many units of a product are produced or sold. Rent, for example, is a fixed cost; it remains the same whether 1 unit or 1000 are produced. **Variable costs** are costs that depend on the number of units produced. The cost of fabricating parts for a stereo receiver is a variable cost. The more units produced, the higher this cost is. The **total cost** of producing a certain number of units is the sum of the fixed costs and the variable costs attributed to those units.

If we assume a particular selling price, we can find the breakeven quantity either graphically or by using a formula. Figure 12.5 shows graphs of the total revenue earned and the total cost incurred with the sale of various quantities of some hypothetical product. With fixed costs of $40,000, variable costs of $60 per unit, and a selling price of $120, the breakeven quantity is 667 units. (The breakeven quantity is the quantity represented by the intersection of the total-revenue and total-cost axes.) If the firm sells more than 667 units, it will earn a profit. If it sells fewer units, it will suffer a loss.

To use this breakeven analysis for pricing, we select several reasonable selling prices and find the breakeven quantity that is associated with each price. For the portable-stereo manufacturer, we might come up with the following results:

Possible price	Breakeven quantity
$100	1000
$110	800
$120	667
$140	500

Next, on the basis of our experience in marketing stereos, along with any additional market data that might be available, we estimate the demand for these stereos. Our goal is to determine, as best we can, how many units we can sell at each possible price. We then combine this demand analysis with our breakeven analysis to set both the price of the stereo and the production quantity.

Suppose we determined that sales would be very weak at the high $140 price, that we could sell 1000 stereos at a price of $100 or 900 stereos at a price of $110. We also estimate that we could sell 800–850 units at $120 each. Based on this information, we would set our basic price at $120

Figure 12.5 *Breakeven Analysis. Breakeven analysis answers the question, "What is the lowest level of production and sales at which a company can break even on a particular product?"*

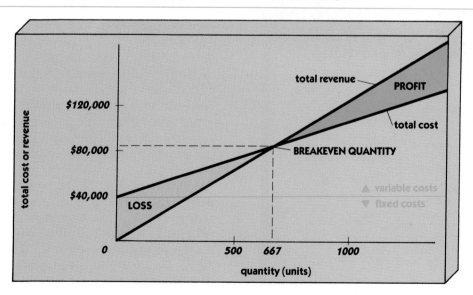

per unit, and we would produce no more than 850 units—not the 1000 units that might be our production capacity.

Competition-Based Pricing

In competition-based pricing, the firm essentially ignores costs and market demand. Instead, it uses competitors' prices as guides in setting its own prices. This method is probably most important when competing products are very similar in nature, or when the market is such that price is the key element of the marketing mix.

Competition-based pricing is popular, especially with retailers, for two main reasons. First, it is simple. There is no need to study demand, to do a breakeven analysis, or even to calculate markups. The firm simply charges the same prices that its competitors charge for similar goods and services. Second, this pricing method is considered fair to both buyer and seller, and it rarely sparks a price war.

PRICING STRATEGIES

Sellers may apply various pricing strategies to their basic prices, either temporarily or permanently, and for individual products or complete product lines. The extent to which particular sellers use any of the following strategies depends on their pricing and marketing goals, the markets for their products, the degree of product differentiation, the life-cycle stage of the product, and other factors. (See Figure 12.6.)

New-Product Strategies

Price Skimming **Price skimming** is the strategy of charging the highest possible price for a product during the introductory stage of its life cycle. The seller essentially "skims the cream" off the market to help cover the high costs of research and development. Many consumers are willing to pay a high price for an innovative product, either because of its novelty or because of the prestige or status that ownership confers.

Penetration Pricing At the opposite extreme, **penetration pricing** is the strategy of setting a very low price for a new product. The idea is to develop a large market for the product quickly. It is hoped that this approach will sell more units during the early life-cycle stages and thus discourage competitors from entering the market.

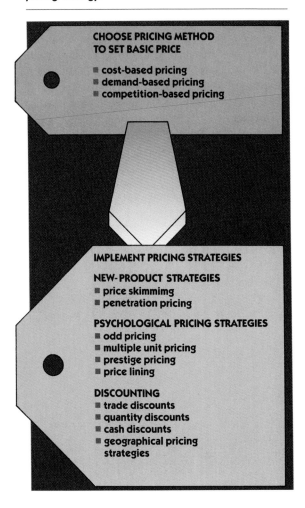

Figure 12.6 *Pricing Strategies. After setting the basic price for a product according to an overall pricing method, the seller adjusts the price according to a pricing strategy.*

CHOOSE PRICING METHOD TO SET BASIC PRICE

■ cost-based pricing
■ demand-based pricing
■ competition-based pricing

IMPLEMENT PRICING STRATEGIES

NEW-PRODUCT STRATEGIES
■ price skimmimg
■ penetration pricing

PSYCHOLOGICAL PRICING STRATEGIES
■ odd pricing
■ multiple unit pricing
■ prestige pricing
■ price lining

DISCOUNTING
■ trade discounts
■ quantity discounts
■ cash discounts
■ geographical pricing strategies

Psychological Pricing Strategies

Odd Pricing Many retailers believe that consumers respond more positively to odd-number prices like $4.99 than to whole-dollar prices like $5. **Odd pricing** is the strategy of setting prices at odd amounts that are slightly below an even or whole number of dollars.

Sellers who use this strategy believe that odd prices will increase sales and hence total revenue and profit. The strategy is not limited to low-priced items. Auto manufacturers may set the price of a car at $9995 rather than $10,000. Odd pricing has been the subject of various psychological studies, but the results have not been conclusive.

Multiple-Unit Pricing Many retailers (and especially supermarkets) practice **multiple-unit pricing.** That is, they set a single price for two or more units, such as two cans for 99 cents rather than 50 cents per can. Especially for products with a rapid turnover, this strategy can increase sales. Customers who see the single price, and who expect eventually to use more than one unit of the product, regularly purchase it in multiple units to save the odd cents.

Prestige Pricing **Prestige pricing** is the strategy of setting a very high price to project an aura of quality and status. Because high-quality items are generally more expensive than those of average quality, many buyers believe that high price *means* high quality (and vice versa). High-priced products such as Rolex watches and stores such as Neiman-Marcus tend to attract quality- and prestige-conscious customers.

Price Lining **Price lining** is selling goods only at certain predetermined prices. For example, a store may sell men's ties only at $7.95 and $12.95. This strategy is widely used in clothing stores and boutiques. It eliminates minor price differences from the buying decision—both for customers and for those who buy merchandise for resale in the store.

Discounting

A **discount** is a deduction from the price of an item. Producers and sellers offer a wide variety of discounts to their customers.

☐ *Trade discounts* are discounts from the list, or retail, price that are offered to middlemen. A furniture retailer, for example, may receive a 40 percent discount from the manufacturer. The retailer would then pay $60 for a lamp carrying a list price of $100. Middlemen, who are discussed in Chapter 13, perform various marketing activities in return for trade discounts.

☐ *Quantity discounts* are discounts that are given to customers who buy in large quantities. The seller's per-unit selling cost is lower for larger purchases. The quantity discount is a way of passing part of this saving on to the buyer.

☐ *Cash discounts* are discounts that are offered for prompt payment. A seller may offer a discount of "2/10 net 30," meaning that the buyer may take a 2 percent discount if the bill is paid within 10 days and that the bill must be paid in full within 30 days.

☐ Various *geographic pricing strategies,* which deal with delivery costs, are a kind of discount. The seller may assume all delivery costs, no matter where the buyer is located. This practice is called *uniform delivered pricing.* Or the seller may share transportation costs with the buyer according to some predetermined policy. The pricing strategy that requires the buyer to pay the greatest part of the delivery costs is called *F.O.B. point of origin pricing.* F.O.B. point of origin stands for "free on board at the point of origin," which means that the seller will pay to load the shipment onto a carrier but the buyer must assume the remaining transportation costs.

Chapter Review

SUMMARY

A product is everything that one receives in an exchange, including all attributes and expected benefits. The basic product may be a good, a service, an idea, or some combination of these. A product line is a group of similar products marketed by a firm. The firm's product mix includes all the products that it offers for sale.

Every product moves through a series of four stages—introduction, growth, maturity, and decline—which together form the product life cycle. As the product progresses through these stages, its sales and the profit it earns increase, reach a peak, and then decline. If a firm does not introduce new products to replace declining products, it will eventually fail.

New products should be developed in a series of six steps. The first two, exploration and screening, are designed to remove from consideration those product ideas that do not mesh with organizational goals or are not feasible. The third step, business analysis, generates information on the marketability and profitability of the proposed good or service. The last three steps, development, testing, and commercialization, actually provide a marketable product and launch it on its life cycle. Most product failures result from inadequate product planning and development.

Branding strategies are used to identify (or not to identify) particular products with existing products, with producers, or with middlemen. Packaging is used to protect goods and to enhance marketing efforts. Labeling provides customers with product information, including some information that is required by law.

Under the ideal conditions of pure competition, an individual seller has no control over the price of its products. Prices are set through the workings of supply and demand. However, in our real economy, sellers do exert some control—primarily through product differentiation.

Before it sets prices for its products, a firm should develop pricing goals that are in line with its organizational and marketing goals. Then it may set prices based on costs, demand, the competition's prices, or some combination of these. Cost-based and competition-based pricing are the simpler, whereas demand-based pricing brings additional marketing factors into the pricing process. Once basic prices are set, the seller may apply various pricing strategies to reach its target markets more effectively.

In this chapter, we discussed two ingredients of the marketing mix. The next chapter is devoted to a third ingredient—distribution. As we will see, distribution includes not only the physical movement of products but also the organizations that facilitate exchanges between the producers and users of products.

KEY TERMS

You should now be able to define and give an example relevant to each of the following terms:

product

product line

product mix

product life cycle

brand

brand name

brand mark

trademark

manufacturer (or producer) brand

middleman's (or store) brand

generic products

individual branding

family branding

packaging

labeling

express warranty

price

supply

demand

product differentiation

markup

breakeven quantity

total revenue

fixed costs

variable costs

total cost

price skimming

penetration pricing

odd pricing

multiple-unit pricing

prestige pricing

price lining

discount

QUESTIONS AND EXERCISES

Review Questions

1. What does the purchaser of a product obtain, besides the good or service itself?
2. What are the products of (a) a bank, (b) an insurance company, and (c) a university?
3. What is the difference between a product line and a product mix? Give an example of each.
4. What are the four stages of the product life cycle? How can a firm determine which stage a particular product is in?
5. Why must firms introduce new products?
6. Briefly describe the six new-product development stages.
7. What is the difference between (a) a producer brand and a store brand, and (b) family branding and individual branding?
8. How can packaging be used to enhance marketing activities?
9. For what purposes is labeling used?
10. What is the primary function of prices in our economy?
11. List and briefly describe the five major pricing goals.
12. What are the differences among markup pricing, pricing by breakeven analysis, and pricing with the competition?
13. In what way is demand-based pricing more realistic than markup pricing?
14. Why would a firm use competition-based pricing?
15. Which pricing strategies are used mainly (a) for new products, (b) by retailers, and (c) in sales to middlemen?

Discussion Questions

1. Why would Coleco, a marketer of electronic devices, take on the Cabbage Patch Kids as a new product?
2. How effective were Coleco's product planning and pricing with respect to the Cabbage Patch Kids? Explain.
3. What factors might determine how long a product remains in each stage of the product life cycle? What can a firm do to prolong each stage?
4. Which steps in the evolution of new products are most important? Which are least important?
5. Do branding, packaging, and labeling really benefit consumers? Explain.
6. To what extent can a firm control its prices in our market economy? What factors limit such control?
7. Can a firm have more than one pricing goal? Can it use more than one pricing method? Explain.
8. What is an "effective" price?

Exercises

1. Suppose you have an idea for a new game called "Oligopoly." Explain how you would shepherd your idea through the four product-development steps between exploration and commercialization.
2. Develop a package for the game described in Exercise 1. Consider the package material, the package design, and the information you would include on the package.
3. As the manager of a clothing store, you have just received a shipment of new "cheese-cloth" T-shirts. The T-shirts cost you $48 per dozen, and your usual markup is 40 percent. However, yours is the only store in town that will be carrying this fashionable product. What price will you set for the T-shirts? Why?

CASE 12-1

Concept Testing at General Foods

Where do ideas for new products come from? There is no one source. At General Foods (GF), most new product ideas originate either in technical research or in marketing research. The people in these areas have years of experience with consumer tastes. (In food industries, product development begins and ends with the consumer.)

Sometimes GF's marketing people bring an idea to the research and production people, saying, "We think we can sell this product if you can make it." At other times, the company gains new technical knowledge before the idea for a product is developed. When R&D achieves an advance in food technology (such as freeze-drying for instant coffee), they may tell marketing, "We think we can make this product if you can sell it."

When an idea for a new product is first proposed, the company tries to make sure that it matches a basic consumer need. The idea may seem attractive, but before too much time and money are invested in it, GF must determine whether the idea appeals to those who will buy it. To find out, the company uses concept testing.

GF's marketing researchers give a small group of consumers a statement describing a product idea. The consumers may also receive product samples. Through interviews, the researchers decide whether the idea is a dud—one in which consumers aren't interested—or one that meets a consumer need but requires modification.

Through concept testing, GF people can usually find out, relatively quickly and inexpensively, whether a new-product idea is unacceptable, right on target, or in need of further thinking.[8]

1. Which statement is more meaningful from the marketing viewpoint: "We think we can sell this product if you can make it," *or* "We think we can make this product if you can sell it"? Explain your position.
2. Is GF's new-product development strategy basically sound? Why?

CASE 12-2

This Box Is More Than a Container

Have you tried an aseptically packaged drink—more commonly called a "drink in a box"? A number of firms are betting that they can get you to accept this new form of packaging.

An aseptic package is a "paper bottle" made of aluminum foil sandwiched within laminated paper and plastic. The container and liquid product are sterilized separately; then the container is filled and sealed air-tight. The product requires no preservatives, and it will remain fresh without refrigeration for five months or more. Because the product-sterilization process uses a short heating period, it is (at least presently) applicable only to liquids and semiliquid products like yogurt.

Aseptic packaging provides a number of advantages to producers and sellers: The packages are less expensive than glass bottles or cans; the product need not be shipped or stored under refrigeration; the box shape takes less space than standard round containers; and the entire packaging process requires less energy than standard packaging. All these advantages translate into savings that can be passed on to consumers.

In this country, aseptic containers are presently manufactured by two firms: Brik Pac Inc., an American subsidiary of a Swedish firm, and Combibloc Inc., a joint venture between R. J. Reynolds and a West German firm. However, packaging manufacturers such as American Can, X-Cello, and International Paper are now developing their own versions of the packages and the process.

Among the first firms to use and heavily promote the paper bottle was Ocean Spray Cranberries Inc. In 1983, its revenues from aseptically packaged juice drinks were about 7 percent of total revenues. This cooperative estimates that 25 percent of its sales will be in aseptic containers by 1987.

The Foods Division of Coca-Cola Inc. was also an early starter; sales of its Hi-C have been increased by almost 20 percent through aseptic packaging. And Borden has already test-marketed orange juice in a box. In addition, producers of both the containers and the food products are looking to aseptic packaging for milk, wine, puddings, and soups. Present aseptic packages are not rigid enough to hold carbonated drinks, so producers are missing out on the very large market for softdrink containers—but they're working on the problem.[9]

1. Aseptic packaging lowers the food producer's costs while providing a number of advantages to purchasers. Should "drinks in a box" be priced higher, lower, or the same as conventionally packaged drinks? Why?

2. Why can't a producer—say, Ocean Spray—simply package all its drinks in aseptic containers, rather than try to build a demand for such packaging?

CHAPTER

THIRTEEN

Wholesaling, Retailing, and Physical Distribution

In Chapter 11, we agreed that a pair of shoes displayed in a Minnesota department store is somehow different from the same pair of shoes in a North Carolina factory. To a great extent, the difference stems from distribution, the subject of this chapter. First we shall examine various channels of distribution—the company-to-company paths that products follow as they move from producer to ultimate user. Then we shall discuss wholesalers and retailers, two important groups of middlemen operating within these channels. Finally, we shall explore the physical distribution function and the major modes of transportation that are used to move goods. After studying the chapter, you should understand:

1. *The various channels of distribution that are used for consumer and industrial goods*
2. *The concept of market coverage*
3. *The types of wholesalers and the services they perform for retailers and manufacturers*
4. *The differences among the major types of retail outlets*
5. *The five most important physical distribution activities*

Consider this:

What is Spiegel? Many people still think of Spiegel as a relatively small mail-order retailer with the usual drab catalog. They associate this catalog with low prices, lots of print, and products ranging from footwear to furnaces and from rugs to refrigerators. But to its management, the new Spiegel is a store that measures 5460 square feet of *paper*—a department store in print.

Spiegel, Inc., has been in operation for more than 75 years. Until the mid-1970s it was a "me too" firm, following the lead of the three largest catalog retailers (Sears, J. C. Penney, and Montgomery Ward). Actually, in terms of catalog sales alone, Spiegel was at or close to the top of the industry. Nonetheless, Spiegel tended to play "follow the leader." Its catalog was aimed at low-income but credit-worthy households. It carried a product mix that would appeal mainly to people living in rural areas. Its primary competitive weapon was price, and it was getting nowhere by competing directly against the big three of non-store retailing.

In 1976 Spiegel began to change all this. The architect of the change was (and still is) Henry Johnson, Spiegel's chairman and chief executive officer. Johnson brought more than 30 years of direct-marketing experience to Spiegel, along with a reputation for creativity and knowledge of his field.

The concept behind the change is almost too simple: the new Spiegel is not just a mail-order firm; it is a retail store without floor space—a department store that displays its merchandise in a catalog. Its competition is no longer Sears and Montgomery Ward, but rather the better department stores, like Bloomingdale's and Saks Fifth Avenue!

How does a "mail order retail store" compete with such established department stores? In the same way any other retailer would. Spiegel began with the target market. Its marketers recognized that one growing segment of our population could and probably would respond to Spiegel's new concept. That segment consists of working women aged 25 to 54, with annual household incomes above $34,000. Along with their jobs, these busy women are involved with family and, often, with

Source: Courtesy of Spiegel, Inc.

civic and political activities and sports. They want quality, value, service, and convenience—which Johnson believes the new Spiegel can deliver.

To direct its product mix toward this new target market, Spiegel dropped bulky, high-freight-charge items such as bargain sofas, do-it-yourself items such as floor tile and furnaces, and most items related to automobiles and construction. Generally, if a product had been competing mainly through price, it was eliminated.

In place of such items, Spiegel took on high-fashion clothing for both men and women, fashionable home furnishings, and small luxury items that can be shipped easily. Spiegel's customers can now choose from fashions by Albert Nipon, Liz Claiborne, Anne Klein, Yves St. Laurent, and Adolfo and from home furnishings by Fieldcrest, Wamsutta, and Cuisinart. In fact, Spiegel's list of suppliers reads like that of any other up-scale department store.

But what about the store itself? Spiegel's "store"—its 600-page full-color catalog—reads like a tour through a high-fashion clothing department. Want to move on to another department? Just flip the catalog upside down and you're in Spiegel's Home World, viewing home furnishings and housewares produced by some of the best manufacturers. Prices are standard retail prices, just as you'd find in competing stores. Even Spiegel's promotion—via television and print media—looks more like that of a department store than a mail-order seller.

Buying from Spiegel's catalog department store does have one disadvantage: the customer cannot see the actual merchandise, or try it on if it is clothing, before making a purchase. But this is true of all catalog sales, and Spiegel makes up for it by guaranteeing every item it sells and providing fast pickup for merchandise being returned. In addition, Spiegel stresses convenience and minimal "shopping" time. A customer need not drive or take public transportation, hunt for a parking space, fight crowds, or wait in line. The store is at her fingertips. She need only dial a toll-free telephone number and give her order. She may use Spiegel's credit-purchase plan or a bank credit card. And orders are delivered within a week.

Is Spiegel's new concept working? It seems to be. The product lines that the firm dropped represented about $40 million worth of sales. Yet sales increased from $268 million in 1976 to about $480 million in 1982. (And this in spite of the fact that 1982 was not a good year for retail sales.) Moreover, sales through direct marketing are expected to double by 1987. By all indications, Spiegel seems to be doing the right thing at the right time.

Johnson expects new competition in the next few years—not from mail-order retailers, but from department stores. Presently, department stores send out an average of ten catalogs each year. Johnson expects to see more catalogs from more department stores, including Neiman-Marcus, Dayton's, and R.H. Macy. But he notes that Spiegel has just opened its "store" and is still in the process of attracting new customers.[1]

Spiegel, Inc., is a retailing middleman—one of more than two million firms in the United States that help move goods and services from producers to consumers. Most of these firms operate stores where consumers take title to, and possession of, their purchases. Some, like Avon and Electrolux, send their salespeople to the homes of customers. Others sell through catalogs or through both catalogs and stores.

In addition, there are more than half a million wholesaling middlemen, or firms that sell merchandise to other middlemen. Most consumers know little about these firms, because they work "behind the scene" and rarely sell directly to consumers.

These and other middlemen are concerned with the transfer of both products and ownership. They thus help create the time, place, and possession utility that are so important in marketing. As we will see, they also perform a number of services for their suppliers and their customers.

Before we look closely at some of these important middlemen, we should get an idea of the various channels—some simple, some complex—by which products are distributed to consumers.

CHANNELS OF DISTRIBUTION

A **channel of distribution** or **marketing channel** is a sequence of marketing organizations that directs a product from the producer to the ultimate user. Every marketing channel begins with the producer and ends with either the consumer or the industrial user.

Marketing organizations that link producer and user within a marketing channel are called **middlemen** or **marketing intermediaries.** For the most part, middlemen are concerned with the transfer of *ownership* of products rather than with the movement of the products themselves. However, in most channels, the products move along with their title of ownership. A **merchant middleman** (or, more simply, a *merchant*) is a middleman that actually buys and then resells products. On the other hand, an **agent middleman** is a middleman that helps in the transfer of ownership of products but does not take title to the products.

Major Marketing Channels

Different channels of distribution are generally used to move industrial and consumer products. The five most commonly used channels are illustrated in Figure 13.1.

Channels for Consumer Products

Producer to Consumer This channel, which is often called the *direct channel,* includes no intermediaries. Practically all services, but very few consumer goods, are distributed through the direct channel. However, the manufacturers of some consumer goods, such as Avon cosmetics, Fuller Brush products, Thom McAn shoes, Goodyear tires, and Sherwin-Williams paints, prefer to sell directly to consumers. The first two

Figure 13.1 *Distribution Channels. Producers use various channels to distribute their products to consumers and industrial users.*

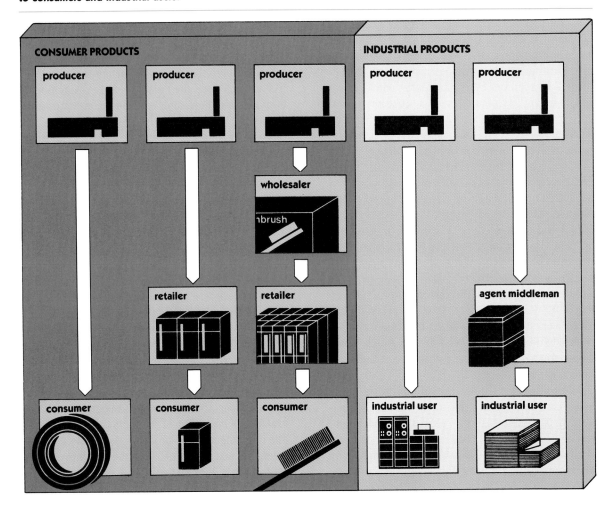

of these firms sell in the consumer's home. The others operate their own stores.

Producers sell directly to consumers for several reasons. They can control the price of their products. They don't have to pay (through discounts) for the services of middlemen. And they can maintain closer ties with the consumer.

Producer to Retailer to Consumer A **retailer** is a middleman that buys from producers or other middlemen and sells to consumers. Producers generally sell directly to retailers in order to maintain a short distribution channel while not actually becoming involved in consumer sales. This channel is most often used for products that are bulky, such as furniture and major appliances, for which additional handling would increase selling costs. It is also the commonest channel for perishable products, such as fruits and vegetables, and for high-fashion products that must reach the consumer in the shortest possible time.

Producer to Wholesaler to Retailer to Consumer
This indirect channel is known as the *traditional* channel, because most consumer goods (especially convenience goods) are routed through wholesalers to retailers. A **wholesaler** is a middleman that sells products to other firms. These firms may be retailers, industrial users, or other wholesalers. Manufacturers use wholesalers when their products are carried by many retailers who would otherwise be difficult to reach.

Often a manufacturer uses different distribution channels to reach different market segments. Multiple channels are also used to increase sales or to capture a larger share of the market. Firestone, for example, markets its tires through its own retail outlets as well as through independent service stations and department stores.

Channels for Industrial Products

Producers of industrial products generally tend to use short channels. We will outline the two that are most commonly used.

Producer to retailer to consumer is the distribution channel most often used for perishable products such as these baked goods. Source: Courtesy of General Foods, Inc.

Producer to Industrial User In this direct channel, the manufacturer's own sales force sells directly to industrial users. Heavy machinery and equipment, large computers, and major installations are usually distributed in this way. The very short channel allows the producer to provide customers with expert and timely services, such as delivery, machinery setup, and repairs.

Manufacturer to Agent Middleman to Industrial User This channel is employed by manufacturers to distribute such items as operating supplies, accessory equipment, small tools, and standardized parts. The agent is an independent intermediary between the producer and the user. Generally, agents may represent either sellers or buyers. They receive payments (in the form of *commissions*) from whichever party they represent.

Market Coverage

How does a producer decide which distribution channels (and which particular middlemen) to use? Like every other marketing decision, this one should be based on all relevant factors. These include the firm's production capability and marketing resources, the target market and the buying patterns of potential customers, and the product itself. After evaluating these factors, the producer can choose a particular *intensity of market coverage*. Then it selects channels and middlemen to implement that coverage. (See Figure 13.2.)

Intensive distribution is the use of all available outlets for a product. The producer that wants to give its product the widest possible exposure in the marketplace chooses intensive distribution. The manufacturer saturates the market by selling to any middlemen of good financial standing who are willing to stock and sell the product. Many convenience goods, including candy, gum, and cigarettes, are distributed intensively.

Selective distribution is the use of only a portion or percentage of the available outlets in each geographic area. Manufacturers of goods such as furniture, major electrical appliances, and clothing typically prefer selective distribution. Franchisers also use selective distribution in granting franchises for the sale of their goods and services.

Exclusive distribution is the use of only a single retail outlet in each geographic area. Exclusive distribution is usually limited to very prestigious products. It is appropriate, for instance, for specialty goods such as expensive pianos, designer clothes, and fine china.

Whatever degree of intensity of market coverage a producer selects, the first link in the distribution chain that connects producer to ultimate user is often the wholesaler.

MARKETING INTERMEDIARIES: WHOLESALERS

Wholesalers may be the most misunderstood of marketing intermediaries. Producers often try to eliminate them from distribution channels by dealing directly with retailers or consumers. Yet wholesalers provide a variety of essential marketing services. It may be true that wholesalers themselves can be eliminated, but their functions cannot. These functions *must* be performed by some organization within the distribution channel.

Figure 13.2 *Market Coverage. How many of the available outlets for a product a producer uses depends on the type of product. Batteries, for example, are distributed intensively.*

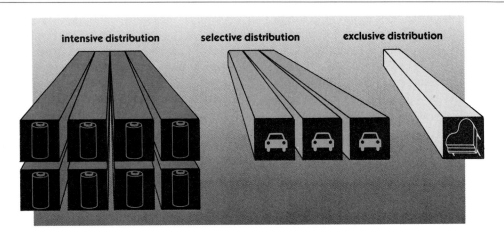

Wholesalers' Services to Retailers

Wholesalers help retailers by buying in large quantities and then selling to retailers in smaller quantities, and by delivering goods to retailers. They also stock—in one place—the variety of goods that retailers would otherwise have to buy from many producers. And wholesalers provide assistance in three other vital areas: promotion, market information, and financial help.

Promotion Most wholesalers help promote the products they sell to retailers. These services are usually either free or performed at cost. Some wholesalers are major sources of display material designed to stimulate "impulse buying" for both producer's and middleman's brands. They may also help retailers build effective window, counter, and bin displays, and they may even donate their own employees to work on the retail sales floor during special promotions.

Market Information Wholesalers are a constant source of market information. Wholesalers have numerous contacts with local businesses and distant suppliers. In the course of these dealings, they accumulate information about consumer demand, prices, supply conditions, new developments within the trade, and even industry personnel. Most of this information is relayed to retailers informally, through the wholesaler's sales force. However, some wholesalers distribute bulletins or newsletters to their customers as well.

Information regarding industry sales and competitive prices is especially important to all firms. Dealing with a number of suppliers and many retailers, a wholesaler is a natural "clearing house" for such information. And most wholesalers are willing to pass it on to their customers.

Financial Aid Most wholesalers provide a type of financial aid that retailers take for granted if they think about it at all. By making prompt and frequent deliveries, wholesalers enable retailers to keep their own inventory investments small in

Most wholesalers help promote the products they sell to retailers—sometimes by providing point-of-sale displays for the product. Source: Courtesy of Schering-Plough Corporation.

relation to sales. Such indirect financial aid reduces the amount of operating capital that retailers need.

In some trades, wholesalers extend direct financial assistance through long-term loans. Most wholesalers also provide help through delayed billing, giving customers 30 to 60 days *after delivery* to pay for merchandise. Wholesalers of seasonal merchandise may offer even longer delays. For example, a wholesaler of lawn and garden supplies may deliver seed to retailers in January but not bill them for it until May.

Wholesalers' Services to Manufacturers

Some of the services that wholesalers perform for producers are similar to those provided to

Black Consumers Equal Profits

While many of America's premier brand-name packaged-goods manufacturers are aware that blacks have a significant amount of purchasing power, they still need help in their marketing efforts. That's where 42-year-old Thomas Dixon, Jr., a native New Yorker, comes in. Dixon's company, Profitable Formulas, Inc. (PFI), has as its mission the promotion and marketing of goods in urban (and usually minority) neighborhoods.

Dixon has been in the marketing field for 18 years, having previously worked with Warner-Lambert Co. "But I always wanted to start my own marketing company," he says. So in 1977 Dixon and a partner pooled $5000 to start PFI.

Profitable Formulas offers valuable services to both the retailer and manufacturer by providing supplementary sales and merchandising help to set up displays, stock shelves, and promote products.

The firm only grossed $60,000 its first year. But after major manufacturers such as Coca-Cola, Hunt-Wesson, and General Foods were sold on the need for supplementary marketing assis-

tance, revenues climbed sharply. In 1983, gross revenues were $372,000, and PFI is predicting a gross of over $500,000 this year. Its 13-member staff is augmented by 24 marketing representatives who conduct sales and merchandising activities in black communities across the nation—New York, Baltimore-Washington, Atlanta, Chicago, Houston, Dallas-Ft. Worth, and Detroit.

"With TV advertising rapidly approaching the million-dollar minute, marketers must begin to maximize the effects of their advertising dollars at store level," Dixon says. He plans to do more of the same marketing to insure future growth as well as to consult with service industries and foreign companies about segmented markets (PFI has landed contracts in India, France, and the Caribbean).

"There's still some reluctance to market to black consumers," notes Dixon. "But today, advertisers realize it's a long way from the TV screen to the supermarket."

Source: *Black Enterprise,* June, 1984, p. 68.

retailers. Others are quite different. See Figure 13.3 for a summary of wholesalers' services.

Providing an Instant Sales Force A wholesaler provides its producers with an instant sales force so that producers' sales representatives need not call on retailers. This can result in large savings for producers. For example, Procter & Gamble and General Foods would have to spend millions of dollars each year to field a sales force that could call on all the retailers that sell their numerous products. Instead, these producers rely on wholesalers to sell and distribute their products to retailers.

Reducing Inventory Costs Wholesalers purchase goods in quantity from manufacturers and store

these goods for resale. By doing so, they reduce the amount of finished-goods inventory that producers must hold and, thereby, the cost of carrying inventories.

Assuming Credit Risks When a producer sells through wholesalers, it is the wholesalers who extend credit to retailers, make collections from retailers, and assume the risks of nonpayment. These services reduce the expenses of the producer and allow it to concentrate on its own marketing activities.

Furnishing Market Information Just as they do for retailers, wholesalers supply market information to the producers they service. Valuable information accumulated by wholesalers may concern consumer demand, the producer's competition, and buying trends.

Types of Wholesalers

Wholesalers generally fall into three categories: merchant wholesalers; commission merchants, agents, and brokers; and manufacturers' sales branches and offices. Of these, merchant wholesalers constitute the largest portion. They account for about 50 percent of sales, 3 of every 4 employees, and 4 of every 5 establishments.[2]

Merchant Wholesalers A **merchant wholesaler** is a middleman that purchases goods in large quantities and then sells them to retailers and to institutional, farm, government, professional, or industrial users. Merchant wholesalers usually operate one or more warehouses where they receive, take title to, and store their goods. They are sometimes called *distributors* or *jobbers*.

Most merchant wholesalers are actually fairly small businesses composed of salespeople, order takers, receiving and shipping clerks, inventory managers, and office personnel. The successful merchant wholesaler must analyze available products and market needs. It must be able to adapt the type, variety, and quality of the products it stocks to changing market conditions.

Commission Merchants, Agents, and Brokers **Commission merchants** usually carry merchandise and negotiate sales for manufacturers, but they do not take title to the goods they sell. In most cases, commission merchants have the power to set the prices and terms of sale. After the sale is made, they either arrange for delivery or provide transportation services. They are generally paid commissions by the manufacturer or producer they represent.

Agents, as we have noted, may represent buyers or sellers. When they represent producers

Figure 13.3 *Wholesalers' Services to Retailers and Producers*

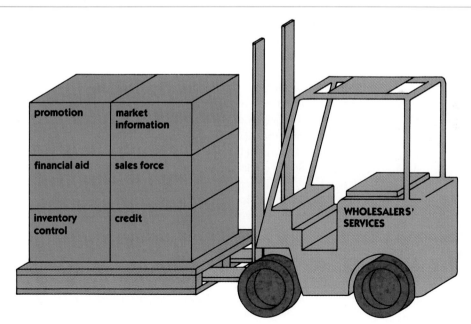

they are known as *sales agents* or *manufacturer's agents*. A sales agent may represent one or several manufacturers, on a commission basis. The agent solicits orders for his or her manufacturers within a specific territory. As a rule, the manufacturer ships the merchandise and bills the customer directly. The manufacturer also sets the prices and other conditions of the sale. What does the manufacturer gain by using a sales agent? The sales agent provides immediate entry into a territory, regular calls on customers, selling experience, and a known, predetermined selling expense (a commission that is a percentage of sales revenue).

A **broker** is a sales agent that specializes in a particular commodity. Brokers usually perform only the selling function for their clients, using established contacts or special knowledge of their field. They are generally paid commissions by the sellers.

Manufacturers' Sales Branches and Offices A **manufacturer's sales branch** is, in essence, a merchant wholesaler that is owned by a manufacturer. Sales branches carry stock, extend credit, deliver goods, and offer help in promoting products. Their customers are retailers, other wholesalers, and industrial purchasers.

Because sales branches are owned by producers, they stock primarily the goods manufactured by their own firms. Selling policies and terms are usually established centrally and then transmitted to branch managers for implementation.

A **manufacturer's sales office** is essentially a sales agent that is owned by a manufacturer. Sales offices may sell not only the products of

Table 13.1 *The Twenty Largest Retail Firms in the United States Ranked by Sales in 1983*

Rank 1982	Company (Headquarters)	Sales in billions of dollars
1	Sears, Roebuck (Chicago)	$35.8
3	K mart (Troy, Mich.)	18.6
2	Safeway Stores (Oakland, Calif.)	18.6
4	Kroger (Cincinnati)	15.2
5	J. C. Penney (New York)	12.1
11	Southland (Dallas)	8.8
8	Federated Department Stores (Cincinnati)	8.7
6	Lucky Stores (Dublin, Calif.)	8.4
9	American Stores (Salt Lake City)	8.0
7	Household International (Prospect Heights, Ill.)	7.9
10	Winn-Dixie Stores (Jacksonville, Fla.)	7.0
14	Dayton Hudson (Minneapolis)	7.0
15	Montgomery Ward (Chicago)	6.0
16	Jewel Companies (Chicago)	5.7
17	BATUS (Louisville)	5.5
12	F.W. Woolworth (New York)	5.5
21	Wal-Marts Stores (Bentonville, Ark.)	4.7
13	Great Atlantic & Pacific Tea (Montvale, N.J.)	4.6
19	Albertson's (Boise)	4.3
20	May Department Stores (St. Louis)	4.2

Source: *Fortune*, "The 50 Largest Retailing Companies," June 11, 1984 issue, 186. By permission.

the owning firm but also certain products of other manufacturers that complement their own product line. For example, Hiram Walker imports wine from Spain to increase the number of products that its sales offices can offer to wholesalers.[3]

MARKETING INTERMEDIARIES: RETAILERS

Retailers are the final link between producers and consumers. Retailers may buy from either wholesalers or producers. They sell not only goods but also such services as repairs, haircuts and hair treatments, and tailoring. Some retailers sell both. Sears, Roebuck sells consumer goods and financial services, and most outlets that sell television sets also provide repair services.

Of the more than 2 million retail firms in the United States, about 15 percent have annual sales under $20,000. On the other hand, there are giants that realize well over $1 million per day in sales revenue. Table 13.1 lists the 20 largest retailing firms, the cities where their headquarters are located, and their approximate 1983 sales revenues. Figure 13.4 shows retail sales by major merchandise category.

Classes of In-Store Retailers

One way to classify retailers is by ownership—in particular, by the number of stores owned and operated by the firm. An **independent retailer** is a firm that operates only one retail outlet. Approximately 85 percent of retailers are independent, and they account for about 55 percent

Figure 13.4 Retail Sales Categorized by Merchandise Type. Source: U.S. Bureau of the Census, 1982.

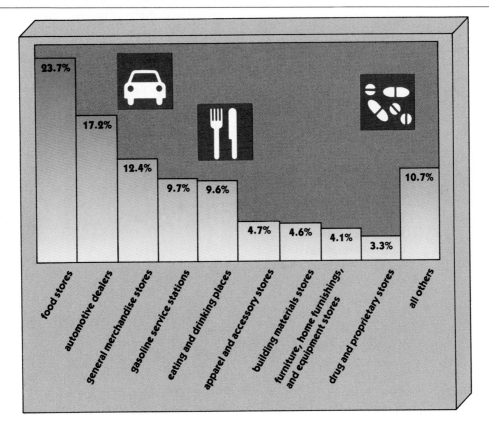

of all retail sales.[4] One-store operators, like all small businesses, generally provide personal service and convenient locations.

A **chain retailer** is a firm that operates more than one retail outlet. By adding outlets, chain retailers attempt to reach new geographic markets. As sales increase, chains may buy in larger quantities and thus take advantage of quantity discounts. They also wield more power in their dealings with suppliers. About 15 percent of retailers operate chains, and they account for about 45 percent of all retail sales revenue.[5]

A better way to classify in-store retailers is by type of store. Each of the following types of stores may be owned independently or by a chain.

Department Stores These are large retail establishments consisting of several parts, or departments, that sell a wide assortment of products. According to the U.S. Bureau of the Census, a **department store** is a retail store that (1) employs 25 or more persons and (2) sells at least

home furnishings, appliances, family apparel, and household linens and dry goods, each in a different part of the store. Macy's in New York, Harrods in London, and Au Printemps in Paris are outstanding examples of large, inner-city department stores.

Department stores are distinctly service-oriented. Along with the goods they sell, they provide credit, delivery, personal assistance, liberal return policies, and a pleasant atmosphere. They are, for the most part, shopping stores. That is, consumers compare merchandise, price, quality, and service in competing department stores before they buy.

Discount Stores **Discount stores** are self-service, general-merchandise outlets that sell goods at prices that are lower than usual. They do so by operating on lower markups, locating their retail showrooms in low-rent areas, and offering minimal customer services. The leading discount department-store chains are listed in Table 13.2.

Table 13.2   The Top Fifteen Discount Department Store Chains

Rank 1982	Chain (Headquarters)	Estimated Sales Volume in billions of dollars	Projected Number of Stores as of 12/83
1	K mart (Michigan)	18.7	2160
2	Wal-Mart (Arkansas)	4.3	635
3	Target (Minnesota)	2.8	206
4	Gemco (California)	2.3	83
5	T.G. & Y. (Oklahoma)	1.8	546
6	Zayre (Massachusetts)	1.8	273
7	Hills (Massachusetts)	1.1	116
8	Caldor (Connecticut)	1.1	96
9	Bradlees (Massachusetts)	1.0	127
10	Meijer (Michigan)	.9	50
11	Pay Less (Oregon)	.8	151
12	Fred Meyer (Oregon)	.8	68
13	Venture (Missouri)	.8	51
14	Rose's (North Carolina)	.7	179
15	Cook United (Ohio)	.6	114

Source: Reprinted with permission from *Discount Store News*, September 19, 1983. Copyright © Lebhar-Friedman, Inc., 425 Park Avenue, New York, N.Y. 10022.

As competition among discount stores has increased, discounters have generally improved their services, store environments, and locations. As a consequence, many of the better-known discount stores have assumed the characteristics of department stores. This has boosted their prices and blurred the distinction between some discount stores and department stores.[6]

Catalog Discount Showrooms **Catalog discount showrooms** are retail outlets that display well-known brands and sell them at discount prices through catalog sales within the store. Colorful catalogs are available in the showrooms (and sometimes by mail). The customer selects the merchandise, either from the catalog or from the showroom display. Then he or she writes up an order on a form provided by the store and hands the order form to a clerk. The clerk retrieves the merchandise from a room that is located away from the selling area and serves as a warehouse.

Catalog showrooms are growing in both number and popularity. Because of their rapid expansion (annual sales are now near $11 billion), the Mass Retailing Institute has labeled these outlets a threat to traditional discounters. Well-known national and regional catalog showrooms include Service Merchandise, McDade's, Consumers Distributing, W. Bell, and Best Products.

Specialty Stores A **specialty store** is a retail outlet that sells a single category of merchandise. Specialty stores may sell shoes, men's or women's clothing, baked goods, children's wear, photo equipment, flowers, or books. Most specialty stores cater to local markets, remain small, and are individually owned. However, there are a few large specialty chains, such as Radio Shack, Toys "Я" Us, Western Auto, and Hickory Farms. Regardless of their size, all specialty stores offer specialized knowledge and service to their customers.

Supermarkets **Supermarkets** are large self-service stores that sell primarily food and household products. They stock canned, fresh, frozen,

A specialty store is a retail outlet that sells a single category of merchandise such as records. Source: © Steve Vidler, Leo deWys, Inc.

and processed foods, paper products, and cleaning products. Supermarkets may also sell such items as housewares, toiletries, toys and games, drugs, stationery, books and magazines, plants and flowers, and small items of clothing.

Supermarkets are large-scale operations that emphasize low prices and one-stop shopping for household needs. The first self-service food market opened 50 years ago. It grossed only $5000 per week, with an average sale of just $1.31.[7] In 1980 supermarkets stocked an average of 14,145 items, up from 9000 items in 1976.[8] Total retail sales reached $252 billion in 1982, an increase of 5.9 percent for the year. Today's top supermarkets include Safeway, Kroger, Winn-Dixie, Jewel, Grand Union, Lucky, and A&P.

Convenience Stores A **convenience store** is a small food store that sells a limited variety of products but remains open well beyond the normal business hours. Almost 70 percent of the people who use convenience stores live within 1 mile of the store. They are popular and are growing in number. White Hen, 7-Eleven, and Open Pantry stores, for example, are found in most areas, as are independent convenience stores. The limited stock that these stores offer and the high prices they must charge in order to stay open for long hours, seven days a week, keep them from becoming a threat to supermarkets.

Warehouse Stores **Warehouse stores** are minimal-service retail food outlets. They appeared in the early 1970s to test discount pricing as a marketing strategy in food retailing. Escalating grocery prices in the 1970s and early 1980s made these low-price outlets extremely appealing. Many were successful.

In warehouse stores, such as Mrs. Clark's Foods and Pick 'N Save, the merchandise is left in packing cases stocked on pallets on the floor. Prices are displayed on the cases but are not individually marked on the items. Customers may be expected to provide the paper bags or cartons in which to take their purchases home. The stores themselves are located in low-rent buildings and have large inventories on the premises.

Kinds of Non-Store Retailers

Non-store retailers are retailers that do not sell in conventional store facilities. Instead they sell door to door, through the mail, or in vending machines.

Door-to-Door Retailers A **door-to-door retailer** is one that sells directly to consumers in their homes. The seller's representative calls on the potential customer at home and demonstrates the product. If a sale is made, she or he writes up the order and often delivers the product to the purchaser. Encyclopedias (Britannica, Americana), cosmetics and toiletries (Avon, Fuller Brush), kitchenware (Tupperware), and vacuum cleaners (Electrolux) have been successfully sold door to door.

Avon is the world's largest direct-selling retailer. Avon representatives sell cosmetics, fragrances and toiletries, jewelry, and accessories in consumers' homes. Avon doesn't tamper with a winning combination: the selling method it uses today was first developed when the firm was founded in 1886.

Mail-Order Retailers A **mail-order retailer** is one that solicits orders by mailing catalogs to potential customers. To make a purchase, the customer fills out an enclosed order form and mails it to the firm. (Lately, more and more mail-order firms are taking orders via toll-free telephone calls and charging the orders to customers' credit cards.)

Avon is a mail-order retailer as well as a door-to-door retailer. The firm markets high-quality, attractively priced women's apparel through nine direct-mailing catalogs annually. Over 62 million catalogs were distributed in 1982.[9]

As a selling technique, catalogs work. According to the Direct Marketing Association, an industry trade group, Americans will buy approximately $50 billion worth of merchandise through the mail this year. And most of this merchandise will be selected from catalogs. In the last five years, mail-order sales have been increasing by about 10 percent a year. This rate is twice that of the annual increase in traditional retail sales. (See Figure 13.5.)

Vending Machines Vending machines dispense convenience goods automatically when customers deposit the appropriate amount of money. Vending machines do not require sales personnel, and they permit 24-hour service. They can be placed in convenient locations in office buildings, educational institutions, motels and hotels, shopping malls, and service stations.

The machines make available a wide assortment of goods. They can supply candy, cigarettes, soups, sandwiches, fresh fruits, yoghurt, chewing gum, postage stamps, hot and cold beverages, perfume and cosmetics, and golf balls. They are even used to sell travel insurance at airports and around-the-clock banking services at convenient urban and suburban locations.

What drawbacks plague the vending-machine business? For one thing, malfunctioning is a costly and frustrating problem, as is vandalism. The machines must also be serviced frequently when they are operating properly. Together, repairs and servicing result in a very high cost for vending-machine selling—often more than one-third of sales revenue.

We have spoken at some length of distribution channels and of the different intermediaries who take charge of, and often title to, products on their way to the consumer or industrial user. Now it is time to discuss the actual physical movement of those products.

PHYSICAL DISTRIBUTION

How do millions of different products, produced in quantities ranging from a single unit to millions of units, get to the homes and businesses of tens of millions of purchasers—all at reasonable cost, almost always in good condition, and at the time when they are needed? The answer, of course, is physical distribution.

Figure 13.5 *Mail-Order Sales. The figures for 1983–1985 are estimates.* Source: All About Mail Order, 1st ed. (Maxwell Sroge Publishing, 1983), p. 8.

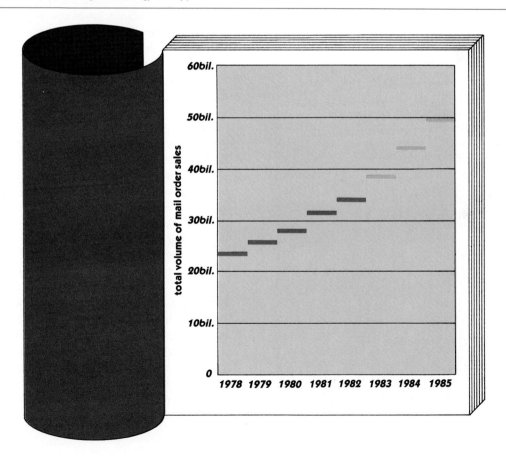

Physical distribution is all those activities concerned with the efficient movement of products from the producer to the ultimate user. Physical distribution is thus the movement of the products themselves—both goods and services—through their channels of distribution. It is a combination of several interrelated business functions. The most important of these are inventory control, order processing, warehousing, materials handling, and transportation. (See Figure 13.6.)

Not too long ago, each of these functions was considered distinct from all the others. In a fairly large firm, one group or department would handle each function. Each of these groups would work to minimize its own costs and to maximize its own effectiveness, but the end result was usually high physical distribution costs.

Various studies of the problem emphasized both the interrelationships among the physical distribution functions *and* the relationship between physical distribution and other marketing functions. Long production runs may reduce per-unit product costs, but they can cause inventory-control and warehousing costs to skyrocket. A new automated warehouse may reduce materials-handling costs to a minimum; but if it is not located properly, transportation time and costs may increase substantially.

There are many more instances of these inter-relationships, and they have made their point. Marketers now view physical distribution as an integrated effort that provides an important marketing service: getting the right product to the right place at the right time and at minimal *overall* cost.

Inventory Management

In Chapter 7 we discussed inventory management from the standpoint of operations. We defined **inventory control** as the process of managing inventories in such a way as to minimize inventory costs, including both holding costs and potential stock-out costs. Both the definition and the objective of inventory control apply here as well.

Holding costs are the costs of storing products until they are purchased or shipped to customers. *Stock-out costs* are the costs of sales that are lost when an item is not in inventory. Of course, holding costs can be minimized by minimizing inventories, but then stock-out costs would ruin the firm. And stock-out costs can be minimized by carrying very large inventories, but then holding costs would be enormous.

Inventory management is thus a sort of "balancing act" between stock-out costs and holding costs. The latter include the cost of money invested in inventory, the cost of storage space, insurance costs, and inventory taxes. Often, even a relatively small reduction in inventory investment can provide a relatively large increase in working capital. And sometimes this can best be accomplished through a willingness to incur a reasonable level of stock-out costs.

Figure 13.6 *The Top Five Functions of Physical Distribution. Source: Photo, © 1984 Leo deWys, Inc.*

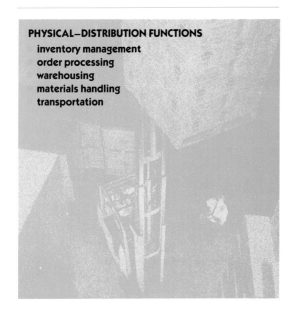

PHYSICAL–DISTRIBUTION FUNCTIONS
inventory management
order processing
warehousing
materials handling
transportation

Order Processing

Order processing consists of those activities that are involved in receiving and filling customers' purchase orders. It may include the means by which customers order products as well as procedures for billing and for granting credit.

Fast, efficient order processing is an important marketing service—one that can provide a dramatic competitive edge. The people who purchase goods for middlemen are especially concerned with their suppliers' promptness and reliability in order processing. To them it means minimal inventory costs as well as the ability to order goods when they are needed rather than weeks in advance.

Warehousing

Warehousing is the set of activities that are involved in receiving and storing goods and preparing them for reshipment. Goods are stored in order to create time utility; that is, they are held until they are needed for use or sale. But along with storage, warehousing includes a number of other activities.[10]

- □ *Receiving goods.* The warehouse accepts delivered goods and assumes responsibility for them.
- □ *Identifying goods.* Records are made of the quantity of each item received. Items may be marked, coded, or tagged for identification.
- □ *Sorting goods.* Delivered goods may have to be sorted before being stored.
- □ *Dispatching goods to storage.* Items must be moved to their own specific storage areas, where they can be found later.
- □ *Holding goods.* The goods are kept in storage under proper protection until needed.
- □ *Recalling, selecting, or picking goods.* Items that are to leave the warehouse must be efficiently selected from storage.
- □ *Marshaling shipments.* The items making up each shipment are brought together, and the

Receiving goods from producers, storing them, and then shipping them to retailers are warehousing activities that can be more efficiently carried out in a computerized warehouse. Source: Courtesy of International Business Machines Corporation.

shipment is checked for completeness. Records are prepared or modified as necessary.
- □ *Dispatching shipments.* Each shipment is packaged suitably and directed to the proper transport vehicle. Shipping and accounting documents are prepared.

A firm may either use its own warehouses or rent space in public warehouses. A *private warehouse,* owned and operated by a particular firm,

An automated warehouse uses self-regulating machines to handle goods. Source: Courtesy of General Foods Corporation.

can be designed to serve the firm's specific needs. However, the firm must take on the task of financing the facility, determining the best location for it, and ensuring that it is fully utilized. Generally, only firms that deal in large quantities of goods can justify private warehouses.

Public warehouses offer their services to all individuals and firms. Most are huge, one-story structures on the outskirts of major cities, where rail and truck transportation are easily available. They provide storage facilities, areas for sorting and marshaling shipments, and office and display spaces for wholesalers and retailers. Public warehouses will also hold—and issue receipts for—goods that are used as collateral for borrowed funds.

Materials Handling

Materials handling is the actual physical handling of goods, in warehousing as well as during transportation. Proper materials-handling procedures and techniques can increase the usable capacity of a warehouse or that of any means of transportation. And proper handling can reduce breakage and spoilage as well.

Modern materials-handling efforts are aimed at reducing the number of times a product is handled. One method of doing so is called *unit loading*. Several smaller cartons, barrels, or boxes are combined into a single standard-sized load that can be handled efficiently by fork lift, conveyor, or truck.

Transportation

As a part of physical distribution, **transportation** is simply the shipment of products to customers. The greater the distance between seller and purchaser, the more important is the choice of the means of transportation and the particular carrier.

Firms that offer transportation services are called **carriers**. A *common carrier* is a transportation firm whose services are available to all shippers. Railroads, airlines, and most long-distance trucking firms are common carriers. A *contract carrier* is a transportation firm that is available for hire by one or several shippers. Contract carriers do not serve the general public. Moreover, the number of firms they can handle at any one time is limited by law. A *private carrier* is one that is owned and operated by the shipper.

In addition, a shipper can hire agents called *freight forwarders* to handle its transportation. Freight forwarders pick up shipments from the shipper, ensure that the goods are loaded onto a selected carrier, and assume responsibility for the safe delivery of the shipment to its destination. Freight forwarders are often able to group a number of small shipments into one large load (which

is carried at a lower rate). This, of course, saves money for shippers.

The two prime elements in choosing a particular mode of transportation—whether railroad, truck, pipeline, or another—are the product itself and the firm's overall distribution system. For some combinations of these two elements, the cost of transportation may be most important. For other combinations, speed may be uppermost. Other factors that enter into this decision are the reliability of the various modes of transportation, their availability at points of shipment and delivery, and their ability to handle particular kinds of shipments. See Figure 13.7 for a breakdown by use of different modes of transportation.

Figure 13.7 Transportation. The graph compares the modes of transportation for products.
Source: *Transportation Policy Associates,* Transportation in America, *March 1983.*

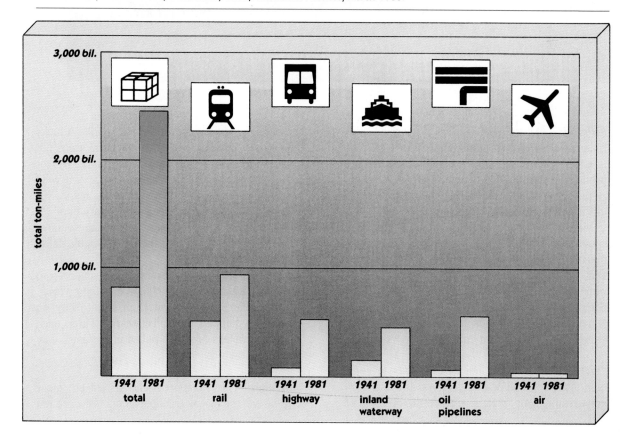

The shipment of goods to customers often involves several means of transportation—ship, railroad, and truck, for example. Source: © James R. Holland, Stock, Boston.

Railroads In terms of total freight carried, railroads are the most important mode of transportation. They are also the least expensive for many products. Almost all railroads are common carriers, although a few coal-mining companies operate their own lines.

Many of the commodities carried by railroads could not easily be transported by any other means. They include a wide range of foodstuffs, raw materials, and manufactured goods. Coal ranks first by a considerable margin. Other major commodities carried by railroads include paper and pulp products, liquids in tank-car loads, heavy equipment, lumber, and cut stone.

Trucks The trucking industry consists of common, contract, and private carriers. It has undergone tremendous expansion since the creation of

a national highway system in the 1920s. Trucks can move goods to suburban and rural areas not served by railroads. They can handle freight quickly and economically, and they carry a wide range of shipments. Many shippers favor this mode of transportation because it offers door-to-door service, less stringent packaging requirements than ships and airplanes, and flexible delivery schedules.

Railroad and truck carriers have teamed up to provide a form of transportation called *piggyback*. Truck trailers are carried from city to city on specially equipped railroad flatcars. Within each city, the trailers are then pulled in the usual way by truck tractors.

Airplanes Air transport is the fastest but most expensive means of transportation. All certified airlines are common carriers. Supplemental or charter lines are contract carriers.

Because of the high cost, the lack of airport facilities in many areas, and their reliance on weather conditions, airlines carry less than 1 percent of all intercity freight. Only high-value or perishable items, such as aircraft parts, electrical equipment, drugs, and fresh fruits and vegetables, are usually shipped by air.

Ships Cargo ships and barges offer the least expensive but slowest form of transportation. They are used mainly for bulky, nonperishable goods such as iron ore, bulk wheat, motor vehicles, and agricultural implements. Of course, shipment by water is limited to cities located on navigable waterways. But ships and barges account for a steady 16 percent of all intercity freight hauling.

Pipelines Pipelines are a highly specialized mode of transportation. They are used primarily to carry petroleum and natural gas. Pipelines have become more and more important as the nation's need for petroleum products has increased. Such products as semiliquid coal and wood chips can also be shipped through pipelines continuously, reliably, and with minimal handling.

Package Carriers The U.S. Postal Service offers *parcel post* delivery, which is widely used by mail-order houses. The Postal Service provides complete geographic coverage at the lowest rates, but it limits the size and weight of the shipments it will accept.

The United Parcel Service (UPS), a privately owned firm, also provides small-parcel services for shippers. Other privately owned carriers, such as Federal Express and Purolator Courier, offer fast—often overnight—parcel delivery both within and outside the United States. There are also many local parcel carriers, including specialized delivery services for various time-sensitive industries, such as publishing.

Nabisco's Risky Plunge

To speed shipments of Fig Newtons, Oreo cookies, Ritz crackers, and other baked goods to supermarkets, Nabisco Inc.'s regional offices have long used telex machines to dispatch orders to the company's factories. But Nabisco's sales have grown so rapidly that its 10-year-old telex system, Western Union's InfoCom, has been pushed to the limit, resulting in an epidemic of irritating and costly communications foulups. Indeed, the situation got so bad at one point that exasperated clerks began routinely telephoning telex recipients to make sure they got their messages.

Now, however, things are looking up again at Nabisco, thanks to a fancy new electronic message system called WINC—for Worldwide Integrated Communications. Developed by Mohawk Data Services Inc., one of Western Union's most ambitious and innovative new rivals, WINC has been up and running at Nabisco since March 1, and Nabisco's executives are beaming. Not only have transmission snafus virtually disappeared, says telecommunications director Walter C. Jacobs, the company has been able to shave $12,000 a month off its telecommunications bill. Marvels Jacobs: "This is really a dynamite system."

Source: John Herrmann, *Management Technology*, May 1984, p. 47.

Chapter Review

SUMMARY

A marketing channel is a sequence of marketing organizations that directs a product from producer to ultimate user. The marketing channel for a particular product is concerned with the transfer of ownership of that product. Merchant middlemen actually take title to products, whereas agents simply aid in the transfer of title.

The channels used for consumer products include the direct channel from producer to consumer; the channel from producer to retailer to consumer; and that from producer to wholesaler to retailer to consumer. The major channels for industrial products are producer to user, and producer to agent to user. Channels and middlemen are chosen to implement a given intensity of distribution from intensive (widest) to exclusive.

Wholesalers are middlemen that purchase from producers or other middlemen and sell to industrial users or other middlemen. Wholesalers provide retailers with help in promoting products, collecting information, and financing. They provide manufacturers with sales help, reduce their inventory costs, furnish market information, and extend credit to retailers. Merchant wholesalers buy and then sell products. Commission merchants and brokers are essentially agents. Manufacturer's sales branches and offices are like merchant wholesalers and agents, respectively.

Retailers are middlemen that buy from producers or wholesalers and sell to consumers. In-store retailers include department stores, discount stores, catalog discount showrooms, specialty stores, supermarkets, convenience stores, and warehouse stores. Non-store retailers sell door-to-door, by mail, or vending machine.

Physical distribution consists of activities designed to move products to ultimate users. Its five major functions are inventory management, order processing, warehousing, materials handling, and transportation. These interrelated functions are integrated into the marketing effort.

In the next chapter we shall discuss the fourth element of the marketing mix—promotion.

KEY TERMS

You should now be able to define and give an example relevant to each of the following terms:

channel of distribution (or marketing channel)
middlemen (or marketing intermediaries)
merchant middleman
agent middleman
retailer
wholesaler
intensive distribution
selective distribution
exclusive distribution
merchant wholesaler
commission merchants
broker
manufacturer's sales branch
manufacturer's sales office
independent retailer
chain retailer
department store
discount store
catalog discount showroom
specialty store
supermarket
convenience store
warehouse store
door-to-door retailer
mail-order retailer
physical distribution
inventory control
order processing
warehousing
materials handling
transportation
carriers

QUESTIONS AND EXERCISES

Review Questions

1. In what ways is a channel of distribution different from the path taken by a product during physical distribution?
2. What are the commonest marketing channels for consumer products? for industrial products?
3. What are the three general approaches to market coverage? What types of products is each used for?
4. What is the basic difference between a merchant wholesaler and an agent?
5. List the services performed by wholesalers. For whom is each service performed?
6. Distinguish between (a) commission merchants and agents and (b) manufacturer's sales branches and manufacturer's sales offices.
7. What is the basic difference between wholesalers and retailers?
8. What is the difference between a department store and a discount store, with regard to selling orientation or philosophy?
9. How do (a) convenience stores and (b) specialty stores compete with other retail outlets?
10. What can non-store retailers offer their customers that in-store retailers cannot offer?
11. What is physical distribution? Which major functions does it include?
12. What activities besides storage are included in warehousing?
13. List the primary modes of transportation, and cite at least one advantage of each.

Discussion Questions

1. Why would Spiegel's management attempt to "position" the firm so that it competes with better department stores rather than with other mail-order firms?
2. As Spiegel's chief executive officer, what would you expect from the firm's overall physical distribution system? What would you expect from each part of the system?
3. Which distribution channels would producers of services be most likely to use? Why?
4. Many producers sell to consumers both directly and through middlemen. How can such a producer justify competing with its own middlemen?
5. In what situations might a producer use agents or commission merchants rather than its own sales offices or branches?
6. Which types of retail outlets are best suited to intensive distribution? to selective distribution? to exclusive distribution? (Explain your answer in each case.)
7. How are the various physical distribution functions related to each other? to the other elements of the marketing mix? to the other parts of the firm's marketing system?

Exercises

1. On the basis of your experience as a consumer, list the services that retailers perform for their customers. Then circle those that could easily be eliminated. Next place a check mark beside those that are most important to you. Finally, summarize your results in a sentence or two.
2. Suppose you have developed and will produce a new golf tee that increases golfers' accuracy and driving distance. Design a marketing channel (or channels) for your product. Explain why your choice of channels would be most effective for this product.
3. For the golf tees described in Exercise 2, answer the following questions:
   a. How would you package your product for sale and for ease in inventory control and handling?
   b. Where would you locate your storage facilities? (Assume nationwide distribution of your product.)
   c. What means of transportation would you use to distribute your product across the nation? Why?

CASE 13-1

Toys "Я" Us Marketing

How could one chain retailer increase its sales by almost one-third and open two dozen new stores in a year in which its competitors experienced decreased sales volume, losses or reduced profits, and even bankruptcy?

For Toys "Я" Us, part of the answer is size. Its 150 stores in 21 states give this chain of discount toy stores the ability to buy extremely well—and to pass on its savings to price-conscious consumers.

Another part of the answer is careful attention to customer convenience. Toys "Я" Us outlets are located near—but not in—large regional shopping malls; each has its own spacious parking lot, separate from that of the mall. For the shopper, this translates into a store that is both easy to get to and free from the overcrowding typical of shopping-center parking lots. Inside, the stores are characterized by wide aisles, colorful displays, eye-level placement of the most popular items, and speedy supermarket-type checkout.

Large stocks of toys and convenient shopping are supplemented by heavy local advertising throughout the year. Together, they permit Toys "Я" Us to achieve half its annual sales during the off-season for toys—the first nine months of the year. (For the typical toy store, the greatest sales occur during the Christmas selling season.) This early selling gives the firm a chance to spot buying trends, so stores are well stocked with "hot" items for the seasonal rush. Moreover, most of the merchandise that the firm sells in the off-season need not be paid for until the following year; thus, the early sales help to finance its Christmas season.

Finally, there is the firm's computerized inventory-control system, which provides extremely accurate monitoring of its operations. Every sale is recorded by a computer as it occurs. Thus the system can provide executives with up-to-the-minute sales figures for every toy sold at every store. If a particular toy turns out to be very popular, buyers can order more from the manufacturer well before they have to worry about being out of stock. If another toy is selling slowly, managers can reduce its price to move it more quickly—and make room for hotter items. And if a particular toy is selling well in one region but slowly in another, inventory can be shifted to the region—or the store—where that item is in demand. [11]

1. Has Toys "Я" Us come up with a unique new formula for success in retailing, or has the firm simply developed an effective marketing mix? Why?
2. Suppose Toys "Я" Us, Inc. wants to expand its product mix by taking on a new non-toy line of products. What product line would you suggest? Why?

CASE 13-2

Absolutely, Positively Federal Express

In the 1960s, while Frederick Smith was a student at Yale, he needed an idea for a project in his management course. The idea he came up with was an overnight package delivery service. Smith argued that there was a definite need for such a service. He believed that a firm whose production line was being held up by a missing part, or whose negotiations were stymied because of missing information, would gladly pay the cost of guaranteed overnight delivery.

As Smith envisioned it, the company offering the service would fly planeloads of packages, from all over the country, to a central distribution point in the early evening—after business hours. Overnight, the packages would be sorted by destination, reloaded onto the same planes, and flown to the appropriate cities for delivery the next day.

Smith's teacher, who was not particularly impressed, told him the idea was impractical and gave him a C for the project.

Nevertheless, Smith liked his idea. In the early 1970s, now a licensed pilot who had flown more than 200 missions in Vietnam, he put the idea into operation. For his distribution point he chose Memphis, Tennessee, whose airport is close to the city and where there was an available building that could serve as a distribution center. Smith's firm purchased its own airplanes, so that it would not be limited by the schedules of commercial carriers. And package weights were held to a maximum of 70 pounds (the amount that one person can carry comfortably), to facilitate loading and sorting. He named his service Federal Express.

Potential investors and transportation industry observers were, at first, skeptical about the firm's chance for success. They could not see why customers would pay an extra $10 to $15 for overnight delivery, when other carriers could deliver in two or three days. But businesses gave the service their hearty approval and used it in droves. From 1974 to 1983, the firm almost doubled in size every two years. Sales in 1983 approached $1 billion. The number of communities served by Federal Express rose from 8,000 in 1979 to 17,000 in 1983, with a reliability rate greater than 99.5 percent. But perhaps the most telling evidence of its success is the rash of competition from both new and established carriers—including the overnight Express Mail service from the U.S. Postal Service.

In 1983, Federal Express began to implement an expansion plan that will double the number of communities it serves. The plan calls for the creation of four regional distribution centers like that in Memphis, and about a 50 percent increase in the size of the firm's fleet of airplanes. In addition, the weight limit on packages was raised to 150 pounds. Then, in 1984, Federal Express instituted a new communications service called Zap Mail—the electronic transmission of documents. Documents up to five pages in length can be duplicated and delivered to selected communities across the nation within two hours; longer documents generally can be delivered the same day they are sent.[12]

1. Is Federal Express presently a service firm, a common carrier, a freight forwarder, a package carrier, a mail service, or some combination of these? Explain.
2. Obviously, businesses are using Federal Express and similar carriers for more than just "emergency" deliveries. In what situations might firms use an overnight carrier on a fairly routine basis?

CHAPTER

FOURTEEN
Promotion

An old adage says, "Build a better mousetrap and the world will beat a path to your door." It does make a nice saying, but it's poor business advice. Having the right product at the right price in the right place is simply not enough. You also need to tell the world that your "mousetrap" is available, why it is better, and where your door is located. In other words, sellers must communicate with their markets. That is the function of promotion. In this chapter we shall discuss four promotion methods—advertising, personal selling, sales promotion, and publicity—and see how they are used to implement the firm's marketing plans. After studying the chapter, you should understand:

1. *The three types of advertising in terms of their purpose*
2. *The advantages and disadvantages of the major advertising media*
3. *The activities involved in personal selling, and the personal-selling process*
4. *The sales-promotion techniques that are used to supplement other promotion methods*
5. *The relationship between public relations and publicity*
6. *How the promotional mix is developed from the firm's marketing objectives*

Consider this:

Source: Courtesy of The Coca-Cola Company.

When the Coca-Cola Company launched diet Coke, it did so with a maximum of hoopla. The company rented Radio City Music Hall in New York for the evening and invited more than 4000 people. These guests were treated to an extravaganza that featured the Rockettes along with pianist Bobby Short leading a 40-piece orchestra. To cap off the evening, a 14-foot replica of a diet Coke container rose slowly from the orchestra pit.

The activities in New York were repeated on a smaller scale throughout the United States. In Detroit, the University of Michigan marching band paraded through a downtown hotel. In Phoenix, a local bottler iced 2-liter bottles of diet Coke in coolers and then served the drink in champagne glasses.

This was just the beginning of a giant promotional campaign intended to make diet Coke an instant success. The company spent $50 million on advertising alone. Another $50 million was spent on promotion. One television commercial portrayed a movie-type premiere of the drink with Radio City as the backdrop. Such celebrities

as Bob Hope, Carol Channing, Joe Namath, Telly Savalas, Ben Vereen, and Glen Ford were very visibly in attendance.

But the Pepsi challenge was not far behind. The Pepsi Cola Company used an "image" theme—with pop superstar Michael Jackson—to blunt the Coca-Cola offensive. Pepsi spent $1 million to produce just one of its seven planned commercials, the one that features the Jackson Brothers in concert. And that figure doesn't include the entertainers' fee, which is a record $5.5 million. Not coincidentally, the Michael Jackson commercial appeared for the first time during the Grammy music awards, for which the 25-year-old entertainer had received 12 nominations.

This campaign is to be Pepsi's most extravagant, reflecting the intensity of its competition with Coca-Cola and other soft-drink producers. Pepsi plans to spend $40 million on air time to launch the campaign. The intention is to saturate the airwaves so thoroughly that, in 3 months, American television viewers will have been exposed to the new ad campaign an average of at least 12 times. Among the new slogans: "Pepsi, the choice of a new generation." Among the commercials that push the slogan: a flying saucer that abducts Pepsi—but not Coca-Cola—vending machines.

It is always difficult to judge whether a new campaign will be a success. Pepsi spent more than $16,000 per second to film the Jackson Brothers concert spot. Yet it hasn't pretested viewer reaction to this or any of the other six "new generation" commercials. Coke, by comparison, tested six different advertising concepts before settling on the "Coke is it!" campaign. Only time will tell which promotional strategy has had the greater impact on American consumers of soft drinks.[1]

For many years, Coke and Pepsi have been involved in an intense struggle for sales. Coke, the "senior competitor," had things its way until 1977, when Pepsi edged Coke out of first place in retail sales. To fight back, Coke doubled its advertising budget between 1977 and 1979. Then, in 1980, the emphasis shifted to point-of-sale displays and price competition.[2] Now it seems the two are back to the advertising battleground.

Promotion is communication that is intended to inform, persuade, or remind an organization's target markets. The promotion with which we are most familiar—like Pepsi's advertising—is intended to inform, persuade, or remind us to buy particular products. But there is more to promotion than advertising, and it is used for other purposes as well. For example, charities use promotion to inform us of their need for donations, to persuade us to give, and to remind us to do so in case we have forgotten. Even the Internal Revenue Service makes use of promotion (in the form of publicity) to remind us of its April 15 deadline for filing tax returns.

At the moment, Coke and Pepsi are stressing advertising in their promotion. But they are not neglecting other promotion methods. Their sales people are calling on firms that sell soft drinks. They are giving away store displays that read "Coke is it!" or "Try the Pepsi Challenge!" And they are trying to generate additional public interest with events like Coke's Radio City extravaganza.

Such activities are part of the promotional campaign developed by these two firms. A **promotional mix** is the particular combination of promotion methods that a firm uses in its promotional campaign to reach a target market. The makeup of a mix depends on many factors, including the characteristics of the target market. We shall discuss these factors toward the end of this chapter, after we have examined the promotion methods of advertising, personal selling, sales promotion, and publicity (which is closely related to public relations).

ADVERTISING

Advertising is any nonpersonal promotional message that is paid for by an identified sponsor and directed to a large audience. The key words in the definition are *nonpersonal,* which excludes personal selling by a sales force, and *paid,* which excludes publicity. The definition also excludes public relations, which usually does not entail a specific message, and sales promotion, which consists of distributing free samples, premiums, and the like.

The largest share of the business advertising dollar goes to newspapers. Other media that are used to deliver the message are television, radio, magazines, outdoor advertising, and direct mail. Figure 14.1 shows how advertising expenditures and employment in advertising have increased since 1972. Total advertising expenditures for 1984 are estimated to be $82.9 billion![3]

Types of Advertising by Purpose

Depending on its purpose—and its message—advertising may be broadly classified into three groups. Selective advertising promotes specific brands of products and services. Institutional advertising is image-building advertising. And primary-demand advertising is industry (rather than brand) advertising.

Selective Advertising **Selective** (or **brand**) **advertising** is advertising that is used to sell a particular brand of product or service. It is by far the commonest type of advertising, and it accounts for the lion's share of advertising expenditures. From Bubble Yum to Buicks, producers use this brand-oriented advertising to convince us to buy their products.

Selective advertising that aims at persuading consumers to make purchases within a short time is called *immediate-response advertising.* Most local advertising is of this type. It generally promotes merchandise with immediate appeal, such as fans or air conditioners during an unusually hot summer. Selective advertising aimed at keeping a firm's name or product before the public is called *reminder advertising.* Most auto makers, for example, show commercials on television week after week, as a reminder of their product line.

A new wrinkle in selective advertising is *comparative advertising.* In such advertising, specific characteristics of two or more brands are compared. Of course, the comparison always shows the advertiser's brand to be best. Comparative advertising is now fairly common among manufacturers of deodorants, toothpaste, butter, tires, and automobiles. Comparisons are often based on the outcome of surveys or research studies. Though competing firms act as effective watchdogs on each other's advertising claims, and regulations on comparative advertising are stringent, a certain sophistication on the consumer's part concerning claims based on "scientific studies" and various statistical manipulations is worth cultivating.

Figure 14.1 *Growth of Advertising Expenditures and of Employment in Advertising. Source: Bureau of Labor Statistics (Employment); 1983–84 estimates by McCann-Erikson, Advertising Age, July 18, 1983, and May 28, 1984.*

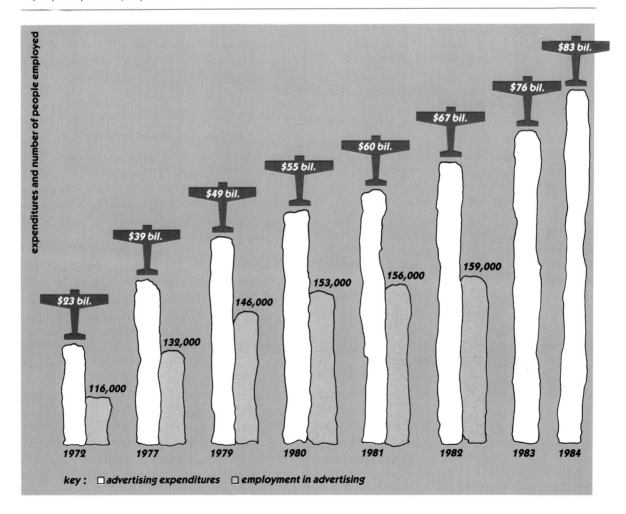

An immediate-response ad (left) attempts to sell a particular brand of product or service within a short period. A
comparative ad (right) attempts to sell a particular brand by
comparing it with other brands. A primary-demand ad
(bottom) tries to increase the demand for all brands of a
product or service. *Sources: Courtesy of Ann & Hope; courtesy of Amoco; courtesy of the Wool Bureau, Inc.*

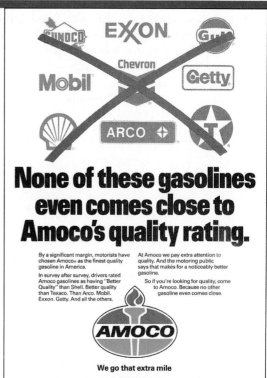

Institutional Advertising Institutional adver-
tising is advertising designed to enhance a firm's
image or reputation. Many public utilities and
larger firms, such as AT&T and the major oil
companies, advertise to build goodwill rather than
to stimulate sales. Perhaps they feel they need
to combat what they see as a negative public
image.

Primary-Demand Advertising Primary-demand
advertising is advertising whose purpose is to
increase the demand for *all* brands of a good or
service. Trade and industry associations, such as
the American Dairy Association ("Drink More
Milk.") and the Association of American Railroads
("Who Needs America's Railroads? We All Do."),
are the major users of primary-demand advertising. Their advertisements promote the product
without mentioning specific brands.

Advertising Media

The **advertising media** are the various forms
of communication through which advertising

reaches its audience. They include newspapers, magazines, television, radio, direct mail, and outdoor displays. Figure 14.2 shows how businesses allocate their advertising expenditures among the various media. The *print media*—which includes newspapers, magazines, direct mail, and billboards—account for about 49 percent of all advertising expenditures. The *electronic media*—television and radio—account for about 28 percent.

Newspapers In 1983 newspapers took in about 27 percent of all advertising expenditures. And more than half of all newspaper advertising was purchased by retailers.

Newspaper advertising is used so extensively by retailers because it is reasonable in cost. Furthermore it provides only local coverage, so advertising dollars are not wasted in reaching people who are outside the store's market area. It is also timely. Ads can usually be placed the day

before they are to appear, and their effectiveness can be measured easily.

There are some drawbacks, however, to newspaper advertising. For one, it has a short life span; newspapers are generally read through once and then discarded. Color reproduction in newspapers is usually poor, so most ads must be run in black and white only. Finally, marketers cannot target specific markets through newspaper ads, except with regard to geographic area.

Newspapers carry more cooperative advertising than other print media. **Cooperative advertising** is advertising whose cost is shared by a producer and one or more local retailers. The costs are shared because the advertising benefits both the producer, whose products are promoted, and the retailer, which reaches its customers through the advertising.

Magazines The advertising revenues of magazines have been climbing dramatically since 1976.

Figure 14.2 *Comparison of Advertising Media in Terms of Advertising Expenditures.*
Source: McCann-Erikson, Advertising Age, May 28, 1984, p. 50.

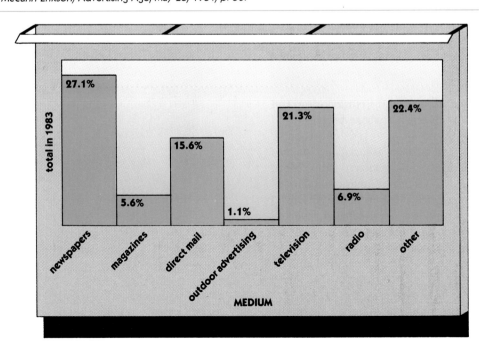

In 1983 they reached $4.2 billion, or about 5.6 percent of all advertising expenditures.

Advertisers can reach very specific market segments through ads in special-interest magazines. A boat manufacturer has a ready-made consumer audience in those who subscribe to *Yachting* or *Sail*. Producers of cameras and photographic equipment advertise primarily in *U.S. Camera* or *Popular Photography*. A number of more general magazines like *Time* and *Cosmopolitan* publish regional editions, which provide advertisers with geographic segmentation as well.

Magazine advertising is more prestigious than newspaper advertising, and it provides high-quality color reproduction. In addition, magazine advertisements have a longer life span than those in other media. Issues of *National Geographic*, for example, may be retained for months or years by subscribers, and the ads they contain are viewed over and over again.

The major disadvantages of magazines are high cost and lack of timeliness. Magazine ads—especially full-color ads—are expensive, although the cost per reader may compare favorably with those of other media. And, because magazine ads must normally be prepared more than a month in advance, they cannot be adjusted to reflect the latest market conditions.

Direct Mail **Direct-mail advertising** is promotional material that is mailed directly to individuals. Direct mail is the most selective medium: mailing lists are available (or can be compiled) to reach almost any target market from airplane enthusiasts to zoologists. The effectiveness of direct-mail advertising can be measured easily because recipients either buy or don't buy the product that is advertised.

But the success of direct-mail advertising depends on appropriate and current mailing lists. More than one direct-mail campaign has failed because the mailing list was outdated and the mailing did not reach the right people. In addition, this medium is relatively costly. Nevertheless direct-mail advertising expenditures amounted to

What's a medium that's overlooked and flashy, yet surprisingly effective? Matchbook advertising.

According to the largest supplier, matchbook advertising is better than the direct mail flyer for building recall of an advertiser's message. Universal Match Corp. recently conducted a recall test among nearly 1000 company presidents, vice presidents, media planners, and marketing managers, and found that observation, retention, and recall of the information on a matchbook outscored customary print materials such as the direct mail flyer or brochure by 3 to 1. Some 32 percent of survey respondents remembered the matchbook's message and only 12 percent remembered the flyer's message, says Patrick Kaiser, senior VP of marketing and sales for Universal Match.

The survey also showed that 14 days after receiving a matchbook in the mail, 64 percent of the respondents had retained the matchbook. After two months, 38 percent still had the information on hand. Comparable figures for the direct mail flyer, identical in color, style, and copy were 22 percent and 8 percent respectively. Moreover, the recall rate for the matchbook information was 59 percent compared with 17 percent for the flyer.

Source: Matthew S. Nadler, "Try Matchbooks for Awareness and Frequency," *Business Marketing,* January, 1984, p. 19.

almost $12 billion in 1983 or about 15.6 percent of the total.

Outdoor Advertising **Outdoor advertising** consists of short promotional messages on billboards, posters, and signs and in skywriting. In 1983 outdoor advertisers spent $794 million, or approximately 1 percent of total advertising expenditures, on outdoor advertising.

Sign and billboard advertising allows the mar-

A company may use several advertising media, each with its own advantages and costs, to reach its target market.
Source: Courtesy of Anheuser-Busch, Inc.

COACHES MONTAGE :30

MUSIC: BUD OLYMPIC FANFARE

ANNCR (VO): Budweiser salutes the coaches and trainers...

...of the 1984 Olympic team.

MUSIC: BUD MELODY THROUGHOUT

SFX: NATURAL SOUNDS THROUGHOUT

ANNCR (VO): To the U.S. Olympic coaches and trainers...

...the team behind the team...

SINGERS: For all you do. ANNCR (VO): This Bud's for you. MUSICAL BUTTON

THIS BUD'S FOR YOU.

The Boston Globe
RETAIL ADVERTISING RATES
EFFECTIVE SEPTEMBER 1, 1984

Advertising Rates
5. ROP/PREPRINT RATES

A. ANNUAL BULK SPACE CONTRACTS
(non-commissionable rates)

	RETAIL RATES	
	Mon.-Fri. R.O.P. Per Col. Inch	Sunday R.O.P. Per Col. Inch
Open Inch Rate	$85.84	$105.72
24 Inches	77.52	97.06
48 Inches	76.62	96.15
96 Inches	76.40	95.92
144 Inches	75.95	95.47
240 Inches	74.83	94.33
480 Inches	74.60	94.10
960 Inches	74.38	93.87
1,440 Inches	74.15	93.65
2,400 Inches	73.93	93.42
3,600 Inches	72.58	92.28
4,800 Inches	71.68	91.37
9,600 Inches	71.23	90.68
19,200 Inches	71.00	90.46
24,000 Inches	70.78	90.23
28,800 Inches	70.11	89.55
33,600 Inches	69.88	89.32
38,400 Inches	69.66	89.09
43,200 Inches	69.43	88.86
48,000 Inches	68.31	87.72
52,800 Inches	67.86	86.81
62,400 Inches	67.63	86.58
72,000 Inches	67.41	86.36
81,600 Inches	65.84	84.53
91,200 Inches	65.39	84.30
100,800 Inches	64.94	83.85
110,400 Inches	64.49	83.39

keter to focus on a particular geographic area, and it is fairly inexpensive. However, because most outdoor advertising is directed toward a mobile audience (and the advertising on buses and taxis is itself mobile), the message must be limited to a few words. The medium is especially suitable for products that lend themselves to pictorial display.

Television Television is the newest advertising medium, but it ranks second only to newspapers in total revenue. In 1983, 21.3 percent of advertising expenditures went to television. Approximately 98 percent of American homes have at least one television set, which is used an average of 7 hours each day.[4] Television obviously provides a massive market for advertisers.

Television advertising is the primary medium for larger firms whose objective is to reach national or regional markets. A national advertiser may buy *network time,* which guarantees that its message will be broadcast by hundreds of local stations that are affiliated with the network. And both national and local firms may buy *local time* on a single station that covers a particular geographic selling area.

Advertisers may *sponsor* an entire show, alone or with other sponsors. Or they may buy *spot*

rea lubar, inc.

15 West 38 Street
New York, New York 10018
212-575-0735
Telex 225579

FOR IMMEDIATE RELEASE

July, 1984

Public Relations
Publicity
Marketing
Advertising

With Her Fall '84 Collection, Claiborne
Celebrates the Rise of the American Woman

Liz Claiborne's fall '84 collection is a celebration of American women and of how far they have come in just the seven years since Liz dedicated herself to designing clothes for them.

That was when Liz and three partners started their own business ⌐lothes for a very particular customer - th⌐

---

time for a single 10-, 20-, 30-, or 60-second commercial during or between programs. To an extent, they may select their audience by choosing the day of the week and the time of day when their ads will be shown. Budweiser advertises its beer and Noxema advertises its shaving cream during the TV football season because the majority of viewers are men, who are likely to use these products.

Television advertising rates are based on the number of people who are expected to be watching when the commercial is aired. During the 1984 Summer Olympics in Los Angeles, a 30-second network commercial cost as much as $250,000. ABC, which had exclusive television rights, sold well over $600 million worth of advertising for the Games.

Unlike magazine advertising, and perhaps like newspaper ads, television advertising has a short life. If a viewer misses a commercial, it is missed forever. Viewers may also become indifferent to commercial messages. Or they may use the commercial time as a break from viewing, thus missing the message altogether. (Remote-control devices make it especially easy to banish at least the sound of commercials from the living room.)

Radio Advertisers spent about $5.2 billion or 7 percent of the total on radio advertising in 1983, up from $4.7 billion in 1982. Like magazine advertising, radio advertising offers selectivity. Radio stations develop programming for—and are tuned in by—specific groups of listeners. There are almost half a billion radio sets in the United States (about six per household), which makes radio the most accessible medium.

Radio is less expensive than other media. Actual rates depend on geographic coverage, the number of commercials contracted for, the time period specified, and whether the station broadcasts on AM, FM, or both. Even small retailers should be able to afford the $60 or less, which will buy a radio spot on most local stations.

Advertising Agencies

Advertisers can plan and produce their own advertising with help from media personnel, or they can hire advertising agencies. An **advertising agency** is an independent firm that plans, produces, and places advertising for its clients. Many larger ad agencies offer help with sales promotion and publicity as well. The media usually pay a commission of 15 percent to advertising agencies, so the cost to the agency's client can be quite moderate. The client, of course, pays for production and other services the agency performs.

Firms that do much advertising may use both an in-house advertising department and an independent agency. This approach gives the firm the advantage of being able to call on the agency's expertise in particular areas of advertising. The agency also brings a fresh viewpoint to the firm's products and advertising plans.

Table 14.1 lists the nation's twenty leading advertisers, in all media.

Social and Legal Considerations in Advertising

There are two main arguments against advertising—that it is wasteful and that it can be deceptive. Although advertising (like any other activity) can be performed inefficiently, it is far from wasteful. Let's look at the evidence.

- Advertising is the most effective and the least expensive means of communicating product information to millions of individuals and firms.
- Advertising encourages competition and is, in fact, a means of competition. It thus leads to the development of new and improved products, wider product choices, and lower prices.
- Advertising revenues support our mass communication media—newspapers, magazines, radio, and television. This means that advertising pays for much of our news coverage and entertainment programming.
- Advertising provides job opportunities in fields ranging from sales to film production. Total employment within the advertising industry stood at 158,600 in 1982.[5]

Along with pure fact, advertising tends to include some exaggeration, stretching of the truth, and occasional deception. Usually, consumers spot such distortion in short order. But various government and private agencies also scrutinize advertising for false or deceptive claims or offers.

At the national level, the Federal Trade Com-

mission, the Food and Drug Administration, and the Federal Communications Commission oversee advertising practices. Advertising may also be monitored by state and local agencies, Better Business Bureaus, and industry associations. These organizations have varying degrees of control over advertising, but their overall effect has been a positive one.

PERSONAL SELLING

Personal selling is the presentation of a promotional message through direct personal communication. It is the most adaptable of all promotion methods, because the person who is presenting the message can modify it to suit the individual buyer. However, personal selling is also

Table 14.1 *The Twenty Leading National Advertisers*

Rank	Company	Total Advertising
1	Procter & Gamble	$726.1 mil.
2	Sears, Roebuck & Co.	631.2 mil.
3	General Motors Corp.	549.0 mil.
4	R. J. Reynolds Industries	530.3 mil.
5	Philip Morris Inc.	501.7 mil.
6	General Foods Corp.	429.1 mil.
7	AT&T Co.	373.6 mil.
8	K mart Corp.	365.3 mil.
9	Nabisco Brands	335.2 mil.
10	American Home Products Corp.	325.4 mil.
11	Mobil Corp.	320.0 mil.
12	Ford Motor Co.	313.5 mil.
13	PepsiCo Inc.	305.0 mil.
14	Unilever U.S.	304.6 mil.
15	Warner-Lambert Co.	294.7 mil.
16	Beatrice Foods Co.	271.0 mil.
17	Johnson & Johnson	270.0 mil.
18	Colgate-Palmolive	268.0 mil.
19	McDonald's Corp.	265.5 mil.
20	Coca-Cola Co.	255.3 mil.

Source: Reprinted with permission from the September 8, 1983 issue of *Advertising Age.* Copyright 1983 by Crain Communications Inc.

Personal selling is the presentation of a promotional message through direct personal contact. Source: © 1982 Robert A. Isaacs, Photo Researchers, Inc.

the most expensive promotion method. The average sales call on an industrial customer costs about $205, and that cost is increasing all the time.[6]

Many selling situations demand the personal contact and adaptability of personal selling. This is especially true of industrial sales, where single purchases may amount to millions of dollars. In just one year, Sears, Roebuck purchases over $1 billion worth of appliances from Whirlpool, $321 million worth of ranges and mowers from Roper, and $389 million worth of clothing and soft goods from Kellwood.[7] Obviously, sales of that size must be based on carefully planned sales presentations, personal contact between buyers and sellers, and thorough negotiation.

Personal-Selling Activities

The variety of activities involved in personal selling can be grouped into three general categories. The first, **order taking,** consists of processing the purchases of customers who have essentially decided what they wish to buy. Many retail clerks are primarily order takers, although they engage in other selling activities as well. Route salespeople, who service retail outlets, are sometimes referred to as *outside order takers.* They may also maintain their customers' inventories, set up in-store displays, and promote new products. For example, when L'eggs hosiery was introduced, route salespeople from L'eggs delivered the merchandise directly to the retail display. These salespeople made sure that a complete choice of sizes and colors was available, kept the display clean and attractive, and rotated the inventory at each location. This sales force also helped with sales promotions at each store.

Creative selling is determining customers' needs and matching products with those needs. Customers may or may not have previously been aware of their need for the product, of what benefits the product offers, or even of the product's existence. Creative selling may require particular technical skills or knowledge. *Sales engineers,* for example, sometimes help develop or modify products to suit the needs of their customers.

Finally, **missionary selling** is personal selling in support of the sales efforts of other middlemen. For example, the manufacturers of prescription drugs sell their products to pharmacies. However, their missionary salespeople call on doctors and hospitals to explain the benefits of their products, provide information, and create goodwill. The manufacturers expect that this promotional effort will eventually result in increased sales by pharmacies.

Most salespeople engage in all three types of activities, to varying degrees. To be successful, they must be able to communicate with people on a one-to-one basis, and they must be strongly motivated. A thorough knowledge of the products they offer for sale is essential. And they must be willing and able to deal with the details involved in handling and processing customers' orders. Sales managers tend to emphasize these qualities in recruiting and hiring, as well as in the other human resources management activities discussed in Chapter 9.

The Personal-Selling Process

No two selling situations are exactly alike, and no two salespeople perform their jobs in exactly the same way. Most salespeople do, however, follow the six-step procedure illustrated in Figure 14.3.

Prospecting   The first step in personal selling is to research potential buyers and choose the most likely customers, who are called *prospects*. Prospects may be suggested by business associates and customers, public records, telephone and trade association directories, and company files. The salesperson concentrates her or his efforts on those prospects who have the financial resources, willingness, and authority to buy the product.

Approaching the Prospect   First impressions are often lasting impressions. Thus the salesperson's

first contact with the prospect is crucial to successful selling. The best approach is one that is based on knowledge—of the prospect, of his or her needs, and of how the product can meet those needs. Salespeople who understand each customer's particular situation are likely to make a good first impression—and to make a sale.

Making the Presentation   The next step is the actual delivery of the sales presentation. In many cases, this includes a demonstration of the product. The salesperson points out the product's features, its benefits, and the ways in which it is superior to competitors' merchandise. If the product has been used successfully by other firms, the salesperson may mention this as part of the presentation.

Figure 14.3   The Six Steps of the Personal-Selling Process

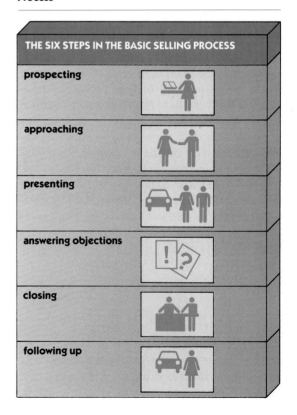

During a demonstration, the salesperson may suggest that the prospect try out the product personally. The demonstration and product trial should underscore specific points made during the presentation.

Answering Objections   The prospect is then given the opportunity to raise objections or ask questions. This gives the salesperson a chance to eliminate objections that might prevent a sale, to point out additional features, or to mention special services that the company offers.

Closing the Sale   To close the sale, the salesperson asks the prospect to buy the product. This is considered the critical point in the selling process. Many experienced salespeople make use of a *trial closing,* in which they ask questions which assume that the customer is going to buy the product. The questions "When would you want delivery?" and "Do you want the standard or the deluxe model?" are typical of trial closings. They allow the reluctant prospect to make a purchase without having to decide all at once.

Following Up   The salesperson must follow up on the order to ensure that the product is delivered on time, in the right quantity, and in good condition. During follow-up, the salesperson also makes it clear that he or she is available in case problems develop before or after delivery. Follow-up leaves a good impression and eases the way to future sales. Hence it is an essential part of the selling process. In a real sense, the salesperson's job does not end with a sale. It continues as long as the seller and the customer maintain a working relationship.

SALES PROMOTION

The American Marketing Association defines **sales promotion** as "those marketing activities, other than personal selling, advertising, and publicity, that stimulate consumer purchasing and dealer effectiveness."[8] Sales-promotion techniques are used primarily to enhance and supplement other promotion methods. In this role they can have a significant impact on sales of consumer products. The dramatic increase in spending for sales promotion over the last several years shows that marketers have recognized the potential of this promotion method. Most firms now include year-round sales promotions as part of their overall promotional mix.

"What's the hot promotion of the 80s?" asks a headline in *Advertising Age.* The answer: cash refunds. What was the hot promotion of the 1970s, according to the same report? Cents-off coupons.[9] Let us briefly discuss these and other important sales-promotion techniques.

Refunding   A **refund** is a return of part of the purchase price of a product. Usually the refund is offered by the producer to those consumers who send in a coupon along with a specific proof of purchase. (Refunds are sometimes called "manufacturer's rebates.") Refunding is a relatively low-cost promotion method. It was formerly used mainly for new product items, but now it is applied to a wide variety of products.

Couponing   A **cents-off coupon** is a coupon that reduces the retail price of a particular item by a stated amount at the time of purchase. These coupons may be worth anywhere from a few cents to well over $1. They are reproduced in newspapers and magazines and/or sent to consumers by direct mail. Approximately 1000 firms now use coupons, and about 90 billion were distributed in 1983. Of these, about 4 billion were redeemed by consumers. They seem to work best for new or improved product items. When L'eggs Products introduced its pantyhose, it sent out introductory direct-mail coupons worth 25 or 35 cents off the purchase price of one pair in order to make people aware of the product and encourage them to try it. This was the hosiery industry's first heavy use of coupons. (Stores in some areas even deduct double the value of manufacturers' coupons from the purchase price, as a sales-promotion technique of their own.)

Coupons may also offer free merchandise, either with or without an additional purchase of the product. Canada Dry recently offered consumers a Thanksgiving holiday gift of two free bottles of Canada Dry with the purchase of four bottles. The offer was publicized via an insert in Sunday newspapers just prior to Thanksgiving.

Sampling A **sample** is a free package or container of a product. Samples may be offered through coupons, by direct mailing, or at *in-store demonstrations*. Although sampling ensures that consumers will try the product, it is the most expensive sales-promotion technique. It gives best results when it is used with new products.

Premiums and Trading Stamps A **premium** is a gift that a producer offers the customer in return for using its product. A producer of packaged foods may, for instance, offer consumers a cookbook as a premium. Most airlines offer free travel to business customers after a certain number of paid trips or air miles.

Trading stamps are stamps that are given out by retailers in proportion to the amount spent. They are redeemable for gifts. They were very popular with supermarkets and service stations in the 1970s, but they seem to be less in vogue at present.

Point-of-Purchase Displays A **point-of-purchase display** is promotional material that is placed within a retail store. The display is usually located near the product that is being promoted. It may actually hold merchandise (as do L'eggs hosiery displays) or inform customers of what the product offers and encourage them to buy it. Most point-of-purchase displays are prepared and set up by manufacturers and wholesalers.

Trade Shows A **trade show** is an industry-wide exhibit at which many sellers display their products. Some trade shows are organized exclusively for dealers—to permit manufacturers and wholesalers to show their latest lines to retailers. Others are consumer promotions designed to stim-

As a type of sales promotion, about 90 billion coupons were distributed in 1983 by U.S. companies; about 4 billion were redeemed by customers. Source: © 1982 Susan McCartney, Photo Researchers, Inc.

ulate buying interest in the general public. Among the latter are the boat shows, home shows, and flower shows that are put on each year in our larger cities.

PUBLICITY AND PUBLIC RELATIONS

Publicity is information about a company, its employees, or its products that is published or broadcast in the mass media. Publicity differs from advertising in two ways: It is not paid for, and it is not controlled by the firm. However, when it enhances the image of the firm or its products, publicity can be an effective form of promotion.

The objective of a public-relations ad is to create or maintain a favorable public image of the company. Source: Courtesy of Bacardi Imports, Inc.

Bacardi rum mixes with everything.

Except driving.

Many firms provide the media with information on a regular basis, hoping that it will be used in news or feature stories. Routine information is usually hand-delivered to the media as a *news release,* which is a page or two of typewritten copy. For special announcements, the firm may invite reporters to a *press conference,* as the Polaroid Corporation did when it unveiled its Sun 600-series cameras.

Public relations consists of all activities whose objective is to create and maintain a favorable public image. In one sense, publicity is a part of public relations—the "information" part. Actually, good public relations generally results in good publicity and a favorable image.

Public-relations activities are many and varied.

They include the sponsorship of programs on public television and radio, the sponsorship of sporting events (including the Olympics), and various informational (rather than product-oriented) advertisements. For example, Du Pont is sponsoring the Du Pont All American Tennis Championships. And, for several decades, Texaco has sponsored weekly broadcasts from the stage of the Metropolitan Opera House in New York, on both commercial and public radio. These and other public-relations efforts tend to build sales indirectly by showing that the sponsor is a "good citizen."

No product is ever promoted via just one of the four promotion methods we have described. Instead, a promotional campaign combining all of them is carefully tailored for every important product.

PROMOTION PLANNING

A **promotional campaign** is a plan for combining and using the four promotion methods—advertising, personal selling, sales promotion, and publicity—in a particular promotional mix to reach one or more marketing goals. Often the campaign is built around a *theme,* such as the "Pepsi Challenge" or Pontiac's "We build excitement."

In planning for promotion, marketers need to answer two basic questions:

- What will be the role of promotion in the overall marketing mix?
- To what extent will each promotion method be used in the promotional mix?

The answer to the first question depends on the firm's marketing objectives since the role of each element of the marketing mix—product, price, distribution, and promotion—depends on these detailed versions of the firm's marketing goals. The answer to the second question depends on the answer to the first as well as on the target market.

Sony's Magic Show

Even for the inimitable Sony Corp., the tiny size of its newest product was astounding: The Super Walkman is no larger than the plastic cases that normally contain audio cassettes. But, as Taizo Ochi, Sony Corp. of America's IR (Industrial Relations) man in New York, points out, "We had to figure out how to make a big splash with a new product that was tiny." The company solved the problem by hiring a professional magician to present the product to a meeting of New York analysts last September.

After warming up the audience by performing some routine illusions showing "large things going into small things," the magician placed a stack of cassettes on a table and asked one analyst to come forward and count them. When the analyst had counted twelve, the magician corrected the number to eleven, reached into the stack himself

and produced the Super Walkman. He then handed out Super Walkmans and cassettes to members of the audience and invited them to discover the "trick" catch that enables Super Walkman to admit a cassette.

But the show was still far from over. Returning to center stage, the magician closed a curtain that appeared to have nothing behind it, recited some mumbo jumbo, and opened the curtain again. Out strode Akio Morita, Sony's cofounder and chairman. And, lest the analysts lapse back into skepticism after the chairman's speech, the magician reached into a fishbowl full of stubs (each analyst had received a raffle ticket for a Super Walkman) and read out a multidigit number: Everyone stood up a winner; every ticket had the same number.

Source: Solveig Jansson and Richard Karp, *Institutional Investor*, April, 1984, p. 160.

Promotion and Marketing Objectives

Promotion is naturally better suited to certain marketing objectives than it is to others. For example, promotion can do little to further a marketing objective such as "reduce delivery time by one-third." (It can, however, be used to inform customers that delivery time has been reduced.) Let's consider some objectives that *would* require the use of promotion as a primary ingredient of the marketing mix.

Providing Information This is, of course, the main function of promotion. It may be used to communicate to target markets the availability of new products or product features. It may alert them to special sales or offers or give the locations of retailers that carry the firm's products. In other words, promotion can be used to enhance the effectiveness of each of the other ingredients of the marketing mix.

Increasing Market Share Promotion can be used to convince new customers to try a product, while maintaining the product loyalty of established customers. Comparative advertising, for example, is directed mainly at those who might— but presently do not—use a particular product. Advertising that emphasizes the product's features also assures those who *do* use it that they are doing the right thing.

Positioning the Product The sales of a product depend, to a great extent, on its competition. The stronger the competition, the more difficult it is to maintain or increase sales. For this reason, many firms go to great lengths to position their products in the marketplace. **Positioning** is the development of an image for a product; relative to competing products.

Promotion is the prime positioning tool. For example, 7 Up has been heavily promoted as the "Uncola," to position it away from the very strong

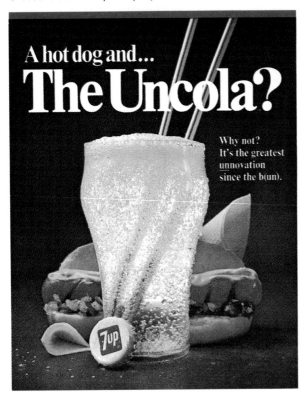

A hot dog and...

The Uncola?

Why not?
It's the greatest
unnovation
since the b(un).

7up

sales of products that are in the declining stage of their life cycle. The object is to keep them going for a little while longer.

Developing the Promotional Mix

Once the role of promotion is established, the various promotion methods may be combined in a promotional campaign. As in so many other areas of business, promotion planning begins with a set of specific objectives. The promotional mix is then designed to accomplish these objectives.

Among the factors that affect the makeup of the promotional mix are

☐ *Campaign objectives.* A firm whose campaign objective is to create awareness of a new product would emphasize advertising in its promotional mix. If its objective were to expand into a new geographic market, the firm might concentrate on personal sales to organize distribution channels within that market.

☐ *Available resources.* Promotion through the mass media (especially television) can be quite expensive. A firm with limited financial resources would tend to rely heavily on its existing sales force, along with some local advertising and sales promotion.

☐ *The target market.* Personal selling is usually the key promotion method for geographically concentrated markets. Advertising and sales promotion are emphasized when markets are scattered throughout the nation.

☐ *The product.* The marketers of consumer goods tend to stress advertising, whereas marketers of industrial goods rely mainly on personal selling. New products are generally heralded with much advertising and sales promotion. Declining products usually demand a heavy emphasis on personal selling, along with various sales promotions.

☐ *Distribution.* A product that is distributed intensively is usually advertised heavily as well. Products that are distributed exclusively or selectively are promoted mainly through personal selling or combined advertising and personal selling.

☐ *The price.* Personal selling is the primary pro-

Coca-Cola and Pepsi Cola. As an uncola, 7 Up avoids competing with these two products. Instead, it is positioned against somewhat weaker, noncola soft drinks. Promotion may also be used to position one product directly against another product, as in the "Pepsi Challenge."

Stabilizing Sales Special promotional effort can be used to increase sales during slack periods, such as the "off season" for certain sports equipment. By stabilizing sales in this way, a firm can use its production facilities more effectively and reduce both capital costs and inventory costs. Figure 14.4 shows part of a long-running AT&T campaign to shift some long-distance telephone usage to evenings and weekends. Telephone equipment and lines are generally underutilized at these times, whereas they may be overloaded during normal business hours.

Promotion is also often used to increase the

motion method for relatively expensive goods. Advertising and sales promotion tend to be emphasized for lower-priced items.

Because all these factors apply to every product, the promotional mix almost always includes all four promotion methods. However, the *amount* of each varies with each campaign.

A Recent Example[10]

For a number of months prior to the 1984 Summer Olympic Games in Los Angeles, Anheuser-Busch's Budweiser brand keyed its promotion to the Games. The Budweiser campaign theme was modified to indicate the firm's support of the American Olympic team: "This Bud's for you . . . the team behind the team." The brand became a general sponsor of the Olympic Games and U.S. Olympic team and, in addition, sponsored the shooting team and the U.S. amateur boxing team.

As a "proud sponsor" of the Games, Budweiser was able to use the Olympic symbol in its advertising. In keeping with its theme, the firm's advertising saluted the workers, coaches, and trainers who help make the Olympics possible—another team behind the team. This advertising was aimed primarily at consumers, in the firm's usual "pull" strategy. A **pull strategy** is a pro-

Figure 14.4 *An Ad from an AT&T Campaign to Stabilize Sales. Special promotional effort can increase sales during slack periods and in that way increase the overall stability of sales. Source: Courtesy of AT&T.*

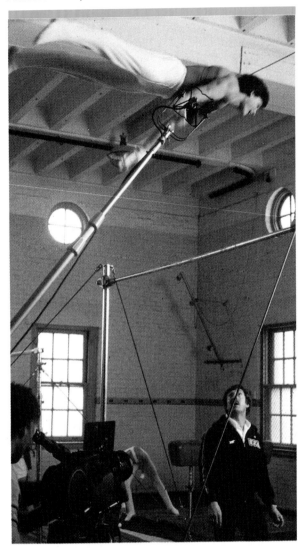

For much of 1984 the Budweiser promotional campaign centered on the 1984 summer Olympics. Source: Courtesy of Anheuser-Busch, Inc.

Their objective was to assist these middlemen in marketing Budweiser aggressively and effectively during the campaign. Here Budweiser was implementing a "push" strategy. A **push strategy** is one in which a firm promotes its products to the next marketing organization along the channel of distribution. The idea is that this marketing organization will continue to *push* the products down the channel to consumers.

Budweiser thus orchestrated all of the promotion methods into its Olympics-theme campaign. Each of the methods was used to its own best advantage. And, at the same time, each supplemented the other promotion methods. Together they formed an integrated and effective promotional mix.

motional strategy that is intended to create consumer demand for a product.

News releases and press conferences kept the mass media informed of Budweiser's activities. Store displays and premiums (mugs, towels, posters, and the like) displayed both the Budweiser symbol and the Olympic symbol.

While all this was going on, the Anheuser-Busch's sales force worked with its wholesalers.

Chapter Review

SUMMARY

Promotion is communication that is intended to inform, persuade, or remind an organization's target markets. The major promotion methods are advertising, personal selling, sales promotion, and publicity (and public relations). A specific combination of promotion methods that is used to reach a specific target market is called a promotional mix.

Advertising is any nonpersonal promotional message that is paid for by an identified sponsor and directed to a large audience. Selective advertising promotes a particular brand of product. Institutional advertising is image-building advertising. Primary-demand advertising promotes the products of an entire industry rather than a single brand.

The major advertising media are newspapers, magazines, direct mail, outdoor advertising, television, and radio. Newspapers account for the greatest part of advertising expenditures, with television running a fairly close second. Magazine advertising is perhaps the most prestigious, and direct mail is certainly the most selective medium. Radio and magazine advertising can also be quite selective, and radio is relatively inexpensive.

A firm may develop its own advertising, hire an advertising agency to plan and produce its ads, or both. Advertising is monitored by federal, state, and local agencies and industry organizations.

Personal selling is the most adaptable promotion method: The message can be modified by the salesperson to fit each buyer. Personal-selling activities are classified as order taking, creative selling, or missionary selling. Different sales jobs require different combinations of these activities. The six steps in the personal-selling process are prospecting, approaching the prospect, making the presentation, answering objections, closing the sale, and following up.

Sales promotion consists of a variety of activities designed to enhance sales. These include refunding, distributing coupons, sampling, offering premiums and trading stamps, setting up point-of-purchase displays, and taking part in trade shows.

Publicity is nonpaid information that is published or broadcast in the mass media. It is transmitted to the media via news releases and press conferences. Public-relations, or image-building, activities include the sponsorship of programs and events that are of interest to the general public.

A promotional campaign is a plan for combining and using advertising, personal selling, sales promotion, and publicity to reach one or more marketing goals. Campaign objectives are developed from marketing objectives. Then the promotional mix is developed on the basis of the campaign objectives, the available resources, and the other ingredients of the marketing mix.

This chapter concludes our discussion of marketing. In the next chapter we shall begin our examination of business finances by discussing money, banks, and the banking system.

KEY TERMS

You should now be able to define and give an example relevant to each of the following terms:

promotion

promotional mix

advertising

selective (or brand) advertising

institutional advertising

primary-demand advertising

advertising media

cooperative advertising

direct-mail advertising

outdoor advertising

advertising agency

personal selling

order taking

creative selling

missionary selling

sales promotion

refund

cents-off coupon

sample

premium

trading stamps

point-of-purchase display

trade show

publicity

public relations

promotional campaign

positioning

pull strategy

push strategy

QUESTIONS AND EXERCISES
Review Questions

1. What is the difference between a marketing mix and a promotional mix? How are they related?
2. How are selective, institutional, and primary-demand advertising different from each other? Give an example of each.
3. What is cooperative advertising? What sorts of firms would use it?
4. List the four major print media, and give an advantage and a disadvantage of each.
5. What types of firms would use each of the two electronic media?
6. Why would a firm use an ad agency if it had its own advertising department?
7. What are the primary differences among the selling activities of salespeople who are engaged in order taking, creative selling, and missionary selling? Give an example of each (other than those discussed in the chapter).
8. Explain how each step in the personal-selling process leads to the next step.
9. In your opinion, what are the three most effective techniques for sales promotion? How does each of these techniques supplement advertising?
10. What is the difference between publicity and public relations? What is the purpose of each?
11. Why is promotion particularly effective in positioning a product? in stabilizing or increasing sales?
12. What factors determine the specific promotional mix that should be used in a campaign?
13. Distinguish between push strategies and pull strategies in promotion.

Discussion Questions

1. Do celebrities (like Michael Jackson) who appear in commercials actually have any effect on what people buy? Explain.
2. Is it really necessary for Coke and Pepsi to spend almost $100 million in their new advertising campaigns? Is their advertising wasteful? Is it deceptive?
3. Discuss the pros and cons of comparative advertising from the viewpoint of (a) the advertiser, (b) the advertiser's competitors, and (c) the target market.
4. Which kinds of advertising—and in which media—influence you most? Why?
5. Which kinds of retail outlets or products require mainly order taking by salespeople? Which require mainly creative selling?
6. Why would a producer offer refunds or cents-off coupons rather than simply lowering the price of its products?
7. How does the publicity that business firms seek help the general public?
8. What kind of promotional mix might be used to extend the life of a product that has entered the declining stage of its life cycle?

Exercises

1. Describe, sketch, or photocopy one example of each of the following types of advertisements. Explain briefly what makes it an example of its particular type.
   a. Immediate-response (selective)
   b. Reminder (selective)
   c. Institutional
   d. Primary-demand
   e. Local
   f. Cooperative
2. Briefly describe four different point-of-purchase displays that you have seen. For each, give the type of display, the product and brand displayed or promoted, and your evaluation of the effectiveness of the display.

3. Choose a particular product that was not discussed in the chapter. From your overall knowledge of the product, outline a promotional mix for it. (That is, determine what percentage of your total promotion budget you would allocate to each promotion method, at whom the promotion would be directed, the media you would use, and why.)

CASE 14-1

Best Promotions

Each year, *Advertising Age,* the advertising-industry newspaper, lists best promotions of the previous year. For 1983, one of the nine winners was General Mills, which sponsored a "Search for Champions" contest to choose six amateur athletes who would be featured on Wheaties packages. Almost 50,000 entries resulted from the promotion, along with a great deal of publicity and a significant increase in sales. Also listed was Red Baron Pizza Service, whose frozen pizzas were promoted with flying exhibitions in thirteen regional markets. To capitalize on the brand name, antique Stearman biplanes were flown in these exhibitions by pilots dressed as the "Red Baron" (World War I ace Baron Manfred von Richthofen).

Another winner was L'eggs Products, whose promotion of L'eggs pantyhouse gave a new twist to the conventional cents-off coupon: Instead of a stated amount, the coupon contained a rub-off square like those on instant-winner game cards. When the square was rubbed gently with a coin, the value of the coupon was revealed. The objective of the campaign was to maintain or increase L'eggs' share of the regular and control-top panty-hose market.

Almost 40 million coupons were distributed nationally in periodicals. Of these,

- 80 percent had a value of 50 cents
- 15 percent had a value of 75 cents
- 5 percent had a value of $1
- An additional 50,000 coupons could be redeemed for a free pair of L'eggs pantyhose

The coupon campaign was reinforced with radio commercials and ads in trade journals. Retailers were also encouraged to advertise the products.

Approximately 1.5 million rub-off coupons (about 3.5 percent of the total) were redeemed. The campaign, which was budgeted at about $1 million, resulted in increased sales of almost 2.9 million pairs of pantyhose. Moreover, during the six months following the start of the campaign, the L'eggs share of the control-top pantyhose market increased by 5.2 percent, and its share of the regular pantyhose market increased by 2.3 percent. [11]

1. Would you expect the Wheaties "Search for Champions" to have a greater sales impact in large or small communities? Why?
2. Did the L'eggs coupon campaign accomplish its objective? Was it worth its cost? Explain.

CASE 14-2

Mary Kay Cosmetics

In the summer of 1963, Mary Kay Ash began to make notes for a book on party-plan selling—direct, personal selling to potential customers gathered at the home of a friend or neighbor. The book was to be based on Mrs. Ash's 25 years of experience in party-plan sales, but it never was written. Instead, the notes developed into a set of innovative party-selling techniques that were put into practice when Mrs. Ash founded Mary Kay Cosmetics that year. Among her innovations, which are still used to sell the firm's line of skin-care products, were the following:

- Utilize parties to teach rather than to sell. Customers who are taught about Mary Kay products will not only buy them but will also use them—and thus obtain their benefits.
- Limit attendance at parties. For more personalized selling, Mary Kay parties were limited to six customers.
- Deliver products immediately, at the party; collect immediately; and don't extend credit (which can become a problem).
- Limit the product mix to the number of products that salespeople can reasonably get to know, demonstrate, and carry for delivery at parties. Even today, the firm offers only forty-five products.
- Provide quality and service to customers. Mary Kay products are generally acknowledged to be of high quality. Unsatisfied customers are given full, unquestioned refunds.

The Mary Kay sales force now consists of almost 200,000 "beauty consultants," supervised by 4,000 full-time sales directors. From the beginning, Mrs. Ash believed in providing full compensation and recognition to her salespeople. She set commissions at a level higher than those of any other party-plan sellers. Salespeople receive recognition for individual effort through gifts ranging from ribbons to diamonds and pink Cadillacs. And Mary Kay's Ladder of Success details exactly what salespeople must achieve in order to advance within the firm.

To help employees climb the ladder, there is a strong emphasis on training. To provide identity with the firm, there are "uniforms"—red blazers for consultants, and gray suits with pink or amethyst blouses for sales directors. (Less than 1 percent of the sales force is male.)

May Kay Ash takes a less active part in running the company nowadays, but her innovations are doing quite well. Sales have risen from about $30,000 in 1963 to $304 million in 1982. Earnings rose by 46 percent in 1982 alone, and in that year the price of Mary Kay stock increased by 202 percent.[12]

1. To what extent are Mary Kay's party-selling techniques applicable to personal selling in general?
2. Evaluate Mrs. Ash's sales-force management concepts in terms of what you learned in Chapters 8 and 9.

Career Profile

John Sculley When he was going to school, John Sculley thought he was headed toward industrial design. But during a summer job at an industrial design firm, Sculley found himself cutting out lettering for an endorsement on the package of a product that had just become the target of a major new marketing strategy. "I realized at that point where the marketing decisions were made, so I took an MBA at Wharton and headed into marketing."

Five years out of Wharton, he joined Pepsi, where he worked for 16 years. He gradually rose to become president of one of Pepsi's major divisions. During his five years as president, the company issued the "Pepsi challenge" and moved up on number-one soft drink maker, Coke. It increased its share of the fountain-syrup business, created the highly successful caffeine-free cola, Pepsi Free, and even passed Coke as the number-one seller in food stores. Sculley succeeded in motivating franchised Pepsi bottlers to sell Pepsi-Cola. His actions helped create the "cola wars," and he seemed destined to succeed Donald Kendall, his former father-in-law, as PepsiCo's chairman.

The growth of the soft drink market has slowed: "It's not as exciting as it was," Sculley said in 1983. When Apple Computer started looking for a new chief, Sculley listened.

Many new high-tech firms are started by entrepreneurs with brilliant technical ideas but limited business experience. Some of these companies falter because they lack the marketing expertise to get the right people to consider their products. Therefore, company after company in the computer industry has hired career marketing experts for top management positions so that the technical innovations won't rot in warehouses. Atari's chief, James J. Morgan, for example, was a marketing executive at Philip Morris. To run its electronics division, Mattel recently hired a former marketer of toiletries and candy.

The challenge faced by Apple is similar to the one Sculley took on at Pepsi. For four years after Steven Jobs and Stephen Wozniak built their first personal computer in a garage, Apple was the leader in this new, fast-growing industry, and the company was successful largely on the strength of its technical innovations and reputation. But with the entry of IBM into the personal computer market, any computer company that wanted to stay afloat had to deal with the IBM challenge, and Apple's technical geniuses realized that they needed marketing help.

During an 18-month search, Apple considered more than 126 executives before they settled on Sculley. Apple felt Sculley was worth the high price it cost to buy him away—$2 million his first year. For his part, Sculley said, "I have to be totally turned on to what I'm doing, and I see the computer business where the soft-drink business was 10 years ago. It's a high-growth business, and competitors are still being formed."

One of Sculley's jobs has been to take a hard look at Apple's distribution network and to try to encourage the kind of dealer loyalty that he motivated at Pepsi. Some dealers were irritated with the way Apple cut advertised prices for its Apple II personal computer without cutting the price to the dealers. Sculley has had to restore relations. Industry observers say Sculley has brought discipline to a chaotic company. He has pared down the staff, rearranged management, reduced overhead, and, most importantly, reorganized Apple's product line. As Sculley put it, "Will the Pepsi generation become the Apple generation?"[1]

The figure in the salary column approximates the expected annual income after two or three years of service.

1 = $12,000–$15,000   2 = $16,000–$20,000   3 = $21,000–$27,000   4 = $28,000–$35,000   5 = $36,000 and up

Job Title	Educational Requirements	Salary Range	Prospects
Advertising account executive	Bachelor's degree in business or liberal arts	2–3	Gradual growth
Advertising manager	Bachelor's degree in business or liberal arts	3	Limited growth
Advertising worker	Some college courses in business and marketing	2	Limited growth
Art director	College degree in art with courses in marketing and advertising	2–3	Gradual growth
Buyer (retail and wholesale trade)	High school diploma; on-the-job experience; some college preferred	3	Limited growth
Commercial/graphic artist	High school diploma; some college preferred	2–3	Limited growth
Manufacturer's salesperson	Some college; degree preferred	2–3	Limited growth
Market research analyst	Bachelor's degree in business, statistics, or math; graduate degree helpful	2–3	Limited growth
Marketing director	Bachelor's degree in business; on-the-job experience	3–4	Limited growth
Marketing researcher	Some college; degree helpful; on-the-job experience	2	Limited growth
Media buyer	Some college; on-the-job experience	2	Limited growth
Order clerk	High school diploma	1–2	Limited growth
Public relations specialist	College degree; on-the-job experience	2–3	Limited growth
Product marketing engineer	College degree; on-the-job experience	2–3	Limited growth
Real estate salesperson	High school diploma plus college work helpful; written state exam	3	Gradual growth
Retail trade salesworker	High school diploma	1–2	Limited growth
Store manager	College degree; on-the-job experience	3–4	Gradual growth
Travel agent	Some college preferred	1–2	Gradual growth
Wholesale trade salesworker	Varies; college preferred; on-the-job experience	3	Gradual growth
Writer/editor	College degree preferred; on-the-job experience	2–3	Limited growth

PART

5
Finance and Investment

In this part we are concerned with still another business resource—money. First we discuss the functions and forms of money and the institutions that are part of the U.S. monetary system. Then we examine the concept and methods of money management, for both firms and individuals. Finally, we discuss the means by which some types of monetary losses can be minimized. Included in this part are:

CHAPTER

FIFTEEN
Money, Banking, and Credit

Money. We work for it, save it, borrow it, and often don't have enough of it. Businesses are built with it. They are formed to earn it, to invest it, or to lend it out. Some people want it so much that they steal it. Yet the only time it has any value is when we give it to someone else. In this chapter we shall take a good look at money and the institutions that create and handle it. After studying the chapter, you should understand:

1. *The functions and important characteristics of money*
2. *The differences among commercial banks and other financial institutions in the banking industry*
3. *The primary services provided by commercial banks and other financial institutions*
4. *How the Federal Reserve System regulates the money supply*
5. *The function of the Federal Deposit Insurance Corporation (FDIC) and the Federal Savings and Loan Insurance Corporation (FSLIC)*
6. *Some important aspects of credit management*

Consider this:

How could the world's fourth-largest oil-producing nation be in financial trouble? The answer to that question is exactly what Mexico's politicians, business leaders, and bankers are trying to figure out.

During the late 1970s, Mexicans were rejoicing about petroleum finds that totaled at least 57 billion proven barrels. With the price of a barrel of oil hovering around $40 and promising to go higher, it looked as though Mexico's nagging economic problems were over. Workers began lining up for jobs in the oil industry. Mexican politicians were concerned with the management of their nation's oil reserves—including restrictions on the amounts to be exported to the United States and other oil-consuming nations. Carefully managed, her economists felt, Mexico's oil reserves should guarantee a healthy national income well into the next century. Some government officials were even concerned about how the country could cope with abundance.

Assuming that world oil prices and the demand for oil would continue to increase, the Mexican government began to spend. Vast amounts of money were spent to expand the production capacity of the government-owned petroleum industry. Huge investments were made to improve the steel industry and to construct four new ports

Because of its debt Mexico had to halt public housing projects. Source: David Woo, Stock, Boston.

in southern Mexico. Mexico also built new and better tourist facilities, and she funded other seemingly worthwhile projects designed to transform Mexico into a supernation almost overnight.

Unfortunately, not even a soon-to-be-rich nation can safely spend more money that it has, but that is exactly what Mexico was doing. The revenues from Mexico's petroleum sales abroad could not keep up with the cost of all the expensive public projects. The result was larger and larger budget deficits, which Mexican authorities made up by borrowing from foreign bankers, mostly in the United States. And suddenly, Mexico was more than $85 billion in debt.

To make matters worse, the price of oil began to fall. Because oil accounts for about three-fourths of Mexico's export trade, the country's revenues declined as well—to the point where Mexico could not make payments on its foreign bank loans. Mexico's borrowing was so widespread that the chance of default (nonpayment) threatened the stability of hundreds of banks, in almost every industrialized nation.

Although no one expects an overnight cure, foreign bankers are working to solve Mexico's financial problems (and, in the process, their own). In particular, Mexico's creditors

☐ Have restructured about one-third of the nation's debt, to allow more liberal repayment terms
☐ Expect to restructure an even larger portion of Mexico's debt, with even more liberal repayment terms
☐ Have extended additional short-term loans to the country to satisfy its immediate needs
☐ Have arranged for $1.7 billion in short-term credits to Mexico through the Bank for International Settlements.

Bankers are still counting on the fact that Mexico is rich in natural resources. According to José Carral, vice president of the Bank of America in Mexico City, "We will pay it all back—with silver, with cement, with shrimp, with petrochemicals, with oil."[1]

Mexico, Argentina, and other underdeveloped countries have run into money problems recently. These countries are rich in natural resources but poor in the financial resources needed to develop them. Banks in the more prosperous industrialized nations have been very willing to lend money to these poorer countries. The interest rate—the "price" for borrowing money—was high, so the banks expected to make a nice profit on their loans. At the same time, the borrowing nations had plenty of natural wealth to back up their borrowing. They would use the borrowed funds to transform their natural resources into financial resources (in Mexico's case, by drilling, pumping, and selling its oil). Then they could easily pay off the loans. So, at the time of negotiation, the loans seemed almost risk-free.

This is no different from the situation in which a business firm or an individual borrows from a bank. A firm (even a new one) may have a valuable asset in the form of a product idea. If the idea is a good one, and the firm (or its founder) has a good reputation, a bank would probably lend it the money to develop, produce, and market the product. The loan—with interest—would be repaid out of future sales revenue. In this way both the firm and the bank would earn a reasonable profit.

Individuals may borrow to buy a home, a car, or some other high-cost item. In this case, labor is the resource that will be transformed into money to repay the loan.

In each of these situations, the borrower needs the money now and has the ability to repay it later. (Mexico ran into trouble partly because its ability to repay the loans was eroded by the drop in world oil prices.) But also, in each situation, the money will be used to *purchase something* and it will be repaid through the use of *resources*. This is in keeping with the concept of money that we developed in Chapter 1. Money is an artificial device that aids in the exchange of resources for goods and services. It is generally very effective in this role.

WHAT IS MONEY?

The members of a primitive society may exchange goods and services through barter, without using money. A **barter system** is a system of exchange in which goods or services are traded directly for other goods or services. One family may raise vegetables and herbs on a plot of land, and another may weave cloth. To obtain food, the family of weavers trades cloth for vegetables, provided that the farming family is in need of cloth.

The trouble with barter is that the two parties to an exchange must need each other's product at the same time, and the two products must be roughly equal in value. It may work well when

Figure 15.1 The Three Functions of Money

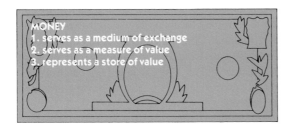

few products, primarily the necessities of life, are available. But even very primitive societies soon develop some sort of money to eliminate the inconvenience of trading by barter.

Money is anything used by a society to purchase goods and services or resources. The members of the society receive money for their products or resources. Then they either hold it or use it to purchase other products or resources, when and how they see fit. Different groups of people have used all sorts of objects as money—whale's teeth, stones, beads, copper crosses, clam shells, and gold and silver, for example. Today, the most commonly used objects are metal coins and paper bills, which together are called *currency.*

The Functions of Money

We have already noted that money aids in the exchange of goods and services for resources. And it does. But that's a rather general (and somewhat theoretical) way of stating money's function. Let us look at three specific functions of money in any society. (See Figure 15.1.)

Serves as a Medium of Exchange A **medium of exchange** is anything that is accepted as payment for products and resources. This definition looks very much like the definition of money. And it is meant to, because the primary function of money is to serve as a medium of exchange. The key word here is *accepted.* As long as the owners of products and resources accept money in an exchange, it is performing this function. Of course, these owners accept it because they know it is acceptable to the owners of other products and resources, which *they* may wish to purchase.

Serves as a Measure of Value A **measure of value** is a single standard or "yardstick" that is used to assign values to, and compare the values of, products and resources. Money serves as a measure of value because the prices of all products and resources are stated in terms of money. It is thus the "common denominator" that we use to compare products and decide which we shall buy. Imagine the difficulty you would have in deciding whether you could afford, say, a pair of shoes if it were priced in terms of yards of cloth or pounds of vegetables—especially if your employer happened to pay you in toothbrushes.

Represents a Store of Value Money that is received by an individual or firm need not be used immediately. It may be held and spent later. Hence money serves as a **store of value,** or a means for retaining and accumulating wealth. This function of money comes into play whenever we hold onto money—in a pocket, a cookie jar, a savings account, or whatever.

Value that is stored as money is affected by fluctuations in the economy. One of the major problems caused by inflation is a loss of stored value: as prices go up in an inflationary period, money loses value because it can buy less. Suppose you can buy a particular stereo system today for $1000. Then we may say that your $1000 now has a value equal to the value of that system.

But let us suppose that you wait a while and don't buy the stereo immediately. If the price goes up to $1100 meantime because of inflation, you can no longer buy the stereo with your $1000. Your money has *lost* value because it is now worth less than the stereo. (See Figure 15.2.)

Important Characteristics of Money

To be acceptable as a medium of exchange, money must be fairly easy to use, it must be trusted, and it must be capable of performing its functions. Together, these requirements give rise to five essential characteristics.

Divisibility The standard unit of money must be capable of division into smaller units in order to accommodate small purchases as well as large ones. Our standard is the dollar, and it is divided into one-hundredths, one-twentieths, one-tenths, one-fourths, and one-halfs through the issuance of coins (pennies, nickels, dimes, quarters, and half-dollars, respectively). These allow us to

Figure 15.2   *Inflation. Inflation causes a loss of money's stored value.* Source: U.S. Bureau of Labor Statistics.

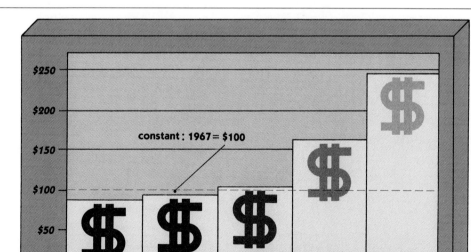

make purchases of less than a dollar and of odd amounts greater than a dollar. Whale's teeth and clam shells are not so easily divisible.

Portability   Money must be small enough and light enough to be carried easily. For this reason, paper currency is issued in larger *denominations*—multiples of the standard unit. Five-, ten-, twenty-, fifty-, and hundred-dollar bills make our money convenient for almost any purchase.

Stability   Money should retain its value over time. When it does not (as happens during periods of high inflation), people tend to lose faith in their money. They may then turn to other means of storing value (such as gold and jewels, works of art, and real estate). In extreme cases, they may use such items as a medium of exchange as well. They may even resort to barter.

Durability   The objects that serve as money should be strong enough to last through reasonable usage. No one would appreciate (or use) dollar bills that disintegrated as they were handled or coins that melted in the sun.

Difficulty of Counterfeiting   If a nation's currency were easy to counterfeit—that is, to imitate or fake—its citizens would be uneasy about accepting it as payment. Even genuine currency would soon lose its value, because no one would want it. Thus the countries that issue currency do their best to ensure that it is very hard to reproduce.

The Supply of Money: M_1 and M_2

How much money is there in the United States? Before we can answer that question, we need to redefine a couple of familiar concepts.

Figure 15.3   The Supply of Money. Two measures of the money supply are M_1, which includes currency and demand deposits, and M_2, which includes currency, demand deposits, and time deposits. Source: Federal Reserve Board, April 1984 Official Reports, May 30, 1984.

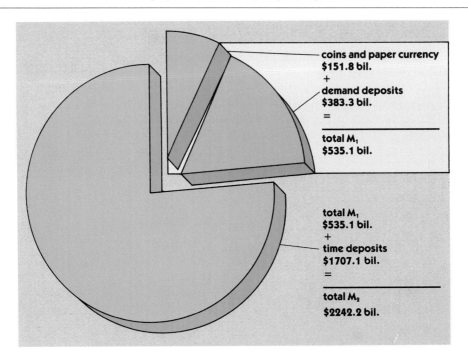

coins and paper currency
$151.8 bil.
+
demand deposits
$383.3 bil.
=

total M_1
$535.1 bil.

total M_1
$535.1 bil.
+
time deposits
$1707.1 bil.
=

total M_2
$2242.2 bil.

Demand deposits are amounts that are on deposit in checking accounts. They are called *demand* deposits because they can be claimed immediately—on demand—by presenting a properly made-out check.

Time deposits are amounts that are on deposit in interest-bearing savings accounts. Savings institutions generally permit immediate withdrawal of money from savings accounts. However, they can require written notice prior to withdrawal. The time between notice and withdrawal is what leads to the name *time* deposits.

Time deposits are not immediately available to their owners, but they can be converted to cash easily. For this reason, they are called *near-monies*. Other near-monies include short-term government securities, government bonds, and the cash surrender values of insurance policies.

The M_1 *supply of money* consists only of currency and demand deposits. (It is thus based on a narrow definition of money.) By law, currency must be accepted as payment for products and resources. Checks are accepted as payment because they are convenient and generally safe.

The M_2 *supply of money* consists of currency, demand deposits, and time deposits. Thus M_2 includes both M_1 and time deposits. It is based on a broader definition of money, under the assumption that time deposits are easily converted to cash for spending. Figure 15.3 shows the elements of the M_1 supply and M_2 supply. About 7 percent is coins and paper currency, about 17 percent is demand deposits, and the remaining 76 percent is time deposits.

We have, then, at least two measures of the supply of money. (Actually, there are other measures as well, which may be broader or narrower than M_1 and M_2.) So the answer to our original question is that the amount of money in the United States depends very much on how we measure it. Generally, economy watchers tend to focus on M_1 or some variation of M_1.

We have seen that a very large part of the money that exists in this country is deposited, by those individuals and firms who possess it, in banks. Let us now examine the banking industry.

THE AMERICAN BANKING INDUSTRY

Commercial Banks

A **commercial bank** is a profit-making organization that accepts deposits, makes loans, and provides related services to its customers. Like other businesses, the bank's primary goal—its purpose—is to earn a profit. Its inputs are money in the form of deposits, for which it pays interest. Its primary output is loans, for which it charges interest. If the bank is successful, its income is greater than the sum of its expenses and it will show a profit.

Because banks deal with money belonging to individuals and other firms, they are carefully regulated. They must also meet certain requirements before they are chartered, or granted permission to operate, by federal or state banking authorities. **National banks** are commercial banks that are chartered by the U.S. Comptroller of the Currency. There are approximately 5500 national banks, and they account for about 70 percent of all bank deposits. These banks must conform to all federal banking regulations and are subject to unannounced inspections by federal auditors.

State banks are commercial banks that are chartered by the banking authorities in the states in which they operate. State banks outnumber national banks by about two to one, but they tend to be smaller than national banks. They are subject to unannounced inspections by both state and federal auditors.

Table 15.1 lists the ten largest banks in the United States. All of these are classified as national banks.

Other Financial Institutions

Savings and Loan Associations   A **savings and loan association** (S&L) is a financial institution that primarily accepts savings deposits and provides home-mortgage loans. Originally they were permitted to offer their depositors *only* savings accounts. But since January 1, 1981, they have

Table 15.1 The Ten Largest Banks in the United States, Ranked by Total Deposits

Rank	Commercial Bank	Deposits
1	Bank of America, San Francisco	$95.9 billion
2	Citibank, New York	72.5 billion
3	Chase Manhattan Bank, New York	58.6 billion
4	Manufacturers Hanover Trust, New York	42.2 billion
5	Morgan Guaranty Trust Co., New York	37.7 billion
6	Chemical Bank, New York	30.7 billion
7	Continental Illinois National Bank, Chicago	29.9 billion
8	First National Bank, Chicago	25.9 billion
9	Security Pacific National Bank, Los Angeles	23.4 billion
10	Bankers Trust Company, New York	23.3 billion

Source: *American Banker*, New York, 1981. Based on deposits as of December 31, 1981. By permission.

been able to offer interest-paying checking accounts (NOW accounts) to attract depositors.

During the early 1980s, high interest rates, coupled with a reduced demand for homes, led to financial difficulties for many S&Ls. Much of their lending is in the form of low-interest, long-term home-mortgage loans that were issued to finance the purchase of homes during the 1960s and 1970s. Those older loans generate very little revenue, compared to more recent loans. In addition, because few people were taking out mortgages, S&Ls were not able to lend money at the higher interest rates of the early 1980s. As a result, the S&Ls were squeezed between the higher interest rates they paid to their depositors and the lower interest rates they received from their loans. Fortunately, interest rates declined somewhat during the mid-1980s, and the demand for mortgage loans increased.

Credit Unions A **credit union** is a financial institution that accepts deposits from, and lends money to, only those people who are its members. Usually the membership is composed of employees of a particular firm, people in a particular profession, or those who live in a community served by a local credit union. Some credit unions require that members purchase at least one share of ownership, at a cost of about $5 to $10. Credit

unions generally pay higher interest than commercial banks and S&Ls, and they may provide loans at lower cost.

Mutual Savings Banks A **mutual savings bank** is a bank that is owned by its depositors. The approximately 500 mutual savings banks in this country have no stockholders. Their profits are distributed to depositors. They operate very much like S&Ls and are controlled by state banking authorities.

Organizations that Perform Banking Functions
There are three types of financial institutions that are not actually banks but that are nevertheless involved in various banking activities to a limited extent.

□ *Insurance companies* provide long-term financing for office buildings, shopping centers, and other commercial real estate projects throughout the United States. They also invest in corporate and government bonds. The funds used for this type of financing are obtained as policyholders' insurance premiums.
□ *Pension funds* are established by employers to guarantee their employees a regular monthly income upon retirement. Contributions to the

fund may come either from the employer alone or from both the employer and the employee. The funds earn additional income through generally conservative investments. Pension funds invest in certain corporate stocks, corporate bonds, government securities, and real estate developments.

□ *Brokerage firms* offer combination savings and checking accounts that pay higher-than-usual interest rates (so-called money-market rates). Many people switched to these accounts, when their existence became widely recognized, to get the higher rates. In the last few years, however, banks have instituted similar types of accounts, hoping to lure their depositors back.

Services Provided by Financial Institutions

If it seems to you that banks and other financial institutions are competing for your business, you're right. That is exactly what is happening. Never before have so many different financial institutions offered such a tempting array of services to attract customers. Let's look briefly at the most important financial services provided by the banking industry. (See Figure 15.4.)

The Deposit Side of Banking Firms and individuals deposit money in checking accounts (demand deposits) so that they can write checks to pay for purchases. A **check** is a written order for a bank or other financial institution to pay a stated dollar amount to the business or person indicated on the face of the check. Today, most goods and services are paid for by check. Most financial institutions charge an activity fee (or service charge) for checking accounts. It is generally somewhere between $5 and $10 per month for individuals. For businesses, monthly charges are based on the average daily balance in the checking account and on the number of checks written.

Most financial institutions also offer NOW accounts (NOW stands for Negotiable Order of Withdrawal). A **NOW account** is an interest-bearing checking account. The usual interest rate is 5.25 percent. However, individual banks may impose certain restrictions on their NOW accounts, including the following:

□ A minimum balance before any interest is paid
□ Fees for accounts whose balances fall below a set minimum balance
□ Restrictions on the number of checks that may be written during each month.

Some financial institutions offer Super NOW accounts. Super NOWs pay somewhat higher interest than NOW accounts and generally include unlimited check-writing privileges. But depositors may be required to maintain a minimum balance as high as $2500 to avoid bank charges that may run up to $7 or $8 per month.

Savings accounts (time deposits) provide a safe place to store money and a fairly conservative means of investing. The usual *passbook savings account* earns about 5.5 percent in commercial banks and S&Ls and slightly more in credit

Figure 15.4 *Services Provided by Financial Institutions*

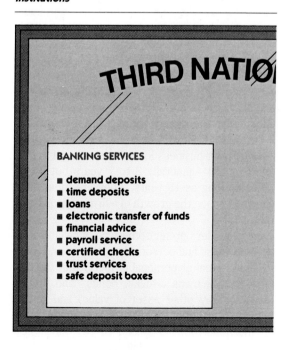

BANKING SERVICES

■ demand deposits
■ time deposits
■ loans
■ electronic transfer of funds
■ financial advice
■ payroll service
■ certified checks
■ trust services
■ safe deposit boxes

unions. Depositors can usually withdraw money from passbook accounts whenever they wish to.

A depositor who is willing to leave money with a bank for a set period of time can earn a higher rate of interest. To do so, the depositor buys a certificate of deposit (CD). A **certificate of deposit** is a document stating that the bank will pay the depositor a guaranteed interest rate for money left on deposit for a specified period of time. The interest rates paid on CDs change weekly; they once briefly exceeded 16 percent. Rates in mid-1984 ranged between 8.5 and 10.5 percent. The rate always depends on how much is invested and for how long. Depositors are penalized for early withdrawal of funds invested in CDs. At present, the penalty is three months' interest.

The Lending Side of Banking Commercial banks, savings and loan associations, credit unions, and other financial institutions provide short-term and long-term loans to both individuals and businesses. *Short-term* loans are those that are to be repaid within one year. For businesses, short-term loans are generally used to provide working capital that will be replaced with sales revenues. To ensure that short-term money will be available when it is needed, many firms establish a line of credit. A **line of credit** is a loan that is approved before the money is actually needed. Because all the necessary paperwork is already completed and the loan is pre-approved, the business can later obtain the money without delay, as soon as it is required.

Long-term business loans have a longer repayment period—generally 3 to 7 years but sometimes as long as 15 years. They are most often used to finance the growth of a firm or its product mix.

Most lenders prefer some type of collateral for both business and personal long-term loans. **Collateral** is real or personal property that the firm or individual owns (stocks, bonds, land, equipment, or any other asset of value) and that is pledged as security for a loan. For example, when an individual obtains a loan to pay for a new automobile, the automobile is the collateral for the loan. If the borrower fails to repay the loan according to the terms specified in the loan agreement, the lender can repossess the collateral pledged as security for that loan.

Repayment terms and interest rates for both short-term and long-term loans are arranged between the lender and the borrower. For businesses, repayment terms may include monthly, quarterly, semiannual, or annual payments. Repayment terms (and interest rates) for personal loans vary, depending on how the money will be used and what type of collateral, if any, is pledged. Borrowers should always "shop" for a loan, comparing the repayment terms and interest rates offered by competing financial institutions.

Electronic Transfer of Funds The newest service provided by financial institutions is electronic banking. An **electronic funds transfer** (EFT) **system** is a means for performing financial transactions through a computer terminal or telephone hookup. Present EFT systems can be used in four ways.

1. *Automated teller machines* (ATMs). An ATM is an electronic bank teller—a machine that provides almost any service a human teller can provide. Once the customer is properly identified, the machine can dispense cash from the customer's checking or savings account or can make a cash advance charged to a credit card. Most ATMs can also accept deposits and provide information about current account balances. ATMs are located in bank parking lots, supermarkets, drugstores, and even a few gas stations. Customers have access to them at all times of the day or night.
2. *Automated clearinghouses* (ACHs). Where ACHs are available, large companies can use them to transfer wages and salaries directly into their employees' bank accounts without making out individual paychecks. The ACH system saves time and effort for both employers and employees and adds a measure of security to the transfer of these payments.
3. *Point-of-sale* (POS) *terminals*. A POS terminal

is a computerized cash register that is located in a retail store and connected to a bank's computer. Once the customer is identified, the POS terminal automatically and immediately transfers the dollar amount of any purchase from the customer's bank account to the store's account. This eliminates both the need to write a check and the chance of nonpayment.

4. *Bill payment by telephone.* Individuals can authorize their banks to make payments to various creditors by using a touch-tone telephone like a computer terminal. The customer simply punches in the required information, and the bank transfers the funds automatically.

Bankers are generally pleased with EFT systems. EFT is fast, and it eliminates some costly processing of checks. However, many bank customers are reluctant to use EFT systems. Some customers simply don't like "the machine," whereas others fear the computer will garble their accounts. Congress has responded to consumer fears by passing the Electronic Funds Transfer Act, which protects the customer in case the bank makes an error or the customer's EFT identification card is lost or stolen. No doubt the use of EFT will increase as people become more familiar with it.

A network as diverse and influential as the banking industry must be subject to uniform regulations and controls. In fact, regulation of banking in this country really amounts to regulation of our economy at large.

THE FEDERAL RESERVE SYSTEM

The **Federal Reserve System** (or simply "the Fed") is the government agency responsible for regulating the United States banking industry. It was created by Congress on December 23, 1913. Its mission is to maintain an economically healthy and financially sound business environment in which banks can operate. The Federal Reserve System is controlled by the 7 members of its Board of Governors, who meet in Washington,

Computerized cash registers—point-of-sale terminals— located in retail stores and connected to banks' computers can transfer funds automatically and immediately from the customer's account to the store's. Source: © Richard Kalvar, Magnum.

D.C. Each governor is appointed by the president and confirmed by the Senate for a 14-year term. The president also selects the chairman and vice chairman of the board from among the board members.

The Federal Reserve System includes 12 Federal Reserve District Banks, which are located throughout the United States, as well as 25 branch territory banks (see Figure 15.5). Each Federal Reserve District Bank is actually owned—but not controlled—by the commercial banks that are members of the Federal Reserve System. All national (federally chartered) banks must be members of the Fed. State banks may join if they choose to and if they meet membership requirements.

The primary function of the Fed is to regulate the supply of money in this country in such a way as to maintain a healthy economy. It does so by controlling bank reserve requirements and the discount rate and by its open-market operations.

Regulation of Reserve Requirements

When money is deposited in a bank, the bank must retain a portion of it to satisfy customers who may want to withdraw money from their accounts. The remainder is available for loans. The **reserve requirement** is the percentage of its deposits that a bank *must* retain, either in its own vault or on deposit with its Federal Reserve District Bank. For example, if a bank has deposits of $20 million and the reserve requirement is 10

Figure 15.5 *Federal Reserve Bank System. Twelve district banks and twenty-five branch banks compose the Federal Reserve Bank System. Source: Board of Governors of the Federal Reserve System,* Federal Reserve Bulletin, *January 1983, p. A88.*

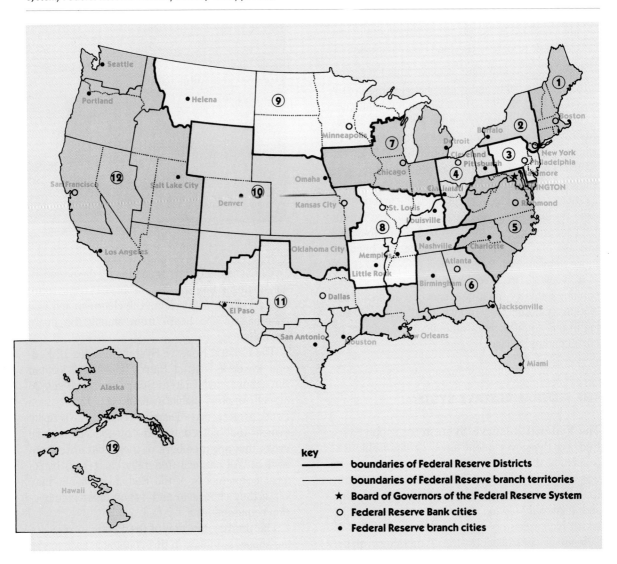

key

—— **boundaries of Federal Reserve Districts**

------ **boundaries of Federal Reserve branch territories**

★ **Board of Governors of the Federal Reserve System**

O **Federal Reserve Bank cities**

● **Federal Reserve branch cities**

percent, the bank must retain $2 million. It may lend or invest the remaining $18 million.

The reserve requirement is set by the Board of Governors of the Fed. When it is increased, banks have less money available for lending. Fewer loans are made, and the economy tends to slow. Thus, increasing the reserve requirement is a powerful anti-inflation weapon. On the other hand, by decreasing the reserve requirement, the Fed can make additional money available for lending, in order to stimulate a slow economy.

The present reserve requirement for time deposits is 3 percent. For NOW accounts it can range from 3 to 12 percent, depending on such factors as the total amount on deposit and the location of the particular member bank. Because this means of controlling the money supply is so very potent and has such far-reaching effects, the Fed seldom changes the reserve requirement.

Regulation of the Discount Rate

Member banks may borrow money from the Fed to satisfy the reserve requirement and to make additional loans to their customers. The interest rate that the Federal Reserve System charges for loans to member banks is called the **discount rate.** It is set by the Fed's Board of Governors.

When the Fed lowers the discount rate, money is easier to obtain. Member banks feel free to make more loans and to charge lower interest rates. This increases the money supply and generally stimulates the nation's economy. When the Fed raises the discount rate, banks begin to restrict loans. They increase the interest rates they charge and tighten their own loan requirements. The overall effect is to slow the economy—to check inflation—by making money more difficult and more expensive to obtain.

Open-Market Operations

The federal government finances its activities partly by selling U.S. government securities. These securities, which pay interest to owners,

may be purchased by any individual, firm, or organization—including the Fed. **Open-market operations** are the buying and selling of U.S. government securities by the Federal Reserve System for the purpose of controlling the supply of money. They are the most frequently used tool of the Fed.

To reduce the nation's money supply, the Fed simply *sells* government securities on the open market. The money it receives from purchasers is taken out of circulation, so less money is available for investment, purchases, or lending. To increase the money supply, the Fed *buys* government securities. The money that it pays for the securities goes back into circulation, so that more money is available to individuals and firms.

The major purchasers of government securities are financial institutions, so open-market operations tend to have an immediate effect on lending and investment. Moreover, this effect can be controlled and adjusted by varying the amount of securities that the Fed sells or buys at any given time.

Table 15.2 summarizes the effects of open-market operations and the other tools used by the Fed to regulate the money supply.

Other Responsibilities

In addition to its regulation of the money supply, the Fed is also responsible for clearing checks, controlling and inspecting currency, and applying selective credit controls.

Clearing Checks   Today people use checks to pay for nearly everything they buy. If all the checks written in one year were taped end to end, they would extend to the moon and back four times.[2] Moreover, it costs approximately 50 cents to *clear* the typical check—that is, to process it for payment.[3]

A check written by a customer of one bank and presented for payment to another bank in the same town may be processed through a local clearinghouse. But the procedure becomes more complicated when the banks are not in the same

Table 15.2 *Methods Used by the Federal Reserve System to Control the Money Supply and the Economy*

Method Used	Immediate Result	End Result
Open-market operations		
1. Fed SELLS government securities and bonds	Less money for banks to lend to customers—reduction in overall money supply	Economic slowdown
2. Fed BUYS government securities and bonds	More money for banks to lend to customers—increase in overall money supply	Increased economic activity
Regulating reserve requirement		
1. Fed INCREASES reserve requirement	Less money for banks to lend to customers—reduction in overall money supply	Economic slowdown
2. Fed DECREASES reserve requirement	More money for banks to lend to customers—increase in overall money supply	Increased economic activity
Regulating the discount rate		
1. Fed INCREASES the discount rate	Less money for banks to lend to customers—reduction in overall money supply	Economic slowdown
2. Fed DECREASES the discount rate	More money for banks to lend to customers—increase in overall money supply	Increased economic activity

town. That's where the Federal Reserve System comes in. The Fed is responsible for the prompt and accurate collection and crediting of intercity checking transactions.

The steps involved in clearing a check through the Federal Reserve System are outlined in Figure 15.6. About half of all the checks written in the United States are cleared in this way. The remainder are either presented directly to the paying bank or processed through local clearinghouses. Through the use of electronic equipment, most checks can be cleared within two or three days.

Control and Inspection of Currency As paper currency is handled, it becomes worn or dirty. The typical dollar bill has a life expectancy of less than one year (larger denominations usually last longer because they are handled less). When member banks deposit their surplus cash in a Federal Reserve Bank, the currency is automatically inspected. Bills that are unfit for further use are

separated and destroyed. The destruction process is usually as follows:

☐ Holes are drilled in each corner of the bills by one group of employees.
☐ The bills are then cut in half by a second group of employees.
☐ Each half is pulverized by a third group.
☐ The end result is barely recognizable as paper. It is baled and sold for use in making such things as wrapping paper and roofing material.

Selective Credit Controls The Federal Reserve System has the power to establish credit terms for loans involving consumer durables (automobiles, appliances, and the like) and for real estate loans. In particular, the Board of Governors can set both the amount of the down payment and the repayment period for these loans. It has not exercised this power in recent years.

The Federal Reserve System is also responsible for setting the margin requirements for certain stock transactions. The *margin* is the minimum portion of the selling price that must be paid in cash. (The investor may borrow the remainder.) The current margin requirement is 50 percent. If an investor purchases $1000 worth of stock, he or she must pay at least $500 in cash. The remaining $500 may be borrowed from the brokerage firm or some other financial institution.

The FDIC and the FSLIC

During the Depression, a number of banks failed and their depositors lost all their savings. To make sure that this does not happen again (and to restore public confidence in the banking industry), Congress organized the *Federal Deposit Insurance Corporation* (FDIC) in 1933. The primary

purpose of the FDIC is to insure deposits against bank failure. All banks that are members of the Federal Reserve System are required to belong to the FDIC. Non-member banks are allowed to join if they qualify. Insurance premiums are paid by the banks.

The FDIC insures all accounts in each member bank for up to $100,000 per depositor. An individual depositor may obtain additional coverage by opening separate accounts in different banks. Individuals who deposit their money in savings and loan associations receive similar protection from the *Federal Savings and Loan Insurance Corporation* (FSLIC).

The FDIC and the FSLIC have improved banking in the United States. When either insures an

Figure 15.6 Clearing a Check Through the Federal Reserve System. Source: Federal Reserve Bank of New York, The Story of Checks, 6th ed., p. 11.

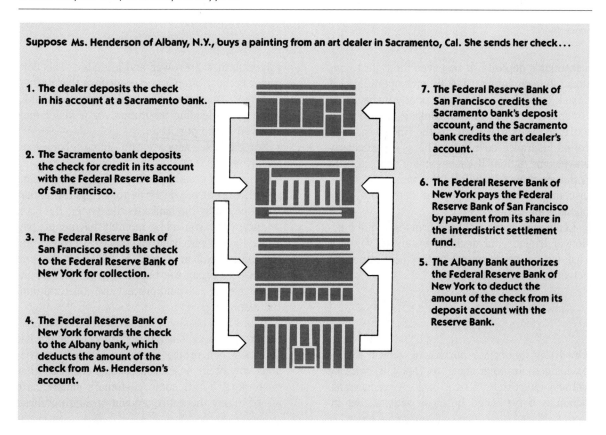

Suppose Ms. Henderson of Albany, N.Y., buys a painting from an art dealer in Sacramento, Cal. She sends her check...

1. The dealer deposits the check in his account at a Sacramento bank.

2. The Sacramento bank deposits the check for credit in its account with the Federal Reserve Bank of San Francisco.

3. The Federal Reserve Bank of San Francisco sends the check to the Federal Reserve Bank of New York for collection.

4. The Federal Reserve Bank of New York forwards the check to the Albany bank, which deducts the amount of the check from Ms. Henderson's account.

7. The Federal Reserve Bank of San Francisco credits the Sacramento bank's deposit account, and the Sacramento bank credits the art dealer's account.

6. The Federal Reserve Bank of New York pays the Federal Reserve Bank of San Francisco by payment from its share in the interdistrict settlement fund.

5. The Albany Bank authorizes the Federal Reserve Bank of New York to deduct the amount of the check from its deposit account with the Reserve Bank.

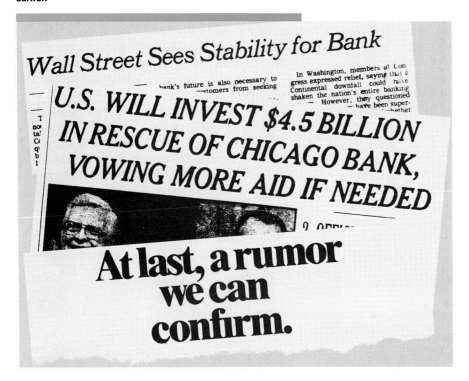

Wall Street Sees Stability for Bank

U.S. WILL INVEST $4.5 BILLION IN RESCUE OF CHICAGO BANK, VOWING MORE AID IF NEEDED

bank's future is also necessary to ...tomers from seeking

In Washington, members of Congress expressed relief, saying that a Continental downfall could have shaken the nation's entire banking ... However, they questioned — have been super—...ther

At last, a rumor we can confirm.

institution's deposits, it reserves the right to periodically examine that institution's operations. If a bank or S&L is found to be poorly managed, it is reported to the proper banking authority. In extreme cases, the FDIC or the FSLIC can cancel its insurance coverage. This is a particularly unwelcome action. It causes many depositors to withdraw their money from the bank or S&L and discourages most prospective depositors from opening an account.

Lending to individuals and firms is a vital function of banks. And deciding wisely to whom it shall extend credit is one of the most important activities of any institution.

EFFECTIVE CREDIT MANAGEMENT

Credit is immediate purchasing power that is exchanged for a promise to repay it, with or without interest, at a later date. A credit transaction is a two-sided business activity that involves both a borrower and a lender. The borrower is most often a person or firm that wishes to make a purchase. The lender may be a bank, some other lending institution, or a middleman involved in the purchase.

For example, suppose you obtain a bank loan to buy a $40,000 Porsche automobile. You, as the borrower, obtain immediate purchasing power. In return, you agree to certain terms that are imposed by the bank. As the lender, the bank requires that you make monthly payments, pay interest, and purchase insurance to protect the car until the loan is paid in full. That is, you promise to repay the purchasing power, pay interest for its use, and protect the collateral until the loan is repaid.

Banks lend money because they are in business for that purpose. The interest they charge is what provides their profit. There are at least two reasons why other businesses extend credit to their customers. First, some customers simply can't afford to pay the entire amount of their purchase immediately, but they *can* repay credit in a number of smaller payments, stretched out over some period of time. Second, some firms are forced to sell goods or services on credit in order to compete effectively when other firms offer credit to their customers.

Today the effective management of credit is a practical necessity for most businesses. Credit terms can be used as a competitive weapon, and firms can realize a profit from interest charges. The major pitfall in granting credit is the possibility of nonpayment and the resulting loss of income. However, if a firm follows the five C's of credit management, it can minimize this possibility.

The Five C's of Credit Management

The primary purpose of any business is to earn a profit by selling goods and services. When a business extends credit to its customers, it must face the fact that some customers will be unable or unwilling to pay for their credit purchases.

Figure 15.7 *Effective Credit Management. Most lenders build their credit policies around the five C's of credit.*

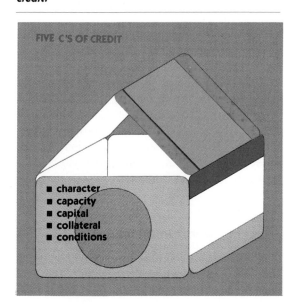

FIVE C'S OF CREDIT

- character
- capacity
- capital
- collateral
- conditions

Customers Paid To Use ATMs

City Savings Bank of Meriden, Conn., recently did an unusual twist on the usual pricing structure for services when it launched a promotion during which it actually paid customers to use its ATMs (Automated Teller Machines).

As part of the promotion, which began in July and was set to run indefinitely, the bank pays customers 25¢ per deposit or bill payment, and 10¢ per withdrawal, up to a total of $3 per month. It also has "sprinkled" a number of $10 and $20 bills in the ATMs cash compartments as a bonus to ATM users. The bills are marked with a sticker saying "Surprise and Thank You. This is not a mistake. Thank you for doing business with us."

"We want to get customers to use their ATM cards and to get used to using them," explained Robert K. Montgomery, president and CEO of the $81 million-assets bank. While the bank only has two ATMs at present, it plans to open a third office October 1 with one drive-up and two interior ATMs.

And from a marketing standpoint, Montgomery said, "The giveaways are peanuts compared to newspaper advertising costs."

Source: *Savings Bank Journal,* October, 1983, p. 58.

With this in mind, credit managers must establish policies for determining who will receive credit and who will not. Most lenders build their credit policies around the five C's of credit: character, capacity, capital, collateral, and conditions (Figure 15.7).

Character By *character* we mean the borrower's attitude toward his or her credit obligations. Experienced credit managers often see this as the most important factor in predicting whether a borrower will make regular payments and ultimately repay a credit obligation.

Typical questions to consider in judging a borrower's character include the following.

1. Is the borrower prompt in paying bills?
2. Have other lenders had to dun the borrower with overdue notices before receiving payment?
3. Have lenders been forced to take the borrower to court to obtain payment?
4. Has the customer ever filed for bankruptcy? If so, did the customer make an attempt to repay debts voluntarily?

Even personal factors such as marital status and drinking or gambling habits may affect an individual's ability to repay a loan or credit obligation. (See Figure 15.8.)

Capacity By *capacity* we mean the borrower's financial ability to meet credit obligations—that is, to make regular loan payments as scheduled in the credit agreement. If the customer is another business, the loan officer or credit manager looks at the firm's income statement. For individuals, the loan officer or credit manager checks salary statements. The borrower's outstanding financial obligations and monthly expenses are also taken into consideration before credit is approved.

Capital The term *capital* as used here refers to the borrower's assets or net worth. In general, the greater the capital, the greater the borrower's ability to repay a loan of a specific size. The capital position of a business can be determined by examining its financial statements. (Most lenders insist that the business borrower's financial statements be prepared or audited by an independent certified public accountant. This helps to ensure that the information contained in the statements is accurate.) For individuals, information on net worth can be obtained by requiring that the borrower complete a credit application. The borrower must also authorize employers and financial institutions to release information to confirm the claims made in the application.

Collateral For large amounts of credit—and especially for large loans—the lender may require some type of *collateral*. If the borrower fails to live up to the terms of the credit agreement, the collateral can be sold to satisfy the debt.

Conditions Here we mean *general economic conditions,* which can affect a borrower's ability to repay a loan or other credit. How well a business firm can withstand an economic storm may depend on the particular industry the firm is in, its relative strength within that industry, and its earnings history and earnings potential. For individuals, the basic question of conditions focuses on security—of both the applicant's job and the firm that he or she works for.

Checking Credit Information

The five C's are concerned mainly with information that is supplied by the applicant. But how can the lender determine whether this information is accurate? That depends on whether the potential borrower is a business or an individual consumer.

Credit information concerning businesses can be obtained from four sources:

- □ Dun & Bradstreet, the most widely used credit-reporting agency in the United States. Its Dun & Bradstreet Reports present detailed credit information about specific firms. It also publishes reference books that include credit ratings for more than three million businesses.
- □ Local credit-reporting agencies. These may require a monthly or yearly fee for providing information on a continual basis.
- □ Industry associations, which also may charge a fee for this service.
- □ Other firms that have given the applicant credit.

Various credit bureaus provide credit information concerning individuals—generally for a fee of from $5 to $20 per request. Following is a list of the five major consumer credit bureaus.

Figure 15.8 Credit Application Form

SECTION 1

NAME — First | Middle | Last

ADDRESS — Street | Apt. | City | State | Zip

HOW LONG AT ABOVE ADDRESS | □ Own | □ Rent | TELEPHONE

FORMER ADDRESS | How Long

NAME OF BUSINESS | TELEPHONE

BUSINESS ADDRESS — Street | City | State | Position | How Long

PREVIOUS EMPLOYER (Please indicate if employed by above less than 3 years, or College/University if recent graduate.) | Years with Firm or Year Graduated

NAME OF BANK □ Reg. Check □ Spec. Check | Branch Address

NAME OF BANK □ Savings | Branch Address

CHARGE ACCOUNTS AT	ACCOUNT NUMBER IF AVAILABLE

OTHERS WHO MAY CHARGE

SPECIAL INSTRUCTIONS

SECTION 2

INFORMATION FOR JOINT APPLICANT OR AUTHORIZED SPOUSE

NAME | Relationship to Applicant (if any) | TELEPHONE

ADDRESS — Street | Apt. | City | State | Zip | □ Own □ Rent | How Long

FORMER ADDRESS | How Long

NAME OF BUSINESS | TELEPHONE

BUSINESS ADDRESS — Street | City | State | Position | How Long

PREVIOUS EMPLOYER (Please indicate if employed by above less than 3 years, or College/University if recent graduate.) | Years with Firm or Year Graduated

NAME OF BANK □ Reg. Check □ Spec. Check | Branch Address

NAME OF BANK □ Savings | Branch Address

How to Establish a Good Credit Rating

More than half of all American families now have at least one credit card, and many have more than one. Credit cards seem to have become a "status symbol." The more a person has, the wealthier and more financially secure he or she seems to be. Gold cards are issued by American Express and Visa. Although these cards have higher credit limits, the biggest attraction of the "gold" is prestige.[1] In fact, an individual who has a large number of credit cards and uses them frequently can easily get even more credit.

But what about people with no credit history? Here are seven specific actions you can take to establish a good credit history.[2]

1. Open both a checking and a savings account at a local bank, savings and loan association, or credit union.
2. Take out a small installment loan at the financial institution where you have your checking and savings accounts.
3. Establish credit with a local department store. Department-store accounts are often easier to obtain than other types of credit accounts.
4. If a bank, department store, or oil company offers you a credit card, take it. Then be sure all payments are made on time.
5. Pay all your bills on time. If you live in an apartment and pay your own utilities, make sure the rent and utilities are paid promptly. These two references may be needed to persuade other potential creditors to give you credit.
6. Don't borrow from a small-loan company (sometimes referred to as a "personal finance company"). A credit reference from this type of company may hurt you more than it can help.
7. If you are married and have a joint credit account, make sure that credit histories are reported in both names. If you are a woman, the account should be reported in your given name.

Once you have obtained credit, make sure you protect it. A good credit rating is even harder to obtain the second time. If an unexpected large expense or a loss of income causes you to miss an installment payment, try to work out alternative arrangements with your creditors. Credit counseling services are also available and some are free. If you need help, take action quickly before your credit rating is damaged.

Sources: [1]"Prestige Plastic—A Gold Rush in Credit," *Time*, June 21, 1982, p. 51; [2]Adapted from "What makes you a good credit risk?" *Consumer Reports*, May, 1983, p. 256, by permission.

- □ TRW Information Services (Orange, California)
- □ Trans Union Credit Information Co. (Chicago)
- □ Credit Bureau Inc. (Atlanta)
- □ Chilton Corp. (Dallas)
- □ Pinger System (Houston)

These and other credit bureaus are subject to the provisions of the Fair Credit Reporting Act of 1970. This Act safeguards consumers' rights in two ways. First, every consumer has the right to know what information is contained in his or her credit bureau file. In most states, a consumer may obtain the information for a $5 or $10 fee. The credit bureau either sends a copy of the file or specifies a local or regional office where it can be obtained.

Second, if a consumer feels that some information in the file is inaccurate, he or she has the right to request that the credit bureau verify it. If the disputed information is found to be correct, the consumer can provide an explanation of up to 100 words, giving his or her side of the dispute. This explanation must become part of the consumer's credit file. If the disputed information is found to be inaccurate, it must be deleted or changed. Furthermore, any lending institution that has been supplied the inaccurate information must be sent a corrected update.

Sound Collection Procedures

The vast majority of borrowers follow the lender's repayment terms exactly. However, some accounts inevitably become overdue for any of a variety of reasons. Experience shows that such accounts should receive immediate attention. The longer an account is overdue, the less likely it is to be paid.

Some firms handle their own delinquent accounts; others prefer to use a professional collection agency. (Charges for an agency's services are usually high—up to half of the amount collected.) Both tend to use the following standard collection techniques, generally in the order in which they are listed.

1. Subtle reminders and overdue notices, such as statements marked "Past Due."
2. Telephone calls to urge prompt payment.
3. Personal visits to stress the necessity of paying past-due amounts immediately.
4. Legal action, although the expense and uncertain outcome of a lawsuit make this action a last resort.

Good collection procedures should be firm, but they should allow for compromise. Harassment is both illegal and bad business. Ideally the customer will be convinced to make up missed payments, and the firm will retain the customer's goodwill.

Chapter Review

SUMMARY

Money is anything that is used by a society to purchase goods and services and resources. It must serve as a medium of exchange, as a measure of value, and as a store of value. To perform its functions effectively, money must be divisible into units of convenient size, light and sturdy enough to be carried and used on a daily basis, stable in value, and difficult to counterfeit.

The M_1 supply of money is made up of coins and bills (currency) and deposits in checking accounts (demand deposits). The broader M_2 supply includes M_1 and deposits in savings accounts (time deposits).

A commercial bank is a profit-making organization that accepts deposits, makes loans, and provides other services to customers. In the United States, commercial banks may be chartered by the federal government or the various state governments. Savings and loan associations, credit unions, and mutual savings banks offer their customers the same basic services that commercial banks provide. Insurance companies, pension funds, and brokerage firms provide some limited banking services.

The Federal Reserve System is responsible for regulating the banking industry and maintaining a sound economic environment. Banks with federal charters must be members of the Fed. State banks may join if they can meet the requirements for membership.

To control the supply of money, the Federal Reserve System regulates the reserve requirement, or the percentage of deposits that a bank must keep on hand. It also regulates the discount rate, or the interest rate the Fed charges member banks for loans. And it engages in open-market operations, in which it buys and sells government securities. The Fed is responsible for clearing checks, controlling currency, and setting credit terms for certain consumer and stock-purchase loans.

The Federal Deposit Insurance Corporation (FDIC) and the Federal Savings and Loan Insurance Corporation (FSLIC) insure all accounts in member banks and S&Ls, up to $100,000 per depositor.

Credit is immediate purchasing power that is exchanged for a promise to repay it, with or without interest, at a later date. Businesses sell goods and services on credit because some customers can't afford to pay cash, and because they must keep pace with competitors who offer credit. Decisions on whether to grant credit to businesses and individuals are usually based on the five C's of credit: character, capacity, capital, collateral, and conditions. Credit information can be obtained from various credit-reporting agencies, credit bureaus, industry associations, and other firms. The techniques used to collect past-due accounts should be firm but flexible enough to maintain customer goodwill.

In the next chapter, our discussions will focus on money as a productive resource. You will see why firms need financing, how they obtain the money they need, and how they ensure that it is utilized efficiently, in keeping with their organizational objectives.

KEY TERMS

You should now be able to define and give an example relevant to each of the following terms:

barter system

money

medium of exchange

measure of value

store of value

demand deposits

time deposits

commercial bank

national bank

state bank

savings and loan association

credit union

mutual savings bank

check

NOW account

certificate of deposit

line of credit

collateral

electronic funds transfer system

Federal Reserve System

reserve requirement

discount rate

open-market operations

credit

QUESTIONS AND EXERCISES

Review Questions

1. How does the use of money solve the problems that are associated with a barter system of exchange?
2. What are the three functions that money must perform in a sound monetary system? Give an example of each.
3. Why must money be (a) divisible, (b) portable, (c) stable, and (d) durable?
4. What is included in the M_1 definition of the supply of money? in the M_2 definition?
5. What is the difference between a national bank and a state bank? What other financial institutions compete with national and state banks?
6. Describe the major depositing and lending services provided by financial institutions today.
7. What is the major advantage of electronic banking? What is its major disadvantage?
8. What is the Federal Reserve System? How is it organized?
9. Explain how the Federal Reserve System uses each of the following to control the money supply.
   a. Reserve requirements
   b. The discount rate
   c. Open-market operations
10. How could the Fed use its control of consumer credit terms and the margin requirement to regulate the supply of money?
11. What is the basic function of the FDIC and the FSLIC? How do they perform this function?
12. List and explain the five C's of credit management.
13. How would you check the information provided by an applicant for credit at a department store? at a heavy-equipment manufacturer's sales office?

Discussion Questions

1. To what extent are Mexico's financial problems due to (a) its own actions, (b) those of the lending banks, and (c) the world economic environment?
2. How and why do the "collection procedures" used with Mexico differ from those suggested in this chapter? Do you think Mexico's creditors acted reasonably? Explain.
3. It is said that financial institutions "create" money when they make loans to firms and individuals. Explain what this means.
4. Is competition among financial institutions good or bad for (a) these institutions, (b) their customers, and (c) the economy?
5. Why would banks pay higher interest on money that is left on deposit for longer periods of time (for example, on CDs)?
6. Why does the Fed use indirect means of controlling the money supply, instead of simply printing more money or removing money from circulation when necessary?
7. Lenders are generally reluctant to extend credit to individuals with no previous credit history (and no outstanding debts). Yet they willingly extend credit to individuals who are in the process of repaying debts. Is this reasonable? Is it fair?

Exercises

1. Devise a form of money, other than coins and bills, that fulfills the functions of money and has all the required characteristics.
2. Obtain a credit application from a store or bank. Fill it out. Then answer the following questions.
   a. Does the application ask for enough information so that a credit manager could apply the five C's? What questions should be added to the application form?
   b. Would you, as a credit manager, extend credit to yourself? Explain.

CASE 15-1

Why Banks Go Broke

The First National Bank of Midland got into serious financial trouble when the oil and gas exploration business slid into a recession in 1982 and 1983. The bank lost $121 million during the first 8 months of 1983. Bad loans climbed to a staggering $314 million (one-fourth of all outstanding loans). And its stock plunged to 30 cents a share from a high of $60 back in mid-1982.[4]

Finally, on October 14, 1983, the Midland bank was declared insolvent. The Federal Deposit Insurance Corporation (FDIC) stepped in and arranged a merger between the First National Bank of Midland and RepublicBank Corporation, a large and prosperous bank holding company located in Dallas.

Unfortunately, the First National Bank of Midland is not the only bank in the nation to become insolvent. In fact nearly 50 U.S. banks failed in 1983. By comparison, bank failures averaged fewer than 10 per year during the 1960s and 1970s. But what is even more frightening is that 617 banks are on the FDIC's "endangered species" list.[5] These banks are regarded as likely to fail unless corrective measures are taken immediately.

At the heart of the problem is the number of bad loans that bankers have made in recent years. At most major banks, problem loans represent about 3 percent of the bank's total loan portfolio. When this percentage increases, the only alternative is for the bank to write off problem loans as a bad-debt expense, which of course lowers the bank's profits.

When a bank fails, customers whose deposits exceed the FDIC coverage face at least partial losses. But the biggest losers of all are the bank's stockholders. Once a bank is declared insolvent, the chance of stockholders getting something back is very slim.[6]

1. Why would the FDIC arrange a merger between a failing bank and a prosperous banking firm? Who does such a merger help?
2. What might have caused the percentage of bad loans at banks to increase so dramatically during the early 1980s?

CASE 15-2
The Float

Suppose you deposit a check in your bank account that is drawn on an out-of-state bank. The check will follow a path similar to that outlined in Figure 15.6. The Federal Reserve System will credit your bank for the amount of the check in one or two days—well before the check itself has returned to the out-of-state bank. Can you then withdraw that amount from your account? In most cases, the answer is no.

The problem, according to the banking industry, is that your bank cannot know whether or not there are sufficient funds in the out-of-state checking account. If there are not, the out-of-state bank will return the check to your bank, unpaid. Your bank will generally not allow you to withdraw the funds until enough time has passed for the check to reach the out-of-state bank and be returned to your bank—if necessary. But bank experience shows that no more than 1 percent of all checks actually do bounce back.

The time lag between the crediting of your bank by the Fed and the time you can withdraw the funds is called the bank's "float." During the float, your bank has access to the amount of the check, but you do not. And most banks earn appreciable interest on depositors' money during the float.

How long should the float be? That depends on the distance between the two banks, among other things. But the holding period is generally set by the individual bank. Investigators in New York State found that it varied from two or three days up to twenty-two days. The longer floats can be inconvenient at the least, and can cause hardship for some depositors.

In response to customer complaints, several states and the federal government have passed or are considering legislation to regulate the float. New York was the first to pass a "float law," giving state bank regulators the authority to set float periods. The new check-crediting periods, which went into effect in March 1984, range from one day (for all checks of less than $100 and government checks of less than $2,500) to six business days (for checks up to $2,500 drawn on out-of-state banks). Banks may still set the float for checks whose amounts are greater than $2,500.[7]

1. Should banks be required to share their float-period earnings with depositors? Justify your answer.
2. Why would float regulations specify a one-day float for small checks but leave the float for large checks (above $2,500) up to the bank's discretion?

CHAPTER

SIXTEEN
Financial Management

Money does for a business what lubricating oil does for a well-designed machine. It keeps things running smoothly. If money is not applied as needed, the business—like an unoiled machine—will grind to a screeching halt. At the other extreme, money is wasted if it is applied too liberally, at the wrong time, or in the wrong way. This chapter is concerned with financial management, and financial management is concerned with the acquisition and efficient use of money. After studying the chapter, you should understand:

1. *The need for financing and financial management in business*
2. *The process of planning for financial management*
3. *How budgets are used in financial planning*
4. *The various means of obtaining short-term financing, and their relative advantages and disadvantages*
5. *The difference between equity financing and debt financing*
6. *How corporations obtain long-term financing by issuing stock and corporate bonds*

Consider this:

For years, U.S. Steel was a wounded giant. Although it was this nation's largest steelmaker—and was spending billions of dollars in an attempt to modernize its steel-making facilities—the firm seemed destined to operate with inefficient production plants and to accept losses or very slim profits.

For one thing, the firm was under increasing competitive pressure from Japan, West Germany, and other countries with expanding steel industries. Firms in these nations were, according to U.S. Steel sources, engaging in unfair international trade practices—sometimes selling their steel in this country at prices that were below the cost of production. Appeals to the U.S. government brought little relief.

For another thing, the recession of the mid and late 1970s, along with a shrinking demand for steel, led to huge losses in steel-making. These losses continued into 1982 and 1983, which were actually the worst recessionary years for the American steel industry. At the time when U.S. Steel was trying to modernize its facilities so as to compete effectively, the firm's steel operations lost as much as $300 million in a single three-

Source: Logo, courtesy of United States Steel; photo, © 1983 Bob Adelman, Magnum.

United States Steel

month period—with its mills operating at about 40 percent of capacity.

The giant was weakened by inefficient facilities; battered by foreign competition; and frustrated in its attempts to finance additional modernization through earnings. David M. Roderick, the chairman of U.S. Steel's board of directors, had to find a way to increase the firm's production efficiency while reducing its expenses. He began, in 1979, by closing all or parts of fifteen antiquated plants. (Later, in 1983, he closed seventy additional operating facilities, in his ongoing attempt to streamline the firm.) Next he centralized accounting, maintenance, production planning, and other managerial functions, in a successful attempt to trim both managerial and production costs. Once these moves were completed, U.S. Steel required only about half its original work force—which cut its wage and salary expenses dramatically.

To counter the effect of the slowing demand for steel, Roderick has stepped up the company's diversification into other areas. For a number of years, U.S. Steel had been increasing its involvement in the chemical and shipping industries. Now the firm is branching out even further. Roderick's boldest move was the $5.93 billion purchase of Marathon Oil Company—the second largest merger in U.S. history at that time.

U.S. Steel had to borrow $3 billion to buy Marathon Oil. And Roderick concedes that it will probably take two more years (a year longer than he thought) to pay off the debt. But Marathon Oil has a 49 percent stake in the giant Yates oil field in west Texas, and in July 1983 it began to produce oil from the Brae field in the British North Sea. According to Roderick, these finds make Marathon "an exceptional business opportunity" that will contribute to U.S. Steel's profitability in the future.[1]

Roderick had to struggle to find the huge sums of money he needed to finance the Marathon purchase and other diversification. And he may have to struggle a while longer: The interest on U.S. Steel's financing amounts to $1 billion per year! To ensure that this is paid, the firm has

☐ Cut in half the cash dividend paid to holders of common stock
☐ Sold two new issues of preferred stock
☐ Deferred some capital spending
☐ Sold such non-steel-making assets as coal mines, real-estate holdings, and electric-cable- and container-manufacturing facilities

This last means of raising needed funds—the sale of assets—is a key part of U.S. Steel's corporate strategy. In fact, a stack of papers labeled "Confidential" sits on Roderick's desk. Roderick says they list assets that the company has already sold and those that are still for sale.[2]

U.S. Steel needed money not just to keep the firm running smoothly, but also to finance a complete overhaul. Such an overhaul seemed absolutely necessary if U.S. Steel was to survive. And, because survival depended on effective financial management, the firm's top executive took on the responsibility himself.

For at least two reasons, it was imperative that Roderick cut the firm's expenses. First, by reducing operating expenses he made funds available for other uses, such as the payment of interest costs. Second, when Roderick reduced the outflow of money, U.S. Steel became a more efficient firm and thus more attractive to the financial community. This enabled Roderick to approach lenders and investors to obtain the needed financing.

The closing of plants and sale of assets are not usual means of raising money. But in U.S. Steel's situation, they seemed to be logical actions. The old and inefficient facilities had to be either modernized—which would take additional funding— or closed and, if possible, disposed of. Since the market for steel and steel products had shrunk, Roderick decided to close them. The sale of the non-steel-making assets generated funds that could be used to modernize U.S. Steel's remaining facilities.

Roderick's other funds-raising methods are more standard. The sale of stock is a means of *equity* financing, and long-term loans are called *debt* financing. Both are discussed later in this chapter. Roderick and his sources of funds were also involved with the uses of the money—for example, the purchase of Marathon Oil. This too is a part of financial management.

WHAT IS FINANCIAL MANAGEMENT?

Financial management consists of all those activities that are concerned with obtaining money and using it effectively. Within a business organization, the financial manager must not only determine the best way (or ways) to raise money.

A designer may use a short-term loan to finance the next season's line and then repay the loan as soon as orders for clothes begin. Source: © David Burnett, Leo deWys, Inc.

She or he must also ensure that projected uses are in keeping with the organization's goals. Effective financial management thus involves careful planning. It begins with determination of the firm's financing needs.

The Need for Financing

Money is needed both to start a business and to keep it going. The original investment of the owners, along with money they may have borrowed, should be enough to get operations under way. Then, it would seem that income from sales could be used to finance the firm's continuing operations and to provide a profit as well.

This is exactly what happens in a successful firm—over the long run. But sales revenue does not generally flow evenly. Both income and expenses may vary from season to season or from year to year. Temporary funding may be needed when expenses are high or income is low. Then too, special situations, such as the opportunity to purchase a new facility, may require more money

than is available within a firm. In either case, the firm looks to outside sources of financing.

Short-Term Financing Needs **Short-term financing** is money that will be used for a period of one year or less and then repaid. A firm might need short-term financing to pay for a new promotional campaign that is expected to increase sales revenue. Or the purchase of a computer-based inventory control system, which will "pay for itself" within a year, might be funded with short-term money.

Speculative production is the manufacture of goods before orders have been received. Firms that engage in speculative production often need short-term financing. The money is used to buy materials and supplies, to pay wages and rent, and to cover inventory costs until the goods are sold. Then the money is repaid out of sales revenue. Wholesalers and retailers may need short-term financing to build up their inventories before peak selling periods. Again, the money is repaid when the merchandise is sold.

Business crises have one commonality: They are almost never acknowledged by management or the board of directors until the company is virtually out of cash. Only when they simply cannot meet the payroll or suppliers refuse to ship or lenders refuse to advance more funds will companies admit that they are in big trouble. Then they call for Gil Osnos. . . .

He doesn't say yes at first to a new assignment—or no. What he wants is two to three weeks to look the company over. If he thinks the situation is hopeless and there will be nothing left worth salvaging, he gives the bad news to the board of directors and moves on. . . .

If Osnos thinks he can do something, those couple of weeks have given him time to prepare himself to act. What he has done is size up the organization and figure out "where to put the tourniquets." That means stopping the hemorrhaging of cash. At that point Osnos can move quickly—he sells cash-draining plants or closes them down. He gets rid of moneylosing product lines. To make his job even more difficult, he is always dealing with angry, frightened, and distrustful people. He terminates executives, sometimes including the chief executive. He renegotiates labor contracts. "I peel a business back to its healthy core," he says. "Success, in this league, is having something meaningful survive."

Osnos goes from one industry to another. He may know nothing about the industry he is asked to work in. It really doesn't matter that much because the first secret is cash flow. That is Gil Osnos's fever chart. . . .

What's next is a business plan. It is not one he devises; it is one that grows out of the business itself and is endorsed by the people who are going to implement it. Osnos the listener starts the process. He listens to top management, and he listens to second-line management; but he finds, it is at the level of third-line management where the problems are truly grasped. It is here also where he often finds the opportunities. Ideas from this level of management often help him start the fleshing out of the new plan. Frequently it is the first real plan the company has ever had. . . .

But what about Gil Osnos? Just how many times can a man handle the crises he thrusts himself into? Osnos isn't sure. The lifestyle is hard—furnished apartments in one city after another, 10- and 12-hour days and always the pressure. At $200 an hour the money is good, but you don't get rich on it, not truly rich. Unlike the glamour set, Osnos isn't working for a piece of the action. "Owning equity," he says, "would compromise my ability to deal with creditors, unions, etc."

Source: Thomas P. Murphy, "Is There a Doctor in the House," *Forbes,* November 7, 1983, pp. 304–305.

Other business practices that affect a firm's cash flow may also create a need for short-term financing. **Cash flow** is the movement of money into and out of an organization. The ideal is to have sufficient money coming into the firm, in any period, to cover the firm's expenses during that period. But the ideal is not always achieved. For example, a firm that offers credit to its customers may find an imbalance in its cash flow. Short-term financing is then needed to pay the firm's bills until customers have paid theirs. An unexpectedly slow selling season or an unanticipated expense may also cause a cash-flow problem.

Long-Term Financing Needs **Long-term financing** is money that will be used longer than one year. Long-term financing is obviously needed to start a new business. It is also needed for effecting business expansions and mergers, for developing and marketing new products, and for replacing equipment that becomes outmoded or inefficient. See Figure 16.1 for a comparison of short- and long-term financing.

The amounts of long-term financing needed by large firms can seem almost unreal. Exxon spends about $10 million to drill an exploratory offshore oil well—without knowing for sure whether oil will be found! Texas Instruments spent millions to develop and produce the TI 99/4A Personal Computer, and millions more to market it, before deciding to abandon the product. And, as we noted earlier, U.S. Steel borrowed $3 billion of long-term money to purchase Marathon Oil.

Figure 16.1 *Comparison of Short-Term and Long-Term Financing. Whether a business will seek short-term or long-term financing depends on what the borrowed money will be used for.*

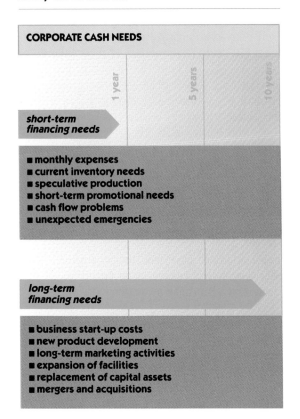

CORPORATE CASH NEEDS

1 year   5 years   10 years

short-term financing needs

- monthly expenses
- current inventory needs
- speculative production
- short-term promotional needs
- cash flow problems
- unexpected emergencies

long-term financing needs

- business start-up costs
- new product development
- long-term marketing activities
- expansion of facilities
- replacement of capital assets
- mergers and acquisitions

The Need for Financial Management

Without financing there would be very little business. Financing gets a business started in the first place. Then financing supports the firm's production and marketing activities; pays its bills; and, when carefully managed, produces a reasonable profit.

Many firms have failed because their managers did not pay enough attention to finances. And many fairly successful firms could be highly successful if they managed their finances more carefully. Often business people tend to take finances for granted. Their first focus may be on production or marketing. As long as there is sufficient funding today, they don't worry about how well it is used or whether it will be there tomorrow.

Proper financial management, on the other hand, can ensure that

☐ Financing priorities are established in line with organizational objectives
☐ Spending is planned and controlled in accordance with established priorities
☐ Sufficient financing is available when it is needed, both now and in the future
☐ Financial resources are obtained and used as efficiently as possible, so that the firm gets the most out of its money

These functions define effective management as applied to a particular resource: money. And, like all effective management, financial management begins with goal setting and planning.

PLANNING—THE BASIS OF SOUND FINANCIAL MANAGEMENT

In Chapter 5, a plan was defined as a course of action intended to achieve specified goals. A **financial plan,** then, is a plan for obtaining and using the money that is needed to implement an organization's goals. Once the plan is developed and put into action, the firm's performance under it must be monitored and evaluated. And, like any other plan, it must be modified if necessary.

Developing the Financial Plan

Financial planning (like all planning) begins with the establishment of a set of valid objectives. Next, planners must assign costs to these objectives. That is, they must determine how much money is needed to accomplish each one. Finally, planners must identify available sources of financing and decide which to use. In the process, they must make sure that financing needs are realistic and that sufficient funding is available to meet those needs.

The three steps involved in financial planning are shown in Figure 16.2.

Establishing Valid Objectives As we have noted, establishing objectives is an important and ongoing management task. Objectives are *specific* statements detailing what the organization intends to accomplish within a certain period of time. If objectives are not specific, they cannot be translated into costs and financial planning cannot proceed. They must also be realistic. Otherwise they may be impossible to finance or achieve.

Budgeting for Financial Needs A **budget** is a statement that projects income and/or expenditures over a specified future period. Once planners know what the firm expects to accomplish over some period of time—say, the next calendar year—they can estimate the various costs the firm will incur and the revenues it will receive. By combining these items into a company-wide budget, financial planners can determine whether they must seek additional funding from sources outside the firm.

Usually the budgeting process begins with the construction of individual budgets for sales and for each of the various types of expenses: production, personnel, promotion, administration, and so on. (A typical sales budget for a retailer is shown in Figure 16.3.) Budgeting accuracy is improved when budgets are first constructed for individual departments and for shorter periods of time. These budgets can easily be combined into a company-wide *cash budget,* such as that shown in Figure 16.4. In addition, they can help managers monitor and evaluate financial performance throughout the period covered by the overall cash budget.

Figure 16.2 *The Three Steps of Financial Planning. After a financial plan has been set up, it must be monitored continually to ensure that it actually fulfills the firm's objectives.*

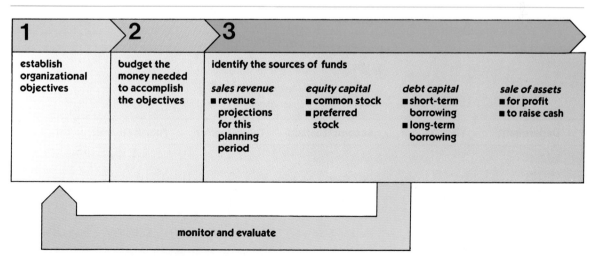

As banks have increased the prices of their cash management services, trying to more accurately gauge each service's cost, some corporations are finding it cost effective to bring their cash management services in-house. Some firms are using their banks only to initiate wire transfers and transactions with the Federal Reserve System.

For many years, firms were content to let their banks do their cash management services, perhaps knowing all along what banks have recently discovered—that inaccurate cost analysis and cross-subsidization of cash management services often resulted in many banks underpricing their services. Most firms only began considering internalizing their cash management services (commonly known as self-provision) when banks increased their prices to cover their costs.

Cash managers and treasurers are also becoming more particular about bank services and are less willing to turn over all cash management operations to their "regular" banks. Instead, they are shopping for the best rates for individual services.

Source: *Cashflow,* January–February 1983, p. 9.

Most firms today use one of two approaches to budgeting. In the *traditional* approach, each new budget is based on the dollar amounts contained in the budget for the preceding year. These amounts are modified to reflect any revised goals, and managers are required to justify only new expenditures. The problem with this approach is that it leaves room for the manipulation of budget items to protect the (sometimes selfish) interests of the budgeter or his or her department.

This problem is essentially eliminated through zero-base budgeting. **Zero-base budgeting** is a budgeting approach in which every expense must be justified in every budget. It can dramatically reduce unnecessary spending, because every budget item must stand on its own merits. However, some managers feel that zero-base budgeting requires entirely too much time-consuming paperwork.

Identifying Sources of Funds The four primary types of funding, as listed in Figure 16.2, are sales revenue, equity capital, debt capital, and proceeds from the sale of assets. Future sales generally provide the greatest part of a firm's financing. Figure 16.4 shows that, for Newton's Clothing Store, sales for the year are expected

Figure 16.3 *Sales Budget for Newton's Clothing Store*

NEWTON'S CLOTHING STORE					
Sales Budget					
For January 1, 198x to December 31, 198x					
Department	First Quarter	Second Quarter	Third Quarter	Fourth Quarter	Totals
Infant's	$ 50,000	$ 55,000	$ 60,000	$ 70,000	$235,000
Children's	45,000	45,000	40,000	40,000	170,000
Women's	35,000	40,000	35,000	50,000	160,000
Men's	20,000	20,000	15,000	25,000	80,000
Totals	$150,000	$160,000	$150,000	$185,000	$645,000

to cover all expenses and to provide a cash gain of about 16 percent of sales. However, Newton's has a problem in the first quarter, when sales are expected to fall short of expenses by $7000.

A second type of funding is **equity capital,** which is money received from the sale of shares of ownership in the business. Equity capital is used almost exclusively for long-term financing. Thus it might be used to start a business and to fund expansions or mergers. It would not be considered for short-term financing needs, such as Newton's first-quarter shortfall.

A third type of funding is **debt capital,** which is money obtained through loans of various types. Debt capital may be borrowed for either short-term or long-term use—and a short-term loan seems made to order for Newton's. The firm would probably borrow the needed $7000 (or perhaps a bit more) at some point during the first quarter and repay it from second-quarter sales revenue. In fact, Newton's might already have established a line of credit at a local bank to cover just such periodic short-term needs.

Once a financial plan is adopted, the company's performance under the plan must be carefully monitored and evaluated. Source: © Tom Tracy, FPG.

Figure 16.4 *Cash Budget for Newton's Clothing Store*

NEWTON'S CLOTHING STORE *Cash Budget* For January 1, 198x to December 31, 198x					
	First Quarter	Second Quarter	Third Quarter	Fourth Quarter	Totals
Cash Sales and Collections	$150,000	$160,000	$150,000	$185,000	$645,000
Less Payments					
Purchases	$110,000	$ 80,000	$ 90,000	$ 60,000	$340,000
Wages/Salaries	25,000	20,000	25,000	30,000	100,000
Rent	10,000	10,000	12,000	12,000	44,000
Other Expenses	4,000	4,000	5,000	6,000	19,000
Taxes	8,000	8,000	10,000	10,000	36,000
Total Payments	$157,000	$122,000	$142,000	$118,000	$539,000
Net Cash Gain or (Loss)	$ (7,000)	$ 38,000	$ 8,000	$ 67,000	$106,000

Our fourth type of funding is the proceeds from the sale of assets. A firm generally acquires assets because it needs them for its business operations, so selling assets is a drastic step. However, it may be a reasonable last resort when neither equity capital nor debt capital can be found. Assets may also be sold when they are no longer needed, as in the case of U.S. Steel. By selling its non-steelmaking assets, U.S. Steel was able to raise needed finances and reduce its expenses while disposing of unneeded assets.

In most cases, the particular funding need clearly suggests the best source of funding. (We shall discuss sources of equity and debt financing later in this chapter.) In all cases, though, the financial manager should identify and verify funding sources in advance to be sure they will be available when they are needed.

Monitoring and Evaluating Financial Performance

It is important to ensure that financial plans are being implemented and to catch minor problems before they become major problems. Accordingly, the financial manager should establish a means of monitoring and evaluating financial performance. Interim budgets (weekly or monthly budgets) may be prepared for this purpose. Then interim reports of sales and expenses can be compared to budgeted amounts. These comparisons will point up areas that require additional or revised planning—or at least those areas where more careful investigation is called for.

Figure 16.5 shows a quarterly comparison of budgeted and actual sales for Newton's Clothing Store. Sales of children's wear are about 7 percent over budget, and sales of infants' wear are about 9 percent below budget. Although neither discrepancy is a cause for immediate alarm, both categories of sales should be watched. The differences may be due to budgeting problems or to non-financial causes. In any case, such comparisons should be routinely reported to department heads and upper-level managers. They may be used as the basis for budgeting, and they may reveal a need to take corrective action (such as promoting infants' wear more vigorously).

It is important to realize that the decision to borrow money does not mean that a firm is in financial trouble. On the contrary, astute financial management often means regular, responsible borrowing of many different kinds. In the next two sections we shall examine the sources of short-term and long-term financing that are available to business firms.

Figure 16.5 *Budget Comparison for Newton's Clothing Store*

NEWTON'S CLOTHING STORE
Sales Budget Update
First Quarter, 198x

Department	First-Quarter Estimate	Actual Sales	Dollar Difference
Infant's	$ 50,000	$ 45,600	$ − 4,400
Children's	45,000	48,200	+ 3,200
Women's	35,000	36,300	+ 1,300
Men's	20,000	21,100	+ 1,100
Totals	$150,000	$151,200	$ + 1,200

SOURCES OF SHORT-TERM FINANCING

Short-term financing is usually easier to obtain than long-term financing for three reasons: The shorter repayment period means there is less risk of nonpayment. The dollar amounts of short-term loans are usually smaller than those of long-term loans. And a close working relationship normally exists between the short-term borrower and the lender.

Most lenders do not require collateral for short-term financing. When they do, it is usually because they are concerned about the size of a particular loan, the borrowing firm's poor credit rating, or the general prospects of repayment. It may be the case that a financially weak firm will have difficulty securing short-term financing even when it is willing to pledge collateral to back up a loan.

Sources of Unsecured Short-Term Financing

Unsecured financing is financing that is not backed by collateral. A company seeking unsecured short-term capital has several options. They include trade credit, promissory notes, bank loans, commercial paper, and commercial drafts.

Trade Credit In Chapter 13 we noted that wholesalers may provide financial aid to retailers by allowing them 30 to 60 days (or more) in which to pay for merchandise. This delayed payment, which may also be granted by manufacturers, is a form of credit known as *trade credit* or the *open-book account*. More specifically, **trade credit** is a payment delay that a firm grants to its customers.

Between 80 and 90 percent of all transactions between businesses involve some trade credit. Typically, the purchased goods are delivered along with a bill (or *invoice*) that states the credit terms. These may include a cash discount for prompt payment.

Promissory Notes Issued to Suppliers A **promissory note** is a written pledge by a borrower to pay a certain sum of money to a creditor at a specified future date. Suppliers that are uneasy about extending trade credit may be less reluctant to offer credit to customers who sign promissory notes. Unlike trade credit, however, promissory notes usually provide that the borrower or buyer on credit shall pay interest.

A typical promissory note is shown in Figure 16.6. Note that the customer buying on credit (or borrowing the money) is called the *maker* and is the party that issues the note. The business selling the merchandise on credit (or lending the money) is called the *payee*.

A promissory note offers two important advantages to the firm extending the credit. First, a promissory note is a legally binding and enforceable document. Second, most promissory notes are negotiable instruments that can be sold when the money is needed immediately. For example, the note shown in Figure 16.6 will be worth $820 at maturity. If it chose, the Shelton Company (the payee) could discount, or sell, the note to its own bank. The price would be slightly less than $820, because the bank charges a small fee for the service—hence the term *discount*. Shelton would have its money immediately, and the bank would collect the $820 when the note matured.

Unsecured Bank Loans Commercial banks offer unsecured short-term loans to their customers at interest rates that vary with the borrower's credit rating. The **prime interest rate** (sometimes referred to as the reference rate) is the lowest rate charged by a bank for a short-term loan. This lowest rate is generally reserved for large corporations with excellent credit ratings. Organizations with good to high credit ratings may pay the prime rate plus 2 percent. Firms with questionable credit ratings may have to pay the prime rate plus 4 percent. Of course, if the banker feels loan repayment may be a problem, the borrower's loan application may be rejected.

Banks generally offer short-term loans through promissory notes, a line of credit, or a revolving credit agreement. *Promissory notes* that are written to banks are similar to those discussed in the last section. Although repayment terms may extend to one year, most promissory notes specify repayment periods of 60 to 180 days.

The *line of credit*—in essence, a prearranged short-term loan—was discussed in Chapter 15. A bank that offers a line of credit may require that a *compensating balance* be kept on deposit at the bank. This balance may be as much as 20 percent of the line-of-credit amount. The bank may also require that every commercial borrower *clean up* (pay off completely) its line of credit at least once each year and not use it again for a period of 30 to 60 days.

Even with a line of credit, a firm may not be able to borrow on short notice if the bank does not have sufficient funds available. For this reason, some firms prefer a **revolving credit agreement,** which is a guaranteed line of credit. Under this type of agreement, the bank guarantees that the money will be available when the borrower needs it. In return for the guarantee, the bank charges a commitment fee ranging from 0.25 to 1.0 percent of the *unused* portion of the revolving credit. The usual interest is charged for the portion that *is* borrowed.

Commercial Paper **Commercial paper** is short-term promissory notes issued by large corporations. Commercial paper is secured only by the reputation of the issuing firm; no collateral is involved. It is usually issued in large denominations, ranging from $5000 to $100,000. Corpo-

Figure 16.6 *A Promissory Note. A promissory note is a written pledge to pay a certain sum of money to a creditor at a specified date. Source: Kelley, McKenzie, and Evans,* Business Mathematics, p. 242.

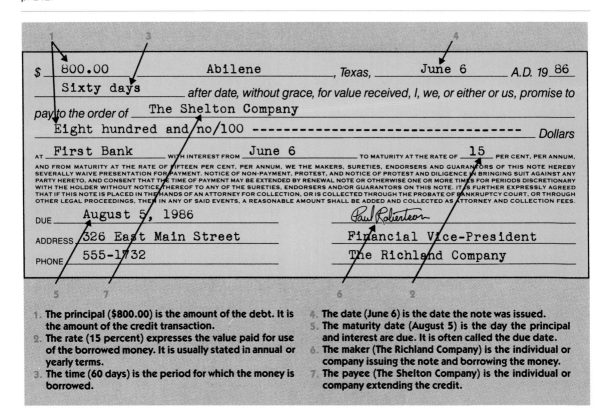

1. The principal ($800.00) is the amount of the debt. It is the amount of the credit transaction.
2. The rate (15 percent) expresses the value paid for use of the borrowed money. It is usually stated in annual or yearly terms.
3. The time (60 days) is the period for which the money is borrowed.
4. The date (June 6) is the date the note was issued.
5. The maturity date (August 5) is the day the principal and interest are due. It is often called the due date.
6. The maker (The Richland Company) is the individual or company issuing the note and borrowing the money.
7. The payee (The Shelton Company) is the individual or company extending the credit.

rations issuing commercial paper pay interest rates slightly below those charged by commercial banks.

Large firms with excellent credit reputations can quickly raise large sums of money in this way. General Motors Acceptance Corporation, for example, may issue commercial paper totaling millions of dollars. (In some cases, the total amount of an issue is more than a bank would be able to lend to a single borrower.) However, commercial paper is not without risks. If the issuing corporation later has severe financial problems, it may not be able to repay the promised amounts. The Penn Central Railroad defaulted on commercial paper worth $80 million when it filed for bankruptcy in 1974.

Commercial Drafts A **commercial draft** is a written order requiring a customer (the *drawee*) to pay a specified sum of money to a supplier (the *drawer*) for goods or services. It is often used when the supplier has reservations about the customer's credit standing. Suppose, for example, that Martin Manufacturing sold merchandise valued at $9800 to Barnes Wholesale Supply and required that Barnes sign a commercial draft. The draft (Figure 16.7) would be completed as follows:

1. The draft form is filled out by the drawer (Martin). The draft contains the purchase price, interest rate, if any, and maturity date.
2. The draft is sent by the drawer to the drawee (Barnes).
3. If the information contained in the draft is correct and the merchandise has been received, the drawee marks the draft "Accepted" and signs it.
4. The customer returns the draft to the drawer. Now the drawer may (a) hold the draft until maturity, (b) discount the draft at its bank, or (c) use the draft as collateral for a loan.

A *sight draft* is a commercial draft that is payable on demand—whenever the drawer wishes to collect. A *time draft* is a commercial draft on which a payment date is specified. Like promissory notes, drafts are negotiable instruments that

Banks providing credit for construction projects often send officers to the site to observe how the money is being used. Source: © David Aronson, Stock, Boston.

may be discounted or used as collateral for a loan. And they are legally enforceable.

Sources of Secured Short-Term Financing

If a business cannot obtain enough capital via unsecured short-term financing, it must put up collateral to obtain the financing it needs. Almost any asset can serve as collateral. However, *inventories* and *accounts receivable* are the assets that are most commonly used for short-term financing.

Loans Secured by Inventory Normally, middlemen and producers have large amounts of money invested in finished-goods or merchandise inventories. In addition, producers carry raw-materials and work-in-process inventories. All three types of inventory may be pledged as collateral for short-term loans. However, lenders prefer the much more salable finished goods to the other inventories.

A lender may insist that inventory that is used as collateral must be stored in a public warehouse. In such a case, the receipt issued by the warehouse is retained by the lender. When the borrowed money is repaid, the lender releases the warehouse receipt—and the merchandise—to the borrower. Because the borrower pays for storage in a public warehouse, the loan will then end up being more expensive than an unsecured loan.

Loans Secured by Receivables Accounts receivable are amounts that are owed to a firm by its customers. They arise primarily from trade credit and are usually due in less than 60 days. It is possible for a firm to pledge its accounts receivable as collateral to obtain short-term financing. A lender may advance 70 to 80 percent of the dollar amount of the receivables. First, however, it conducts a thorough investigation to determine the *quality* of the receivables. (The quality of the receivables is the credit standing of the firm's customers.) If a favorable determination is made and the loan is approved, then whenever the borrowing firm collects from a customer whose account has been pledged as collateral, the money must be turned over to the lender as partial repayment of the loan.

Figure 16.7 *A Commercial Draft. A commercial draft is a written order requiring a customer to pay a specified sum of money to a supplier for goods or services.*

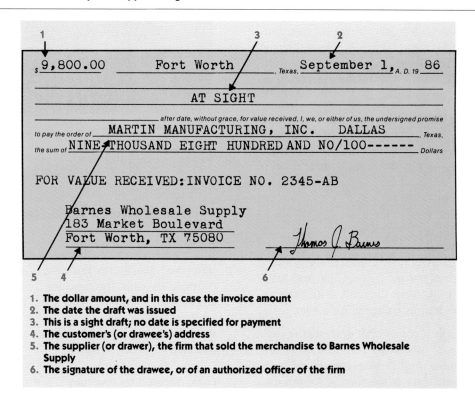

1. The dollar amount, and in this case the invoice amount
2. The date the draft was issued
3. This is a sight draft; no date is specified for payment
4. The customer's (or drawee's) address
5. The supplier (or drawer), the firm that sold the merchandise to Barnes Wholesale Supply
6. The signature of the drawee, or of an authorized officer of the firm

Table 16.1 *Comparison of Short-Term Financing Methods*

Type of Financing	Cost	Repayment Period	Businesses That May Use It	Comments
Trade credit	Low, if any	30 to 90 days	All businesses	Usually no finance charge
Promissory note	Moderate	1 year or less	All businesses	Usually unsecured, but requires legal document; issued by borrower
Unsecured bank loan	Moderate	1 year or less	All businesses	A line of credit or revolving credit agreement may be used
Commercial paper	Moderate	1 year or less	Large corporations with high credit ratings	Available only to large firms
Commercial draft	Moderate	1 year or less	Manufacturers and wholesalers	Issued by seller and accepted by buyer; has value and can be sold
Secured loan	High	1 year or less	Firms with questionable credit ratings	Inventory may have to be stored in a public warehouse
Factoring	High	None	Firms that have large numbers of credit customers	Accounts receivable are sold to a factor

Factoring Accounts Receivable

Accounts receivable may be used in one other way to help raise short-term capital: They can be sold to a factoring company, or factor. A **factor** is a firm that specializes in buying other firms' accounts receivable. The factor buys the accounts receivable for less than their face value, but it collects the full dollar amount when each account is due. The factor's profit is thus the difference between the face value of the accounts receivable and what the factor has paid for them.

Even though the selling firm gets less than face value for its accounts receivable, it does receive needed cash immediately. Moreover, it has shifted both the task of collecting and the risk of nonpayment to the factor, which now owns the receivables. Generally, customers whose accounts receivable have been factored are given instructions to make their payments directly to the factor.

Cost Comparisons

Table 16.1 compares the various types of short-term financing. As you can see, trade credit is the least expensive, but it also has the shortest term. Generally, the less favorable a firm's credit rating, the more likely that it will have to use a higher-cost means of financing. Factoring of accounts receivable is the highest-cost method shown.

For many purposes, short-term financing suits the firm's needs perfectly. In other cases, however, some means of long-term financing may be more appropriate.

SOURCES OF LONG-TERM FINANCING

Sources for long-term financing vary with the size and type of business. For corporations, equity-financing options include the sale of stock and the

use of profits not distributed to owners. The available debt-financing options are long-term loans and the sale of corporate bonds.

Equity Financing

Some equity capital is used to start every business—sole proprietorship, partnership, or corporation. If the business is a sole proprietorship or partnership, equity capital is acquired by the business when the owners invest their own money in the business. In the case of corporations, equity capital is provided by stockholders who buy shares of stock in the company. In general, however, only corporations turn to equity capital as a source of financing once they are established. They do so by selling additional shares of stock.

There are at least two reasons why equity financing is attractive to large corporations. First, the corporation need not repay money obtained from the sale of stock, and it need not repurchase

the shares of stock at a later date. Thus equity funding does not have to be repaid. Occasionally a corporation buys its own stock, but only because such an investment is in its own best interest. Recently IBM Corporation purchased thousands of shares of its own stock with uninvested profits. The firm's top management believed the purchase was the best investment available at that particular time.

A second advantage of equity funding is that a corporation is under no legal obligation to pay dividends to stockholders. **Dividends** are distributions of earnings to the stockholders of a corporation. Investors purchase the shares of stock of many corporations primarily for the dividends they pay. However, if a company should have a bad year (or, actually, for any other reason), its board of directors can vote to omit dividend payments. Earnings are then retained for use in funding business operations. Thus a corporation need not even pay for the use of equity capital. Of course, the corporate management may hear from unhappy stockholders if expected dividends are omitted too frequently.

There are two types of stock: common and preferred. (A specimen certificate is shown in Figure 16.8.) Each type has advantages and drawbacks as a means of long-term financing.

Common Stock   A share of **common stock** represents the most basic form of corporate ownership. By law, every corporation must hold an annual meeting, at which the holders of common stock may vote for directors and approve (or disapprove) major corporate actions. Among such actions are (1) amendments of the corporate charter or by-laws, (2) the sale of certain assets, (3) mergers, (4) the issuing of preferred stock or bonds, and (5) changes in the amount of common stock issued.

Many states require that a provision for pre-emptive rights be included in the charter of every corporation. **Pre-emptive rights** are the rights of current stockholders to purchase any new stock that the corporation issues before it is sold to the general public. By exercising their pre-emptive rights, stockholders are able to maintain their current proportion of ownership of the corporation. This may be important when the corporation is a small one and management control is a matter of concern to stockholders.

Money that is acquired through the sale of

Figure 16.8   *Common Stock. Capital is provided to the company by stockholders when they purchase shares of stock (equity) in the company. Source: Courtesy of the American Bank Note Company and Union Carbide.*

common stock is thus essentially cost-free, but few investors will buy common stock if they cannot foresee some return on their investment. We'll examine common stock from the point of view of the investor in Chapter 17.

Preferred Stock As we noted in Chapter 3, the owners of **preferred stock** usually do not have voting rights, but their claims on profit and assets precede those of common-stock owners. Thus holders of preferred stock must receive their dividends before holders of common stock are paid, provided dividends are distributed at all. Moreover, they have first claim (after creditors) on corporate assets if the firm is dissolved or declares bankruptcy. Even so, like common stock, preferred stock does not represent a debt that must legally be repaid.

The dividend to be paid on a share of preferred stock is known before the stock is purchased. It is stated, on the stock certificate, either as a percentage of the par value of the stock or as an amount of money. The **par value** of a stock is an assigned (and often arbitrary) dollar value that is printed on the stock certificate. To see just how arbitrary a par value can be, consider stock recently issued by Mattel, Inc. This particular preferred stock has a par value of $1 but pays a dividend of $2.50 per year!

A corporation may issue only one common stock, but it may issue many types of preferred stock with varying dividends or dividend rates. To make their preferred stock particularly attractive to investors, some corporations include cumulative, participating, convertible, and callable features in various issues.

Cumulative preferred stock is preferred stock on which any unpaid dividends accumulate and must be paid before any cash dividend is paid to the holders of common stock. Suppose the Bartlett-Jones Corporation has issued cumulative preferred stock that pays $4 per year. In 1985 Bartlett-Jones is faced with a substantial loss, and the board of directors votes to omit dividends on both common and preferred stock. In 1986, however, the board of directors decides that profits

are high enough to pay the required preferred dividend, as well as a $2-per-share dividend on its common stock. The holders of the cumulative preferred stock must first receive $8 per share ($4 for 1985 and $4 for 1986). Then and only then, holders of common stock can receive the $2-per-share dividend declared for 1986.

Participating preferred stock is preferred stock whose owners share in the corporation's earnings, along with the owners of common stock. Here's how it works: First, the required dividend is paid to holders of the preferred stock. Then a declared dividend is paid on the common stock. Finally, any remaining earnings that are available for distribution are shared by both preferred and common stockholders.

Convertible preferred stock is preferred stock that can be exchanged *at the stockholder's option* for a specified number of shares of common stock. This conversion feature provides the investor with the safety of preferred stock and the hope of greater speculative gain through conversion to common stock.

Callable preferred stock is preferred stock that the corporation may exchange *at the corporation's option* for a specified amount of money. Generally, a corporation calls in an issue of preferred stock when management believes it can issue new preferred stock at a lower dividend rate—or possibly common stock with no specified dividend. The price the corporation pays is usually higher than the original par value for the preferred stock.

Retained Earnings Most large corporations distribute only a portion of their after-tax earnings to shareholders. The remainder, the portion of a corporation's profits that is not distributed to stockholders, is called **retained earnings.** Retained earnings are reinvested in the business. Because they are undistributed profits, they are considered a form of equity financing.

Retained earnings represent a large pool of potential equity financing that does not have to be repaid. The amount of a firm's earnings that is to be retained in any year is determined by

Table 16.2 *Total Retained Earnings for Exxon and Coca-Cola, Since Founding*

Exxon Corporation		Coca-Cola Corporation
$25,629.8 million	Total retained earnings as of 1981	$2,109.5 million
+1,581.5 million	Plus after-tax profits retained in 1982	+190.7 million
$27,211.3 million	Total retained earnings as of 1982	$2,300.2 million

Sources: *Exxon Corporation 1982 Annual Report*, p. 21; and *The Coca-Cola Company Annual Report for 1982*, p. 31.

corporate management and approved by the board of directors. As Table 16.2 shows, it can add up to a hefty bit of financing.

Most small and growing corporations pay no cash dividend—or a very small dividend—to their shareholders. All or most earnings are reinvested in the business. Stockholders don't actually lose because of this. Reinvestment tends to increase the value of their stock while it provides essentially cost-free financing. More mature corporations may distribute 40 to 60 percent of their after-tax profits as dividends. Utility companies and other corporations with very stable earnings often pay out as much as 80 to 90 percent of what they earn.

Debt Financing

For a small business, long-term debt financing is generally limited to loans. Large corporations have the additional option of issuing corporate bonds.

Corporate Bonds A **corporate bond** is a corporation's written pledge that it will repay a specified amount of money, with interest. Figure 16.9 shows a typical bond. Note that it includes the interest rate and the maturity date. The **maturity date** is the date on which the corporation is to repay the borrowed money. It also has spaces for the amount of the bond and the bond owner's name.

Large corporations issue bonds in denomina-

tions of from $1000 to $50,000. The total face value of all the bonds in an issue usually runs into the millions of dollars. An individual or firm buys a bond (generally through a securities broker) usually by paying the amount stated on the bond. Between the time of purchase and the maturity date, the corporation pays interest to the bond owner—usually every six months—at the stated rate. At the maturity date, the bond owner returns the bond to the corporation and receives cash equaling its face value.

Maturity dates for bonds generally range from 15 to 40 years after the date of issue. When compared to stockholders, bond owners have first claim on the assets of the corporation in the event that the interest is not paid or the firm becomes insolvent. Some bonds are *callable*, which means that the corporation can buy them back before the maturity date. Usually the corporation must then pay the bond owner a *premium,* or an additional amount above the face value. The amount of the premium is specified, along with other provisions, in the bond indenture. The **bond indenture** is a legal document that details all the conditions relating to a bond issue.

Financing through a bond issue differs considerably from equity financing. Interest must be paid periodically, and the bonds must be redeemed for their face value at maturity. If the corporation defaults on (does not pay) either of these payments, owners of bonds could force it into bankruptcy.

A corporation may use one of two methods to ensure that it has sufficient funds available to redeem a bond issue. First, it can issue the bonds as **serial bonds,** which are bonds of a single issue that mature on different dates. For example, Seaside Productions used a 25-year, $50 million bond issue to finance its expansion. None of the bonds matures during the first 15 years. Thereafter, 10 percent of the bonds mature each year, until all the bonds are retired at the end of the twenty-fifth year. Second, the corporation can establish a sinking fund. A **sinking fund** is a sum of money to which deposits are made each year for the purpose of redeeming a bond issue.

A corporation that issues bonds must also appoint a **trustee,** which is an independent firm or individual that acts as the bond owners' representative. Trustees' duties are most often handled by commercial banks. The corporation must report to the trustee periodically regarding its ability to make interest payments and eventually redeem the bonds. In turn, the trustee transmits this information to the bond owners, along with its own evaluation of the corporation's ability to pay.

Most corporate bonds are **debenture bonds,** which are bonds that are backed only by the reputation of the issuing corporation. To make its

Figure 16.9 *A Corporate Bond. A corporate bond is a corporation's written pledge that it will repay on the date of maturity a specified amount of money, with interest. Source: Used by permission of the LTV Corporation.*

Table 16.3 *Comparison of Long-Term Financing Methods*

Type of Financing	Repayment?	Repayment Period	Interest/Dividend Rate	Businesses That May Use It
Equity				
1. Common stock	No	None	Dividends not required	All corporations that sell their stock to investors
2. Preferred stock	No	None	Dividends not required, but must be paid before common stockholders receive any dividends	Larger corporations that have an established investor base of common stockholders
Debt				
1. Corporate bond	Yes	Usually 15 to 40 years	Interest rates range between 8 and 15%, depending on economic conditions and the risks involved	Larger corporations that investors trust
2. Long-term loan	Yes	Usually 3 to 7 years (up to 15 years)	Interest rates range between 10 and 17%, depending on economic conditions and the risks involved	All firms that can meet the lender's repayment and collateral requirements

bonds more appealing to investors, however, a corporation may issue mortgage bonds. **Mortgage bonds** are corporate bonds that are secured by various assets of the issuing firm. Or the corporation can issue **convertible bonds,** which are bonds that can be exchanged, at the owner's option, for a specified number of shares of the corporation's common stock. The corporation can gain in two ways by issuing convertible bonds. They usually carry a lower interest rate than non-convertible bonds. And once a bond owner converts a bond to common stock, the corporation no longer has to redeem it.

Long-Term Loans Many businesses finance their long-range activities with loans from commercial banks, insurance companies, pension funds, and other financial institutions. Manufacturers and suppliers of heavy equipment and machinery may also provide long-term financing by granting extended credit terms.

When the loan repayment period is longer than one year, the borrower must sign a term-loan agreement. A **term-loan agreement** is a promissory note that requires a borrower to repay a loan in monthly, quarterly, semiannual, or annual installments.

Long-term business loans are normally repaid in 3 to 7 years. Although they may occasionally be unsecured, in most cases the lender requires some type of collateral. Acceptable collateral includes real estate, machinery, and equipment. Lenders may also require that borrowers maintain a minimum amount of working capital. The interest rate and other specific terms are often based on such factors as the reasons for borrowing, the borrowing firm's credit rating, and the collateral.

Cost Comparisons

Table 16.3 compares the different types of equity and long-term debt financing. Obviously, the least expensive type of financing is through an issue of common stock. The most expensive is a long-term loan.

A WORD ABOUT THE USES OF FUNDS

We have mentioned a variety of business uses of funds in this chapter. They range from the payment of recurring expenses, such as rent, wages, and the cost of raw materials, to the payment of such one-time costs as plant expansion and mergers. In general, a business uses funds to pay for the resources it needs to produce and market its products. Even the interest a business pays is really the cost of a resource—money.

The effective use of finances, as we have noted, is an important function of financial management. For the most part, the manner in which funds are used is dictated by the needs of the business. However, financial managers must ensure that funds are available for these uses and that they are obtained at the lowest possible cost. They must also ensure that financing is used as efficiently as possible. This responsibility may involve them in the purchasing practices of various operating departments within a firm. And, finally, financial managers must ensure that funds are available for the repayment of debts in accordance with lenders' financing terms. Prompt repayment is essential to protect the firm's credit rating and its ability to obtain financing in the future.

Chapter Review

SUMMARY

Financial management consists of those activities that are concerned with obtaining money and using it effectively. Short-term financing is money that will be used for one year or less. Speculative production and cash-flow problems may lead to the need for short-term financing. Long-term financing is money that will be used longer than one year. Such financing may be required for expansion, new-product development, and replacement of production facilities. Proper financial management can ensure that money is available when it is needed and that it is used efficiently, in keeping with organizational goals.

A financial plan begins with the organization's objectives. Next these objectives are "translated" into budgets that detail expected income and expenses. From these budgets, which may be combined into an overall cash budget, the financial manager determines what funding will be needed and where it may be obtained. The four principal sources of financing are sales revenue, equity capital (derived from the sale of ownership shares), debt capital, and proceeds from the sale of assets. Once the needed funds have been obtained, the financial manager is responsible for ensuring that they are properly used. This is accomplished through a system of monitoring and evaluating the firm's financial activities.

Most short-term financing is unsecured. That is, no collateral is required. Sources of unsecured short-term financing include trade credit, promissory notes issued to suppliers, unsecured bank loans, commercial paper, and commercial drafts. Sources of secured short-term financing include loans that are secured by inventory or accounts receivable and the outright sale of receivables to factors. Trade credit is the least expensive source of short-term financing; there is no interest charge. The cost of financing through other sources generally depends on the source and on the credit rating of the firm that requires the financing. Factoring is generally the most expensive approach.

Long-term financing may be obtained as equity capital or debt capital. For a corporation, equity capital is obtained by selling either common stock or preferred stock. Common stock is voting stock; holders of common stock elect the corporation's directors and must approve equity funding plans. Holders of preferred stock do not vote on corporate matters, but they must be paid a specified dividend before holders of common stock are paid. Another source of equity funding is retained earnings, which are undistributed earnings that are reinvested in the corporation.

Sources of long-term debt financing are the sale of corporate bonds and long-term loans. Money that is realized from the sale of bonds must be repaid when the bonds mature. In addition, interest must be paid on that money from the time the bonds are sold until maturity. Bonds may mature in up to 40 years, but long-term loans are generally repaid in 3 to 7 years. The rate of loan interest usually depends on the financial status of the borrower and on the kind of collateral that is pledged to back up the loan.

To a great extent, firms are financed through the investments of individuals—money that people have deposited in banks or have used to purchase stocks and bonds. In the next chapter, we shall look at this "flip side" of finance—personal investment. You will see why people invest their money in business and how they go about it.

KEY TERMS

You should now be able to define and give an example relevant to each of the following terms:

financial management	bond indenture
short-term financing	serial bonds
speculative production	sinking fund
cash flow	trustee
long-term financing	debenture bonds
financial plan	mortgage bonds
budget	convertible bonds
zero-base budgeting	term-loan agreement
equity capital	
debt capital	
unsecured financing	
trade credit	
promissory note	
prime interest rate	
revolving credit agreement	
commercial paper	
commercial draft	
accounts receivable	
factor	
dividends	
common stock	
pre-emptive rights	
preferred stock	
par value	
cumulative preferred stock	
participating preferred stock	
convertible preferred stock	
callable preferred stock	
retained earnings	
corporate bond	
maturity date	

QUESTIONS AND EXERCISES
Review Questions

1. How is short-term financing distinguished from long-term financing? Give two business uses of each of these types of financing.
2. What is financial management concerned with? How can it help a business?
3. What is the function of budgets in financial planning?
4. How does a financial manager monitor and evaluate a firm's financing?
5. What are the four general sources of financing?
6. How is unsecured financing different from secured financing?
7. How important is trade credit as a source of short-term financing? How is trade credit different from other kinds of short-term financing?
8. What is the difference between a line of credit and a revolving credit agreement?
9. Distinguish between a commercial draft and a promissory note. Why would a supplier require either of these?
10. Explain how factoring works. Of what benefit is factoring to a firm that sells its receivables?
11. What are the advantages of financing through the sale of stock? What are pre-emptive rights?
12. Explain each of the following features of preferred stock: (a) the cumulative feature, (b) the participating feature, and (c) the convertible feature.
13. Where do a corporation's retained earnings come from? What are the advantages of this type of financing?
14. Describe the two methods used to ensure that funds are available to redeem corporate bonds at maturity.

Discussion Questions

1. Among other actions, U.S. Steel closed fifteen plants, laid off workers, and deferred some capital spending. In what way are such actions a part of financial management?
2. How would you justify U.S. Steel's purchase of Marathon Oil in light of its financial problems—especially the losses it had suffered?
3. Discuss the pros and cons of zero-base budgeting from the point of view of (a) the department heads who must do the budgeting and (b) the financial manager who must approve departmental budgets.
4. Why would a supplier offer both trade credit and cash discounts to its customers?
5. In what circumstances might a large corporation sell stock rather than bonds to obtain long-term financing? In what circumstances would it sell bonds rather than stock?
6. Why would a lender offer unsecured loans when it could demand collateral?
7. As the financial manager of Newton's Clothing Store, what would you do with the excess cash that the firm expects to have in the second and fourth quarters? (See Figure 16.4.)

Exercises

1. Suppose you are responsible for setting a bank's interest rates. Your prime rate is 12 percent. What interest rate would you charge a new, medium-sized firm for:
   a. A 6-month unsecured loan?
   b. Loans on a revolving credit agreement? (Also specify the commitment fee.)
   c. A 3-month loan secured by the firm's accounts receivable?
   d. A 5-year loan secured by the firm's land and buildings?

Explain briefly how you arrived at each interest rate.

2. You want to borrow funds to finance next year's college expenses. Set up a budget showing your expected income and expenses, and determine how much money you will need to borrow. Then outline a plan for repaying the borrowed funds. Provide enough detail to convince your financing source to advance you the money.

CASE 16-1

The Timing Aspect of Financial Planning at Chrysler

On February 25, 1983, Chrysler Corporation registered a public offering of 10 million shares of common stock with the Securities and Exchange Commission. Chrysler's stock offering led to three unexpected events. First, the price of Chrysler's existing stock jumped almost $2 per share in one day. Second, there was so much investor interest in the new issue that Chrysler was able to sell not just 10 million shares, as originally planned, but 26 million shares. Third, only four weeks after the new stock was issued, the price of Chrysler stock had risen by more than 50 percent.

Clearly, Chrysler's management had picked an almost perfect time to sell additional stock. In February 1983, interest rates were lower than they had been for at least a year. This factor alone made stock a more attractive investment than bonds, certificates of deposit, or U.S. Government Treasury Bills. In addition, all major stock averages were on the rise, and the volume of stock traded on a daily basis was heavy. Both were signs of a strong investor interest in stocks.

Moreover, Chrysler's financial condition had improved considerably, owing to brisk sales of its new K-car line. The future for Chrysler looked much brighter than it had in the early 1980s, when Chrysler was forced to obtain government guarantees to secure long-term debt financing.

Chrysler was not the only large corporation to sell stock in early 1983. In fact, American corporations raised over $21.7 billion during the first 6 months of that year. Although 75 percent of the new stock issues were sold by large corporations with stock already available, 25 percent were sold by firms offering stock for the first time. One market analyst was prompted to ask, "Why are all these corporations selling common stock?"[3]

1. Why *were* so many corporations selling stock in early 1983?
2. How do general economic conditions influence the means that a firm uses to obtain long-term financing?

CASE 16-2

"Greenmail" Is Not a Firm Name

Early in 1984, Saul P. Steinberg and his Reliance Group Holdings, Inc. began to accumulate shares of Walt Disney Productions common stock. At about the same time, Roy E. Disney, a nephew of company founder Walt Disney, resigned from the firm's board of directors and began to increase his own holdings in Disney Productions. Industry analysts suggested that Steinberg, either alone or with Roy Disney, was preparing for a hostile takeover of the firm. (A hostile takeover is, essentially, the acquisition of a controlling interest in a firm—by purchasing common stock—in opposition to the wishes of the present management.)

To counter a possible takeover, Disney management took several steps. Among these were the tripling of its line of bank credit to $1.3 billion, and the issuing of $538 million worth of new stock. The new stock, which had the effect of diluting Steinberg's holdings, was used to purchase a real-estate development firm and a greeting-card producer.

Disney Productions' income had been dropping—by 16 percent in 1982 and 7 percent in 1983. So the question arises as to why anyone would want to take over the firm. A possible reason is the value of its film library (over $500 million) and its 28,000 acres of Florida land (which could be worth from $1,000 to $1,000,000 per acre). According to one estimate, the company's assets may be worth as much as $100 per share. Steinberg and his associates, who already owned 11.1 percent of Disney, offered to buy another 37.9 percent of the firm's common stock at $67.50 per share. Naturally, the market price of the stock took an upward course.

Disney's management reacted with "all the steadfast coolness of a flock of sheep at the first whiff of wolf."[4] In June 1984, the firm agreed to pay Steinberg and his associates about $77 per share for their stock, plus $28 million for Steinberg's "out-of-pocket expenses." The profit on the stock sale alone came to $31.7 million. Within days, the market price of Disney common stock tumbled from $65 to about $51.

The process in which stock is repurchased from particular investors at a premium, in order to prevent a hostile takeover, is called "greenmail." (The connection with the term "blackmail" is fairly evident.) The Disney case was far from the first. Other recent above-market-price buyouts involved Texaco (10 percent of its common stock yielded a $400 million profit to the sellers); Quaker State (9 percent of its stock yielded an $11 million profit); and Warner Communications (9 percent yielded a profit of $50 million).

The Disney buyout, however, may be one of the last. Several stockholders who could not sell their stock at a premium—and who lost when the value of their stock decreased—have filed suit against Disney's management. They claim that the premium paid to Steinberg is actually a dividend; they want the firm to distribute a similar dividend to all other stockholders. At the same time, Congress and the Securities and Exchange Commission are investigating methods of eliminating greenmail—which is, at present, perfectly legal.[5]

1. What might be some consequences of Disney Productions' action in combating the takeover, especially with regard to its financial position and financial planning?
2. What steps can Disney management take to improve its financial position?

CHAPTER

SEVENTEEN
Personal Investment

Corporations sell stocks and bonds to raise money. Firms or individuals buy these pieces of paper as investments. People also buy pieces of paper that give them only the right to purchase stocks at some later time, if they should decide to do so. And they invest in commodities ranging from gold to pork bellies—with absolutely no intention of ever accepting delivery of these products. In fact, there are investments to please just about every taste, from ultra-conservative to wildly speculative. In this chapter we shall examine a number of them. And we shall see how they might be used to help achieve an individual's personal investment goals. After studying the chapter, you should understand:

1. Why it is necessary to develop a personal investment plan, and how to do so

2. The three factors—safety, income, and growth—that link investment planning to the various types of investments

3. The traditional investment alternatives: savings accounts, stocks, bonds, and mutual funds

4. More speculative investment techniques, including buying on margin and trading in options and commodities

5. How securities are bought and sold through brokerage firms and securities exchanges

6. The various sources of financial information, especially newspaper stock quotations and stock indexes

7. How federal and state authorities regulate trading in securities

Consider this:

Victor Kiam says he tried a Remington electric shaver and liked it so much that he bought the company. Now he does television commercials in a bathrobe, and he seems to be enjoying himself while his investment grows.

Marvin Jensen had a similar experience, but on a much smaller scale. In early November of 1983, he bought his family an Intellivision cartridge-driven home video console. The Jensens enjoyed it tremendously. Marvin's two sons—aged 14 and 12—seemed particularly good at the skill games. Marvin and his wife Louise liked an adventure game that Jensen had purchased as an extra cartridge. Within two weeks of purchasing the console, the Jensens had bought four additional Intellivision cartridges.

At the time they purchased the Intellivision console, the Jensens had about $8000 invested in a money market account. The interest they earned on the account had been falling throughout 1983, as the economy improved and interest rates declined. They were considering a shift in investments—perhaps to a stock, because stock prices were going up as interest rates went down. Their enjoyment of Intellivision, along with the general hoopla over home video games and home computers, led them to consider Mattel, Inc., the producer of Intellivision, as a possibility for investment.

The Jensens decided that Mattel must be rolling in profits from its popular and exciting games. Marvin "researched" the firm's common stock in the Sunday newspaper. He found that its price had been more than $16 per share earlier in 1983 but had dropped to about $6 per share. At that bargain price, the Jensens could afford to buy 1000 shares. They did exactly that. And, to save on the commission, they purchased their stock through a discount brokerage house. (Discount stock brokers charge lower commissions to buy and sell securities for their clients, but most offer little investment advice.)

Marvin and Louise probably would not have spent $6000 in any other way without first shopping carefully and learning all they could about their purchase. But, like many other amateur investors, they seemed to feel it was reasonable to jump into the stock market almost blindly. If the Jensens had done a little homework before taking the plunge, they would have found out that Mattel (1) was not doing very well with Intellivision and (2) was expected to abandon the home electronics and computer business.

At this point, the Jensens had made two common investing errors. First, they had arbitrarily decided to invest, without considering what they wanted to accomplish through their investing. Second, they had not considered any investment alternatives other than the Mattel stock. Conscientious investors—even amateurs—spend hours each week evaluating possible investments. The information they need is readily available from periodicals, corporate reports, stock brokers and financial planners, and investment services. The cost of obtaining this information—in both time and money—is well worth the difference it makes in the success of their investment activities.

An Ohio housewife, for example, unexpectedly inherited $50,000 in 1972. Ten years later, she had transformed her inheritance into a portfolio of 88 stocks worth almost $250,000. Her investment secret is simple: She spends 10 to 15 hours each week evaluating stocks and maintaining comprehensive records on several hundred corporations.[1]

But what happened to Marvin and Louise Jensen and their Mattel stock? In spite of their lack of investing knowledge, the Jensens seemed to have done well. The market price of their stock began to increase. By the end of February 1984, it had reached $9.25 per share. If they had sold the stock at that time, they would have realized a profit of about $3000, or 50 percent of their investment—and in only three months' time.

But the Jensens had bought Mattel stock in ignorance, and for the wrong reasons. Now they remained in ignorance. As they watched the price rise to $9.25, they took that increase as a sign that their "analysis" was correct: Mattel stock would go even higher. Here the Jensens made a third common mistake. They decided to sit back and let their investment manage itself. They didn't bother to find out why the stock had increased in price, whether it was expected to increase further because of some actions the firm had taken, or how the experts thought the stock might behave in the long run. They simply watched newspaper coverage of the price of Mattel's common stock.

Unfortunately, what the Jensens watched was a slow but steady decline. By early May of 1984, the price of Mattel common was down to $7.50 per share. Half their "paper profit" was lost. Now they started thinking about alternatives. Should they sell at that point in order to salvage at least some profit? Or should they continue to sit on the stock, expecting its price to start increasing again at any time? And why was the price going down anyway?

This last question bothered Marvin Jensen so much that he finally consulted a brokerage firm. The first consultation led to another, and eventually to a realistic investment plan for the Jensens—a plan based on their own financial situation and investment goals. As part of that plan, the Jensens sold their Mattel stock at $7 per share and used the proceeds to begin a balanced investment portfolio.[2]

The Jensens (that's not their real name) were lucky. They made a few dollars from their investment. (Actually, when brokers' commissions are taken into account, they would have done about as well—with much less risk—by leaving their money in the money market account.) Over the long run, though, people who invest on the basis of hunches or tips generally lose. An investment—even a small one—is a business venture. And success in business requires knowledge, skill, and experience. Moreover, like other business ventures, investing must begin with one or more objectives and a plan for attaining these objectives. Only when the investor's resources are carefully managed according to the plan is there a good chance of reaching the goal.

THE CONCEPT OF PERSONAL INVESTMENT

Personal investment is the use of one's personal funds to earn a financial return. Thus, in the most general sense, the objective of investing is to earn money with money. But that objective is completely useless for the individual, because it is so vague and so easily attained. If you place $100 in a savings account paying 5.5 percent annual interest, your money will earn 46 cents in 1 month. If your objective is simply to earn money with your $100, you will have attained that objective at the end of the month. Then what do you do?

Investment Objectives

To be useful, an investment objective must be specific and measurable. It must also be tailored to the individual so that it takes into account his or her particular financial circumstances and needs. Further, it must be oriented toward the future, because investing is, in general, a long-term undertaking. And finally, an investment goal must be realistic in terms of the economic conditions that prevail and the investment opportunities that are available.

Some counselors suggest that investment
goals be stated in terms of money: "By January
1, 1995, I will have total assets of $80,000."
Others believe that people are more motivated
to work toward goals that are stated in terms of
the particular things they desire: "By May 1,
1990, I will have accumulated enough money so
that I can take a year off from work to travel
around the world." Like the objectives themselves, how they are stated depends on the individual to whom they apply.

The following can be helpful in establishing
valid investment objectives.

1. Why do I want to obtain some specific amount
   of money?
2. How much money will I need, and when?
3. What are the consequences if I don't obtain it
   all?
4. Is it reasonable to assume that I can obtain
   the amount of money I will need?
5. Do I expect my financial or personal situation

to change in a way that will affect my investment goals?
6. Am I willing to make the sacrifices that are
   necessary to ensure that my financial goals
   are met?

A Personal Plan of Action

Once specific goals have been formulated, investment planning for an individual is similar to
planning for a business. If the goals are realistic,
investment opportunities will be available to implement them. Investment planning begins with
the assessment of these opportunities—including
the potential return and the risk involved in each.
At the very least, this requires some expert advice and careful study. (There are many companies and individuals now providing financial services. Two professional associations, the College
for Financial Planners in Denver and the International Association for Financial Planning in Atlanta, have about 16,000 members.) Then, gen-

erally through a process of comparison and elimination, particular alternatives are chosen and combined into an investment plan.

Many investment counselors suggest that an investment program begin with the accumulation of an "emergency fund"—a certain amount of money that can be obtained quickly in case of immediate need. This money should be deposited in a savings account at the highest available interest rate. (Although savings accounts are actually time deposits, the money can almost always be withdrawn immediately. By comparison, it may take a week or more to exchange stocks or bonds for cash.) The amount of money that should be salted away in the emergency fund varies from person to person. However, most investment planners agree that an amount equal to three months' salary (after taxes) is reasonable.[3]

Once the emergency account is established, additional funds may be invested according to the individual's investment plan. Some additional funds may already be available, or money for further investing may be saved out of earnings. In either case, savings is an important part of the typical investment plan.

Once a plan has been put into operation, it must be monitored and, if necessary, modified. As we noted earlier, the most successful investors spend hours each week evaluating their own investments and investigating new investment opportunities. A particular personal investment plan may or may not need such close supervision. In fact, some people prefer investments that are monitored by professionals—mutual funds, for example.

However, both the investor's circumstances and economic conditions are subject to change. Hence all investment programs should be re-evaluated regularly. An investor may take a new job at a substantially higher salary. As a result, his or her investment goals may change, and the present investment plan may become obsolete. Other investors may want to shift some of their investments in response to a general increase or decrease in interest rates.

Three Important Factors in Personal Investment

To implement a personal investment plan, an individual can choose from thousands of specific investments. How can the individual (or an investment counselor) tell which investments are "right" for the plan and which are not? One way to do so—or at least to start doing so—is to match potential investments with investment goals in terms of three factors: safety, income, and growth potential. (See Figure 17.1.)

The Safety Factor Safety in an investment means minimal risk of loss. Investment goals that require a steady increase in value or a fairly certain annual return are those that stress safety. In general, they are implemented with the more conservative investments, such as savings accounts, whose safety is guaranteed up to $100,000 by the FDIC or FSLIC.

Other relatively safe investments include highly rated corporate and municipal bonds and the stocks of certain highly regarded corporations—sometimes called "blue-chip stocks." These corporations are generally industry leaders that have provided stable earnings and dividends over a number of years. Examples include Du Pont, Xerox, Texaco, and General Electric.

To implement goals that stress a high return on their investment, investors must generally give up some safety. How much risk should they take in exchange for how much return? This question is almost impossible to answer for someone else, because the answer depends so much

Figure 17.1 Criteria for Personal Investment

on the individual and his or her investment goals. However, in general, *the potential return should be directly related to the risk that is assumed.* That is, the greater the risk, the greater the potential monetary reward should be.

As we will see shortly, there are a number of risky—and potentially profitable—investments. They include some stocks, commodities, and stock options. The securities issued by new and growing corporations usually fall in this category.

Not too long ago, the stock of Computer-Tabulating-Recording Company was considered a risky investment. Today the company is known as International Business Machines (IBM), and its stock is part of most conservative investment portfolios.

The Income Factor Savings accounts, bonds, and certain stocks pay a predictable amount of interest or dividends each year. Such investments are generally used to implement investment goals that stress periodic income.

The investor in savings accounts and bonds knows exactly how much income he or she will receive each year. The dividends paid to stockholders can and do vary, even for the largest and most stable corporations. However, a number of corporations have built their reputations on a policy of paying dividends every three months. (Those listed in Table 17.1 have paid dividends to their owners for at least 80 years.) The stocks of these corporations are often purchased primarily for income.

The Growth Factor A corporation that is in the process of growing usually pays a small cash dividend or no dividend at all. Instead, profits are reinvested in the business (as retained earnings) to finance additional expansion. Such a corporation's stockholders receive little or no income from their investments. However, the value of their stock increases as the corporation grows.

Investment goals that stress growth, or an increase in the value of the investment, can be implemented by purchasing the stocks of such "growth corporations." Investors should realize, however, that they are giving up present income in return for this potential growth. During the first part of the 1980s, firms in the electronics, energy, health care, and financial services industries showed the greatest growth. They are expected to continue to grow at least through the remainder of this decade. Individual firms within these industries may grow at a slower or a faster rate than the industry as a whole—or they may not grow at all.

Table 17.1 *Corporations That, Through 1983, Had Made Consecutive Dividend Payments for at Least 80 Years*

Corporation	Dividends Since	Type of Business
Allied Corporation	1887	Chemical & Petroleum Products
American Telephone and Telegraph	1881	Telephone Utility
Borden, Inc.	1899	Foods
Burroughs Corporation	1895	Computers
Commonwealth Edison Company	1890	Electric Utility
Continental Corporation	1854	Insurance
Exxon Corporation	1882	Chemical & Petroleum Products
General Electric Company	1899	Electrical Equipment
Nabisco Brands, Inc.	1899	Foods
Norfolk & Western Railway Co.	1901	Railroad
PPG Industries, Inc.	1899	Glass
Procter & Gamble Company	1891	Soap Products
Standard Oil Co. (Indiana)	1894	Chemical & Petroleum Products
Union Pacific Corporation	1900	Railroad

Source: *Standard & Poor's 500 Stock Market Encyclopedia*, Vol. 6, No. 1, February 1984. Used by permission.

Different kinds of investments offer different combinations of the safety, income, and growth factors that we have discussed. Keep the nature of that important "mix" in mind as we go on to consider various investment alternatives.

TRADITIONAL INVESTMENT ALTERNATIVES

In this section and the next, we shall look at some of the types of investments that are available to investors. A number of them have already been discussed. Others have only been mentioned and will be examined in more detail. Still others may be completely new to you. (See Figure 17.2.)

Bank Accounts

Bank accounts that pay interest—and are therefore investments—include passbook savings accounts, certificates of deposit, and NOW accounts. These were discussed in Chapter 15. They are the most conservative of all investments, and they provide safety and either income or growth. That is, the interest paid on bank accounts can be withdrawn to serve as income,

or it can be left on deposit to earn additional interest and increase the size of the bank account. Figure 17.3 shows how a $5000 deposit will grow at various interest rates, when both the principal amount and the interest remain in the account.

Figure 17.2 *Investment Alternatives. Traditional investments involve less risk than speculative, or high-risk, investments.*

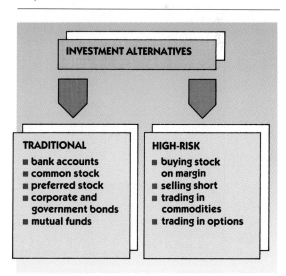

INVESTMENT ALTERNATIVES

TRADITIONAL
- bank accounts
- common stock
- preferred stock
- corporate and government bonds
- mutual funds

HIGH-RISK
- buying stock on margin
- selling short
- trading in commodities
- trading in options

The banking industry was deregulated in 1980. This meant that banks were free of certain government regulations and could compete more aggressively for customers. Besides offering higher rates on deposits and more types of accounts, banks have started to market their products and advertise their services in ways that were once used only by more "glamorous" industries. For example, Houston's Med Center Bank offers the weekend use of a seven-passenger plane and crew—for the cost of fuel only—to customers with accounts over $100,000.

Common Stock

We discussed common stock in Chapters 3 and 16. Now it is time to look at them specifically from the investor's viewpoint.

□ Common stock represents a share in the ownership of a corporation.
□ Corporations need not pay dividends on their

common stock, although many firms have long records of making consecutive dividend payments.
□ Cash dividends are paid out of profits, so investors who intend to buy stock for income must evaluate the firm's earning potential.
□ An increase (or decrease) in the market value of a certain stock increases (or decreases) the value of an investment in that stock.

The **market value** of a stock is the price of one share of the stock at a particular time. It is determined solely by the interaction of buyers and sellers in the various stock markets. (Note that market value is different from *par value,* which, as we noted in Chapter 16, is an arbitrary value that the issuing corporation assigns to a stock.)

Stock Dividends   A corporation may pay stock dividends in place of—or in addition to—cash dividends. A **stock dividend** is a dividend in the form of additional stock. It is paid to shareholders

Figure 17.3   Investment in a Bank Account. This chart shows how $5000 will grow depending on the duration of the deposit and on the rate of interest (when both the original amount—or principal—and the interest remain in the account).

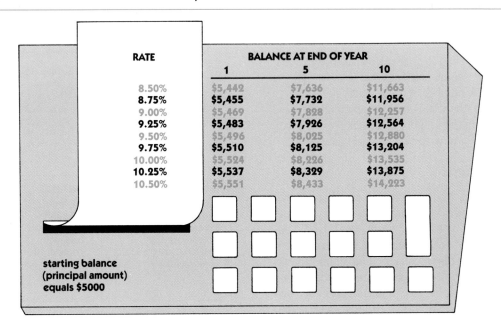

RATE	BALANCE AT END OF YEAR		
	1	5	10
8.50%	$5,442	$7,636	$11,663
8.75%	$5,455	$7,732	$11,956
9.00%	$5,469	$7,828	$12,257
9.25%	$5,483	$7,926	$12,564
9.50%	$5,496	$8,025	$12,880
9.75%	$5,510	$8,125	$13,204
10.00%	$5,524	$8,226	$13,535
10.25%	$5,537	$8,329	$13,875
10.50%	$5,551	$8,433	$14,223

starting balance
(principal amount)
equals $5000

just as cash dividends are paid: in proportion to the number of shares they own. An individual stockholder may sell the additional stock to obtain income or retain it to increase the total value of her or his stock holdings.

Stock Splits As a corporation prospers and grows, its stock becomes worth more. In other words, the market value of the stock tends to grow along with the company. The directors of many corporations feel that there is an optimal price range within which their firm's stock is most attractive to investors. When the market value increases beyond that range, they may declare a *stock split* to bring the price down. A **stock split** is the division of each outstanding share of a corporation's stock into a greater number of shares. A stock split, in and of itself, does not increase the value of any investor's holdings, although it is probably more likely to take place during a prosperous period for the company.

The commonest stock splits result in one, two, or three new shares for each original share. (See Figure 17.4.) The value of an original share is then reduced proportionally. As an example, IBM's common stock had a market value of $280 per share in 1979. The corporation's directors declared a four-for-one stock split and issued three additional shares to the owner of each original share of IBM. Because there were then four times as many shares as there were before, each share was worth only $280 ÷ 4, or $70. Every shareholder retained his or her proportional ownership of the firm. But, at the lower price, the stock was more attractive to the investing public because there is a greater potential for a rapid increase in dollar value.

Preferred Stock

As we noted in Chapter 16, the owners of a firm's preferred stock must receive their cash dividends before the owners of common stock are paid any dividends. Moreover, preferred-stock dividends are specified on the stock certificates. And the owners of preferred stock have first claim, after

One out of every six Americans—about 42 million of them—now own shares in companies or in equity mutual funds, according to the latest (mid-1983) survey conducted by the New York Stock Exchange. The typical adult shareowner is a 44½-year-old woman, who has a portfolio worth $5100, says Stock Exchange Chairman William M. Batten.

In mid-1983, 24 percent of all shareholders owned equity mutual funds, compared to the 16 percent in the last survey two years ago. More than 7.3 million shareholders bought stock for the first time in the last two years. The largest proportion of new investors (34.7 percent) bought their stock through a broker-dealer. But the next largest group (32.8 percent) became investors through company-sponsored stock purchase plans. Another significant share (8 percent) was accounted for by Individual Retirement Accounts.

Not surprisingly, considering the large number of first-time investors, who probably bought less than round-lots, the size of the average portfolio declined to $5100 from $5450 two years ago.

Source: *Dun's Business Month,* January 1984, p. 32.

Figure 17.4 *Stock Split. When the market value of a company's stock increases beyond the range that the company's board of directors believes is most attractive to investors, then the directors may declare a stock split, such as one to four, to bring down the price.*

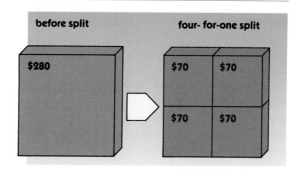

bondholders, on the assets of the issuing corporation. These features tend to provide the holders of preferred stocks with safety and a predictable income.

In addition, holders of *cumulative* preferred stocks are assured that omitted dividends will be paid to them before holders of common stock receive any dividends. Holders of *participating* preferred stock may earn more than the specified dividend if the firm has a good year. The participating feature enables preferred stockholders to share in surplus profit, along with common stockholders, after the designated amounts have been paid to both classes of stockholders. And holders of *convertible* preferred stock may profit through growth as well as from dividends: if the value of a firm's common stock increases, the market value of its convertible preferred stock also grows. Convertibility allows the owner of convertible preferred stock to combine the lower risk of preferred stock with the possibility of greater speculative gain through conversion to common stock.

Corporate and Government Bonds

In Chapter 16 we discussed the issuing of bonds by corporations to obtain financing. The United States government and state and local governments also issue bonds, and for the same reason. In addition, many government and municipal bonds are tax free, which enables owners to earn income that is exempt from federal income taxes.

Bonds are generally considered a more conservative investment than either preferred or common stocks. But they are less conservative than bank accounts. They are primarily income-producing investments. However, when interest rates are rising, the market value of existing bonds typically declines. They may then be purchased for less than their face value. By holding such bonds until maturity, or until interest rates decline (causing their market values to increase), bond owners can realize some profit through the growth of their investments.

Convertible bonds generally carry a lower interest rate than nonconvertible bonds—by about 2 percent. In return for accepting a lower interest rate, holders of convertible bonds have the opportunity to benefit through investment growth. Consider, for example, the White Consolidated Industries convertible bond that pays 5.5 percent interest annually and matures in 1992. Each $1000 bond may be converted (exchanged), at the owner's option, for 39 shares of White common stock. If the price of White common stock increases, the value of the convertible bond will increase as well—and vice versa.

The safety of a particular bond, issued by a particular firm or government, depends very much on the financial strength of the issuer. For example, in 1983 the Washington Public Power Supply could not pay off their debt on municipal bonds worth more than $2 billion dollars and thousands of investors lost money. Several years ago, New York City was on the verge of *defaulting* on (failing to redeem) an issue of bonds that was about to mature. Strong financial measures and new loans saved the city and the bondholders, but the experience affected the market value of all New York City bonds. In addition, the city had to pay higher-than-usual interest rates to attract investors to new issues of bonds.

Mutual Funds

Mutual funds combine and invest the funds of many individual investors, under the guidance of professional managers. Their major advantages are this professional management and their *diversification,* or investment in a wide variety of securities. Diversification spells safety, because an occasional loss incurred with one security is usually offset by gains from other investments.

Mutual-Fund Shares and Fees A *closed-end* mutual fund sells shares (in the fund) to investors only when the fund is organized. And only a specified number of shares are made available at that time. Once all the shares are sold, an investor

With some 600 mutual funds looking to lure investors' dollars, the decision to launch a new fund carries with it substantial risk. In the best of all possible worlds, one would first spot a niche that no one else has entered and then be able to convince wary underwriters, and the public, that the fund's managers have an especially keen eye for picking winners in the fund's chosen sector. But in today's competitive environment, that's a highly unlikely scenario.

Hundreds of funds already trade daily under the headings "capital appreciation," "growth," "small-company growth," "growth and income," and "equity-income." And, spurred by the technology stocks' year-long surge that started in late 1982, scores of special-purpose funds have been rushed to market, with the scientific and technological sectors of the economy as their primary underpinning.

For new-fund managers, then, the question remains the same: What do you bring to market that's new?

To Marc Klee, the 29-year-old vice president and co-manager of the National Telecommunications & Technology Fund Inc. (Teletech), a closed-end growth fund inaugurated in January 1983, the answer was clear: a chance to invest in the rough-and-tumble world of information and data processing while enjoying the protection afforded by a diversified portfolio and, one hoped, meticulous management.

"More so in the telecommunications field than in perhaps any other," says Klee, a graduate of the University of Pennsylvania's Wharton business school, "investors need time to do the research and the resources to play the game. These companies have more rapidly changing fundamentals because of their more rapidly changing product life cycles."

Source: Robert Sonenclar, *Financial World,* March 21–April 3, 1984, p. 38.

can purchase shares only from some other investor who is willing to sell them. The mutual fund itself is under no obligation to buy back shares from investors.

An *open-end* mutual fund issues and sells new shares to any investor who requests them. It also buys back shares from owners who wish to sell all or part of their holdings. For this reason, open-end funds are the more popular.

With regard to costs, there are again two types of mutual funds. An individual who invests in a *load fund* pays a sales charge every time he or she purchases shares. This charge is typically 7 to 8.5 percent of the investment. The purchaser of shares in a *no-load fund*, on the other hand, pays no sales charges at all.

In addition, most funds (of either type) collect a management fee of about 0.5 to 1 percent of the total dollar amount invested. No-load funds generally have higher management fees, primarily because they assess no sales charges.

Mutual-Fund Investments The managers of mutual funds tailor their investment portfolios to provide growth, income, or a combination of both. Most mutual funds are fairly conservative and relatively safe, although there are some speculative mutual funds. The major categories of funds, in terms of the types of securities they invest in, are as follows:

□ *Balanced funds,* which apportion their investments among common stocks, preferred stocks, and bonds

By pooling money from a large number of investors under professional management and investing in a diversified group of securities, mutual funds can offer stable investment returns. Source: Courtesy of Dreyfus Corp.

□ *Income funds,* which invest in stocks and bonds that pay high dividends and interest

□ *Growth–income funds,* which invest in common and preferred stocks that pay good dividends *and* are expected to increase in market value

□ *Growth funds,* which invest in the common stock of well-managed, rapidly growing corporations

□ *Money market funds,* which invest in short-term corporate obligations and government securities that offer high interest

Recently, the most popular mutual funds have been the money market funds, primarily because they offer high returns with less risk than comparable investments. Another attractive feature is the investor's ability to withdraw money from these funds quickly if necessary—by making a phone call, sending a telegram, or writing a check.

MORE SPECULATIVE INVESTMENT TECHNIQUES

A **speculative investment** is an investment that is made in the hope of earning a relatively large profit in a short time. (See the high-risk investment categories in Figure 17.2.) Some securities may be speculative by their very nature; that is, they are quite risky. (In this sense, a bet on a roulette wheel in a Las Vegas casino is a speculative investment.) However, most speculative investments become so because of the methods that are used by investors to earn a quick profit. These methods can lead to large losses as well as to gains. They should not be used by anyone who does not fully understand the risks that are involved.

The investor should also realize that the tax on short-term capital gains (such as money earned by buying securities and selling them within one year) is considerably higher than the tax on profit earned upon selling securities that the investor has held more than one year.

Buying Stock on Margin

An investor buys stock *on margin* by borrowing part of the purchase price, usually from a stock brokerage firm. As we noted in Chapter 15, the **margin requirement** is the proportion of the price of a stock that cannot be borrowed. This requirement, which is set by the Federal Reserve System, is currently 50 percent.

Thus, investors can presently borrow up to half the cost of a stock purchase. But why would they want to do so? Simply because they can buy twice as much stock by buying on margin. Suppose an investor expects the market price of a certain stock to increase in the next month or two. Let's say this investor has enough money to purchase 1000 shares of the stock. But if she buys on margin, she can purchase an additional 1000 shares. If the price of the stock increases by $5 per share, her profit will be $5 × 1000, or $5000, if she pays cash. But it will be $5 × 2000, or $10,000, if she buys on margin. That is, she will earn double the profit (less the interest she pays on the borrowed money) by buying her shares on margin.

The use of borrowed funds to increase the return on an investment is called **leverage.** Profit is earned by both the borrowed funds and the borrower's own money. The borrower retains all the profit and pays only interest for the temporary use of the borrowed funds. Note that the stock purchased on margin serves as collateral for the borrowed funds.

If all goes as expected, investors can increase their profits by using leverage—buying stocks on margin. However, margin buyers are subject to two problems. First, if the market price of the purchased stock does not increase as quickly as expected, interest costs mount and will eventually drain away the investor's profit. Second, if the price of the purchased stock falls, the leverage works against the investor. That is, because the margin buyer has purchased twice as much stock, he or she loses twice as much money.

Moreover, any decrease in the value of the stock is considered to come out of the investor's own funds, not out of the borrowed funds. If the stock's market value decreases to approximately half of the original price, the investor will receive a margin call from the brokerage firm. To satisfy the margin call, the investor must then provide additional cash or securities. If he or she cannot do so, the stock is sold and the proceeds are used to pay off the loan.

Selling Short

Normally, investors buy stocks expecting that they will increase in value and can then be sold at a profit. This procedure is referred to as **buying long.** However, many securities decrease in value, for various reasons. More risk-oriented investors can use a procedure called *selling short* to make a profit when the price of an individual security is falling. **Selling short** is the process of selling stock that an investor does not actually own but has borrowed from a stock broker and will repay at a later date. The idea is to sell at today's higher price and then buy later at a lower price.

To make a profit from a short transaction, the investor must proceed as follows:

1. Arrange to borrow a certain number of shares of a particular stock from a stock broker.
2. Sell the borrowed stock immediately, assuming that its price will drop in a reasonably short time.
3. Once the price does drop, buy the same number of shares as was sold in step 2.
4. Give the newly purchased stock to the stock broker, in return for the borrowed stock.

The investor's profit is the difference between the amount received in step 2 and the amount paid in step 3, less the broker's commission. Of course, if the market price of the stock increases after the investor has sold it in step 2, he or she loses money.

Trading in Commodities

The ownership of certain commodities (including cattle, hogs, pork bellies, various grains, sugar, coffee, frozen concentrated orange juice, cotton, gold, silver, and copper) is traded on a regular basis. The buying and selling of commodities for immediate delivery is called **spot trading.** However, most commodities transactions involve a future delivery date. A **futures contract** is an agreement to buy or sell a commodity at a guaranteed price on some specified future date.

Commodity trading is much more risky than trading in securities, because prices fluctuate widely. Almost any change in economic conditions, supply and demand, or even the weather affects commodity prices. An unexpected freeze in Florida can cause the price of orange juice futures to soar. An exceptionally good harvest can have the opposite effect on grain and cattle futures. Rumors, natural disasters, and political events can also propel commodity prices up or down very quickly. These continual price movements and the relatively low margin requirements tend to attract numbers of speculators to the

This "stock" is a relatively risky investment. Commodity prices are affected by many changeable conditions, including general economic trends, politics, and the weather.
Source: © 1982 Ken Kaufman, Black Star.

commodity markets. The same characteristics make these markets too risky for most investors.

Trading in Options

An **option** is the right to buy or sell a specified amount of stock at a specified price within a certain period of time. Options are purchased and sold by investors who expect the price of a stock to change. The Chicago Board Options Exchange (CBOE) is an established exchange for the trading of options on selected stocks. The CBOE provides more liquidity and uniformity in options trading than is found in the traditional over-the-counter options market.

A *call option* gives the purchaser the right to *buy* the stock at a specified price within a specified time. Call options are sold by owners of stock. They are purchased by investors who expect the market price of the stock to increase beyond the amount specified in the call. If this occurs, the call purchaser exercises the call (buys the stock at a specified price) and then sells it on the open market for a profit. If the call purchaser does not exercise the call before it expires, she or he loses the cost of the option.

A *put option* gives the purchaser the right to *sell* the stock at a specified price within a specified time. Put options are purchased by investors who expect the market price of the stock to fall below the guaranteed price. If this occurs before the option expires, the put purchaser buys the stock at the lower market price and then sells it at the higher price guaranteed by the put. Again, if the put is not exercised before it expires, the purchaser loses the cost of the option.

Now that we know something about the traditional and the more speculative investments that are available, let's take a look at the actual process of buying and selling securities and at the people involved.

BUYING AND SELLING SECURITIES

To purchase a sweater, you simply walk into a store that sells sweaters, choose one, and pay for it. To purchase stocks or bonds (and to sell them), you have to work through a representative—your stock broker. In turn, your broker must buy or sell for you in a securities marketplace, which is either a securities exchange or the over-the-counter market.

Securities Exchanges

A **securities exchange** is a marketplace where member brokers meet to buy and sell securities. The securities sold at a particular exchange must first be *listed,* or accepted for trading, at that exchange. Generally, securities issued by nationwide corporations are traded at either the New York Stock Exchange or the American Stock Exchange. The securities of regional corporations are traded at smaller *regional exchanges.* These are located in Chicago, San Francisco, Philadelphia, Boston, and several other cities. The securities of very large corporations may be traded at more than one of these exchanges. And American firms that do business abroad may also be listed on foreign securities exchanges—in Tokyo, London, or Paris, for example.

The largest and best-known securities exchange is the *New York Stock Exchange* (NYSE). It handles about 80 percent of all stock bought and sold through organized exchanges in the United States. On June 30, 1982, the NYSE listed 2214 securities issued by 1547 corporations, with a total value of $1.02 trillion![4] The actual *trading floor* of the NYSE, which is where listed securities are bought and sold, is approximately the size of a football field.

Before a corporation's stock is approved for listing on the New York Stock Exchange, the firm must meet five criteria.

1. Its annual earnings before taxes must be at least $2.5 million.
2. At least 1 million shares of its stock must be held publicly.
3. The market value of its publicly held stock must equal or exceed $16 million.
4. At least 2000 stockholders must each own 100 or more shares of its stock.
5. The firm must own tangible assets valued at $16 million or more.[5]

The American Stock Exchange handles about 10 percent of U.S. stock transactions, and the regional exchanges account for the remainder.

These exchanges have generally less stringent listing requirements than the NYSE.

The Over-the-Counter Market

The **over-the-counter (OTC) market** is a network of stock brokers who buy and sell the securities of corporations that are not listed on a securities exchange. Usually each broker specializes, or *makes a market,* in the securities of one or more specific firms. The securities of each firm are traded through its specialist, who is generally aware of their prices and of investors who are willing to buy or sell them. Most OTC trading is conducted by telephone. Since 1971, the brokers and dealers operating in the OTC markets have used an electronic quotation system called NASDAQ—the letters stand for the National Association of Securities Dealers Automated Quotation System. NASDAQ is a computerized system that displays current price quotations on a terminal in the subscriber's office.

The Role of the Stock Broker

An **account executive** or **stock broker** is an individual who buys or sells securities for clients. (Actually, *account executive* is the more descriptive title, because account executives handle all securities—not only stocks. Most also provide securities information and advise their clients regarding investments.) Account executives are employed by stock brokerage firms, such as Merrill Lynch and Prudential-Bache. To trade at a particular exchange, a brokerage firm must be a member of that exchange. In 1981 a membership (or *seat*) on the NYSE cost $220,000 and up.

The Typical Transaction Once an investor and his or her account executive have decided on a particular transaction, the investor gives the account executive an order for that transaction. A **market order** is a request that a stock be purchased or sold at the current market price. The broker's representative on the exchange's trading floor

will try to get the best possible price, and the trade will be completed as soon as possible.

A **limit order** is a request that a stock be bought or sold at a price that is equal to or better (lower for buying, higher for selling) than some specified price. Suppose you place a limited order to *sell* General Dynamics common stock at $49 per share. Then the broker's representative sells the stock only if the price is $49 per share or *more*. If you place a limited order to *buy* General Dynamics at $49, the representative buys it only if the price is $49 per share or *less*. Limit orders may or may not be transacted quickly, depending on how close the limit price is to the current market price.

Figure 17.5 shows how a market order to sell is actually executed. Two things should be noted. First, every stock is traded at a particular *trading post,* which is a desk on the trading floor. Generally, around ten or twelve issues are traded at each trading post. Second, each transaction is recorded, and the pertinent information (stock name, number of shares, and price) is transmitted to interested parties through a communications network called a *ticker tape.*

Commissions Brokerage firms are free to set their own commission charges. Like other businesses, however, they must be concerned with the fees charged by competing firms. *Full-service brokers*—those that provide information and advice as well as securities-trading services—generally charge higher fees than *discount brokers,* which buy and sell but may offer less advice and information to their clients.

On the trading floor, stocks are traded in **round lots,** which are units of 100 shares of a particular stock. Table 17.2 shows typical commission charges for some round-lot transactions. An **odd lot** is fewer than 100 shares of a particular stock. Brokerage firms generally charge higher per-share fees for trading in odd lots, primarily because several odd lots must be combined into round lots before they can actually be traded.

Commissions for trading bonds, commodities, and options are usually lower than those for trading stocks. The charge for buying or selling a $1000 corporate bond is typically between $5 and $10. No matter what kind of security is traded, the investor generally pays a commission when buying *and* when selling. Payment for the securities and for commissions is generally required within five business days of each transaction.

Even the investor who pays (in the form of commissions) for the advice and guidance of a full-service broker must become familiar with numerous sources of financial information. It is important to remember that brokers have *two* goals: to help the investor achieve his or her financial objectives *and* to promote their own interests and those of the brokerage firm they represent. (These interests do not conflict with one another, but the fact that broker and brokerage house receive a commission on every trade may sometimes lead to recommendations to trade more frequently than necessary.) The investor alone makes financial decisions with *only* her or his own interests in view. It is obvious, then, that investors should keep themselves as well informed as possible on financial matters.

Figure 17.5 *The Steps of a Typical Stock Transaction. The entire process, from receipt of the selling order to confirmation of the completed transaction, takes about twenty minutes.*

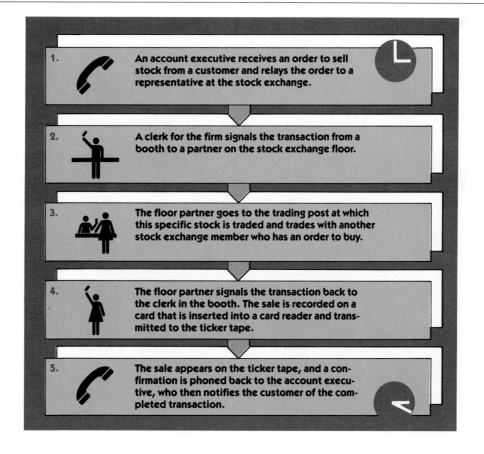

1. An account executive receives an order to sell stock from a customer and relays the order to a representative at the stock exchange.

2. A clerk for the firm signals the transaction from a booth to a partner on the stock exchange floor.

3. The floor partner goes to the trading post at which this specific stock is traded and trades with another stock exchange member who has an order to buy.

4. The floor partner signals the transaction back to the clerk in the booth. The sale is recorded on a card that is inserted into a card reader and transmitted to the ticker tape.

5. The sale appears on the ticker tape, and a confirmation is phoned back to the account executive, who then notifies the customer of the completed transaction.

Table 17.2 *Typical Commission Charges for Round-Lot Stock Transactions*

	Stock Dollar Cost	Commission	
		Full-Service Broker	Discount Broker
100 shares @ $40 per share	$ 4,000	$ 82	$ 35
100 shares @ $60 per share	$ 6,000	$ 90	$ 35
200 shares @ $35 per share	$ 7,000	$136	$ 70
400 shares @ $40 per share	$16,000	$268	$140

SOURCES OF FINANCIAL INFORMATION

A wealth of information is available to investors. Sources include newspapers and business periodicals, corporate reports, and investors' services. Most local newspapers carry several pages of business news, including reports of securities transactions. *The Wall Street Journal* (which is published on weekdays) and *Barron's* (which is published once a week) are devoted almost entirely to financial and economic news. Both include complete coverage of transactions on all major securities exchanges.

Newspaper Coverage of Securities Transactions

Securities transactions are reported as long tables of figures that tend to look somewhat forbidding. However, they are easy to decipher once you know what to look for. Because transactions involving listed stocks, OTC stocks, and bonds are reported differently, we shall examine all three types of reports.

Listed Common and Preferred Stocks Transactions involving listed common and preferred stocks are reported together in the same table. This table usually looks like the top section of Figure 17.6. Parts of a dollar are traditionally quoted as fractions rather than as cents. Thus 1/8 means $0.125, or 12.5 cents, and 3/4 means $0.75, or 75 cents. Stocks are listed alphabetically, so your first task is to move down the table

to find the stock you're interested in. Then, to read the transactions report, or *stock quotation,* you simply read across the table. For U.S. Industries, the third stock down from the top in Figure 17.6, you would find the following information. (The numbers in this list refer to the column numbers that have been added to the figure.)

1. The highest price paid for a share of U.S. Industries during the past 52 weeks was $15 5/8, or $15.625.
2. The lowest price paid for a share of U.S. Industries during the past 52 weeks was $7 3/4, or $7.75.
3. The abbreviated name of the corporation is USInd.
4. The dividend paid to holders of U.S. Industries common stock over the past year was $0.76 per share.
5. The current annual yield for U.S. Industries is $0.76 ÷ $14.50 = 0.052, or 5.2 percent.
6. The current price of U.S. Industries common stock is 12 times the firm's per-share earnings.
7. On this day, 33,400 shares of U.S. Industries were traded.
8. The highest price paid for a share of U.S. Industries on this day was $14 7/8, or $14.875.
9. The lowest price paid for a share of U.S. Industries on this day was $14 3/8, or $14.375.
10. The price of the last share of U.S. Industries traded on this day was $14 1/2, or $14.50.

11. The last price paid for a share of U.S. Industries on this day was $0.125 higher than the last price paid on the previous trading day. In Wall Street terms, U.S. Industries "closed up 1/8" on this day.

If a corporation has more than one stock issue, the common stock is always listed first. Note that there are three listings for U.S. Steel in Figure 17.6. The first is for the company's common stock. The others are for its preferred stock, as

Figure 17.6 *Reading Stock Quotations for Common and Preferred Stocks. Source: Newspaper at top of the figure is* The Wall Street Journal, *April 5, 1983, p. 55. Copyright Dow Jones & Company, Inc., 1983. Reprinted by permission of* The Wall Street Journal. *All rights reserved.*

52 Weeks High 1	Low 2	Stock 3	Div 4	Yld % 5	P-E Ratio 6	Sales 100s 7	High 8	Low 9	Close 10	Net Chg 11
49¾	24½	USGy	pf 1.80	3.6	..	7	u50	50	50	+ ¾
32⅛	11	USHom	.32	1.1	47	191	30	29⅞	29⅞	− ⅛
15⅝	7¾	USInd	.76	5.2	12	334	14⅞	14⅜	14½	+ ⅛
41½	21	USLeas	.68	1.7	11	20	40½	40⅜	40⅜	.....
72	27¾	USShoe	1.36	1.9	13	115	71¼	70	70	− 1¼
25⅜	16	USSteel	1	4.4	..	2249	22⅞	22⅜	22½	− ¼
52	44	USSteel	pf 3.61	7.5	..	14	48⅛	48⅛	48⅛	+ ⅛
119⅞	113⅛	USSteel	pf12.75		..	3	118⅜	118⅜	118⅜	+ ¼

1. Highest price paid for one share during the past year.
2. Lowest price paid for one share during the past year.
3. Abbreviated name of the corporation.
4. Total dividends paid per share during the last 12 months; *pf* denotes a preferred stock.
5. Yield percentage, or the percentage of return based on the current dividend and current price of the stock.
6. Price-to-earnings ratio: the price of a share of the stock divided by the corporation's earnings per share of stock outstanding over the last 12 months.
7. Number of shares traded during the day, expressed in hundreds of shares.
8. Highest price paid for one share during the day; *u* denotes unchanged.
9. Lowest price paid for one share during the day.
10. Price paid in the last transaction for the day.
11. Difference between the price paid for the last share today and the price paid for the last share on the previous day.

indicated by the letters pf in the dividend column (column 4).

Over-the-Counter Stocks   A typical newspaper report of daily over-the-counter stock transactions is shown in the top part of Figure 17.7. Note that less information is given for OTC stocks than for listed stocks. However, many of the columns have the same meaning in both newspaper reports. Thus, for Aaron Rents common stock, Figure 17.7 shows that 2700 shares were traded on this day. The first price quotation, or the bid price, is the amount a seller could receive for a share of stock at the end of the trading day. The second, or asked price, is the amount at which the buyer could purchase a share

of stock. Aaron Rents, had a bid price of $20.75 and an asked price of $21.50. In addition to price, information about current dividends and net change is also included.

Bonds   Purchases and sales of bonds are reported in tables like that shown at the top of Figure 17.8. In bond quotations, prices are given as a *percentage* of the face value, which is usually $1000. Thus, to find the actual price paid, you must multiply the quoted price by 10. For example, a price that is quoted as 92 means a selling price of $92 \times 10 = 920. The fourth row of Figure 17.8 gives the following information (again, by column number) for the Aetna Life and Casualty bond.

Figure 17.7   *Reading Stock Quotations for Over-the-Counter Stocks. Source: Newspaper at top of the figure is* The Wall Street Journal, *April 5, 1983, p. 52. Copyright Dow Jones & Company, Inc., 1983. Reprinted by permission of* The Wall Street Journal. *All rights reserved.*

Stock & Div 1	Sales 100s 2	Bid 3	Asked 4	Net chg 5
Aaron Rents	27	20¾	21½	+ ¾
Acapulco Rest	55	7	7¼	. . . . . .
AcclrtnCp .05d	80	7⅞	8	. . . . .
AccurayCp .14	392	18⅝	18¾	+ ⅛

1. Abbreviated name of the company and dividends, if any, paid by the company during the last 12 months.
2. Number of shares traded during the day, expressed in hundreds of shares.
3. The amount a seller could receive for a share of stock.
4. The amount for which a buyer could purchase a share of stock.
5. The difference between the bid price today and the bid price on the previous day.

1. The abbreviated name of the issuing firm is AetnaLf. The bond pays annual interest at the rate of 8.125 percent of its face value, or $1000 \times 0.08125 = \$81.25$ per year. It matures in the year 2007.
2. The annual yield, or return, based on today's market price is $\$81.25 \div \$695$, or 12 percent.
3. Six $1000 bonds were traded on this day.
4–6. The highest price, the lowest price, and the last price paid for the bond on this day were all $\$69.5 \times 10$, or $695.

7. The last price paid on this day was the same as the last price paid on the previous day.

Other Sources of Financial Information

Brokerage Firm Reports Brokerage firms employ financial analysts to prepare detailed reports on individual corporations and their securities. Such reports are based on the corporation's sales, earnings, management, and planning, plus other information on the company, its industry, and demand for its products. The reports may include

Figure 17.8 Reading Bond Quotations. *Source: Newspaper at top of the figure is* The Wall Street Journal, *February 23, 1984, p. 42. Copyright Dow Jones & Company, 1984. Reprinted by permission of* The Wall Street Journal. *All rights reserved.*

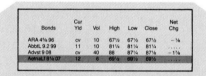

Bonds 1	Cur Yld 2	Vol 3	High 4	Low 5	Close 6	Net Chg 7
ARA 4⅝ 96	cv	10	67½	67½	67½	− ⅛
AbbtL 9.2 99	11	10	81¼	81¼	81¼	. . . . .
Advst 9 08	cv	40	88	87¼	87⅛	− 1⅞
AetnaLf 8⅛ 07	12	6	69½	69½	69½	. . . . .

1. Abbreviated name of the corporation, the bond's interest rate, and the year of maturity.
2. Current yield, determined by dividing the annual interest in dollars by the current price of the bond. The "cv" for ARA indicates that this bond is convertible into a specified number of shares of common stock.
3. Number of bonds traded during the day.
4. Highest price paid for one bond during the day.
5. Lowest price paid for one bond during the day.
6. Price paid in the last transaction for the day.
7. Difference between the price paid for the last bond today and the price paid for the last bond on the previous day.

Table 17.3 The 30 Corporations Whose Common Stock Is Included in the Dow Jones Industrial Average

Allied Chemical	General Foods	Owens-Illinois
Aluminum Company of America	General Motors	Procter & Gamble
American Brands	Goodyear	Sears, Roebuck
American Can	Inco, Ltd.	Standard Oil of California
American Telephone & Telegraph	International Business Machines	Texaco
Bethlehem Steel	International Harvester	Union Carbide
Du Pont	International Paper	U.S. Steel
Eastman Kodak	Johns-Manville	United Technologies
Exxon	Merck & Company	Westinghouse Electric
General Electric	Minnesota Mining & Manufacturing	Woolworth

buy or sell recommendations, and they are usually provided free to the brokerage firm's clients. Firms offering this service include E. F. Hutton, Prudential-Bache, and Merrill Lynch.

Business Periodicals Most business periodicals are published weekly, so that the financial information they contain is up to date. Financial magazines like *Business Week, Fortune, Forbes,* and *Dun's Review* provide not only general economic news, but also detailed financial information about individual corporations. Business periodicals like *Advertising Age* and *Business Insurance* may include some information about the firms in a specific industry. And news magazines like *U.S. News & World Report, Time,* and *Newsweek* feature financial news regularly. These periodicals are available at libraries and by subscription.

Corporate Reports Publicly held corporations must send their stockholders annual and quarterly reports on their operations. In addition, a corporation issuing a new security must—by law—prepare a prospectus and ensure that copies are distributed to potential investors. A **prospectus** is a detailed written description of a new security, the issuing corporation, and the corporation's top management. Both prospectuses and annual reports are usually available to the general public.

Investors' Services For fees ranging from $30 to $300 or more per year, various investors' serv-

ices will provide financial information to subscribers. Three of the most widely accepted investors' services are Standard & Poor's Reports, Value Line, and Moody's Investment Service. All are fairly expensive, but their reports may be available from brokerage firms or libraries.

Stock Averages

Investors often gauge the stock market through the stock averages that are reported in newspapers and on television news programs. A **stock average** (or **stock index**) is an average of the current market prices of selected stocks. Over a period of time, these averages indicate price trends, but they cannot predict the performance of individual stocks. At best, they can give the investor a "feel" for what is happening to stock prices generally.

The *Dow Jones Industrial Average,* established in 1897, is the oldest index in use today. This average is composed of the prices of the common stocks of 30 leading industrial corporations. (These firms are listed in Table 17.3.) In addition, Dow Jones & Company publishes

☐ A *transportation average,* computed from the prices of 20 transportation-industry stocks
☐ A *utility average,* computed from the prices of 15 utility stocks
☐ A *composite average,* computed from the prices of the 65 stocks included in the industrial, transportation, and utility averages

The Standard & Poor's 500 Stock Index and the New York Stock Exchange Index include more stocks than the Dow Jones averages. Thus they tend to reflect the stock market more fully. The *Standard & Poor's 500 Stock Index* is an average of the prices of 400 industrial stocks, 40 utility stocks, 40 financial stocks, and 20 transportation stocks. The *New York Stock Exchange Price Index* (Figure 17.9) is computed from the prices of all common stocks listed on the NYSE, weighted to reflect the number and value of outstanding shares.

It should be apparent by now that vast sums of money are involved in securities trading and that following and interpreting changes in the securities markets is a complex undertaking. In an effort to protect investors from unfair treatment, both federal and state governments have acted to regulate securities trading.

REGULATION OF SECURITIES TRADING

Government regulation of securities trading began as a response to abusive and fraudulent practices in the sale of stocks and bonds. The states were the first to react, early in this century. Later, federal legislation was passed to regulate the interstate sale of securities.

State Regulation

The first state law regulating the sale of securities was enacted in Kansas in 1911. Within a few years, several other states had followed suit. Today, most states require that new issues be registered with a state agency and that brokers and securities dealers operating within the state be licensed. The states also provide for the prosecution of individuals accused of the fraudulent sale of stocks and bonds.

The state laws that regulate securities trading are often called **blue-sky laws.** They are designed to protect investors from purchasing securities that are backed up by nothing but the "clear blue sky."

Federal Regulation

The *Securities Act of 1933,* sometimes referred to as the Truth in Securities Act, provides for full disclosure of important facts about corporations issuing new securities. Such corporations are required to file a *registration statement* containing specific information about the corporation's earnings, assets, and liabilities; its products or services; and the qualifications of its top management. Publication of the prospectus, which is a summary of information contained in the registration statement, is also required by this act.

The *Securities Exchange Act of 1934* created the **Securities and Exchange Commission (SEC),** which is the agency that enforces federal securities regulations. The operations of the SEC are directed by five commissioners, who are appointed by the president of the United States and approved by a two-thirds vote of the Senate. The 1934 securities act gave the SEC the power to regulate trading on the NYSE and the American Stock Exchange. It empowered the SEC to make

Figure 17.9 *New York Stock Exchange Price Index. This index of current stock prices averages the prices of all stocks listed on the NYSE. Source: Chart produced by STOCK GRAPHIC, Ricky D. Woods, owner.*

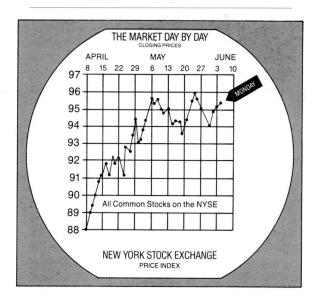

In this nineteenth-century cartoon, W. H. Vanderbilt watches complacently as rival speculator Jay Gould is undone by his own stock-market manipulations. Today, state and federal regulation of securities trading works to prevent dishonest dealings. Source: The Bettmann Archive.

brokers and securities dealers pass an examination before they are allowed to sell securities. And it requires that registration statements be brought up to date periodically.

Four other federal acts were passed primarily to protect investors.

□ The *Maloney Act of 1938* established the **National Association of Securities Dealers (NASD),** to be responsible for the self-regulation of the over-the-counter securities market.

□ The *Investment Company Act of 1940* placed investment companies that sell mutual funds under the jurisdiction of the SEC.

□ The *Federal Securities Act of 1964* extended the SEC's jurisdiction to include companies whose stock is sold *over the counter,* if they have total assets of at least $1 million or have more than 500 stockholders of any one class of stock.

□ The *Securities Investor Protection Act of 1970* created the *Securities Investor Protection Corporation* (SIPC). This organization provides insurance of up to $500,000 for securities and up to $100,000 for cash left on deposit with a brokerage firm that later fails. The SIPC is, in essence, the securities-market equivalent of the FDIC and the FSLIC (Chapter 15).

Chapter Review

SUMMARY

Personal investment planning begins with formulating measurable and realistic investment goals. The investment plan itself is then designed to implement those goals. Many counselors suggest, as a first step, the establishment of an emergency fund equivalent to three months' salary after taxes. Then additional funds may be invested according to the investment plan. Finally, all investments should be carefully monitored and, if necessary, modified.

Depending on their particular investment goals, investors seek varying degrees of safety, income, and growth from their investments. Safety is, in essence, freedom from the risk of loss. Generally, the greater the risk, the greater should be the potential return on an investment. Income is the periodic return from an investment. Growth is an increase in the value of the investment.

Among the traditional investment alternatives are bank accounts, common stock, preferred stock, corporate bonds, government bonds, and mutual funds. More speculative investment techniques can provide greater returns, but they entail greater risk of loss. They include buying stock on margin, selling short, and trading in commodities and options.

Securities exchanges are marketplaces where members buy and sell securities for their clients. The New York Stock Exchange is the largest in the United States; it accounts for about 80 percent of stock traded on an organized exchange. Other securities exchanges include the American Stock Exchange and several regional exchanges. The over-the-counter market is a network of stock brokers who buy and sell the securities that are not traded in exchanges. If you invest in securities, the chances are that you will use the services of an account executive who works for a brokerage firm. Most account executives not only process your orders to buy and sell securities but also provide valuable information and advice. For these services, they are paid a commission based on the size and value of the transaction.

Information on securities and the firms that issue them can be obtained from local newspapers, business periodicals, brokerage firms, corporate reports, and investors' services. Most local newspapers report daily securities transactions and stock indexes, or averages. The averages indicate price trends but reveal nothing about the performance of individual stocks.

State and federal regulations protect investors from unscrupulous securities trading practices. Federal laws, which are enforced by the Securities and Exchange Commission, require the registration of new securities, the publication and distribution of prospectuses, and the licensing of brokers and securities dealers. They apply to securities listed on the NYSE and the American Stock Exchange, to mutual funds, and to some OTC stocks.

In the next chapter we shall discuss the protection of finances and other assets from the hazards involved in simply existing. As you will see, these hazards include fire, theft, accident, and the legal liability for injury to others. Their potential effect on firms and individuals can be minimized through effective risk management.

KEY TERMS

You should now be able to define and give an example relevant to each of the following terms:

personal investment

market value

stock dividend

stock split

mutual fund

speculative investment

margin requirement

leverage

buying long

selling short

spot trading

futures contract

option

securities exchange

over-the-counter (OTC) market

account executive (or stock broker)

market order

limit order

round lot

odd lot

prospectus

stock index (stock average)

blue-sky laws

Securities and Exchange Commission

National Association of Securities Dealers

QUESTIONS AND EXERCISES

Review Questions

1. What steps are involved in personal investing?
2. What is an investment "emergency fund," and why is it recommended?
3. What is meant by the safety of an investment? What is the trade-off between safety and return on the investment?
4. In general, what kinds of investments provide income? What kinds provide growth?
5. How can interest on savings accounts be used either as income or for growth?
6. How does a stock dividend differ from a stock split, from an investor's point of view?
7. Characterize the purchase of corporate bonds as an investment, in terms of safety, income, and growth.
8. An individual may invest in stocks either directly or through a mutual fund. How are the two investment methods different?
9. What are the risks and rewards of purchasing stocks on margin?
10. When would a speculator sell short? buy a call option? buy a put option?
11. What is the difference between a securities exchange and the over-the-counter market?
12. What steps are involved in the purchase of a stock that is listed on the NYSE?
13. What use are newspaper stock quotations to investors? What use are stock averages?
14. What is the Securities and Exchange Commission? What are its principal functions?

Discussion Questions

1. What was wrong with the investment planning of the Jensens? How would you improve it?
2. What might make a particular investment—say, Mattel common stock—a good investment for one person and a poor investment for another person?
3. What personal circumstances might lead some investors to emphasize income rather than growth in their investment planning?

What might lead them to emphasize growth rather than income?
4. Suppose you have just inherited 500 shares of IBM common stock. What would you do with or about it, if anything?
5. For what reasons might a corporation's executives be *unwilling* to have their firm's securities listed on an exchange?
6. What kinds of information would you like to have before you invest in a particular common stock? Where can you get that information?
7. A federal law prohibits corporate managers from making investments that are based on "inside information"—that is, special knowledge about their firms that is not available to the general public. Why is such a law needed?

Exercises

1. Using recent newspaper stock quotations, fill in the following table for common stocks only.

Newspaper: _____

Date: ____	Annual Dividend	P–E Ratio	Closing Price	Net Change
American Can Co. (AmCan)	_____	_____	_____	_____
Detroit Edison (DetEd)	_____	_____	_____	_____
Texaco, Inc. (Texaco)	_____	_____	_____	_____

   a. Which of the three stocks would be the best investment for someone whose investment plan stresses income? Why?

   b. Which stock would seem to be best for an investment plan that stresses growth? (If you need more information to answer this, explain what information you need.)

   c. Can you tell from this information which stock offers the most safety? Explain.

2. Municipal bonds (those issued by cities) generally pay a lower rate of interest than corporate bonds. Through library research, determine why this is so—and why municipal bonds are still attractive to investors.

CASE 17-1

Washington Public Power Supply System

What could be a more attractive investment than a municipal bond—issued and backed by local government and providing interest payments that are free of federal income tax? For those investors who bought Series 4 and 5 bonds of the Washington Public Power Supply System (WPPSS), the answer may be "almost anything," because WPPSS has defaulted on these bonds. Because scheduled interest payments have not been made, the owners of the bonds have already lost more than $2 billion in market value, in addition to the interest. And Wall Street is now referring to the issuer of the bonds as "Whoops."

Revenues from the WPPSS Series 4 and 5 bonds were to be used to erect two nuclear power plants. They, like most municipal bonds, seemed as safe as could be—and their 13 percent tax-free interest was extremely attractive. But that exceptionally high interest rate should have served as a warning that the bonds were far from super-safe; in other words, the less safe a bond is, the higher the interest rate that is needed to attract investors.

Municipal bonds are not regulated by the SEC, as are corporate stocks and bonds. However, the SEC is looking into the default, for evidence of possible fraud. Some irregularities may have been involved in the disclosure of information concerning the bonds, and in their sale. In addition, several brokers are being sued by unhappy bondholders; the suits charge that brokers were selling the WPPSS bonds to clients even after they knew, or should have known, that there were problems.[6]

1. Does the experience of holders of WPPSS Series 4 and 5 bonds mean that high-interest-rate bonds are generally poor investments? Explain.
2. Should stock brokers be held legally responsible for the advice they give to their clients? Explain.

CASE 17-2

Investing in "Art"

The C. V. J. Corporation has an annual cash flow in the millions, a $500,000 revolving credit line from Citibank of New York, and a $300,000 loan from the same bank. Its chief asset is the artist Christo, and its task is to finance his super-large-scale art, or projects, or events.

Christo was the force behind a work called "Surrounded Islands," in which eleven islands in Miami's Biscayne Bay were surrounded by 6.4 million square feet of pink fabric. That project, which cost over $3.5 million, was done in 1983. Earlier works included "Running Fence" (1976), a 24-mile long strip of nylon hung across northern California farmland; and "Valley Curtain" (1971–1972), in which 200,000 square feet of orange nylon was suspended across a valley in Rifle, Colorado. Future projects include wrapping a 200-foot-high statue in Barcelona with rose-colored fabric, and—if C. V. J. can get permission—arranging 11,000 nylon sheets on gates in New York's Central Park.

Raising funds is a continual problem for the firm, so investments would seem to be welcome. However, C. V. J. sells no stock. The money that finances Christo's projects comes primarily from the sale of paintings, drawings, and collages of his works. These are sold to collectors *before* the projects are constructed, at discounted prices. Before Christo did "Surrounded Islands," a hundred or so collectors were given the chance to buy about $70,000 worth of Christo's art for $50,000. Those who purchased the art essentially became investors in C. V. J. They realized about 40 percent on their investments, while C. V. J. obtained financing—interest free—for the project.[7]

1. How does an "investment" in C. V. J. Corporation differ from an investment in, say, IBM stock? How are they similar?
2. Evaluate the C. V. J. "investment" with regard to safety, income, and growth. What types of investors might it attract?

CHAPTER

EIGHTEEN
Risk Management and Insurance

In Chapters 1 and 17 we discussed one kind of risk: the risk that entrepreneurs and investors assume when they put their money on the line in the hope of earning a profit. Here we shall examine a second kind of risk—a kind that is difficult or impossible to avoid. The risks we are about to discuss can result only in loss. But fortunately, they can be managed so that the effect of a loss is minimized. In this chapter, you will see how firms and individuals go about this risk management and how they make use of the services of insurance firms. After studying the chapter, you should understand:

1. *What risk is, and the difference between a pure risk and a speculative risk*

2. *The four general techniques of risk management: avoidance, reduction, assumption, and the shifting of risk to an insurer*

3. *The principles underlying insurance and the insurability of risks*

4. *The types of insurance that can be used to protect businesses and individuals against property and casualty losses*

5. *The advantages and disadvantages of term, whole, endowment, and universal life insurance*

Consider this:

What do Marlene Dietrich's legs and Elizabeth Taylor's eyes have in common with a $60 million supertanker? If you happen to be in the insurance business, the answer is simple: they have all been insured at Lloyd's of London.

Chances are that Lloyd's will pay out on an insurance claim if the winner of the Kentucky Derby breaks a leg or if hailstones ruin the California wine crop. Yet Lloyd's of London is not an insurance company at all, but rather an association of insurance underwriters. Each of its 446 underwriters represents a syndicate that is made up of an average of 40 members. The members are all private individuals—not firms—who take on insurance contracts for personal profit. Members are sole proprietors, so each is liable for losses to the full extent of his personal assets.

Lloyd's of London is the world's largest insurance market.
Source: © Ian Berry, Magnum.

Because of this unique structure, you don't buy insurance *from* Lloyd's, but rather you buy it *at* Lloyd's. The procedure works like this:

1. Suppose a large shipping company—the prospective policyholder—wants to insure a supertanker and its cargo for $60 million. The firm contacts an insurance broker, who writes a proposal and presents it to a Lloyd's underwriter.
2. The underwriter, representing his or her syndicate of individual members, carefully examines the proposal. If it is acceptable, the underwriter and the broker negotiate a fee (or premium) for accepting part of the $60 million risk. Usually an underwriter will accept 5 to 10 percent of the total risk. In this case, the underwriter may be willing to accept 10 percent, or $6 million of the risk, for a premium of $100,000.
3. The broker then presents the proposal to other Lloyd's underwriters, and negotiates with each, until the full $60 million policy is subscribed. In all, 15 to 20 syndicates may be involved.

This intimate approach has made Lloyd's the world's largest insurance market, with approximately $4.5 billion in annual income. Policies are written for any legitimate insurable risk, no matter how unusual. As a result, almost every catastrophe (in Great Britain, America, and elsewhere) tends to cause shock waves for Lloyd's underwriters. And lately there seem to have been many shock waves.

☐ The $80 million loss caused by President Carter's Olympic Games boycott. Lloyd's had insured NBC's television contract.
☐ A $400 million loss when customers broke their leasing contracts with Itel Corporation and other California computer companies because the leased equipment was obsolete.
☐ A $300 million claim involving three liquid-natural-gas tankers that failed Coast Guard inspection.[1]

Source: Chip Hires, Gamma-Liaison.

As a result of these claims and others, Lloyd's may show a loss for the first time since 1967. But Peter Green, chairman of Lloyd's says, "If you don't have claims, people aren't going to insure, are they?"[2]

The underwriters and members of Lloyd's of London provide a service that satisfies a need—the need for safety and protection from the unknown. (You may recall, from Chapter 8, that Maslow considered this a very basic human need. He placed it second only to the need for food, clothing, and shelter.) To the owners of a $60 million supertanker, buying insurance is a practical way to fill that need. Although the insurance cannot make their ship safe from storms and other hazards, it does safeguard their investment.

Most firms insure their resources and products against the hazards of doing business: damage, liability, theft, injury, and others. Similarly, individuals purchase insurance coverage to protect their families, their property, and themselves. In fact, the average American family spends over $1800 each year for insurance to satisfy its need for safety.

Firms and individuals make use of other risk-management methods as well. One example is the periodic inspection of production facilities to discover and eliminate hazards that could lead to injury. Another example is the use of smoke alarms in homes and businesses. Together, the various techniques of risk management are intended to reduce both the possibility of loss and the impact of any losses that do occur.

THE ELEMENT OF RISK

Risk is the possibility that a loss or injury will occur. It is impossible to escape some types of risk in today's world. For individuals, driving an automobile, investing in stocks or bonds, and even jogging along a country road involve some risk. For businesses, risk is a part of every decision. In fact, the essence of business decision making is weighing the potential risks and gains involved in various courses of action.

There is obviously a difference between, say, the risk of losing money that one has invested and the risk of being hit by a car while jogging. This difference leads to the classification of risks as either speculative risks or pure risks. (See Figure 18.1.)

A **speculative risk** is a risk that accompanies the possibility of earning a profit. Most business decisions, such as the decision to market a new product, involve speculative risks. If the new product succeeds in the marketplace, there are profits; if it fails, there are losses. For example, Liquid Paper is a typewriter correction fluid that was invented and then marketed by Betty Graham. The product worked well, and it would earn a profit for Graham if it was accepted by typists. However, there was a distinct possibility that office workers would reject the idea of correcting typing errors with fluid from a bottle. Hence this was one speculative risk that accompanied the chance to earn a profit with the new product.

A **pure risk** is a risk that involves only the possibility of loss, with no potential for gain. The possibility of damage due to a hurricane, fire, or auto accident is a pure risk, because there is no gain if such damage does not occur. Another pure risk is the risk of large medical bills due to a serious illness. Again, if there is no illness, there is no monetary gain.

Let us now look at the various techniques that are available for managing risk.

RISK MANAGEMENT

Risk management is the process of evaluating the risks faced by a firm or an individual and then minimizing the costs involved with those risks. Any risk entails two types of costs. The first is the cost that will be incurred if a potential loss becomes an *actual* loss. An example is the cost of rebuilding and re-equipping an assembly plant

Figure 18.1 *Classification of Risks. A speculative risk is a risk that accompanies the possibility of profit; a pure risk is a risk that involves only the possibility of loss.*

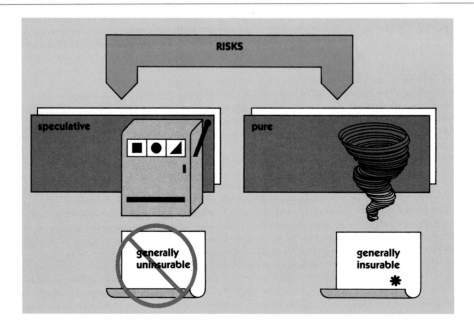

that burns to the ground. The second type consists of the costs of reducing or eliminating the risk and the potential loss. Here we would include the cost of purchasing insurance against loss by fire or the cost of not building the plant at all (this cost is equal to the profit that the plant might have earned). These two types of costs must be balanced, one against the other, if risk management is to be effective.

Most people tend to think of risk management as simply buying insurance. But, although insurance is an important part of risk management, it is not the only means of dealing with risk. Other methods may be less costly in specific situations. And some kinds of risks are uninsurable—not even Lloyd's will issue a policy to protect against them. In this section, we shall examine the four general risk-management techniques. Then, in the following sections, we shall look more closely at insurance.

Risk Avoidance

An individual can avoid the risk of an automobile accident by not riding in a car. A manufacturer can avoid the risk of product failure by refusing to introduce new products. Both would be practicing risk avoidance—but at a very high cost. The person who avoids automobile accidents by forgoing cars may have to give up his or her job to do so. The business that does not take a chance on new products will probably fail when the product life cycle catches up with it.

There are, however, situations in which risk avoidance is a practical technique. At the personal level, individuals who stop smoking or refuse to walk through a high-crime neighborhood are avoiding risks. Jewelry stores lock their merchandise in vaults at the end of the business day to avoid losses through robbery. And, to avoid the risk of a hold-up, many gasoline stations accept only credit cards or the exact amount of the purchase for sales made during the hours they are open after dark.

Obviously no person or business can eliminate

Reducing risks, as this worker's safety goggles do, is one of four risk-management techniques; the others are avoiding risks, assuming risks, and shifting risks. Source: © Lou Jones.

all risks. But, by the same token, no one should assume that all risks are unavoidable.

Risk Reduction

If a risk cannot be avoided, perhaps it can be reduced. For example, an automobile passenger can reduce the risk of injury in an auto accident by wearing a seat belt. A manufacturer can reduce the risk of product failure through careful product planning and market testing. In both these situations, the cost of reducing the risk would seem to be well worth the potential saving.

Businesses face risks as a result of their operating procedures and as a result of management decision making. An analysis of operating procedures—by company personnel or outside consultants—can often point up areas where risk can be reduced. Among the techniques that can be used are

□ The establishment of an employee safety program to encourage awareness of safety among employees
□ The purchase *and use* of proper safety equipment, from hand guards on machinery to goggles and safety shoes for individuals
□ Burglar alarms, security guards, and even guard dogs that protect warehouses from burglary
□ Fire alarms, smoke alarms, and sprinkler systems to reduce the risk of fire and the losses due to fire
□ Accurate and effective accounting and financial controls, to protect the firm's inventories and cash from pilfering

The risks involved in management decisions can be reduced only through effective decision making. These risks *increase* whenever a decision is made hastily or is based on less than sufficient information. However, the cost of reducing these risks goes up when managers take too long to make decisions. It also increases when they require an overabundance of information before they are willing to decide. Among other things, effective management means balancing these two opposing costs.

Risk Assumption

An individual or firm will—and probably must—take on certain risks as part of living or doing business. Individuals who drive to work *assume* the risk of having an accident, but they wear a seat belt to reduce the risk of injury in the event of an accident. The firm that markets a new product *assumes* the risk of product failure—after first reducing that risk through market testing.

Risk assumption is, then, the act of taking on

responsibility for the loss or injury that may result from a risk. Generally, it makes sense to assume a risk when one or more of the following conditions exist:

1. The potential loss is too small to worry about.
2. Effective risk management has reduced the risk.
3. Insurance coverage, if available, is too expensive.
4. There is no other way of protecting against a loss.

Large firms that own many facilities often find that a particular kind of risk assumption called self-insurance is a practical way to avoid high insurance costs. **Self-insurance** is the process of establishing a monetary fund that can be used to cover the cost of a loss. For instance, Southland Corporation may own 2000 7-Eleven convenience stores, each worth $200,000, scattered around the country. For Southland, a logical approach to self-insurance against fire losses would be to collect a certain sum—say, $200—from each store every year. The money that is collected is placed in an interest-bearing reserve fund and used as necessary to repair any fire damage that occurs to 7-Eleven stores. Money that is not used remains the property of the firm. And eventually, if the fund grows, the yearly assessment can be reduced.

Self-insurance does not eliminate risks; it only provides a means for covering losses. And it is, itself, a risky practice—at least in the beginning. Southland would suffer a considerable financial loss if more than two stores were destroyed by fire in the first year the self-insurance program was in effect.

Shifting Risks

Perhaps the most commonly used method of dealing with risk is to shift, or transfer, the risk to an insurance company. An **insurer** (or **insurance company**) is a firm that agrees, for a fee, to assume financial responsibility for losses that may result from a specific risk. The fee charged by an insurance company is called the **premium.** A contract between an insurer and the person or firm whose risk is assumed is known as an **insurance policy.** Generally, an insurance policy is written for a period of one year. Then, if both parties are willing, it is renewed each year. It specifies exactly which risks are covered by the agreement, the dollar amounts that the insurer will pay in case of a loss, and the amount of the premium.

Insurance is thus the protection against loss that is afforded by the purchase of an insurance policy. Insurance companies will not, however, assume every kind of risk. Those risks that insurance companies will assume are called **insurable risks.** We shall discuss insurable risks in

Figure 18.2 *Insurable Risks for Businesses and Individuals*

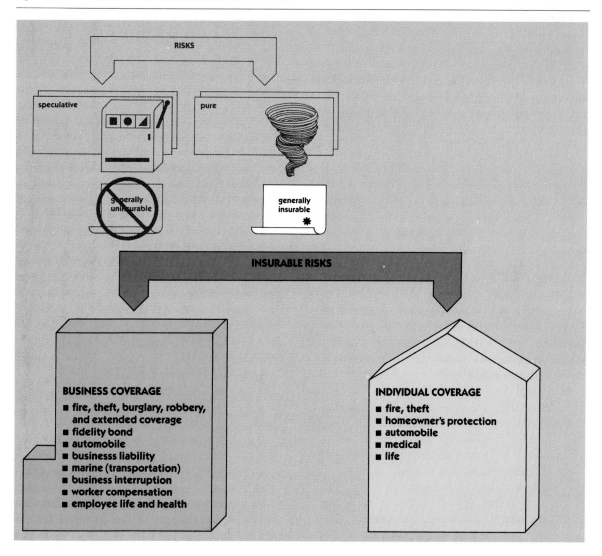

The risk of injury or death while racing cars is an example of an uninsurable risk. Source: © Vicki Lawrence, Stock, Boston.

INSURANCE AND INSURANCE COMPANIES

An insurance company is a business. Like other businesses, an insurer provides a product—protection from loss—in return for a reasonable fee. Its sales revenues are the premiums it collects from the individuals and firms that it insures. (Insurance companies typically invest the money that they have on hand at any time, so we should include interest and dividend income as part of their revenues.) Its expenses are the costs of the various productive resources—salaries, rent, utilities, and so on—*plus* the amounts that the insurance company pays out to cover the losses of its clients.

Pricing and product are very important and exacting issues to an insurance company. This is primarily because it must set its price (its premiums) before the specific cost of its product (how much money it will have to pay out in claims) is known. For this reason, insurance companies employ mathematicians called *actuaries* to predict the likelihood of losses and to determine the premiums that should be charged. Let us look at some of the more important concepts on which insurance (and the work of actuaries) is based.

Basic Insurance Concepts

The Principle of Indemnity The purpose of insurance is to provide protection against loss; it is neither speculation nor gambling. This concept is expressed in the **principle of indemnity**: in the event of a loss, an insured firm or individual cannot collect, from the insurer, an amount greater than the actual dollar amount of the loss. Suppose you own a home that is valued at $100,000. However, you purchase $150,000 worth of fire insurance on your home. Even if it is totally destroyed by fire, the insurer will pay you only $100,000. That is the actual amount of your loss.

The premiums that are set by actuaries are based on the amount of risk involved and the amount to be paid in case of a loss. Generally,

some detail shortly. They include the risk of loss by fire and theft, the risk of loss by automobile accidents, and the risks of sickness and death. Risks that insurance firms will not assume are called **uninsurable risks.**

In general, pure risks are insurable, whereas speculative risks are uninsurable. An insurance company will protect General Electric's locomotive assembly plant against losses due to fire or tornadoes. It will not, however, protect General Electric against losses due to a lack of sales orders for locomotives. (See Figure 18.2.)

The next section provides an overview of the basic principles of insurance and the kinds of companies that provide insurance.

Unemployment Insurance for Execs

While executives and their employers look for ways to protect individuals against an uncertain employment picture, a New York benefits consultant is marketing an unemployment insurance product that may fill that need.

Ron Adler, a Baldwin Harbor, NY, benefits consultant, has taken an idea that has already had limited success in Canada, and is packaging it for the American market as part of a benefits plan for salaried employees.

In Canada, Gestas Inc., has been selling a product called CareerGuard, which protects individuals against unemployment—up to 100 percent after taxes for a year—at a premium equal to 1.6 percent of the pre-tax salary. Reports are, however, that CareerGuard is having trouble, because premiums are not covering losses when the policy is sold to individuals.

Adler's idea is to shift the concept from a coverage sold to individuals to one sold to companies. A company-based plan would have more participants, and would be more easily controlled than one in which the employer is not involved.

Such insurance provides a reasonable level of security for high-level executives without the exorbitant costs associated with "golden parachute" arrangements now predominant in many firms thought to be takeover targets. (A golden parachute is a special employment contract whereby an executive receives a generous severance package if control of the firm changes hands.) Such golden parachutes are unpopular among stockholders because they make top executives wealthy at the company's expense, should those executives be terminated. Mr. Adler believes, however, that the insurance has more promise for lower-salaried employees and for high-level executives in small but growing companies.

The insurance is an attractive alternative to severance pay, Mr. Adler claims, because it is paid out gradually and payments stop when the covered individual becomes re-employed.

Source: Jay Pridmore, *Cashflow*, June 1983, p. 20.

---

the greater the risk and the amount to be paid, the higher the premium. (See Figure 18.3.)

Insurability of the Risk As we noted earlier, insurers will accept responsibility for only certain risks. To be insurable, a risk must meet at least the following conditions:

1. Losses must not be under the control of the insured. Losses due to fire, windstorm, or accident are generally insurable, but gambling losses are not. Moreover, an insurer will not pay a claim for damage that was intentionally caused by the insured person. For example, a person who sets fire to an insured building cannot collect on a fire insurance policy.

2. The insured hazard must be widespread. That is, the insurance company must be able to write many policies, covering the same specific hazard, throughout a wide geographic area. This condition allows the insurer to reduce its own risk: the risk that it will have to pay huge sums of money to clients within a particular area in the event of a catastrophe caused by, say, a tornado.

3. The probability of a loss should be predictable. Insurance companies cannot tell which particular clients will suffer losses. However, their actuaries must be able to determine, statistically, what *fraction* of their clients will suffer each type of loss. They can do so, for insurable risks, by examining records of losses for

past years. They can then base their premiums, at least in part, on the number and value of the losses that are expected to occur.

4. Losses must be measurable. Property that is insured must have a value that is measurable in dollars, because insurance firms reimburse losses with money. Moreover, premiums are based partly on the measured value of the insured property. As a result of this condition, insurers will not insure an item for its emotional or sentimental value, but only for its actual monetary value.

Figure 18.3 *A Comparison of Insurance Rates. Generally the greater the risk and the amount to be paid, the greater the premium. In cities the risks and costs are higher than they are in small towns.* Sources: All-Industry Research Advisory Council, Geographical Differences in Automobile Insurance Costs, *October 1982, pp. 19–21; photo © Craig Aurness, Woodfin Camp.*

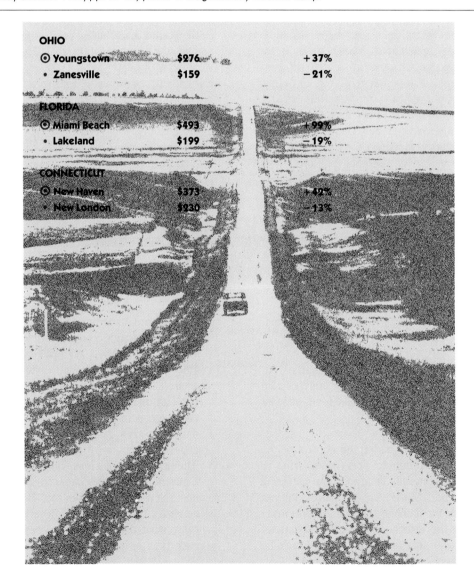

OHIO
⊙ Youngstown $276   +37%
• Zanesville $159   −21%

FLORIDA
⊙ Miami Beach $493   +99%
• Lakeland $199   −19%

CONNECTICUT
⊙ New Haven $373   +42%
• New London $230   −13%

5. The policyholder must have an insurable interest. That is, the individual or firm that purchases an insurance policy must be the one that would suffer from a loss. You can purchase insurance on your own home, but you cannot insure your neighbor's home in the hope of making a profit if it should burn down! Generally, individuals are considered to have an insurable interest in their family members, so a person can insure the life of a spouse, a child, or a parent. Corporations may purchase "key executive" insurance covering certain corporate officers. The proceeds from this insurance help offset the loss of the services of these key people if they die or become incapacitated.

Low-Cost, Affordable Coverage   Price is usually a marketing issue rather than a technical concept. However, the price of insurance is intimately tied to the risks and potential losses that are involved in a particular type of coverage. Insurers would like to "produce" insurance at a very low cost to their policyholders, but they must charge enough in premiums to cover their expected payouts. (See Figure 18.4.)

Customers purchase insurance when they feel that premiums are low enough in relation to the possible dollar loss. For certain risks, premiums can soar so high that insurance is simply not cost-effective. A $1000 life insurance policy for a 99-year-old male would cost about $910 per year. Clearly, a man of that age would be better off if he invested the premium amount in a bank. By this means he would use self-insurance rather than shifting the risk. Although this is an extreme example, it illustrates the fact that insurers must compete, through their prices, with alternative methods of managing risk.

Ownership of Insurance Companies

Insurance companies are owned either by stockholders or by policyholders. A **stock insurance**

Figure 18.4   The Premium Dollar. *For each dollar that property and casualty insurance businesses received in premiums in 1982, they spent $1.10. Investment of premium dollars, not the premiums themselves, is the major income for insurance businesses and the reason they can afford to spend more than the premium dollars add up to.* Source: Insurance Information Institute, Insurance Facts: 1983–1984 Edition, p. 18.

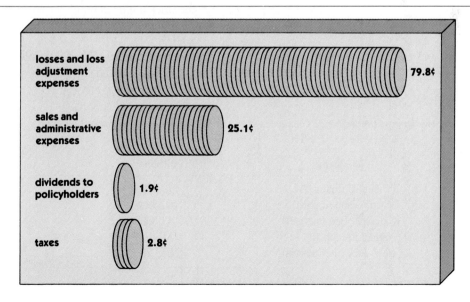

company is owned by stockholders and is operated to earn a profit. Like other profit-making corporations, stock insurance companies pay dividends to stockholders from the surplus of income over operating expenses. Most of the approximately 5000 insurance companies in the United States are stock insurance companies.

A **mutual insurance company** is an insurance company that is collectively owned by its policyholders and is thus a cooperative. Because a mutual insurance company has no stockholders, its policyholders elect the board of directors. The members of the board, in turn, choose the executives who manage the firm. Any surplus of income over expenses is distributed to policyholders as a return of part of their premiums. (This return may take the form of a reduced premium at the start of the policy year or that of a "dividend" at the end of the policy year.)

Both stock and mutual insurance companies must maintain cash reserves to cover future obligations and policyholders' claims. Cash reserves are typically invested in certificates of deposit, stocks, bonds, and real estate. As Table 18.1 shows, four of the five largest life insurance firms are mutual companies. By prudent investment of reserves, insurance firms can develop sizable incomes for their owners.

PROPERTY AND CASUALTY INSURANCE

In this section and the next, we shall examine the major types of insurance coverage offered by insurers. Here, our subject will be insurance against loss of property and against losses due to accident. In the following section we shall discuss the various kinds of life insurance.

Insurance is available to cover most pure risks, but specialized or customized policies can be expensive. A part of effective risk management is to ensure that, when insurance is purchased, the coverage is proper for the individual situation. Three questions can be used as guidelines in this regard: What hazards must be insured against? Is the cost of insurance coverage reasonable in this situation? What other risk-management techniques can be used to reduce insurance cost?

Fire Insurance

Fire insurance is insurance that covers losses due to fire. The standard fire insurance policy provides protection against partial or complete loss of a building and/or its contents when that loss is caused by fire or lightning. Premiums depend on the construction of the building, its use and contents, whether risk-reduction devices (such as smoke and fire alarms) have been installed in the building, and other factors. If a fire does occur, the insurance company reimburses the policyholder for either the actual dollar loss or the maximum amount stated in the policy, whichever is lower.

Coinsurance Clause To reduce their insurance costs, individuals and businesses sometimes in-

Table 18.1 *The Five Largest Life Insurance Companies in the United States in 1983, Ranked by Assets*

Rank	Company	Assets (millions)	Net Investment Income (millions)
1	Prudential (mutual)	$72,249	$4,265
2	Metropolitan (mutual)	60,599	4,749
3	Equitable Life (mutual)	43,306	2,581
4	Aetna Life (stock)	31,414	1,588
5	New York Life (mutual)	24,228	1,811

Source: *Fortune,* "The 50 Largest Life Insurance Companies," June 11, 1984 issue, 184.

Premiums for fire insurance depend on the construction of the building, its use and contents, whether smoke and fire alarms have been installed, and so forth. Source: Courtesy of Liberty Mutual Insurance.

sure property for less than its actual cash value. Their theory is that fire rarely destroys a building completely, so they need not buy full insurance. However, if the building is partially destroyed, they expect their insurance to cover all the damage. This places an unfair burden on the insurance company, which receives less than the full premium but must cover the full loss. To avoid this problem, insurance companies include a coinsurance clause in most fire insurance policies.

A **coinsurance clause** is a part of a fire insurance policy that requires the policyholder, in order to obtain full reimbursement for losses, to purchase coverage at least equal to a specified percentage of the replacement cost of the property. In most cases, the required percentage is 80 percent of the replacement cost. Suppose the owners of a $600,000 building decide to purchase only $300,000 worth of fire insurance. If the building is totally destroyed, the insurance company must pay the policy's face value of $300,000. However, if the building is only partially destroyed, and the damage amounts to $200,000, the insurance company will pay only $125,000. This dollar amount is calculated in the following manner:

1. The coinsurance clause requires coverage of at least 80 percent of $600,000, or $480,000.
2. The owners have purchased only $300,000 of insurance. Thus they have insured for only a portion of any loss. That portion is $300,000 ÷ $480,000 = 0.625, or 62.5 percent.
3. The insurance company will therefore reimburse the owner for only 62.5 percent of any loss. In the case of a $200,000 loss, the insurance company will pay 62.5 percent of $200,000, or $125,000.

If the owners of the building had insured it for $480,000, the insurance company would have covered the entire $200,000 loss.

Extended Coverage **Extended coverage** is insurance protection against damage caused by windstorm, hail, explosion, riots or civil commotion, aircraft, vehicles, and smoke. Extended coverage is available as an *endorsement,* or addition, to some other insurance policy—usually a fire insurance policy. The premium for extended coverage is generally quite low (much lower than the total cost of separate policies covering each individual hazard). Normally, losses caused by war, nuclear radiation or contamination, and water (other than in storms) are excluded from extended-coverage endorsements.

Burglary, Robbery, and Theft Insurance

Burglary is the illegal taking of property through forcible entry. A kicked-in door, a broken window pane, or pry marks on a window sill are evidence of a burglary or attempted burglary. *Robbery* is the unlawful taking of property from an individual by force or threat of violence. A thief who uses a gun to rob a gas station is committing robbery. *Theft* (or *larceny*) is a general term that means the wrongful taking of property that belongs to another. Insurance policies are available to cover burglary only, robbery only, theft only, or all three. Premiums vary with the type and value of the property covered by the policy.

Burglary, robbery, and theft are crimes that are committed by outsiders. Business owners must also be concerned about crimes that employees may commit. A **fidelity bond** is an insurance policy that protects a business from theft, forgery, or embezzlement by its employees. If such a crime does occur, the insurance company reimburses the business for financial losses up to the dollar amount specified in the policy. Individual employees or specific positions within an organization may be bonded. It is also possible to purchase a "blanket" policy that covers the entire work force. Fidelity bonds are most commonly purchased by banks, savings and loan associations, finance companies, and other firms whose employees handle cash on a regular basis.

Motor Vehicle Insurance

Individuals and businesses purchase automobile insurance because it is required by state law, because it is required by the firm financing purchase of the vehicle, or because they want to protect their investment. The commonest types of automobile coverage can be broadly classed as either liability insurance or physical damage insurance. Figure 18.5 shows the distinction.

Automobile Liability Insurance **Automobile liability insurance** is insurance that covers financial losses resulting from injuries or damages caused by the insured vehicle. Liability insurance *does not* pay for the repair of the insured vehicle.

Property damage liability coverage pays for the repair of damage that the insured vehicle does to the property of another person. Such damage is covered up to the amount specified in the policy. Payment for additional damage is the responsibility of the insured. Insurance companies generally recommend at least $50,000 worth of property damage liability.

Bodily injury liability coverage pays medical bills and other costs in the event that an injury or death results from an automobile accident in which the policyholder is at fault. Bodily injury liability coverage protects the person in the other car and is usually specified as a pair of dollar amounts, such as "$20,000 each person, $50,000 each occurrence." This means the insurance company will pay up to $20,000 to each person injured in an accident and up to a total of $50,000 to all those injured in a single accident. In view of the cost of medical care today, and considering the size of legal settlements resulting from automobile accidents, insurance companies recommend coverage of at least $100,000 per person and $300,000 per occurrence.

Along with their automobile liability insurance, most car owners also purchase protection for the passengers in their own cars. A *medical payments endorsement* can be included in automobile coverage for a small additional premium. This endorsement provides for the payment of medical bills, up to a specified amount, for passengers (including the policyholder) injured in the policyholder's vehicle.

Automobile Physical Damage Insurance **Automobile physical damage insurance** is insurance that covers damage to the insured vehicle. *Collision insurance* pays for the repair of damage resulting from an accident. Most collision coverages include a *deductible amount*—anywhere from $50 up—that the policyholder must pay. The insurance company then pays either the remaining cost of the repairs or the actual cash value of the vehicle (when the vehicle is "totaled"), whichever is less. For most automobiles, collision insurance is the most costly coverage. Premiums can, however, be reduced by increasing the deductible amount.

Comprehensive insurance covers damage to the insured vehicle that is caused by fire, theft, hail, dust storm, vandalism, and almost anything else that could damage a car, except collision and normal wear and tear. With the exception of CB radios and tape decks, even the contents of the car are insured. For example, comprehensive coverage will pay for a broken windshield, stolen hubcaps, or small dents caused by a hailstorm. Like collision coverage, comprehensive coverage includes a deductible amount, usually $50 or $100.

Figure 18.5 *Automobile Insurance Coverage. Liability insurance covers financial losses resulting from injuries or damages caused by the insured vehicle; physical damage insurance covers damage to the insured vehicle.*

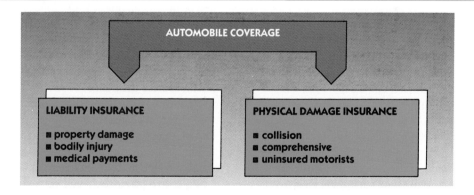

Public liability insurance covers injury or death due to hazards at a place of business, such as the 1981 collapse of the "skybridge" at the Hyatt Regency Hotel in Kansas City.
Source: Hank Young, Black Star.

Uninsured motorists insurance covers the insured vehicle and its passengers in the event that they are damaged or injured by a vehicle with no liability insurance. It also covers damages caused by a hit-and-run driver. Premiums are generally quite low. Also a deductible amount of $50 or $100 is quite common.

No-Fault Automobile Insurance No-fault auto **insurance** is a method of paying for losses suffered in an automobile accident. It is enacted by state law and requires that those suffering injury or loss be reimbursed by their own insurance companies, without regard to who was at fault in the accident. Although there are numerous exceptions, most no-fault laws also limit the rights of involved parties to sue each other.

Massachusetts enacted the first no-fault law in 1971, in an effort to reduce both auto insurance premiums and the crushing caseload in its court system. Since then, at least 27 states have followed suit. Every state with a no-fault law requires liability coverage for all vehicles registered in the state.

Business Liability Insurance

Business liability coverage protects the policyholder from financial losses resulting from an injury to another person or damage to another person's property. During the past ten years or so, both the number of liability claims and the size of settlements have increased dramatically. The result has been heightened awareness of the need for liability coverage—along with quickly rising premiums for this coverage.

Public liability insurance is insurance that protects the policyholder from financial losses due to injuries suffered by others, as a result of negligence on the part of a business owner or employee. It covers injury or death due to hazards at the place of business or resulting from the actions of employees. For example, liability claims totaling more than $2 billion were filed on behalf of the victims of the 1981 skybridge collapse in the Hyatt Regency Hotel in Kansas City, Missouri. *Malpractice insurance,* which is purchased by physicians, lawyers, accountants, engineers, and other professionals, is a form of public liability insurance.

Product liability insurance is insurance that protects the policyholder from financial losses due to injuries suffered by others as a result of using the policyholder's products. Recently, court settlements for individuals injured by defective products have been extremely large.

Many firms are unknowingly vulnerable to excessive employee discrimination damage payouts because such liability is covered neither by directors and officers liability coverage nor by a firm's umbrella coverage.

Firms, however, are becoming more aware of this exposure, which cost them $112 million in 1981—more than triple the amount from a year earlier—and they are moving quickly to insure the risk. Both the number of grievance suits filed and the size of damages asked have accelerated sharply in recent years as judgments, like the one in an employee discrimination case against Harris Bank in Chicago, gain wide publicity.

"Right now, (discrimination) coverage is very hard to get," says Ronald Boggs, a risk management consultant with the Wyatt Company, Chicago. "That is because the underwriters don't understand it." Firms with large volumes of insurance, however, should be able to negotiate some kind of discrimination coverage with their broker.

Although employers generally rely on their umbrella liability policies for coverage in this area, only 10 percent of the 70 policies he recently surveyed indicated they cover discrimination suits. In the case of a large retailer, although discrimination coverage was mentioned in the umbrella policy, the insurer balked at paying the cost of an employee's discrimination suit. The insurer said its policy covered only discrimination suits brought by customers and that its coverage didn't extend to employee discrimination cases.

Employee discrimination settlements can be very costly. Although federal guidelines usually limit damages to back pay, the class action nature of many suits leads to extremely large settlements. Motorola some years ago paid $10 million to 10,000 employees in a case in which the firm was charged with racial discrimination.

Source: *Cashflow*, May 1983, p. 12.

A recent product liability case involved the Ford Motor Company and Richard Grimshaw. Grimshaw was injured when he was a passenger in a Ford Pinto that was hit from behind and burst into flames. He was so severely burned that over 50 operations were required to treat him. He sued and was awarded $128.5 million by a jury, which decided that his injuries resulted from poor product design on the part of Ford. (Later, on appeal, the award was reduced to $6 million.)

Some juries have found manufacturers and retailers guilty of negligence even when the consumer used the product incorrectly. This development and the very large awards given to injured consumers have caused management to take a hard look at product hazards. As part of their risk-management efforts, most manufacturers now take the following precautions.

1. Include thorough and explicit directions for product use with their products
2. Warn customers on the hazards of using their products incorrectly.
3. Remove from the market those products that are considered hazardous
4. Test their products in-house to determine whether safety problems can arise from either proper *or* improper use[3]

Such precautions can reduce both the risk of product-liability losses and the cost of liability insurance.

Marine (Transportation) Insurance

Marine or transportation coverage provides protection against the loss of goods that are being shipped from one place to another. It is the oldest type of insurance—and the type that Lloyd's of London was originally established to provide. The term *marine insurance* was coined at a time when only goods transported by ship were insured.

Today marine insurance is available for goods shipped over water or land. **Ocean marine insurance** protects the policyholder against loss or damage to a ship or its cargo on the high seas. **Inland marine insurance** protects against loss or damage to goods shipped by rail, truck, airplane, or inland barge. Both types cover losses resulting from fire, theft, and most other hazards.

Business Interruption Insurance

Business interruption insurance provides protection for a business whose operations are interrupted because of a fire, storm, or other natural disaster. It is even possible to purchase coverage to protect the firm in the event that its employees go out on strike. For most businesses, interruption coverage is available as an endorsement to a fire insurance policy. Premiums are determined by the amount of coverage and the risks that are covered.

The standard business interruption policy reimburses the policyholder for both loss of profit and fixed costs in the event that it cannot operate. Profit payments are based on the profits earned by the firm during some specified period. Fixed-cost payments cover expenses that the firm incurs even when it is not operating. Employee salaries are normally not covered by the standard policy. However, they may be included for an increased premium.

Worker's Compensation

Worker's compensation insurance is insurance that covers medical expenses and provides salary continuation for employees who are injured while they are at work. This insurance also pays benefits to the dependents of workers who are killed on the job. Today, every state requires that employers provide some form of worker's compensation insurance, with benefits that are established by the state.

Salary continuation benefits are paid to employees who are unable to work because of injuries sustained on the job. These payments normally range from 60 to 75 percent of an employee's usual wage, but they may be limited to a specified number of payments. In all cases, they stop when the employee is able to return to work.

Worker's compensation premiums are paid by the employer and are generally computed as a small percentage of each employee's wages. The percentage varies with the type of job and is, in general, higher for jobs that involve greater risk of injury.

Medical Insurance

Almost every employer pays, as an employee benefit, part or all of the cost of medical insurance for its employees. **Medical insurance** is insurance that covers the cost of medical attention, including hospital care, physicians' and surgeons' fees, prescription medicines, and related services.

The cost of medical care has been increasing at an alarming rate over the last decade or so. In an attempt to keep medical insurance premiums from rising just as quickly, insurers have developed a variety of insurance plans that are less expensive than full-coverage plans. Some plans have deductibles of up to $500. Some require that the policyholder pay 20 percent of the first $1000 to $3000 of medical bills. And some pay the entire hospital bill but only a percentage of other medical expenses. *Major medical insurance* can also be purchased to extend medical coverage beyond the dollar limits of the standard medical insurance policy.

Along with medical insurance, some firms provide employees with life insurance coverage. The amount of this coverage varies from one company to another. And, in addition, some firms include dental insurance, which covers the cost of dental care.

LIFE INSURANCE

Life insurance is insurance that pays a stated amount of money upon the death of the insured individual. The money obviously cannot be paid to the person who is insured. Instead, it is paid to one or more **beneficiaries**—individuals or organizations named in a life insurance policy as recipients of the proceeds of that policy upon the death of the insured.

Life insurance thus provides protection for the beneficiaries of the insured. And the amount of insurance that is needed depends very much on *their* situation. For example, a wage earner with three small children generally needs more life insurance than someone who is single. Moreover, the need for life insurance changes as a person's situation changes. Once our wage earner's children are grown and on their own, they need less

protection (through their parent's life insurance) than they did when they were young. Life insurance in the United States reached a record $4,476.7 billion at the end of 1982. That breaks down to $49,300 per family, or 25 months of income per family—one-third the coverage recommended by experts.[4]

For a particular dollar amount of life insurance, premiums depend primarily on the age and sex of the insured and on the type of insurance. The older a person is, the higher the premium. (On the average, older people are less likely to survive each year than younger people.) And females generally pay lower premiums than males of the same age, because (again, on the average) they live longer. Finally, insurers offer several different types of life insurance for customers with varying insurance needs. The price of each type depends on the benefits it provides.

Term Life Insurance

Term life insurance is life insurance that provides protection to beneficiaries for a stated period of time. Because term life insurance includes no other benefits, it is the least expensive form of life insurance. It is especially attractive to young married couples who want as much protection as possible but cannot afford the higher premiums charged for other types of life insurance.

Most term life policies are in force for a period of one year. At the end of each policy year, a term life policy can be renewed at a slightly higher cost—to take into account the fact that the insured individual has aged one year. In addition, some term policies can be converted to other forms of life insurance at the option of the policyholder. This feature permits policyholders to modify their insurance protection to keep pace with changes in their personal circumstances.

Whole Life Insurance

Whole life insurance is life insurance that provides both protection and savings. In the begin-

ning, premiums are generally higher than those for term life insurance. However, premiums for whole life insurance remain constant for as long as the policy is in force.

A whole life policy builds up savings over the years. These savings are in the form of a **cash surrender value,** which is an amount that is payable to the holder of a whole life insurance policy if the policy is canceled. In addition, the policyholder may borrow from the insurance company, at a relatively low interest rate, amounts up to the policy's surrender value.

Whole life insurance policies are sold in three forms:

- *Straight life insurance,* for which the policyholder must pay premiums as long as the insured is alive
- *Limited-payment life insurance,* for which premiums are paid for only a stated number of years
- *Single-payment life insurance,* for which one lump-sum premium is paid at the time the insurance is purchased

Which of these is best for a given individual depends, as usual, on that individual's particular situation.

Endowment Life Insurance

Endowment life insurance is life insurance that provides protection and guarantees the payment of a stated amount to the policyholder after a specified number of years. Endowment policies are generally in force for 20 years or until the insured person reaches age 65. If the insured dies while the policy is in force, the beneficiaries are paid the face amount of the policy. However, if the insured survives through the policy period, the stated amount is paid to the policyholder.

The premiums for endowment policies are generally higher than those for whole life policies. In return, though, the policyholder is guaranteed a future payment, so the endowment policy includes a sort of "enforced saving." In addition, endowment policies have cash surrender values that are usually higher than those of whole life policies.

Universal Life Insurance

Universal life insurance is life insurance that provides protection and offers a tax-deferred savings account that pays a flexible interest rate. Insurers guarantee only a minimum interest rate on the savings (usually 4 percent), but the rates currently being paid by universal life policies range from 9 to 12 percent.[5]

Universal life insurance is the newest product available from life insurance companies. It offers policyholders several options that are not available with other types of policies. For example, policyholders may choose to make larger or smaller premium payments, to increase or decrease their insurance coverage, or even to withdraw the policy's cash value without canceling the policy. Universal life generally offers lower premiums and higher cash values than whole life insurance. However, companies that offer universal life insurance may charge a fee when the policy is first purchased, each time an annual premium is paid, and when funds are withdrawn from the policy's cash value.[6] Such fees tend to decrease the return on the savings-account part of the policy.

Chapter Review

SUMMARY

Risk—or the possibility of loss or injury—is a part of everyday life for both businesses and individuals. Speculative risks are those that accompany the chance of earning a profit. Pure risks are those that involve only the possibility of loss, without any potential gain.

Individuals and businesses must evaluate the risks they face, and they should minimize the costs involved with those risks. Four general techniques of risk management are risk avoidance, risk reduction, risk assumption, and the shifting of risk. Usually, pure risks that cannot be avoided or reduced, and that are too large to be assumed, can be shifted to insurance companies.

Insurance companies, for a fee, assume risks that meet certain insurability criteria. They do so through contracts called insurance policies. An important condition in the issuing of an insurance policy is that the insured individual or firm cannot profit from the policy. That is, the payment in the event of a loss cannot exceed the actual amount of the loss. Insurance company fees, or premiums, must be affordable. At the same time, they must be high enough to cover expected payouts and other expenses.

Stock insurance companies are profit-making corporations that are owned by stockholders. Mutual insurance companies are cooperatives that are owned by their policyholders.

Property and casualty insurance protects the policyholder against loss of property and loss due to accident. Included in this category is insurance that protects against loss of property due to fire, theft, and various natural hazards; against liability due to injury to employees or customers; and against damage and liability resulting from automobile accidents. Employers may also purchase insurance to cover the medical expenses of their employees and their employees' families.

All life insurance provides a stated amount of money, which is paid to beneficiaries upon the death of the insured individual. Term insurance provides this single benefit. Whole life insurance provides some savings as well—in the form of a cash surrender value. Endowment insurance also provides a guaranteed payment at the end of some specified period of time. And universal life insurance combines protection with a tax-deferred savings account.

This chapter concludes our discussion of finance and risk management for firms and individuals. The next part of the book deals with another of the four business resources—information. We begin our discussion of information with an examination of accounting, which is the major source of internal information about the firm itself.

KEY TERMS

You should now be able to define and give an example relevant to each of the following terms:

risk

speculative risk

pure risk

risk management

self-insurance

insurer (or insurance company)

premium

insurance policy

insurance

insurable risks

uninsurable risks

principle of indemnity

stock insurance company

mutual insurance company

fire insurance

coinsurance clause

extended coverage

fidelity bond

automobile liability insurance

automobile physical damage insurance

no-fault auto insurance

public liability insurance

product liability insurance

ocean marine insurance

inland marine insurance

business interruption insurance

worker's compensation insurance

medical insurance

life insurance

beneficiaries

term life insurance

whole life insurance

cash surrender value

endowment life insurance

universal life insurance

QUESTIONS AND EXERCISES

Review Questions

1. What is the difference between a speculative risk and a pure risk? Why are speculative risks generally uninsurable?
2. List the four general risk-handling techniques and give an example of how each is used to handle risk.
3. Under what conditions is self-insurance a practical risk-management method?
4. How does the principle of indemnity affect:
   a. The amount that an insurer will pay in the event of a loss?
   b. The maximum amount for which property should be insured by its owner?
5. What are the five principal conditions that determine whether a risk is insurable?
6. Distinguish between a stock insurance company and a mutual insurance company.
7. What is the general effect of the coinsurance clause in a fire insurance policy?
8. What is extended insurance coverage, and what does it usually "extend"?
9. For what purpose are fidelity bonds used?
10. What is the difference between automobile liability insurance and automobile physical damage insurance? List three liability coverages and three physical damage coverages.
11. What is the difference between public liability insurance and product liability insurance? Why would a business need these two coverages?
12. How are the premiums determined for worker's compensation insurance? Who pays them?
13. What or whom does life insurance protect?
14. List and briefly describe four different kinds of life insurance.

Discussion Questions

1. In what ways is Lloyd's of London different from the usual type of insurer? How do the differences affect customers of Lloyd's?
2. Discuss the question asked by Peter Green, the chairman of Lloyd's: "If you don't have claims, people aren't going to insure, are they?" Must an insurer have claims in order to survive?
3. Suppose you were the owner of a retail clothing store. To what extent could you use risk avoidance, risk reduction, and risk assumption in your risk-management program? Cite specific applications of each of these three techniques.
4. As the owner of the retail store described in Question 3, which insurance coverages would you purchase for your business? How would you determine how much of each coverage to purchase?
5. The principle of indemnity does not seem to apply to life insurance, because people can, within reason, purchase as much or as little of this coverage as they wish. Why should this be so?

Exercises

1. Find and read an article or two on homeowner's or renter's insurance. From your reading, answer the following questions:
   a. Which hazards are generally covered by these policies?
   b. How does the cost of homeowner's or renter's insurance compare to the cost of fire insurance alone?
   c. Which additional coverages are available as endorsements?
2. The owner of a $500,000 building has purchased $300,000 worth of fire insurance on the building. How much will the owner collect from the insurance company under each of the following conditions?
   a. The building is totally destroyed by fire.
   b. A fire does $300,000 worth of damage to the building.

CASE 18-1

Unisex Insurance May Be Next

First came unisex hair styles, and then we got unisex clothing. Or was it the other way around? In any case, the National Organization for Women is now lobbying for unisex insurance premiums— that is, equal premiums for men and women of the same age and in the same general circumstances.

Congress may, in fact, soon enact legislation that would end the practice of charging males and females different premiums for the same insurance coverage. But would unisex rates help women, or would women be hurt by the proposed legislation?

According to insurance company officials, women would be hurt. Present insurance premiums are based on statistics which show that women live longer than men and are better drivers than men. Such statistics result in lower premiums for female policyholders. If the proposed legislation is enacted, women will have to pay higher premiums in the future. Insurance officials predict that the increase will amount to at least $700 million per year for automobile insurance coverage and $360 million per year for life insurance.

Supporters of unisex pricing admit that women would pay higher insurance premiums, but they contend that premiums are not the real issue. The key issue, they say, is benefits. For example, women now receive less in monthly retirement and pension benefits than men, again because women live longer. Unisex pricing would eliminate this type of discrimination. In addition, supporters note that unisex pricing would mean bigger benefits for widows, because men would get more life insurance for the same dollar.

The final argument for unisex pricing is a simple one: Unisex pricing is already practiced in the insurance industry. For example, many medical insurance policies spread the cost of pregnancy and childbirth among all policyholders—male and female, young and old—instead of charging only young women for this type of coverage. Supporters believe that it is time to extend equality to all insurance and insurance premiums.[7]

1. In what ways would women benefit from unisex insurance premiums? In what ways would they lose?
2. Should Congress enact legislation to require unisex pricing of insurance policies? Defend your position.

CASE 18-2

Boise Cascade Corporation

The payment of worker's compensation benefits to job-injured employees is mandatory in all fifty states. However, a firm is permitted either to purchase worker's compensation insurance or to self-insure against this risk. A number of states sell the insurance in competition with insurance companies; and, in six states, worker's comp. insurance can be purchased only from the state.

On the average, worker's comp. insurance costs about $2 per $100 of wages per employee. (In California, a high-premium state, the cost is about 50 percent greater.) Many larger firms feel they can reduce this cost through self-insurance—by setting up their own worker's comp. funds. Now, self-insuring firms are examining the benefits of careful management of their worker's compensation programs.

An example is the wood products division of Boise Cascade Corporation. With the help of Dr. Phillip Haber of the Minneapolis-based Metropolitan Rehabilitation Services, the division has implemented a three-part strategy to reduce its worker's comp. costs. Total savings over five years have been almost $11 million:

- □ Workers who have been injured are given limited-duty jobs when (and if) they can return to work. This requires a matching of the worker's present abilities with available jobs; the goal is eventually to move the returned worker to his or her previous job or to one like it. Boise has been able to save $1.6 million in this way.
- □ Permanently disabled workers are helped to obtain Social Security and other government benefits to which they are entitled. By working with disabled employees to present thorough and complete evidence of their disabilities to government agencies, Boise has been able to save $8.6 million in benefits payments.

- □ Injured workers who can work but who refuse legitimate job offers are cut off from disability benefits. Boise has found that almost all people who can hold a job will accept one. But lawsuits against the occasional shirker have resulted in savings of $0.7 million.

Altogether, Boise's management strategy has reduced its worker's compensation liability from about $13 million to $2.4 million—for a cost reduction of over 80 percent. Not bad for a firm whose only insurance client is itself![8]

1. Does Boise's three-part strategy seem reasonable and fair to both the injured worker and the firm? Explain.
2. Could insurance companies devise and implement similar cost-reduction plans? If not, why not? If so, why haven't they?

Career Profile

Muriel Siebert   Thirty years ago, Muriel Siebert, a dentist's daughter from Cleveland, arrived on Wall Street looking for a job. Because she was a few units short of earning her accounting degree, she was turned down by the first firm she applied to. Eventually Bache & Co. hired her as a $65-a-week assistant to research the airline industry, which was then considered a low-return investment. Siebert did some sharp analyses, earned clients a good deal of money, and began building an excellent reputation. She has been surprising people and adding to that reputation ever since.

Because banks and brokerages have long been dominated by men, Siebert confronted many barriers in her rise to the top. "I left jobs because they were paying the men more," she says. Such discrimination, she claims, "gave me my strength. Besides, I had knowledge and I could carry that with me." Throughout her years on Wall Street, Siebert has retained her own character, gaining recognition for her straight, blunt talk and for a flamboyant style of dress that stands out in the grey-suited bankers' world.

Siebert's long career has been marked by innovation and integrity. In 1967 she gained considerable public attention when she became the first woman to buy a seat on the New York Stock Exchange—a purchase that cost almost half a million dollars. She also established her own firm, Muriel Siebert & Co. Then in 1975, when new laws made it possible for brokers to work for lower, "discount" commissions, Siebert's firm was the first to offer lower rates. Some on Wall Street were so irritated that the firm that had cleared Siebert's transactions stopped dealing with her. "When you take a stand on something, a lot of people aren't going to like you," she says. "Of course, firms that didn't like me then now say I had foresight."

Siebert also took many unpopular stands while serving as New York's banking superintendent. In that position, she kept an eye on more than 200 American savings and commercial banks and on American branches of 139 foreign banks. Many observers credit her with dealing successfully with the greatest set of state banking problems since the Depression of the 1930s.

The list of Siebert's accomplishments as banking superintendent is very long. She championed the cause of savings banks, which she sees as one of the major forces providing the country with economic and political stability. She fought for the establishment of international banking zones, which have brought hundreds of billions of dollars into the United States, mostly into New York. And in a case that revealed her typically evenhanded judgment, she worked out a compromise that outlawed "redlining"—the practice by which banks refuse to give mortgage loans for property in a whole section of a city—and at the same time, lifted interest-rate ceilings that many banks felt were too strict.

Siebert resigned her position in 1982 to run unsuccessfully for a Senate seat. But she hasn't stayed out of the news. In 1983, her company opened a branch in First Women's Bank, becoming the first discount brokerage firm to open an actual branch in a bank. Her ability to take bold, progressive action without limiting her individuality or her principles is sure to serve as a model for many who come after her.[1]

The figure in the salary column approximates the expected annual income after two or three years of service.

1 = $12,000–$15,000   2 = $16,000–$20,000   3 = $21,000–$27,000   4 = $28,000–$35,000   5 = $36,000 and up

Job Title	Educational Requirements	Salary Range	Prospects
Actuary	Bachelor's or master's degree in math, business, or statistics	3–4	Gradual growth
Bank clerk	High school diploma	1	Gradual growth
Bank officer and manager	College degree; master's degree preferred; on-the-job experience	2–3	Limited growth
Bank teller	High school diploma; some college preferred	1	Limited growth
Brokerage clerk	High school diploma; some college preferred	1–2	Limited growth
Claims adjuster	Some college preferred; on-the-job training	2	Gradual growth
Claims clerk	High school diploma	1	Gradual growth
Collection worker	High school diploma	1–2	Limited growth
Credit clerk	High school diploma; some college preferred	1–2	Greatest growth
Credit manager	College degree; on-the-job experience	2–3	Limited growth
Credit reporter	Some college preferred; on-the-job experience	2	Greatest growth
Financial analyst	College degree; on-the-job experience; master's degree helpful	4–5	Limited growth
Insurance agent	Bachelor's degree preferred	2–3	Limited growth
Insurance clerk	High school diploma; some college preferred	1–2	Gradual growth
Insurance underwriter	Bachelor's degree in insurance; on-the-job experience	2–3	Limited growth
Investment banker	College degree; on-the-job experience	4–5	Limited growth
Mortgage loan officer	Some college courses; bachelor's degree helpful; on-the-job experience	2–3	Limited growth
Portfolio/trust officer	College degree; on-the-job experience	3	Limited growth
Stockbroker	Bachelor's degree; on-the-job experience	4–5	Gradual growth
Tax preparer or consultant	College degree; on-the-job experience	3–4	Greatest growth

PART

6
Information for Business Decision Making

The subject of this part is information, the fourth of our business resources. First we discuss the firm's financial information: how it is collected, processed, and presented. Then we do the same for the various other kinds of information that are necessary for effective management decision making. Included in this part are:

CHAPTER

NINETEEN
Accounting

The function of accounting is to produce useful information about the financial operation of the firm. Without this information, the firm's managers would be blind to what was going on. There could be no meaningful planning, and decision making would be almost pure guesswork. Investors wouldn't invest in the firm, because they would know nothing about it. Lenders wouldn't lend it money, and the Internal Revenue Service would be camping at its front door. In this chapter, you will see what this vital accounting information is like, how it is produced, and how it is used. After studying the chapter, you should understand:

1. *What accounting is, and what accountants do*
2. *The difference between accounting and bookkeeping*
3. *The accounting equation and the concept of double-entry bookkeeping*
4. *The five steps of the accounting cycle*
5. *How to read and interpret a statement of financial position*
6. *How to read and interpret an income statement*
7. *The various financial ratios that reveal how a business is doing*

Consider this:

In 1967, Equity Funding Life Insurance Company reported sales of $54 million and insurance in force totaling $109 million. By 1972, sales had grown to $1.32 billion and insurance in force had jumped to $6.5 billion. In the same five-year period, corporate profits increased nearly eightfold. For at least the first nine months of 1972, Equity Funding was ranked among the top ten American life insurance companies. It was the fastest-growing life insurance company in the United States.

In early March 1973, acting on a tip from a former employee, investigators began to look into the company's activities. By March 27, trading in Equity's stock was suspended by the New York Stock Exchange. The price of the stock had dropped almost 10 points in a week, to less than $15 a share. Shortly after that, the stock was declared to be of "no value." Equity's 7000 stockholders had lost at least $114 million.

The investigators found that, of the 97,000 policies listed on the books of an Equity Funding subsidiary, approximately 58 percent were nonexistent. Moreover, other insurance companies that had bought these policies as reinsurers had paid millions of dollars for nothing. This defrauding of other insurance companies had gone on for four years.

Reinsurance is not unusual in the insurance business. It is a practice whereby a company issues an insurance policy to a customer and then sells the policy to another insurance company in order to acquire cash. What was unusual in the Equity Funding case was that there were no policyholders behind most of the policies. Nearly two-thirds of what the company claimed as its insurance business was based on bogus policies!

The chairman and president of Equity Funding received an annual salary of $100,000. In addition, in 1972 he was given a stock bonus then worth over $150,000. He was a respected Los Angeles business leader who, until January 1972, had served as chairman of the business conduct committee of the Los Angeles branch of the National Association of Securities Dealers. He had a home with a gymnasium and tennis courts, a Rolls Royce, and a 35-foot yacht. On November 1, 1973, he and 18 other executives of Equity Funding were indicted on 105 criminal counts. They were charged with committing felonies that included securities fraud, mail fraud, bank fraud, interstate transportation of counterfeit securities and other securities obtained by fraud, electronic eavesdropping, and filing of false documents with the Securities and Exchange Commission.

At the time, Equity Funding had a highly computerized accounting system that facilitated the mixing of phony policies with genuine policies. However, the hoax could easily have been discovered if the policies on the books had been verified with their supposed owners. (This is a standard practice in banking.) Unfortunately, not one auditor for an outside accounting firm ever confirmed a policy directly with a policyholder until after the rumors of fraud began to circulate.

It is not surprising that traditional auditing techniques failed to detect the phony policies. The company made the policies look valid, and auditors generally tend to believe the computer, according to Peter Louderback, the head of the Peat, Marwick, Mitchell & Co. banking-auditing training program.[1] In the wake of the Equity Funding scandal, the American Institute of Certified Public Accountants formed a committee to study the techniques used in auditing insurance companies and to determine how they should be changed. One almost certain change will be to require that auditors obtain policy confirmation directly from policyholders.[2]

The vast majority of business firms are legitimate enterprises whose managers would much rather earn profits than steal from other firms. However, in a negative way, the Equity Funding case does show just how much the business world relies on financial information—and it also demonstrates the great power of this information.

Most businesses prepare at least two financial reports each year: the statement of financial position and the income statement. Each of these statements is usually no more than about one page in length. Together, they report the results of perhaps tens of thousands of transactions that have occurred during the reporting period.

These two financial statements are thus concise summaries of the firm's activities during a specific time period. The standard unit of measurement for business operations is the dollar, but sometimes other units are used as well. The raw data are the day-to-day items of income and expense: every sale to a customer and every payment for rent, wages, raw materials, inventory, interest, and so on.

Standard accounting methods (described later) have been developed for summarizing and presenting data in financial reports. This is so that each item in each report means the same thing to everyone who reads it. Moreover, the form of the financial statements is pretty much the same for all businesses, from a neighborhood video arcade to giant conglomerates like Exxon. This information has a variety of uses, both within the firm and outside it. However, accounting information is, first and foremost, management information. As such, it is of most use to those who are responsible for the operation of the firm.

ACCOUNTING AND ACCOUNTANTS

Accounting is the process of systematically collecting, analyzing, and reporting financial information. Because of its great value, business owners have been concerned with financial information for hundreds of years: the first book of

The first book of accounting principles was written almost five hundred years ago by an Italian monk named Paciolo. Source: Scala, Art Resources.

accounting principles was written in 1494, by an Italian monk named Paciolo.

Modern accounting in the United States can be traced back to the establishment of the American Institute of Certified Public Accountants (AICPA) in 1887. By the early 1900s, accounting instruction was offered (but was optional) at many colleges and universities. Today, accounting courses are required for virtually every type of business degree.

Accounting or Bookkeeping?

Many people confuse accounting with bookkeeping, but there are important differences between the two. Accounting deals with the entire system for providing accurate and up-to-date financial information—from the design of the system through its operation to interpretation of the information that is obtained. To become an accountant, an individual must undergo years of training and chalk up a great deal of practical experience.

Bookkeeping, on the other hand, is the routine, day-to-day recordkeeping that is a necessary part of accounting. Bookkeepers are responsible for obtaining the financial data that the accounting system processes. An accounting system cannot operate without good, accurate bookkeeping, but a bookkeeper can generally be trained within a year or so.

Classification of Accountants

Accountants are people who are trained and experienced in the methods and systems of accounting. They are generally classified as private accountants or public accountants.

A **private** (or *non-public*) **accountant** is an accountant who is employed by a specific organization. A medium-sized or large firm may employ one or several private accountants to design its accounting system, manage its accounting department, prepare the variety of reports that are required either by management or by law, and provide managers with advice and assistance. Private accountants provide their services only to their employers.

Smaller firms and larger firms that don't require full-time accountants can hire the services of public accountants. A **public accountant** is an accountant whose services may be hired by individuals or firms. Public accountants may be self-employed, or they may work for accounting firms. Accounting firms range in size from one-person operations to huge international firms with hundreds of accounting partners and thousands of employees. Table 19.1 lists the eight largest accounting firms in the United States and some of their clients.

Most accounting firms include on their staffs at least one **certified public accountant** (CPA), an individual who has met state requirements for accounting education and experience and has passed a rigorous three-day accounting examination. State requirements usually include a college accounting degree and from one to five years of on-the-job experience. Certification as a CPA brings both status and responsibility. Only an independent CPA can officially verify the financial contents of a corporation's annual report and express an opinion—as required by law—regarding the acceptability of the corporation's accounting practices.

The Users of Accounting Information

As we have noted, the primary users of accounting information are *managers*. The firm's accounting system provides a range of information dealing with revenues, costs, accounts receivable,

Table 19.1 *The Eight Largest Certified Public Accounting Firms in the United States*

Firm	Home Office	Some Major Clients
Arthur Andersen & Co.	Chicago	ITT, Texaco, United Airlines
Arthur Young & Co.	New York	Mobil, Sperry Corp., McDonald's
Coopers & Lybrand	New York	AT&T, Ford, Firestone
Deloitte Haskins & Sells	New York	General Motors, Procter & Gamble
Ernst & Whinney	Cleveland	McDonnell-Douglas, Coca-Cola
Peat, Marwick, Mitchell & Co.	New York	General Electric, Xerox
Price Waterhouse & Co.	New York	IBM, Exxon, Du Pont
Touche Ross & Co.	New York	Chrysler, Boeing, Sears

Source: Needles/Anderson/Caldwell, *Principles of Accounting*, Second Edition, p. 14. Copyright © 1984 by Houghton Mifflin Company. Used by permission.

amounts borrowed and owed, profits, return on investment, and the like. This information can be compiled for the entire firm; for each product; for each sales territory, store, or individual salesperson; by division or department; and generally in any way that will help those who manage the organization. At a company like General Foods Corporation, for example, financial information is gathered for all of its hundreds of food products: Maxwell House Coffee, Birds Eye Frozen Foods, Post Cereals, Jell-O Desserts, Tang Instant Breakfast Drink, and so on. The president of the company would be interested in the combined sales for all these products. The marketing manager for desserts would be interested in sales for Birds Eye Frozen desserts and Jell-O. The northeastern sales manager might want to look at sales figures for Tang in New England. For a large, complex organization like General Foods, the ac-

counting system must be flexible and complete because managers at different levels must be able to get the information they need.

Much of this accounting information is *proprietary;* it is not divulged to anyone outside the firm. However, certain financial information is demanded by individuals and organizations that the firm must deal with. (See Figure 19.1.)

☐ *Lenders* require at least the information that is contained in the firm's financial statements before they will commit themselves to either short-term or long-term loans.
☐ *Suppliers* generally ask for this same information before they will extend trade credit to a firm.
☐ *Stockholders* must, by law, be provided with a summary of the firm's financial position in each annual report. In addition, *potential investors*

Figure 19.1 *Accounting Information. The primary users of accounting information are managers; but certain financial information is demanded by outside individuals and organizations that the company deals with.*

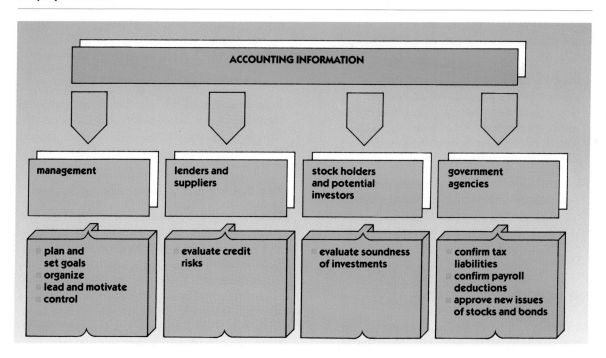

must be provided with financial statements in the prospectus for each securities issue.
- *Government agencies* require a variety of information pertaining to the firm's tax liabilities, payroll deductions for employees, and new issues of stocks and bonds.

The firm's accounting system must be able to provide all this information, and in the required form. An important function of accountants is to ensure that such information is accurate and thorough enough to satisfy these outside groups.

THE ACCOUNTING PROCESS

Accounting can be viewed as a system for transforming raw financial *data* into useful financial

information. In this section, we shall see how such a system operates, beginning with the collection of the raw data. Then, in the next two sections, we shall describe the two most important financial statements provided by the accounting process. And we shall discuss the information they contain.

The Accounting Equation

The accounting equation is a simple statement that forms the basis for the accounting process. It shows the relationship among the firm's assets, liabilities, and owners' equity.

- **Assets** are the things of value that a firm owns. They include cash, inventories, land, equipment, buildings, patents, and the like.
- **Liabilities** are the firm's debts and obligations—what it owes to others.
- **Owners' equity** is the difference between a firm's assets and its liabilities—what would be left over for the firm's owners if its assets were used to pay off its liabilities.

The relationship among these three is almost self-evident: Owners' equity = assets − liabilities. By moving terms algebraically, we obtain the standard form of the **accounting equation:**

$$\text{Assets} = \text{liabilities} + \text{owners' equity}$$

Implementation of this equation begins with the recording of raw data—that is, the firm's day-to-day financial transactions. It is accomplished through the double-entry system of bookkeeping.

The Double-Entry Bookkeeping System

Double-entry bookkeeping is a system in which each financial transaction is recorded as two separate accounting entries in order to maintain the balance shown in the accounting equation. Most often, one entry changes the left (assets) side of the equation, and the other entry changes the right (liabilities + owners' equity) side in the same way. However, for a few types of transactions, the two entries change only one side of the equation, but in opposite ways. This occurs, for example, when cash (an asset) is used to purchase equipment (another asset).

Suppose that John Thompson and Mark Martin each invest $25,000 in cash to start a new business. Before they make these investments, both sides of the accounting equation are equal to zero. The firm has no assets, no liabilities, and no owners' equity. The results of their investments are shown as transaction A in Figure 19.2. Cash (an asset) is increased by $50,000; owners' equity is also increased by $50,000 to balance the increase in assets.

Note that the entries for this transaction are not lumped together as one asset increase and one owners' equity increase. Instead, the entries are placed in separate *accounts,* which show exactly what is being increased. Here the investments are cash, so the *cash* account is increased.

Similarly, under owners' equity, there is one account for Thompson and one for Martin.

Three additional transactions are shown in Figure 19.2:

□ In transaction B, a bank loan of $10,000 was used to purchase equipment. The loan is a liability, and the equipment is an asset.
□ In transaction C, inventory worth $5000 was purchased on credit. The inventory is an asset, and the amount owed is a liability.
□ In transaction D, $5000 in cash was used to pay off part of the bank loan. The payoff decreases cash, an asset; the reduction of the loan amount decreases a liability.

Follow through each of these transactions in the figure to make sure you understand why each entry is recorded as shown. Also note that, after all four transactions, the books are still balanced.

Figure 19.2 *Four Business Transactions Recorded Using the Double-Entry System. Double-entry bookkeeping is used to balance the accounting equation (assets equal liabilities plus owners' equity).*

	ASSETS			**= LIABILITIES**		**+ OWNERS' EQUITY**	
	Cash	Equipment	Inventory =	Bank Loans	Suppliers	Thompson	Martin
Transaction A (*cash investment*)	$50,000	–0–	–0–	–0–	–0–	$25,000	$25,000
	$50,000 +	–0– +	–0– =	–0– +	–0– +	$25,000 +	$25,000
Transaction B (*equipment purchase via bank loan*)	–0–	$10,000	–0–	$10,000	–0–	–0–	–0–
	$50,000 +	$10,000 +	–0– =	$10,000 +	–0– +	$25,000 +	$25,000
Transaction C (*credit purchase of inventory*)	–0–	–0–	$5,000	–0– +	$5,000	–0–	–0–
	$50,000 +	$10,000 +	$5,000 =	$10,000 +	$5,000 +	$25,000 +	$25,000
Transaction D (*partial payoff of loan*)	– $ 5,000	–0–	–0–	– $ 5,000	–0–	–0–	–0–
	$45,000	$10,000 +	$5,000 =	$ 5,000	$5,000 +	$25,000 +	$25,000

That is, assets are indeed equal to liabilities plus owners' equity.

The Accounting Cycle

In the typical accounting system, raw data are transformed into financial statements in five steps (Figure 19.3). The first three—analysis, journalizing, and posting—are performed on a continual basis throughout the accounting period. The last two—preparation of the trial balance and of the financial statements—are performed at the end of the accounting period.

Analyzing Source Documents   The basic accounting data are contained in *source documents,* which are the receipts, invoices, sales slips, and other documents that show the dollar values of day-to-day business transactions. The accounting cycle begins with the analysis of each of these documents. The purpose of the analysis is to determine which accounts are affected by the documents and how they are affected.

Each transaction results in two or more debits and credits. A **debit** is an increase in an asset account or a decrease in a liability or owners' equity account. A **credit** is a decrease in an asset account or an increase in a liability or owners' equity account. The terms *debit* and *credit* do not mean anything negative or positive. *Debit* simply means "left," and *credit* means "right." The terms tell the bookkeeper which of two columns (left or right) to place entries in when journalizing the transactions.

Journalizing the Transactions   Every financial transaction is next recorded in a journal—a process that is called *journalizing.* Transactions must be recorded in the firm's general journal. The **general journal** is a book of original entry in which all transactions are recorded in order of their occurrence.

Figure 19.4 shows the general journal entries that correspond to the transactions listed in Figure 19.2. Note the two columns and the placement of the entries in those columns.

An accounting system may also include *specialized journals* for specific types of transactions that occur frequently. Thus a retail store might have a cash receipts, cash disbursements, purchases, and a sales journal in addition to its general journal.

Posting Transactions   Next the information entered in the general journal is transferred to the general ledger. The **general ledger** is a book of accounts that contains a separate sheet or section for each account. The process of transferring journal entries to the general ledger is called **posting.**

Figure 19.5 shows how the first general journal entry of Figure 19.4 would be posted in the three affected ledger accounts. Note that the ledger has four columns for entries. Each new entry is posted in the first two columns, and a running balance is kept in the last two columns on the right. Notice also that credits are equal to debits in both Figures 19.4 and 19.5. If they are not equal, a mistake has been made. Finally, the notation "GJ-1" in the ledger entries indicates that these entries originate on page 1 of the firm's general journal.

Figure 19.3   The Accounting Cycle

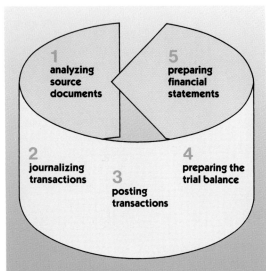

Preparing the Trial Balance A **trial balance** is a summary of the balances of all ledger accounts at the end of the accounting period. To prepare a trial balance, the accountant

1. Determines and lists the balances for all ledger accounts
2. Totals all debit balances
3. Totals all credit balances
4. Compares the total of the debit balances with the total of the credit balances

If the totals in step 4 are equal, the accountant can proceed to the financial statements. If not, there is a mistake somewhere. The accountant must find and correct it before proceeding.

Preparing Financial Statements The firm's financial statements are prepared from the information contained in the trial balance. This information is presented in a standardized format in order to make the statements as generally accessible as possible to the various parties who may be interested in the firm's financial affairs.

Once these statements have been prepared and checked, the firm's books are "closed" for the accounting period. A new accounting cycle is then begun for the next period.

Now let us consider the two most important financial statements generated by the accounting process, the statement of financial position and the income statement.

Figure 19.4 *Journalizing. Every financial transaction is recorded in a journal, as part of the accounting cycle.*

General Journal		DEBIT	CREDIT
198x			
JAN 12	CASH	50000--	
	JOHN THOMPSON, OWNERS' EQUITY		25000--
	MARK MARTIN, OWNERS' EQUITY		25000--
	TO RECORD ORIGINAL INVESTMENT		
JAN 12	EQUIPMENT	10000--	
	LIABILITY - BANK LOAN		10000--
	TO RECORD LOAN FROM BANK USED TO		
	PURCHASE EQUIPMENT		
JAN 13	INVENTORY	5000--	
	LIABILITY - SUPPLIER		5000--
	TO RECORD THE PURCHASE OF INVENTORY		
	ON CREDIT		
JAN 14	LIABILITY - BANK LOAN	5000--	
	CASH		5000--
	TO RECORD PARTIAL REPAYMENT OF BANK		
	LOAN		

THE STATEMENT OF FINANCIAL POSITION

A **statement of financial position** is a summary of a firm's accounts at a particular time, showing the various dollar amounts that enter into the accounting equation. Also called the **balance sheet,** the statement of financial position must demonstrate that the accounting equation does indeed balance. That is, it must show that the firm's assets are equal to its liabilities plus its owners' equity. As we noted, the balance sheet is prepared at the end of the accounting period, which usually covers one year. Some firms also have balance sheets prepared semiannually, quarterly, or monthly.

Figure 19.6 shows the statement of financial position for Northeast Art Supply, a small corporation that sells picture frames, paints, canvases, and other artists' supplies to retailers in New England. Note that assets are reported at the top of the statement, followed by liabilities and owners' equity. This is the standard format for these statements. Let us work through the accounts in Figure 19.6, from top to bottom.

Assets

On a balance sheet, assets are listed in order, from the *most liquid* to the *least liquid.* The **liquidity** of an asset is the ease with which it can be converted into cash.

Figure 19.5 ***Posting. The process of transferring entries from journals to the general ledger is called posting.***

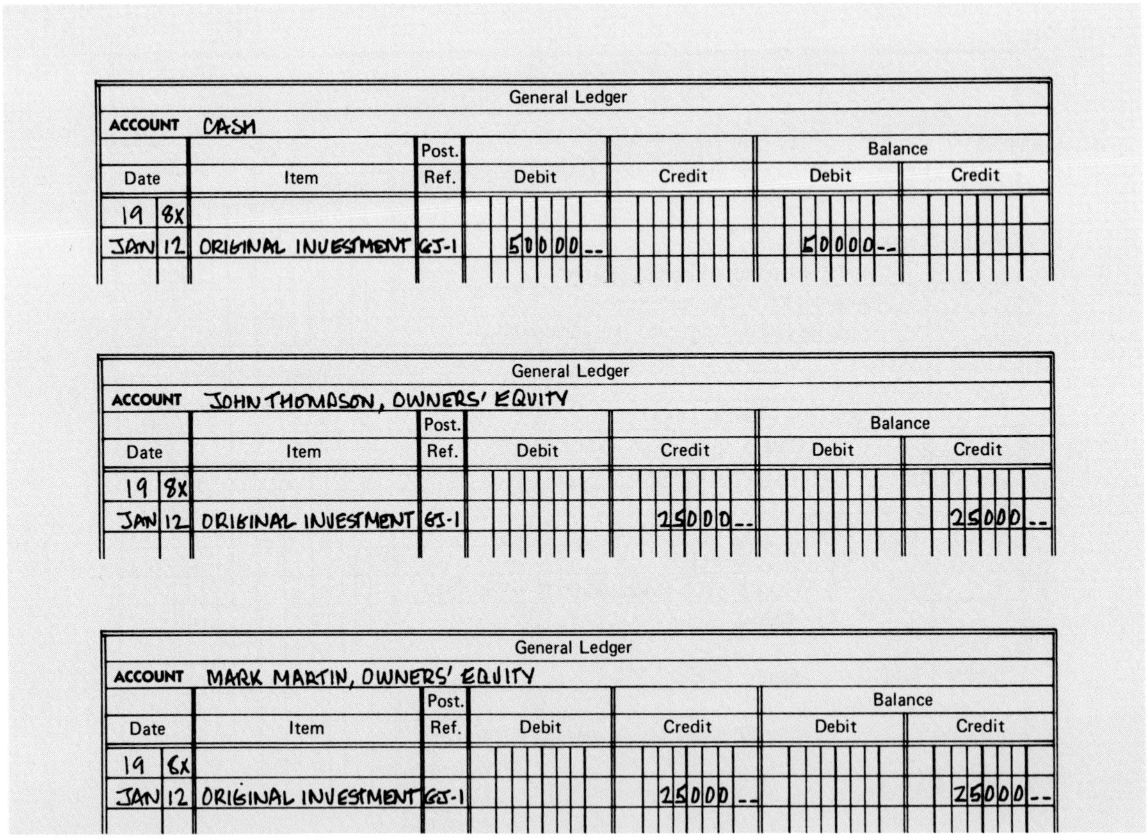
General Ledger

ACCOUNT CASH

Date		Item	Post. Ref.	Debit	Credit	Balance Debit	Balance Credit
19	8X						
JAN	12	ORIGINAL INVESTMENT	GJ-1	50000--		50000--	

General Ledger

ACCOUNT JOHN THOMPSON, OWNERS' EQUITY

Date		Item	Post. Ref.	Debit	Credit	Balance Debit	Balance Credit
19	8X						
JAN	12	ORIGINAL INVESTMENT	GJ-1		25000--		25000--

General Ledger

ACCOUNT MARK MARTIN, OWNERS' EQUITY

Date		Item	Post. Ref.	Debit	Credit	Balance Debit	Balance Credit
19	8X						
JAN	12	ORIGINAL INVESTMENT	GJ-1		25000--		25000--

Figure 19.6 *Statement of Financial Position. A statement of financial position summarizes the firm's accounts at a particular time, showing the various dollar amounts that enter into the accounting equation and showing that the equation balances.*

Northeast Art Supply, Inc.

Statement of Financial Position
December 31, 198x

ASSETS

Current Assets

Cash		$ 59,000	
Marketable Securities		10,000	
Accounts Receivable	$40,000		
Less Allowance for Doubtful Accounts	2,000	38,000	
Notes Receivable		32,000	
Merchandise Inventory		41,000	
Prepaid Expenses		2,000	
Total Current Assets			$182,000

Fixed Assets

Delivery Equipment	$110,000		
Less Accumulated Depreciation	20,000	$ 90,000	
Furniture and Store Equipment	62,000		
Less Accumulated Depreciation	15,000	47,000	
Total Fixed Assets			137,000

Intangible Assets

Patents		$ 6,000	
Goodwill		15,000	
Total Intangible Assets			21,000
Total Assets			$340,000

LIABILITIES AND OWNERS' EQUITY

Current Liabilities

Accounts Payable	$ 35,000		
Notes Payable	25,000		
Salaries Payable	4,000		
Taxes Payable	6,000		
Total Current Liabilities		$ 70,000	

Long-Term Liabilities

Mortgage Payable on Store Equipment	$ 40,000		
Total Long-Term Liabilities		40,000	
Total Liabilities			$110,000

Owners' Equity

Common Stock, 10,000 shares at $15 Par Value		$150,000	
Retained Earnings		80,000	
Total Owners' Equity			230,000
Total Liabilities and Owners' Equity			$340,000

A business's assets may include intangible assets such as the reputation of this famous deli. Source: © Andy Levin, Black Star.

Current Assets Current assets are cash and other assets that can be quickly converted into cash or that will be used within one year. Cash is the most liquid asset, so it is listed first. Following that are *marketable securities*—stocks, bonds, and so on—that can be converted into cash in a matter of days.

Next are the firm's receivables. Its *accounts receivable,* which result from the issuance of trade credit, are generally due within 60 days. However, the firm expects that some of these debts will not be collected, so it has reduced its accounts receivable by a 5 percent *allowance for doubtful accounts.* The firm's *notes receivable* are receivables for which customers have signed promissory notes. They are generally repaid over a longer period of time.

Northeast's *merchandise inventory* represents the value of goods that are on hand for sale to customers. These goods are listed as current assets because they will be sold within the year.

Northeast's last current asset is **prepaid expenses,** which are assets that have been paid for in advance but not yet used. An example is insurance premiums. They are usually paid at the beginning of the policy year for the whole year. The unused portion (say, for the last 4 months of the policy year) is a prepaid expense—a current asset.

Fixed Assets Fixed assets are assets that will be held or used for a period longer than one year. They generally include land, buildings, and equipment. Although Northeast owns no land or buildings, it does own *delivery equipment* that originally cost $110,000. It also owns *furniture and store equipment* that originally cost $62,000.

Note that the values of these fixed assets are decreased by their *accumulated depreciation.* **Depreciation** is the process of apportioning the cost of a fixed asset over the period during which it will be used. The amount that is allotted to each year is an expense for that year, and the value of the asset must be reduced by that expense. In the case of Northeast's delivery equipment, $20,000 of its value has been depreciated (or used up) since it was purchased. Its value at this time is thus $110,000 less $20,000, or $90,000. In a similar fashion the value of furniture and store equipment has been reduced by accumulated depreciation of $15,000.

Intangible Assets Intangible assets are assets that do not exist physically but that have a value based on legal rights or advantages that they confer on a firm. They include patents, copyrights, trademarks, franchises, and goodwill. By their nature, intangible assets are long-term assets. They are of value to the firm for a number of years.

Northeast Art Supply lists two intangible assets. The first is a *patent* for an oil paint that the company has developed. The firm's accountants estimate that it has a current market value of $6000. The second intangible asset, **goodwill,** is the value of a firm's reputation, location, earning capacity, and other intangibles that make the business a profitable concern. Goodwill is not normally listed on a statement of financial position unless the firm has been purchased from previous owners. In this case, the purchasers have actually paid an additional amount (over and above the value of the previous owners' equity) for this intangible asset.

Liabilities and Owners' Equity

Like its assets, the firm's liabilities are separated into two groups—current and long-term—on the statement of financial position. These and the owners' equity accounts complete the statement of financial position.

Current Liabilities A firm's **current liabilities** are debts that will be repaid within one year. Northeast Art Supply purchased merchandise from its suppliers on credit, so its statement of financial position includes an entry for accounts payable. **Accounts payable** are short-term obligations that arise as a result of making credit purchases.

Notes payable are obligations that have been secured with promissory notes. They are usually short-term obligations, but they may extend beyond one year. Only those that must be paid within the year are listed under current liabilities.

Northeast also lists *salaries payable* and *taxes payable* as current liabilities. These are both expenses that have been incurred during the current accounting period but will be paid in the next accounting period. Such expenses must be shown as debts for the accounting period in which they were incurred.

Long-Term Liabilities Long-term liabilities are debts that need not be repaid for at least one year. Northeast lists only a $40,000 *mortgage payable* in this group. Bonds and other long-term loans would be included here as well, if they existed.

Owners' Equity For a sole proprietorship or partnership, the owners' equity is shown as the dif-

Of all the intangible "assets" or "advantages" enjoyed by a selling company in a merger and acquisition deal, the hardest to value are those that produce non-economic benefits. These may include publicity, prestige, influence, and access to circles otherwise closed to the buyer. James B. Kobak, a consultant specializing in appraisal of magazine values, calls this the "glamor factor."

Kobak estimates that the glamor factor alone could account for $20 million of the purchase price (estimated at $300 million-plus prior to the sale) of U.S. News & World Report Inc., weekly news-magazine publisher. "There are only three weekly news magazines [in the United States], only one of which was available for sale," he says. "It offered a position to influence the world." Kobak says the glamor factor is most prevalent in acquisitions in the media, entertainment, and sports fields, where traditional rules of thumb on cash flow, returns, and other financial criteria often don't justify the deals. But, he maintains, the glamor factor works its way into other industries where these rules are more strictly applied. He cites brand-name consumer products and retailing as examples, but says even the more mainstream industrialized industries can have a touch of the glamor factor in final purchase prices.

While acknowledging that the glamor factor exists, Kobak concedes there is no real way to divorce it from the rest of the purchase price. Asked if there are methods to determine or price the glamor factor, Kobak replies, "Don't ask me."
Source: *Mergers & Acquisitions*, Spring 1984, p. 48.

ference between assets and liabilities. For a corporation, the owners' equity is shown as the total par value of its stock, plus retained earnings that have accumulated to date. Northeast Art Supply has issued only common stock. Its value is shown as its par value ($15) times the number of shares outstanding (10,000). In addition, $80,000 of

"The more I own of it, the more I realize what a beautiful country it is."

Northeast's earnings have been reinvested in the business since it was founded.

Other names for owners' equity include *shareholders' equity* and *partners' equity.* For a partnership, each partner's share of the ownership is reported separately.

As the two grand totals show, Northeast's assets and the sum of its liabilities and owners' equity are equal—in this case, $340,000.

THE INCOME STATEMENT

An **income statement** is a summary of a firm's revenues and expenses during a specified accounting period. The income statement is sometimes called the *earnings statement* or the *statement of income and expenses.* It may be prepared monthly, quarterly, semiannually, or annually. An income statement covering the previous year must be included in a corporation's annual report to its stockholders.

Figure 19.7 shows the income statement for Northeast Art Supply. Note that it consists of four sections. Generally, revenues *less* cost of goods sold *less* operating expenses *equals* net income from operations.

Revenues

Revenues are dollar amounts received by the firm. Northeast obtains its revenues solely from the sale of its products. The revenues section of its income statement begins with gross sales. **Gross sales** are the total dollar amount of all goods and services sold during the accounting period. From this are deducted the dollar amounts of

- *Sales returns,* or merchandise returned to the firm by its customers
- *Sales allowances,* or price reductions offered to customers who accept slightly damaged or soiled merchandise

Figure 19.7 *Income Statement. An income statement summarizes the firm's revenues and expenses during a specified accounting period—monthly, quarterly, semiannually, or annually.*

Northeast Art Supply, Inc.
Income Statement
For the Year Ended December 31, 198x

Revenues

Gross Sales		$465,000	
Less Sales Returns and Allowances	$ 9,500		
Less Sales Discounts	4,500	14,000	
Net Sales			$451,000

Cost of Goods Sold

Beginning Inventory, January 1, 198x		$ 40,000	
Purchases	$346,000		
Less Purchase Discounts	11,000		
Net Purchases		335,000	
Cost of Goods Available For Sale		$375,000	
Less Ending Inventory, December 31, 198x		41,000	
Cost of Goods Sold			334,000
Gross Profit on Sales			117,000

Operating Expenses

Selling Expenses

Sales Salaries	$ 30,000		
Advertising	6,000		
Sales Promotion	2,500		
Depreciation–Store Equipment	3,000		
Miscellaneous Selling Expenses	1,500		
Total Selling Expenses		$ 43,000	

General Expenses

Office Salaries	$ 18,500		
Rent	8,500		
Depreciation–Delivery Equipment	4,000		
Depreciation–Office Furniture	1,500		
Utilities Expense	2,500		
Insurance Expense	1,000		
Miscellaneous Expense	500		
Total General Expenses		36,500	
Total Operating Expenses			79,500

Net Income from Operations	$ 37,500
Less Interest Expense	2,000
Net Income Before Taxes	$ 35,500
Less Federal Income Taxes	5,640
Net Income After Taxes	$ 29,860

In 1979 the Supreme Court ruled that businesses must pay taxes on the full-sale value of their inventory instead of the lesser value they had been allowed. Consequently some businesses find it more economical to destroy their inventory. *Source:* © 1984 T. Molinski.

☐ *Sales discounts,* or price reductions offered by manufacturers and suppliers to customers who pay their bills promptly

The remainder is the firm's net sales. **Net sales** are the actual dollar amount received by the firm for the goods and services it has sold, after adjustment for returns, allowances, and discounts.

Cost of Goods Sold

According to Figure 19.7, Northeast began its accounting period with a merchandise inventory that cost $40,000 (see *beginning inventory* under *cost of goods sold*). During the period, the firm purchased, for resale, merchandise worth $346,000. But, after taking advantage of *purchase discounts,* it paid only $335,000 for this merchandise. Thus, during the year, Northeast had *goods available for sale* valued at $40,000 + $335,000 = $375,000.

At the end of the accounting period, Northeast had an *ending inventory* of $41,000. Thus it had sold all but $41,000 worth of the available goods. The *cost of goods sold* by Northeast was therefore $375,000 *less* $41,000, or $334,000.

This is the standard method of determining the cost of the goods sold by a retailing or wholesaling firm during an accounting period. It may be summarized as follows:

Cost of goods sold

$$= \frac{\text{beginning}}{\text{inventory}} + \frac{\text{net}}{\text{purchases}} - \frac{\text{ending}}{\text{inventory}}$$

A manufacturer must include its raw-materials inventories, work-in-process inventories, and direct manufacturing costs in this computation.

A firm's **gross profit on sales** is its net sales *less* the cost of goods sold. For Northeast, this was $117,000.

Inventory Valuation The prices that a firm pays for the goods it sells (or the materials it uses in manufacturing) are likely to change during an accounting period. However, the goods (or materials) all look alike, whether they were purchased at the beginning of the period or at the end. How, then, should the firm determine the value of its ending inventory?

Either of two approximations may be used for this purpose. The first, called **FIFO** (for "first in, first out") is the valuation of inventories under the assumption that the first goods purchased by the firm are the first to be sold or used. To use this approximation, a firm evaluates its ending inventories as though they consist of the last goods purchased.

The second means of determining the value of ending inventory, called **LIFO** (for "last in, first out"), is the valuation of inventories under the assumption that the last goods purchased are the first to be sold or used. Under this assumption, a firm evaluates its ending inventories as though they consist of the beginning inventory and the earliest purchases made during the accounting period.

In a time of rising prices, LIFO results in a higher cost of goods sold than FIFO. This leads to a lower taxable income. The Internal Revenue Service permits firms to use either LIFO or FIFO consistently, year after year. However, before a firm can change from one to the other, it must obtain permission from the IRS.

Operating Expenses

A firm's **operating expenses** are those costs that do not result directly from the purchase or manufacture of the products it sells. They are generally classed as either selling expenses or general expenses.

Selling expenses are costs that are related to the firm's marketing activities. They include salaries for members of the sales force, advertising and other promotion expenses, and the costs involved in operating stores.

General expenses are costs that are incurred in managing a business. They are sometimes called *administrative expenses.* Typical general expenses are the salaries of office workers and the costs of maintaining offices. A catch-all account called *miscellaneous expense* is usually included in the General Expenses section of the income statement.

Net Income

Net income is the profit earned (or the loss suffered) by a firm during an accounting period, after all expenses. In Figure 19.7, Northeast's *net income from operations* is computed as gross profit on sales *less* total operating expenses.

From this, an *interest expense* of $2000 is deducted to give a *net income before taxes* of $35,500. The interest expense is deducted here because it is not an operating expense. It is, rather, an expense that results from the financing of the business.

Northeast's *federal income taxes,* based on its before-tax income, are $5640. Although these taxes may or may not be payable immediately, they are definitely an expense that must be deducted from income. This leaves Northeast with a *net income after taxes* of $29,860. This amount may be used to pay a dividend to stockholders, help finance the firm's operations, reduce its debts, or all three.

ANALYZING FINANCIAL STATEMENTS

As we have seen, a firm's statement of financial position provides a "picture" of the firm at a particular time. Its income statement summarizes its operations during one accounting period. Both can be used to answer a variety of questions about the firm's ability to do business and stay in business, its profitability, its value as an investment, and its ability to repay its debts.

Even more information can be obtained by comparing present financial statements with those prepared for past accounting periods. Such comparisons permit managers (and other interested people) to (1) pick out trends in growth, borrowing, income, and other business variables and (2) determine whether the firm is on the way to accomplishing its long-term goals. Most corporations include, in their annual reports, comparisons of the important elements of their financial statements for recent years. One such comparison is shown in Figure 19.8.

Many firms also compare their financial results with those of competing firms and with industry averages. These comparisons give managers a

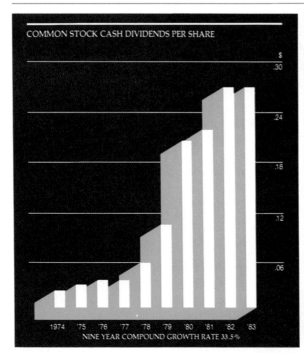

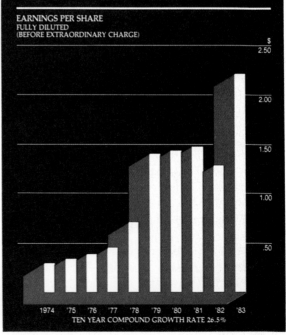

general idea of the firm's relative effectiveness and its standing within the industry. For example, a manager at IBM would read the financial reports for Digital Equipment Corporation, Wang Laboratories, and Data General Corporation to give her a good idea of IBM's position within the office automation market. Competitors' financial statements can be obtained from their annual reports—if they are public corporations. Industry averages are published by reporting services such as Dun & Bradstreet and Standard & Poor's, as well as by some of the industry associations.

Still another type of analysis involves computation of the financial ratios discussed in the next section. Like the individual elements in the financial statements, these ratios can be compared with the firm's past ratios, with those of competitors, and with industry averages.

FINANCIAL RATIOS

A **financial ratio** is a number that shows the relationship between two elements of a firm's financial statements. Many of these ratios can be formed, but only about a dozen or so have real meaning. Those that we shall discuss are generally grouped as profitability ratios, short-term financial ratios, and long-term debt ratios. The information required to form these ratios is contained in the statement of financial position and the income statement.

Profitability Ratios

A firm's net income after taxes indicates whether the firm is profitable. It does not, however, indicate how effectively the firm's resources are being used. For this later purpose, three ratios can be computed.

Figure 19.8 *Comparison of Present and Past Financial Statements. Most corporations include in their annual reports comparisons of the important elements of their financial statements of recent years.* Source: James River Corporation, Annual Report, 1983.

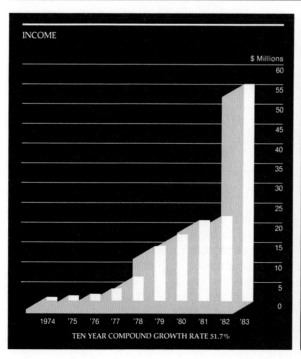

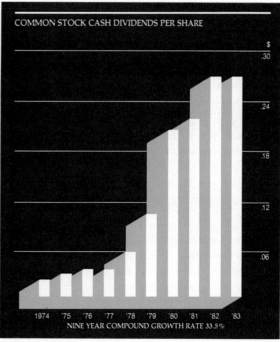

Net Profit Margin Net profit margin is a financial ratio that is calculated by dividing net income after taxes by net sales. For Northeast Art Supply,

$$\text{Net profit margin} = \frac{\text{net income after taxes}}{\text{net sales}}$$

$$= \frac{\$\ 29,860}{\$451,000} = 0.066, \text{ or } 6.6\%$$

The net profit margin indicates how effectively the firm is transforming sales into profits. Today, the average net profit margin for all business firms is between 4 and 5 percent. With a net profit margin of 6.6 percent, Northeast Art Supply is well above average. A low net profit margin can be increased by reducing expenses or by increasing the size of the average sale.

Return on Equity Return on equity is a financial ratio that is calculated by dividing net income after taxes by owners' equity. Again, for Northeast Art Supply,

$$\text{Return on equity} = \frac{\text{net income after taxes}}{\text{owners' equity}}$$

$$= \frac{\$\ 29,860}{\$230,000} = 0.13, \text{ or } 13\%$$

Return on equity indicates how much income is generated by each dollar of owners' equity. Northeast is providing income of 13 cents per dollar invested in the business; the average for all businesses is between 12 and 15 cents. The only practical way to increase return on equity is to increase net income after taxes. This means either reducing expenses or increasing sales, or both.

Earnings per Share From the point of view of stockholders, this is one of the most widely used indicators of a corporation's success. **Earnings per share** is calculated by dividing net income after taxes by the number of shares of common stock outstanding. For Northeast,

$$\text{Earnings per share} = \frac{\text{net income after taxes}}{\text{common stock shares outstanding}}$$

$$= \frac{\$29,860}{10,000} = \$2.99 \text{ per share}$$

Earnings per share is, obviously, a measure of the amount earned (after taxes) per share of common stock owned by investors. There is no meaningful average for this measure, mainly because the number of outstanding shares of a firm's stock is subject to change via stock splits and stock dividends. As a general rule, however, an increase in earnings per share is a healthy sign for any corporation. For the stockholder, such an increase may mean that common-stock dividends will also be increased.

Short-Term Financial Ratios

The three short-term financial ratios permit managers (and lenders) to evaluate the ability of a firm to cover its current liabilities. Before we discuss these ratios, we should examine one other easily determined measure: working capital. Although it is not a ratio, it is an important indicator of a firm's ability to pay its short-term debts.

Working Capital Working capital is the difference between current assets and current liabilities. It indicates how much would remain if a firm paid off all its current liabilities with cash and other current assets. For Northeast,

Current assets	$182,000
Less current liabilities	70,000
Equals working capital	$112,000

The "proper" amount of working capital depends on the type of firm, its past experience, and its particular industry. A firm with too little working capital may have to borrow money to finance its operations. A firm with too much— that is, more working capital than it needs to operate smoothly—may be able to invest its excess working capital in order to earn interest over the short term.

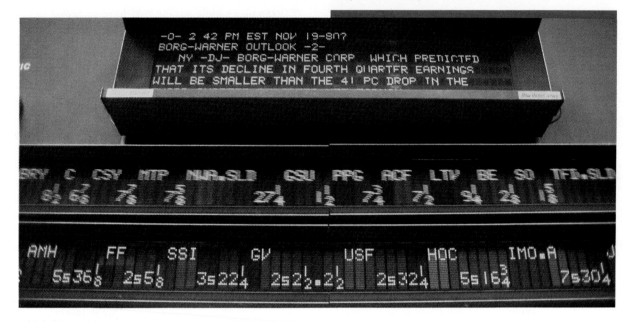

A corporation's "earnings per share" is calculated by dividing net income after taxes by the number of shares of common stock owned by investors. Source: © 1980 Robert McElroy, Woodfin Camp.

Current Ratio A firm's **current ratio** is computed by dividing current assets by current liabilities. For Northeast,

$$\text{Current ratio} = \frac{\text{current assets}}{\text{current liabilities}}$$

$$= \frac{\$182,000}{\$\ 70,000} = 2.6$$

This means that Northeast Art Supply has $2.60 of current assets for every $1 of current liabilities. The average current ratio for all industries is 2.0, but it varies greatly from industry to industry. Each firm should compare its current ratio with those of its own industry, to determine whether it is high or low. A low current ratio can be improved by repaying current liabilities, by converting current liabilities to long-term liabilities, or by increasing the firm's cash balance by reducing dividend payments to stockholders.

Acid-Test Ratio This ratio, sometimes called the *quick ratio,* is a measure of the firm's ability to pay current liabilities quickly—with its cash, marketable securities, and receivables. The **acid-test ratio** is calculated by dividing the sum of cash, marketable securities, accounts receivable, and notes receivable by current liabilities. It is similar to the current ratio, except that the values of the firm's inventories and prepaid expenses do not enter into the calculation. Inventories are "removed" from current assets because they are not converted into cash as easily as other current assets. And prepaid expenses may not be recoverable at all. For Northeast Art Supply,

$$\frac{\text{Acid-test}}{\text{ratio}} = \frac{\begin{array}{l}\text{cash + marketable securities}\\+ \text{ accounts receivable}\\+ \text{ notes receivable}\end{array}}{\text{current liabilities}}$$

$$= \frac{\begin{array}{l}\$59,000 + \$10,000\\+\ \$38,000 + \$32,000\end{array}}{\$70,000}$$

$$= \frac{\$139,000}{\$\ 70,000} = 1.99$$

The average acid-test ratio for all businesses is 1.0. Northeast Art Supply is above average with a ratio of 1.99, and the firm should be well able to pay its current liabilities. To increase a low ratio, a firm would have to repay current

To pay current liabilities a company may have to obtain cash by selling off inventory. *Source: © 1982 Ken Robert Buck, The Picture Cube.*

liabilities, obtain additional cash from investors, or convert current liabilities to long-term debt.

Inventory Turnover A firm's **inventory turnover** is the number of times the firm sells and replaces its merchandise inventory in one year. It is approximated by dividing the cost of goods sold in one year by the average value of the inventory.

The average value of the inventory can be found by adding the beginning and ending inventory values (as given on the income statement) and dividing the sum by 2. For Northeast, this comes out to $40,500. Then,

$$\text{Inventory turnover} = \frac{\text{cost of goods sold}}{\text{average inventory}}$$

$$= \frac{\$334,000}{\$\ 40,500} = 8.2$$

Northeast Art Supply sells and replaces its merchandise inventory 8.2 times each year, or about once every month and a half.

The higher a firm's inventory turnover, the more effectively it is using the money invested in inventory. The average inventory turnover for all firms is about 9 times per year, but turnover rates vary widely from industry to industry. For

example, supermarkets may have turnover rates near 20, whereas turnover rates for furniture stores are generally well below the national average.

Long-Term Debt Ratios

Two financial ratios are of particular interest to lenders of long-term funds. They indicate the degree to which the firm's operations are financed through borrowing.

Debt-to-Assets Ratio The **debt-to-assets ratio** is calculated by dividing total liabilities by total assets. It indicates the extent to which the firm's borrowing is backed by its assets. For Northeast Art Supply,

$$\text{Debt-to-assets ratio} = \frac{\text{total liabilities}}{\text{total assets}}$$

$$= \frac{\$110,000}{\$340,000} = 0.32$$

Northeast's debt-to-assets ratio of 0.32 means that slightly less than one-third of its assets are financed by creditors. For all businesses, the average debt-to-assets ratio is 0.33.

The lower this ratio is, the more assets the firm has to back up its borrowing. Northeast has $3 in assets with which to repay each $1 of borrowing. A high debt-to-assets ratio can be reduced by restricting both short-term and long-term borrowing, by securing additional financing from stockholders, or by reducing dividend payments to stockholders.

Debt-to-Equity Ratio The **debt-to-equity ratio** is calculated by dividing total liabilities by owners' equity. It compares the amount of financing provided by creditors with the amount provided by owners. For Northeast Art Supply,

$$\text{Debt-to-equity ratio} = \frac{\text{total liabilities}}{\text{owners' equity}}$$

$$= \frac{\$110,000}{\$230,000} = 0.48$$

Table 19.2 Summary of Financial Ratios for Northeast Art Supply

Ratio	Formula	Northeast Art Supply	Overall Business Average
Profitability Ratios			
Net profit margin	$$\frac{\text{net income after taxes}}{\text{net sales}}$$	6.6 percent	4–5 percent
Return on equity	$$\frac{\text{net income after taxes}}{\text{owners' equity}}$$	13 percent	12–15 percent
Earnings per share	$$\frac{\text{net income after taxes}}{\text{common stock shares outstanding}}$$	$2.99 per share	—
Short-Term Financial Ratios			
Working capital	current assets *less* current liabilities	$112,000	—
Current ratio	$$\frac{\text{current assets}}{\text{current liabilities}}$$	2.6	2.0
Acid-test ratio	$$\frac{\text{cash + marketable securities + accounts receivable + notes receivable}}{\text{current liabilities}}$$	1.99	1.0
Inventory turnover	$$\frac{\text{cost of goods sold}}{\text{average inventory}}$$	8.2	9
Long-Term Debt Ratios			
Debt-to-assets ratio	$$\frac{\text{total liabilities}}{\text{total assets}}$$	0.32	0.33
Debt-to-equity ratio	$$\frac{\text{total liabilities}}{\text{owners' equity}}$$	0.48	0.33–0.50

A debt-to-equity ratio of 0.48 means that creditors have provided about 48 cents of financing for every dollar provided by owners. In other words, about one-third of Northeast's total financing comes from creditors.

The debt-to-equity ratio for business in general ranges between 0.33 and 0.50. The larger this ratio, the riskier the situation is for lenders. A high debt-to-equity ratio can be reduced by paying off debts or by increasing the owners' investment in the firm.

Northeast's Financial Ratios: A Summary

The formulas that we used in analyzing Northeast Art Supply's financial statements are listed in Table 19.2, along with the ratios we calculated. Northeast seems to be in good financial shape.

Its net profit margin, current ratio, and acid-test ratio are all above average. Its other ratios are about average, although its inventory turnover could be improved. To do so, Northeast might consider ordering smaller quantities of merchandise at shorter intervals. Of course, the resulting decrease in inventory holding costs would have to be balanced against increased ordering costs and the possible cost of stockouts.

Chapter Review

SUMMARY

Accounting is the process of systematically collecting, analyzing, and reporting financial information. Bookkeeping is essentially recordkeeping or a part of the overall accounting process. A private accountant is employed by a specific organization to operate its accounting system and to interpret accounting information. A public accountant performs these functions for various individuals or firms, on a professional-fee basis. Accounting information is used primarily by management, but it is also of interest to creditors, suppliers, stockholders, and government.

The accounting process is based on the accounting equation: Assets = liabilities + owners' equity. Double-entry bookkeeping ensures that the balance shown by this equation is maintained.

There are five steps in the accounting process: (1) Source documents are analyzed to determine which accounts they affect. (2) Each transaction is recorded in a journal. (3) Each journal entry is posted in the affected ledger accounts. (4) At the end of each accounting period, a trial balance is prepared to make sure that the accounting equation is in balance for the period. (5) Financial statements are prepared from the trial balance.

The statement of financial position, or balance sheet, is a summary of a firm's accounts at a particular time. This statement consists of assets, liabilities, and owners' equity, and it must demonstrate that the equation is in balance. On the balance sheet, assets are categorized as current (convertible to cash within a year), fixed (to be used or held for more than one year), or intangible (valuable solely because of rights or advantages that they confer). Similarly, current liabilities are those that are to be repaid within one year, and long-term liabilities are debts that will be repaid after one year. For a sole proprietorship or partnership, owners' equity is reported by the owner's name in the last section of the statement of financial position. For a corporation, the value of common stock, preferred stock, and retained earnings is reported in the owners' equity section.

An income statement is a summary of a firm's financial operations during the accounting period. On this statement, the firm's gross profit on sales is computed by subtracting the cost of goods sold from net sales. Operating expenses are then deducted to compute net income from operations. Finally, non-operating expenses and income taxes are deducted to obtain the firm's net income after taxes.

The information contained in these two financial statements becomes more meaningful when it is compared with corresponding information for previous years, for competitors, and for the industry in which the firm operates. A number of financial ratios can also be formed with this information. These ratios provide a picture of the firm's profitability, its short-term financial position, and its long-term debt financing. Like the information on the firm's financial statements, the ratios can and should be compared with those of past accounting periods, those of competitors, and those representing the average of the industry as a whole.

In the next chapter we shall extend our discussion of information to include *all* the information required to manage a business. We shall see what kinds of information are needed, how data are obtained, and how they are processed by a computer-based management information system.

KEY TERMS

You should now be able to define and give an example relevant to each of the following terms:

accounting

bookkeeping

private accountant

public accountant

certified public
   accountant (CPA)

assets

liabilities

owners' equity

accounting equation

double-entry
   bookkeeping

debit

credit

general journal

general ledger

posting

trial balance

statement of financial
   position
   (or balance sheet)

liquidity

current assets

prepaid expenses

fixed assets

depreciation

intangible assets

goodwill

current liabilities

accounts payable

notes payable

long-term liabilities

income statement

revenues

gross sales

net sales

cost of goods sold

gross profit on sales

FIFO

LIFO

operating expenses

selling expenses

general expenses

net income

financial ratio

net profit margin

return on equity

earnings per share

working capital

current ratio

acid-test ratio

inventory turnover

debt-to-assets ratio

debt-to-equity ratio

QUESTIONS AND EXERCISES
Review Questions

1. What is the difference between accounting and bookkeeping? How are they related?
2. What are certified public accountants? What functions do they perform?
3. List five groups that use accounting information, and briefly explain why each has an interest in this information.
4. State the accounting equation, and list two specific examples of each term in the equation.
5. How is double-entry bookkeeping related to the accounting equation? Briefly, how does it work?
6. Briefly describe the five steps of the accounting cycle, in order.
7. What is the principal difference between a statement of financial position and an income statement?
8. How are current assets distinguished from fixed assets? Give two examples of each.
9. Why are fixed assets depreciated on a balance sheet?
10. Can a single debt (for example, a promissory note) be part current liability and part long-term liability? Explain.
11. Explain how a retailing firm would determine the cost of the goods it sold during an accounting period.
12. How does a firm determine its net income after taxes?
13. Explain the calculation procedure for, and the significance of (a) one profitability ratio, (b) one short-term financial ratio, and (c) one long-term debt ratio.

Discussion Questions

1. Can strict accounting requirements stop fraudulent business practices? What group or groups should develop such requirements? Who should implement them?
2. How might an employee at Equity Funding have discovered the fraud? What would you have done if you were that employee?
3. What can be said about a firm whose owners' equity is a negative amount? How could such a situation come about?
4. Why is it so important to compare a firm's financial statements and ratios with those of previous years, those of competitors, and the average of all firms in the industry in which the firm operates?
5. Do the statement of financial position and the income statement contain all the information you might want as a potential lender or stockholder? What other information would you like to have?
6. Which do you think are the two or three most important financial ratios? Why?

Exercises

1. Table 19.3 lists the ledger account balances for the Green Thumb Garden Shop, which was started just one year ago. From that information, prepare a statement of financial position and an income statement for the business.
2. Using the financial statements you prepared in Exercise 1, evaluate the financial health of the Green Thumb Garden Shop. Explain how the firm's finances could be improved.

Table 19.3 *Account Balances for Green Thumb Garden Shop*

Accounts	Amounts
Cash	$ 7,500
Accounts Receivable	3,500
Inventory	20,000
Equipment	15,000
Accumulated Depreciation	2,000
Accounts Payable	11,000
Long-Term Debt—Equipment	10,000
Owners' Equity	23,000
Sales	48,000
Cost of Goods Sold	23,000
Sales Salaries Expense	8,500
Advertising Expense	1,500
Depreciation Expense	2,000
Rent Expense	6,000
Utilities Expense	1,500
Insurance Expense	1,000
Miscellaneous Expense	500
Income Taxes	600

CASE 19-1

Campbell Soup Company

The Campbell Soup Company, which was founded in 1869, is today one of the world's leading producers and marketers of consumer food products. The firm employs 42,000 people and sells its products in approximately 120 nations. Net sales are over $3 billion.

Campbell's income statement and statement of financial position for 1983 are reproduced in Figures 19.9 and 19.10.[3]

1. Explain what kinds of information you might expect to be included in each of the following entries in Campbell's statement of financial position.
   a. Temporary Investments
   b. Prepaid Expenses
   c. Other Liabilities
   d. Capital Surplus
2. Based on your analysis of available information, how would you describe Campbell's current financial condition? What actions, if any, would you consider taking to improve it? Explain your recommendations. (Compute any financial ratios you think you might need to know before you can answer these questions critically.)

Figure 19.9 *Income Statement for Campbell Soup Company.* Source: Campbell Soup Company, Annual Report, 1983.

Campbell Soup Company

Income Statement
For the Year Ended, July 31, 1983
(Reported in thousands – 000 omitted)

Net Sales		$3,292,433
Costs and Expenses		
Cost of Products Sold	$2,444,213	
Marketing and Sales Expenses	367,053	
Administrative and Research	135,855	
Interest – Net	39,307	2,986,428
Income Before Taxes		$ 306,005
Taxes On Earnings		141,000
Net Income After Taxes		$ 165,005

Figure 19.10 *Statement of Financial Position.* Source: Campbell Soup Company, Annual Report, 1983.

Campbell Soup Company
Statement of Financial Position
July 31, 1983
(Reported in thousands – 000 omitted)

ASSETS

Current Assets

Cash	$ 34,102	
Temporary Investments	178,977	
Accounts Receivable	237,271	
Inventories	456,484	
Prepaid Expenses	25,265	
Total Current Assets		$ 932,099

Fixed Assets

Plant Assets, After Depreciation Is Deducted	$ 889,156	
Total Fixed Assets		889,156
Other Assets		170,271
Total Assets		$1,991,526

LIABILITIES

Current Liabilities

Payable to Suppliers and Others	$ 255,795	
Notes Payable	44,624	
Payrolls and Taxes Payable	152,781	
Total Current Liabilities		$ 453,200
Long-Term Debt		267,465
Other Liabilities		121,457
Total Liabilities		$ 842,122

OWNERS' EQUITY

Owners' Equity

Capital Stock	$ 20,343	
Capital Surplus	35,400	
Earnings Retained in the Business	1,178,620	
Less Capital Stock Not Issued	(54,734)	
Less Cumulative Adjustments	(30,225)	
Total Owners' Equity		$1,149,404
Total Liabilities and Owners' Equity		$1,991,526

CASE 19-2

Tandy Corporation

Tandy Corporation is the owner of more than 5,500 Radio Shack retail stores, the franchisor of an additional 3,000 Radio Shack outlets, the manufacturer of a wide variety of electronic products, and the producer and distributor of the TRS-80 microcomputer. The firm's annual report for 1982 includes the "investment equation" shown in Table 19.4. According to the report, the equation is the framework for discussions of the corporation's philosophies regarding investment and shareholder returns.[4]

1. Explain the significance of each of the following ratios.
   a. Asset-turnover ratio
   b. Return-on-assets ratio
   c. Financial-leverage ratio
2. What, if anything, do the ratios in the equation tell you about Tandy's concern with return on shareholders' investments?

Table 19.4 *Investment Equation and Ratios for Tandy Corporation, 1982*

Asset Turnover	×	Return On Sales	=	Return On Assets	×	Financial Leverage	=	Return On Equity
$\dfrac{\text{Sales}}{\text{Average Assets}}$	×	$\dfrac{\text{Net Income}}{\text{Sales}}$	=	$\dfrac{\text{Net Income}}{\text{Average Assets}}$	×	$\dfrac{\text{Average Assets}}{\text{Average Equity}}$	=	$\dfrac{\text{Net Income}}{\text{Average Equity}}$
1.88	×	11.0	=	20.7	×	1.56	=	32.3

Source: Tandy Corporation, *Annual Report 1982*, p. 16.

CHAPTER

TWENTY
Management Information and Computers

We have been dealing with information throughout this book. Every word, figure, and table in the book is here solely to transmit information to you, the reader. And much of that information is about information: we discussed information as a business resource in Parts 1 and 2. We saw how information is used to recruit, hire, and appraise employees in Part 3. In Part 4 we discussed the need for (and uses of) marketing information. And we emphasized the role of information as the basis for sound money management in Part 5.

In the last chapter, we discussed the development of accounting information from raw data. In this chapter we shall do the same for management information in general. After studying the chapter, you should understand:

1. What information is, and how it differs from data
2. The information requirements of management
3. Why computers are so well suited to being used in management information systems
4. The various sources of business data
5. The basic statistical measures
6. The four functions of a management information system: collecting data, storing and updating data, processing data, and presenting information

Consider this:

Westinghouse Electric Corporation is changing the way its executives and their assistants process information. For years, the firm has had a traditional management information system. This system is capable of maintaining and updating records on a variety of company activities. Operations managers, for example, use it to keep tabs on production levels and on the flow of materials and work in process. Marketing personnel use it to store information on the current prices and inventories of Westinghouse's wide range of products. It is used by the personnel department, by accounting and financial managers, and by administrators throughout the company.

The usefulness of such a system is directly proportional to the amount of information it makes available to executives. Top managers at Westinghouse have realized that, if the firm is to remain competitive, its management information system—and its information-management effort as well—must be extended to other, less traditional areas.

Thus far, the most revolutionary approach to information management at Westinghouse has been taken by the firm's Construction Group in Pittsburgh. In early 1982, every Construction Group typewriter except one was removed, despite the fact that secretaries typically spend one-third of their time at their typewriters. The single exception was a typewriter that was left close to the office of the group president, for use in making minor corrections. And people who use that typewriter must log in their time, to ensure that the machine is not overused.

In place of the typewriters, a computer terminal was issued to every secretary and every boss. The terminal gives them direct access to the information system for immediate input or retrieval of information. This computerized system not only extends the Construction Group's data base; it also eliminates some annoying or time-wasting chores.

Executives who are away from their desks for even a few minutes often return to find a small stack of memos about telephone calls they

missed. Each of these calls has to be returned, and often the original caller is no longer at his or her desk. Now, people who call the Construction Group can record their messages in the information system. Whenever an executive has a few minutes of free time, he or she simply dials the message center. All messages addressed to that executive are then displayed on his or her own computer screen. The executive can, in turn, use the system to reply to inquiries or transmit additional messages.

Along with the typewriters, the Construction Group eliminated the standard dictation equipment. Now managers dictate their letters and reports into a central word-processing system. A clerical pool then performs any necessary editing and routes the communication to the appropriate person.

At first there was some concern among secretaries that these changes would eliminate their jobs. Once they realized that this was not the firm's purpose in installing the new system, they themselves became more productive. For one thing, turnover among clerical employees declined substantially. The secretaries also began to look for and discover ways to cut costs in their own work. For example, the secretaries realized that they were duplicating each other's efforts every day, when they distributed packets of information to various locations within the company. They responded by devising a system that consolidated all communications going to each specific location.

All things considered, the new system seems to be working well for Westinghouse. Managers report that they now have more time to spend on substantive matters. And the clerical staff has a greater sense of responsibility and added pride in its work.[1]

Source: Courtesy of The Westinghouse Electric Corporation.

As noted in Chapter 5, managers spend about 75 percent of their time communicating with others. On a typical day, a manager is likely to be bombarded with telephone calls, letters, reports, meetings, and visitors—in other words, with information. If the manager is lucky, he or she is able to spend the rest of the workday using this information. (Managers who are less fortunate or less efficient can end up processing information well after normal working hours.)

Information is the basic material from which plans are developed and decisions are made. To help their managers obtain and use information, most firms establish management information systems. The recent "computer revolution" has expanded the capabilities and capacities of such systems and, therefore, their usefulness.

Westinghouse already had a traditional management information system—one that accepted and processed the data that are of interest to executives. To many firms, updating such a system would simply mean installing one or more computers in order to store more information, to glean it from more sources, and to process it more quickly.

Westinghouse, however, is using the latest technology to bring its information system directly to those who use it and to provide them with information faster. This same technology also takes most of the drudgery out of information transmission and data processing. Westinghouse's new system is designed to automate the process of everyday communication. The firm is concerned with both the 25 percent of the day when managers *use* information and the 75 percent of the day during which they *transmit* information.

We shall examine management information systems from the roots up—beginning with the information requirements of the typical manager. You will see what management information systems are, what they must do, and why the computer has become so very important to these systems.

MANAGEMENT INFORMATION

In Chapter 19 we noted that an accounting system converts financial data into financial information. There is an important difference between data and information, although in many contexts the two terms are used interchangeably. Let us first look at this difference. Then we shall briefly discuss the information requirements of management.

Data versus Information

Data are numerical or verbal descriptions that usually result from measurements of some sort. (The word *data* is plural; the singular form is *datum*.) An individual's current wage level, a firm's net after-tax profit last year, and the names of automobiles currently produced in the United States are all data. Most people think of data as being numerical only, but they can be nonnumerical as well. A description of an individual as a "tall, sturdily built female with short, dark hair" would certainly qualify as data.

Information is data of a particular sort. Specifically, **information** is data that are presented in a form that is useful for a specific purpose. Suppose a personnel manager wants to compare the wages paid to male and female employees by the firm over the past four years. The manager might begin with a stack of computer output listing every person employed by the firm, along with his or her current and past wages. But such a printout would consist of data rather than information. The manager would be hard pressed to make any sense of the mass of names and numbers.

Now suppose the manager goes back to the computer and has it compute and graph the average wage paid to males and that paid to females in each of the four years. The resulting graph (Figure 20.1) is information, because the manager can use it for the purpose at hand—to compare wages paid to males and females over the four-year period.

The wage data became information when they were summarized in the chart given in Figure 20.1. Often, a large set of data must be summarized if they are to be at all useful, but this is not always the case. For example, suppose the manager had wanted to know only the wage history of a specific employee. That information would be contained in the original computer output. The manager would only have to find the employee's name in the listing to locate the required information. That is, the data would already be in the most useful form for the manager's purpose; they would need no further processing.

Managers' Information Requirements

What information do managers need? They need all the information they can get about their firm and the environment in which it operates. Managers have to plan for the future, implement their plans in the present, and evaluate the results against what has been accomplished in the past. Thus they need access to information that summarizes future possibilities, the present situation, and past performance. Of course, the specific types of information they need depend on their area of management and on their level within the firm.

Figure 20.1 Data versus Information. Data are numerical or verbal descriptions that usually result from measurements; information is data presented in a form useful for a specific purpose.

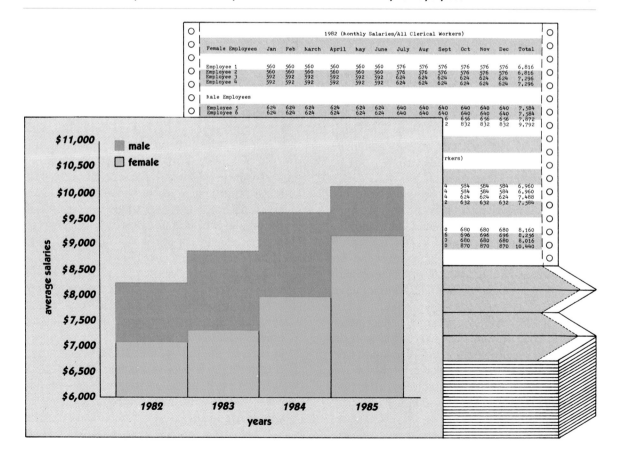

Management Information by Area In Chapter 5 we identified five areas of management: financial, operations, marketing, personnel, and administrative. Financial managers are obviously most concerned with the firm's finances. They ponder its debts and receivables, cash flow, future capitalization needs, financial ratios, and other accounting information. Of equal importance to financial managers is information about the present state of the economy and predictions of business conditions for the near future.

Operations managers are concerned with present and future sales levels and with the availability of the resources required to meet sales forecasts. They need to know the cost of producing the firm's goods and services, including inventory costs. And they are involved with new-product planning. They must also keep abreast of any new production technology that might be useful to their firm.

Marketing managers need to have available detailed information about their firm's product mix and the products offered by competitors. Such information includes prices and pricing strategies, new and projected promotional campaigns, and new products that are being test-marketed by competitors. Information concerning target markets and changes in those markets, market share, new and pending product legislation, and developments within marketing channels is also important to marketing managers.

Personnel managers must be aware of anything that pertains to the firm's employees and employment in general—from plant safety to the unemployment rate. Key examples include current wage levels and benefits packages both within the firm and in firms that compete for valuable employees; current legislation and court decisions that affect employment practices; union activities; and the firm's plans for growth, expansion, or merger.

Administrative managers are responsible for the overall management of the organization. Thus they are concerned with the coordination of information—just as they are concerned with the coordination of other business resources. First,

All five areas of management—financial, operational, marketing, human resources, and administrative—require information from many sources. Source: Courtesy of Televideo Systems, Inc.

administrators must ensure that subordinates have access to the information they need in order to do their jobs. Second, they are concerned that area managers make use of this information. And third, they must ensure that the information is used in a consistent manner. Suppose, for example, that the operations group is designing a new plant to be opened in five years. Is the capacity of the plant consistent with marketing plans, on the basis of economic projections? Will personnel managers be able to staff the plant, on the basis of their employment forecasts? And will projected sales generate enough income to cover the expected cost of financing?

Management Information by Level We also noted in Chapter 5 that there are three general levels of management: top, middle, and lower. Information requirements vary across these management levels, just as they vary from area to area.

Top managers need information that reflects a broad perspective, deals with the long term, and is presented in a very succinct or condensed form. Middle managers require narrower, less condensed information that deals with the relatively near future as well as the present. Lower-level managers are most concerned with short-term, detailed information with a fairly narrow focus.

As an illustration of these differences, consider a top-level, a middle-level, and a lower-level marketing manager within a large, multiproduct firm. In managing the firm's overall marketing effort, the top marketing executive has to deal with projected sales levels for all the firm's products for, say, the next five years. These huge numbers of data must be summarized radically to have any informational value at all. Weekly or monthly fluctuations in sales—either present or projected—

Figure 20.2 *Management Information System (MIS)*. Source: Adapted from Ricky W. Griffin, Management, p. 51.

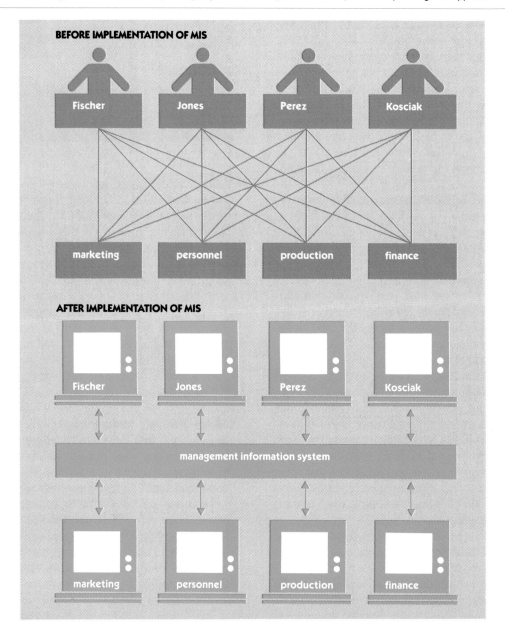

are of minimal concern to this executive as long as no problems arise.

In a firm that is departmentalized by product, the middle manager may be responsible for sales of one particular line of products. Hence he or she is concerned with sales of that one line, over a period extending perhaps two years into the future. Sales trends for specific products or sales districts are a constant concern in the administration of the product line.

Finally, a lower-level manager—say, a regional sales manager—may be responsible for ten sales representatives within one geographic area. This manager's attention is focused on the weekly and monthly sales generated by those employees. Specific information on the number of sales calls made, dollar volume of sales, and so on—the details—are of most interest here. This manager's planning horizon is probably limited to one year.

It should be clear that managers in different areas and at different levels in the firm need a great deal of information of various kinds. We shall now consider how a single management information system can work for all of them.

THE MANAGEMENT INFORMATION SYSTEM

Where do managers get the information they need? In many organizations, the answer lies in a **management information system** (MIS), which is a means of providing managers with the information they need to perform their functions as effectively as possible. (See Figure 20.2.)

If this sounds like the marketing information system discussed in Chapter 11, the similarity is intended. A well-designed MIS operates very much as a good marketing information system does, but it is considerably wider in scope. In many firms, the MIS is combined with a marketing information system so that it can provide information based on a wide variety of data. Accounting data should be included in the MIS as well. In fact, it makes little sense to have separate information systems for the various management areas. After all, the goal is to provide needed information to all managers.

Functions of the System

In order to provide information, a management information system must perform four specific functions. It must collect data, store and then update them as necessary, process stored data into information, and present information to users of the system. (See Figure 20.3.)

Obviously, data must be collected if they are to be available for processing and presentation. The data that are entered into the system must be *relevant* to both the operation of the firm and

the needs of its managers. And, perhaps most important, these data must be *accurate*. Irrelevant data are simply useless; inaccurate data can be disastrous.

The system must be capable of storing data until they are needed. And it must be able to update stored data to ensure that the information presented to managers is *timely*. An operations manager cannot produce finished goods with last week's work-in-process inventory. She or he needs to know what is available today.

Much of the power of a management information system stems from its ability to transform data into useful information. The system must be capable of processing data in different ways in order to meet the particular needs of different managers. Where this processing requires condensation or summarizing, the accuracy, relevance, and timeliness of the data must be maintained.

Finally, the system must be capable of presenting the information in a *usable form*. That is, the method of presentation—tables, graphs, or charts, for example—must be in keeping with the information itself and with the uses to which it will be put.

We shall explore each of these functions in more detail, later in this chapter.

Size and Complexity of the System

A management information system must be tailored to the needs of the organization it serves. For example, the system should be designed to fill the information requirements of managers at all levels and in all areas of the firm. This is especially true with regard to storage and data-processing capability.

In some firms there may be a tendency to save on initial costs by purchasing a system that is too small or simple. Such a system generally ends up serving only one or two management levels or a single department—the one that gets its data into the system first. Managers in other departments "give up" on the system as soon as they find that it cannot accept or process their data. They either look elsewhere for information or do without.

Figure 20.3 *Four MIS Functions*

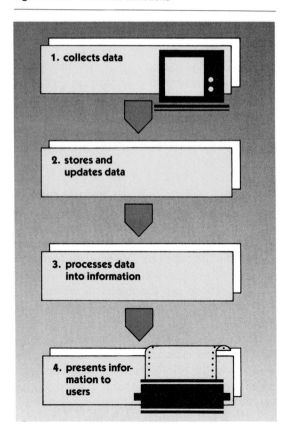

1. collects data

2. stores and updates data

3. processes data into information

4. presents information to users

One of the nation's "Big Eight" accounting firms recently learned that guarding against a minor problem can result in major savings.

Arthur Young & Co. offices provide accounting and auditing service to businesses across the country. Because of its location in the heart of Northern California's Silicon Valley, the San Jose office deals almost exclusively in high-tech clients. The office uses more than two dozen computers, including Apple IIIs, Lisas, Eagles, Altos, and IBM. A year ago, Chris Veal, director of computer audit, began hearing reports of machine failures and disappearing data. "I got tired of people coming to me with complaints that machines didn't work, had died, or done something to the data diskette," he said.

Mr. Veal felt certain the problem lay neither with the machines nor the programs, but with electrostatic discharge. Static electricity, which builds up on clothing and computer enclosures and plastics, emits tiny bolts of microlightning. Most of the time, people are not aware of its occurrence.

This discharge is responsible for a host of data processing problems: hardware and software damage, glitches, ghost bytes, and loss of memory.

The operators were unintentionally creating the discharges by "shuffling across carpets and zapping the machine or diskette," Mr. Veal discovered. Discharge is more prevalent in colder weather, and the number of complaints rose during Northern California's heavy winter season last year. He tried a couple of methods to solve the problem, both unsuccessfully. Then a chance conversation on an airplane led the director to the right solution. One of his audit people was seated beside scientist Rollin McCraty, developer of an electronic antistatic device known commercially as StatKleer, marketed by the Evans Specialty Co., Richmond, Va.

A small device measuring $5\frac{3}{8}'' \times 4\frac{1}{4}''$, Stat-Kleer emits a constant stream of positive and negative ions that prevent static discharge from occurring. A single unit can sit on a desk or computer table.

Mr. McCraty and consultant Tom Watkins inspected the San Jose office, whose computer section is in a large open area. Their recommendation was to install 12 machines and continue applying antistatic sprays to carpets and furniture. The installation took place last August, and Mr. Veal reports the units have been operating as promised.

Source: "Static Electricity Can Become a Major Problem," *The Office*, March 1984, p. 31.

Almost as bad is an MIS that is too large or too complex for the organization. Unused size and complexity do nothing but increase the cost of owning and operating the system. In addition, a system that is difficult to use may not be used at all. Managers may find that it is easier to maintain their own records and to seek general business information from periodicals. Or, again, they may try to operate without information that could be helpful in their decision making.

Obviously, much is expected of an effective MIS. Let us see how the computer has come to fit naturally into the recording and manipulation of information that managers need.

COMPUTERS AND THE MIS

Nowadays, the key component of an effective MIS is a computer or a computer network. This was not always the case, however. Even after computers were developed and mass-produced, most were too large and too expensive to use in an MIS. Until perhaps 15 years ago, most MISs

Just fifteen years ago, most records were kept in written form, requiring clerks to do the computer's job by hand.
Source: © Ellis Herwig, The Picture Cube.

were manual systems. Records were kept in written form, and clerical personnel were responsible for collecting, filing, retrieving, and processing the data required by managers.

The change to the computer-based MIS came about with the advent of low-cost computers that were produced in a range of sizes and especially designed for business use. This "computer revolution" put computers—and the computer-based MIS—within reach of nearly every business.

A **computer** is a machine that can accept, store, manipulate, and transmit data in accordance with a set of specific instructions. A computer can thus perform all four functions of an MIS. Moreover, it can store large amounts of data, process them very rapidly with perfect accuracy, and transmit (or present) results in a variety of ways. In other words, the computer is almost a ready-made MIS. For example, Carter Hawley Hale Stores, Inc., is a large corporation that owns several retail companies: Neiman-Marcus in Dallas, Bergdorf Goodman in New York, Waldenbooks based in Stamford, Connecticut, and John Wanamaker in Philadelphia, to name a few. Altogether, Carter's management must keep track of more than 1000 stores and more than 8 million items of merchandise. To deal with all this,

Carter's management invested $75 million in a computer center near Los Angeles to keep track of all the buying, pricing, and inventory-control data and to provide management with the information it needs to run the retail network.

The Vocabulary of Computers

It is not our purpose here to teach you how to use computers. (In fact, you may already be quite proficient in computer use. More and more people are becoming "computer literate" each day.) However, we should identify the main components of the computer and define the basic computer terms.

Computer Components Most computers and computer systems consist of five basic components. (See Figure 20.4.) The **input unit** is the device to enter data into a computer. In the past, data were fed to computers on punched cards, which were "read" by the input unit. Few systems use this method now. Instead, data are entered through a keyboard (much like a typewriter keyboard) or on magnetic tapes or disks that the input unit can read.

The **memory unit** (or **storage unit**) is the

part of a computer that stores all data entered into the computer and processed by it. One measure of a computer's power is the amount of data that can be stored within it at one time. This memory capacity is given in *bytes*: One byte is the capacity to store one character, and K bytes is the capacity to store 1024 characters. A personal computer with a 256K memory is thus capable of storing almost 60 pages of this book.

The **control unit** is the part of a computer that guides the entire operation of the computer. It transfers data and sends processing directions to the various other units, in the proper sequence to carry out the instructions of the user.

The **arithmetic-logic unit** is the part of a computer that performs mathematical operations,

comparisons of data, and other types of data transformations.

The **output unit** is the mechanism by which a computer transmits processed data to the user. Most commonly, computer output is printed on paper or displayed on a television-like screen called a *monitor*.

Hardware and Software Computer **hardware** is the electronic equipment or machinery used in a computer system. Hence, a keyboard used to enter data, the arithmetic/logic, control, and storage units, and the monitor are all hardware. **Software,** on the other hand, is the set of instructions that tells a computer what to do. These instructions are called the computer *program*.

Figure 20.4 *How a Computer Works. A computer is a machine that can accept, store, manipulate, and transmit data in accordance with a set of specific instructions. Most computers consist of five basic components. Source: Adapted from George J. Brabb and Gerald W. McKean,* Business Data Processing, *p. 21.*

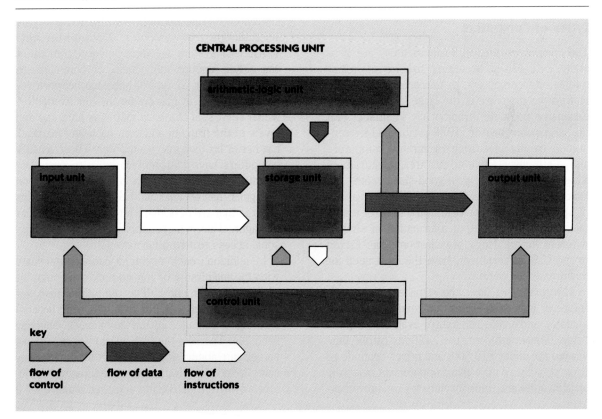

The manner in which a computer processes data is controlled through the program.

Types of Computers

The computers used in business today are generally categorized according to size as mainframes, minicomputers, or microcomputers. The *mainframe computer* is the large, powerful, and expensive computer traditionally identified with the largest businesses. IBM established its reputation by manufacturing mainframe computers and is still very active in this area. Mainframes, which may be as big as a good-sized room, can handle huge quantities of data, perform a variety of operations on these data in fractions of a second, and provide output information in several different forms. Huge organizations, like Exxon or the U.S. government, have the most need for mainframe computers.

Minicomputers are the smaller computers (more or less desk-sized) that revolutionized the industry and made computers available to most firms. These self-contained systems can be purchased for under $10,000, and prices continue to drop steadily. With a minicomputer and specially written software, most businesses can now maintain very sophisticated information systems that were beyond their reach before. Digital Equipment's VAX series are extremely powerful minicomputers used by many businesses today.

The *microcomputer,* the latest breakthrough, is a desk-top computer. It was made possible by the development of microprocessor *chips,* a fraction of an inch in size, that contain all the electronic circuitry required to perform large-scale data processing. Microcomputers, which are also referred to as personal computers, sell for as little as several hundred dollars or as much as a few thousand dollars. Although microcomputers are often purchased for use in the home, many smaller firms find them completely satisfactory for their limited needs. Companies like IBM, Wang, Digital, and Apple make microcomputers for the small-business market.

Computer Networks

The concept of networking is perhaps the greatest boon to management information systems since the low-cost computer. A **computer network** is a system in which several computers can either function individually or communicate with each other. A typical business network revolves around a mainframe or minicomputer, which serves as the basic MIS for all areas and levels of the firm. In addition, each key manager has her or his own microcomputer. These smaller computers have sufficient capacity to store up-to-date information that the managers require on a regular basis. That is, each micro maintains records that are of primary interest to a particular manager. This manager has immediate and personal access to that information.

In addition, each manager can communicate with the mainframe or minicomputer through his or her microcomputer. The operations manager in charge of shipping, for example, may be considering a change in the company's shipping schedule. To make the change, he needs to know something about sales patterns in the various sales territories. Rather than requesting the information from marketing and then waiting for it to be prepared, he can simply tie into the main-frame and extract the information he needs.

Similarly, the microcomputers can communicate directly with each other. Once the new shipping schedule has been drafted, the shipping manager is able to transmit it to other managers—computer to computer—to get their opinions.

The system now being used by Westinghouse's Construction Group (described at the beginning of this chapter) is a computer network. As you can see, networking opens the standard MIS to a wide range of new uses.

Now that we know what an MIS is and how important computers have become in MIS applications, it is time to examine in detail the four functions of an MIS: collecting data, storing and updating data, processing data, and presenting information.

COLLECTING DATA

A computer network provides the most flexibility that is presently available in a management information system. On the other hand, a microcomputer-based MIS may be fully adequate for many small firms. What is important is (1) that the MIS be compatible with the needs of the firm and (2) that it be used.

The first step in using an MIS is to gather the information needed to establish the system—that is, the firm's *data bank*. This data bank should include all past and current data that may be useful in managing the firm. The data themselves can be obtained from within the firm and from outside sources.

Internal Sources of Data

Typically, the majority of the data gathered for an MIS come from internal sources. The most common internal sources of information include company records, reports, managers, and conferences and meetings.

Past and present accounting data can be obtained from ledgers or from financial statements.

Union College, located in Lincoln, Neb., is the first in the nation to provide its students with computer terminals in every dormitory room at no additional cost.

According to Tom Becker, the college's director of computer services, "the school wants to make students as comfortable with computers as with a telephone. We want to take away the mystery of the computer and enable all students, music majors as well as math majors, to use it as a tool."

The terminals in each of the college's 410 dormitory rooms access a Hewlett-Packard 3000 through a data PABX from Micom Systems, Chatsworth, Calif. The system is called Micro600 and provides the students with password protection for privacy.

Now, many students who had never worked with a computer before are using a word processor to revise term papers and are drawing on a variety of databases in the comfort of their own dormitory rooms.

Source: *Office Administration & Automation,* January 1984, p. 42.

Accounting source documents can be used to obtain information about the firm's customers, creditors, and suppliers. Similarly, sales reports are a source of data on sales and sales patterns, pricing strategies, and level and effectiveness of promotional campaigns during past years. Various management reports and the minutes of committee meetings can also yield valuable information to include in an MIS.

Personnel records are useful as a source of data on wage and benefits levels, hiring patterns, employee turnover, and other human-resource variables. Production and inventory records can be used to reconstruct patterns of production, inventory movement, costs, and the like.

Present and past forecasts should also be included in the MIS, along with data indicating how well these forecasts predicted actual events. Similarly, specific plans and management decisions—regarding capital expansion and new product development, for example—should be made a part of the system.

The firm's managers can supply additional data concerning its economic and legal situation. For instance, financial managers can provide information about the firm's credit rating and insurance. Legal personnel can add data regarding lawsuits and the firm's compliance with pertinent government regulations, especially in the areas administered by OSHA.

External Sources of Data

External sources of management data include customers, suppliers, bankers, trade and financial publications, industry conferences, and firms that specialize in gathering data for organizations.

Again, these data take various forms, depending on the needs and requirements of the firm and its managers. A marketing research company may be used to acquire forecasts pertaining to product demand, consumer tastes, and other marketing variables. Suppliers are an effective source of information about the future availability and costs of the raw materials and parts used by the firm.

Bankers can often provide valuable economic insights and projections. The information furnished by trade publications and industry conferences is usually concerned as much with the future as with the present. Both are valuable sources of data on competitors and production technology.

Legal issues and court decisions that may affect the firm are occasionally discussed in local newspapers and, more often, in specialized publications such as *The Wall Street Journal, Fortune,* and *Business Week.* Such publications provide a variety of other useful information as well. Government publications like the *Monthly Labor Review* and the *Federal Reserve Bulletin* are also quite useful as sources of information.

Cautions in Collecting Data

Three cautions should be observed in collecting data for an MIS. First, the cost of obtaining data from such external sources as marketing research firms can be quite high. And in all cases, the cost of obtaining data should be weighed against the potential benefit that having the data will confer on the firm.

Second, although computers do not make mistakes, the people who program them can make or cause errors. By simply pushing the wrong key on a computer keyboard, a technician can change an entire set of data, along with the information it contains. Data—from whatever source—should always be viewed in light of the manager's judgment and intuition. Where there is a disagreement between data (or information) and judgment, the data should be checked.

Third, outdated or incomplete data usually yield inaccurate information. Data collection is an ongoing process. New data must be added to the data bank as they are obtained, or they should be used to update the existing store of data regularly.

STORING AND UPDATING DATA

Data should be entered into the data bank as they are collected. Computers are especially well suited for both storing and rapidly updating MIS data.

Storing data is simply holding them for future use. A computer can store vast quantities of data in a very small space. Depending on the particular type of computer, the data may be stored on magnetic tapes or disks. Magnetic tapes and hard disks can hold the most data. They are generally associated with mainframes and some minicomputers. Floppy (soft) disks are used with some minicomputers and with almost all microcomputers.

Large mainframes can store millions of bytes. However, that storage capacity is generally used for the particular data that are being processed at any given time (and for the processing instructions). When data are stored for an MIS, the

computer is used only to transfer the data to tapes or disks: The programmer enters the data into the computer, which transfers it to a tape or disk in a form that can be read by a special input device. When the tape or disk is full, the programmer removes it from the machine, makes a note about which data it contains, stores the tape or disk on a shelf, and (if necessary) continues with another tape or disk. When the data stored on a particular disk are needed, the disk is inserted into an input device that enters it into the computer.

Manual Updating   To update stored data manually, a programmer inserts the proper tape or disk into the computer, locates the data that are to be changed, and provides the new data. The computer automatically replaces the older data with the new.

The frequency with which data are updated depends on how fast they change and how often they are used. When it is vital to have current data, updating may occur daily. Otherwise, new data may be collected and held for updating at a certain time each week, or perhaps each month.

Automatic Updating   In automatic updating, the system itself updates the existing data bank as new information becomes available. The data bank, usually in the form of hard disks, is permanently connected into the MIS. The computer automatically finds the proper disk and replaces the existing data with the new data.

Many larger supermarkets have installed cash registers that automatically transmit, to a central computer, information regarding each item sold. The computer adjusts the store's inventory records accordingly. At any time of day, the manager can get precise, up-to-the-minute information on the inventory of every item sold by the store. In some systems, the computer may even be programmed to reorder items whose inventories fall below some specified level!

Forms of Updating   We have been discussing the type of updating in which new data are *substituted for* old data. Although this is an efficient type of

updating in terms of the use of storage, it does result in the loss of the old data. In a second form of updating, new data are *added to* the old data—much as a new file folder is placed between two folders that are already in a drawer. (In fact, on a magnetic tape or disk, existing data are actually spread apart by the computer to accommodate the new data.) The form of updating used depends entirely on whether the existing data will be needed in the future.

PROCESSING DATA

Data are collected, stored in an MIS, and updated under the assumption that they will be of use to managers. Some data are used in the form in which they are stored. This is especially true of verbal data—a legal opinion, for example. Other data require processing of some sort to extract,

Figure 20.5 *Statistics. Statistics are numbers that summarize the characteristics of an entire group of numbers.*

```
RONDEX CORPORATION
Daily billings for the week
of June 4, 1984

DATE                    BILLINGS
=================================
June 4              $4,427.00
June 5              $4,168.00
June 6              $3,904.00   < median
June 7              $3,807.00
June 8              $3,619.00
---------           ----------
Total               $19,925.00
```

$$\text{arithmetic mean} = \frac{\text{total}}{\text{number of items}} = \$3{,}985.000$$

range = difference between highest and lowest entries = $808.00

no frequency distribution, since each entry appears only once

no mode, since each entry appears only once

highlight, or summarize the information they contain. We shall define **data processing** as the transformation of data into a form that is useful for a specific purpose. In other words, data processing transforms data into information. For verbal data, this processing consists mainly of extracting the pertinent material from storage and combining it into a report.

Most business data, however, are in the form of numbers—large groups of numbers, such as daily sales volumes or annual earnings of workers in a particular city. Such groups of numbers are difficult to handle and to comprehend, but their information content can be summarized through the use of statistics.

Statistics as Summaries

A **statistic** is a measure of a particular characteristic of a group of numbers. The statistic itself is a number that summarizes the characteristic for the entire group. We shall discuss the most commonly used statistics (or statistical measures). For this purpose, we shall use the data given in Figure 20.5. This table contains only five items of data, which will simplify our discussion. In most business situations, we would be dealing with tens or hundreds of items. Fortunately, computers can be programmed to process such large groups of numbers quickly. Managers are free to concern themselves mainly with the information that results.

The number of items in a set of data can be reduced by developing a frequency distribution. A **frequency distribution** is a listing of the number of times each value appears in the data set. Each of the dollar values in Figure 20.5 appears only once, so such a listing would not do us any good. However, we can group the data to obtain the *grouped frequency distribution:*

Billing, $	Number of Items
4000 to 4499	2
3500 to 3999	3

By summarizing the data in this way, we have reduced the number of data items by 60 percent.

Measures of Size and Dispersion

Perhaps the most familiar statistic is the arithmetic mean, which is commonly called the *average*. The **arithmetic mean** of a set of data is the sum of all the data values, divided by the number of items in the set. The sum of the daily billings given in Figure 20.5 is $19,925. Because there are five items, the average (arithmetic mean) daily billing is $19,925 ÷ 5, or $3985.

The arithmetic mean is a measure, or summary, of the sizes of the items in a data set. Two other summaries of size (or magnitude) are the median and the mode. The **median** of a set of data is the value that appears at the exact middle of the data when they are arranged in order from the highest value to the lowest. The data in Figure 20.5 are already arranged from the highest value to the lowest value. Their median is thus $3904, which is exactly halfway between the top and bottom values.

The **mode** of a set of data is the value that appears most frequently in the set. Each value appears only once in Figure 20.5, so that data set has no mode.

Size, of course, is an important characteristic of the items in a data set. But size alone does not describe the set. Another characteristic that is often summarized is the dispersion, or spread, of the items within the set. The simplest measure of disperson is the **range,** which is the difference between the highest value and the lowest value in a set of data. The range of the data in Figure 20.5 is $4427 − $3619 = $808.

The smaller the range of a data set, the closer the values are to the mean—and, thus, the more effective the mean is as a measure of those values. Other measures of dispersion that are used to describe business data are the *variance* and the *standard deviation*. These are somewhat more complicated than the range, and we shall not define or calculate them here. However, you should remember that larger values of both the variance and the standard deviation indicate a greater spread among the values of the data.

With the proper software, a computer can provide these and other statistical measures almost as fast as a programmer can ask for them. How they are used is then up to the manager. Although statistics provide information in a much more manageable form than raw data, they can be interpreted incorrectly. Note, for example, that the average of the daily billings given in Figure 20.5 is $3985, yet not one of the billings is exactly equal to that amount. This distinction between actual data and the statistics that describe them is an important one that should never be disregarded.

PRESENTING INFORMATION

Processed data should be presented in the form in which they have the most informational value. Verbal information may be presented in list or paragraph form. Numerical information, and combinations of numerical and verbal information, are most easily and effectively presented in visual and tabular displays.

Visual Displays

A **visual display** is a diagram that represents several items of information in a manner that makes comparison easier or reflects trends among the items. The most accurate visual display is a *graph*, in which values are plotted to scale on a set of axes. Graphs are most effective for presenting information about a single variable that changes with time (such as variations in the gross national product over the last 40 years). They tend to emphasize trends as well as peaks and low points in the value of the variable.

In a *bar chart,* each value is represented as a vertical or horizontal bar. The longer a bar, the greater the value. This type of display is useful for presenting values that are to be compared. The eye can quickly pick out the longest or shortest bar, or even those that seem to be of average size.

A *pie chart* is a circle (the "pie") that is divided into "slices," each of which represents a different item. The circle represents the whole—for example, a total cost. The size of each slice shows

Data should be presented in a form that provides the most information such as graphs, bar charts, and pie charts.
Source: Courtesy of Quadram Corporation.

the contribution of that item to the whole. The larger the slice, the larger the contribution. By their nature, pie charts are most effective in displaying the relative size or importance of various items of information.

Tabular Displays

A **tabular display** is an array of verbal or numerical information in columns and rows. It is most useful in presenting information about two or more related variables (for example, variations in both sales volume and size of sales force by territory).

Tabular displays generally have less impact than visual displays. Moreover, the data contained in most two-column tables (like Figure 20.5) can be displayed visually. However, to display the information in, say, a three-column table, several bar or pie charts would be required. In such a case, the items of information are easier to compare when they are presented in a table. Also, information that is to be manipulated—used, for example, to calculate interest payments—is most often displayed in tabular form.

Chapter Review

SUMMARY

Data are numerical or verbal descriptions, whereas information is data that are presented in a form that is useful for a specific purpose. Managers in different areas of a business generally require information pertaining to their own areas. Managers at higher levels usually need more general, longer-range information. Lower-level managers are concerned mainly with more specific, near-term information.

A management information system is a means of providing managers with the information they need to perform their functions as effectively as possible. The data that are entered into the system must be relevant, accurate, and timely. The information provided by the system must be all of these—and it must be in usable form as well. The system itself should be designed to match the firm it serves in size and complexity.

At the heart of most management information systems is a computer—a machine that can perform all the functions of an MIS. Firms can choose mainframe computers, minicomputers, or microcomputers to match their information needs. Each of these machines consists of at least one input unit (perhaps along with tape or disk readers), a memory unit, an arithmetic/logic unit, a control unit, and an output unit. In addition, computers require software, or programs, which are operating instructions.

The four functions performed by an MIS are collecting data, storing and updating data, processing data, and presenting information. Data may be collected from such internal sources as accounting documents and other financial records, sales and production records, and conferences and meetings. External sources include customers, suppliers, bankers, publications, and information-gathering organizations.

With a computer, data can be stored on magnetic tapes and disks and used whenever they are needed. Data should be updated in order to maintain their timeliness and accuracy. Updating can also be accomplished via the computer.

Data processing is the MIS function that transforms stored data into a form that is useful for a specific purpose. Large groups of numerical data are usually processed into summary numbers called statistics. The mean, median, and mode are measures of the sizes of the values in a set of data. The range is a measure of the dispersion, or spread, of the data values.

Finally, the processed data (which can now be called information) must be presented for use. Verbal information is generally presented in list or paragraph form. Numerical information is most often displayed in graphs and charts or tables.

The next chapter opens a series of discussions on the environment in which businesses operate. In Chapter 21 we shall examine the legal environment, placing emphasis on the laws that have been enacted primarily to regulate business activities.

KEY TERMS

You should now be able to define and give an example relevant to each of the following terms:

data

information

management information system

computer

input unit

memory (or storage) unit

control unit

arithmetic-logic unit

output unit

hardware

software

computer network

data processing

statistic

frequency distribution

arithmetic mean

median

mode

range

visual display

tabular display

QUESTIONS AND EXERCISES
Review Questions

1. What is the difference between data and information? Give one example of accounting data and one example of accounting information.
2. How do the information requirements of managers differ by management area?
3. What general types of information are of most interest to top managers? to middle managers? to lower-level managers?
4. List the four functions of a management information system.
5. What is meant by "tailoring" an MIS to the firm?
6. List the five primary units within a computer, and briefly state the function of each.
7. What is meant by the term *computer networking*?
8. List several internal and several external sources of data.
9. In a computer-based MIS, must the computer have a large enough memory to store the entire data bank? Explain.
10. What kinds of data might be updated by substituting new data for old data? by adding new data to old data?
11. What are the differences among the mean, median, and mode of a set of data? In what way are they alike?
12. Data set A has a mean of 20 and a range of 10; data set B has the same mean and a range of 4. In which data set are the values closer to each other in size? How do you know?
13. When should information be presented in tabular form rather than in a visual display?

Discussion Questions

1. What is your conception of a "traditional" management information system?
2. The new MIS at Westinghouse's Construction Group would seem to be expensive to purchase, install, and operate. What benefits are derived from the system? Are they worth the cost?
3. How can confidential data (such as the wages of individual employees) be kept confidential but be made available to managers who need them?
4. Why are computers so well suited to management information systems? What are some things that computers *cannot* do in dealing with data and information?
5. Do managers really need all the kinds of information discussed in this chapter? If not, which kinds can they do without?

Exercises

1. Leaf through a few magazines to find advertisements for three different brands of computers. For each brand, list the product attributes that are stressed in the ads. Then state whether each attribute would be important in an MIS, and why.
2. Construct a bar chart, a pie chart, and a graph to display the data given in Figure 20.5. Which method of presentation is most effective? Why?

CASE 20-1

"Information, Please!" at Butler Distributing

Butler Distributing Company is a medium-sized warehousing and distributing firm located in Texas. The company serves as a clearinghouse for three major hardware chains. It purchases approximately 150 different products directly from the manufacturers in quantity, stores them until they are needed, and then ships them to each individual hardware store as they are ordered.

Butler Distributing was founded by Henry Butler eleven years ago, and it grew from a modest operation into a major distribution center under his leadership. Butler himself supervised all phases of the company's operations, and he always knew what was going on. He could tell employees exactly what was in inventory at any time, when new stock was due to arrive, and when orders were supposed to be shipped out.

About three months ago, poor health forced Butler to sell the business. It was bought by a local investor who knew nothing about the business except that it was very profitable. He hired a professional manager to operate the facility. The new manager had several years of retail experience, but none as a warehouse manager.

The manager, who expected to find a smoothly running operation, instead found that no one really knew what was going on. None of Butler's employees knew exactly what products were in stock and in what quantities. And no one had any idea when new inventory was supposed to arrive or when orders were expected from the firm's customers. One employee told the new manager that "without Mr. Butler, we just don't have any way of keeping on top of things."

1. What does Butler Distributing need in the way of information?
2. How might the company go about establishing a management information system?

CASE 20-2

An MIS for Cook Luggage?

Everyone at Cook Luggage seems to be taking sides. Jack Cook, the owner of the firm, has just returned from a three-day seminar on management development at the local university. The seminar was entitled "Making MIS Work for You," and Cook now believes that his firm must have a management information system to survive.

Cook Luggage was founded 20 years ago by William Cook, Jack's father. The firm has prospered by manufacturing quality luggage for major firms like Samsonite and American. Luggage parts are ordered from several very dependable local suppliers. (Actually, very little ordering is needed. Sales representatives from the suppliers periodically visit Cook and simply place orders for parts whose inventories are getting low.)

The luggage is produced by 40 luggage makers, each working at his or her own workbench. When a luggage maker is given a customer's order to fill, he or she first goes to the stockroom to pick up all the required parts. Then the luggage maker assembles as many pieces as have been ordered. Finished goods are periodically moved to a storeroom, and orders are shipped to customers as soon as they have been completed.

Cook now believes, however, that an MIS will improve the firm's efficiency. He wants a completely automated inventory and ordering system. Moreover, he wants each luggage maker to have access to a computer terminal. The luggage makers will enter their current activities into the system periodically. This way, Cook reasons, everyone will know exactly what everyone else is doing. He also wants the finished-goods inventory and shipping system to be part of the MIS.

The luggage makers argue that things are working fine now. The proposed system, they believe, will complicate matters unnecessarily.

1. What are the pros and cons of the proposed MIS at Cook Luggage?
2. Do you think Cook should proceed with his plans? Why or why not?

Career Profile

Dr. An Wang "I'm there to impart the philosophy I value . . . to serve a useful purpose to society at large, and to make sure the people we serve—stockholders, employees, and customers—get a fair return." So says Dr. An Wang, the most successful individual in the information-processing world. Wang's philosophy, entrepreneurial skills, and technical genius have led his company, Wang Labs, to establish an astonishing record of growth in a highly competitive field.

"The Doctor," as everyone at his company refers to him, was born in Shanghai in 1920, the son of an English teacher. He came to the United States in 1945 to study applied physics at Harvard. He received his Ph.D. and taught at Harvard and at age 28 invented the magnetic core, the device necessary to all computer memory until it was replaced by the semiconductor in the late 1960s. He sold his core-memory patent to IBM and started Wang Labs in 1951. For years he personally designed everything his company sold. He still spends some time in the labs. In its first two decades, his company specialized in one-of-a-kind products, like the first digital scoreboard, built for New York's Shea Stadium in 1964.

By the early 1970s, the company's main products were calculators. But unlike many of his competitors in the calculator industry who eventually went under, Wang saw that semiconductor giants would move into the field and cut prices with their mass-production technology, so he began to focus on other products. The company reached a crossroads in 1976, when it faced the question of whether to concentrate on word or data processing. Wang decided to pursue both, a decision that enabled the company to take the lead in developing integrated office equipment.

It was the first company to have a product line that featured all three types of technology needed in modern office systems—word processing, data processing, and communications. The key to its system is Wangnet, a cable network system that links word processors, computers, and telephones. It therefore had a lead over its giant competitors—IBM, Digital Equipment, and Xerox.

Analysts attribute some problems with product lines and service and slowed growth to the lack of a professional management team. Wang's very strength at being what some have called a "benevolent dictator" over his company has led the company to experience growing pains. The management system that worked well for a small entrepreneurial company is no longer sufficient now that that company has revenues of over $1 billion each year. Wang himself says, "Since we are growing so fast, our organization is weaker than it should be. Paperwork procedures and systems are always behind." The company has succeeded by being able to change and adapt more quickly than the giants with larger inventories and overheads. But now it, too, is a giant. "We work hard to create an atmosphere where good people can motivate themselves," says Wang spokesman John Cunningham. The company gives employees access to stock option plans, a country club, and a day-care center.

As he reaches the normal retirement age and gradually withdraws from his one-man management of the company, An Wang devotes more time to education. He has advisory positions at three colleges and on the Massachusetts Board of Regents. And his family organized the Wang Institute of Graduate Study, which now grants degrees in software engineering. "The schools just aren't turning out the practical, development-oriented people we need," Wang says.

The figure in the salary column approximates the expected annual income after two or three years of service.

1 = $12,000–$15,000   2 = $16,000–$20,000   3 = $21,000–$27,000   4 = $28,000–$35,000   5 = $36,000 and up

Job Title	Educational Requirements	Salary Range	Prospects
Accountant—corporate	Bachelor's degree in accounting; master's degree preferred	3–4	Greatest growth
Accountant—private practice	Bachelor's degree in accounting; state exam for Certified Public Accountant status	4–5	Gradual growth
Auditor	Bachelor's degree; master's degree helpful; on-the-job experience	3–4	Gradual growth
Bookkeeper	High school diploma; some college preferred	1–2	Limited growth
Computer application engineer	Bachelor's degree in business and computer science	3	Gradual growth
Computer operator	Two years of college in data processing; on-the-job experience	1–2	Greatest growth
Computer programming coordinator	Bachelor's degree; on-the-job experience	2–3	Gradual growth
Computer-service technician	High school diploma; some technical training required	2	Greatest growth
Computer-systems analyst	College degree preferred; on-the-job experience	3–4	Gradual growth
Controller	College degree; on-the-job experience	4–5	Limited growth
Cost accountant	College degree; on-the-job experience	3–5	Limited growth
Engineering programmer	College degree in engineering	3–4	Gradual growth
File clerk	High school diploma	1	No growth
Information systems programmer	College degree in business and computer science	3–4	Gradual growth
Mail clerk	High school diploma	1	Limited growth
Office machine operator	High school diploma; some college helpful	1–2	Limited growth
Payroll clerk	High school diploma; some college preferred	1–2	Gradual growth
Process control programmer	College degree in computer science; on-the-job experience	3–4	Gradual growth
Salesperson—computer software or hardware	Some college; degree helpful	3–4	Gradual growth
Scientific programmer	College degree in computer science or engineering	3–4	Gradual growth

PART

7
The Business Environment

This final part of Business covers two topics that affect the operations of every firm: the legal aspects of business and the relationship between business and government in the United States. It also treats a topic that is steadily increasing in importance: the benefits, problems, and methods of international trade. Included in this part are:

CHAPTER

TWENTY-ONE
Business
Law

Whether you realize it or not, the book you are now reading is subject to perhaps ten different kinds of laws and an uncounted number of individual laws. For example, the book is copyrighted, so it comes under copyright law. When you purchased it, that transaction was subject to contract law and property law. If anyone steals it, it becomes the object of public law. And if you have a bookstore sell it for you, agency law comes into the picture.

Should you worry about all this law? Probably not—unless you happen to manage a business. If you do (or if you expect to), you should be aware of the myriad laws that affect almost every business activity. Actually, many of these laws were passed primarily to govern the way in which businesses deal with each other and with customers. In this chapter we shall examine these types of laws and discuss their most important provisions. After studying the chapter, you should understand:

1. How law comes into being and how it is administered by the courts

2. What the Uniform Commercial Code is, and why it has been adopted, in whole or in part, by all 50 states

3. What constitutes a valid and enforceable contract, and the principal remedies for breach of contract

4. The major provisions of property law, especially those regarding the transfer of title to property

5. What a negotiable instrument is, and how it is endorsed for transfer

6. The agent-principal relationship

7. How bankruptcy is initiated and resolved

Consider this:

In 1976 two major motion picture studios, Disney and Universal, brought legal action against the Sony Corporation. Lawyers for the studios argued that Sony's Betamax videocassette recorder (VCR) enables home viewers to record movies without paying a royalty to the studios and that home videotaping violates the federal copyright laws. They contended that consumers are using the VCRs to build home video libraries, which reduces the value of the studios' copyrighted material. For example, the lawyers maintained that no sponsor would want to purchase commercial time during the annual television showing of *The Ten Commandments* if 30 to 40 million viewers had already taped it.

The studios' proposed remedy was simple: all VCR manufacturers should pay a royalty of $25 to $100 on each new videocassette recorder manufactured. In addition, the producers of video tapes should pay a royalty of up to $1 for each blank tape they sold.

Lawyers representing Sony argued that a manufacturer should not be held responsible for how consumers use its products. They also introduced consumer-use studies to prove that most videotaping is done for the purpose of "time-shifting." (Time-shifting is recording a television program in order to watch it later, at a time more convenient for viewing than the original broadcast time.)

Further, Sony's lawyers contended that time-shifting actually benefits television advertisers, because it increases the number of people who see a television program (and, presumably, its commercials). Charles Ferris, a former FCC chairman who is currently employed as legal counsel for the Home Recording Rights Coalition, reasoned that a viewer who uses a VCR for time-shifting either was unable to watch the show when it was broadcast or is watching it for the second time. Either way, time-shifting increases the number of people who see the program.

A great deal of money was at stake in the suit, because VCRs show every sign of being a very successful product. In 1983 alone, 3.5 million units were sold—at prices ranging from $300 to $1000—to bring the total sold to around 9 million. By 1990 an estimated 45 million VCRs will have

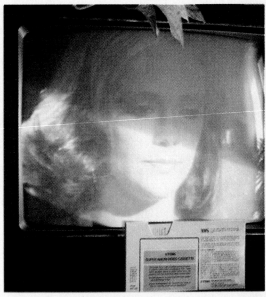

Source: © 1984 T. Molinski.

been sold. This is just about one VCR for every two homes with television sets!

After eight years of legal battles, the United States Supreme Court ruled on January 17, 1984, that videotaping for home use does not violate current federal copyright laws. In its decision, the court held that time-shifting constituted "fair use" of copyrighted material. Justice John Paul Stevens wrote, "One may search the Copyright Act in vain for any sign that the elected representatives of the millions of people who watch television every day have made it unlawful to copy a program for later viewing at home."[1] He added, however, that current copyright laws would be violated if a VCR were used to make tapes and those tapes were sold for a profit.

Although they lost this battle, the motion picture studios have not given up the war. They are now expected to alter their approach and lobby Congress for a change in the copyright law.

Ironically, some major Hollywood motion picture studios have begun to profit from the sale of movies distributed in videocassette form, for showing on home television sets. One major production, *Raiders of the Lost Ark,* sold half a million videocassettes at about $40 each in 1983.[2]

The court case brought against Sony is fairly typical of disputes that arise out of business law. Actually, there is no sharp distinction between business law and other kinds of law. The term *business law* is simply taken to mean those laws that primarily affect business activities and practices.

Such laws set standards of behavior for both businesses and individuals. They set forth the rights of the parties in exchanges and various types of agreements. And they provide remedies in the event that one business (or individual) believes it has been injured by another. The motion picture studios believed that they were injured when Sony provided individuals with a means of violating the studios' rights under the copyright laws. The injury was, of course, monetary—the loss of revenues. The studios' remedy was to sue Sony, asking that the court order Sony to reimburse them for their losses.

The U.S. Supreme Court decided that the taping of television shows for personal use is not a violation of the copyright laws. That is, the taping does not violate the studios' rights under those laws. Because their rights were not violated, the studios were not injured and there was nothing to reimburse.

Three ideas are critical here. First, the studios' case against Sony was based on *existing laws.* Second, they sought a remedy within the *court system,* which exists for that purpose. And third, having failed in their suit, the studios are expected to urge Congress to pass *new laws* that will provide them with increased protection. In the first section of this chapter, we will see what laws are, where they originate, and how the courts settle disputes according to the law. Then, in the following sections, we shall discuss the major categories of business law.

LAWS AND THE COURTS

Laws are the rules developed by a society to govern the conduct of, and relationships among, its members. In the United States, laws are developed and administered at all three levels of government: federal, state, and local. The entire group of laws dealing with a particular subject, or arising from a particular source, is often called a *body of law* or, more simply, *law.* Some examples are business law, contract law, and common law.

Sources of Laws

Each level of government derives its laws from three major sources. These are judges' decisions, legislative bodies, and administrative agencies. (See Figure 21.1.)

Common Law **Common law** is the body of law created by the court decisions rendered by judges. The common law began as custom and tradition in England, and it was enlarged by centuries of English court decisions. It was transported to America during the colonial period and, since then, has been further enlarged by the decisions of American judges.

This growth of the common law is founded on the doctrine of *stare decisis,* a Latin term that is

Figure 21.1 Sources of Law. *Source: Photo, © John Urban, Stock, Boston.*

SOURCES OF LAW
- judges' decisions (COMMON LAW)
- legislative bodies (STATUTORY LAW)
- administrative agencies

Manufacturers have a duty to do all that is commercially feasible to avoid unintended, but foreseeable, use of their products in ways that could injure, a U.S. district court says. A maker of artificial fibers for wigs is thus open to a suit by patients of a doctor who implanted the fibers into their scalps, causing medical problems. The court says the manufacturer could have warned persons with access to the fibers that the material had not been tested for scalp implantation and could be dangerous if used in that way.

Source: *U.S. News & World Report,* May 21, 1984, p. 86.

translated as "to stand by the decisions." It means that a judge's decision in a case may be used by other judges as the basis for later decisions. The earlier decision thus has the strength of law and is, in effect, a source of law.

Statutory Law A **statute** is a law that is passed by the U.S. Congress, a state legislature, or a local government. **Statutory law**, then, consists of all the laws that have been enacted by legislative bodies. Statutory law is written law, so it is easier to interpret and apply than common law. Many aspects of common law have been incorporated into statutory law and, in the process, made more precise.

The Uniform Commercial Code For businesses, one very important part of statutory law is the Uniform Commercial Code (UCC). The **Uniform Commercial Code** is a set of laws designed to eliminate differences among state regulations affecting business and to simplify interstate commerce. The UCC consists of ten articles, or chapters, that cover sales, commercial paper, bank deposits and collections, transfers of title, securities, and transactions that involve collateral. It has been adopted in its entirety by all the states except Louisiana, which has adopted only part of it. The statutes that were replaced by the UCC generally varied from state to state. These vari-

ations tended to cause problems for firms that did business in more than one state.

Administrative Law **Administrative law** consists entirely of the regulations created by government agencies that have been established by legislative bodies. The Nuclear Regulatory Commission, for example, has the power to set specific requirements for nuclear power plants. It can even halt the construction or operation of plants that do not meet those requirements. These requirements thus have the force and effect of law.

Most regulatory agencies hold hearings that are similar to court trials. Evidence is introduced, and those involved are represented by legal counsel. Moreover, the decisions of these agencies may be appealed in state or federal courts.

Public Law and Private Law: Crimes and Torts

Public law is the body of law that deals with the relationships between individuals or businesses and society. A violation of a public law is called a **crime.** Among the crimes that can affect a business are the following:

- Burglary, robbery, and theft (discussed in Chapter 18)
- Embezzlement, or the unauthorized taking of money or property by an employee, agent, or trustee
- Forgery, or the false signing or changing of a legal document with the intent to alter the liability of another person
- The use of inaccurate weights, measures, or labels
- The use of the mails to defraud, or cheat, an individual or business

Those accused of crimes are prosecuted by federal, state, or local government.

Private law is the body of law that governs the relationships between two or more individuals or businesses. A violation of a private law (which is, in essence, a violation of another's rights) is called a **tort.** A single illegal act—shoplifting, for example—can be both a crime and a tort.

The purpose of private law is to provide a remedy for the party that is injured by a tort. In most cases, the remedy is monetary damages to compensate the injured party and punish the person committing the tort. (Recall the motion picture studios' suit against Sony.)

Generally, torts may result either from intentional acts or from negligence. Such acts as shoplifting and embezzlement are intentional torts. **Negligence** is a failure to exercise reasonable care, resulting in injury to another. Suppose the driver of a delivery truck loses control of the truck, and it damages a building. A tort has been committed, and the owner of the building may sue the driver's employer to recover the cost of the necessary repairs.

An important area of tort law deals with *product liability*—the responsibility of manufacturers for negligence in designing, manufacturing, or providing operating instructions for their products. In some cases, product liability has been extended to mean strict product liability. **Strict product liability** is the legal concept which holds that a manufacturer is responsible for injuries caused by its products even if it was not negligent. An injured party need only prove that the product was defective, that an injury occurred because of the defect, and that the defect caused the product to be unsafe. A lawn mower manufacturer was sued under this concept by a man who was injured while using a rotary mower as a hedge trimmer. The jury decided the man was entitled to monetary damages, because the manufacturer had not sufficiently warned him of the danger of using the mower incorrectly.

The Court System

The United States has a dual court system. The federal court system consists of the Supreme Court of the United States, which was established by the Constitution, and other federal courts that were created by Congress. In addition, each of the 50 states has established its own court system. Figure 21.2 shows the makeup of both the federal court system and a typical state court system.

Product liability law makes manufacturers responsible for providing both operating instructions and warnings about misuses of their products. Source: © Ray Ellis, Photo Researchers, Inc.

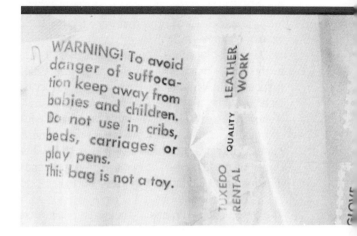

The Federal Court System Federal courts generally hear cases that involve

☐ Questions of constitutional law
☐ Federal crimes or violations of federal statutes
☐ Property valued at $10,000 or more, between citizens of different states or between an American citizen and a foreign nation
☐ Bankruptcy, the Internal Revenue Service, the postal laws, or copyright, patent, and trademark laws

The United States is divided into judicial districts. Each state includes at least one district court, and more populous states have two or more. A district court is a **court of original jurisdiction,** which is the first court to recognize and hear testimony in a legal action. The court decision is rendered by a jury, unless both parties involved in the action waive their right to a jury trial. In that case, the decision is rendered by the judge.

If the losing party is not satisfied with the decision reached in the district court, the decision may be appealed to a higher court. A court which hears cases that are appealed from lower courts is called an **appellate court.** Generally, an appellate court does not hear witnesses. Instead it examines the original trial record to decide whether some legal principle has been violated. If the appellate court finds the lower court's ruling to be in error, it may reverse that ruling, modify the decision, or return the case to the lower court for a new trial. Currently, there are twelve U.S. Courts of Appeal.

The U.S. Supreme Court—the highest court in the land—consists of nine justices (the Chief Justice of the United States and eight associate justices). The Supreme Court has original jurisdiction in cases that involve ambassadors and consuls and in certain cases involving one or more states. However, its main function is to review decisions made by the U.S. Courts of Appeal and, in some cases, by state supreme courts.

The State Court Systems The state court systems are quite similar to the federal system in structure. All have courts of original jurisdiction and supreme courts, and most have appellate courts as well. In a state that does not have an appellate court, decisions of the court of original jurisdiction are appealed directly to the state supreme court. The decision of a state supreme court may be appealed to the U.S. Supreme Court if it involves a question of constitutional or federal law.

Other Types of Courts Other courts have been created to meet special needs at both the federal and state levels. These **courts of limited jurisdiction** are courts that hear only specific types of cases. At the federal level, for example, Congress has created a Customs Court, a Court of International Trade, a Tax Court, and a Bankruptcy Court. At the state level, there are small-claims courts, which hear cases involving claims

Figure 21.2 The Court System. The United States has a dual court system illustrated here by the federal court system and a typical state court system.

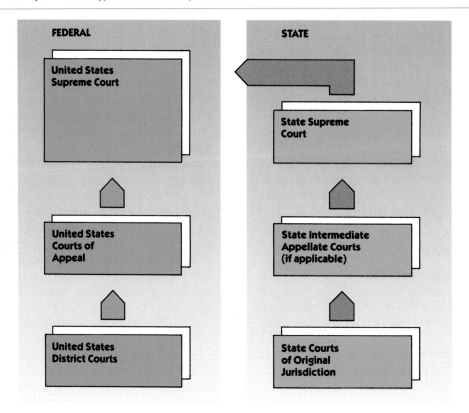

Steps in a Court Suit

Suppose Arthur Maddox slips on a wet floor and injures his arm, leg, and back while shopping in a Montgomery Ward department store. The following steps would be involved in bringing suit for his injuries.

Step 1—Commencement of Action. The person who initiates a legal action is called the *plaintiff*. In this case, Arthur Maddox, the plaintiff, talks to an attorney and describes the accident and his injuries. The attorney then files a complaint against Montgomery Ward in the state trial court. The complaint contains a description of the problem and a request for damages.

Step 2—The Summons. A *summons* is the legal document that serves notice that a legal action has been commenced against the defendant. The *defendant* is the party that is sued for damages by the plaintiff. In this case Montgomery Ward, the defendant, is notified by an officer of the court that Arthur Maddox slipped and fell while shopping in a Montgomery Ward store, causing personal injuries and hospital expenses of $25,000, for which Maddox requests reimbursement.

Step 3—The Defendant's Response. The defendant must respond to the summons within 15 to 30 days, depending on individual state requirements. Here, Montgomery Ward will respond by filing an answer. An *answer* is a legal document that contains admissions, denials, defenses, or counterclaims. Generally, the answer merely denies the plaintiff's allegations. If the defendant does not reply, the court may order a default judgment against the defendant and declare the plaintiff the winner.

Step 4—Pretrial Procedures. The main purpose of pretrial procedures is to discover all the facts prior to the actual trial. Each party has the right to obtain evidence or facts—a legal procedure called *discovery*. The discovery procedure includes

1. Pretrial depositions consisting of sworn testimony from the opposing party
2. Written interrogatories, which consist of sworn answers to questions prepared in advance by the opposing party
3. A motion for the opposing party to produce documents and other evidence that are relevant to the case
4. Physical or mental examination of the opposing party, if relevant
5. Demands for admission of facts given by one party (under oath) at the request of the other

The evidence obtained in the discovery procedure may be so conclusive that a trial becomes unnecessary. In this situation, either party may move for a *summary judgment,* which means that a judge will decide the case on the basis of the evidence obtained in the discovery procedure. Also, a pretrial conference among all lawyers and the judge is normally held in a final attempt to settle the case before it goes to trial.

Step 5—The Court Trial. If either Maddox or Montgomery Ward is unwilling to settle out of court, and if it is impossible for the judge to decide the case on the basis of discovery procedure evidence, the only alternative is a court trial. A jury is selected and the attorneys make their opening statements concerning the facts that they expect to prove during the trial. Witnesses are called by the plaintiff and the defendant, and all evidence relating to the case is presented. Finally, both attorneys make their summation statements. In the summation statement, each attorney reviews the evidence brought forth in the trial and urges a verdict in favor of his or her client. The judge then gives instructions, which are sometimes called a *charge,* to the jury, outlining the rules of law that are applicable to this case. The jury retires to the jury room to deliberate the case and reach a decision. If the jury decides in favor of the defendant, Montgomery Ward *is not* liable for Maddox's injuries. On the other hand, if the jury decides for the plaintiff, Montgomery Ward *is* liable for Maddox's injuries. Of course, the party who loses the case may appeal to an appellate court.

for less than a specified dollar amount (usually $500 or $1500, depending on the state); traffic courts; divorce courts; and juvenile courts.

Let us now briefly discuss the major categories of business law. These are contract law, property law, laws relating to negotiable instruments, agency law, and bankruptcy law.

CONTRACT LAW

Contract law is perhaps the most important area of business law, because contracts are so much a part of doing business. Every business person should understand what a valid contract is and how contracts are fulfilled or violated.

A **contract** is a legally enforceable agreement between two or more parties who promise to do, or not to do, a particular thing. The parties to a contract may be individuals or businesses. An *implied contract* is an agreement that results from the actions of the parties rather than from specific promises. For example, a person who orders dinner at a local restaurant assumes that the food will be served within a reasonable time and will be fit to eat. The restaurant owner, for his or her part, assumes that the customer will pay for the meal.

Most contracts are more explicit and formal than that between a restaurant and its customers: An *express contract* is one in which the parties involved have made oral or written promises about the terms of their agreement.

Requirements for a Valid Contract

To be valid and legally enforceable, an implied or express contract must meet five specific requirements, which may be characterized as follows: (1) voluntary agreement, (2) consideration, (3) legal competence of all parties, (4) lawful subject matter, and (5) proper form.

Voluntary Agreement **Voluntary agreement** consists of both an *offer* by one party to enter into a contract with a second party and *acceptance* by the second party of all the terms and conditions of the offer. If any part of the offer is not accepted, there is no contract. And, if it can be proved that coercion, undue pressure, or fraud was used to obtain a contract, it may be voided by the injured party.

Unless the method of acceptance is specified in the offer, a contract can be accepted orally or in writing. Generally, acceptance must occur within a certain time. If the offer calls for acceptance by a specific date, acceptance after that date does *not* result in a binding contract. Both the offer and the acceptance should be given in specific terms that would enable a reasonable person to understand the agreement.

Consideration A contract is a binding agreement only when each party provides something of value to the other party. The value or benefit that one party furnishes to the other party is called **consideration.** This consideration may be money, property, a service, or the promise not to exercise a legal right. However, the consideration given by one party need not be equal in dollar value to the consideration given by the other party. As a general rule, the courts will not void a contract just because one party got a bargain.

Legal Competence All parties to a contract must be legally competent to manage their own affairs *and* must have the authority to enter into binding agreements. Aliens, convicts, and corporations limited by their charters may have restricted ability to enter into contracts. And the courts generally will not require minors, persons of unsound mind, or those who entered into contracts while they were intoxicated to comply with the terms of their contracts. The intent is to protect individuals who may not have been able to protect themselves. In particular, minors can void (or nullify) contracts to which they are parties (except contracts for such necessities of life as food and shelter) at any time before they reach the age of majority. In some states, minors may void a contract even after reaching the age of majority. The businessperson, on the other hand, is bound by the terms and conditions of the contract.

Lawful Subject Matter A contract is not legally enforceable if it involves an unlawful act. Certainly, a person who contracts with an arsonist to burn down a building cannot go to court to obtain enforcement of the contract. Equally unenforceable is a contract that involves **usury,** which is the practice of charging interest in excess of the maximum legal rate. In many states, a lender who practices usury is denied the right to recover any interest at all. In a few states, such a lender may recover the maximum legal interest.

Proper Form of Contract Although contracts may be oral, it is safer to commit them to writing. A written contract is visible evidence of its terms, whereas an oral contract is subject to the memories and interpretations of the parties involved.

Businesses generally draw up all contractual agreements in writing so that differences can be resolved readily if a dispute develops. Figure 21.3 shows that a contract need not be complicated to be legally enforceable.

A written contract must contain the names of the parties involved and their signatures, the purpose of the contract, and all terms and conditions to which the parties have agreed. Changes to a written contract should be made in writing and should be initialed by all parties. They should either be written directly on the original contract or attached to it.

The *Statute of Frauds,* which has been passed in some form by all states, requires that certain

Figure 21.3 *Contract Between a Business and a Customer. Notice that the requirements for a valid contract are satisfied and that the contract takes the proper form by containing the names of the parties involved, the purpose of the contract, and all terms and conditions.*

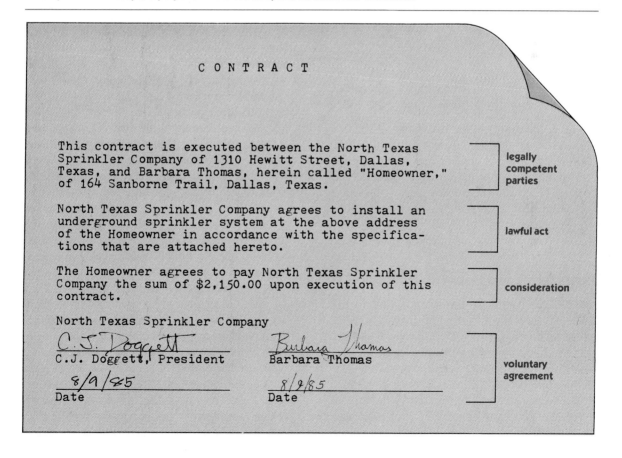

Lynn Redgrave claimed her acting contract was breached when Universal Television fired her from CBS's House Calls. *Breastfeeding her daughter at work, she claimed, was not a legal reason for breaking a contract. Source: AP/Wide World Photos.*

types of contracts be in writing to be enforceable. These include contracts dealing with

- The exchange of land or real estate
- The sale of goods, merchandise, or personal property valued at $500 or more
- Acts that will not be performed within one year after the agreement is made
- A promise to assume someone else's financial obligation
- A promise made in contemplation of marriage

Performance and Nonperformance

Ordinarily, a contract is terminated by **performance,** which is the fulfillment of all obligations by all parties to the contract. Occasionally, however, performance may become impossible. Death, disability, or bankruptcy, for example, may legally excuse one party from a contractual obligation. And a contract may be terminated by the mutual agreement of all parties involved. But what happens when one party simply does not perform according to a legal contract?

A **breach of contract** is the failure of one party to fulfill the terms of a contract when there is no legal reason for that failure. Other parties to the contract may then bring legal action to discharge the contract, obtain monetary damages, or require specific performance.

Discharge is the termination of a contract because one party refuses to fulfill a contractual obligation. Other parties are then excused from their obligations under the contract. Any consideration received by the parties must be returned when a contract is discharged.

Damages are a monetary settlement awarded to a party that is injured through breach of contract. In awarding damages, an attempt is made to place the injured parties in the position they would be in if the contract had been performed. Suppose A contracts to paint B's house for $1500. Then A breaches the contract, and B must hire C to paint the house for $2000. B can sue A for $500, the additional cost she or he had to pay to achieve what was expected as a result of the original contract—a newly painted house.

Specific performance is the legal requirement that the parties to a contract fulfill their obligations according to the contract (as opposed to settlement via payment of damages). Generally, the courts will require specific performance when the contract calls for a unique service or product that cannot be obtained from another source. For example, only one artist may be capable of designing and creating a specific piece of art. In this case, the court may order the artist to create the artwork at the price agreed upon in the original contract.

Most individuals and firms enter into a contract because they expect to live up to its terms. Very few end up in court. When they do, it is usually because one or more of the parties did not understand all the conditioins of the agreement. Thus it is imperative to know what you are signing before you sign it. If there is any doubt, get legal help! Once a contract is signed, it is very difficult—and often very costly—to void.

Sales Agreements

A **sales agreement** is a special (but very common) type of contract by which ownership is transferred from a seller to a buyer. Because sales agreements are contracts, they are generally subject to the conditions and requirements we have discussed.

Article 2 of the UCC (entitled "Sales") provides much of our sales law, which is derived from both common and statutory law. It covers the sale of goods only. It does *not* cover the sale of stocks and bonds, personal services, or real estate. Among the topics included in Article 2 are rights of the buyer and seller, acceptance and rejection of an offer, inspection of goods, delivery, transfer of ownership, and warranties.

Article 2 provides that a sales agreement may be binding even though one or more of the general contract requirements is omitted. For example, a sales agreement is legally binding when the selling price is left out of the agreement. Article 2 requires that the buyer pay the reasonable value of the goods at the time of delivery. Key considerations in resolving such issues are the actions and business history of the parties and any customary sales procedures within the particular industry.

Article 2 also deals with warranties—both express and implied. As we saw in Chapter 12, an **express warranty** is a written explanation of the responsibilities of the producer (or seller) when a product is found to be defective or otherwise unsatisfactory. It may also include the seller's representations concerning such product characteristics as age, durability, and quality.

An **implied warranty** is a guarantee that is imposed or required by law. In general, the buyer is entitled to assume that

1. The merchandise offered for sale has a clear title and is not stolen.
2. The merchandise is as advertised.
3. The merchandise will serve the purpose for which it was manufactured and sold.

Any limitation to an express or implied warranty must be stated in writing.

PROPERTY LAW

Property is anything that can be owned. The concept of private ownership of property is fundamental to the free-enterprise system. Our Constitution guarantees to individuals and businesses the right to own property and to use it in their own best interest.

Kinds of Property

Property is legally classified as either real property or personal property. **Real property** is land and anything that is permanently attached to it. Thus a house, a factory, a garage, and a well are all considered real property.

The degree to which a business is concerned with real-property law depends on the size and type of business. The owner of a small jewelry store needs only a limited knowledge of the law. But a national jewelry store chain might employ several real estate experts with extensive knowledge of real-property law, property values, and real estate zoning ordinances throughout the country.

Personal property is all property other than real property. Personal property such as inventories, equipment, store fixtures, an automobile, or a book has physical or material value. It is thus referred to as *tangible personal property*. Property that derives its value from a legal right or claim is called *intangible personal property*. Examples include stocks and bonds, receivables, trademarks, patents, and copyrights.

As we noted in Chapter 12, a **trademark** is a brand that is registered with the U.S. Patent and Trademark Office. Registration guarantees the owner the exclusive use of the trademark for 20 years. At the end of that time, the registration can be renewed for additional 20-year periods. If necessary, the owner must defend the trademark from unauthorized use—usually through legal action. McDonald's was recently forced to do exactly that, when the brand name "Big Mac" was used by another fast-food outlet in a foreign country.

A recent Tennessee law gives the Presley estate the right to control the use of Elvis Presley's name and likeness. Source: © *Theo Westenberger, Sygma.*

A **patent** is the exclusive right to make, use, or sell a newly invented product or process. Patents are granted by the U.S. Patent and Trademark Office for a period of 17 years. After that time has elapsed, the invention becomes available for general use. A patent holder may license others to use the patented invention, in return for a fee.

A **copyright** is the exclusive right to publish, perform, copy, or sell an original work. Copyright laws cover fiction and nonfiction, plays, poetry, musical works, photographs, films, and—nowadays—computer programs. For example, the copyright on this textbook is held by the publisher, Houghton Mifflin Company. The copyright on the record album *Born in the U.S.A.* is held by the recording artist, Bruce Springsteen. A copyright is granted to the creator of the work by the U.S. Copyright Office. It generally holds for the lifetime of the creator plus 50 years.

Transfer of Ownership

Real Property As we noted earlier, the Statute of Frauds requires that exchanges of real estate be in writing. A **deed** is a written document by which the ownership of real property is transferred from one person or organization to another. The deed must contain the names of the previous owner and the new owner, as well as a legally acceptable description of the property. However, consideration is not required.

A **lease** is an agreement by which the right to use real property is temporarily transferred from its owner, the landlord, to a tenant. In return for the use of the property, the tenant generally pays rent on a weekly, monthly, or yearly basis. A lease is granted for a specific period of time, after which a new lease may be negotiated. If the lease is terminated, the right to use the real property reverts to the landlord.

Personal Property Suppose you go into a Neiman-Marcus department store and buy a sweater. When, exactly, do you own it? The answer depends on how you pay for it. The sale of the sweater is, in essence, a contract. The seller's consideration is the title to, or ownership of, the sweater. The buyer's consideration is the full price of the sweater.

When the buyer pays the *full cash price* at the time of purchase, the title to personal property passes to the buyer immediately. When a buyer purchases goods on an *installment plan,* the title passes to the buyer when he or she takes possession of the goods. Although the full cash price has not been paid, the buyer has made a legally enforceable promise to pay it. This is sufficient consideration for the transfer of ownership. Moreover, if the purchased goods are stolen from the buyer, the buyer is still responsible for the full purchase price.

Goods that are purchased on a *C.O.D.* (collect on delivery) *basis* are paid for at the time of delivery. Usually title passes to the buyer when goods are delivered to the carrier. (In this type of sale, however, the buyer is generally allowed a reasonable time after delivery to inspect the goods and, if they are damaged, to reject them.)

When goods are purchased on an *F.O.B. point of origin basis,* the buyer, rather than the seller, is responsible for shipping them. Thus, title passes to the buyer when the goods are accepted by a carrier. If the goods are damaged in transit, the buyer must attempt to collect for the damage from the carrier. On the other hand, if the merchandise is shipped *F.O.B. destination basis,* title passes to the buyer when the goods reach their final destination. If the goods are damaged in transit, the seller must attempt to collect from the carrier.

LAWS RELATING TO NEGOTIABLE INSTRUMENTS

A **negotiable instrument** is a written document that (1) is a promise to pay a stated sum of money and (2) can be transferred from one person or firm to another. In effect, a negotiable instrument is a substitute for money. Checks are the most familiar form of negotiable instruments. However, the promissory notes, bank drafts, certificates of deposit, and commercial paper discussed in Chapter 16 are also negotiable. Even a warehouse receipt can qualify as a negotiable instrument if certain conditions are met.

Requirements for Negotiability

The UCC establishes the following conditions for negotiability.

☐ The credit instrument must be in writing and signed
☐ It must contain an unconditional promise or order to pay a stated sum of money
☐ The instrument must be payable on demand or at a specified future date
☐ It must be payable to a specified person or firm or to the bearer

If a financial document does not meet all these requirements, it is not negotiable. It may still be valid and legally enforceable, but it cannot be transferred.

The negotiability of these documents helps facilitate credit transactions. A supplier who accepts, say, a promissory note, knows that if the need arises, the note can be sold to a bank in return for immediate cash. The supplier can obtain payment at any time—and so is more willing to extend credit to customers.

Endorsements

To transfer a negotiable instrument, the payee must sign it. The payee's signature on the back of a negotiable instrument is called an **endorsement.** There are four types of endorsements, as shown in Figure 21.4.

A *blank endorsement* consists only of the payee's signature. It is quick, easy, and dangerous, because it makes the instrument payable to anyone who gets possession of it—legally or otherwise. A blank endorsement should be used only when the instrument is signed in the presence of the next holder.

A *restrictive endorsement* states the purpose for which the instrument is to be used. It is probably the safest endorsement, because it renders the instrument useful only for that purpose.

A *special endorsement* identifies the person or firm to whom the instrument is payable. Like the restrictive endorsement, the special endorsement protects the negotiable instrument in case it is lost or stolen.

A *qualified endorsement* limits the liability of the payee in the event that the instrument is not honored. The words "without recourse" in Figure 21.4 indicate that the person who originally signed the instrument—and not the endorser—is responsible for payment.

AGENCY LAW

An **agency** is a business relationship in which one party (called the *principal*) appoints a second party (called the *agent*) to act on behalf of the principal. Most often, agents are hired to apply their special knowledge to a specific purpose. For example, real estate agents are hired to sell or buy real property. Insurance agents are hired to sell insurance. And booking agents are hired to obtain engagements for entertainers. The officers of a firm, lawyers, accountants, and stock brokers also act as agents.

Most agents are independent business people or firms. They are paid for their services with either set fees or commissions.

Almost any legal activity that can be accomplished by an individual can also be accomplished through an agent. (The exceptions are voting, giving sworn testimony in court, and making a will.) Moreover, under the law, the principal is bound by the actions of the agent. The principal can be held liable even if the agent acts contrary to the principal's instructions or ventures into areas not covered by a written contract of agency. However, if the agent performs an unauthorized act, he or she may be sued for damages by the principal. For this reason, a written contract describing the conditions and limits of the agency relationship is extremely important to both parties.

A **power of attorney** is a legal document which serves as evidence that an agent has been appointed to act on behalf of a principal. A power of attorney is required in agency relationships involving the transfer of real estate, as well as in other specific situations.

An agent is responsible for carrying out the principal's instructions in a professional manner, for acting reasonably and with good judgment, and for keeping the principal informed of progress according to their agreement. The agent must also be careful to avoid a conflict involving the interests of two or more principals. The agency relationship is terminated when its objective is accomplished, at the end of a specified period, or in some cases, when either party renounces the relationship.

BANKRUPTCY LAW

Bankruptcy is a legal procedure designed both to protect an individual or business that cannot

Figure 21.4 Endorsements. The payee's signature on the back of a negotiable instrument is called an endorsement. There are four types of endorsements.

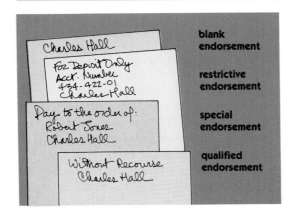

Charles Hall — blank endorsement

For Deposit Only Acct. Number 434-422-01 Charles Hall — restrictive endorsement

Pay to the order of: Robert Jones Charles Hall — special endorsement

Without Recourse Charles Hall — qualified endorsement

meet its financial obligations and to protect the creditors involved. In principle, the assets of the individual or business are sold to satisfy the claims of creditors. The debtor is then relieved of all its remaining debts.

The Bankruptcy Reform Act was enacted in 1978 and was subsequently amended in July of 1984; and this act is divided into eight separate parts, called chapters, which explain the procedures for resolving a bankruptcy case. Under the act, bankruptcy proceedings may be initiated either by the person or business that is in financial difficulty or by the creditors.

Initiating Bankruptcy Proceedings

Voluntary bankruptcy is a bankruptcy procedure initiated by an individual or business that can no longer meet its financial obligations. To declare bankruptcy, the debtor must have debts exceeding both $1000 *and* the total value of its assets. Individuals, partnerships, and most corporations may file for voluntary bankruptcy. However, railroads, banks, savings and loan associations, insurance companies, credit unions, and municipalities may *not* file for bankruptcy.

Involuntary bankruptcy is a bankruptcy procedure initiated by creditors. The creditors must be able to prove that the individual or business has debts in excess of $5000 and cannot pay its debts as they come due. If there are more than 12 creditors, a petition for involuntary bankruptcy must be signed by 3 or more creditors whose claims total at least $5000. If there are fewer than 12 creditors, 1 or more creditors with claims of at least $5000 need to sign the petition.

Today most bankruptcies are voluntary. Creditors are wary of initiating bankruptcy proceedings, because they usually end up losing most of the money that is involved. They generally feel it is better to wait and to hope the debtor will eventually be able to pay.

Resolving a Bankruptcy Case

A petition for bankruptcy is filed with the court that has jurisdiction over bankruptcy cases. If the

Lynn Watner is an agent—someone who acts as a business representative—for several baseball players. Source: © Gene Sweeney, Sports Illustrated.

court declares the individual or business to be bankrupt, three means of resolution are available. These are liquidation, reorganization, and repayment.

Liquidation Chapter 7 of the Bankruptcy Reform Act concerns *liquidation*, the sale of assets of a bankrupt individual or business to pay its debts. Chapter 7 specifies the order in which claims are to be paid. First, creditors with secured claims are allowed to repossess (or assume ownership of) the collateral for their claims.

Next, unsecured claims are paid in the following order:[3]

1. The costs involved in the bankruptcy case
2. Claims that arose in the course of the debtor's business activities, after the commencement of the case
3. Claims for wages, salaries, or commissions, up to a limit of $2000 per claimant
4. Claims for contributions to employee benefits plans
5. Claims by consumer creditors, arising from the purchase of products that have not been delivered, up to $900 per claimant
6. Federal and state taxes

The remaining cash and assets—if any—are divided among creditors with unsecured claims, in

Figure 21.5 Steps Involved in Chapter 7 of the Bankruptcy Reform Act—Liquidation of Assets

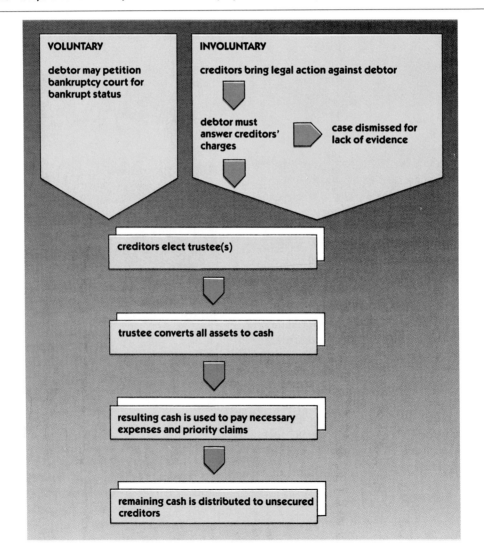

proportion to the size of their various claims. (See Figure 21.5.)

Reorganization   Chapter 11 of the Bankruptcy Reform Act outlines the procedure for reorganizing a bankrupt business. The idea is simple: The distressed business will be preserved by correcting or eliminating the factors that got the firm into financial trouble. To implement this idea, a plan to reorganize the business is developed. Only the debtor may file a reorganization plan for the first 120 days unless a trustee has been appointed by the court. If a trustee has been appointed, the trustee may file a reorganization plan. After 120 days any interested party may file a reorganization plan. After the plan has been filed with the court, both the plan and a written disclosure statement are distributed to all individuals and businesses with claims against the bankrupt firm. These people and firms may testify at a hearing that is held for the purpose of confirming the plan. If the plan is confirmed, the reorganized business emerges from bankruptcy with only the financial obligations that are imposed on it by the plan. This is exactly what occurred when Braniff International Corporation filed for protection under Chapter 11 in the spring of 1982.

Repayment   Chapter 13 of the Bankruptcy Reform Act permits a bankrupt individual to file, with the courts, a plan for paying off specific debts. (Only individuals with a regular income, less than $100,000 in unsecured debts, and less than $350,000 in secured debts are eligible to file for repayment under Chapter 13.) The plan must provide for the repayment of specified amounts in up to 3 years. If the plan is approved by the court, the individual usually pays the money to a court-appointed trustee in monthly installments. The trustee, in turn, pays the individual's creditors.

The bankruptcy of a large corporation such as Braniff involves human feelings as well as money and regulations.
Sources: Top, © 1982 Phil Huber, Black Star; bottom, © Shelly Katz, Black Star.

Chapter Review

SUMMARY

Laws are the rules that govern the conduct of, and relationships among, the members of a society. In the United States, laws originate in judicial decisions (common law), in the enactments of legislative bodies (statutory law), and in the regulations of government agencies (administrative law). An important body of business law is contained in the statutory Uniform Commercial Code, which has been adopted, in whole or in part, by all 50 states.

Public law is concerned with the relationships between a society and its members. Private law is concerned with relationships among the society's members. The private law dealing with negligence, or the failure to exercise reasonable care, is of particular interest to businesses.

The United States has a dual court system made up of the federal court system and the court systems of the 50 states. At both the federal level and the state level, court cases are first heard in courts of original jurisdiction. The decisions of these courts may be appealed to appellate courts.

A contract is a legally enforceable agreement. The conditions for a valid contract include voluntary agreement between the parties, consideration, the legal competence of all parties, subject matter that is legal, and proper contract form. Usually a contract is terminated through fulfillment of all obligations contained in the contract. If one party to a contract does not fulfill its obligations, the other party or parties may request the courts to discharge the contract, to award damages for nonperformance, or to require that the terms of the contract be fulfilled.

A sales agreement is a contract by which ownership is transferred from a seller to a buyer. Exchanges of the title to real property must be in writing. In general, the title to personal property is exchanged when the property is paid for.

A negotiable instrument is a written document that is a promise to pay a stated sum of money and can be transferred from one person or firm to another. To be negotiable, the instrument must meet certain requirements and must be endorsed by the payee.

An agency is a business relationship in which an agent acts on behalf of a principal. The principal is generally responsible for, and bound by, all actions of the agent. The agent is responsible for carrying out the instructions of the principal in a reasonable and professional manner.

Bankruptcy laws are designed to protect both a person or firm that cannot pay its debts and the creditors involved. Bankruptcy proceedings may be initiated by either the creditors or the person or firm that cannot cover its liabilities. Bankruptcy proceedings may be resolved through liquidation of the debtor's assets, reorganization of a bankrupt firm, or repayment of specific debts incurred by an individual.

In this chapter we have been concerned with relationships among businesses—and, in particular, with the legal aspects of those relationships. In the next chapter we shall examine the relationship between business and government in the United States. The three areas of primary concern will be government assistance to, regulation of, and taxation of business.

KEY TERMS

You should now be able to define and give an example relevant to each of the following terms:

laws

common law

statute

statutory law

Uniform Commercial
    Code

administrative law

public law

crime

private law

tort

negligence

strict product liability

court of original
    jurisdiction

appellate court

court of limited
    jurisdiction

contract

voluntary agreement

consideration

usury

performance

breach of contract

discharge

damages

specific performance

sales agreement

express warranty

implied warranty

property

real property

personal property

trademark

patent

copyright

deed

lease

negotiable instrument

endorsement

agency

power of attorney

bankruptcy

voluntary bankruptcy

involuntary bankruptcy

QUESTIONS AND EXERCISES
Review Questions

1. What are the differences among common law, statutory law, and administrative law?
2. What is a tort? How does the law punish those who commit torts?
3. How is the concept of strict product liability different from the concept of product liability?
4. What are the three levels of courts in the federal and state court systems? What kinds of cases are heard at each level?
5. List and describe the conditions for a legally enforceable contract.
6. When a contract is breached, what remedies are available to the injured party or parties?
7. What are the differences between an express warranty and an implied warranty? What is implied by an implied warranty?
8. How does real property differ from personal property? Give a specific example of real property, intangible personal property, and tangible personal property, all owned by an independent service station.
9. What is the principal basis on which a court decides when the title to personal property passes from the seller to the buyer? Illustrate your answer with an example.
10. What requirements must be met for a financial instrument to be negotiable? Why is negotiability important?
11. Identify the four types of endorsements discussed in this chapter. Explain the advantages and disadvantages of each.
12. What is the relationship between an agent and a principal?
13. How is voluntary bankruptcy different from involuntary bankruptcy?
14. Briefly describe the three means of resolving a bankruptcy case under the 1984 bankruptcy law.

Discussion Questions

1. In the case brought by the Disney and Universal studios, lawyers representing Sony argued that a manufacturer should not be responsible for how consumers use its products. Do you agree? Does this concept apply to all products?
2. In your opinion, should Congress change the federal copyright law to protect the motion picture studios from loss of income due to taping of television shows?
3. Does the United States really need both federal and state court systems? What are the advantages and disadvantages of this dual court arrangement?
4. Why should the law specifically require written contracts for exchanges of real estate, sales over $500, and long-term obligations?
5. Suppose you are a party to a contract that has been breached by the other party. Under what circumstances would you sue for discharge? for damages? for specific performance?
6. In your opinion, is there a social stigma attached to bankruptcy nowadays? Should there be?

Exercises

1. Find two or more articles describing a recent court case that involved two or more businesses.
   a. State the exact nature of the issue or issues involved in the case.
   b. Describe how these issues were resolved.
   c. State whether the resolution seems fair, and justify your answer.
2. Draw up a standard contract form for a company that sells and installs burglar alarm systems in homes. The average cost of the alarm system, including installation, is $750. Include everything required for a valid contract.
3. Obtain or draw a check, and note on it the various items that fulfill the requirements for negotiability.

CASE 21-1
Penn Central

When the Penn Central Transportation Corporation (PCT) went bankrupt in 1970, its primary business was railroad transportation, although it also owned hotels and other assets. The reorganization of the firm was considered by some to be close to impossible, given the vast number of creditors and the size of its debts. PCT's bankruptcy was the biggest ever.

But the firm was indeed reorganized, by a group that included its present board chairman, Richard Dicker. As part of the reorganization of PCT, a new firm—called Penn Central Corporation—was formed. Creditors of the old PCT were given 96 percent of the stock of the new firm, and the remaining 4 percent was awarded to PCT shareholders. In 1976, almost all of PCT's railroad assets were transferred to the Consolidated Rail Corporation (ConRail)—a corporation that was formed by the federal government to take over and operate the failing railroads that had served the northeastern part of the country. (All six of those railroads eventually went bankrupt.) At the same time, a three-member Special Court was established to decide how much Penn Central should be paid for these assets.

The deadline for the decision was to be 1987. Nonetheless, the Special Court urged Penn Central and the federal government to come to an out-of-court settlement at a much earlier date. The two parties were, however, far apart in their valuations of PCT's railroad assets. Penn Central valued them at about $3.2 billion, their book value. The government was willing to pay only $550 million, the estimated scrap value of the transferred assets.

Meanwhile, the reorganized Penn Central—now out of the railroad business and primarily in energy, recreation, and real estate—was doing fairly well. It earned profits in 1977 and 1978; and in October 1979 its stock was selling at about $17.50 per share. However, the firm still had about $2 billion in PCT preferred stock, notes, and corporate bonds to pay off. The bankruptcy settlement specified that these were to be re-deemed, at par value, with the first $2 billion of any award given Penn Central by the Special Court. (Other means of paying off or converting these debts were to be used in the event the award was less than $2 billion.)

In November 1980, Penn Central Corporation and the federal government agreed to an out-of-court settlement of $2.1 billion for PCT's railroad assets.[4]

1. Comment on the amount of the Penn Central settlement, and its effect on the firm.
2. Were creditors, bondholders, stockholders, and other interested parties treated fairly in the PCT reorganization? Explain.

CASE 21-2

Vlases v. Montgomery Ward

Because much of our law is based on previous court decisions, those decisions are carefully analyzed by both students and practicing attorneys. Here is the outline of a simple but typical business case, as presented in a business-law textbook:

> Plaintiff [Vlases] purchased 2000 chickens from defendant [Montgomery Ward] in order to start a chicken-raising business. After a few weeks, the chickens showed signs of illness and were found to be suffering from avian leukosis, or bird cancer. Plaintiff brought an action based upon breach of implied warranties. Defendant contended that there was no way of detecting the disease in baby chicks, and the testimony bore this out. It was defendant's position that the birds might have contracted the disease subsequent to the sale, but the jury returned a verdict in favor of plaintiff. Defendant appealed.[5]

Before you read on, put yourself in the position of the appeals-court judge by answering the following questions:

1. Does the principle of implied warranty apply in this case? Explain.
2. Should the lower-court verdict be affirmed or reversed? Why?

In its decision, the appeals court noted that two implied warranties were involved: "the implied warranty of merchantability and the implied warranty of fitness for a particular purpose." According to the court, the purpose of the implied-warranty sections of the Uniform Commercial Code is to "hold the seller responsible when inferior goods are passed along to the unsuspecting buyer." And the seller is responsible if the delivered goods are not saleable or fit for their particular purpose. The seller's inability to detect the disease had no bearing on that responsibility; only the quality of the goods was of importance. The lower-court verdict was affirmed.[6]

CHAPTER

TWENTY-TWO
Government Assistance, Regulation, and Taxation

The relationship between government and business is a controversial one. Some observers argue that government does too much, especially in the regulation of business activities and in the taxation of business profits. Others believe there is much more that government could do to create a healthy business environment, promote competition, and protect the interests of citizens. Regardless of the controversy surrounding it, the relationship between business and government does exist, and it is the subject of this chapter. After studying the chapter, you should understand:

1. The ways in which government can assist business firms
2. The reasons for—and content of—the major federal antitrust laws
3. How and why the federal government regulates natural monopolies
4. The nature of government's response to the current deregulation movement
5. The various taxes through which the federal, state, and local governments are financed

Consider this:

On January 8, 1982, the U.S. Department of Justice settled one of the largest antitrust suits it had ever brought against an American firm. The defendant in the suit was American Telephone & Telegraph (AT&T), the owner of the Bell telephone system and the nation's largest regulated monopoly.

AT&T's legal problems actually began in 1949, when the Justice Department tried to separate Western Electric from the rest of the company. Western Electric, the manufacturing subsidiary of AT&T, was accused of keeping competing manufacturers from selling telephone equipment that could be used with the Bell system. That case was resolved in 1956, when AT&T's management signed a consent decree that restricted the company to the government-regulated telephone business. The firm retained Western Electric, but it was legally barred from entering such unregulated and competitive markets as that for computers and word-processing equipment.

Then, in 1974, the Justice Department began another antitrust suit against AT&T. This time the firm was accused of being "too big" and of monopolizing the entire telephone industry, including portions in which competition could thrive.

In 1982, after a total of 33 years of legal battles, AT&T's management signed another consent decree. This one required the firm to sever its relationship with 22 of its operating companies. (An AT&T operating company is a subsidiary that provides local phone service to consumers in a specific geographic area.) The 22 operating companies were grouped into 7 independent regional firms, owned by those persons and organizations that were AT&T shareholders at the time of the breakup. These 7 firms continue to be regulated monopolies, each providing local telephone service in its own region.

The new, smaller AT&T consists primarily of

☐ Western Electric, which provides phone and switching equipment to a large part of the telephone industry
☐ Bell Laboratories, which does AT&T's research and development
☐ AT&T Communications, which is a new subsidiary that provides long-distance telephone service
☐ AT&T Information Systems, which will market communications and information services and equipment to businesses, government, and residential customers
☐ AT&T International, which will market AT&T's products and services overseas

Because the new AT&T is not a regulated monopoly, its subsidiaries must compete for sales dollars in the various communications markets.

AT&T's agreement to break up its telephone empire looks like a surrender to government pressure, but the economics of the agreement seem to favor the firm. Although AT&T retained only one-third of its former assets (roughly $49 billion out of $137 billion), the retained businesses are the fastest-growing and potentially most profitable. In addition, an important restriction in the 1956 agreement was removed: AT&T can now enter the high-technology markets, which promise to be very profitable in the future. As a result, most financial analysts predict that the new, slimmed-down Ma Bell will do just fine.[1]

Source: Courtesy of AT&T.

The breakup of AT&T resulted in the total separation of local telephone service—a natural monopoly—from other communications services. Obviously, the federal government felt that customers would benefit from competition in the markets for long-distance calling, telephones, and general communications equipment and services. AT&T must now compete with a variety of firms—from Panasonic to Muraphone—that sell telephones for home and business use. And, although AT&T still takes in about 90 percent of all long-distance calling revenue, it is facing increased competition in that area from such firms as MCI and GTE Sprint. In fact, as part of the breakup, AT&T must provide telephone customers with "equal access" to all firms that sell long-distance calling services. That is, long-distance customers must be able to use, say, Sprint, as easily as they can use AT&T.

The encouragement and protection of competition is, of course, a prime reason for government involvement in business. As you have seen throughout this book, there are other reasons as well. They are, in general, based on the needs of business, government, and the American public. We shall look first at the various ways in which our government is supportive of American business.

GOVERNMENT SUPPORT OF BUSINESS

Government regulations and actions that restrict certain business activities may, at the same time, support other activities. The breakup of AT&T, for example, was calculated to restrict the operations of that firm. But it also opened up new markets to the firms that are now producing telephone equipment in competition with Western Electric. And the "equal access" portion of the consent decree directly benefited such firms as Sprint and MCI. These firms are now able to compete with AT&T on a more or less equal footing.

Obviously, not all government regulations are of this nature. Many of them (and some critics say *too many* of them) are intended primarily to restrict business activities, for various reasons. We shall discuss government regulation and deregulation in some detail later in the chapter. Here, our main point is simply that at least some government regulations do function in support of business activities.

In addition, government supports business by providing information and assistance, by funding research, and by acting as the largest customer of American business firms.

Providing Information and Assistance to Business

The U.S. Government may be the world's largest collector and user of information. Much of this information is of value to businesses and is available at minimal cost.

The U.S. Census Bureau, for example, collects and can provide a wealth of marketing data:

☐ Demographic data showing the population distribution by age, sex, race, geographic area, educational level attained, occupation, and income
☐ Housing data by type and year of construction, size, building materials, and the like

The Census Bureau also provides information on manufacturing and agricultural activity, government spending, and the availability of natural resources. To inform businesses of the types of data and reports that are available, the bureau publishes an annual *Catalog of U.S. Census Publications*.

Other U.S. government publications that can be valuable sources of business information include the *Survey of Current Business* from the Department of Commerce, the *Monthly Labor Review* from the Department of Labor, and the *Federal Reserve Bulletin*.

The Internal Revenue Service and the Small Business Administration provide not only information, but also direct assistance. (As we saw in Chapter 4, the SBA provides management assistance and financial help to qualifying businesses.)

Finally, state and local governments provide information and aid (including tax reductions and help with low-cost financing) to firms that are, or expect to be, located within their borders.

Funding Research

Each year the federal government and business spend about $6 billion on basic and applied research and the government spends about $11 billion on developmental research. Some government-funded research is done at federal installations such as the Center for Disease Control in Atlanta. However, the greatest portion of government-funded research is performed independently at colleges and universities under government grants.

The federal government is (and has been, for some time) funding research into the causes and potential cures of cancer. This research, which is taking place at a number of institutions around the country, is simply too expensive to be funded by individual firms. Because the research is being financed with public funds, the results it yields become part of the *public domain*. That is, they become the property of all citizens—and, in particular, of those who can use the results to produce cancer-fighting drugs and apparatus.

Figure 22.1 Budget of the United States by Department. The U.S. government as a whole is the largest single purchaser of goods and services in the world. Source: Executive Office of the President and Office of Management and Budget, Budget of the United States Government—Fiscal Year 1984.

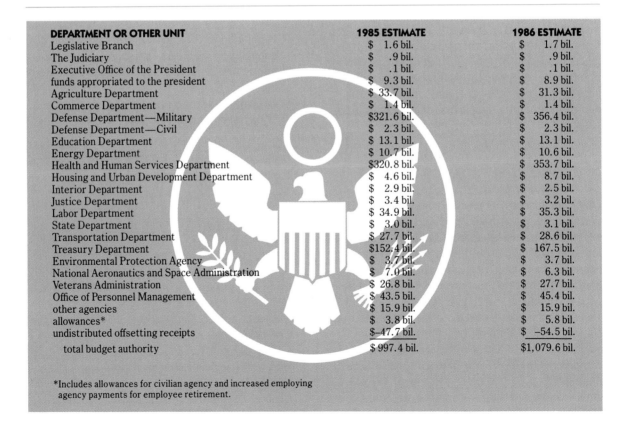

DEPARTMENT OR OTHER UNIT	1985 ESTIMATE	1986 ESTIMATE
Legislative Branch	$ 1.6 bil.	$ 1.7 bil.
The Judiciary	$ .9 bil.	$ .9 bil.
Executive Office of the President	$ .1 bil.	$ .1 bil.
funds appropriated to the president	$ 9.3 bil.	$ 8.9 bil.
Agriculture Department	$ 33.7 bil.	$ 31.3 bil.
Commerce Department	$ 1.4 bil.	$ 1.4 bil.
Defense Department—Military	$321.6 bil.	$ 356.4 bil.
Defense Department—Civil	$ 2.3 bil.	$ 2.3 bil.
Education Department	$ 13.1 bil.	$ 13.1 bil.
Energy Department	$ 10.7 bil.	$ 10.6 bil.
Health and Human Services Department	$320.8 bil.	$ 353.7 bil.
Housing and Urban Development Department	$ 4.6 bil.	$ 8.7 bil.
Interior Department	$ 2.9 bil.	$ 2.5 bil.
Justice Department	$ 3.4 bil.	$ 3.2 bil.
Labor Department	$ 34.9 bil.	$ 35.3 bil.
State Department	$ 3.0 bil.	$ 3.1 bil.
Transportation Department	$ 27.7 bil.	$ 28.6 bil.
Treasury Department	$152.4 bil.	$ 167.5 bil.
Environmental Protection Agency	$ 3.7 bil.	$ 3.7 bil.
National Aeronautics and Space Administration	$ 7.0 bil.	$ 6.3 bil.
Veterans Administration	$ 26.8 bil.	$ 27.7 bil.
Office of Personnel Management	$ 43.5 bil.	$ 45.4 bil.
other agencies	$ 15.9 bil.	$ 15.9 bil.
allowances*	$ 3.8 bil.	$ 5.8 bil.
undistributed offsetting receipts	$ –47.7 bil.	$ –54.5 bil.
total budget authority	$ 997.4 bil.	$1,079.6 bil.

*Includes allowances for civilian agency and increased employing agency payments for employee retirement.

Government funding is not limited to research into diseases. In the 1940s, for example, the federal government began to finance basic research into a phenomenon called semiconduction. This research eventually led to development of the transistor, which has become the basis of the modern electronics industry. It may well be that present government-funded research will lead to entirely new industries and jobs in the decades to come.

Buying the Products of Business

The U.S. government is the largest single purchaser of goods and services in the world. Figure 22.1 shows projected federal spending for 1985 and 1986, by department. A single purchase may range in size from a few hundred dollars for office supplies or furniture to over a billion dollars for new aircraft. The federal government is the largest customer of many firms, and it is the only customer of some.

In addition, there are 50 state governments, 3000 county governments, 18,000 cities, 17,000 townships, 21,000 school districts, and 21,000 special districts in this country.[2] Together, their total expenditures *exceed* the federal budget. Their needs run from paper clips to highways, from janitorial services to the construction of high-rise office buildings. And they purchase what they need from private business. Through its protection of competition, the government provides business with support of another sort. And the protection and encouragement of competition have become prime motives in the involvement of government in business.

FEDERAL REGULATIONS TO ENCOURAGE COMPETITION

A body of federal law—both statutory and administrative—has been developed to guard against monopolies, price fixing, and similar restraints of competition. These laws protect consumers by ensuring that they have a choice in the market-place. The same laws protect businesses by ensuring that they are free to compete. (See Figure 22.2.)

The need for such laws became apparent in the late 1800s, when monopolies or trusts were developed in the sugar, whiskey, tobacco, shoe, and oil industries, among others. A **trust** is a business combination that is created when one firm obtains control of competing firms by purchasing their stock or their assets. Eventually, the trust gains control of the entire industry and can set prices and manipulate trade to suit its own interests.

One of the most successful trusts was the Standard Oil Trust, created by John D. Rockefeller in 1882. Until 1911 the Standard Oil Trust controlled between 80 and 90 percent of the petroleum industry. The firm earned extremely high profits at the expense of smaller oil companies and consumers, primarily because it had obtained secret price concessions from the railroads that shipped its products. Very low shipping costs, in

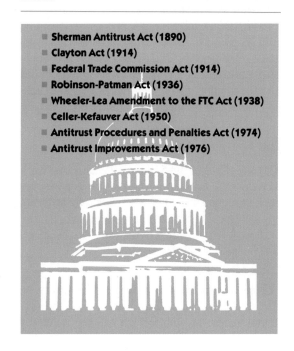

Figure 22.2 *Federal Laws to Protect Free Enterprise. Free enterprise protects both consumers and businesses.*

- Sherman Antitrust Act (1890)
- Clayton Act (1914)
- Federal Trade Commission Act (1914)
- Robinson-Patman Act (1936)
- Wheeler-Lea Amendment to the FTC Act (1938)
- Celler-Kefauver Act (1950)
- Antitrust Procedures and Penalties Act (1974)
- Antitrust Improvements Act (1976)

turn, enabled the firm to systematically eliminate most of its competition by holding prices down deliberately. Once this was accomplished, increasing prices followed quickly.

In response to public outcry against such practices—and prices—Congress passed the Sherman Antitrust Act in 1890. Since then, it has enacted a number of other laws designed to protect American business from monopoly.

The Sherman Antitrust Act (1890)

The objectives of the *Sherman Antitrust Act* were to encourage competition and to prevent the creation of monopolies. The act specifically prohibits any contract or agreement entered into for the purpose of restraining trade. Its two most important provisions are

☐ *Section 1:* Every contract, combination in the form of trust or otherwise, or conspiracy, in restraint of trade or commerce among the several states, or with foreign nations, is hereby declared to be illegal.

☐ *Section 2:* Every person who shall monopolize, or attempt to monopolize, or combine or conspire with any other person or persons to monopolize any part of the trade or commerce . . . shall be deemed guilty of a misdemeanor.

Power to enforce the Sherman Act was given to the Department of Justice, which may bring legal action against businesses suspected of violating its provisions. In 1911, for example, under the Sherman Act the Standard Oil Trust was broken up into 39 independent companies, to restore an acceptable level of competition within the oil industry. The Sherman Act was also used to break up the Northern Securities Company in 1904 and the American Tobacco Company in 1911. It was, in fact, part of the basis for the Justice Department's 1949 and 1974 suits against AT&T.

A much more recent law, the *Antitrust Procedures and Penalties Act* of 1974, made violation of the Sherman Act a felony rather than a misdemeanor. (A felony is a more serious crime than a misdemeanor.) It provides for fines of up to

$100,000 and prison terms of up to 3 years for individuals convicted of antitrust violations. The same act makes corporations subject to fines of up to $1 million. It also provides that a guilty corporation may be sued by competitors or customers for monetary damages.

The Clayton Act (1914)

Because the wording of the Sherman Antitrust Act is somewhat vague, it could not be used to halt specific monopolistic tactics. Congress therefore enacted the *Clayton Act* in 1914. This legislation identified and prohibited five distinct practices that had been used to weaken trade competition:

☐ **Price discrimination,** the practice in which producers and wholesalers charge larger firms a lower price for goods than they charge smaller firms. The price differential had been used by large firms to gain a competitive edge and, in many cases, to force small firms out of business. (The Clayton Act does, however, allow quantity discounts.)

☐ The **tying agreement,** which is a contract that forces a middleman to purchase unwanted products along with the products it actually wants to buy. This practice was used to "move" a producer's slow-selling merchandise along with its more desirable merchandise. Twentieth Century–Fox, for example, was fined under the Clayton Act for forcing theater chains to rent a less popular motion picture along with one that promised to be highly successful.[3]

☐ The **binding contract,** an agreement that requires a middleman to purchase products from a particular supplier, not from the supplier's competitors. In return for signing a binding contract, the middleman was generally given a price discount.

☐ The **interlocking directorate,** in which members of the board of directors of one firm are also directors of a competing firm. Thus, for example, a person may not be a director of American Airlines and Delta Airlines at the

same time. The threat to competition that such a situation creates is obvious.

☐ The **community of interests,** or the situation in which one firm buys the stock of a competing firm in order to reduce competition between the two. This is the tactic that was used to create the giant trusts of the late 1800s.

The Federal Trade Commission Act (1914)

In spite of the Sherman and Clayton Acts, abuses continued. In 1914 Congress passed the *Federal Trade Commission Act,* which states that "Unfair methods of competition in commerce are hereby declared unlawful." This act also created the **Federal Trade Commission** (FTC), a five-member committee charged with the responsibility of investigating illegal trade practices and enforcing antitrust laws.

At first the FTC was limited to enforcement of the Sherman, Clayton, and FTC Acts. However, in 1938, in the Wheeler–Lea Amendment to the FTC Act, Congress gave the FTC the power to eliminate deceptive business practices—including those that are aimed at consumers rather than competitors. This early "consumer legislation" empowered the FTC to deal with a variety of unfair business tactics without having to prove that they endanger competition.

In 1982 the U.S. government withdrew its antitrust case against IBM, giving IBM's defense lawyers a reason to celebrate. Source: © 1982 P. F. Bentley, Photo Reporters.

The FTC may act on its own or on complaints lodged by businesses or individuals. The first step is to investigate the accused firm and its business practices. After its investigation, the commission can issue a **cease and desist order,** which is an order to refrain from an illegal practice. If the practice is continued, the FTC may, with the aid of the Justice Department, bring suit against the violating firm.

The Robinson-Patman Act (1936)

Although the Clayton Act prohibits price discrimination, it does permit quantity discounts. This provision turned out to be a major loophole in the law: It was used by large chain retailers to obtain sizable price concessions that gave them a strong competitive edge over independent stores. To correct this imbalance, the *Robinson-Patman Act* was passed by Congress in 1936. This law specifically prohibits

□ Price differentials that "substantially" weaken competition, unless they can be justified by the actual lower selling costs associated with larger orders
□ Advertising and promotional allowances (a form of discount), unless they are offered to small retailers as well as large retailers

The Robinson-Patman Act is more controversial than most antitrust legislation. Many economists believe that the act tends to discourage price competition rather than to eliminate monopolies. In any case, so far there have been relatively few convictions under the act because the burden of proof is on the injured party—and that is most often small business owners, who have limited time and financial resources necessary to take legal action.

The Celler-Kefauver Act (1950)

The Clayton Act prohibited building a trust by purchasing the stock of competing firms. To get around that prohibition, however, a firm could still purchase the *assets* of its competitors. The result was the same: the elimination of competition.

This gigantic loophole was closed by the *Celler-Kefauver Act,* which prohibits mergers through the purchase of assets if these mergers will tend to reduce competition. The act also requires that all mergers be approved by the FTC and the Justice Department before they are completed. The recent proposed merger between Lykes-Youngstown Corporation and the LTV Corporation (both of which are producers of steel) was touch-and-go for some time, although it finally received approval.

The Present Antitrust Environment

The laws we have discussed were enacted "after the fact"—to correct abuses. In 1976 Congress passed the *Antitrust Improvements Act* to strengthen previous legislation. This law provided additional time for the FTC and the Justice Department to evaluate proposed mergers, and it expanded the investigative powers of the Justice Department. It also authorized the attorneys general of the states to prosecute firms accused of price fixing and to recover monetary damages for *consumers.*

The problem with antitrust legislation and its enforcement is that it is hard to define exactly what an appropriate level of competition is. For example, a particular merger may be in the public interest because it increases the efficiency of an industry. But it may be harmful at the same time because it reduces competition. There is really no rule of law (or of economics) that can be used to determine which of these two considerations is more important in a given case.

Three factors tend to influence the enforcement and effectiveness of antitrust legislation at the present time. The first is the growing presence of foreign firms in American markets. These firms have increased competition and thus have made it more difficult for any firm to monopolize an industry. Second, most antitrust legislation must be interpreted by the courts, because it is often vague and open-ended. Thus the attitude of the courts has a lot to do with the effectiveness of these laws. And third, political considerations often determine how actively the FTC and the Justice Department pursue antitrust cases. For example, a number of pending cases were resolved only after Ronald Reagan took office as president. This political factor may very well be the primary determinant of the antitrust environment at any given time.

But what about those monopolies that our government *does* allow to exist and flourish? In the next section, we will see what makes them different and how they are regulated.

FEDERAL REGULATION OF NATURAL MONOPOLIES

In Chapter 1, a **natural monopoly** was defined as an industry that requires a huge capital investment and within which the duplication of facilities would be wasteful. In such an industry the government may permit one or very few firms to operate. Then it carefully regulates their activities, prices, and profits. Such regulation is aimed at ensuring that the natural monopolist earns a reasonable profit but does not take advantage of its unique position. The three major regulated

monopolies are the public utility, communications, and transportation industries.

Public Utilities

To provide electricity to homes and businesses within an area requires the installation of expensive generating equipment, transmission lines, transformers, and protective equipment. Constant maintenance of these installations is also necessary. Moreover, electricity is most efficiently generated in large quantities. Duplication of equipment for generating and distributing electricity within a geographic area would be wasteful. Prices would be higher than they are at present, but profits would be lower. Quality of service would eventually deteriorate.

For these reasons, a single supplier of electricity is licensed to operate in each geographic area. Its operations are generally controlled by a city or state utility commission that must, for example, approve any proposed rate increases. The Federal Energy Regulatory Commission oversees the *interstate* operations of firms that sell electricity or natural gas or operate gas pipelines. The nuclear power plants operated by public utilities are licensed and regulated by the Nuclear Regulatory Commission.

Communications

Radio and television stations are monopolies in the sense that each has the exclusive right to broadcast on a particular frequency within a specified area. Telephone and telegraph companies both fall within our definition of a regulated monopoly. All are regulated by either state or federal agencies.

The **Federal Communications Commission** (FCC) was created by Congress in 1934, primarily to license radio stations and set rates for interstate telephone and telegraph services. At present, the FCC is also responsible for the licensing and regulation of television stations, cable television networks, and ham and CB radio operators. Recently the FCC has abolished scores of regulations ranging from required radio-program logs to the amount of time that TV stations can use for commercial messages. Given the current deregulatory movement, this trend will probably continue.

Transportation

Various abuses in the late nineteenth century—primarily by the railroads—led to passage of the Interstate Commerce Act in 1887. This act was really the first major piece of federal regulatory legislation. It created the **Interstate Commerce Commission** (ICC), whose main function was to police the railroads. Since then its scope has been expanded to include all interstate carriers. The ICC is responsible for licensing carriers to operate in specific geographic areas, for establishing safety standards for interstate carriers, and for approving mergers of transportation firms.

The Civil Aeronautics Board (CAB) was created in 1938 to regulate the new airline industry. It sets or approves fares, licenses airlines to serve particular airports, and establishes standards of service for air carriers.

Critics have argued that regulation of the transportation industry tends to benefit the carriers rather than their customers. In fact, both the ICC and the CAB have been criticized for not paying enough attention to the needs of consumers. As a result, their activities have been affected by the current deregulation movement (which we shall discuss shortly). Deregulation of the airline industry is already in progress, and the CAB is scheduled to be phased out of existence on December 31, 1984.

OTHER AREAS OF REGULATION

It is impossible to manage even a small business without being affected by local, state, and federal regulations. And it is just as impossible to describe all the government regulations that affect

business. In addition to the two broad areas discussed here, we have examined a variety of regulations in other chapters (and there are more in the next chapter). Figure 22.3 is provided as both a cross-reference and an illustration of the wide range of government regulation.

Even as we read about the extensive regulation that business is subject to, however, a committed deregulation movement is afoot. Let us examine its roots, its goals, and its accomplishments so far.

THE DEREGULATION MOVEMENT

Deregulation is the process of removing existing regulations, forgoing proposed regulations, or reducing the rate at which new regulations are enacted. A movement to deregulate business began in the 1970s and has gained momentum lately. The primary aim of the movement is to cut down on the complexity of regulations that affect business and the cost of complying with them all.

Perhaps equally important is the goal of reducing the size of the U.S. government. It has been estimated that, in 1985, the government will

☐ Employ approximately 3 million civilian workers (in addition to 2 million military personnel)
☐ Spend almost $1 trillion, which is approximately $4000 for every person in the United States

As the federal government has grown, the number of regulatory agencies has increased as well. In the 1970s alone, 20 new federal agencies were formed. (The average for the previous 60 years was about 6 new agencies per decade.) At least 16 federal agencies now have a direct impact on business activities. These agencies are listed in Table 22.1, with the activities they regulate.

The Cost of Regulation

It has been estimated that federal spending for enforcing regulations cost the taxpayers $4 billion in 1980, whereas compliance with all of these

Figure 22.3 *Additional Discussions of Government Regulations That Affect Business*

CHAPTER 2		
	physical environment	regulations enacted mainly during the 1960s and 1970s to deal with air, water, and land pollution
CHAPTER 9	consumerism	regulations designed to protect consumers from unfair and deceptive business practices
CHAPTER 10	personnel and employee relations	laws to eliminate discrimination in employee selection, compensation, and advancement
CHAPTER 17	union-management relations	early legislation enacted to promote union growth; later legislation designed to curb union growth
CHAPTER 21	securities	state and federal laws that regulate the exchange of securities
CHAPTER 23	trademarks, patents, and copyrights	regulations protecting the inventions, written works, and trademarks of individuals and businesses
	international trade	duties and other restrictions on importing foreign goods

regulations costs businesses $100 billion dollars each year.[4]

The Business Roundtable is an organization of 187 of America's leading corporations. In 1979 it completed a detailed research study to determine how much its members spend in order to comply with government regulations. Forty-eight corporations participated in the study. Each kept track of all costs incurred as a result of specific regulations, for a period of one year. Only costs that could be attributed to regulation were recorded. Any expense that might be incurred for sound business reasons, whether or not a regulation existed, was eliminated.

The results were staggering. Government regulations had cost the 48 corporations a total of $2,621,593,000. This dollar amount represented

☐ 16 percent of the corporations' after-tax profits
☐ 43 percent of their research and development costs
☐ 10 percent of their total capital expenditures[5]

One corporation involved in the study, Whirlpool, incurred regulatory costs of more than $20 million. Moreover,

☐ Whirlpool's after-tax earnings were 22 cents per share lower as a result of government regulations
☐ Whirlpool employees spent over 287,000 hours to comply with these regulations
☐ Whirlpool submitted more than 13,200 pages of documentation to 6 government agencies[6]

The large corporations, such as those involved in the Business Roundtable study, can cope with government regulation. They have been doing so for some time. In essence, coping means passing the cost of regulation along to stockholders in the form of lower dividends and to consumers in the form of higher prices.

Smaller firms bear a smaller regulatory burden, but they may find it harder to cope with that burden. Some are not aware of all the applicable regulations, and that can lead to legal difficulties.

Table 22.1 *Government Agencies and What They Regulate*

Government Agency/Commission	Regulates
Civil Aeronautics Board (CAB)	Airline industry
Consumer Product Safety Commission (CPSC)	Consumer protection
Environmental Protection Agency (EPA)	Pollution control
Equal Employment Opportunity Commission (EEOC)	Discrimination in employment practices
Federal Aviation Administration (FAA)	Airline industry
Federal Communications Commission (FCC)	Radio, television, telephone, and telegraph
Federal Energy Regulatory Commission (FERC)	Electric power and natural gas
Federal Marine Commission (FMC)	Ocean shipping
Federal Trade Commission (FTC)	Antitrust, consumer protection
Food and Drug Administration (FDA)	Consumer protection
Interstate Commerce Commission (ICC)	Rail, bus, trucking, pipelines, and waterways
Mine Safety and Health Administration (MSHA)	Worker safety and health in the mining industry
National Highway Traffic Safety Administration (NHTSA)	Vehicle safety
Nuclear Regulatory Commission (NRC)	Nuclear power and nuclear industry
Occupational Safety and Health Administration (OSHA)	Worker safety and health
Securities and Exchange Commission (SEC)	Corporate securities

Others may not have the staff necessary to comply with the various documentation requirements. And, for many small businesses, stiff competition for customers requires that they pass the cost of compliance directly to their owners.

Current Attempts at Deregulation

Presidents Ford and Carter tried to control the activities of federal agencies and commissions, but they had only limited success. President Reagan began a deregulation effort almost immediately after taking office in 1981. Nine days after his inauguration, he postponed the implementation of all regulations not yet in effect. In addition, his administrators set about removing or slowing the enforcement of many existing regulations. (See Table 22.2.) The principal guidelines for Reagan's deregulation efforts were as follows:

□ Impose regulations only if their benefits exceed their costs
□ Choose the least expensive method of achieving the goals of regulation
□ Tailor regulatory burdens to the size and nature of the affected firms
□ Reduce unnecessary paperwork and regulatory delays[7]

President Reagan also created the Presidential Task Force on Regulatory Relief, whose purpose is to reduce the amount of time, money, and effort required to comply with government regulations. The Task Force has estimated that, in its first 18 months, the Reagan administration saved industry more than $15 billion by revoking or revising regulations that had been issued during the previous decade.[8]

The deregulation drive is continuing, but there is a question as to how far it can—or should—go. Many federal agencies operate outside the immediate control of the president and Congress. If they choose, they may issue regulations without answering to any government institution except the courts. Moreover, support for deregulation is mixed. According to a recent Roper

The popularity of Mexican food in the United States is hardly news. So, acknowledging that Mexican food is here to stay, the U.S. Department of Agriculture (USDA) has for the first time funded a full-scale investigation into the nutritional content of South-of-the-Border food.

The USDA has granted the University of Arizona, Tucson over $90,000 to sample food from local Mexican restaurants for caloric value, protein content, and so on.

According to Charles Peyton, associate vice president of research for the university, the study was the result of an unsolicited proposal by the school, which noticed that the USDA's annual nutrition study had a glaring omission: Mexican food.

"What better place to study Mexican food," says Peyton. "Graduate students conducting the study have a lot of opportunity to sample Mexican foods in Tucson."

Results of the study, which should take about a year to complete, will be used by the USDA to update its study. This data is used as a standard by nutritionists and food researchers nationwide.

Source: *Restaurant Business*, July 1, 1984, p. 10.

Table 22.2   President Reagan's Regulatory "Hit List," Compiled in 1981

Government Agency/Commission	Action
Consumer Product Safety Commission [CPSC]	Emphasize dangerous-product warnings over product regulation
Environmental Protection Agency [EPA]	Move away from technology-forcing standards, such as smokestack scrubbers for all coal-fired plants, toward performance standards
Equal Employment Opportunity Commission [EEOC]	Look for case-by-case discriminatory practices rather than seek industry-wide patterns of discrimination
Federal Energy Regulatory Commission [FERC]	Speed up decontrol of natural gas
Food and Drug Administration [FDA]	Review the law that prohibits food additives that may cause cancer—no matter how low the risk
National Highway Traffic Safety Administration [NHTSA]	Postpone rule requiring air bags or passive seat belts in autos
Nuclear Regulatory Commission [NRC]	Streamline licensing of nuclear power plants
Occupational Safety and Health Administration [OSHA]	Emphasize personal-protection devices rather than costly engineering controls to achieve workplace safety
Securities and Exchange Commission [SEC]	Prosecute major offenders vigorously rather than file numerous cases now often settled out of court
Agriculture Department [USDA]	Ease meat-labeling requirements
Energy Department [DOE]	Relax requirements for utilities and industry to convert to coal power
Interior Department [DOI]	Accelerate leasing of mineral and energy resources on federal land
Urban Mass Transportation Administration [UMTA]	Review requirement that subways and buses be fully accessible to the handicapped

Source: "Deregulation: A Fast Start for the Reagan Strategy," reprinted from the March 9, 1981 issue of *Business Week* by special permission, © 1981 by McGraw-Hill, Inc.

public-opinion survey, a growing number of people say government agencies aren't doing enough to protect the public.[9]

Deregulation may also create problems for business. For example, the government has been in the process of deregulating the airline industry since 1978. Now airline officials admit that some government regulations are needed to maintain an orderly market. For the airlines, deregulation has led to price wars and other very aggressive marketing strategies. These have resulted in operating losses for even the strongest air carriers.

Many politicians and consumers believe the deregulation movement has gone far enough. They argue that further deregulation could result in inferior products, dangerous working conditions, polluted air, and other problems that were prevalent during the 1960s and 1970s. Perhaps what is needed now is not more deregulation but a fresh look at present regulation, its goals and costs, and its effectiveness. Another worthwhile goal would be a reworking of the regulatory structure to create a "livable" environment for consumers, workers, and businesses.

Now that we have discussed both regulation and the move to deregulate, let us examine the sources of the revenues that government draws on to fund its activities, regulatory and otherwise.

GOVERNMENT TAXATION

Whether you believe there is too much government regulation or too little, you are required to help pay for it. In one way or another, each of us helps pay for everything that government does— from regulating business to funding basic research into the causes and cures of cancer. We pay taxes to our local, state, and federal governments on the basis of what we earn, what we own, and even what we purchase.

Federal Taxes

It takes a lot of money to run something as big as the U.S. government. Each year vast sums are spent for human services, national defense, and interest on the national debt. In addition, the federal government must pay the salaries of its employees, cover its operating expenses, and purchase equipment and supplies that range from typewriter ribbons to aircraft carriers. Most of the money comes from taxes.

Taxes and Deficits Figure 22.4 shows that the federal government had revenues of $666.1 billion in 1983. About 95 percent of that sum was obtained through taxation. However, the government actually spent more than it took in that year. In other words, there was a **budget deficit,** which is an excess of spending over income. In fact, the U.S. government has had budget deficits in every year since 1960, with the exception of 1969 (see Figure 22.5).

What is disturbing about the information given in Figure 22.5 is the increasing size of the budget deficits. Because deficits must be financed by borrowing, the outstanding debt of the U.S. government has grown to more than $1 trillion! The interest on this debt is enormous, and the government's continued borrowing has been blamed for the high interest rates of the 1970s and 1980s.

A number of politicians have proposed a Constitutional amendment requiring that federal spending be limited to total federal revenues. If it were ratified, this amendment would either curtail government spending or lead to an increase in taxes.

Another deficit-reducing suggestion is a complete overhaul of the federal income tax structure. What is suggested is a much simpler tax structure that allows no tax shelters and only minimal deductions. According to its advocates, such a tax structure would produce enough income to cover federal expenses without unduly burdening taxpayers.

Neither proposal seems to have wide support. At least for the present, we appear to be left with both budget deficits and the federal tax structure as it now stands.

Individual Income Taxes The individual (or personal) income tax is derived from the Sixteenth

Amendment to the Constitution, which was ratified in 1913. It states that "The Congress shall have the power to lay and collect taxes on incomes, from whatever source derived, without apportionment among the several states and without regard to any census or enumeration." A person's individual income tax liability is computed from his or her taxable income, which is gross income less various authorized deductions from income. In 1914, the first year of the individual income tax, the federal government collected an average of 28 cents per taxpayer. Today that average is over $1200 per person.

The federal income tax is a progressive tax. A **progressive tax** requires the payment of an increasing proportion of income as the individual's income increases. For example, a single individual with a taxable income of $20,000 must presently pay a federal income tax of $3376, or 17 percent of taxable income. A single taxpayer with a taxable income of $40,000 must pay $10,323, or 26 percent of that income.

Taxpayers who own sole proprietorships or partnerships pay their income taxes to the Internal Revenue Service in four quarterly installments. Employees pay a specified amount each pay period. That amount is withheld (deducted from the employee's paycheck) by the employer and sent to the IRS. In addition, every taxpayer must file an annual tax return by April 15 of each year, for the previous calendar year. The return shows the income, deductions, and computations on which the taxpayer's tax liability is based.

Corporate Income Taxes Corporations pay federal income tax only on their taxable income, which is what remains after deducting *all* legal business expenses from net sales. (This is net income before taxes, discussed in Chapter 19.)

Currently, the federal corporate tax rate is 15 percent of the first $25,000 of before-tax profit; 18 percent of the second $25,000; 30 percent of the third $25,000; 40 percent of the fourth $25,000; and 46 percent of profits in excess of

Figure 22.4 *Federal Revenues from Taxes. In 1983 the largest source of federal tax revenue was the individual income tax.* Source: Office of Management and Budget, Budget of the United States Government: FY 1983, p. 4.2.

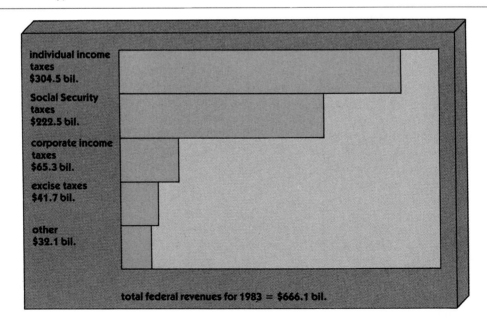

individual income taxes $304.5 bil.

Social Security taxes $222.5 bil.

corporate income taxes $65.3 bil.

excise taxes $41.7 bil.

other $32.1 bil.

total federal revenues for 1983 = $666.1 bil.

$100,000. A corporation with a taxable income of $400,000 must pay a total of $163,750 to the federal government, as shown in Table 22.3.

Corporate income taxes provide approximately 10 percent of total federal revenues. The effectiveness and fairness of the corporate income tax are, however, the subject of continual debate. For example, President Reagan created a stir when he suggested, in 1983, that the corporate income tax should be eliminated because the money that corporations pay in taxes should be reinvested in American business. Actually, many economists advocate elimination of the corporate income tax, for two reasons. First, corporate profits are subject to double taxation: The corporation pays a tax on its profits before they are distributed to stockholders. Then each stockholder pays a personal income tax on those dividends that are distributed. Second, economists consider the tax on corporate profits to be an added expense of doing business. In effect, this cost is borne by workers through lower wages, by consumers in the form of higher prices, and by stockholders through lower dividends.

Figure 22.5 *Federal Budgets, Surplus and Deficit, 1960 to 1986. Figures for 1983–1986 are estimates. Source: Executive Office of the President and Office of Management and Budget,* Budget of the United States Government: FY 1982, p. 611, *and* Special Analyses, Budget of the United States: FY 1985, p. E-5.

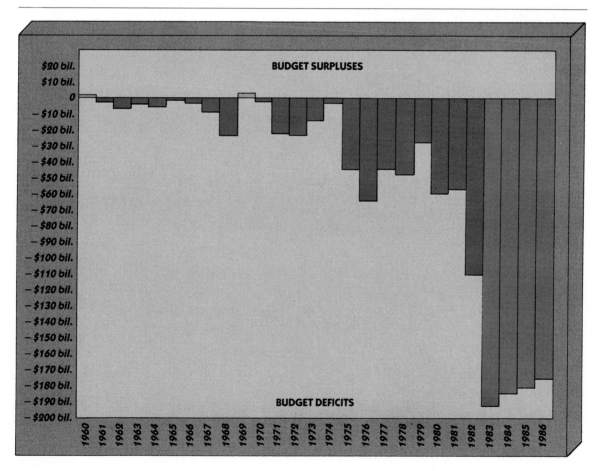

What Happens in a Tax Audit?

"If nothing strikes terror into a taxpayer's heart like the thought of an audit, it can only be because of the Internal Revenue Service's bully boy reputation."[1] Yet there are certain things you should know about the IRS's audit procedures. Your changes of getting audited are not so great as you might think. Actually, the IRS audits about 1.4 million income tax returns each year, for an overall average of approximately 1.5 percent of all returns filed.

The IRS selects returns to be audited by computer analysis, using a closely guarded formula that scores returns on their potential for an upward adjustment in taxes owed by the taxpayer. This system compares specific figures on your return with "normal" amounts for all taxpayers. If, for instance, your charitable deductions are "scored" much higher than average, the IRS's computer will kick out your return for special attention and perhaps an audit.

If you are audited, the burden of proof is on you, not on the IRS. You should bring along checks, receipts, or whatever documentation you need to substantiate your claim. If you cannot document your deduction, the IRS will throw it out.

You may represent yourself or you may be represented by an attorney, a CPA, or an "enrolled practitioner"—a person who either is a former IRS employee or has passed the stiff IRS tax exam.

Finally, if you lose the first round, you may decide to appeal the decision to the auditor's supervisor. If the immediate supervisor refuses to overturn the decision, you may decide to take the IRS to court. You may choose the U.S. District Court, the U.S. Court of Claims, or the U.S. Tax Court. Many taxpayers choose the U.S. Tax Court because it is possible to petition the court for a hearing without paying the IRS. If the dis-puted amount is less than $5000 for the year in question, you can go to the tax court's Small Tax Case Division. Of course, at any point you may decide to negotiate a settlement with the IRS or agree with the IRS's findings and arrange to pay the full amount.

The chances of an IRS audit have been decreasing.
Source: Internal Revenue Service.

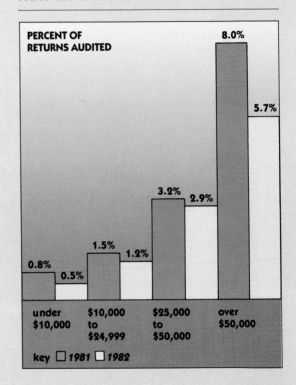

PERCENT OF RETURNS AUDITED

- under $10,000: 0.8% (1981), 0.5% (1982)
- $10,000 to $24,999: 1.5% (1981), 1.2% (1982)
- $25,000 to $50,000: 3.2% (1981), 2.9% (1982)
- over $50,000: 8.0% (1981), 5.7% (1982)

key ☐ 1981 ☐ 1982

[1]"What Happens to Your Tax Return Now," *U.S. News & World Report,* April 18, 1983, pp. 52–53.

Sources: Harry Anderson and Rich Thomas, "The Coming Tax Crackdown," *Newsweek,* April 11, 1983, pp. 54–55. Leonard Weiner, "What to Do When the IRS Comes Calling," *U.S. News & World Report,* May 2, 1983, pp. 71–72. Julian Block, "Tax Audit Tightrope," *Vogue,* October 1982, p. 206.

The arguments against corporate taxation seem quite reasonable. However, if these taxes were abolished, the federal government would have to make up for the lost revenue somehow. The burden would probably fall on the same people who are bearing it now: workers, consumers, and stockholders.

Other Federal Taxes Additional sources of federal revenue include Social Security, unemployment, and excise taxes, as well as customs duties. One objective of all taxes is to raise money, but excise taxes and customs duties are also designed to regulate the use of specific goods and services.

The second largest source of federal revenue is the *Social Security tax,* which is collected under the Federal Insurance Contributions Act (FICA). This tax provides funding for retirement, disability, and death benefits for contributing employees. FICA taxes are paid both by the employer and the employee. The employee's share is withheld from his or her salary by the employer and sent to the federal government with the employer's share. For 1984 the annual FICA tax was 13.7 percent of the first $37,800 earned.

Under the provisions of the Federal Unemployment Tax Act (FUTA), employers must pay an *unemployment tax* equal to 1.1 percent of the

The FUTA tax is paid by employers for federal aid to unemployed workers such as this family who have lost their house and now live in their car. Source: AP/Wide World Photos.

first $7000 of each employee's annual wages. The tax is paid to the federal government to fund benefits for unemployed workers. Unlike the Social Security tax, the FUTA tax is levied only on employers.

An **excise tax** is a tax on the manufacture or sale of a particular domestic product. Excise taxes are used to help pay for government services directed toward the users of these products and, in some cases, to limit the use of potentially harmful products. For example, there are federal excise taxes on alcoholic beverages ($10.50 per gallon), cigarettes ($4 per thousand), and gasoline ($0.09 per gallon).[10] Alcohol and tobacco products are potentially harmful to consumers; they are taxed to raise their prices and thus discourage consumption. The federal excise tax on gasoline is a source of income that can be used to build and repair highways. Although manufacturers and retailers are responsible for paying excise taxes, these taxes are usually passed on the consumer in the form of higher retail prices.

A **customs** (or **import**) **duty** is a tax on a particular foreign product entering a country. Import duties are designed to protect specific domestic industries by raising the prices of competing imported products. They are first paid by

Table 22.3 *Federal Corporate Income Tax on an Income of $400,000*

tax on first $25,000:	
$25,000 × 15% =	$ 3,750
second $25,000:	
25,000 × 18% =	4,500
third $25,000:	
25,000 × 30% =	7,500
fourth $25,000:	
25,000 × 40% =	10,000
excess:	
300,000 × 46% =	138,000
total corporate tax	$163,750

the importer, but then they are passed on to consumers through higher—and less competitive—prices.

State and Local Taxes

Like the federal government, state and local governments are financed primarily through taxes. As illustrated in Figure 22.6, sales taxes provide about 50 percent of state tax revenues, whereas property taxes account for about 76 percent of local tax revenues. Most states and some cities also levy taxes on the incomes of individuals and businesses.

Sales Taxes   Sales taxes are levied by both states and cities and are paid by the purchasers of consumer products. Retailers collect sales taxes as a specified percentage of the price of each taxed product and then forward them to the taxing authority. At present, the highest sales tax (7.5 percent) is paid by residents of Connecticut. In several states, no state or city sales taxes are levied at all.

A sales tax is a regressive tax. A **regressive tax** is one that takes a greater percentage of a lower income than of a higher income. The regressiveness of the sales tax stems from the fact that lower-income households generally spend a greater proportion of their income on taxable products such as food, clothing, and other essentials. Consider the impact of a 5 percent sales tax on food items purchased by a low-income family. If this family earns $10,000 a year and spends $3000 for food, they will pay sales taxes of $150, or 1.5 percent of their total earnings. By comparison a family that earns $40,000 a year

Figure 22.6   Sources of Tax Revenues for State and Local Governments. *Source: Bradley R. Schiller, The Economy Today, 2d ed., (New York: Random House, 1983), p. 64. Copyright © 1983 by Random House, Inc.*

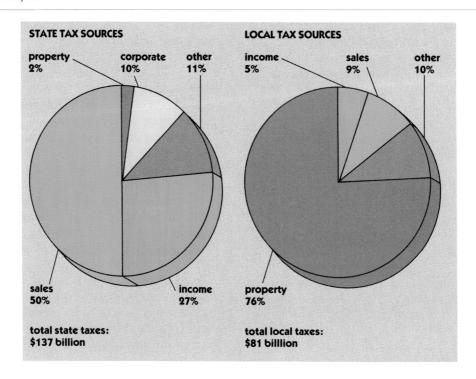

STATE TAX SOURCES

property 2%
corporate 10%
other 11%
sales 50%
income 27%

total state taxes: $137 billion

LOCAL TAX SOURCES

income 5%
sales 9%
other 10%
property 76%

total local taxes: $81 billion

and spends $5000 for food will pay sales taxes of $250, or 0.625 percent of their total earnings.

Property Taxes Property taxes are levied on the real estate and personal property owned by businesses and individuals.

Real estate taxes are usually computed as a percentage of the assessed value of the real property. (The assessed value is determined by the local tax assessor as the fair market value of the property, a portion of its fair market value, or its replacement cost.) For example, suppose the city council has established a real estate tax rate of $2.10 per $100 of assessed valuation. Then the property tax bill for an office building with an assessed value of $200,000 will be $200,000 × $2.10/$100, or $4200.

Certain personal property owned by businesses and individuals is also subject to local taxation. For businesses, taxable personal property normally includes machinery, equipment, raw materials, and finished inventory. In some cases, local authorities also tax the value of stocks, bonds, mortgages, and promissory notes held by businesses. For individuals, such items as trucks, automobiles, and boats may be classified as personal property and taxed as such by local authorities. Taxes on personal property are usually computed as a percentage of some assessed value.

Chapter Review

SUMMARY

Government's relationship with business is based on the needs of business, government, and the general public. Government supports business by enacting some of its regulations, by providing information and assistance to business, by funding much of the basic research that leads to new products and jobs, and by purchasing goods and services that businesses produce. At the same time, government regulates business activity in such a way as to promote competition and protect the interests of individuals.

Congress passed the Sherman Antitrust Act in 1890 as a means of restoring a reasonable level of competition within industries that had become dominated by trusts. Later antitrust legislation was intended mainly to close loopholes in previous laws and to prohibit specific practices that had been used to weaken competition. Enforcement of these laws is the responsibility of the Federal Trade Commission and the U.S. Justice Department.

Natural monopolies are industries in which the duplication of production facilities (which competition would require) would be wasteful. Government regulation of natural monopolies consists of the licensing of firms to operate in natural monopolies and the supervision of their activities. The principal natural monopolies are the public utility, communications, and transportation industries.

Government regulation extends to a wide range of business activities, and compliance can be very costly. In response to a call for deregulation, the federal government has slowed the enactment and enforcement of some regulations and has removed others. There is, however, a question as to how much regulation—or deregulation—is most effective in maintaining orderly markets.

Federal, state, and local governments finance their activities primarily by collecting taxes. For the federal government, individual income taxes are the major source of funding. Other sources include corporate income taxes, Social Security, unemployment, excise and customs taxes. In spite of its huge tax revenues, however, the U.S. government continues to operate at a deficit.

The major source of tax revenues for the states is the sales tax, which is levied on purchases of consumer goods. Local governments are financed mainly by property taxes, which are based on the value of the real estate and/or personal property owned by individuals and businesses.

So far in this text, we have been concerned only with American business within American markets. In the next chapter, we shall extend our discussion to business that is conducted across national borders. As we will see, international trade can be both a necessary and an exciting facet of business.

KEY TERMS

You should now be able to define and give an example relevant to each of the following terms:

trust

price discrimination

tying agreement

binding contract

interlocking directorate

community of interests

Federal Trade Commission

cease and desist order

natural monopoly

Federal Communications Commission

Interstate Commerce Commission

deregulation

budget deficit

progressive tax

excise tax

customs (or import) duty

regressive tax

QUESTIONS AND EXERCISES

Review Questions

1. In what ways does government provide assistance or support to business?
2. How do federal antitrust regulations work to support American business?
3. What situation led to passage of the Sherman Antitrust Act?
4. What was the major loophole in the Sherman Antitrust Act? How was it closed?
5. The Clayton Act specifically prohibited five practices. List these practices and briefly explain how each weakens competition.
6. Describe the process by which the Federal Trade Commission acts to halt an illegal business practice.
7. Why does the federal government go to great lengths to curb monopolies like the Standard Oil Trust but readily license natural monopolies like Florida Power & Light?
8. Cite the responsibilities of (a) the Federal Communications Commission, (b) the Interstate Commerce Commission, and (c) the Federal Energy Regulatory Commission.
9. What are the principal reasons for the current deregulation movement? What forces may slow it down?
10. Which single tax provides the most income for the federal government? for state governments? for local governments?
11. What is "regressive" about a regressive tax?
12. Why are excise taxes and customs duties sometimes referred to as regulatory taxes? What do they regulate?

Discussion Questions

1. What are the probable long-term effects of the AT&T breakup on AT&T itself? on the firms that the new AT&T will be competing with? on consumers?

2. Should the Justice Department bring suit to break up other giant corporations in order to promote competition? Explain.
3. What benefits and what problems can result from the requirement that the FTC and the Justice Department approve mergers before they take place?
4. Is there any competition at all among public utilities? Would such competition benefit or harm consumers?
5. How might legislators and regulatory agencies determine whether deregulation is needed in a particular area? How might they determine where additional regulation is needed?
6. Are budget deficits necessary, or harmful, or both? Should there be a Constitutional amendment that requires a balanced budget? Explain your opinion.

Exercises

1. Outline a plan for the removal of all graduation requirements (other than the number of credit hours required) at your school over the next two years. List three advantages and three disadvantages of such deregulation.
2. Suppose a certain state levies a 4 percent sales tax on all consumer products. Develop, in detail, a method for modifying the sales tax to make it less regressive. Explain how your method would be applied, and show that your tax would actually be less regressive than the present tax.

Do The Airlines Need Fixing?

In February 1982, Robert Crandall, president of American Airlines, and Howard Putnam, president of Braniff International, had a telephone conversation that was of great interest to the U.S. Justice Department. In that conversation, which was taped by Putnam, Crandall suggested that the two airlines raise fares by 20 percent. The suggestion, documented by Putnam's tape, was enough evidence for the Justice Department to file a civil antitrust suit against Crandall and American Airlines.

The actual complaint quoted Mr. Crandall as saying, "I think it's dumb as hell . . . to sit here and pound . . . each other and neither one of us making a (expletive) dime." When Mr. Putnam asked, "Do you have a suggestion?" Mr. Crandall replied: "Yes, I have a suggestion for you. Raise your (expletive) fares 20 percent. I'll raise mine the next morning . . . You'll make more money and I will too."[11] At this point Putnam said, "We can't talk about pricing." Crandall replied, "Oh (expletive), Howard. We can talk about any (expletive) thing we want to talk about."[12]

The government antitrust suit sought an injunction barring Crandall from serving as president of American Airlines. It also requested that the court bar American Airlines officials from discussing price with the competition for ten years. Actually, the suit was the climax of a ten-month investigation of unfair business practices, which Braniff accused American of using in retaliation for Braniff's low fares. Among the alleged "dirty tricks" were delays of Braniff flights, caused by American's pilots, and the delayed reimbursement for Braniff tickets that had been purchased through American Airlines.

Eighteen months after Crandall's telephone call, the government's case was dismissed. United States District Court Judge Robert M. Hill said in his ruling that "No actual attempt at price fixing occurred, despite the fact that Crandall's 'conduct was at best unprofessional and his choice of words distasteful.'"[13] Judge Hill went on to say that, because Putnam declined Crandall's offer, there was no agreement on a price conspiracy.[14]

1. Before the airlines were deregulated, minimum fares were set by the federal government. Is price fixing between corporations different from price setting by government agencies? Explain.
2. The government case was dismissed because there was no agreement between Crandall and Putnam. Do you agree with Judge Hill's ruling? On what body of law was it probably based?

CASE 22-2

Federal Income Tax Laws

The present federal income tax laws are a maze of regulations, deductions, brackets, exclusions, shelters, credits, and alternative computations. As one result of this complex tax structure, many corporations and high-income individuals seem to expend more effort on reducing their taxes than on increasing their productivity and income. Another result is that individuals with incomes in the hundreds of thousands of dollars may pay less in taxes than those with much lower incomes.

A variety of tax reforms have been proposed by taxpayer groups and members of the Congress. Those that are receiving the most attention at present are the so-called "flat-tax" plans—those that include either a single tax rate for all individuals and corporations, or few tax-rate steps. Proponents claim that such tax structures would close the many loopholes in the existing tax laws and ensure that all individuals and corporations assume a fair share of the nation's tax burden.

Two flat-tax proposals now being seriously considered by the Congress are known as the Fair Tax plan and the Fair and Simple Tax (FAST) plan. Neither one is, however, a purely flat income tax.

Under the Fair Tax plan, individual income tax rates would be either 14, 26, or 30 percent, depending on income (the current maximum is 50 percent of taxable income). Deductions for mortgage interest, charitable contributions, and state and local taxes—among others—would remain, but most loopholes would be closed. Corporations would pay a straight 30 percent of income (down from the 46 percent maximum); here, too, most special provisions and loopholes would be eliminated. Proponents claim that the Fair Tax plan would result in lower tax rates for most taxpayers; people earning the same income would pay about the same amount of tax no matter how the income was earned; and federal tax revenues would not be decreased by the plan.

The FAST plan features a single rate—25 percent—for all taxable income and eliminates many (but not all) deductions and credits. It includes, as well, a provision that guards against increases in income taxes due to the effects of inflation.

Flat-tax plans have developed both supporters and opponents. Many observers feel they would benefit businesses and individuals, while shifting the tax burden only slightly—to those who are now carrying less than their fair share. However, a preliminary study by the Joint Committee on Taxation of the U.S. Congress indicates that:

☐ The FAST plan would reduce the taxes of high-income taxpayers by about 15 percent, but raise the taxes of middle-income taxpayers by 2 to 3 percent.
☐ The Fair Tax plan would not appreciably shift the tax burden among income groups. [15]

1. What would be the advantages and disadvantages of Congress's enacting some sort of flat tax plan?
2. Which of the two plans (FAST or Fair Tax) do you think is the better one? Why? (If you feel strongly about either, you might want to make your feelings known to Sen. Robert Dole, Chairman, Senate Finance Committee, Washington, D.C. 20510.)

CHAPTER

TWENTY-THREE
International Business

Twelve thousand years ago, European and Asiatic tribes met and began to trade goods with each other. In one way or another, humanity has been engaged in international business ever since. Somewhat more "recently," for example, Marco Polo's expeditions into China and England's colonization of America had as their primary objectives the expansion of international trade.

In this chapter we shall discuss the present international business environment, as well as the methods by which firms may enter international markets. After studying the chapter, you should understand:

1. *The economic basis for international business*

2. *The restrictions that nations place on international trade, the objectives of these restrictions, and their results*

3. *The extent of international trade, and the organizations that are working to foster it*

4. *The methods by which a firm can organize for and enter international markets*

5. *The main considerations in international marketing*

6. *The institutions that help firms and nations to finance international business*

Consider this:

From 1976 to 1980, sales of Japanese automobiles in this country increased from fewer than 1 million units per year to almost 2 million. In the same period, sales of American-made cars decreased by 2.1 million units per year. More than 200,000 workers in the U.S. auto industry and related industries became unemployed. American car manufacturers experienced losses in the billions of dollars.

To a great extent, the U.S. auto industry's problems could be blamed on consumers' shift away from large American cars to the smaller Japanese cars, in the wake of rising gasoline prices. Nevertheless, these problems led to a demand for restrictions on the import of Japanese autos. In 1980, under the threat of formal restrictions, the Japanese government agreed to "voluntarily" limit exports to the United States. For

photos, © 1984 T. Molinski.

a three-year period beginning in April 1981, the number of Japanese cars exported to this country was limited to 1.68 million per year.

As expected, the Japanese auto makers exported primarily their higher-priced cars—those that would provide the most profit. The demand for Japanese cars remained high, so dealers had no difficulty selling the cars at their sticker prices.

The number of Japanese autos sold in the United States increased rapidly until Japanese auto makers limited their exports to the United States in 1981. Source: Data, Predicasts Inc.

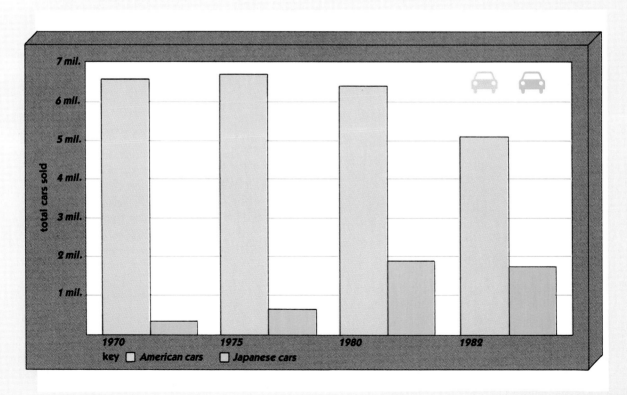

During this three-year period, American auto manufacturers began to turn out smaller cars in an effort to compete directly with the Japanese imports. The high prices of the imports and consumer acceptance of Detroit's smaller cars worked in favor of American auto firms. Sales of American-made automobiles rose substantially, month by month. Workers were rehired, and losses turned into profits. The voluntary restriction on the import of Japanese cars had worked well: The American auto industry was back on its feet. Yet in 1984, when the import restriction was to have run out, it was extended for at least another year. This time the number of Japanese cars to be exported to this country was limited to 1.8 million cars per year.

Japanese auto makers fear that the import restriction may become more or less permanent—at least for the near future. Yet they believe they can sell many more cars in the United States than their quotas allow. Honda, for example, has a quota of 350,000 cars per year under the import restriction. Yet the firm's management feels that it can eventually sell a million cars here each year. To make up the difference, some Japanese firms have established, or are in the process of establishing, production facilities in the United States. (Autos produced in this country are not counted as part of their import quotas.) Honda's first American plant, in Ohio, was able to produce autos at the rate of 150,000 per year by mid-1984. That capacity is expected to double by 1988. In addition, the firm, which began by producing motorcycles, has opened a motorcycle engine plant in Ohio and a lawn mower factory in North Carolina.

The larger Japanese auto producers (including Toyota, Nissan, and Mitsubishi) have been more wary of using this direct method of competing in the American market. However, Nissan already has a production facility in Tennessee, which is producing 120,000 pickup trucks each year. The excess capacity of that plant (another 120,000 vehicles per year) has been committed to the production of Nissan Sentras, beginning in April 1985.[1]

International trade is not, of course, limited to the sale of foreign products in the United States. World trade currently totals around $2 trillion annually, and U.S. exports account for about 11 percent of that amount. Every nation is involved in international business to some degree.

Theoretically, international trade is every bit as logical and worthwhile as, say, trade between Indiana and Ohio. Yet nations tend to restrict the import of certain goods for a variety of reasons, just as the United States effectively restricted the import of Japanese autos in order to protect the faltering American auto industry.

In spite of such restrictions, international trade has increased almost steadily since World War II. Many of the industrialized nations have signed trade agreements that are intended to eliminate problems in international business and to help less developed nations participate in world trade. Individual firms around the world have seized this opportunity to compete in foreign markets through exporting and foreign production, as well as by other means.

THE BASIS FOR INTERNATIONAL BUSINESS

International business is all business activities that involve exchanges across national boundaries. Thus a firm is engaged in international business when it buys some portion of its input from, or sells some portion of its output to, an organization that is located in a foreign country. (A small retail store may sell goods that were produced in some other country. However, because it purchases these goods from American distributors, it is not considered to be engaged in international trade.)

Absolute and Comparative Advantage

Some countries are better equipped than other countries to produce particular goods or services.

The reason may be a country's natural resources, its labor supply, or even custom or historical accident. Such a country would be best off if it could *specialize* in the production of such products, because it can produce them most efficiently. The country would use what it needed of these products and then trade the surplus for products that it could not produce efficiently.

Saudi Arabia has thus specialized in the production of crude oil and petroleum products, South Africa in diamonds, and Australia in wool. Each of these countries is said to have an absolute advantage with regard to a particular product. An **absolute advantage** is the ability to produce a specific product more efficiently than any other nation.

One country may have an absolute advantage with regard to several products, whereas another country may have no absolute advantage at all. Yet it is still worthwhile for these two countries to specialize and trade with each other. To see why this is so, consider the following situation: You are the president of a successful manufacturing firm, and you can accurately type 90 words per minute. Your secretary can type 80 words per minute, but would run the business poorly. You thus have an absolute advantage over your secretary in both typing and managing. But you cannot afford to type your own letters, because your time is best spent in managing the business. That is, you have a comparative advantage in managing. A **comparative advantage** is the ability to produce a specific product more efficiently than any other products.

Your secretary, on the other hand, has a comparative advantage in typing, because he or she can do that better than managing the business. So you spend your time managing, and you leave the typing to your secretary. Overall, the business is run as efficiently as possible, because you are each working in accordance with your own comparative advantage.

The same is true for nations: Goods and services are produced most efficiently when each country specializes in the products for which it has a comparative advantage. Moreover, by definition, every country has a comparative advantage in *some* product.

Exporting and Importing

Suppose the United States specializes in producing, say, corn. It will then produce a surplus of corn, but perhaps it will have a shortage of wine. France, on the other hand, specializes in producing wine but experiences a shortage of corn. To satisfy both needs—for corn and for wine—the two countries should trade with each other. That is, the United States should export corn and import wine. France should export wine and import corn.

Exporting is selling and shipping raw materials or products to other nations. Boeing, for example, exports its airplanes to a number of countries, for use by their airlines.

Importing is purchasing raw materials or products in other nations and bringing them into one's own country. Thus, buyers for Macy's department stores may purchase rugs in India or raincoats in England and have them shipped back to the United States for resale.

Importing and exporting are the principal activities involved in international trade. They give rise to an important concept called the balance of trade. A nation's **balance of trade** is the total value of its exports *less* the total value of its imports, over some period of time. If a country imports more than it exports, its balance of trade is negative and is said to be *unfavorable*. (A negative balance of trade is unfavorable because the country must export money to pay for its excess imports.) In 1983 the United States imported $258 billion worth of merchandise and exported $200.5 billion worth. It thus had a trade deficit of $57.5 billion.[2] A **trade deficit** is an unfavorable balance of trade. (See Figure 23.1.)

The United States exports a wide variety of industrial and consumer products to a diverse international market. Here the shelves of a Japanese grocery are stocked with Tide detergent. Source: © Richard Kalvar, Magnum.

On the other hand, when a country exports more than it imports, it is said to have a *favorable* balance of trade. This has consistently been the case for Japan over the last two decades or so.

A nation's **balance of payments** is the total flow of money into the country *less* the total flow of money out of the country, over some period of time. Balance of payments is thus a much broader concept than balance of trade. It includes imports and exports, of course. But it also includes investments, money spent by foreign tourists, payments by foreign governments and aid to foreign governments, and all other receipts and payments.

A continual deficit in a nation's balance of payments (a negative balance) can cause other nations to lose confidence in its economy. A continual surplus can indicate that the country encourages exports but limits imports by imposing trade restrictions.

RESTRICTIONS TO INTERNATIONAL BUSINESS

Specialization and international trade can result in the efficient production of want-satisfying goods and services, on a worldwide basis. And, as we have noted, total international business is generally increasing. Yet the nations of the world continue to erect barriers to free trade. They do so for reasons ranging from internal political and economic pressures to simple mistrust of other nations. We shall examine first the types of restrictions that are applied and then the arguments for and against trade restrictions.

Types of Trade Restrictions

Nations are generally eager to export their products. They want to provide markets for their industries and to develop a favorable balance of trade. Hence, most trade restrictions are applied to imports from other nations.

Tariffs Perhaps the most commonly applied trade restriction is the customs duty, or import duty, discussed in Chapter 22. As defined there, an **import duty** is a tax that is levied on a foreign product entering a country. This tax, which is also called a **tariff,** has the effect of raising the

Figure 23.1 *Balance of Trade. A nation's balance of trade is the value of its exports minus the value of its imports, during a given time. When a country exports more than it imports, it has a favorable balance of trade. Source: Federal Reserve Bank of Chicago,* International Letter No. 521, *March 9, 1984.*

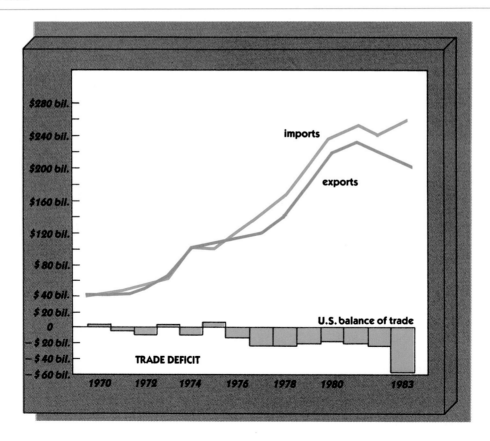

price of the product in the importing nation. Because fewer units of the product will be sold at the increased price, fewer units will be imported.

Quotas An **import quota** is a limit on the amount of a particular good that may be imported into a country during a given period of time. The limit may be set in terms of either quantity (so many pounds of beef) or value (so many dollars worth of shoes). See Figure 23.2.

Quotas may also be set on individual products imported from specific countries, or on worldwide imports. For example, if the Japanese had not voluntarily limited their exports of autos to this country, the government might have placed an import quota on Japanese autos. Or the government could simply have ruled that no more than,

say, three million autos per year would be imported into this country, no matter where they were manufactured.

Once an import quota has been reached, imports are halted until the specified time has elapsed.

Embargoes An **embargo** is a complete halt to trading with a particular nation or in a particular product. Most often the embargo is used as a political weapon. At present, the United States has import embargoes against Cuba and Vietnam—both as a result of extremely poor political relations.

Foreign-Exchange Control A **foreign-exchange control** is a restriction on the amount of a par-

Figure 23.2 Import Quotas. Data shows 1984 U.S. limits on imports of chocolate containing over 5.5 percent butterfat. Source: Office of District Director of Customs.

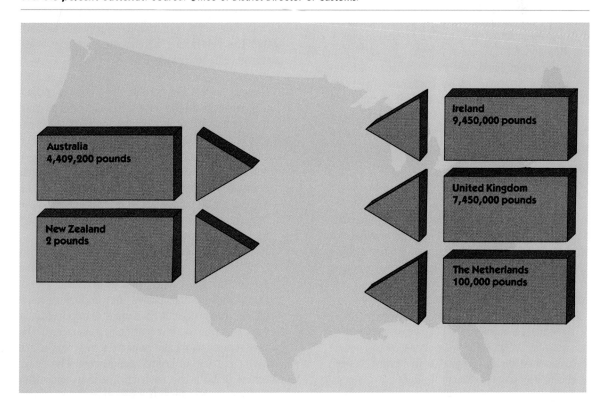

ticular foreign currency that can be purchased or sold. By limiting the amount of a foreign currency that importers can obtain, a government limits the amount of goods that importers can purchase with that currency. This has the effect of limiting imports from the country whose foreign exchange is being controlled.

Currency Devaluation   A nation can increase or decrease the value of its money, relative to the currency of other nations. **Currency devaluation** is the reduction of the value of a nation's currency relative to the currencies of other countries.

Devaluation increases the cost of foreign goods, and it decreases the cost of domestic goods to foreign firms. For example, suppose the English pound is worth $4. Then an American-made $4000 computer can be purchased for £1000. But if the pound is devalued so it is worth only $2, that same computer will cost £2000. The increased cost, in pounds, will reduce the import of American computers—and all foreign goods—into England.

On the other hand, before devaluation a £500 set of English bone china costs an American $2000. After the devaluation, the set of china will cost only $1000. The decreased cost will make the china—and all English goods—much more attractive to foreign purchasers.

Arguments For Trade Restrictions

Various reasons are advanced for trade restrictions either on the import of specific products or on trade with particular countries. We have noted that political considerations are usually involved in trade embargoes. Other frequently cited reasons for restricting trade include the following:

☐ To equalize a nation's balance of payments. This may be considered necessary to restore confidence in the country's monetary system and in its ability to repay its debts.
☐ To protect new or weak industries. A new, or *infant,* industry may not be strong enough to withstand foreign competition. Temporary trade restrictions may be used to give it a chance to grow and become self-sufficient.
☐ To protect national security. Restrictions in this category are generally on exports, to keep the nation's technology out of the hands of potential enemies. For example, strategic and defense-related goods cannot be exported to unfriendly nations.
☐ To protect the health of citizens. Products that are dangerous or unhealthy (for example, farm products that are contaminated with insecticides) may be embargoed for this reason.
☐ To retaliate for another nation's trade restrictions. A country whose exports are taxed by another country may respond by imposing tariffs on imports from that country.

Arguments Against Trade Restrictions

Trade restrictions lead to certain immediate and certain long-term economic consequences—both within the restricting nation and in world trade patterns. These include

☐ Higher prices for consumers. Higher prices may result from the imposition of tariffs or from the elimination of foreign competition. One result of the voluntary import quota on Japanese cars was a general increase in the level of automobile prices in the United States. Some estimates suggest that this cost may have been as high as $9 billion per year as a result of the higher prices consumers were forced to pay for cars they purchased.[3]
☐ Restriction of consumers' choices. Again, this is a direct result of the elimination of some foreign products from the marketplace, and of the artificially high prices that importers must charge for products that *are* still imported.
☐ Misallocation of international resources. The protection of weak industries results in the inefficient use of limited resources. The economies of both the restricting nation and other nations eventually suffer because of this waste.

□ Loss of jobs. The restriction of imports by one nation must lead to cutbacks—and the loss of jobs—in the export-oriented industries of other nations. The U.S. Department of Commerce estimates that one job is generated directly, and one job indirectly, by each $40,000 of American exports.[4]

THE EXTENT OF INTERNATIONAL BUSINESS

Restrictions or not, international business is growing. Figure 23.3 shows the value of world trade and the degree to which it increased through the decade that ended in 1982. (The decreases in 1981 and 1982 resulted from the worldwide recession—the worst since the 1930s. Yet, in spite of the recession, the declines were only about 3 or 4 percent each.) Despite an increase in volume of world trade in 1983, the value of world trade in terms of U.S. dollars decreased 2 percent (due to currency fluctuation).

During the period covered by Figure 23.3, West Germany, France, and Japan experienced the greatest growth in exports. United States exports grew in dollar value as well, but at a slower rate. Thus the overall effect was a shrink-

Figure 23.3 *A Decade of World Trade. The declines in world trade volume in 1981 and 1982 reflect the occurrence of a worldwide recession.* Source: Federal Reserve Bank of Chicago, International Letter No. 495, *March 11, 1983, and* International Letter No. 528, *June 15, 1984.*

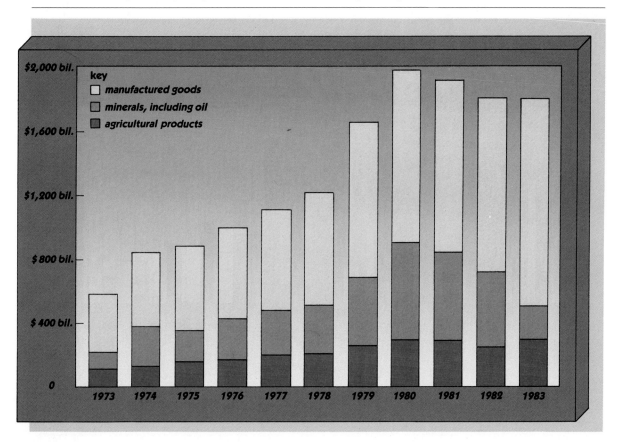

ing of the United States's "Share" of the world market.

Figure 23.4 shows the value of U.S. exports to, and imports from, each of its major trading partners, and the resulting trade balance. Figure 23.5 shows the major U.S. export and import categories. Our major exports are machinery and agricultural products. Our major import (to no one's surprise) is oil.

The General Agreement on Tariffs and Trade

At the end of World War II, the United States and 22 other nations organized the body that came to be known as GATT. The **General Agreement on Tariffs and Trade** (GATT) is an international organization whose goal is to reduce or eliminate tariffs and other barriers to

Figure 23.4 U.S. Trade with Major Partners. Source: *Federal Reserve Bank of Chicago,* International Letter No. 521, *March 9, 1984.*

Figure 23.5 U.S. Trade by Category of Goods. Source: *Federal Reserve Bank of Chicago,* International Letter No. 521, *March 9, 1984.*

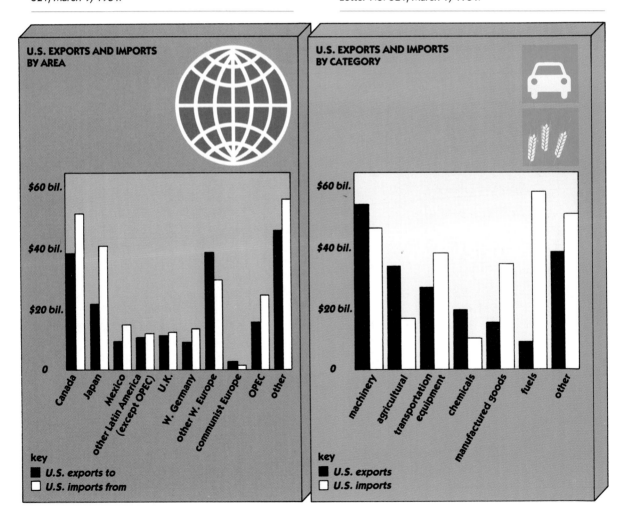

International trade shows demonstrate the success of the General Agreement on Tariffs and Trade in opening new world markets by reducing trade barriers. *Source: AP/Wide World Photos.*

world trade. GATT is headquartered in Geneva, Switzerland. It provides a forum for tariff negotiations and a means for settling international trade disputes and problems. Since 1947 it has sponsored seven "rounds" of negotiations to reduce trade restrictions. Two of the most fruitful were the Kennedy Round and the Tokyo Round.

The Kennedy Round In 1962 the U.S. Congress passed the *Trade Expansion Act.* This law gave President Kennedy the authority to negotiate reciprocal trade agreements that could reduce U.S. tariffs by as much as 50 percent. Armed with this authority, which was granted for a period of 5 years, President Kennedy called for a round of negotiations through GATT.

These negotiations, which began in 1964, have since become known as the *Kennedy Round.* They were aimed at reducing tariffs and other barriers to trade in both industrial and agricultural products. The participants were very successful in reducing tariffs—by an average of more than

35 percent. They were less successful in removing other types of trade barriers.

The Tokyo Round In 1973 representatives of some 100 nations gathered in Tokyo for another round of GATT negotiations—the *Tokyo Round,* which was completed in 1979. The participants negotiated tariff cuts of 30 to 35 percent, which were to be implemented over an 8-year period. In addition, they were able to remove or ease such nontariff barriers as import quotas, unrealistic quality standards for imports, and unnecessary red tape in customs procedures.

International Economic Communities

The primary objective of GATT is to remove barriers to trade on a worldwide basis. On a smaller scale, an **economic community** is an organization of nations formed to promote the free movement of resources and products among its members and to create common economic

Table 23.1 *Members of Major International Economic Communities*

European Economic Community (EEC, Common Market)	European Free Trade Association (EFTA)	Latin American Free Trade Association (LAFTA)	Organization of Petroleum Exporting Countries (OPEC)
France	Austria	Argentina	Venezuela
Federal Republic of Germany	Iceland	Brazil	Algeria
Italy	Norway	Chile	Libya
Belgium,	Portugal	Colombia	Iraq
Netherlands	Sweden	Ecuador	Iran
Luxembourg	Switzerland	Mexico	United Arab Emirates
United Kingdom	Finland	Paraguay	Ecuador
Ireland	(associate member)	Peru	Nigeria
Denmark		Uruguay	Gabon
Greece			Saudi Arabia
Turkey			Kuwait
(associate member)			Qatar
			Indonesia

policies. A number of economic communities now exist. Table 23.1 lists the members of the four that are most familiar.

The *European Economic Community* (EEC), which is also known as the *Common Market,* was formed in 1957 by the first six countries listed in Table 23.1. Its objective was freely conducted commerce among these nations and others who might later join the EEC. Most of the trade restrictions that existed among EEC members before the EEC was formed have been abolished, and a common tariff policy has been developed. In essence, the EEC trades with the rest of the world as a single unit.

The *European Free Trade Association* (EFTA) was organized in 1960 in response to the formation of the Common Market. The original members included the United Kingdom and Denmark, both of whom later withdrew to join the EEC. Like the EEC, EFTA has eliminated many restrictions on trade among its members and has developed a number of common trade policies. Unlike the EEC, however, individual EFTA members determine tariffs on goods imported from and exported to nonmembers.

The *Latin American Free Trade Association* (LAFTA) was formed in 1960. Its primary objective was completely free trade among its members, without any restrictions. This goal has not yet been achieved.

The *Organization of Petroleum Exporting Countries* (OPEC) was founded in 1960 in response to reductions in the prices that oil companies were willing to pay for crude oil. The organization was conceived as a collective-bargaining unit, to provide oil-producing nations with some control over oil prices. A second goal was to reduce the oversupply of oil, which was forcing prices downward. At first, OPEC members had difficulty agreeing on prices or production limits. Most wanted to expand production to balance their growing national budgets. However, since their oil embargo of 1973, they have effectively controlled both production and the price of oil—which has risen from $2 per barrel to around $30 at this writing.

Although economic communities enhance the freedom of trade among member nations, cooperation in such communities also restricts the independence of each individual country. Source: © Dave Bellak, Jeroboam, Inc.

ORGANIZING FOR INTERNATIONAL BUSINESS

A firm that has decided to enter international markets can do so in several ways. We shall discuss five different methods (or, more accurately, organizational structures). (See Figure 23.6.) These different approaches require varying degrees of involvement in international business. Typically, a firm begins its international operations at the simplest level. Then, depending on its goals, it may progress to higher levels of involvement.

Licensing

At a fairly basic level of international business is licensing. **Licensing** is a contractual agreement in which one firm permits another to produce and market its product and use its brand name, in return for a royalty or other compensation. For example, an American candy manufacturer might enter into a licensing arrangement with a British firm. The British producer would be entitled to use the American firm's candy formulas, brand name, and packaging and to advertise the product as though the candy were its own. In return, the British firm would pay the American firm a certain percentage of its income from sales of the product.

The advantage of licensing is that it provides a simple method of expanding into a foreign market with virtually no investment. On the other hand, if the licensee does not maintain the licensor's product standards, the product's image may be damaged. Another disadvantage is that a licensing arrangement does not usually provide the original producer with any foreign marketing experience.

Exporting

A firm may also manufacture its products in its home country and export them for sale in foreign markets. Like licensing, exporting can be a relatively low-risk method of entering foreign markets. It does, however, open up several levels of involvement to the exporting firm.

At the most basic level, the exporting firm may sell its products to an *export/import merchant,* which is essentially a merchant wholesaler. The

Figure 23.6   Five Approaches to Entering the International Market

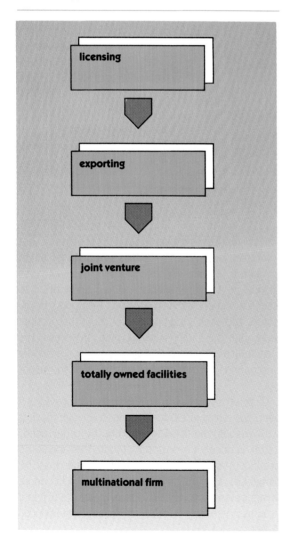

merchant assumes all the risks of product ownership, distribution, and sale. It may even purchase the goods in the producer's home country and assume responsibility for exporting the goods.

The exporting firm may instead ship its products to an *export/import agent,* which arranges the sale of the products to foreign middlemen for a commission or fee. The agent is an independent firm—like other agents—that sells and may perform other marketing functions for the exporter. The exporter, however, retains title to the products during shipment and until they are sold.

An exporting firm may also establish its own *sales offices or branches* in foreign countries. These installations are international extensions of the firm's distribution system. They represent a deeper involvement in international business than the other exporting techniques that we have discussed—and thus they carry a greater risk. The exporting firm maintains control over sales, and it gains both experience and knowledge of foreign markets. Eventually, the firm might also develop its own sales force to operate in conjunction with foreign sales offices or branches.

The Joint Venture

As we noted in Chapter 3, a joint venture is a partnership that is formed to achieve a specific goal or to operate for a specific period of time. A joint venture with an established firm in a foreign country provides immediate market knowledge and access, reduced risk, and control over product attributes. However, joint-venture agreements established across national borders can become extremely complex. As a result, such agreements generally require a very high level of commitment from all of the parties that may be involved.

A joint venture may be used to produce and market an existing product in a foreign nation or to develop an entirely new product. American Motors has entered into an unusual joint venture with the People's Republic of China, under which the new Beijing Jeep Corporation began to build Jeep vehicles in China in 1984.[5]

What Is a Free Trade Zone?

Congress defines them as: "An isolated, enclosed, or policed area, operated as a public utility … with facilities for loading, unloading, handling, storing, manipulating, manufacturing, and exhibiting goods, and for reshipping them by land, water, or air … (it's a place) where foreign or domestic merchandise, except merchandise prohibited by law for reasons of safety or health, can be bought without being subject to the customs laws of the United States."

In other words, you may not be able to package or puff Havana Havana's there, but other merchandise can be stored, shown, mixed, or manipulated in any manner, then exported, destroyed, or sent out of the zone and into U.S. Customs territory. Only when the merchandise crosses into the U.S. are duties and excise taxes due or do quota restrictions take hold. The savings can be enormous.

For example, a company in Kansas City annually imports some $2 million worth of bone china. The customs duty is 17½ percent. While the firm still has to pay those duties eventually, it doesn't have to put out $350,000 up front, because the china is shipped into its FTZ office. Since breakage plays a significant role in this business, the company can then sort out and throw away the broken pieces before any duties are due on them—for an annual tax savings of $17,500.

An FTZ needn't look any different from a fenced-in industrial park. There are the usual offices and warehouses and loading bays and railroad sidings. But instead of an ordinary guard at the front gate, there is a customs inspector.

In the U.S. today, there are 77 operating FTZs, plus 18 sub-zones specifically for manufacturing. Five years ago, there were 52 FTZs, only about half of which were operational. Companies working out of FTZs do an estimated $7 billion worth of business. Ten years ago, it was less than $200 million. A sampling of what happens in some of the zones shows the possibilities.

- In the old Brooklyn Navy Yard, there is a one-million-square-foot warehouse and processing space that is home to 160 firms, 60 percent of which are re-exporters. Products they repackage for foreign markets include cassettes, caviar, feathers, and paper. One company deals in piece goods, with no customs duties on whatever imported fabrics wind up on the cutting room floor.
- In New Orleans, a company ages wine in its FTZ, delaying customs taxes for years.
- In Little Rock, Ark., Timex used an FTZ warehouse to store production machinery reclaimed from a closed plant overseas. By putting the equipment in an FTZ, the company was able to take its time fitting it into domestic facilities.

Marshall V. Miller, who helped found the National Association of FTZs, reports that there are more than 29,000 people currently employed inside FTZs, and at least 50 percent of the activities in the zones involve exports. In Miami, for example, FTZ No. 32 houses operations directed almost solely toward Latin and South America. Goods are brought in, mainly from Europe, and 95 percent are then shipped out as re-exports.

And Nissan is moving into FTZ No. 78 outside Nashville, Tenn. In fact, its $600 million plant there constitutes the largest single Japanese investment in the U.S.

Source: Adapted from *Barron's*, June 20, 1983, p. 18.

Marketing Mistakes

Pepsodent was unsuccessful in Southeast Asia because it promised white teeth to a culture where black or yellow teeth are symbols of prestige.

In Quebec, a canned fish manufacturer tried to promote a product by showing a woman dressed in shorts, golfing with her husband, and planning to serve canned fish for dinner. These activities violated cultural norms.

Maxwell House advertised itself as the "great American coffee" in Germany. It found out that Germans have little respect for American coffee.

In Puerto Rico, the Chevrolet Nova (meaning "star") was translated as "no va"—"it doesn't go."

General Motors' "Body by Fisher" slogan became "Corpse by Fisher" when translated into Japanese.

In Brazil, Gerber could not convince mothers that baby food was a good alternative to food the mothers made themselves.

African men were upset by a commercial for men's deodorant that showed a happy male being chased by women. They thought the deodorant would make them weak and overrun by women.

Source: Evans and Berman, *Essentials of Marketing* (New York: Macmillan, 1984). p. 431.

Totally Owned Facilities

At a still deeper level of involvement in international business, a firm may develop its own production and marketing facilities in one or more foreign nations. This *direct investment* provides complete control over operations, but it carries a greater risk than the joint venture. The firm is really establishing a subsidiary in a foreign country. Most firms do so only after they have acquired some knowledge of the host country's markets.

Direct investment may take either of two forms. In the first, the firm builds or purchases manufacturing and other facilities in the foreign country. It uses these facilities to produce its own established products and to market them in that country and perhaps in neighboring countries. For example, the Polaroid Corporation owns manufacturing facilities in the Netherlands and in Scotland. These plants, in turn, supply Polaroid products to subsidiaries in twelve European countries.[6]

A second form of direct investment in international business is the purchase of an existing firm in a foreign country. When Nestlé (a Swiss corporation) decided to enter the frozen food business in the United States, it purchased Stouffer's rather than starting a new product line from scratch.

The Multinational Firm

A **multinational enterprise** is a firm that operates on a worldwide scale, without ties to any specific nation or region. The multinational firm represents the highest level of involvement in international business. It is equally "at home" in most countries of the world. In fact, as far as its operations are concerned, national boundaries exist only on maps. It is, however, organized under the laws of its home country.

Table 23.2 lists the largest U.S. industrial, multinational corporations. Nestlé, based in Switzerland, is the forty-second largest industrial corporation in the world and is a good example of a multinational firm. Nestlé operates more than 300 plants throughout the world. About 41 percent of its revenues are derived from sales in Europe, 19 percent from North America, 19 percent from Central and South America, 14 percent from Asia, and 5 percent from Africa.

According to the chairman of the board of directors of Dow Chemical Company, a multinational firm of United States origin, "The emergence of a world economy and of the multinational corporation has been accomplished hand in hand."[7] He sees multinational enterprises moving

Table 23.2 The 25 Largest U.S. Multinationals

Rank	Company	Foreign revenue (millions)	Total revenue (millions)	Foreign revenue as % of total
1	Exxon	$61,815	$88,651	69.7%
2	Mobil	32,629	55,609	58.7
3	Texaco	25,157	40,068	62.8
4	Phibro-Salomon	20,100	29,757	67.5
5	IBM	17,058	40,180	42.5
6	Ford Motor	16,080	44,455	36.2
7	General Motors	14,913	74,582	20.0
8	Gulf	11,535	26,581	43.4
9	Standard Oil Calif	10,952	27,342	40.1
10	E. I. du Pont de Nemours	10,816	35,173	30.8
11	Citicorp	9,650	17,037	56.6
12	ITT	7,808	20,249	38.6
13	BankAmerica	5,943	13,299	44.7
14	Dow Chemical	5,726	10,951	52.3
15	Standard Oil Indiana	5,363	27,937	19.2
16	Chase Manhattan	4,943	8,523	58.0
17	General Electric	4,758	27,681	17.2
18	Occidental Petroleum	4,544	19,709	23.1
19	Safeway Stores	4,528	18,585	24.4
20	Sun Co	4,282	14,928	28.7
21	Procter & Gamble	3,685	12,452	29.6
22	J. P. Morgan	3,446	5,764	59.8
23	Xerox	3,393	8,464	40.1
24	Eastman Kodak	3,270	10,170	32.2
25	Sears, Roebuck	3,246	35,883	9.0

Source: "The 100 Largest Industrial Companies in the World," *Forbes*, July 2, 1984, pp. 129–130. © 1984 Time Inc. All rights reserved.

toward what he calls the "anational company," a firm that has no nationality but belongs to all countries. In recognition of this movement, there have already been international conferences devoted to the question of how such enterprises would be controlled.

Any firm that chooses to go into business internationally beyond the licensing level encounters new challenges as well as enlarged opportunities. Many of these challenges arise in the area of marketing.

INTERNATIONAL MARKETING

A firm's marketing program—the strategies it uses to accomplish its marketing goals—must generally be modified and adapted to foreign markets. Within each foreign nation, the firm is likely to find a combination of marketing environment and target markets that is different from those of its home country and other foreign countries. Product, pricing, distribution, and promotion strategies must be adapted accordingly.

Nations protect their industries and technology by enforcing trade regulations. In the photo below U.S. agents confiscate microchips stolen from a U.S. electronics firm for illegal export to other countries. Source: © Ron Burda, San Jose Mercury News.

The Marketing Environment

Cultural, social, economic, and legal forces within the host country must be clearly understood. Even so simple a thing as the color of a product or its package can present a problem. In Japan, black and white are the colors of mourning, so they should not be used in packaging. In Brazil, purple is the color of death. And in Egypt, green is never used on a package because it is the national color.[8]

An important economic consideration is the distribution of income (especially discretionary income), which may vary widely from nation to nation. International marketers tend to concentrate on higher-income countries, for obvious reasons. However, some producers have found that their products sell best in countries with a low income per capita. As in domestic marketing, the determining factor is how well the product satisfies its target market.

The legal and political atmosphere also varies across national borders. Gifts to authorities— sometimes quite large ones—are standard business procedure in some countries. In others, including the United States, they are called bribes or payoffs and are strictly illegal. Moreover, mar-

keting activities may be regulated to varying degrees. In Japan, new brands of cigarettes must be test-marketed in 60 scattered retail outlets, and test marketing is allowed only once a year. A new brand must surpass a certain sales level before it can be mass-marketed. Further, each American firm can spend no more than $660,000 per year on advertising, and a single brand can no longer be advertised after it has been on the market for three years.

Marketing information is often difficult to obtain. Consumers in some countries believe it is simply nobody else's business whether a new product tastes better to them than an old one, or which television program they watched last night. And most governments don't provide population and other statistics as freely as the U.S. government does. Some may not even have collected such data.

The Marketing Mix

An international marketer can adopt any of several strategies regarding its product and promotion. The possibilities include

- Marketing one product via a single promotional message worldwide. This strategy can be effective for products that have a more or less standardized appeal for most people—chewing gum or soft drinks, for example. It is also the least expensive strategy.
- Marketing one product but varying the promotion. This strategy is used when it is hard to translate promotional messages or to adapt any overall promotion to local customs or social usages.
- Adapting the product but using the same promotional mix. For example, Kraft uses slightly different formulas for the Philadelphia cream cheese it markets in different countries, to please local tastes.[9]
- Adapting both the product and its promotion. This most expensive strategy may be required when neither the existing product nor its promotion would appeal to foreign markets. In

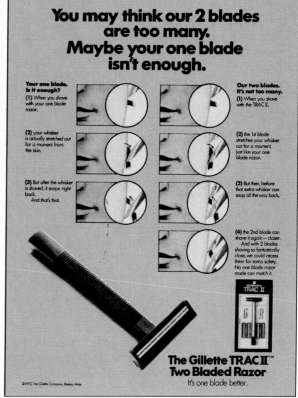

some cases, the international firm may develop a completely new product for a foreign market.

Distribution strategies depend on the firm's international organization—whether it is licensing, exporting, or manufacturing in the host country. For the most part, however, the international marketer uses existing distribution channels.

Cost-based pricing is more common in international marketing than in domestic marketing. The added costs of shipping, paying import duties, and complying with various regulations tend to make this the most logical pricing method. Prices are also affected by exchange rates, and especially by changes in these rates. Because of these added costs and the uncertainties in the exchange rate, prices tend to be higher in foreign markets than in domestic markets.

Marketing is not the only aspect of operations that is significantly affected by entering the arena of international business. Another factor to be considered is financing.

FINANCING INTERNATIONAL BUSINESS

International trade compounds the concerns of financial managers. Currency exchange rates, tariffs and foreign-exchange controls, and the tax structures of host nations all affect international operations and the flow of cash. In addition, financial managers must be concerned both with the financing of their international operations and with the means available to their customers to finance purchases.

The Champagne of Soft Drinks

The list of Howard Lapides's qualifications to import exotic soft drinks was extremely short when he launched International Soft Drinks, Inc., in 1982.

He was only 23, with no experience in business and no money. But he did have enthusiasm and persistence—qualities that helped him double sales in a year and led to recognition from Minnesota Governor Rudy Perpich for his forays into international trade.

Starting a business was far from Lapides's mind when he visited a friend in Bergen, Norway, in the summer of 1981. He was a student at the University of Minnesota majoring in criminal justice and sociology and thinking of going to law school. But then he sampled Champagne Brus (it rhymes with juice), Norway's third-best-selling soda pop.

Lapides drank so much of the bubbly yellow beverage—which he describes as "a cross between fruity cream soda and Juicy Fruit gum"—that he jokingly said he should import it to America.

When he returned to Minnesota, the thought seemed less and less silly. Lapides wrote a "To Whom It May Concern" letter to the drink's manufacturer, A/S Hansa Bryggeri, in which he described Champagne Brus as "the greatest drink I have ever had" and offered to introduce it to America.

For six weeks, he heard nothing. He followed up with a phone call and soon received a reply thanking him for his enthusiasm and asking what experience he had in marketing. He told the truth: nothing.

"The marketing director was somewhat taken aback," recalls Lapides, but nonetheless shipped him 10 cases of soda to test.

Lapides tried Champagne Brus on 400 customers in a cross-section of Twin Cities stores in November 1981. About 80 percent liked it.

The Norwegian marketing director, excited by the results, gave Lapides the green light to break into the U.S. market. But Lapides's original idea of making a commission on sales to various bottling companies fell flat. "A lot of bottlers just laughed at me" because of his youth and lack of money, he says. By March, his own enthusiasm began to fizzle.

Fortunately, though, he had hooked his father on Champagne Brus. Jerry Lapides, a real estate developer, secured a $60,000 bank loan for his son, and they incorporated the business in Minneapolis, with Howard as president and Jerry as chairman.

Howard Lapides found a bottler, PepsiCo. He began ordering drink concentrate from Norway, and he had PepsiCo package Champagne Brus in newly designed magenta, purple, and yellow cans. He priced the product "very competitively," he says, at $1.99 for six.

Lapides peddled his wares to buyers himself until he found a food broker, First Brokerage Company in Minnesota, to do much of the legwork. He expanded his territory from Minnesota to North Dakota, Florida, Indiana, Illinois, Texas, Wisconsin, and Missouri and is hoping to reach at least six more states by the end of 1984.

Sales went from 30,000 cases in 1982 to 60,000 in 1983, and Lapides expects them to total 400,000 in 1984. Gross income rose from $300,000 in 1982 to almost $500,000 in 1983, and the fledgling company expects to be in the black at the end of 1984, with a gross of $2 million.

Source: Mary-Margaret Wantuck, *Nation's Business*, April 1984, pp. 93–94.

Fortunately, a number of larger banks have become international in scope, along with business in general. Many have established branches in major cities around the world. Thus, like firms in other industries, they are able to provide their services where and when they are needed. In addition, financial assistance is available from U.S. government and international sources.

The Export-Import Bank of the United States

The **Export-Import Bank of the United States** is an independent agency of the U.S. government whose function is to assist in financing the exports of American firms. *Eximbank,* as it is commonly called, extends and guarantees credit to overseas buyers of American goods and services, guarantees short-term financing for exports, and discounts negotiable instruments that arise from export transactions. It also cooperates with commercial banks in helping American exporters offer credit to their overseas customers.

Multilateral Development Banks

All the **multilateral development banks** (MDBs) are internationally supported banks that provide loans to developing countries to help them grow. The most familiar is the World Bank, which operates worldwide. Three other MDBs operate primarily in Africa, Asia, and Central and

The International Monetary Fund (IMF) provides loans to nations with balance of payment deficits. Recipients of aid are required to repay their IMF loans responsibly, and voting procedures within the organization give more power to the lending nations. Source: © 1982 Dilip Mehta, Woodfin Camp.

South America. All four are supported by the industrialized nations, including the United States.

The four MDBs are, together, the largest single source of advice and assistance to the developing nations. In 1982, for example, they provided approximately $16.9 billion in loans. Much of this money was used to finance purchases from firms in the industrialized nations.

The International Monetary Fund

The **International Monetary Fund** (IMF) is an international bank that makes short-term loans to countries experiencing balance-of-payments deficits. This financing is contributed by member nations, and it must be repaid with interest. It is provided primarily to fund international trade.

In 1983, a few months before the House of Representatives increased the United States's contribution to the IMF, President Reagan noted that

Expanding trade is the answer to our most pressing international financial problem—the mounting debt of many developing countries. Without the opportunity to export, debt-troubled countries will have difficulty servicing, and eventually reducing, their large debts. Meanwhile, the U.S. will support the efforts of the international financial community to provide adequate financing to sustain trade and to encourage developing countries in the efforts they are making to improve the basic elements of their domestic economic programs. Lending by the IMF has a direct impact on American jobs and supports continued lending by commercial institutions. If such lending were to stop, the consequences for the American economy would be very negative.[10]

Chapter Review

SUMMARY

International business is all business activities that involve exchanges across national boundaries. The basis for international trade is specialization, whereby each country produces those goods and services that it can produce more efficiently than any other goods and services. A nation is said to have a comparative advantage relative to these goods. International trade develops when each nation trades its surplus products for those that are in short supply.

A nation's balance of trade is the difference between the value of its exports and the value of its imports. Its balance of payments is the difference between the flow of money into the nation and the flow of money out. Generally, a negative balance is considered unfavorable.

In spite of the benefits of world trade, nations tend to use tariffs, import quotas, embargoes, and other restrictions to limit trade. These restrictions are typically justified as being needed to protect a nation's economy, industries, citizens, or security. They can result in the loss of jobs, higher prices, fewer choices in the marketplace, and the misallocation of resources.

World trade totals around $2 trillion annually and is generally increasing. Trade between the United States and other nations is increasing in dollar value but decreasing in terms of our share of the world market. The General Agreement on Tariffs and Trade and various economic communities have been formed to dismantle trade barriers and provide an environment in which international business can grow even faster.

A firm may enter international markets in several ways. It may license a foreign firm to produce and market its products. It may export its products and sell them through foreign middlemen or its own sales organization. It may enter into a joint venture with a foreign firm. It may establish its own foreign subsidiaries. Or it may develop into a multinational enterprise. Generally, each of these methods represents a deeper involvement in international business than those that precede it in this list.

A firm's domestic marketing program must be adapted to foreign markets in order to account for differences in the business environment and target markets from nation to nation. Social, cultural, economic, and legal differences may require modification of elements of the marketing mix—especially the product and its promotion. Various additional costs involved in foreign marketing tend to increase the prices of exported goods.

The financing of international trade is more complex than that of domestic trade. Institutions such as the Eximbank and the International Monetary Fund have been established to provide financing and ultimately increase world trade for American and international firms.

This is the final chapter of the book. We hope that we have been able to convey to you some of the excitement and challenge of the world of business. We hope, too, that you will read and make use of the epilogue that follows. It is included to help you begin your business career.

KEY TERMS

You should now be able to define and give an example relevant to each of the following terms:

international business
absolute advantage
comparative advantage
exporting
importing
balance of trade
trade deficit
balance of payments
import duty (or tariff)
import quota
embargo
foreign-exchange control
currency devaluation
General Agreement on Tariffs and Trade
economic community
licensing
multinational enterprise
Export–Import Bank of the United States
multilateral development banks
International Monetary Fund

QUESTIONS AND EXERCISES

Review Questions

1. Why do firms engage in international trade?
2. What is the difference between absolute advantage and comparative advantage in international trade? How are they related to the concept of specialization?
3. What is a favorable balance of trade? In what way is it "favorable"?
4. List and briefly describe the principal restrictions that may be applied to a nation's imports.
5. What reasons are generally given for imposing trade restrictions?
6. What are the general effects of import restrictions?
7. What are (a) GATT and (b) economic communities? What are the main objectives of each?
8. Which nations are the principal trading partners of the United States? What are our major imports and exports?
9. The methods of engaging in international business may be categorized as either direct or indirect methods. How would you classify each of the methods described in this chapter? Why?
10. In what ways is a multinational enterprise different from a large corporation that does business in several countries?
11. List some specific environmental factors that can affect the marketing mix that a company develops for marketing in a foreign nation.
12. Under what circumstances might a firm modify (a) its product, (b) its promotion, or (c) both its product and its promotion for marketing in a foreign nation?
13. In what ways do Eximbank, multilateral development banks, and the IMF enhance international trade?

Discussion Questions

1. Which groups tend to benefit from the "voluntary" agreement to limit imports of Japanese autos into the United States? Which groups tend to lose? Should the quota be extended or lifted?
2. The United States restricts imports but, at the same time, supports GATT and international banks whose objective is to enhance world trade. As a member of Congress, how would you justify this contradiction to your constituents?
3. What effects might the devaluation of a nation's currency have on its business firms? on its consumers? on the debts it owes to other nations?
4. Should imports to the United States be curtailed by, say, 20 percent so as to eliminate our trade deficit? What might happen if this were done?
5. When should a firm consider expanding from strictly domestic trade to international trade? When should it consider becoming further involved in international trade? What factors might affect the firm's decisions in each case?
6. How can a firm obtain the expertise needed to produce and market its products in, say, the EEC?

Exercises

1. Use Table 23.3 to answer the following questions. Assume a two-nation, two-product world economy.
   a. Which country has an absolute advantage in the production of cloth? of beef?
   b. Which country has a comparative advantage in the production of cloth? of beef?
   c. How many units of cloth and how many units of beef would be produced by the 30 workers if both countries specialized? if both didn't specialize?
2. Explain how you would modify the domestic marketing mix (as you know it) in order to market (a) Wrigley's Doublemint chewing gum in China, (b) Timex watches in Algeria, and (c) Hires root beer in France. Use the library to obtain information you might need to know about these countries.

Table 23.3

Country	Cloth		Beef	
	Number of Workers	Output per Hour	Number of Workers	Output per Hour
X	5	100 units	7	100 units
Y	10	100 units	8	100 units

CASE 23-1

Mirvis Unlimited

Mirvis Unlimited is a large clothing manufacturer and distributor located in a midwestern state. The firm was founded over 50 years ago by Edward Mirvis and was known as Mirvis Clothing, Inc. Its major products were men's work clothing and other "heavy-duty" clothes (such as outdoor apparel). The company was generally successful and grew steadily.

When Mirvis retired, however, the company began to flounder. Finally it was sold to a woman named Debra Henderson, who had several years of apparel-related experience.

After a couple of years of "marking time," Henderson began to alter the firm's basic product line. She retained the basic heavy-duty look but began to strive for style as well as function. For example, recent popular items included a man's shooting jacket and a safari shirt. Henderson also changed the name of the firm to Mirvis Unlimited, to give the firm's image a more contemporary flavor.

Thus far, Henderson's actions have been uniformly successful—to the point where she is now considering a move into international retailing. The idea actually came from an English tourist. The tourist bought one of the safari shirts at a fashionable department store and found that everybody loved it back home. He wrote Mirvis a letter asking if it published a catalog for mail order or if it had any plans to begin selling its products abroad.

After consulting with her banker and attorney, Henderson thinks that she should, in fact, proceed with international distribution. Her first step has been to engage the services of a management consultant with experience in international business.

1. Given your knowledge of international marketing and your understanding of the firm's background, do you think Mirvis should go international? Why or why not?
2. Assuming that Henderson proceeds, what advice would you give her about where and how she should enter the international markets? What do you think would be a realistic goal for the firm to expect to achieve in its international marketing efforts?

CASE 23-2

Globalization, Anyone?

The latest thing in international marketing is "globalization," or "global marketing." Definitions of the term vary—primarily because the concept is still so new to many business people. Generally, however, it implies the development, production, and marketing of a single product to satisfy a worldwide market.

If this loose definition sounds a bit familiar, there is good reason: Globalization looks very much like the "one product, one message" international marketing strategy, with perhaps a bit more emphasis on the "one product" part. In the past, it has been used successfully to market a number of products, including diamonds, cameras, and soft drinks. Now, however, it is being applied to a wide variety of products. And manufacturers are now thinking globally from the product-development stage onward; that is, they are designing their products to be global from the start.

The current popularity of globalization stems from a number of factors. Perhaps the most important are (1) the emergence of international markets that have many characteristics in common with American markets, and (2) the production economies that can be realized by manufacturing the same product for both American and foreign markets. Along with manufacturers, a number of large advertising agencies are "going global," so as to be in a position to provide international marketing services to their "globalized" clients.

In spite of the rush to globalization, experts warn that it is not for everyone. In general, its effectiveness (and its profitability) depends very much on the product and the market. For example, IBM has been "global" for some time—and successfully so—because its products do not

have to overcome cultural barriers in foreign markets. On the other hand, Nabisco's Oreo cookies did not appeal to European tastes, and they were much less successful when they were marketed in Europe a few years ago.[11]

1. Is globalization simply a fad, or is it a necessary and important part of international marketing? Explain.
2. Procter & Gamble expects that global marketing will get its products into world markets faster. How can global marketing help in that regard?

EPILOGUE

Our Future, Your Future

Everyone who manages must plan. And, because plans will be implemented in the future, they must try to take into account what will be happening in the future. Thus we need some way of looking to the future, whether we are managing a business, a personal investment portfolio, or a career. This epilogue contains a brief peek at the future of business, along with some ideas on how you can begin to take part in it. After reading the epilogue, you should understand:

1. Some of the changes that are expected to occur in American business
2. How these changes will affect the job market
3. How to plan for your future in business, and how to start implementing your plans

There are individuals who claim to be able to see the future in dreams or visions. Well, maybe. But most of us need something more concrete. For business people, the most fruitful source of information about the future is an examination of the past and the present. The idea is to pick out trends that have been strong in the recent past and are still strong at present. Such trends are likely to continue into the future. Then the future will be shaped, at least in part, by those trends.

Because of the importance of the future in business planning, much effort is devoted to this analysis of trends. The results of different studies may vary in many ways, but they all agree that the one overriding trend is *change*. American business (and, in fact, our entire society) has been changing since it began. Moreover, the rate of change has been increasing over the past several decades. It is not very difficult, then, to predict that the years ahead will be characterized by continued—and perhaps accelerated—change.

It is more difficult to predict the form this change will take. In today's business environment, a single unexpected occurrence, such as the oil crisis of the 1970s, can have far-reaching consequences. However, we cannot include the unexpected in our predictions. The best we can do is allow for what we know—the trends that will probably continue to affect business as we approach the twenty-first century.

CONTINUING TRENDS IN AMERICAN BUSINESS: A REVIEW

In the various parts of this book we have already discussed the major trends that bear on business and its environment. It would be worthwhile to review them briefly here, as part of our look to the future.

The Business Environment

In Parts 1 and 7 we noted that free enterprise and competition are alive and thriving. Antitrust legislation, now almost one hundred years old, continues to be reinforced and used to promote competition. Government involvement in business may have reached its peak and may now be on the decline, thanks to the continuing deregulation movement. However, some observers believe that additional deregulation can result in the loss of hard-won gains in the areas of consumer and environmental protection. This deregulation controversy, then, promises to continue for some time.

Increasing international trade is, on the one hand, helping to foster competition in American markets. Moreover, the presence of foreign firms is forcing American firms to improve both product quality and productivity, in order to compete effectively. On the other hand, new foreign markets are being opened to American businesses. While it is enhancing international trade, the slow but continual reduction of trade barriers and a large appetite for imported oil also seem to be leading to increasing trade deficits for the United States.

The late 1970s were characterized by increasing energy prices, inflation rates, interest rates, unemployment, and business failures. All these trends were halted or reversed in the early 1980s. In particular, the price of crude oil has dropped from its peak and is fairly steady—in large part because of a reduction in demand at the higher prices. The U.S. inflation rate has been holding steady, well below its double-digit peak. Interest rates, however, which had fallen substantially, are again on the rise. Unemployment is down, and U.S. industrial output is up. These factors, which are determinants of business activity as well as indicators of its effectiveness, are extremely volatile. Predictions for even the near future are difficult and acutely subject to error.

Business Operations and Resources

A variety of factors has produced a continuing attempt to use business resources more effectively. In Part 2 we noted that the business organization itself is being made trimmer and more

adaptable. New organizational structures are being developed to fit the particular operations of the business—either on a company-wide basis or department by department in larger firms. Along with these new organizational structures have come new management techniques that seem to be proving their worth—and thus are here to stay.

Productive Resources Inflation has increased the prices of material resources, and high interest rates have pushed up the cost of financial resources. As a result, both of these resources are receiving—and will continue to receive—increased attention from businesses. The expanding interest in robotics, for example, stems from a need to extract as much efficiency, productivity, and quality as possible from business investments. Financial planning, as discussed in Part 5,

is catching up with, and surpassing, production planning in perceived importance.

Firms are also looking to their employees for increased productivity—as well as for help in increasing productivity. A variety of new techniques, including quality circles, flexible workweeks, and new types of reward systems, seem to be working well for both employers and their employees. Continued and expanded use of these nontraditional management techniques, discussed in Part 3, is expected to enhance the effectiveness of the business organization and the motivation and productivity of its employees.

Finally, the computer "revolution" is both emphasizing the importance of management information and making that information available. As we noted in Part 6, management information systems are now within reach of even the smallest firms. New or expanding industries are providing

Understanding computer information systems has become an integral part of the management function. Many training programs have been instituted to acquaint managers with computer operations. Source: © 1983 Robert Isear, Photo Researchers Inc.

computer hardware and software, communications links, and information for use in management decision making. And managers are increasingly expected to make full and effective use of these resources.

Marketing   We have already noted the ongoing expansion of international markets and international marketing. Two additional trends are of particular importance to domestic marketing. The first trend is the continuing expansion of service industries in what is now our service economy. The second trend is made up of a number of shifts in our social values and our population. Among these changes, which were discussed in Part 4, are

☐ An increase in the average age of the population, due primarily to an increasing proportion of older citizens and a declining birth rate

☐ A continuing shift in population to the "sun belt" of the South and Southwest
☐ An increasing number of women in the work force, and particularly in management, as part of the continuing effort to eliminate sex discrimination
☐ An increasingly better informed and more affluent population
☐ A shorter workweek and more flexible working hours, with an increasing emphasis on leisure pursuits

These and similar patterns add up to a fairly hefty change in the markets for consumer products, as well as in the derived markets for industrial goods. They may foreshadow other changes as well, such as a southward move by business firms, in order to be closer to both the expanding markets and the ready supply of labor in southern regions.

Table 1 Occupations for the Future

Position	New Jobs to Be Created by the Year 2000
Telemarketing (sales) workers	8,000,000
CAD/CAM workers (computer-aided design and manufacturing)	1,220,000
Software writers	1,000,800
Geriatric social workers	600,000
Housing-rehabilitation workers	490,000
Energy conservation technicians	400,000
Emergency medical technicians	375,000
Gerontological aides	300,000
Hazardous waste technicians	300,000
Energy auditors	180,000

Source: Reprinted from *U.S. News & World Report* issue of May 9, 1983, p. A-25. Copyright, 1983, U.S. News & World Report, Inc. By permission.

TRENDS IN EMPLOYMENT

As you look ahead to your own career, you are probably most interested in the effects that these trends will have on employment and employment opportunities. At least some of these effects seem fairly obvious (although, as we noted earlier, predictions are subject to change without notice).

□ Jobs in service industries will account for an increasing proportion of total employment.
□ Training—and retraining—will become increasingly important, as firms require their employees to understand and utilize the latest technology. Good jobs will generally require strong educational qualifications.
□ Automation of factories and offices will create new types of jobs. Many of these will be computer-related. In some cases, employees will be able to complete assignments at home on remote computer terminals.
□ The number of women in the workforce, the number of two-income families, and the number of older workers will increase. There will be greater emphasis on job sharing, flexible

hours, and other innovative work practices to accommodate employees' special circumstances.

What, exactly, will the jobs be? A 1984 survey by *Changing Times* indicates that engineering graduates are most in demand, followed closely by computer-science graduates and those whose majors are accounting, business, marketing, and economics.[1] There will be fewer manufacturing jobs, and those that remain will require "high-tech" skills.

The new types of jobs that are created over the next decade or so will be related to technological and medical advances. Table 1 lists projections of the numbers of workers that will be needed in such fields. Note the projected need for energy-conservation and hazardous-waste technicians, as part of the solution to two contemporary problems.

YOUR FUTURE IN BUSINESS

It is generally agreed that competition for the better jobs will get tougher and tougher. The key

Internships and other student programs sponsored by corporations can provide work experience that will make a participant more attractive to future employers. Source: Courtesy of E. I. du Pont de Nemours and Company.

to landing the job you want is planning and preparation—and planning begins with goals. In particular, it is important to determine your *personal* goals, to decide on the role your career will play in reaching those goals, and then to develop your career goals. Once you know where you are going, you can devise a reasonable plan for getting there.

Career Planning and Preparation

The time to begin planning is as early as possible. A good way to start is to match your interests and skills with those required by various occupations or occupational areas. The career perspectives at the ends of the parts of this book can be helpful. You can obtain additional help from your school's placement office and from a variety of publications: the *College Placement Annual* and the *Occupational Outlook Handbook* published by the U.S. Department of Labor, for example. Most people find that planning to enter a general occupational area is more effective than targeting a specific job.

You must, of course, satisfy the educational requirements for the occupational area you wish to enter. Early planning will give you the opportunity to do so. But those people with whom you

will be competing for the better jobs will also be fully prepared. Can you do more?

The answer is yes. Corporate recruiters say that the following give job candidates a definite advantage:

☐ Work experience in cooperative work/school programs, during summer vacations, or in part-time jobs during the school year. Experience in the chosen occupational area carries the most weight, but even unrelated work experience is important.
☐ The ability to communicate well. Verbal and written communication skills are increasingly important in all aspects of business. Yours will be tested in your letters to recruiters, in your résumé, and in interviews. They will be of use throughout your career.
☐ Clear and realistic job and career goals. Recruiters feel most comfortable with candidates who know where they are headed and why they are applying for a specific job.[2]

Here again, early planning can make all the difference in getting your goals together, in sharpening your communication skills (through elective courses, if necessary), and in obtaining solid work experience.

Letter and Résumé

Preparation again becomes important when it is time to apply for a position. Your college placement office and various publications (including such directories as *Standard & Poor's Register of Corporations* and *Thomas' Register*) can be helpful—in your task of finding firms to apply to for jobs. Help-wanted ads and employment agencies may also provide leads.

Your first contact with a prospective employer will probably be through the mail—in a letter expressing your interest in working for that firm. This letter should be clear and straightforward, and it should be cast in proper business-letter form. It (and any other letters that you write to potential employers) will be considered part of your employment credentials. See Figure 1.

This first letter should be addressed to the personnel or human resources manager, by name if possible. You may include in this letter—very briefly—some information regarding your qualifications and your reason for writing to that particular firm. You should request an interview and, if the firm requires it, an employment application.

You may wish to include a copy of your résumé

Figure 1 Letter of Application. A letter of application should give your qualifications and your reasons for applying to that particular company. *Source: Adapted from Rinehart and Moncrieff, "Résumé Preparation Guide," 6th printing, p. 21. College of DuPage, Glen Ellyn, Ill.*

16 Wescott Lane
Collinsville, IL 62547

November 25, 1985

Mr. A. J. Rumney
Director of Personnel
Marriot Corporation
34 Lake Shore Drive
Chicago, IL 60606

Dear Mr. Rumney:

I am sending this letter and résumé in application for the position of Banquet Manager with your corporation. I think you will find my qualifications very compatible with those that you listed in the Hotel and Motel Journal.

For the last three years, I have been very excited about and involved in the restaurant training program at College of DuPage in Glen Ellyn, Illinois. Under the direction of George Macht, restaurant training coordinator, I became involved in both on- and off-campus educational experiences. After obtaining basic skills in the food service area, I supplemented my educational work with many volunteer food service related experiences at various clubs, civic organizations, and trade shows (NRA). I feel confident that my practical experiences coupled with my educational background have well prepared me for the position you have available.

My interest in Marriot Corporation began years ago when Marriot's fine reputation was discussed in classes and has continued through my own dining experiences. I recognized your interest in cultivating good employees when I read about your six-month management training program. This program seems well designed to provide just the right exposure to the total operation of your banquet facilities.

I would appreciate the opportunity to visit with you and further explain some of the information contained on the enclosed résumé. I'll be giving you a call within the next week to see if you have a few minutes to spend with me.

Sincerely yours,

Helen DeCarlis

Helen DeCarlis

Enclosure

with your first letter (most applicants do so). In any case, you should already have prepared the résumé, which is a summary of all your employment credentials and capabilities. Your goal in preparing both the letter and the résumé is to leave the potential employer with the feeling that you are someone who deserves an interview.

The résumé should fit on a single sheet of

Figure 2 *Résumé. A résumé summarizes your employment objectives, education, work experience, and major activities.*

```
                          MARY GASSNER
                        612 Brookhaven St.
                        Dallas, TX 75233
                        (214) 339-2617

PERSONAL DATA
     Single                       Age: 22
     Birthdate: March 3, 1962     Health: Excellent

EMPLOYMENT OBJECTIVE
     An accounting position that will provide involvement in
     all facets of the accounting cycle.

EDUCATIONAL BACKGROUND
     North Texas State University, Bachelor of Business
     Administration, May, 1984. Major in Management,
     Minor in Accounting. Grade point average: 3.4 based
     on a 4.0 scale.

     El Centro Community College, Associate of Applied Science
     in Accounting, May, 1982. Major emphasis on accounting
     and general business. Grade point average: 3.6 based on
     a 4.0 scale.

     South Oak Cliff High School - High School Diploma, 1980.

WORK EXPERIENCE
     6/84 - Present: Accounting clerk for Murphy
                     Manufacturing, Inc. Prepared
                     customer invoices, accounts payable, and
                     accounts receivable.

     6/82 - 8/83:    Accounting clerk for Murphy
     (summers)       Manufacturing, Inc. Prepared employee tax
                     records and payroll information.

     6/81 - 8/81:    General office clerk for Barton Foods
                     Company. Prepared customer invoices,
                     performed typing and receptionist duties.

EXTRACURRICULAR ACTIVITIES
     Outstanding Young Women of America, 1984
     President of the Phi Beta Lambda chapter, North Texas
        State University
     Member of the Future Accountants Club
     Served as Youth Director for Underprivileged Children's
        Association in Denton, Texas

REFERENCES (by permission)
     Dr. Harold Putter                 Mrs. Patti Church
     Chairman, Department of Accounting Office Supervisor
     North Texas State University      Barton Foods Company
     Denton, TX 76244                  802 Houston Street
                                       Dallas, TX 75201
     Miss Sarah Fleetwood
     Murphy Manufacturing, Inc.
     1246 McKinney Avenue
     Dallas, TX 75201
```

Table 2   Typical Job-Interview Questions

1. What can you tell me about yourself?
2. Why do you want to change jobs?
3. What kind of job are you looking for now?
4. What are your long-range objectives?
5. What are your salary requirements?
6. When could you be available to start here?
7. What can you tell me about your present company?
8. What kind of manager are you (or would you be)?
9. How would you describe yourself?
10. What are your strengths and weaknesses?
11. How would you describe your present boss?
12. To whom may I talk about your present job performance?
13. Are you willing to relocate?
14. How long have you been looking for a new job?
15. Why are you interested in this company?

Source: Thomas M. Camden and Nancy Bishop, *How to Get a Job in Dallas–Fort Worth,* Surrey Books, 1983, pp. 157–158. Reprinted by permission.

standard letter paper. It should be carefully thought out and reworked as many times as necessary to get it right—to put your best foot forward. Your résumé should be concise, but everything important should be noted on it. You need not include explanations or details, because you will have an opportunity to discuss your qualifications in your interviews.

Figure 2 shows a typical résumé. Items that should be included are your name, address, and telephone number; your employment and/or career objectives; your educational background; your work experience; any awards you have won; and the principal activities you take part in outside of school or work. You may either include the names and addresses of references or add a note to the effect that references will be furnished on request. (If you do include your references, make sure you have their permission to do so.) You are not obliged to include personal data (such as age, marital status, and state of health). However, in some cases the omission of these data may raise questions in the minds of personnel managers.

The Job Interview

Your résumé and first letter are, in essence, an introduction. The deciding factor in the hiring process is the interview (or several interviews) with representatives of the firm. It is through the interview that the firm gets to know you and your qualifications. At the same time, the interview provides a chance for you to learn about the firm.

Here again, preparation is the key to success. Research the firm before your first interview. Learn all you can about its products, its subsidiaries, the markets it operates in, its history, the locations of its facilities, and so on. If possible, obtain and read the firm's most recent annual report. Be prepared to ask questions about the firm and the opportunities it offers. Interviewers welcome such questions. They expect you to be interested enough to spend some time thinking about your potential relationship with their firm.

Prepare also to respond to questions that the interviewer may ask. Table 2 is a list of typical interviewer questions. But don't expect interviewers to stick to the list given in the table or

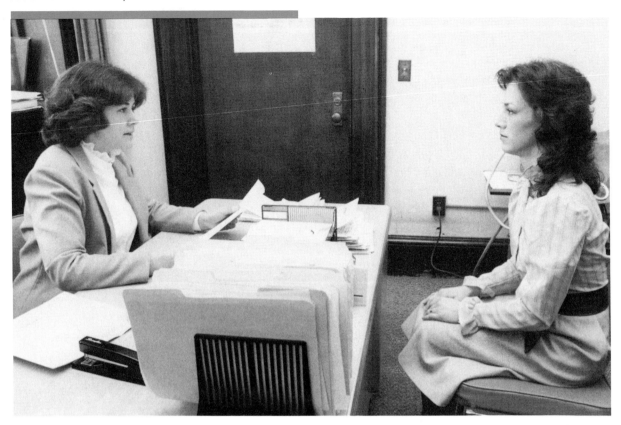

to the items appearing in your résumé. They will be interested in anything that helps them decide what kind of person and worker you are.

Make sure you are on time for your interview and are dressed and groomed in a business-like manner. Punctuality and appearance, like other personal qualities, are judged as part of the interviewing process. Have a copy of your résumé with you, even if you have sent one to the firm before. You may also want to bring a copy of your course transcript and letters of recommendation.

Consider the interview itself as a two-way conversation, rather than as a question-and-answer session. Volunteer any information that is relevant to the interviewer's questions. If an important point is skipped in the discussion, don't hesitate to bring it up. Be yourself, but emphasize your strengths. Good eye contact and posture

are important too. They should come naturally if you take an active part in the interview.

At the conclusion of the interview, thank the recruiter for taking the time to see you. Then, a day or two later, follow up by sending him or her a short letter of thanks. In this letter, you can ask a question or two that may have occurred to you after the interview or add pertinent information that may have been overlooked.

In most cases, the first interview is used to *screen* applicants, or choose those that are best qualified. These applicants are then given a second interview, and perhaps a third—usually with one or more department heads. If the job requires relocation to a different area, applicants may be invited there for these later interviews. After the interviewing process is completed, applicants are told when to expect a hiring decision.

Accepting an Offer

"We'd like to offer you the job" may be the best news a job applicant can hear. To take the job, you should send the firm a letter in which you express your appreciation, accept the offer, and restate the conditions of employment as you understand them. These conditions should include the starting salary and a general description of the job (responsibilities, immediate superior, training, and such). If you have any concerns regarding the job, make sure they are cleared up before you send your letter of acceptance: The job offer and your acceptance constitute a contract between you and the firm.

Less exciting is the news that begins "We thank you for your interest in our firm, *but. . . .*" The fact is that there are many more applications for jobs than there are jobs. (This is because most people apply for several jobs at the same time.) As a result, most people are turned down for some jobs during their careers. Don't be discouraged if you don't get the first position you apply for. Instead, think back over the application process, analyze it, and try to determine what might be improved. In other words, learn from your experience—and keep trying. Success will come if you persevere.

Career Profile

Patricia Roberts Harris   Patricia Roberts Harris influences some of the nation's largest companies, including IBM, Chase Manhattan Bank, Scott Paper Company, and Genex. Yet she is not a businesswoman in the traditional sense of entrepreneur or executive. Rather it is as a public official and as a board member of a number of important corporations that she has made decisions that affect millions of people as well as thousands of businesses from real estate companies to farmers.

Now 60, Harris was raised in Mattoon, Illinois, the daughter of a school teacher and a railroad dining-car waiter. She graduated *summa cum laude* from Howard University in 1945 and was first in her class at George Washington University's National Law Center in 1960. By 1970 she was a partner in a prestigious Washington, D.C., law firm. By training, Harris is a lawyer; but she is also an educator. She has taught at Howard University Law School and is currently professor of law at George Washington University. She served briefly as dean of law at Howard.

Harris's influence in the business world grew largely out of her involvement in politics. During the Johnson administration, she was appointed ambassador to Luxembourg—the first black woman to become an ambassador. Jimmy Carter appointed her the first black woman to hold a cabinet post. At different times in his administration, she headed three different cabinet departments: Housing and Urban Development; Health, Education, and Welfare; and Health and Human Services. She was instrumental in directing more aid to older, distressed cities and in revitalizing the public housing program.

Her work in the Carter administration made her into one of the nation's leading experts on how the government serves the most basic needs of its people. Such expertise is highly valued by businesses, especially those that are affected by government social policies. So when Harris left office, she was elected to the boards of directors of a number of corporations. Such directors sel-dom get involved in the day-to-day workings of a company, but they are often responsible for making, or at least passing judgment on, a company's most important decisions. They provide companies with opinions and expertise from the "outside," relatively free of the biases which company loyalties and paychecks naturally create in company presidents and other executives.

Harris can provide companies with valuable insights from at least four different perspectives. As a former cabinet head she knows how government functions at the highest level and can predict how government policy is likely to affect a company's actions. Her many contacts in Washington are sources both of information and of lobbying power, if a company should wish to influence government policy. As a knowledgeable and well-respected lawyer her opinions on legal matters carry a lot of weight. A company's leaders can feel better about making a controversial decision if they know that Harris supports it. Harris's opinions are also important because she is a leading black woman. She has spoken out on both racial and feminist matters.

You probably won't see Patricia Harris mentioned next time IBM opens a new plant or Genex announces a new product. But she's there, behind the scenes, using her knowledge and beliefs to influence decisions and having a greater effect than if she were a chief executive officer in one particular company.[1]

The figure in the salary column approximates the expected annual income after two or three years of service.

1 = $12,000–$15,000   2 = $16,000–$20,000   3 = $21,000–$27,000   4 = $28,000–$35,000   5 = $36,000 and up

Job Title	Educational Requirements	Salary Range	Prospects
Agent/broker— imports	No college required; related training and experience essential	3–5	Gradual growth
Antitrust attorney	Bachelor's degree plus at least three years of law school; on-the-job experience	4–5	Limited growth
City manager	College degree in business or public administration; on-the-job experience	4	Limited growth
Contract lawyer	Bachelor's degree plus at least three years of law school	4–5	Limited growth
Corporate attorney	Bachelor's degree plus at least three years of law school; on-the-job experience	4–5	Gradual growth
Corporate environmental officer	College degree in business; on-the-job experience	4	Limited growth
Court clerk	High school diploma; some college preferred	1–2	No growth
Court reporter	High school diploma; technical training	2–3	Limited growth
Economist	Bachelor's degree in economics; graduate degree preferred	3–4	Gradual growth
Eligibility worker— welfare	Some college preferred	1–2	Limited growth
Foreign exchange positions clerk	High school diploma; math ability required; on-the-job experience	1	Limited growth
Health and regulatory inspector	High school diploma; some college helpful	2–3	Limited growth
Importer, foreign buyer	High school diploma; math ability required; on-the-job experience	1–2	Limited growth
Legal assistant	Two- or four-year college degree	2–3	Greatest growth
Legal secretary	Some college preferred; on-the-job experience	2	Gradual growth
Patent attorney	Bachelor's degree plus at least three years of law school; on-the-job experience	4	Limited growth
Real estate attorney	Bachelor's degree plus at least three years of law school; on-the-job experience	4–5	Limited growth
Statistician	College degree preferred	2–3	Limited growth
Tax examiner, collector, and revenue agent	Some college preferred; on-the-job experience	2–3	No growth
Urban and regional planner	Master's degree; on-the-job experience	3–4	Gradual growth

All rights reserved. **103** "They Rescue Rockers from Heartbreak Hotels," by Gerri Hirshey reprinted from the January 24, 1984 issue of Family Circle Magazine. © 1984 The Family Circle, Inc. **104** "Computer Junkyards" from *Forbes,* January 16, 1984, page 8. By permission. **107** Adapted from "Operating a Franchise Often Pays But Demands on Buyer Are Great" by Sanford Jacobs reprinted by permission of *The Wall Street Journal,* © Dow Jones & Company, Inc. 1980. All rights reserved. **110** "Concern Fights to Stay Small So It Can Keep U.S. Contracts," reprinted by permission of *The Wall Street Journal,* © Dow Jones & Company, Inc. 1982. All rights reserved. **111** Reprinted from the July, 1983 issue of *Venture,* The Magazine for Entrepreneurs, by special permission. © 1983 Venture Magazine, Inc., 35 West 45th St., New York, NY 10036.

Art **90** National Federation of Independent Business Research and Education Foundation, "Small Business in America," (150 W. 20th Avenue, San Mateo, CA 94403, 1981). Copyright © National Federation of Independent Business Research and Education Foundation. **93** National Federation of Independent Business Research and Education Foundation, "Small Business in America," (150 W. 20th Avenue, San Mateo, CA 94403, 1981). Copyright © National Federation of Independent Business Research and Education Foundation. **98** National Federation of Independent Business Research and Education Foundation, "Small Business in America," (150 W. 20th Avenue, San Mateo, CA 94403, 1981). Copyright © National Federation of Independent Business Research and Education Foundation. **106** Bureau of Industrial Economics, U.S. Department of Commerce, "Franchising in the Economy, 1982–1984," (Washington, D.C.: Government Printing Office, 1984) p. 2.

Chapter Five

Text **130** "Her Paycheck" from *New England Business,* March 19, 1984, page 11. By permission. **133** "Reversing Performance Review" from *Psychology Today,* March 1984, page 80 reprinted from *Psychology Today Magazine.* Copyright 1984 American Psychological Association.

Art **122** Henry Mintzberg, "The Manager's Job," 53 *Harvard Business Review* (July–August, 1975): pp. 49–61.

Chapter Six

Text **150** "Risky Shifts" from *Psychology Today,* January 1984, page 52 reprinted from *Psychology Today Magazine.* Copyright 1984 American Psychological Association. **162** "Telecommuting—more than a fad" reprinted from *Management World,* with permission from the Administrative Management Society, Willow Grove, PA 19090. Copyright 1984 AMS.

Art **164** Ricky W. Griffin, *Management* (Boston: Houghton Mifflin, 1984), p. 337.

Chapter Seven

Text **190** "Square Holes for Quality Circles" from *Psychology Today,* February 1984, page 17 reprinted from *Psychology Today Magazine.* Copyright 1984 American Psychological Association.

Art **177** Bureau of Labor Statistics, U.S. Department of Labor, "Employees in Nonagricultural Establishments" (Washington, D.C.: Government Printing Office, 1984).

Chapter Eight

Text **206** "Killing Creativity" reprinted from *Infosystems,* March

1984, page 101, by permission. Copyright Hitchcock Publishing Company. **212** Adaptation from "The Invasion of the Pronoids" from *Psychology Today,* February 1984, page 18 reprinted from *Psychology Today Magazine.* Copyright 1984 American Psychological Association.

Chapter Nine

Text **235** "Faked Credentials" republished with permission from *Administrative Management* copyright © December, 1982 by Geyer-McAllister Publications, Inc., New York. **240** "Tough Interviews" reprinted by permission of *The Wall Street Journal,* © Dow Jones & Company, Inc. 1984. All rights reserved. **250** *Inc.,* September 1983, p. 86. By permission.

Art **238** CBS Personnel Record form used courtesy of CBS, Inc. **242** © 1984, Jeff MacNelly. Reprinted by permission of the Tribune Media Service, Inc.
246 R. Wayne Mondy and Robert M. Noe III, *Personnel: The Management of Human Resources* (Boston: Allyn and Bacon, 1984), p. 262. Copyright © 1984 by Allyn and Bacon, Inc. Reprinted with permission.

Chapter Ten

Text **266** "Keeping Unions Out" from *United States Banker,* February 1984, page 44, by permission.
Art **256** Bureau of Labor Statistics. **261** Courtney D. Gifford, ed., *Directory of U.S. Labor Organizations, 1982–1983 Edition,* (Washington, D.C.: The Bureau of National Affairs, 1982) p. 7. Copyright © by The Bureau of National Affairs, Inc., Washington, D.C. **265** Courtesy of the National Labor Relations Board.

Chapter Eleven

Text **295** "Slow Music Sells" from *Psychology Today,* January 1983, page 56 reprinted from *Psychology Today Magazine.* Copyright 1983 American Psychological Association. **299** "VDT Maps" from *New England Business,* December 5, 1983, page 9. By permission. **308** Adapted from an article by Michael Schrage; used by permission of *The Washington Post.* **309** Adapted from *Viewpoint,* Vol. 11, 1982, by permission of Ogilvy & Mather and Stephen Arbeit.

Art **292** William M. Pride and O. C. Ferrell, *Marketing,* 3d ed. (Boston: Houghton Mifflin, 1983), p. 46. **295** William M. Pride and O. C. Ferrell, *Marketing,* 3d ed. (Boston: Houghton Mifflin, 1983), p. 19. **297** William M. Pride and O. C. Ferrell, *Marketing,* 3d ed. (Boston: Houghton Mifflin, 1983), p. 19. **301** Bureau of Labor Statistics, U.S. Department of Labor, "Survey of Consumer Expenditures, 1960–1961," p. 17. **302** U.S. Bureau of the Census.

Chapter Twelve

Text **318** "Hitting the Singles Market" from *Dairy Record,* April 1984, page 42. By permission. **320** From *Marketing Definitions: A Glossary of Marketing Terms,* 1960, page 8. By permission of the American Marketing Association. **334** Adapted from "About General Foods" and reprinted with permission of General Foods Corporation. **344** "Black Consumers Equal Profits" from *Black Enterprise,* June 1984, page 68. Copyright June 1984, The Earl G. Graves Publishing Co., Inc., 130 Fifth Avenue, New York, NY 10011. All rights reserved.

Art **317** William M. Pride and O. C. Ferrell, *Marketing,* 3d ed. (Boston: Houghton Mifflin, 1983), p. 149.

Chapter Thirteen

Text **357** Extract from "Nabisco's Risky Plunge into Electronic

Mail" from *Management Technology,* May 1984, page 47. By permission.

Art **347** U.S. Bureau of the Census, 1982. **351** *All About Mail Order,* 1st ed. Colorado Springs, Colo.: Maxwell Sroge Publishing, 1983), p. 8. **355** Transportation Policy Associates, *Transportation in America* (March 1983).

Chapter Fourteen

Text **369** Extract from "Try matchbooks for Awareness and Frequency" from *Business Marketing,* January 1984, page 19. By permission. **376** From *Marketing Definitions: A Glossary of Marketing Terms,* 1960, page 20. By permission of the American Marketing Association. **379** "Sony's Magic Show" from *Institutional Investor,* April 1984, page 160. By permission. **386** Reprinted with permission from the May 31, 1984 issue of *Advertising Age.* Copyright 1984 by Crain Communications Inc.

Art **366** Bureau of Labor Statistics. McCann-Erickson,. *Advertising Age,* July 18, 1984 and May 28, 1984. **368** McCann-Erickson, *Advertising Age,* May 28, 1984, p. 50.

Chapter Fifteen

Text **409** "Customers Paid for Using ATMs," from *Savings Bank Journal,* October 1983, p. 58. By permission.

Art **397** Bureau of Labor Statistics. **398** Federal Reserve Board, *April 1984 Official Reports,* May 30, 1984. **404** Board of Governors of the Federal Reserve System, *Federal Reserve Bulletin* (January 1983), p. A88. **407** Federal Reserve Bank of New York, *The Story of Checks,* 6th ed., (New York: Federal Reserve Board) p. 11.

Chapter Sixteen

Text **426** Reprinted from the January-February 1983 issue of *Cashflow* Magazine, 1807 Glenview Rd., Glenview, IL 60025. Copyright 1983 by *Cashflow* Magazine Venture.

Art **430** Kelley, McKenzie, and Evans, *Business Mathematics* (Boston: Houghton Mifflin, 1982), p. 242.

Chapter Seventeen

Text **455** "42 Million Own Shares in America" reprinted with the permission of Dun's Business Month (formerly Dun's Review), January 1984, Copyright 1984, Dun & Bradstreet Publications Corporation.

Art **465** *The Wall Street Journal,* April 5, 1983, p. 55. Copyright Dow Jones & Company, Inc., 1983. Reprinted by permission of *The Wall Street Journal.* All rights reserved. **466** *The Wall Street Journal,* April 5, 1983, p. 52. Copyright Dow Jones & Company, Inc., 1983. Reprinted by permission of *The Wall Street Journal.* All rights reserved. **467** *The Wall Street Journal,* February 23, 1984, p. 42. Copyright Dow Jones & Company, Inc., 1984. Reprinted by permission of *The Wall Street Journal.* All rights reserved. **469** *Dallas Morning News,* "Business Today," June 7, 1983, p. 140. Chart produced by Stock Graphic, Ricky D. Woods, owner.

Chapter Eighteen

Text **483** Reprinted from the June 1983 issue of *Cashflow* Magazine, 1807 Glenview Rd., Glenview, IL 60025. Copyright 1983 by *Cashflow* Magazine Venture. **491** Reprinted from the May 1983 issue of *Cashflow* Magazine, 1807 Glenview Rd., Glenview, IL 60025. Copyright 1983 by *Cashflow* Magazine Venture.

Art **484** All-Industry Research Advisory Council, *Geographical Differences in Automobile Insurance Costs* (1200 Harger Road, Suite 22, Oak Brook, Illinois 60521, 1982), pp. 19–21. **485** *Insurance Facts: 1983–1984 Edition* (New York: Insurance Information Institute, 1983), p. 18.

Chapter Nineteen

Text **506** Haskell and Yablonsky: *Criminology: Crime and Criminality,* Second Edition, Copyright © 1983 by Houghton Mifflin Company. Used by permission. **517** From *Mergers and Acquisitions,* Spring 1984, p. 48. By permission. **521** Reprinted from the January-February 1981 issue of *Cashflow* Magazine, 1807 Glenview Rd., Glenview, IL 60025. Copyright 1981 by *Cashflow* Magazine Venture.

Art **522–523** James River Corporation, *Annual Report,* 1983. **531** Campbell Soup Company, Annual Report, 1983. **532** Campbell Soup Company, Annual Report, 1983. **533** Tandy Corporation, Annual Report, 1983, p. 16.

Chapter Twenty

Text **543** From *The Office,* March 1984, p. 31. By permission. **547** Republished with permission from *Office Administration and Automation,* copyright © January 1984 by Geyer-McAllister Publications, Inc., New York.

Art **540** Ricky W. Griffin, *Management* (Boston: Houghton Mifflin, 1984), p. 51. **545** George J. Brabb and Gerald W. McKean, *Business Data Processing* (Boston: Houghton Mifflin, 1982), p. 21.

Chapter Twenty-two

Text **596** From *Restaurant Business,* July 1, 1984, p. 10. By permission.

Art **586** Executive Office of the President and Office of Management and Budget, *Budget of the United States Government— Fiscal Year 1984* (Washington, D.C.: Government Printing Office, 1983). **598** Office of Management and Budget, *Budget of the United States Government: Fiscal Year 1983* (Washington, D.C.: Government Printing Office, 1982), p. 4.2. **599** Executive Office of the President and Office of Management and Budget, *Budget of the United States Government: Fiscal Year 1982,* p. 611; Office of the President and Office of Management and Budget, *Special Analysis, Budget of the United States Government: Fiscal Year 1985,* p. E-5. **600** Internal Revenue Service. **602** Bradley R. Schiller, *The Economy Today,* 2nd ed. (New York: Random House, 1983), p. 64. Copyright © 1983 by Random House, Inc.

Chapter Twenty-three

Text **623** From "Next Best Thing to Haven" by Jeffrey Robinson, reprinted by permission of *Barron's,* © Dow Jones & Company, Inc. 1983. All rights reserved. **628** "The Champagne of Soft Drinks" from *Nation's Business,* April 1984, pp. 93–94. By permission.

Art **610** Predicasts, Inc. 1984. **614** Federal Reserve Bank of Chicago, *International Newsletter No. 521:* (March 9, 1984), p. 1. **615** U.S. Customs Service, *Tariff Schedule of the U.S. (Annotated)* (Washington, D.C.: Government Printing Office). **617** Federal Reserve Bank of Chicago, *International Letter No. 495:* (March 11, 1983), pp. 1–2. Federal Reserve Bank of Chicago, *International Letter No. 528,* (June 15, 1984), p. 3. **618** Federal Reserve Bank of Chicago, *International Letter No. 521:* (March 9, 1984), p. 2.

Epilogue

Art **643** Rinehart and Moncrieff, "Résumé Preparation Guide," 4th printing (Glen Ellyn, Ill.: College of DuPage, 1984), p. 21.

Notes

Chapter 1

[1] Sharman Stein, "Pizza a Zesty Investment," *Boston Sunday Globe,* September 18, 1983, p. A12. [2] For more information, see *Venture,* November 1982, p. 6; and *Boston Sunday Globe,* September 18, 1983, p. A12. [3] Adapted from "The Origins of Enterprise in America," Exxon U.S.A., third quarter 1976, pp. 8–11. [4] For more information, see D. Gale Johnson, "Cracks in the Iron Rice Bowl," *Across the Board,* February 1984, pp. 34–41; "China's So-Called Capitalism," *Fortune,* May 28, 1984, p. 6; "China Turns to Grassroots Free Enterprise to Help Solve Youth Unemployment Problems," *International Management,* July 1982, p. 12; Edward R. Cony, "Beansprout Capitalism," *Barron's,* June 14, 1982, pp. 20, 32; and Albert Keidel, "Incentive Farming," *The China Business Review,* November–December 1983, pp. 12–14. [5] For more information, see Milton Moskowitz, Michael Katz, and Robert Levering (eds.), *Everybody's Business.* (San Francisco: Harper & Row, 1980), pp. 454–455; and the Chase Manhattan Bank Annual Reports.

Chapter 2

[1] Judith B. Gardner, "When a Brand Name Gets Hit by Bad News," *U.S. News & World Report,* November 8, 1982, p. 71. [2] For more information, see Samuel F. O'Gorman, "New Stress on Product Safety," *Senior Scholastic,* January 7, 1983, p. 4; Thomas Moore, "The Fight to Save Tylenol," *Fortune,* November 29, 1982, p. 47; Judith B. Gardner, "When a Brand Name Gets Hit by Bad News," *U.S. News & World Report,* November 8, 1982, p. 71; "J&J Will Pay Dearly to Cure Tylenol," *Business Week,* November 29, 1982, p. 37; and "Tylenol Comes Back as Case Grows Cold," *Newsweek,* April 25, 1983, p. 18. [3] Colgate-Palmolive Company, *Annual Report,* 1981, p. 26. [4] Robert Kreitner, *Management,* 2nd ed. (Boston: Houghton Mifflin, 1983), p. 286. [5] *Ibid.* [6] John L. Hysom and William J. Bolce, *Business and Its Environment* (New York: West, 1983), p. 270. [7] Bill Richards, "Something Terrible Has Happened in Idaho. Was It Lead?" *The Washington Post,* October 7, 1979, p. A21. [8] Margaret Hornblower, "Herbicide, Birth Defects Linked for House Panel," *The Washington Post,* June 22, 1979, p. A8. [9] "The Nation Awakens to a New Danger," *U.S. News & World Report,* February 28, 1983, p. 28. [10] For more information, see Sandra Porter with Janice DeGooyer,

"What is Comparable Worth Anyway," *The Secretary,* May, 1983, p. 19; "Beyond 'Equal Pay for Equal Work,'" *Business Week,* July 18, 1983, p. 169; and *Harassment and Compensation—Today's Sex Discrimination Issues* (Chicago: Commerce Clearing House, 1983), pp. 12–13. [11] For more information, see "Ethics and Infant Formula," *The Boston Globe,* February 6, 1984, p. 10; "Nestle Complying with WHO Code for Infant Formulas," *Science,* October 28, 1983, p. 400; and "Campus Crunch," *Newsweek,* November 27, 1978, p. 115.

Chapter 3

[1] For more information, see Apple Computer Company, *Third Quarter Report,* July 27, 1983; Apple Computer Company, "Press Information"; and various materials promoting IBM computers. [2] *U.S. News & World Report,* January 16, 1984, p. 65. [3] *Ibid.* [4] "Converse Trying a Full Court Press in Athletic Shoes," *Business Week,* May 7, 1984, p. 52. [5] *Fortune,* April 30, 1984, p. 270. [6] Pabst Brewing Company, *Annual Report,* 1983. [7] *Ibid.* [8] *Ibid.* [9] For more information, see Milton Moskowitz, Michael Katz, and Robert Levering, *Everybody's Business* (San Francisco: Harper & Row, 1980), pp. 86–88; David Avery, "Hedge Gives the Edge in Cargill's Grain Picture," *Futures: The Magazine of Commodities and Options,* vol. 13, no. 3, March, 1984, pp. 82, 84; and "Putting Sizzle into Safety Programs," *Industry Week,* May 17, 1982, pp. 60–64.

Chapter 4

[1] *The Wall Street Journal,* February 7, 1983, p. 19. [2] For more information, see *The Wall Street Journal,* February 7, 1983, p. 19; and *InfoWorld,* November 7, 1983, p. 109. [3] Arnold C. Cooper, "Entrepreneurship: Starting a New Business," (San Mateo, Calif.: National Federation of Independent Business, 1980). [4] Robert A. Schaefer, "Starting and Managing a New Business," (Washington, D.C.: U.S. Small Business Administration, 1981), p. v. [5] Richard Greene, "A Boutique in Your Living Room," *Forbes,* May 7, 1984, p. 86. [6] This section draws heavily from *The Pitfalls in Managing a Small Business* (New York: Dun & Bradstreet, 1976) and from a brochure published by the National Federation of Independent Business. [7] *Hearings on Small Business and Innovation,* held before the Subcommittee on Antitrust, Consumers and Employment, and the

Senate Select Committee on Small Business, on August 9 and 10, 1978. [8]*Hearings on Job Creation and Small Business,* held by the Subcommittee on Antitrust, Consumers and Employment on September 25 and 26, 1978. [9]*Hearings on Job Creation and Small Business,* part 1, p. 310. [10]*Franchising in the Economy 1981–83,* U.S. Department of Commerce, Bureau of Industrial Economics. [11]This section is adapted from *The Wall Street Journal,* November 3, 1980, p. 27. [12]From "Concern Fights to Stay Small So It Can Keep U.S. Contracts," *The Wall Street Journal,* December 13, 1982, p. 5. [13]From *Venture,* July 1983, p. 19.

Chapter 5

[1]For more information, see "How International Harvester Hopes to Return to the Black," *Fortune,* January 25, 1982, pp. 7–8; and "International Harvester Lives," *Fortune,* December 26, 1983, pp. 64–70. [2]Margaret Loeb, "Staid Delta Air Tries to Stem Losses by Following Other Carriers' Moves," *The Wall Street Journal,* September 6, 1983, p. 29. [3]Steven Flax, "How to Snoop on Your Competitors," *Fortune,* May 14, 1984, p. 29. [4]Henry Mintzberg, "The Manager's Job: Folklore and Fact," *Harvard Business Review,* July–August 1975, pp. 49–61. [5]*Ibid.* [6]William Ouchi, *Theory Z* (Reading, Mass.: Addison-Wesley, 1981). [7]Michael Cieply, "Meanwhile, Back in Marysville," *Forbes,* March 12, 1984, p. 127. [8]Terrence Deal and Allan Kennedy, *Corporate Culture* (Reading, Mass.: Addison-Wesley, 1982). [9]Thomas Peters and Robert Waterman, *In Search of Excellence* (New York: Harper & Row, 1982). [10]For more information, see Ann Morrison, "Revlon's Surprising New Face," *Fortune,* November 2, 1981, pp. 72–80; "The Other Side of Revlon," *Forbes,* August 18, 1980, p. 130; "Revlon: A Painful Case of Slow Growth and Fading Glamour," *Business Week,* April 12, 1982, pp. 116–119; and Ray Rowan, "Business Triumphs of the Seventies," *Fortune,* December 31, 1979, pp. 30–34. [11]For more information, see "The $5 Billion Man—Pushing the New Strategy at GE," *Fortune,* April 18, 1983, p. 6; "GE Promotes Factory Automation, but Some Doubt Big Market Exists," *The Wall Street Journal,* October 21, 1982, p. 33; "GE's Wizards Turning from Bottom Line to Share of the Market," *The Wall Street Journal,* July 12, 1982, pp. 1, 14; and Ann Morrison, "Trying to Bring GE to Life," *Fortune,* January 25, 1982, pp. 50–57.

Chapter 6

For more information, see "Levi Strauss Is Stretching Its Wardrobe," *Fortune,* November 19, 1979, pp. 86–89; and "Adding Koracorp to Levi's Wardrobe," *Business Week,* June 4, 1979, pp. 69–70. [2]For more information, see "The Bigness Cult's Grip on Beatrice Foods," *Fortune,* September 20, 1982, pp. 122–129; and "Beatrice Revamps," *Fortune,* March 21, 1983, p. 7. [3]See "Texas Instruments in Midlife," *Forbes,* March 15, 1982, pp. 64–65; and "Texas Instruments Regroups," *Fortune,* August 9, 1982, pp. 40–45.

Chapter 7

[1]For more information, see "Can Detroit Catch Up?" *Fortune,* February 8, 1982, pp. 34–39; and "Ford Is on a Roll in Europe," *Fortune,* October 18, 1982, pp. 182–191. [2]Robert Kreitner, *Management,* 2nd ed. (Boston: Houghton Mifflin, 1983), p. 520. [3]The least-cost order quantity is found by applying the equation $EOQ = \sqrt{2RC/S}$, where R is the yearly requirement in units, C is the cost of placing an order, and S is the storage cost per unit. [4]For more information, see "Flexible Manufacturing—Another Step towards the Automated Plant," *Automotive Industries,* November 1981, pp. 61–63; and "Planting Deep and Wide at John Deere," *Forbes,* March 14, 1983, pp. 119–122. [5]For more information, see "Turnaround Update: Pizza Hut," *Restaurant Business,* January 1, 1981, p. 104; Peter Berlinski, "Pizza Hut's Turnaround Strategists," *Restaurant Business,* January 1, 1982, pp. 117–133; and "Pizza Hut Tries a New Recipe for Success," *Business Week,* January 18, 1982, pp. 87–88.

Chapter 8

For more information, see "Data Processing: What Makes Tandem Run," *Business Week,* July 24, 1980, p. 73; and "Managing by Mystique at Tandem Computers," *Fortune,* June 28, 1982, pp. 84–91. [2]Douglas McGregor, *The Human Side of Enterprise* (New York: McGraw-Hill, 1960). [3]George A. Weimer, "Is RMI's Best Asset Its Chief Executive?" *Iron Age,* September 24, 1982, p. 59. [4]For more information, see *Iron Age,* September 24, 1982, pp. 59, 61; Thomas J. Peters and Robert H. Waterman, Jr., *In Search of Excellence,* (New York: Harper & Row, 1982), pp. 242–243; and "'Big Jim' Daniell, Ex-RMI Chief, Is Dead at 65" *American Metal Market,* December 16, 1983, p. 1.

Chapter 9

[1]For more information, see "Arbitration's Clout," *Dallas Morning News,* January 16, 1984, pp. 1B, 6B; and *Official Baseball Guide—1983.* (St. Louis: The Sporting News, 1983). [2]"U.S. Job Security in the Japanese Style," *Business Week,* April 20, 1981, p. 36. [3]John Greenwald, "The Colossus That Works," *Time,* July 11, 1983, p. 47. [4]"Curtailing the Freedom to Fire," *Business Week,* March 19, 1984, p. 29. [5]Ellen Wojan, "A Touch of Class," *Inc.,* September 1983, p. 86. For more information, see *Inc.,* September 1983, pp. 79–86. [6]Greenwald, *op. cit.* pp. 44–54. [7]For more information, see *Business Week,* February 20, 1984, pp. 66–77; *Esquire,* December 1983, pp. 194–202; and *Time,* July 11, 1983, pp. 44–54.

Chapter 10

[1]For more information, see "Anatomy of an Auto-Plant Rescue," *Fortune,* April 4, 1983, pp. 108–113; and "Chrysler on the Brink," *Fortune,* February 9, 1981, pp. 38–44. [2]"Labor's Voice on Corporate Boards: Good or Bad?" *Business Week,* May 7, 1984, pp. 151–153. [3]Adapted from "The New Work Spirit in St. Louis," *Fortune,* November 16, 1981, pp. 92–106. [4]Adapted from "An Airline Boss Attacks Sky-High Wages," *Fortune,* January 9, 1984, pp. 66–73.

Chapter 11

[1]*Marketing News,* January 21, 1983, sec. 1, p. 8. [2]*Marketing News,* January 21, 1983, sec. 1, p. 9. For more information, see *Marketing News,* January 21, 1983, sec. 1, pp. 8–9; *Fortune,* March 8, 1982, p. 7; and Eastman Kodak Company, *Annual Report,* 1982, p. 6. [3]*The Wall Street Journal,* September 12, 1983, p. 1. [4]*The Mustang Story,* Ford Corporate Studies No. 10 (Dearborn, Mich: Ford Motor Company). [5]*National Economic Trends,* Federal Reserve Bank of St. Louis, December 23, 1982. [6]Stanton, *Marketing.* (New York: McGraw-Hill, 1984), p. 92. [7]*Financial World,* September 15, 1983, p. 20. [8]*Survey of Current Business,* U.S. Department of Commerce, March 1984, p. 5–1. [9]"Letter from the Lion," The Dreyfus Corporation, Fall 1983. [10]*Roundup,* Federal Reserve Bank of Dallas, October 1983. [11]*Chicago Sun-Times,* March 14, 1983, p. 1. [12]*Boston Sunday Globe,* April 1, 1984, p. 44. For more information, see *Boston Sunday Globe,* April 1, 1984, p. 44; and *The Wall Street Journal,* September 12, 1983, p. 12. [13]For more information, see *Viewpoint,* vol. 11, 1982, Ogilvy & Mather.

Chapter 12

[1]For more information, see *Newsweek,* December 12, 1983, pp. 81–85; *Barron's,* December 5, 1983, p. 8; and *Time,* December 12, 1983, pp. 64–67. [2]*Nielson Researcher,* no. 1, 1983, pp. 8–9. [3]*Marketing Times,* July–August 1981, p. 2. [4]Adapted from *Marketing Definitions: A Glossary of Marketing Terms* (Chicago: American Marketing Association, 1960), p. 8. [5]Campbell Soup Company, *Annual Report,* 1982. [6]ConAgra, *Annual Report,* 1982. [7]Ford Motor Company, *Annual Report,* 1982, p. 3. [8]Taken from *About General Foods,* a booklet published by General Foods, White Plains, N.Y. [9]For more information, see "Who'll Buy a Drink in a Box," *Marketing & Media Decisions,* April 1982, pp. 74–75, 184; and *Business Week,* January 16, 1984, pp. 56–57.

Chapter 13

[1]For more information, see *Chain Store Age Executive,* May 1983, pp. 125–126; *Business Week,* October 4, 1982, p. 68; *Direct Marketing,* August 1982, p. 58; and *Madison Avenue,* September 1982, pp. 49–55. [2]*U.S. Industrial Outlook 1983* (Washington, D.C.: U.S. Government Printing Office), p. 47–1. [3]William M. Pride and O. C. Ferrell, *Marketing,* 3rd ed. (Boston: Houghton Mifflin, 1983), p. 247. [4]*Retailing,* Small Business Bibliography No. 10 (Washington, D.C.: U.S. Small Business Administration). [5]*Ibid.* [6]Pride and Ferrell, *op. cit.,* p. 247. [7]*Chain Store Age/Supermarkets,* July 1983, p. 11. [8]*The Wall Street Journal,* September 10, 1981, p. 27. [9]Avon, *Annual Report,* 1982, p. 23. [10]Adapted from John F. Magee, *Physical Distribution Systems* (New York: McGraw-Hill, 1967), p. 73. [11]For more information, see Subrata N. Chakravarty, "Toys 'Я' Fun," *Forbes,* March 28, 1983, pp. 58–60; Peter Kerr, "The New Game at Toys 'Я' Us," *The New York Times,* September 4, 1983, sec. 3, p. 7; Claudia Ricci, "Children's Wear Retailers Brace for Competition from Toys 'Я' Us," *The Wall Street Journal,* August 25, 1983, p. 21; and Toys "Я" Us, Inc., *Annual Report,* 1983. [12]For more information, see Eugene Kozicharow, "Federal Express Plans Regional Hubs," *Aviation Week & Space Technology,* April 11, 1983, pp. 39–42; Joani Nelson-Horchler, "The Overnight Race: Airborne's Flying Right at Federal Express," *Industry Week,* March 19, 1984, pp. 67–69; and Roy Rowan, "Business Triumphs of the Seventies," *Fortune,* December 3, 1979, p. 34.

Chapter 14

[1]For more information, see *U.S. News & World Report,* December 5, 1983; *The Wall Street Journal,* February 28, 1984; and the various advertising materials produced by Coke and Pepsi. [2]William M. Pride and O. C. Ferrell, *Marketing, 3rd ed.* (Boston: Houghton Mifflin Company, 1983), p. 23. [3]*Advertising Age,* May 28, 1984, p. 50. [4]*Chicago Sun-Times,* January 25, 1984, pp. 1, 26. [5]*U.S. Industrial Outlook 1983* (Washington, D.C.: Bureau of Labor Statistics). [6]*The Wall Street Journal,* June 7, 1984, p. 1. [7]Milton Moscowitz, Michael Katz, and Robert Levering (eds.) *Everybody's Business* (San Francisco: Harper & Row, 1982), p. 49. [8]*Marketing Definitions: A Glossary of Marketing Terms* (Chicago: American Marketing Association, 1960), p. 20. [9]Kenneth Roman, "A Coupon May Be a Good Idea, But It's Not a Promotion," *Viewpoint: By, For, and About Ogilvy and Mather,* vol. 1, 1982, p. 12. [10]Adapted from Anheuser-Busch Companies, *Annual Report 1983,* February 6, 1984, pp. 11–12. [11]For more information, see William A. Robinson, "The Best Promotions of 1983," *Advertising Age,* May 31, 1984, pp. 10–12. [12]For more information, see "Leaders in Sales and Sales Management," *Journal of Personal Selling & Sales Management,* May 1983, pp. 51–53; "Mary Kay Cosmetics," *Business Week,* March 28, 1983, p. 130; and Solveig Jansson, "Who Spotted Last Year's Hottest Stocks?", *Institutional Investor,* p. 84.

Chapter 15

[1]*Fortune,* January 9, 1984, p. 97. For more information, see *USA Today,* September 1983, p. 17; *Reader's Digest,* December 1983, p. 144; and *Fortune,* January 9, 1984, p. 97. [2]David R. Kamerschen and Eugene S. Klise, *Money and Banking.* (Cincinnati: South-Western, 1976), p. 268. [3]Tony J. Salvaggio, "Changing Pattern in Check Collection," *Voice of the Federal Reserve Bank of Dallas,* April 1978, p. 1. [4]*Newsweek,* October 24, 1983, p. 106. [5]*Time,* August 29, 1983, p. 47. [6]For more information, see *Newsweek,* October 24, 1983, p. 106; *U.S. News & World Report,* October 31, 1983, p. 89; *Time,* August 29, 1983, p. 47; and *Forbes,* December 5, 1983, p. 148. [7]For more information, see "The Banks Had It Coming," *Business Week,* April 23, 1984, p. 124; "New Rules on Check Clearing," *Dun's Business Month,* April 1984, p. 25; and Peter Kerr, "Clearing Checks: Waiting Time Varies," *The New York Times,* April 2, 1983, p. 18.

Chapter 16

[1]*Business Week,* April 26, 1982, p. 34. [2]For more information, see *Business Week,* April 26, 1982, pp. 34–35; *Business Week,* October 18, 1982, p. 154; *Business Week,* November 15, 1982, p. 44; and *The Wall Street Journal,* February 1, 1983, p. 1. [3]For more information, see *Forbes,* June 20, 1983, p. 158; *Business Week,* August 15, 1983, p. 26; *U.S. News & World Report,* August 15, 1983, p. 31; and *Forbes,* August 1, 1983, pp. 31–32. [4]Shirley Hobbs Scheibla, "A Mickey for Greenmail?", *Barron's,* June 18, 1984, pp. 8–9, 28. [5]For more information, see Shirley Hobbs Scheibla, "A Mickey for Greenmail?", *Barron's,* June 18, 1984; "Disney Rumors Percolate," *Dun's Business Month,* May 1984, p. 32; "'Greenmail'—It's Legal, but Is It Right?", *U.S. News & World Report,* June 25, 1984, pp. 75–76; "Problems in Walt Disney's Magic Kingdom," *Business Week,* March 12, 1984, pp. 50–54; and "While the Shareholders Watch," *The New York Times,* June 25, 1984, p. A14.

Chapter 17

[1]Robert H. Runde, "What to Do When It's Time to Invest," *Money,* October 1982, p. 84. [2]For more information on the dos and don'ts of investing, see *Money,* October 1982, p. 84; *Forbes,* May 9, 1983, p. 338; and *The NASD: What It Does to Protect the Public,* a pamphlet published by the National Association of Securities Dealers, Inc. [3]Robert H. Runde, *op. cit.,* p. 83. [4]*The World Almanac & Book of Facts 1983* (New York: Newspaper Enterprise Association, 1981), p. 123. [5]Courtesy of the New York Stock Exchange. [6]For more information, see Ray Brady, "Those Tempting Municipal Bonds," *Nation's Business,* January 1984, p. 16; Richard L. Stern, "Malpractice for Brokers," *Forbes,* March 26, 1984, pp. 38, 39; and "SEC Looks into Possible Whoops Fraud," *Dun's Business Month,* March 1984, p. 32. [7]For more information, see Ann Monroe, "Prime Property," *The Wall Street Journal,* July 12, 1984, p. 1; Carter Ratcliff, "Unwrapping Christo," *Saturday Review,* December 1980, pp. 18–22; and L. Nilson, "Christo's Blossoms in the Bay," *Art News,* January 1984, pp. 54–62.

Chapter 18

[1]Maurice Barnfather, "For Whom the Bell Tolls," *Forbes,* March 16, 1981, p. 36. [2]*Ibid.* For more information, see *Forbes,* March 16, 1981, p. 36; *Smithsonian,* March 1981, p. 82; and Robert I. Mehr and Emer-

son Cammack, *Principles of Insurance* (Homewood, Ill.: Irwin, 1972), p. 74. [3]"Proper Precautions Trim Product Liability Risks," *Inc.*, May 1980, p. 131. [4]"Financial Planning Guide, Personal Finance," *The New York Times*, May 20, 1984, Section 12, p. 74. [5]"An Array of New Products to Woo the Policyholder," *Business Week*, December 27, 1982, p. 126. [6]Margaret Daly, "Universal Life Insurance: A Good Idea for Your Family?", *Better Homes and Gardens*, April 1983, p. 25. [7]For more information, see *Time*, June 20, 1983, p. 62; *Forbes*, April 25, 1983, p. 14; *Fortune*, July 25, 1983, p. 22; and *Newsweek*, July 4, 1983, p. 52. [8]For more information, see "Companies Using a 'Managed' Approach Find Dollar Savings in Workers' Comp Costs," *Management Review*, July 1984, pp. 39, 40; "Ohio's Pivotal Contest over Workers' Comp," *Business Week*, October 26, 1981, p. 68; and "On-the-Job Injuries: Now, Suits against the Boss," *Business Week*, January 25, 1982, p. 114.

Chapter 19

[1]"Conning by Computer," *Newsweek*, April 23, 1973, p. 90. [2]For more information, see *Fortune*, August 1973, p. 132; *Newsweek*, April 16, 1973, p. 82; and *Newsweek*, April 23, 1973, p. 90. [3]Campbell Soup Company, *Annual Report*, 1983. [4]Tandy Corporation, *Annual Report*, 1982.

Chapter 20

[1]For more information, see *Fortune*, June 15, 1981, pp. 74–93; and *Fortune*, June 28, 1982, pp. 58–65.

Chapter 21

[1]Richard Stengel, "Decision: Tape It to the Max," *Time*, January 30, 1984, p. 67. [2]For more information, see *U.S. News & World Report*, February 13, 1984, p. 50; *Time*, January 30, 1984, p. 67; *Newsweek*, January 30, 1984, p. 57; and *U.S. News & World Report*, January 30, 1984, p. 10. [3]Summarized from 11 *USC* 507 (1–6). [4]For more information, see Bernard Shakin, "Alive and Kicking," *Barron's*, March 14, 1979, pp. 9, 14; Robert J. Flaherty and Alyssa A. Lappen, "It Comes in All Shapes and Sizes," *Forbes*, October 15, 1979, pp. 83–84; and Heinz H. Biel, "The New Penn Central," *Forbes*, February 16, 1981, p. 124. [5]Vlases v. Montgomery Ward & Co., 377 F.2d 846 (1967), as given in Robert N. Corley and William J. Robert, *Principles of Business*, 10th ed. (Englewood Cliffs; N.J.: Prentice-Hall, 1975), p. 343. [6]Corley and Robert, *Ibid.*

Chapter 22

[1]For more information, see *Dun's Business Month*, February 1982, p. 13; *Fortune*, February 8, 1982, p. 59; *U.S. News & World Report*, October 24, 1983, p. 51; and *AT&T Annual Report*, 1982, p. 3. [2]Bradley R. Schiller, *The Economy Today*, 2nd ed. (New York: Random House, 1983), pp. 61–62. [3]Keith Davis, William C. Frederick, and Robert L. Blomstrom, *Business and Society*, 4th ed. (New York: McGraw-Hill, 1980), pp. 263–264. [4]Marvin Stone, "Will Self-Regulation Work?" *U.S. News & World Report*, December 13, 1982, p. 96. [5]John L. Hysom and William J. Bolce, *Business and Its Environment* (St. Paul, Minn.: West, 1983), pp. 308–309. [6]*CORS Report: A Closer Look at the Cost of Government Regulation* (Benton Harbor, Mich.: Whirlpool Corporation, 1979). [7]"Deregulation: A Fast Start for the Reagan Strategy," *Business Week*, March 9, 1981, p. 63. [8]"Deregulation Still Has a Long Way to Go," *Business Week*, August 23, 1982, p. 24. [9]Felicity Barringer, "Overregulation? Public Finds Agencies Not Guilty," *The Washington Post*, November 10, 1981, p. H1. [10]Bradley R. Schiller, *The Economy Today*, 2nd ed. (New York: Random House, 1983), p. 63. [11]Dean Rotbart, "American Air, Its President Gets Trust Suit Voided," *The Wall Street Journal*, September 14, 1983, p. 2. [12]John DeMott, "Dirty Tricks in Dallas," *Time*, March 7, 1983, p. 66. [13]Mary Lenz and Dan Piller, "American Unscathed," *The Dallas Times Herald*, September 14, 1983, p. B1. [14]For more information, see *The Wall Street Journal*, September 14, 1983, p. 2; *Time*, March 7, 1983, p. 66; and *The Dallas Times Herald*, September 14, 1983, p. B1. [15]For more information see Jonathon Fuerbringer, "Tax Shifts Assayed as Hearings Start," *The New York Times*, August 8, 1984, pp. D1, D5; Al Santoli, "Does This Tax Plan Make Sense," *Parade*, August 12, 1984, pp. 8, 10; and Harry A. Jacobs Jr., "A Flat Tax Can Help Growth Firms," *The Wall Street Journal*, July 12, 1983, p. 38.

Chapter 23

[1]For more information, see Federal Reserve Bank of Chicago, *International Letter*, No. 512, November 4, 1983; *Chicago Sun-Times*, January 19, 1984; *The Wall Street Journal*, January 18, 1984; *Fortune*, February 20, 1984, pp. 104–108; and *Newsweek*, May 21, 1984, p. 70. [2]Federal Reserve Bank of Chicago, *International Letter*, No. 521, March 9, 1984. [3]*International Letter* No. 527, Federal Reserve Bank of Chicago, June 1,

1984. [4]Manufacturers Hanover Bank, *Financial Digest,* August 8, 1983. [5]American Motors Corporation, *Annual Report,* 1983, p. 12. [6]Polaroid Corporation, *Annual Report,* 1983, p. 11. [7]Carl A. Gerstacker, *A Look at Business in 1990* (Washington, D.C.: U.S. Government Printing Office, November 1972), pp. 274–275. [8]Adapted from *Business Week,* December 6, 1976, pp. 91–92. [9]*Chicago Tribune,* August 4, 1983, sec. 3, p. 11. [10]"The Trade Challenge for the 1980s," an address delivered by President Ronald Reagan before the Commonwealth Club, San Francisco, March 4, 1983. [11]For more information, see Christopher Lorenz, "The World as a Marketplace," *Boston Sunday Globe,* July 29, 1984, pp. 79, 80; Dennis Chase, "Global Marketing: The New Wave," *Advertising Age,* June 25, 1984, p. 49; and "P&G Moving Fast on World Market Entry," *Advertising Age,* June 25, 1984, p. 50.

Epilogue
[1]*Changing Times,* February 1984, p. 38. [2]*Changing Times,* February 1984, p. 42.

Part One
[1]Jill Bettner and Christine Donahue, "Now They're Not Laughing," *Forbes,* November 21, 1983, pp. 116–119; "A Friendly Frontier for Female Pioneers," *Fortune,* June 25, 1984, p. 78; Sharon Nelton, "The People Who Take the Plunge," and "Lorraine Mecca's Story: She Saw an Opportunity and Took It," *Nation's Business,* June 1984, p. 22.

Part Two
[1]"A Retirement Changes the Guard at Exxon," *Business Week,* July 7, 1975, 19; "A New Face for Exxon's New Role in Oil," *Business Week,* July 14, 1975, p. 136; "One Thing You'll See About Us Is Flexibility," *Fortune,* August 1975, p. 35; "New Faces at Exxon," *Time,* July 7, 1975, p. 58.

Part Three
[1]John F. Stacks, "Plain Vanilla, But Very Good," *Time,* July 11, 1983, p. 48; John Greenwald, "The Colossus That Works," *Time,* July 11, 1983, p. 44; "Other Maestros of the Micro," *Time,* January 3, 1983, p. 28; "Cary Steps Down at IBM," *Business Week,* March 7, 1983, p. 38; James A. White, "IBM, As Expected, Taps John Opel, 58, As New Chairman," *The Wall Street Journal,* February 23, 1983, p. 36.

Part Four
[1]Janet Guyon and Erik Larson, "New Apple Chief Expected to Bring Marketing Expertise Gained at Pepsi," *The Wall Street Journal,* April 11, 1983, Sec. 2, p. 29; Janet Guyon, "Apple Lured President from Pepsi with Patient Persuasion and Cash," *The Wall Street Journal,* April 15, 1983, Sec. 2, p. 33; "Conflict, Conquest Mark Newsmakers" and "What Was Your First Job?" *Advertising Age,* January 2, 1984, p. 18; "Apple Reaches Out for a Marketing Pro" and "Why Sculley Gave Up the Pepsi Challenge," *Business Week,* April 25, 1983, p. 27.

Part Five
[1]Julie Salamon, "Muriel Siebert's Style in Overseeing Banks Is Hardly Banker's Gray," *The Wall Street Journal,* December 18, 1981, p. 1; Robert A. Bennett, "Muriel Siebert, Bank 'Pioneer,'" *The New York Times,* June 10, 1982, D1; "Siebert Opens Branch in Bank," *The New York Times,* May 26, 1983, D6.

Part Six
[1]"The Doctor's Winning Formula," *Forbes,* January 7, 1980, p. 170; "Wang Labs' Run for a Second Billion," *Business Week,* May 17, 1982, p. 100; "Winging With Wang," *Forbes,* October 15, 1976, p. 103; "The Guru of Gizmos," *Time,* November 17, 1980, p. 81; Jeff Blyskal, "Dr. Wang's Next Test," *Forbes,* February 15, 1982, p. 36.

Part Seven
[1]Lawrence Feinberg, "Patricia Harris Named Professor of Law at GW," *The Washington Post,* March 9, 1983, C3; "How Much More Federal Aid Can Cities Expect?" *U.S. News & World Report,* December 12, 1977, p. 63; "Two for One Deal," *Time,* January 3, 1977, p. 44.

Glossary

absolute advantage a nation's ability to produce a specific product more efficiently than any other nation (page 612)

accountability the obligation of a subordinate to accomplish an assigned job or task (page 155)

accountant a person trained and experienced in the methods and systems of accounting (page 508)

account executive an individual who buys or sells securities for clients (page 461)

accounting the process of systematically collecting, analyzing, and reporting financial information (page 507)

accounting equation the basis for the accounting process: assets = liabilities + owners' equity (page 510)

accounts payable short-term obligations that arise as a result of credit purchases (page 517)

accounts receivable amounts owed to a firm by its customers (page 432)

acid-test ratio the financial ratio calculated by dividing the sum of cash, marketable securities, and accounts and notes receivable by current liabilities (page 525)

Active Corps of Executives (ACE) a group of active managers who counsel small-business owners on a volunteer basis, under the auspices of the Small Business Administration (page 99)

ad hoc committee a committee created for a specific short-term purpose (page 161)

administrative law the regulations created by government agencies that have been established by legislative bodies (page 564)

administrative managers managers who are not associated with any specific area, but instead provide overall administrative guidance and leadership; also called general managers (page 128)

advertising any nonpersonal promotional message that is paid for by an identified sponsor and directed to a large audience (page 365)

advertising agency an independent firm that plans, produces, and places advertising for its clients (page 372)

advertising media the various forms of communication through which advertising reaches its audience (pages 367–368)

affirmative-action program a plan designed to increase the number of minority employees at all levels within an organization (page 44)

agency a business relationship in which one party (called the *principal*) appoints a second party (called the *agent*) to act on behalf of the principal (page 574)

agency shop a firm in which employees can choose not to join the union, but must pay dues to the union (page 267)

agent middleman a middleman that helps in the transfer of ownership of products, but does not take title to the products (page 339)

analytic skills the ability to identify the relevant issues or variables in a situation, determine how they are related, and assess their relative importance (page 130)

appellate court a court that hears cases which are appealed from lower courts (page 565)

arbitration the process in which a neutral third party hears the two sides of a dispute and renders a decision. The decision is binding when arbitration is part of the grievance procedure, but may not be binding when arbitration is used to settle labor-contract disputes (pages 269, 273)

arithmetic/logic unit the part of a computer that performs mathematical operations, comparisons of data, and other data transformations (page 545)

arithmetic mean of a set of data, the sum of all data values, divided by the number of items in the set (page 551)

assets the things of value that a firm owns (page 510)

authority the power needed to accomplish an assigned job or task within an organization (page 155)

automobile liability insurance insurance that covers financial losses resulting from injuries or damages brought about by the insured vehicle (page 488)

automobile physical damage insurance insurance that covers damage to the insured vehicle (page 489)

average *see* arithmetic mean

balance of payments the total flow of money into a country *less* the total flow of money out of the country, over some period of time (page 613)

balance of trade the total value of a nation's exports *less* the total value of its imports, over some period of time (page 613)

balance sheet *see* statement of financial position

bankruptcy a legal procedure designed to protect an individual or business that cannot meet its financial obligations, as well as the creditors involved (page 574)

bargaining unit the specific group of employees that a union represents (page 264)

barter system a system of exchange in which goods or services are traded directly for other goods or services (page 396)

behavior modification the use of a systematic program

of reinforcement to encourage desirable organizational behavior (page 219)

beneficiaries individuals or organizations named in a life-insurance policy as the recipients of the proceeds of the policy (page 493)

binding contract an agreement that requires a middleman to purchase products from a particular supplier, and not from the supplier's competitors (page 589)

blue-sky laws state laws that regulate securities trading (page 469)

board of directors the top governing body of a corporation, elected by the shareholders (page 73)

bond see corporate bond

bond indenture a legal document that details all the conditions relating to a bond issue (page 437)

bonus a payment in addition to wages, salary, or commissions, usually as an extra reward for job performance (page 242)

bookkeeping the routine, day-to-day recordkeeping that is a necessary part of accounting (page 508)

boycott a refusal to do business with a particular firm (page 272)

brand a name, term, symbol, or design—or any combination of these—that identifies a seller's products and distinguishes them from competitors' products (page 320)

brand advertising see selective advertising

brand mark the part of a brand that is a symbol or distinctive design (page 320)

brand name the part of a brand that can be spoken; it may include letters, words, numbers, and pronounceable symbols (page 320)

breach of contract the failure of one party to fulfill the terms of a contract when there is no legal reason for that failure (page 570)

breakeven quantity the number of units of a product which must be sold in order that the total revenue from all units sold is equal to the total cost of all units sold (page 328)

broker a sales agent (wholesaler) that specializes in a particular commodity (page 346)

budget a statement that projects income and/or expenditures over a specified future period (page 425)

budget deficit an excess of spending over income (page 597)

bureaucratic structure a management system based on a formal framework of authority that is carefully outlined and precisely followed (page 163)

business the organized effort of individuals to produce and sell, for a profit, the goods and services that satisfy society's needs (page 6)

business ethics the application of moral standards to business decisions and actions (page 52)

business interruption insurance insurance that provides protection for a business whose operations are interrupted because of fire, storm, or other natural disaster or a strike by its employees (page 492)

buying acquiring through the value of money; an exchange function of marketing that includes obtaining raw materials to make products, knowing how much merchandise to keep on hand, and selecting suppliers (page 289)

buying long buying a stock in the expectation that it will increase in value and can then be sold at a profit (page 459)

callable preferred stock preferred stock that a corporation may exchange, at the corporation's option, for a specified amount of money (page 436)

capacity the amount of input that a production facility can process or the amount of output it can produce in a given time (page 181)

capital/capital goods the materials, factories, machinery, and transportation equipment needed to create wealth; also the money needed to purchase these tools (page 10)

capital-intensive technology a technology in which machines and equipment do most of the work (page 182)

carriers firms that offer transportation services (page 354)

cash flow the movement of money into and out of an organization (page 423)

cash surrender value an amount that is payable to the holder of a whole life insurance policy if the policy is canceled (page 494)

catalog discount showrooms retail outlets that display well-known brands and sell them at discount prices through catalog sales within the store (page 349)

caveat emptor a Latin phrase meaning "let the buyer beware" (page 37)

cease and desist order an order to refrain from an illegal practice (page 590)

centralized organization an organization that systematically works to retain authority at the upper levels of management (page 156)

cents-off coupon a coupon that reduces the retail price of a particular item by a stated amount at the time of purchase (page 376)

certificate of deposit (CD) a document which specifies that a bank will pay a depositor a guaranteed interest rate for money left on deposit for a specified period of time (page 402)

certified public accountant (CPA) an individual who has met state requirements for accounting education and experience and has passed a rigorous three-day accounting examination (page 508)

chain of command the line of authority that extends from the highest to the lowest levels of an organization (page 147)

chain retailer a firm that operates more than one retail outlet (page 348)

channel of distribution a sequence of marketing organizations that directs a product from the producer to the ultimate user; also called a marketing channel (page 339)

check a written order for a bank or other financial institution to pay a stated dollar amount to the business or person indicated on the face of the check (page 401)

closed corporation *see* private corporation

closed shop a firm in which workers must join the union before they are hired; outlawed by the Taft-Hartley Act (page 267)

coinsurance clause a part of a fire-insurance policy that requires the policyholder to purchase coverage at least equal to a specific percentage of the replacement cost of the property in order to obtain full reimbursement for losses (page 487)

collateral real or personal property that a firm or individual owns and that is pledged as security for a loan (page 402)

collective bargaining the process of negotiating a labor contract with management (page 269)

commercial bank a profit-making organization that accepts deposits, makes loans, and provides other services to its customers (page 399)

commercial draft a written order requiring a customer (the drawee) to pay a specified sum of money to a supplier (the drawer) for goods or services (page 431)

commercial paper short-term promissory notes issued by large corporations (page 430)

commission a payment that is some percentage of sales revenue (page 242)

commission merchants wholesalers that carry merchandise and negotiate sales for manufacturers, but do not take title to the goods they sell (page 345)

common law the body of law created by the court decisions of judges (page 563)

common stock stock whose owners may vote on corporate matters, but whose claim on profit and assets is subsidiary to the claims of others (pages 73, 435)

community of interests the situation in which one firm buys the stock of a competing firm to reduce competition between the two (page 589)

comparative advantage the ability to produce a specific product more efficiently than other products (page 612)

compensation the payment that employees receive in return for their labor (page 240)

compensation system the policies and strategies that determine employee compensation (page 240)

competition a rivalry among businesses for sales to potential customers (page 6)

compressed workweek an arrangement whereby an employee works forty hours per week, but in fewer than the standard five days (page 160)

computer a machine that can accept, store, manipulate, and transmit data in accordance with a set of specific instructions (page 544)

computer network a system in which several computers can either function individually or communicate with each other (page 546)

conceptual skills the ability to think in abstract terms (page 129)

consideration the value or benefit that one party to a contract furnishes to another party (page 568)

consumer goods products purchased by individuals for personal consumption (page 24)

consumerism all activities intended to protect the rights of consumers in their dealings with business (page 41)

consumer product a good or service intended primarily for personal or household use (page 293)

consumers individuals who purchase goods or services for their own personal use rather than to resell them (page 7)

contract a legally enforceable agreement between two or more parties (either individuals or businesses) who promise to do or not to do a particular thing (page 568)

controlling the process of evaluating and regulating ongoing activities to ensure that goals are achieved (page 125)

control unit the part of a computer that guides the entire operation of the computer (page 545)

convenience goods those consumer goods that have a low unit price, are purchased frequently, and are purchased with a minimum of effort (page 293)

convenience store a small food store that sells a limited variety of products but offers extended business hours (page 350)

convertible bonds bonds that can be exchanged, at the owner's option, for a specified number of shares of the issuing corporation's common stock (page 439)

convertible preferred stock preferred stock that can be exchanged, at the stockholder's option, for a specified number of shares of common stock (page 436)

cooperative an association of individuals or firms for the purpose of performing some business function for all its members (page 81)

cooperative advertising advertising whose cost is shared by a producer and one or more local retailers (page 368)

copyright the exclusive right to publish, perform, copy, or sell an original work (page 572)

corporate bond a corporation's written pledge that it will repay a specified amount of money, with interest (page 437)

corporate charter a contract between a corporation and the state of incorporation, in which the state recognizes the formation of the artificial person that is the corporation (page 72)

corporate code of ethics a guide to acceptable and ethical behavior (page 53)

corporate culture the inner rites, rituals, heroes, and values of a firm (page 136)

corporation an artificial person created by law, with most of the legal rights of a real person, including the right to start and operate a business, to own or dispose of property, to borrow money, to sue or be sued, and to enter into binding contracts (page 70)

cost of goods sold the cost of the goods a firm has sold during an accounting period; equal to beginning inventory *plus* net purchases *less* ending inventory (page 520)

court of original jurisdiction the first court to recognize and hear testimony in a legal action (page 565)

courts of limited jurisdiction courts that hear only specific types of cases, such as small-claims courts (page 566)

craft union an organization of skilled workers in a single craft or trade (page 256)

creative selling determining customers' needs and matching products with those needs (page 374)

credit immediate purchasing power that is exchanged for a promise to repay it, with or without interest, at a later date, also, in accounting, a decrease in an asset account or an increase in a liability or owners' equity account (pages 408, 512)

credit union a financial institution that accepts deposits from, and lends money to, its members only (page 400)

crime a violation of a public law (page 564)

cumulative preferred stock preferred stock whose unpaid dividends accumulate and must all be paid before any cash dividend is paid to the holders of common stock (page 436)

currency devaluation the reduction of the value of a nation's currency relative to that of other countries (page 616)

current assets cash and other assets that can be quickly converted to cash or that will be used within one year (page 516)

current liabilities debts that will be repaid within one year (page 517)

current ratio the financial ratio computed by dividing current assets by current liabilities (page 525)

customs duty *see* import duty

damages a monetary settlement awarded to a party that is injured through breach of contract (page 570)

data numerical or verbal descriptions, usually resulting from measurements of some sort (page 537)

data processing the transformation of data into a form that is useful for a specific purpose (page 550)

debenture bonds bonds that are backed only by the reputation of the issuing corporation (page 438)

debit an increase in an asset account or a decrease in a liability or owners' equity account (page 512)

debt capital money obtained through loans of various types (page 427)

debt-to-assets ratio a financial ratio calculated by dividing total liabilities by total assets; it indicates the extent to which a firm's borrowing is backed by its assets (page 526)

debt-to-equity ratio a financial ratio calculated by dividing liabilities by owners' equity; it compares the amount of financing provided by creditors with the amount provided by owners (page 526)

decentralized organization an organization in which management consciously attempts to push authority down into the lower organizational levels (page 156)

decisional roles roles that involve various aspects of management decision making (page 130)

deed a written document by which the ownership of real property is transferred from one person or organization to another (page 572)

delegation of authority the assigning of a portion of a manager's work and power to a subordinate (page 155)

demand the quantity of a product that buyers are willing to purchase at each of various prices (pages 17, 325)

demand deposits amounts that are on deposit in checking accounts (page 399)

departmentalization the process of grouping jobs into manageable units according to some reasonable scheme (page 151)

departmentalization basis the scheme or criterion according to which jobs are grouped into units (page 151)

departmentalization by customer the grouping of activities according to the needs of various customer groups (page 153)

departmentalization by function the grouping together of all jobs that relate to the same organizational activity (page 153)

departmentalization by location the grouping of activities according to the geographic area in which they are performed (page 153)

departmentalization by product the grouping together of all activities related to a particular product or product group (page 153)

department store a retail store that employs 25 or more persons and sells at least home furnishings, appliances, family apparel, and household linens and dry goods, each in a different part of the store (page 348)

depreciation the process of apportioning the cost of a fixed asset over the period during which it will be used (page 516)

deregulation the process of removing existing regulations, forgoing proposed regulations, or reducing the rate at which new regulations are enacted (page 592)

design planning the development of a plan for converting a product idea into an actual commodity ready for marketing (page 180)

development *see* management development

diagnostic skills the ability to assess a particular situation and identify its causes (page 130)

direct-mail advertising promotional material that is mailed directly to individuals (page 369)

discharge the termination of a contract because one party refuses to fulfill a contractual obligation (page 570)

discount a deduction from the price of an item (page 331)

discount rate the interest rate that the Federal Reserve System charges for loans to member banks (page 405)

discount store self-service, general merchandise retail outlets that sell goods at lower than usual prices (page 348)

discretionary income disposable income *less* savings and expenditures on food, clothing, and housing (page 300)

disposable income personal income *less* all personal taxes levied by local, state, and federal governments (page 300)

dividends distributions of earnings to the stockholders of a corporation (page 434)

domestic corporation within any state, a corporation that is incorporated in that state (page 71)

domestic system a method of manufacturing in which an entrepreneur distributes raw materials to homes where families use these materials to manufacture finished goods (page 19)

door-to-door retailer a retailer that sells directly to consumers in their homes (page 350)

double-entry bookkeeping a system in which each financial transaction is recorded as two separate accounting entries, so as to maintain the balance shown in the accounting equation (page 510)

earnings per share a financial ratio calculated by dividing net income after taxes by the number of shares of common stock outstanding (page 524)

economic community an organization of nations formed to promote the free movement of resources and products among its members and to create common economic policies (page 619)

economic model of social responsibility the concept that society will benefit most when business is left alone to produce and market profitable products (page 38)

economics the study of how wealth is created and distributed (page 9)

economy the means by which a society answers the three economic questions—what, how, and for whom (page 9)

electronic funds transfer (EFT) system a means for performing financial transactions through a computer terminal or telephone hookup (page 402)

embargo a complete halt to trading with a particular nation or in a particular product (page 615)

employee benefits nonmonetary rewards provided to employees, consisting mainly of services paid for by employers and employee expenses reimbursed by employers (page 243)

employee training the process of teaching operating and technical employees how to do their present jobs more effectively and efficiently (page 244)

endorsement the payee's signature on the back of a negotiable instrument (page 573)

endowment life insurance life insurance that provides protection and guarantees the payment of a stated amount to the policyholder after a specified number of years (page 494)

entrepreneur a person who risks time, effort, and money to start and operate a business (page 7)

Environmental Protection Agency (EPA) the federal agency charged with the responsibility of enforcing laws concerning the environment (page 48)

Equal Employment Opportunity Commission (EEOC) a government agency that has the power to investigate complaints of discrimination and sue firms that practice discrimination in employment (page 46)

equity capital   money received from the sale of shares of ownership of a business (page 427)

equity theory   a theory of motivation based on the premise that people are motivated first to achieve and then to maintain a sense of equity (page 210)

esteem needs   the human requirements for respect and recognition as well as a sense of personal accomplishment and worth (page 208)

ethics   the study of right and wrong and of the morality of choices made by individuals (page 52)

exchange functions   buying and selling are the exchange functions of marketing (page 289)

excise tax   a tax on the manufacture or sale of a particular domestic product (page 601)

exclusive distribution   the use of only a single retail outlet in each geographic area (page 342)

expectancy theory   a complex model of motivation based on the assumption that motivation depends on how much a person wants something and how likely that person thinks he is of getting it (page 210)

Export-Import Bank of the United States (Eximbank)   an independent agency of the U.S. government whose function is to assist in financing the exports of American firms (page 629)

exporting   selling and shipping raw materials or products to other nations (page 613)

express warranty   a written explanation of the responsibilities of a producer or seller in the event a product is found to be defective or otherwise unsatisfactory (pages 323, 571)

extended coverage   insurance protection against damage caused by windstorm, hail, explosion, riots or civil commotion, aircraft, vehicles, and smoke; usually available as an addition to some other insurance policy (page 488)

external recruiting   the attempt to attract job applicants from outside an organization (page 235)

facilitating functions   financing, standardizing, grading, risk taking, and gathering market information are the facilitating functions of marketing (page 289)

factor (factoring company)   a firm that specializes in buying other firms' accounts receivable (page 433)

factors of production   land, labor, and capital (page 24)

factory system   the method of manufacturing in which all the materials, machinery, and workers required to manufacture a product are assembled in one place (page 20)

family branding   the strategy in which a firm uses the same brand for all or most of its products (page 322)

Federal Communications Commission (FCC)   the federal agency responsible for the supervision of interstate communications, including radio, television, telephone, and telegraph (page 591)

Federal Reserve System   the government agency responsible for regulating the banking industry (page 403)

Federal Trade Commission (FTC)   a five-member committee charged with investigating illegal trade practices and enforcing antitrust laws (page 589)

fidelity bond   an insurance policy that protects a business from theft, forgery, or embezzlement by its employees (page 488)

FIFO ("first in, first out")   the valuation of inventories under the assumption that the first goods purchased are the first to be sold or used (page 520)

financial management   all the activities concerned with obtaining and effectively using money (page 421)

financial managers   those managers whose primary responsibility is an organization's financial resources (page 127)

financial plan   a plan to obtain and use the money needed to implement an organization's goals (page 424)

financial ratio   a number that shows the relationship between two elements of a firm's financial statements (page 523)

financing   a facilitating function of marketing; borrowing from a bank or receiving credit from a supplier, manufacturer, or retailer (page 289)

fire insurance   insurance that covers losses due to fire (page 486)

fixed assets   assets that will be held or used for a period longer than one year (page 516)

fixed costs   costs incurred no matter how many units of a product are produced or sold (page 328)

flexible workweek   an arrangement in which each employee chooses the hours during which he or she will work, subject to certain limitations (page 160)

foreign corporation   within any state, a corporation that has been incorporated in some other state (page 72)

foreign-exchange control   a restriction on the amount of a particular foreign currency that can be purchased or sold (page 615)

form utility   utility created by converting production inputs to finished products (page 286)

franchise   a license to operate an individually owned business as though it were part of a chain of outlets or stores (page 102)

franchisee   the person or firm purchasing a franchise (page 104)

franchising the granting of a franchise; essentially a method of distributing goods or services (page 102)

franchisor the individual or firm granting a franchise (page 104)

free enterprise the system of business in which individuals are free to decide what to produce, how to produce it, and at what price to sell it (page 5)

free-market economy an economic system in which individuals and firms are free to enter and leave markets at will (page 10)

frequency distribution a listing of the number of times each value appears in a data set (page 550)

futures contract an agreement to buy or sell a commodity at a guaranteed price at some specified future date (page 459)

gathering market information a facilitating function of marketing; searching for comparative data necessary for use in making marketing decisions (page 289)

General Agreement on Tariffs and Trade (GATT) an international organization whose goal is to reduce or eliminate tariffs and other barriers to world trade (page 618)

general expenses costs incurred in managing a business; sometimes called administrative expenses (page 521)

general journal a book of original entry in which all transactions are recorded in order of occurrence (page 512)

general ledger a book of accounts that contains a separate sheet or section for each account (page 512)

general partner a person who assumes full co-ownership of a business; *compare* limited partner (page 67)

generic products ("brands") products with no brand at all (page 321)

goal an end state that an organization is expected to achieve (page 122)

goal setting the process of developing and committing an organization to a set of goals (page 122)

goodwill the value of a firm's reputation, location, earning capacity, and other intangibles that make the business a profitable concern (page 516)

government-owned corporation a corporation owned and operated by local, state, or federal government to provide a service that the business sector is reluctant or unable to offer (page 76)

grading a facilitating function of marketing; classifying products by size and quality, usually through a sorting process (page 289)

grapevine the informal communications network within an organization (page 166)

grievance procedure a formally established course of action for resolving employee complaints against management (page 268)

gross national product (GNP) the total value of all goods and services produced by a nation in a certain period of time, usually one year (page 24)

gross profit on sales net sales less the cost of goods sold (page 520)

gross sales the total dollar amount of all goods and services sold during an accounting period (page 518)

hard-core unemployed workers with little education or vocational training and a long history of unemployment (page 47)

hardware the electronic equipment or machinery used in a computer system (page 545)

hierarchy of needs Maslow's sequence of human needs in the order of their importance (page 207)

hourly wage a specific amount of money paid for each hour of work (page 242)

human-resource planning the development of strategies to meet a firm's future human-resource needs (page 231)

human resources management all the activities involved in acquiring, maintaining, and developing an organization's human resources (page 227)

hygiene factors job factors that decrease dissatisfaction when present to an acceptable degree, according to the motivation-hygiene theory, but do not necessarily result in high levels of motivation (page 209)

implied warranty a guarantee that is imposed or required by law (page 571)

import duty a tax on a particular foreign product entering a country (pages 601, 614)

importing purchasing raw materials or products in other nations and bringing them into one's own country (page 613)

import quota a limit on the amount of a particular good that may be imported during a given period of time (page 615)

income statement a summary of a firm's revenues and expenses during a specified accounting period (page 518)

incorporation the process of forming a corporation (page 70)

indemnity, principle of *see* principle of indemnity

independent retailer a firm that operates only one retail outlet (page 347)

individual branding the strategy in which a firm uses a different brand for each of its products (page 322)

industrial product a good or service intended primarily for use in producing other goods or services (page 294)

industrial union an organization of both skilled and unskilled workers in a single industry (page 259)

inflation a general rise in prices (page 23)

informal group a group created by the members themselves to accomplish goals that may or may not be relevant to the organization (page 165)

informal organization the pattern of behavior and interaction that stems from personal rather than official interrelationships (page 165)

information data presented in a form that is useful for a specific purpose (page 537)

informational roles the roles a manager assumes when gathering or providing information (page 131)

injunction a court order requiring a person or group either to perform or refrain from performing some act (page 262)

inland marine insurance insurance that protects against loss or damage to goods shipped by rail, truck, airplane, or inland barge (page 492)

input unit the device used to enter data into a computer (page 544)

inspection the examination of production output for the purpose of controlling quality (page 188)

institutional advertising advertising designed to enhance a firm's image or reputation (page 367)

insurable risks those risks that insurance companies will assume (page 481)

insurance the protection that is afforded by the purchase of an insurance policy (page 481)

insurance company see insurer

insurance policy a contract between an insurer and the person or firm whose risk it assumes (page 481)

insurer a firm that agrees, for a fee, to assume financial responsibility for losses that may result from a specific risk (page 480)

intangible assets assets that do not exist physically but that have a value based on legal rights or advantages that they provide to a firm (page 516)

intensive distribution the use of all available outlets for a product (page 342)

interlocking directorate the situation in which members of the board of directors of one firm are also directors of a competing firm (page 589)

internal recruiting considering present employees as applicants for available positions (page 235)

international business all business activities that involve exchanges across national boundaries (page 611)

International Monetary Fund (IMF) an international bank that makes short-term loans to countries experiencing balance-of-payments deficits (page 630)

interpersonal roles the roles a manager assumes when dealing with people (page 130)

interpersonal skills skills associated with the ability to deal effectively with other people, both inside and outside the organization (page 129)

Interstate Commerce Commission (ICC) the federal agency responsible for the licensing and supervision of interstate carriers (page 592)

inventories stocks of goods and materials (page 186)

inventory control the process of managing inventories to minimize inventory costs, including both holding costs and potential stock-out costs (pages 187, 352)

inventory turnover the number of times a firm sells and replaces its merchandise inventory in one year; it is approximated by dividing the cost of goods sold in one year by the average value of the inventory (page 526)

involuntary bankruptcy a bankruptcy procedure that is initiated by creditors (page 575)

job analysis a systematic procedure for studying jobs to determine their various elements and requirements (page 233)

job description a listing of the elements that make up a particular job (page 233)

job enlargement giving a worker more tasks to do within the same job (page 150)

job enrichment providing workers with both more tasks to do and more control over how they do their work, thereby increasing their sense of responsibility and providing motivating opportunities for growth and advancement (page 151)

job evaluation the process of determining the relative worth of the various jobs within a firm (page 241)

job rotation the systematic shifting of employees from one job to another (page 150)

job security protection against the loss of employment (page 267)

job sharing an arrangement whereby two people essentially share one full-time position (page 161)

job specialization see specialization

job specification a listing of the qualifications required to perform a particular job (page 233)

joint venture a partnership that is formed to accomplish a specific objective or to operate for a specific period of time (page 82)

jurisdiction the right of a particular union to organize particular workers (page 264)

labeling the presentation of information on a product or its package (page 323)

labor-intensive technology a technology that requires people to do the major portion of the work (page 182)

labor relations the dealings between labor unions and management, both in the bargaining process and beyond it; also called union-management relations (page 255)

labor union an organization of workers, acting together to negotiate their wages and working conditions with employers (page 255)

laissez-faire capitalism an economic system characterized by private ownership of property, free entry into markets, and the absence of government intervention (page 9)

laws the rules developed by a society to govern the conduct of, and relationships among, its members (page 563)

leading the process of influencing people to work toward a common goal (page 125)

lead time the time that elapses between the placement of an order and the receipt of the ordered material (page 186)

lease an agreement by which the right to use real property is temporarily transferred from its owner, the landlord, to a tenant (page 572)

leverage the use of borrowed funds to increase the return on an investment (page 459)

liabilities a firm's debts and obligations—what it owes to others (page 510)

licensing a contractual agreement in which one firm permits another to produce and market its product and use its brand, in return for a royalty or other compensation (page 621)

life insurance insurance that pays a stated amount of money upon the death of the insured individual (page 493)

LIFO ("last in, first out") the valuation of inventories under the assumption that the last goods purchased are the first to be sold or used (page 520)

limited liability the limitation of an owner's financial liability to the amount of money he or she has paid for a corporation's stock (page 74)

limited partner a person who contributes capital to a partnership but is not active in managing it; his or her liability is limited to the amount that has been invested (page 67)

limit order a request that a stock be bought or sold at a price that is equal to or better than some specified price (page 462)

line management position a position that is part of the chain of command and that includes direct responsibility for achieving the goals of the organization (page 158)

line of credit a loan that is approved before the money is actually needed (page 402)

liquidity the ease with which an asset can be converted to cash (page 514)

lockout refusal by management to allow employees to enter the workplace (page 272)

long-term financing money whose use will extend beyond one year (page 423)

long-term liabilities debts that need not be repaid for at least one year (page 517)

lower-level managers managers who coordinate and supervise the activities of operating employees (page 127)

mail-order retailer a retailer that solicits orders by mailing catalogs to potential customers (page 350)

maintenance shop a firm in which an employee who joins the union must remain a union member as long as he or she is employed by the firm (page 267)

management the process of coordinating the resources of an organization to achieve the primary goals of the organization (page 119)

management by objectives (MBO) a motivation technique in which a manager and his or her subordinates collaborate in setting goals (page 216)

management development the process of preparing managers and other professionals to take on increased responsibility in both present and future positions (page 244)

management ethics *see* business ethics

management excellence theory the point of view that promotes a feeling of excellence in employees (page 136)

management information system (MIS) a means of providing managers with the information they need to perform their functions as effectively as possible (page 541)

managerial hierarchy the arrangement that provides increasing authority at higher levels of management (page 161) manufacturer brand a brand owned by a manufacturer; also called producer brand (page 321)

manufacturer's sales branch a merchant wholesaler owned by a manufacturer (page 346)

manufacturer's sales office a sales agent owned by a manufacturer (page 346)

margin requirement the proportion of the price of a stock that cannot be borrowed (page 458)

marine insurance see inland marine insurance, ocean marine insurance

market people who have a need, along with money and the desire and authority to spend it on goods and services (page 291)

marketing the performance of business activities that direct the flow of goods and services from producer to consumer or user (page 285)

marketing channel see channel of distribution

marketing concept a total approach to marketing that includes the entire business organization in the process of satisfying customers' needs while achieving the organization's goals (page 288)

marketing information system a computer-based system for managing marketing information that is gathered from internal and external sources (page 289)

marketing intermediaries see middlemen

marketing managers those managers responsible for facilitating the exchange of products between the organization and its customers or clients (page 128)

marketing mix a combination of product, price, distribution, and promotion created to reach a particular target market (page 295)

marketing orientation see marketing concept

marketing plan an outline of actions intended to accomplish a specific set of marketing goals (page 296)

marketing program a set of strategies aimed at accomplishing a firm's marketing objectives (page 298)

marketing research the process of systematically gathering, recording, and analyzing data concerning a particular marketing problem (page 290)

market order a request that a stock be purchased or sold at the current market price (page 461)

market price in pure competition, the price at which the quantity demanded is exactly equal to the quantity supplied (page 17)

market segment a group of individuals or firms within a market that share one or more common characteristics (page 291)

market segmentation the process of dividing a market into market segments (page 291)

market value the price of one share of stock at a particular time, determined by the interaction of buyers and sellers in the various stock markets (page 454)

markup the amount that a seller adds to the cost of a product to determine its basic price (page 327)

materials handling the actual physical handling of goods, in warehousing as well as during transportation (page 354)

matrix structure the structure that results when product departmentalization is superimposed on a functionally departmentalized organization (page 163)

maturity date the date on which a corporation must repay money that it has borrowed by selling a bond (page 437)

measure of value a single standard or "yardstick" used to assign values to, and compare the values of, products and resources (page 396)

median of a set of data, the value that appears at the exact middle of the data when they are arranged in order from the highest value to the lowest (page 551)

mediation the use of a neutral third party to assist management and a union during negotiations (page 272)

medical insurance insurance that covers the cost of medical attention, including hospital care, physicians' and surgeons' fees, prescription medicines, and related services (page 492)

medium of exchange anything that is accepted as payment for products and resources (page 396)

memory unit the part of a computer that stores all data entered into and processed by the computer; also called storage unit (page 544)

merchant middleman a middleman that actually buys and then resells products (page 339)

merchant wholesaler a middleman that purchases goods in large quantities and then sells them to retailers, and institutional, farm, government, professional, or industrial users (page 345)

merger The purchase of one corporation by another (page 79)

middle managers managers who implement the strategy and major policies developed at the top level of the organization (page 127)

middleman's brand a brand that is owned by an individual wholesaler or retailer; also called a store brand (page 321)

middlemen marketing organizations that link producer and user within a marketing channel; they are, for the most part, concerned with the transfer of ownership of products rather than the physical movement of products; also called marketing intermediaries (page 339)

minority a group of people who have been singled out

on the basis of race, age, religion, sex, or national origin for prejudicial, selective, or unfavorable treatment (page 44)

mission   the means by which an organization fulfills its purpose (page 122)

missionary selling   personal selling in support of a customer's sales efforts (page 375)

mixed economy   an economy that contains elements of both capitalism and socialism (page 24)

mode   of a set of data, the value that appears most frequently (page 551)

money   anything used by a society to purchase goods and services or resources (page 396)

monopolistic competition   a market situation in which there are many buyers, along with relatively many sellers who differentiate their essentially similar products through minor differences in packaging, warranty, etc. (page 17)

monopoly   a market or industry with only one producer (page 18)

morale   an employee's attitude toward his or her job, superiors, and the firm (page 203)

mortgage bonds   corporate bonds secured by various assets of the issuing firm (page 439)

motivating   the process of providing reasons for people to work in the best interests of an organization (page 125)

motivation   the individual, internal process that energizes, directs, and sustains behavior; the personal "force" that causes a person to behave in a particular way (page 203)

motivation factors   job factors that increase motivation, but their absence does not necessarily result in dissatisfaction according to the motiviation-hygiene theory (page 209)

motivation-hygiene theory   the idea that satisfaction and dissatisfaction are separate and distinct dimensions (page 209)

multilateral development banks (MDBs)   internationally supported banks thtat provide loans to developing countries to assist in their growth (page 629)

multinational enterprise   a firm that operates on a world-wide scale, without practical ties to a specific nation or region (page 624)

multiple-unit pricing   the strategy of setting a single price for two or more units of a product (page 331)

mutual fund   a firm that combines and invests the funds of many individual investors, under the guidance of professional managers (page 456)

mutual insurance company   an insurance company owned by its policy holders and, thus, a cooperative (page 486)

mutual savings bank   a bank owned by its depositors (page 400)

National Alliance of Businessmen (NAB)   a joint business-government program to train the hard-core unemployed (page 47)

National Association of Securities Dealers (NASD)   the organization responsible for the self-regulation of the over-the-counter securities market (page 470)

national banks   commercial banks chartered by the U.S. Comptroller of the Currency (page 399)

National Labor Relations Board (NLRB)   the federal agency that enforces the provisions of the Wagner Act (page 262)

natural monopoly   an industry requiring huge investments in capital and for which duplication of facilities would be wasteful and, thus, not in the public interest (pages 18–19, 591)

needs   personal requirements, either physiological or psychological in nature (page 207)

negligence   a failure to exercise reasonable care, resulting in injury (page 565)

negotiable instrument   a written document that (1) is a promise to pay a stated sum of money and (2) may be transferred from one person or firm to another (page 573)

negotiable order of withdrawal   see NOW account

net income   the profit earned (or the loss incurred) by a firm during an accounting period, after all expenses (page 521)

net profit margin   a financial ratio calculated by dividing net income after taxes by net sales (page 524)

net sales   the actual dollar amount received by a firm for the goods and services it has sold, after adjustment for returns, allowances, and discounts (page 520)

no-fault automobile insurance   a method of paying for losses suffered in an automobile accident; it is enacted by state law and requires that those suffering injury or loss be reimbursed by their own insurance companies, without regard for who was at fault in the accident (page 490)

not-for-profit corporation   a corporation organized to provide a social, educational, religious, or other non-business service rather than to earn a profit (page 77)

notes payable   obligations that have been secured with promissory notes (page 517)

NOW account   an interest-bearing checking account;

NOW stands for negotiable order of withdrawal (page 401)

objectives   specific statements detailing what an organization intends to accomplish as it goes about fulfilling its mission (page 122)

ocean marine insurance   insurance that protects the policyholder against loss or damage to a ship or its cargo on the high seas (page 492)

odd lot   fewer than 100 shares of a particular stock (page 462)

odd pricing   the strategy of setting prices at odd amounts that are slightly below a whole or even number of dollars (page 331)

oligopoly   a market situation (or industry) in which there are few sellers (page 18)

open corporation   *see* public corporation

open-market operations   the buying and selling of U.S. government bonds by the Federal Reserve System, to control the supply of money (page 405)

operating expenses   costs that do not result directly from a firm's purchase or manufacture of the products it sells (page 521)

operational planning   the development of plans for the utilization of production facilities (page 183)

operations management   all the activities that managers engage in to create goods and services (page 174)

operations managers   those people who create and manage systems that convert resources into goods and services (page 128)

option   the right to buy or sell a specified amount of stock at a specified price within a certain period of time (page 460)

order processing   those activities involved in receiving and filling customers' purchase orders (page 353)

order taking   processing the purchases of customers who have essentially decided what they wish to buy (page 374)

organic structure   a management system founded on cooperation and knowledge-based authority (page 163)

organization   a group of two or more people working together in a predetermined fashion to achieve a common set of goals (page 145)

organizational height   the number of layers, or levels, of management in a firm; a *tall* organization has many layers of management; a *flat* organization has few layers of management (page 158)

organizational structure   a fixed pattern of (1) positions within the organization and (2) relationships among those positions (page 146)

organization chart   a diagram that represents the positions and relationships within an organization (page 146)

organizing   the process of grouping resources and activities to accomplish some end result in an efficient and effective manner (pages 124, 146)

orientation   the process of acquainting new employees with the organization (page 239)

outdoor advertising   short promotional messages on billboards, posters, signs, and in skywriting (page 369)

output unit   the mechanism by which a computer transmits processed data to the user (page 545)

over-the-counter (OTC) market   a network of stock brokers who buy and sell the securities of corporations that are not listed on a securities exchange (page 461)

overtime   time worked in excess of forty hours in one week (page 267)

owners' equity   the difference between a firm's assets and liabilities (page 510)

packaging   all those activities involved in developing a container for a product (page 322)

participating preferred stock   preferred stock whose owners share in the corporation's earnings, along with owners of common stock (page 436)

partnership   an association of two or more persons to act as co-owners of a business for profit (page 66)

par value   an assigned (and often arbitrary) dollar value that is printed on a stock certificate (page 436)

patent   the exclusive right to make, use, or sell a newly invented product or process (page 572)

penetration pricing   the strategy of setting a very low price for a new product (page 330)

performance   the fulfillment of all obligations by all parties to a contract (page 570)

performance appraisal   the evaluation of employees' current and potential levels of performance within a firm (page 245)

personal income   the income an individual receives from all sources *less* social security taxes (page 300)

personal investment   the use of one's personal funds to earn a financial return (page 449)

personal property   all property other than real property (page 571)

personal selling   the presentation of a promotional message through direct personal communication (page 373)

personnel managers   the people charged with managing an organization's formal human-resources programs (page 128)

PERT (Program Evaluation and Review Technique)   a

technique for scheduling a process or project and maintaining control of the schedule (page 187)

physical distribution all those activities concerned with the efficient movement of products from the producer to the ultimate user (page 352)

physical distribution functions transportation and storage are the physical distribution functions of marketing (page 289)

physiological needs a human's requirements for survival and biological functioning (page 208)

picketing the marching back and forth by strikers in front of their place of employment with signs informing the public that a strike is in progress (page 271)

piece-rate system a system under which employees are paid a certain amount for each unit of output they produce (page 205)

place utility utility created by making a product available at a location where customers wish to purchase it (page 286)

plan an outline for actions intended to accomplish the goals of an organization (page 123)

planned economy an economy in which the answers to the three basic economic questions (what, how, and for whom) are determined, to some degree, through centralized government planning (page 12)

planning the processes involved in developing plans (page 123)

planning horizon the time period over which a plan will be in effect (page 183)

plant layout the arrangement of machinery, equipment, and personnel within a facility (page 182)

point-of-purchase display promotional material that is placed within a retail store (page 377)

policy a general guide for action in a situation that occurs repeatedly (page 124)

pollution the contamination of water, air, or land through the actions of people in an industrialized society (page 47)

positioning the development of an image for a product, relative to competing products (page 379)

possession utility utility created by transferring title (or ownership) of a product to the buyer (page 286)

posting the process of transferring journal entries to the general ledger (page 512)

power of attorney a legal document which serves as evidence that an agent has been appointed to act on behalf of a principal (page 574)

pre-emptive rights the rights of current stockholders to purchase any new stock that the corporation issues, before it is sold to the general public (page 435)

preferred stock stock whose owners usually do not have voting rights, but whose claim on profit and assets has precedence over that of common stock owners (pages 73, 436)

premium the annual fee charged by an insurance company; also, a gift that is offered by a producer in return for using its product (pages 377, 481)

prepaid expenses assets that have been paid for in advance but not yet used (page 516)

prestige pricing the strategy of setting a very high price to project the image of quality and status (page 331)

price the amount of money a seller is willing to accept in exchange for his product, at a given time and under given circumstances (page 324)

price discrimination the practice in which producers and wholesalers charge larger firms a lower price for goods than smaller firms (page 589)

price lining the strategy of selling goods only at certain predetermined prices to eliminate minor price differences from the buying decision (page 331)

price skimming the strategy of charging the highest possible price for a product during the introductory stage of its life cycle (page 330)

primary-demand advertising advertising whose purpose is to increase the demand for all brands of a good or service (page 367)

prime interest rate the lowest rate charged by a bank for a short-term loan (page 429)

principle of indemnity in the event of a loss, an insured firm or individual cannot collect from the insurer an amount greater than the actual dollar amount of the loss (page 482)

private accountant an accountant employed by a specific organization (page 508)

private corporation a corporation whose stock is owned by relatively few people and is not traded openly in stock markets; also called a closed corporation (page 70)

private law the body of law that governs the relationships between two or more individuals or businesses (page 564)

producer brand see manufacturer brand

product everything that one receives in an exchange, including all tangible and intangible attributes and expected benefits (page 313)

product design the process of creating a set of specifications from which a product can be produced (page 181)

product differentiation the process of developing and

promoting differences between one firm's product and all similar products (page 326)

production the process of converting resources into goods and services (page 175)

productivity the average output per hour for all workers in the private business sector (pages 134, 189)

product liability insurance insurance that protects the policyholder from financial losses due to injuries suffered by others, as a result of the use of the policyholder's products (page 490)

product life cycle a series of stages in which a product's sales revenue and profit increase, reach a peak, and then decline (page 315)

product line a group of similar products, differing only in relatively minor characteristics (pages 180, 314)

product mix all the products that a firm offers for sale (page 314)

profit the amount of money that remains after all business expenses have been deducted from sales revenue (page 8)

profit sharing the distribution of a percentage of a firm's profit among employees (page 242)

progressive tax a tax that requires the payment of an increasing proportion of income as the individual's income increases (page 598)

promissory note a written pledge by a borrower to pay a certain sum of money to a creditor at a specified future date (page 429)

promotion communication intended to inform, persuade, or remind an organization's target markets (page 365)

promotional campaign a plan for combining and using the various promotion methods to reach one or more marketing goals (page 378)

promotional mix the particular combination of promotion methods a firm uses to reach a target market (page 365)

property anything that can be owned (page 571)

prospectus a detailed written description of a new security, the issuing corporation, and the corporation's top management (page 468)

proxy a legal form that lists issues to be decided at a stockholders' meeting and requests that stockholders transfer their voting rights to some other individual or individuals (page 73)

public accountant an accountant whose services may be hired by individuals or firms (page 508)

public corporation a corporation whose stock is traded openly in stock markets and may be purchased by any individual; also called an open corporation (page 70)

publicity information about a company, its employees, or its products published or broadcast in the mass media (page 377)

public law the body of law that deals with the relationships between individuals or businesses and society (page 564)

public liability insurance insurance that protects the policyholder from financial losses due to injuries suffered by others, as a result of negligence on the part of a business owner or employee (page 490)

public relations all activities whose objective is to create and maintain a favorable public image (page 378)

pull strategy a promotional strategy intended to create consumer demand for a product (pages 381–382)

purchasing all those activities involved in obtaining required materials, supplies, and parts from other firms (page 185)

pure competition the market situation in which there are many buyers and sellers of a product, and no buyer or seller is powerful enough to affect the price of that product (page 15)

pure risk a risk that involves only the possibility of loss, with no potential for gain (page 478)

purpose the reason for an organization's existence (page 122)

push strategy a promotional strategy in which a firm promotes its products to the next marketing organization along the channel of distribution (page 382)

quality circle a group of employees who meet periodically, on company time, to solve problems relating to product quality (page 191)

quality control the process of ensuring that goods and services are produced in accordance with product-design specifications that reflect an organization's goals and strategies regarding quality (page 188)

quasigovernment corporation a business owned partly by the government and partly by private citizens or firms (page 77)

range the difference between the highest and lowest values in a set of data (page 551)

ratification approval of a contract by a vote of the union membership; the final step in collective bargaining (page 270)

real property land and anything that is permanently attached to it (page 571)

recruiting the process of attracting qualified job applicants (page 233) refund   a return of part of the purchase price of a product (page 376)

regressive tax   a tax that takes a greater percentage of a lower income than of a higher income, such as a sales tax (page 602)

reinforcement theory   the theory of motivation based on the premise that behavior that is rewarded is likely to be repeated, whereas behavior that is punished is less likely to be repeated (page 211)

replacement chart   a list of key personnel along with possible replacements within the firm (page 232)

research and development   an organized set of activities intended to identify new ideas and technical advances that have the potential to result in new goods and services (page 177)

reserve requirement   the percentage of its deposits that a bank must retain, either in its own vault or on deposit with its Federal Reserve District Bank (page 404)

responsibility   the duty to do a job or perform a task (page 155)

retailer   a middleman that buys from producers or other middlemen and sells to consumers (page 341)

retained earnings   the portion of a corporation's profits that is not distributed to stockholders (page 436)

return on equity   a financial ratio calculated by dividing net income after taxes by owners' equity (page 524)

revenues   dollar amounts received by a firm (page 518)

revolving credit agreement   a guaranteed line of credit (page 430)

reward system   an organization's formal mechanism for defining, evaluating, and rewarding employee performance (page 214)

risk   the possibility that a loss or injury will occur (page 477)

risk management   the process of evaluating the risks faced by a firm or an individual, and then minimizing the costs involved with those risks (page 478)

risk taking   a facilitating function of marketing; encountering possibilities of loss not prevented by management and insurance (page 289)

round lot   a unit of 100 shares of a particular stock (page 462)

safety needs   a human's requirements for physical and emotional security (page 208)

salary   a specific amount of money paid for an employee's work during a set calendar period, regardless of the actual number of hours worked (page 242)

sales agreement   a special but very common type of contract by which ownership is transferred from a seller to a buyer (page 571)

sales promotion   those marketing activities, other than personal selling, advertising, and publicity, that stimulate consumer purchasing and dealer effectiveness (page 376)

sample   a free package or container of a product (page 377)

savings and loan association   a financial institution that primarily accepts savings deposits and provides home-mortgage loans (page 399)

scheduling   in operations control, the process of ensuring that materials are at the right place at the right time (page 187)

scientific management   the application of scientific principles to the management of work and workers (page 204)

S-corporation   a corporation that is taxed as though it were a partnership; specific restrictions limit S-corporation status; formerly called subchapter-S corporation (page 78)

Securities and Exchange Commission (SEC)   the agency that enforces federal securities regulations (page 469)

securities exchange   a marketplace where member brokers meet to buy and sell securities (page 461)

selection   the process of gathering information about applicants for a position, and then using that information to choose the most appropriate applicant (page 236)

selective advertising   advertising used to sell a particular brand of product; also called brand advertising (page 365)

selective distribution   the use of only a portion of the available outlets in each geographic area (page 342)

self-insurance   the process of establishing a monetary fund that can be used to cover the cost of a loss (page 480)

self-realization needs   the human requirements for personal growth and development (page 208)

selling   an exchange function of marketing; creating ownership utility through the transfer of title from seller to customer (page 289)

selling expenses   costs related to a firm's marketing activities (page 521)

selling short   the process of selling stock that an investor does not actually own, but has borrowed from a stock broker and will repay at a later date (page 459)

seniority   the length of time an employee has worked for an organization (page 267)

serial bonds   bonds of a single issue that mature on different dates (page 438)

Service Corps of Retired Executives (SCORE)   a group of retired business people who volunteer their services to small businesses through the Small Business Administration (page 99)

service economy an economy in which more effort is devoted to the production of services than to the production of goods (page 176)

shopping goods those consumer goods that have a relatively high unit price, are purchased infrequently, and are usually purchased only after comparison with competing products (page 293)

shop steward an employee who is elected by union members to serve as their representative (page 269)

short-term financing money that will be used for a period of one year or less, and then repaid (page 422)

sinking fund a sum of money to which deposits are made each year, for the purpose of redeeming a bond issue (page 438)

skills inventory a computerized data bank containing information regarding the skills and experience of all present employees within an organization (page 232)

slowdown a job action in which workers report to their jobs but work at a slower pace than normal (page 272)

small business a business that is independently owned and operated for profit and is not dominant in its field (page 89)

Small Business Administration (SBA) a government agency created to assist, counsel, and protect the interests of small businesses in the United States (page 89)

Small Business Development Centers (SBDCs) university-based groups that provide individual counseling and practical training to owners of small businesses (page 100)

Small Business Institute (SBI) a group of senior and graduate business administration students who provide management counseling to small businesses, under the guidance of a faculty advisor (page 100)

Small Business Investment Companies (SBICs) privately owned firms that provide venture capital to small enterprises which meet their investment criteria (page 101)

social audit a comprehensive report of what an organization has done and is doing with regard to social issues that affect it (page 55)

social needs the human requirements for love and affection and a sense of belonging (page 208)

social responsibility the recognition that business activities have an impact on society, and the consideration of that impact in business decision making (page 35)

socioeconomic model of social responsibility the concept that business should emphasize not only profits,

but also the impact of its decisions on society (page 38)

software the set of instructions that tells a computer what to do (page 545)

sole proprietorship a business that is owned (and usually operated) by one person (page 63)

span of management the number of subordinates who report directly to one manager; also called span of control (pages 156–157)

specialization (of labor) the separation of a manufacturing process into distinct tasks, and the assignment of different tasks to different individuals (pages 21, 148)

specialty goods those consumer goods for which buyers have a strong personal preference, so that price is not a major purchase consideration; these goods are purchased infrequently and often require extra purchase effort from the consumer (page 293–294)

specialty store a retail outlet that sells a single category of merchandise (page 349)

specific performance the legal requirement that the parties to a contract fulfill their obligations according to the contract (page 570)

speculative investment an investment made in the hope of earning a relatively large profit in a short time (page 458)

speculative production the manufacture of goods before orders have been received (page 422)

speculative risk the risk that accompanies the possibility of earning a profit (page 478)

spot trading the buying and selling of commodities for immediate delivery (page 459)

staff position a position created to provide support, advice, and expertise within an organization (page 158)

standardizing a facilitating function of marketing; setting uniform specifications for products or services (page 289)

standard of living a subjective measure of how well off an individual or a society is, mainly in terms of want satisfaction through goods and services (page 23)

standard operating procedure (SOP) a plan that outlines the steps to be taken in a repetitive situation (page 124)

standing committee a relatively permanent committee charged with the performance of some recurring task (page 161)

state banks commercial banks chartered by the banking authorities in the states in which they operate (page 399)

statement of financial position a summary of a firm's accounts at a particular time, showing the various dollar amounts that enter into the accounting equation; also called a balance sheet (page 514)

statistic a measure of a particular characteristic of a group of numbers (page 550)

statute a law that is passed by the U.S. Congress, a state legislature, or a local government (page 564)

statutory law all the laws that have been enacted by legislative bodies (page 564)

stock the shares of ownership of a corporation (page 70)

stock average *see* stock index

stock broker *see* account executive

stock dividend a dividend in the form of additional stock paid to shareholders in proportion to the number of shares they own (page 454)

stockholders the people who own a corporation's stock and who thus own the corporation; also called shareholders (page 70)

stock index an average of the current market prices of selected stocks (page 468)

stock insurance company an insurance company owned by stockholders and operated to earn a profit (pages 485–486)

stock split a division of each outstanding share of a corporation's stock into a greater number of shares (page 455)

storage unit *see* memory unit

store brand *see* middleman's brand

store of value a means for retaining and accumulating wealth (page 397)

storing a physical distribution function of marketing; housing goods in order to sell them at the best selling time (page 289)

strategy an organization's broadest set of plans, developed as a guide for major policy- and decision-making; it defines what business the company is in or wants to be in, and the kind of company it is or wants to be (page 123)

strict product liability the legal concept that holds a manufacturer responsible for injuries caused by its products even if it was not negligent (page 565)

strike a temporary work stoppage by employees to add force to their demands (page 258)

strikebreakers non-union employees who perform the jobs of striking union members (page 272)

subchapter-S corporation *see* S-corporation

supermarket a large self-service store that sells primarily food and household products (page 349)

supply the quantity of a product that producers are willing to sell at each of various prices (pages 16, 324)

syndicate a temporary association of individuals or firms organized to perform a specific task that requires a large amount of capital (page 82)

tabular display an array of verbal or numerical information in columns and rows (page 552)

tactical plans small-scale, short-range plans developed to implement a strategy (page 124)

target market a market segment toward which a firm directs its marketing effort (page 292)

tariff *see* import duty

task force a committee established to investigate a major problem or pending decision (page 161)

technical skills specific skills needed to accomplish specialized activities (page 129)

technology a process used by a firm to transform input resources into output goods or services (page 175)

term life insurance life insurance that provides protection to beneficiaries for a stated period of time, but includes no other benefits (page 494)

term-loan agreement a promissory note that requires a borrower to repay a loan in monthly, quarterly, semiannual, or annual installments (page 439)

Theory X a set of assumptions regarding employee motivation that are generally consistent with Taylor's scientific management (page 206)

Theory Y a set of assumptions regarding employee motivation that are generally consistent with the concepts of the human-relations movement (page 207)

Theory Z the belief that some combination of Ouchi's Type A and Type J practices is best for American business (page 135)

time deposits amounts that are on deposit in interest-bearing savings accounts (page 399)

time utility utility created by making a product available when customers wish to purchase it (page 286)

top managers the small group of upper-level executives who guide and control the overall fortunes of an organization (page 127)

tort a violation of a private law (page 564)

total cost the sum of variable costs and fixed costs (page 329)

total revenue the total amount received from sales of a product (page 328)

trade credit a payment delay granted by a firm to its customers (page 429)

trade deficit an unfavorable, or negative, balance of trade (page 613)

trademark a brand that is registered with the U.S. Patent and Trademark Office and thus is legally protected from use by anyone except its owner (pages 321, 571)

trade show an industry-wide exhibit at which many sellers display their products (page 377)

trading stamps stamps that are given out by retailers in proportion to the amount spent, and that are redeemable for gifts (page 377)

training *see* employee training

transportation the shipment of products to customers (page 354)

transporting a physical distribution function of marketing; selecting and using a mode of transport that provides an acceptable speed of delivery at an acceptable price (page 289)

trial balance a summary of the balances of all ledger accounts at the end of the accounting period (page 513)

trust a business combination that is created when one firm obtains control of competing firms by purchasing their stock (page 587)

trustee an independent firm or individual that acts as representative for bond owners (page 438)

tying agreement a contract that forces a middleman to purchase unwanted products along with the products it actually wishes to buy (page 589)

Uniform Commercial Code (UCC) a set of statutory laws designed to eliminate differences in state regulations affecting business and to simplify interstate commerce (page 564)

uninsurable risks risks that insurance firms will not assume (page 482)

union-management relations the dealings between labor unions and management, both in the bargaining process and beyond it; also called labor relations (page 255)

union security the protection of a union's position as employees' bargaining agent (page 267)

union shop a firm whose new employees need not be union members, but must join the union after a specified probationary period (pages 263, 267)

universal life insurance life insurance that provides protection and offers a tax-deferred savings account that pays a flexible interest rate (page 495)

unlimited liability a legal concept that holds a sole proprietor personally responsible for all the debts of his or her business (page 65)

unsecured financing financing not backed by collateral (page 429)

usury the practice of charging interest in excess of the maximum legal rate (page 569)

utility the power of a good or service to satisfy a human need (page 286)

variable costs costs that depend on the number of units produced (pages 328–329)

venture capital money invested in small (and sometimes struggling) firms that have the potential to become very successful (page 101)

visual display a diagram that represents several items of information in a manner that facilitates comparisons or conveys trends among the items, such as a graph, bar chart, or pie chart (page 551)

voluntary agreement a contract requirement consisting of an *offer* by one party to enter into a contract with a second party and an *acceptance* by the second party of all the terms and conditions of the offer (page 568)

voluntary bankruptcy a bankruptcy procedure initiated by an individual or business that can no longer meet its financial obligations (page 515)

wage survey a collection of data on prevailing wage rates within an industry or a geographic area (page 241)

warehouse stores minimal-service retail food outlets (page 350)

warehousing those activities involved in receiving and storing goods and preparing them for re-shipment (page 353)

warranty *see* express warranty, implied warranty

whistle blowing the act in which an employee informs the press or government officials of his or her firm's unethical practices (page 53)

whole life insurance life insurance that provides both protection and savings (page 494)

wholesaler a middleman that sells products to other firms (page 341)

wildcat strike a strike that has not been approved by the union (page 272)

worker's compensation insurance insurance that covers medical expenses and provides salary continuation for employees injured at work; it also pays benefits to the dependents of workers who are killed on the job (page 492)

working capital the difference between current assets and current liabilities (page 524)

zero-base budgeting a budgeting approach in which every expense must be justified in every budget (page 426)

Index of Names

Index of Subjects

Federal Savings and Loan Insurance Corporation (FSLIC), 407–408
Federal Securities Act (1964), 470
Federal Trade Commission (FTC), 589–590
Federal Trade Commission Act (1914), 589–590
Federal Unemployment Tax Act (FUTA), 601
FICA, *see* Federal Insurance Contributions Act
Fidelity bond, 488
FIFO (first-in, first-out), 520
Figurehead, manager as, 130–131
Financial aid, from wholesalers, 343
Financial information, 464, 539
   in brokerage firm reports, 467–468
   in business periodicals, 468
   in corporate reports, 468
   from investors' services, 468
   from newspapers, 464–467
   from stock averages, 468–469
Financial institutions, 399–401
   deregulation and, 454
   FDIC and FSLIC and, 407–408
   international business and, 629–630
   open-market operations and, 405
   services provided by, 401–403
Financial management
   definition of, 421–422
   financial plan and, 424–428
   monitoring and evaluating performance and, 428
   need for, 424
Financial managers, 127–128
   information used by, 539
Financial plan, 424–425
   budgeting and, 425–426
   objectives and, 425
   sources of funds and, 426–428
Financial ratios, 523
   long-term, 526–527
   profitability, 523–524
   short-term, 524–526
Financial resources, 7, 119–120
Financial statements, 468, 507. *See also* Balance sheet; Income statement; Statement of financial position
   analyzing, 522–523
   preparation of, 513
Financing
   debt, 437–439
   equity, 434–437
   international business and, 627–630
   long-term, 423–424, 433–439
   need for, 422–424
   secured, 431–432
   short-term, 422–423, 429–433
   unsecured, 429–431
Fire insurance, 486–488
Fixed assets, 516
Fixed costs, 328

Fixed-rate system, 215
Flexibility, of sole proprietorship, 64
Flexible time, 161
Floppy disks, 548, 549, 549 (illus.)
F.O.B. (free-on-board) destination basis, 573
F.O.B. (free-on-board) point of origin basis, 331, 573
Follow-up
   in operations control, 187
   on sale, 376
Foreign corporation, 72. *See also* International business
Foreign Corrupt Practices Act (1977), 52
Foreign-exchange control, 615–616
Formation
   of corporation, 70–73, 75–76
   of partnership, 69
   of sole proprietorship, 64
Form utility, 286
Franchise, definition of, 102
Franchisee, 104
   advantages to, 107
   disadvantages to, 107
Franchise fee, 107
Franchising, 102–104
   advantages of, 106–107
   disadvantages of, 107
   growth of, 104–105
   real estate industry and, 105
   success of, 105–106
Franchisor, 104
   advantages to, 106–107
   disadvantages to, 107
Free enterprise, 5–6
   competition and, 6
Free-market economy, *see* Laissez-faire capitalism
Free Trade Zone (FTZ), 623
Freight forwarders, 355
Frequency distribution, 550
FSLIC, *see* Federal Savings and Loan Insurance Corporation
FTC, *see* Federal Trade Commission
FTZ, *see* Free Trade Zone
Full-service brokers, 462
Function, departmentalization by, 153
Functional authority, 159
Funds
   income, 458
   sources of, 426–428
   uses of, 430
Furniture, as asset, 516
FUTA, *see* Federal Unemployment Tax Act
Futures contract, 459

General Agreement on Tariffs and Trade (GATT), 618–619
General expenses, 521
General journal, 512

General ledger, 512
General managers, 128
General partners, 67
Generic products, 321
   price and, 17
Goal(s), 122
   career, 641
   conflicting, 123
Goal setting
   in management by objectives, 217–218
   as management function, 122–123
Good(s), 313
   available for sale, 520
   consumer, 24
   convenience, 293–294
   distribution of, 12
   durable, 300
   shopping, 293–294
   specialty, 293–294
Goodwill, as asset, 516–517
Government. *See also* Tax(es)
   in American business system, 26–27
   cost of pollution control and, 50–52
   as customer, 587
   information and assistance provided by, 585–586
   involvement in business, 23
   research funded by, 586–587
   role in laissez-faire capitalism, 10–11
   services provided by, 26–27
   in socialist economy, 12
   as user of accounting information, 510
Government-owned corporations, 76–77
Government regulation
   affirmative action and, 46–47
   of corporations, 76
   cost of marketing and, 298
   deregulation and, 592, 594–596
   to encourage competition, 587–591
   environmental, 48 (table), 48–50
   of monopolies, 18–19, 591–592
   since 1960, 43 (table)
   before 1930s, 37, 37 (table)
   since 1930, 43 (table), 44
   productivity and, 191
   product safety and, 41
   under Roosevelt, 37
   of securities trading, 469–470
Grapevine, 166
Graph, 551
Great Depression, 23
Grievance procedures, 268–269
Gross national product, 23–24
Group(s), informal, 165–166
Growth
   corporate, *see* Corporate growth
   of franchise, 104–105
   personal investment and, 452–453
Growth funds, 458
Growth-income funds, 458

Loan(s). *See also* Borrowing; Financing
  to business, 395
  credit history and, 412
  guaranteed by SBA, 101
  to individuals, 395
  long-term, 402, 439
  from personal finance company, 412
  to poorer countries, 395
  short-term, 402
  sole proprietorship and, 65
  unsecured, 429–430
  from wholesalers, 343
Local time, 371
Location
  business failures and, 95
  departmentalization by, 153
  incorporation and, 70–72
Lockout, 272
Loss, 8

Magazines, 368–369
Magnetic tapes, 548, 549, 549 (illus.)
Mail-order retailer, 350
Mainframe computer, 546
Maintenance shop, 267
Major medical insurance, 492
Maker, of note, 429
Maloney Act (1938), 470
Malpractice insurance, 490
Management, 22, 119–120
  areas of, 127–128
  attitudes toward affirmative action, 46–47
  attitudes toward social responsibility, 38, 40–41
  business failures and, 89
  commitment to social responsibility program, 55
  cooperation with unions to improve productivity, 191
  courses and workshops on, 99
  definition of, 119
  disagreements of partners regarding, 69
  Japanese, 134–135
  levels of, 127
  of productivity, 189–191
  proxy fight and, 73
  rights of, 267–268
  role in management by objectives, 217
  span of, 148, 156–158, 163
  during strike, 272
  telecommuting and, 162
  weapons against unions, 272
Management by objectives (MBO), 217–218
Management development, 244
Management ethics, *see* Business ethics
Management excellence, 136–137
Management functions, 121–122
  controlling as, 125–126

goal setting as, 122–123, 217–218
leading and motivating as, 125, 131. *See also* Motivation
organizing as, 124–125
planning as, 123–124
Management information
  by area, 539
  by level, 539–541
Management information system (MIS), 541–542
  cautions in collecting data for, 548
  computers and, 543–547
  external sources of data and, 548
  functions of, 542
  internal sources of data and, 547–548
  presenting information and, 551–552
  processing data and, 550–551
  size and complexity of, 542–543
  storing and updating data in, 548–550
Management skills
  analytic, 130
  business failures and, 94–95
  conceptual, 129
  in corporation, 75
  diagnostic, 130
  of entrepreneur, 93
  franchisor support for, 107
  interpersonal, 129–130
  in partnership, 69
  in small business, 98
  in sole proprietorship, 65–66
  technical, 129
Management theory
  corporate culture and, 136
  management excellence and, 136–137
  theories X and Y and, 206–207
  theory Z and, 134–135
Management training programs, 134
Manager(s)
  activities of, 121
  administrative, 128, 539
  assessment centers for selection of, 239
  on board of directors, 74
  communication by, 537
  decentralization of authority and, 156
  decisional roles of, 130
  delegation of authority by, 155–156
  employee creativity and, 206
  financial, 127–128
  informational roles of, 131
  information requirements of, 508–509, 538–541
  interpersonal roles of, 130–131
  marketing, 128
  operations, 128
  personnel, 128
  of project, 163
  sources of, 131–134, 232

subordinates' performance appraisal of, 133
top, middle, and lower-level, 127
treatment of grapevine by, 166
Managerial hierarchy, 161
Managerial roles
  decisional, 130
  informational, 131
  interpersonal, 130–131
Manufacturer(s), 7
  wholesalers' services to, 343–345
Manufacturer brand, 321
Manufacturer's agents, 346
Manufacturer's sales branch, 346
Manufacturer's sales office, 346–347
Manufacturing, guidelines to smallness for, 89
Margin requirements, 406–407, 458
Marine insurance, 491–492
Market(s), 290–291
  competitive, 10
  consumer, 292–294
  industrial, 292–293, 294–295
  making, 461
  over-the-counter, 461, 466
  for small companies, 96
  target, 292, 298, 380
Market coverage, 342
Marketing, 285
  costs and benefits of, 298–299
  functions of, 288, 289 (table)
  international, 624, 625–627
  trends in, 640
  utility and, 285–287
Marketing analysis, new products and, 318
Marketing channels, 340. *See also* Distribution channels
Marketing concept, 287
  evolution of, 287–288
  implementing, 288–289
Marketing information, 289
  for international business, 626
  in marketing plan, 298
  research and, 290, 291 (table)
  wholesalers and, 343, 344
Marketing information system, 289–298
Marketing intermediaries, *see* Middlemen
Marketing managers, 128
  information used by, 539
Marketing mix, 295–296
  controllable and uncontrollable elements in, 296
  elements of, 295
  international business and, 626–627
  in marketing plan, 298
Marketing objectives
  in marketing plan, 298
  promotion and, 379–380
Marketing orientation, *see* Marketing concept